STUDIES OF THE INTERNATIONAL INSTITUTE
OF TEACHERS COLLEGE, COLUMBIA UNIVERSITY

NUMBER 4

# THE REORGANIZATION OF EDUCATION IN PRUSSIA

# THE REORGANIZATION
# OF EDUCATION IN PRUSSIA

## BASED ON OFFICIAL DOCUMENTS
## AND PUBLICATIONS

TRANSLATED BY

## I. L. KANDEL, Ph.D.

PROFESSOR OF EDUCATION AND ASSOCIATE
IN THE INTERNATIONAL INSTITUTE OF TEACHERS COLLEGE,
COLUMBIA UNIVERSITY

AND

## THOMAS ALEXANDER, Ph.D.

PROFESSOR OF EDUCATION AND ASSOCIATE
IN THE INTERNATIONAL INSTITUTE OF TEACHERS COLLEGE,
COLUMBIA UNIVERSITY

Bureau of Publications
𝔗eachers 𝔠ollege, 𝔠olumbia 𝔘niversity
NEW YORK CITY
1927

*Printed in the United States of America by*
J. J. LITTLE AND IVES COMPANY, NEW YORK

# PREFACE

The educational systems of Germany have always been of interest to students of education in the United States. To-day when Germany is approaching the whole problem of education in the light of the new situation consequent on the Revolution and the adoption of a democratic constitution, what she does and thinks in education should be of additional interest. As in 1806 after the defeat at Jena, so in 1918 Germany recognized that the most important resource at her command, if she were to regain the ground that she has lost, is through a reorganization of her educational system. Students familiar with the history of German education will recognize many parallels and analogies between the situations in 1806 and 1918, just as they will realize that in the main Germany is taking up the threads of educational theory which were broken in 1819 and again in 1848 by the encroachment of political authority in the field of education. Allowing for differences due to the development of a science of education, the present philosophy of German education has its roots in the philosophies current in the days of Herder, Goethe, Schiller, Kant and Fichte and of the Neohumanistic movement.

The present volume is devoted to a study of the Prussian reorganization, partly because Prussia still seems destined to give the lead to the rest of Germany, partly because the situation appears to be more stable than in the other states. There are many, both in Prussia and in other German states, who are not satisfied with the solution. And, indeed, if the proposals and practices of the radical reformers as illustrated by the new systems established soon after the Revolution in Hamburg and Thuringia are compared with the reorganized system in Prussia, there may be reason for disappointment. Largely because it illustrates the difficulties that confronted the educational statesmen and administrators in this reorganization, it was considered that a translation of *Prussian Educational Systems* by Dr.

O. Boelitz, former Minister of Education in Prussia, would throw a great deal of light on the situation. This volume does not neglect to mention and discuss the more radical proposals and suggestions, but at the same time it discusses the possibility of putting them into practice in the light of conditions, political and economic, as they actually are at present. It is difficult to prophesy the future development of German education; more will depend on the economic and financial situation of the future than on the political, for from the point of view of the discussions in education the principles of democracy appear to be thoroughly established.

The study of education in Germany at the present time is valuable not merely to those who are interested in the readjustment of an educational system to new political and social conditions; it is interesting in many ways from the point of view of comparative education. Many of the problems with which educators in this country are concerned are being discussed and experiments are being made to find solutions. To cite only a few, the American student will find much to interest him in the attempts to solve the problem of educational opportunity and the use of tests and measurements for the purpose. The treatment of the difficult question of the curriculum is also of interest, starting with the first year of school with integrated instruction *(Gesamtunterricht)* and based throughout the elementary school on the utilization and interpretation of the environment *(Heimatkunde und Lebenskunde)*. The reorganization of the curriculum and the consequent effect on methods of instruction involve the still more serious problem of preparation of teachers. Nor are the discussions and experiments in the fields of intermediate or junior high school education and of secondary education suitable for modern needs without their suggestions. Each of these questions is considered in detail in Dr. Boelitz' book. In order to present the concrete discussions this book has been supplemented by a translation of all the pertinent regulations which have been issued since 1918 and which constitute the basis of the present Prussian system.

No attempt is made in the present volume to offer a critical evaluation of the new system; each criticism can be valuable only if based on an intensive study in the schools themselves. The International Institute plans to make a study of this type during

the present year and to embody the results in a further supplementary volume.  The present book is, therefore, presented as a
picture of the hopes and aspirations of the Prussian educational
authorities and of the tendencies and general direction that the
system is to follow during the next few years.

I. L. K.
T. A.

*New York, 1927*

# CONTENTS

## INTRODUCTION

## PART I

### RECONSTRUCTION OF THE PRUSSIAN EDUCATIONAL SYSTEM SINCE THE REVOLUTION

# PART II

## COURSES OF STUDY, SUGGESTIONS AND REGULATIONS

### SECTION I

### SUGGESTIONS FOR THE COURSES OF STUDY OF THE VOLKSSCHULEN

# CONTENTS

## SECTION II

### REGULATIONS CONCERNING THE MIDDLE SCHOOLS IN PRUSSIA

## SECTION III

### SUGGESTIONS FOR THE COURSES OF STUDY OF THE SECONDARY SCHOOLS OF PRUSSIA

### SECTION IV

### THE DEUTSCHE OBERSCHULE AND AUFBAUSCHULE

# CONTENTS

# INTRODUCTION

## THE PRUSSIAN EDUCATIONAL SYSTEM

### FEDERAL PARTICIPATION

The administration of education in Germany is a state affair, and federal laws on education, when they are passed, are carried out by the state authorities. While the Constitution was under consideration and for a few years thereafter there was a strong movement in favor of greater federal participation than had existed before the War. Not only was it desired that the Federal Government should issue legislation in education binding on all the states, but it was hoped that it would coöperate with the states in the support of education.

The Constitution adopted in 1919 limited itself to defining certain general principles to guarantee educational rights and equality with a promise of subsequent federal legislation on specific points. Thus Article 10 provided that "the Federal Government may by law prescribe fundamental principles with respect to . . . (2) Education, including higher education and scientific libraries." The whole of Section IV (Articles 142 to 150) of the Constitution is devoted to Education and Schools. The Section provides that "art, science and instruction in them are free"; that education shall be furnished in public institutions; that the training of teachers shall be uniformly regulated; that the states are responsible for the conduct of education; that compulsory education shall be universal, full-time for eight years of the elementary period, followed by part-time education up to eighteen; that a common foundation school shall be established for all children; that schools may be organized on a denominational, interdenominational, or secular basis; that neither teacher nor pupils be compelled to give or participate in religious instruction; that private preparatory schools should be established; and that emphasis be placed on civic and manual training in the schools.

To carry out these fundamental principles the Federal Gov-

ernment through the *Kulturabteilung* of the Ministry of the Interior drafted a law which was passed on April 20, 1920, for the
general establishment of the foundation school (*Grundschule*)
and for the abolition of the preparatory school (*Vorschule*).
This law was followed by Suggestions (*Richtlinien*) issued on
February 25, 1921, for putting it into effect and on April 18,
1925, by Suggestions on the Curriculum of the *Grundschule*.
Beyond this no further action has been taken by the Federal
Government such as was expected, for example, on the training
of teachers. There has, however, been established in the Ministry of the Interior a Committee on Educational Affairs of eight
members (1924) to consult on common standards especially in
the field of secondary education and the training of teachers,
while "the states are required to submit for examination by the
Committee before they come into force any decisive measures of
a fundamental character that affect the educational system of
other states."

That any further action of a regulative character will be
taken by the Federal Government is doubtful and in 1924 the
Federal Chancellor stated in Section 42 of the Third Tax Ordinance that "the conduct of the school and educational systems
will in accordance with the regulations of a forthcoming federal
law be left to the states to be regulated independently." Such
a law has not yet been passed and the states have proceeded to
organize their systems within the general provisions of the
Constitution. While there is a considerable party that is still
in favor of some federal regulations, there is a stronger party
opposed to it through fear of uniformity and standardization.
The Federal Educational Conference (*Reichsschulkonferenz*),
held in 1920, pronounced in favor of federal uniformity in such
matters as teacher preparation, minimum essentials in each type
of school, minimum requirements leading toward the establishment of the *Einheitsschule*, length of school year, nomenclature,
reciprocity of certificates, and statistics; it recommended decentralization of administration, each state legislating for itself in
accordance with federal principles, and an arbitration board
(*Reichskontrolle*) to decide on disputes between the Federal
Government, states, and localities. So much in general has
already been adopted, but there is no likelihood that the further
suggestion that the Federal Government give financial assistance

to the states for educational purposes will be adopted in the near future.

## THE ADMINISTRATION OF EDUCATION IN PRUSSIA

### THE MINISTRY

The central authority for the administration of education in Prussia is the Ministry for Science, Art and Popular Education (*Ministerium für Wissenschaft, Kunst und Volksbildung*) at the head of which is the Minister appointed by the president of the state. The work of the Ministry is divided among eight departments:—personnel, general, universities and scientific institutions, secondary education, elementary education and training of teachers, physical education, art education, and adult education. The officials in charge are known as *Referenten* and *Ministerialräte*. The Ministry also has the assistance of an expert in public health (*Landesgesundheitsrat*). A departure has been made from former practices, when the majority of the officials were experts with a legal or administrative training, in the direction of employing more officials with educational preparation and experience.

The function of the Ministry is to prepare bills and the budget, to issue decrees, regulations, and suggestions, to outline courses of study, to approve textbooks and school materials, to supervise the training of teachers and of teachers in service, to provide funds for education, and to select some of the higher officials in the various branches of the educational service. The official organ of the Ministry is the *Zentralblatt für die gesamte Unterrichtsverwaltung in Preussen*. Associated with the Ministry but not a constituent part of it is the *Zentralinstitut für Erziehung und Unterricht,* which serves as a clearing-house for information on education, conducts research, institutes lectures and courses in education and allied fields, and organizes tours for educational investigations in different parts of the country, and so on. (See pp. 157 ff.) The state also maintains a State Bureau for Educational Information.

Besides the Ministry for Science, Art, and Popular Education, other Ministries are concerned in the administration of special branches of education. Thus the Ministry of Commerce is responsible for industrial and commercial education, and the Ministry of Agriculture for agricultural education. The Ministry of Public Welfare (*Volkswohlfahrtsministerium*) has charge of child welfare and the care of young children and children of school age outside of the schools, supervises institutions for orphan and defective children, and coöperates with the Ministry for Science, Art, and Popular Education in the medical inspection of schools. The actual supervision of schools apart from the general welfare of the children is in the hands of the Ministry for Science, Art, and Popular Education.

## PROVINCIAL SCHOOL BOARDS

For general administrative purposes Prussia is divided into thirteen provinces, each under an *Oberpräsident*. For educational purposes the supervisory authority in each province is the Provincial School Board (*Provinzialschulkollegium*) ; the *Oberpräsident* is technically the chairman of this board but his duties are as a rule delegated to a vice-president whose preparation may be in the field of law or of education. The members of the board (*Oberschulräte*) are educators in increasing numbers, while others are legally trained administrators; recently women have become eligible for membership on the Provincial School Boards.

The chief function of these Boards is the supervision of secondary education and the exercise of certain disciplinary authority over teachers in elementary schools. The supervision of the training of elementary school teachers, formerly entrusted to the Provincial School Board, has now been transferred to the Ministry.

## COUNTY SCHOOL BOARDS

A further administrative subdivision of the provinces is found in the counties (*Regierungen*) of which there are thirty-four. The supervision of education in each county is in the hands of a Section for School Affairs (*Abteilung für Schulwesen*) at the head of which is the county president (*Regierungspräsident*) or the director of the section (*Abteilungsdirigent*) in his place. The members consist of county councillors (*Regierungsräte*), school councillors (*Schulräte*), architects (*Bauräte*), physicians (*Medizinalräte*), and legal experts appointed by the county president.

The directors of the Section for School Affairs are increasingly men of experience in education rather than in law.

The functions of the County Section for School Affairs are the appointment and supervision of elementary school teachers, the supervision of public and private elementary schools and of certain extra-school matters, and the administration of school property and endowments. The Section publishes its regulations in the *Regierungsamtsblatt,* where they must appear to have legal force, or in some official educational journal.

## INSPECTION

For purposes of inspection the counties (*Regierungen*) are divided into inspection districts (*Kreise*), each under an inspector (formerly known as *Kreisschulinspektor* but now as *Schulrat*). Article 144 of the Constitution removed one of the chief grievances of the teaching body by the provision that inspection should be solely in the hands of professional educators and in 1920 the number of inspectors was increased and full-time positions were everywhere made available. Another grievance of long standing was removed by a law of July 18, 1919, which abolished the position of local school inspector (*Ortsschulinspektor*), who was most usually the local pastor and very rarely a man of professional training.

The *Schulräte* are state officials appointed by the Minister. The position is open directly to elementary school teachers, the former preliminary examinations having been abolished by the decree of September 1, 1919. The inspectors are responsible for the complete supervision of the external and internal affairs of public and private elementary schools, and of rural continuation schools, unless there are special officials for these. They are the professional leaders in elementary education; they approve courses of study and lesson plans, conduct conferences of teachers and principals, and exercise disciplinary power over the professional and outside conduct of teachers with the right to warn and censure.

Inspectors may be present at meetings of school deputations and committees, but, although they have no vote, they may object to local resolutions that appear to conflict with laws and regulations or with the interests of the state.

*Cities.* The administration of education in cities is shared between the mayor, the administrative officers (*Magistrate*), the city council, and the School Deputation (*Schuldeputation*). The first three of these authorities are responsible for the budget, the provision of school materials, the administration of school property, and appointments. For the rest educational matters affecting elementary schools are delegated to the *Schuldeputation,* which consists of representatives of the permanent city officials, of the city council, of the teachers, and of the public. The teacher representatives are elected by and from the local teaching body; the public representatives are elected by the city council. In addition the *Schuldeputation* includes official representatives of the Protestant, Catholic, and Jewish denominations. The city health officer and other public officials may be invited to serve in an advisory capacity. Women may serve as members. The term of office is six years. The chairman of the deputation is the mayor or a deputy nominated by him. The *Schuldeputation* may appoint committees for individual schools or to look after the interests of any particular denomination. Berlin is an independent school union divided into districts each with its own *Schuldeputation.*

City educational authorities may establish secondary schools but only with the approval of the Ministry, which in such cases considers the need for such schools and the ability of the locality to support them. The local authorities in turn must undertake the provision of suitable sites, buildings, and equipment, must designate the type, number, and salaries of the teachers, and must organize a suitable system of administration. After a school is established and approved the supervision of both its external and its internal affairs is in the hands of the pertinent Provincial School Board. With the internal affairs, the actual direction and the teachers, the local authority has no right to interfere except in minor matters, such as the remission or reduction of fees, and granting teachers leave of absence, or permission to undertake outside work or to live outside of the city limits.

*Rural Areas.* In the rural communities that constitute school areas (*Schulverbände*) the preparation of the budget, the administration of school property, and the supervision of school accounts are entrusted to the general administrative authorities. For educational purposes, however, there is established a school committee (*Schulvorstand*) responsible to the general administration and to the superior authority for elementary education. Unlike the *Schuldeputation* the *Schulvorstand* is an independent unit consisting of the president of the community, elected teachers, and representatives of the public and of the religious denominations appointed by the local council. The chairman of the committee is appointed. The function of the committee is to exercise general superintendence over the external welfare of the schools under them and to promote sound relations between the school and the home.

Several rural communities may combine to organize a union school district (*Gesamtschulverband*) under a single *Schulvorstand,* constituted in the same way as the committee of a single community.

### PARENTS' COUNCILS

A Ministerial decree of November 11, 1919, required the establishment of parents' councils for every school. The councils are elected by parents who have children in a school, and their function is to promote the best possible relations between the school and the home. The councils are advisory and express the views of the parents on such matters as discipline, the physical, intellectual and moral development of the children, and other matters of general rather than individual interest. A further activity of the councils is to organize parent-teacher meetings, lectures, and school exhibitions.

### TEACHERS' COUNCILS

Teachers' councils have been established in country areas and in other districts, coterminous with political or school inspection boundaries. Regulations on the constitution and powers of these councils (*Bezirkslehrerräte* and *Kreislehrerräte*), which have been established by law, have not as yet been defined. The *Bezirkslehrerräte* are established to act in an advisory capacity to the *Regierungen* on general educational matters, such as the regulation of questions affecting teachers, which they do by presenting petitions, memoranda, and reports; they coöperate in selecting one of the three members of the committees for the final appointment of teachers; and they report on the qualifications of candidates for inspectorships. The authorities of the *Regierungen* may send representatives to the meetings of the councils, which may also be attended by the inspectors.

The functions of the *Kreislehrerräte*, which cover a smaller area, are, in general, functions similar to those of the *Bezirkslehrerräte*.

## SCHOOL SUPPORT

The cost of education is borne by the state and the school districts, the state undertaking an important share of the cost of the salaries of teachers and the school districts the remaining costs with aid from the state, if necessary. In order to equalize the burden for the salaries of elementary school teachers there was established a *Landesschulkasse* (State Elementary School Fund Bureau) by the *Volksschullehrerdiensteinkommengesetz* (law of December 17, 1920, amendments of January 1, 1925, and regulations of June 3, 1921). The Bureau acts as a central organization to administer funds contributed by the state and local authorities. The Bureau is not technically a state office but an organization created to relieve the educational authorities of direct relations with the teachers in such matters as the securing of personal records. It is administered by a treasurer appointed by representatives of the local authorities. Payments are made by the Bureau either directly, as in the case of pensions and allowances for dependents, or through the office of the treasurer of the school or general local administration.

The funds from the Bureau are made up of grants from the state, miscellaneous incomes, and grants from the school districts to make up the balance needed to meet the obligations. The state contributes one-fourth of the salaries of all teachers on the basis of one teacher for sixty pupils, one-fourth of the cost for pensions and allowances for dependents, and a contribution determined in the budget annually for emergency needs. The total amount of the state's contributions to the *Landesschulkasse* is not expected to exceed more than one-fourth of the estimated cost of salaries, pensions, dependent allowances, and other grants. The local authorities are required to contribute the balance. For any activities beyond a certain minimum, such as the provision of advanced work in the elementary schools, reduction of the size of classes, payment of substitutes and so on, the local authorities must raise additional funds themselves.

In addition to the contribution made by the state to the *Landesschulkasse*, it also contributes a sum, not exceeding half of the cost of salaries and maintenance, calculated on the basis of pupil enrollment (*Beschulungsgeld*). School districts that are unable to support the cost of education even with the contributions coming directly from the state and indirectly from the state through the *Landesschulkasse* may resort to the state for additional assistance.

The state may further grant assistance toward the cost of school buildings under certain conditions, mainly the size and need of the school district. The amount of such assistance is limited to one-third of the cost, the details of which are carefully defined and scrutinized.

For the payment of salaries in middle schools an arrangement somewhat similar to the *Landesschulkasse* has been established. The cost of secondary education, except in the case of state schools, is borne by the local authorities.

### PREPARATION OF TEACHERS

From the provision of Article 143 of the Constitution it was expected that the preparation of teachers would ge regulated by the Federal Government. Since the Federal Government took no steps in this direction, each state began to establish its own system, based, however, on one uniform requirement that the preliminary preparation of future teachers should be in a secondary school and up to the level of university entrance standards. For the rest the important question that remained to be solved was whether the professional preparation should be given in the universities or in special institutions of a university grade but not constituent parts of the universities. Saxony and Thuringia decided on the former course; Prussia adopting the latter has established *Pädagogische Akademien*. Three such pedagogical academies have already been established.

The purpose of the two-year course there offered is to give pedagogical training, a mastery of educational values in relation to intellectual, religious, moral, technical, and artistic development, the recognition of the origin of educational values in popular culture, and the cultivation of a strong professional sense. The academic training is to give a mastery of the educational materials to be used in the elementary schools; the practical preparation is to be given through observation, discussions, conferences, and practice teaching; in addition provision is made for training in skill (technical) and art subjects. A professional examination, on the result of which teachers are admitted to temporary appointment only, is held at the end of the two-year course.

Permanent appointment of elementary school teachers can be obtained either by passing a second examination after two years and before the completion of five years of service, or by completing an approved course in a coöperative study group (*Arbeitsgemeinschaft*).

The system of training teachers for secondary schools remains unchanged except in a few details. Candidates are required to have spent a number of years in a university, to pass the state examination, and then to spend two years in professional preparation (*Vorbereitungsjahre*) in a designated secondary school.

# PART I

## RECONSTRUCTION OF THE PRUSSIAN EDUCATIONAL SYSTEM SINCE THE REVOLUTION

# CHAPTER I

## POLITICS AND EDUCATION AT THE PRESENT TIME

The educational authority of a large country rich in diversity
of opinions, if it is fully conscious of its heavy responsibilities,
must above all else realize the limits of the resources at its
disposal.  Not only is this true in periods of peaceful development, when new problems are to be solved and carried out, but
it is particularly true after the tremendous upheavals that we
have experienced in the recent war and political revolution.
When Descartes initiated the great revolution of the modern
spirit with full consciousness of the ramifications of his ideas,
he stated that the difficulty of a reformation lay in the restoration, once they have been shattered, or even in the maintenance,
when they have been shaken, of the mighty fabric of institutions
that have become historical.  When a reconstruction is planned
it is not enough to tear down the house in which we live in order
to rebuild it, nor is a carefully devised plan for the reconstruction adequate, but a livable dwelling must be retained during
the process of building.

During the War and the Revolution, attempts were not lacking
to level to the ground the fabric of our Prussian school system.
Nor were there wanting plans for a new construction on a large
scale laid out in all possible styles frequently enough after the
pattern of castles in the air.  Even if the resources had existed
for tearing down the old construction, the resources for a new
building were not available.  They were not available because
the new school must rise out of the ethos of the whole people,
because we are still lacking a new cultural ideal to give style
and form to popular education.

The inspiring and impassioned educational conflict of the
recent past and of the present has, however, revealed to its
innermost the tremendous crisis in the education of our times;
it has also stirred up in the consciousness of the masses a yearning for cultural unity, for a genuinely national system of edu-

3

cation. But an ideal, emerging from the depths of our terrible experience, an ideal that would consolidate all in Fichte's sense in a great unified whole, is not yet at hand. The storms of the revolution have not inspired the creative spirit in education.

It is generally known, however, that such an educational ideal cannot be artificially created; above all, the state cannot create it; nor does such creation lie within the power of educational theory. Educational ideals of universal applicability, of which radical thinkers speak, do not exist. The theories of many of the most up-to-date reformers in education furnish a classical example of the truth of this statement. Superficial contempt of history, attempts to found education on laws of nature, the severest criticism, scorn for the present and negation of tried methods, none of these in any way alter the fact that the absolute applicability of these reforms that are implied is but an expression of a tendency that is historically determined. The one thing that is proved by this storm and stress in modern education which is dragging the young into the conflicts of the cultural agitation is that we are striving for a new epoch in the training of the German nation. Hence the error of those who imagine that they could simply delete the last ten years in which we passed through war and revolution, and debated from every angle the aims and ideals of education, and recall to life or artificially preserve the past, the old-fashioned, the dead. Such attempts at resurrection or artificial preservation are as naïve as the ideals of the radical reformers who do not believe in history. The education of a people can only blossom forth out of the natural life and experiences of a generation.

The full content of contemporary life cannot, however, be comprehended. So far no poet has given expression to it; no philosopher has formulated an intellectual statement about it; no educational genius has based a new educational ideal on it. The pedagogical genius will first arise in the schoolroom in living association with the young, will first flourish with all the genuine characteristics of creative power. "Genuine reforms," Dilthey once maintained correctly, "are brought to fruition only through constant, persistent pedagogical activity in schoolrooms. Regulations can only smooth the path and can then render useful the results of this research completed in the schoolroom. More they cannot accomplish. Educational conditions they can never create.''

Educational administrators must remain conscious of these limitations, particularly to-day, when from all sides demands are made on them that cannot be accomplished and responsibilities are laid on their shoulders that they cannot in any way carry. All that the state can do is to organize available resources. In the schoolroom, the center of real reform, it can supply light and air. But of itself it cannot raise up creative forces. The power of the state does not extend into the depths of inner personality, from which alone new ideals develop. Demands should not be made on it which because of its nature it cannot heed. Its task is indeed more difficult to-day than it was formerly, for our young are painfully bewildered by the clash of parties fighting for their possession, by the conflicting philosophies, secular and religious. In the midst of the noisy demands of different groups many forget the right of the child, his inalienable claim on all the cultural possessions of the nation and every opportunity for development that slumbers in the soul of every child according to its ability. Many also forget the peculiar right of the school, which, as the trustee of the child and the guardian of national culture, has the duty of organizing education in accordance with principles appropriate to it. Hence the state must set a limit to the claim of all groups that demand control in the school. Neither the family, nor the church, nor any party, nor any other group of any kind should demand sole authority in the school. The state must assure to every group, including itself, the measure of influence that is its due. Every group has a right to the child, but it has this right only in proportion to its importance within the limits of national culture. A group that enjoys superior or sole authority in the school is a menace not only to the peculiar right of the child, but also to the existence of our whole national culture.

A sound distribution of the rights of groups concerned in education has always been an educational problem as significant as it is difficult. The destruction of all that is fundamental at the present time has intensified these difficulties to an extraordinary degree. The separation of church and state provided in the Constitution has not only imposed on the authorities responsibility for a series of questions that cannot be solved once and for all, but has aroused in the hearts and minds of large masses of the people pangs of conscience and deep unrest, and has put before them the whole question of political agitation. No less passionately do parents demand participation in the school which they would permit to serve merely as an institution to supplement parental education. Various sections of Prussia demand home rule in educational politics while from another side there appear stormy movements in favor of a centralized imperial policy in education. Parties again wish to find expression in education for their own points of view, their political articles of faith, and where they suspect in the school a spirit that is not pleasing to them, they attempt to get hold of the pupils outside of school hours. Action of this kind deprives the school of that spirit of quiet without which nothing can prosper. The young themselves, shaken by the terrible experience of war and revolution, drawn into the chaos of the present, surrounded by the buzz of slogans, mistrusting the older generation, school and home, the church, state and society, no less loudly and vociferously demand their right in education and set up educational utopias which in spite of their variety and contradiction betray a strong impulse and unquenched yearning for education. In the midst of the unhappy discord in our social life, of the incomplete reorganization of the relations between the social classes, of the conflict between educational interests, justifiable in themselves, it is, in spite of all the pressure, an almost insoluble task for the state to restore the balance of powers and to reconcile all conflicting claims in a unified strong system of German national education. The pressure of this task is so great because state consciousness itself can no longer be assumed as a sound fact or be taken for granted and because the destruction of the idea of the state is particularly acceptable to the young. It is apparent that the relation between the state and church, state and society, state and nationalism, the idea of the state and the constitution no longer operates in large, settled, historical types but that all possibilities, even the most radical kind, have already been experienced by the young.

Educational administration must ever and again prove in this period of stress and turmoil that the school cannot solve cultural problems that have not been solved by society itself. The school need not permit itself to lag behind the times; on the other hand, it should not attempt to move in advance of the times.

If the educational politician carefully observes all the living expressions of the cultural effort of the nation, he should not overlook the law which is also applicable here, that all aggressive, importunate, revolutionary forces make themselves more strongly and noisily noticeable than the powers that are great and silent and have developed historically and organically. New tendencies, alluring slogans, radical theories often appear to claim the field almost without opposition and yet they only affect the surface. The waters underneath flow on undisturbed and the surface rippled by the wind of contemporary tendencies is soon smoothed out. Frequently, however, the attack of the new calls out the strongest reaction from the old, which then shows amazing vitality and not only wards off the attack, but itself advances as aggressor.

The educational discussions of recent years are rich in such surprising changes and vicissitudes. Disillusion, setbacks, and reaction have accordingly resulted in all cases where attempts at reform have not been commensurate with the resources actually available. Almost everywhere the strong educational demands have had to be watered down; almost everywhere the slower, more organic method of reform has been substituted. It has been proved that really new educational ideas of wide sweep and of genuinely attractive force have not met with success in spite of the Revolution, indeed that almost in all cases they could be and of necessity were bound up with ideas and movements that could be observed before the War and made rapid advancement during the War. Some of these reform ideas have been so strengthened by the War and the Revolution and have become so widespread that they could be incorporated in school practice and be made the subject of administrative measures by the educational authorities. Others still remain to be tested, evaluated, and carefully proved to see whether an idea that may perhaps have seemed sound in a small and narrow compass should be introduced into the short life of a great state. Nowhere else perhaps does so much depend on the human element as in the field of education and instruction. The door that opens quickly and readily at the touch of the magic wand of the gifted educator generally remains closed to the average teacher. Admin-

istrative measures should not start with the assumption that
every teacher is a master.  This is too often forgotten in cheap
criticisms of reforms: their incompleteness is condemned on one
hand, and their extravagance is blamed on the other, while the
element of soundness is recognized by but few.

# CHAPTER II

## THE DEVELOPMENT AND ORGANIZATION OF THE COMMON SCHOOL

The idea of the common school *(Einheitsschule)* appears to be completely matured. Gneisenau once praised the French Republic because it translated the power of the French people as a nation into action. "What infinite powers," he said, "slumber undeveloped and unutilized in the bosom of a nation. In the hearts of thousands upon thousands of men there lies a great genius whose soaring wings are crippled by profound causes." During the War and the period of collapse, the opinion was shared by all of us that the still unawakened forces in our people must be aroused, that many barriers that hitherto kept apart large sections of our nation must be torn down, and that all must be consolidated into a great democratic society. For the last century, since Süvern in the time of Prussia's greatest need first formed a clear conception of the idea of the common school and carefully planned its organization, the idea was never again laid aside. Süvern regarded the universal school as an institution for national education and aimed to this end to establish a uniform system from the elementary school to the university; unfortunately the proposal was defeated owing to the objections of a weaker period. It came to the fore again in full vigor in 1848 as the expression, picture, and hope of the German unity, to which we had to come ultimately. There was call for the common school to create the unity of our people. Here again, as in Süvern's day, there developed disillusion, objections, reaction. When at last the long desired unity was secured through Bismarck, when we had attained what had been our dream and hope, we forgot, in our power, strength, and unity, the need of pressing forward to cultural unity. The idea of the common school as a necessary cultural principle was pushed into the background. The common school was, it is true, demanded in the programs of the elementary school teaching body, which,

9

though fighting boldly and energetically for it for decades, met
with no response either with the great public or among leading
educators.  It was not until the World War, when there was a
glimmering recognition among our young men in the trenches
of the terrible disruption in our culture, that there arose again
a yearning for spiritual unity among our people, for cultural
unity, for educational unity, and for the common school; when,
finally, the catastrophe of defeat revealed to us the weakness of
our spiritual life while indicating hope of salvation, that the
common school as the means to spiritual unity of our people
was placed on the program of the widely scattered groups in
the country.  At the great Federal Educational Conference [1]
of 1920 the possibility of its organization was discussed.  Here,
too, objections were raised, but the idea was too sound and
simple to be neglected again on this occasion.  After the Federal
Law had laid the foundation for the organization of the common
school by creating the foundation school, Prussia devoted herself enthusiastically to the task.  If it was denied us at that
early stage to permeate our school system immediately with an
educational ideal common to us all, at least there could be created
an educational organization which, on the one hand, assures to
everybody the cultural possessions according to his intellectual
capacity and promotes the development and most appropriate
employment in appropriate positions of all the powers of our
people, and, which, on the other hand, removes barriers and
places the common elements in the foreground to a greater
extent than ever before.

Greatly admired and reviled, often misunderstood and confused by party hate or party favor, this important administrative idea of the common school has remained victorious.  Educational opportunity for each in accordance with intellectual
ability; articulation of schools on psychological principles which
does not demand premature determination of curriculum or
school type but assures even to the older pupils the possibility
of transfer and access to higher education, and removes blind

[1] See *Die Reichsschulkonferenz, ihre Vorgeschichte und Vorbereitung und
ihre Verhandlungen.  Amtlicher Bericht erstattet vom Reichministerium des
Innern.*  1920.  See also *Die deutsche Schulreform,* and *Die Reichsschulkonferenz in ihren Ergebnissen, Zentralinstitut für Erziehung und Unterricht.*  Quelle und Meyer, Leipzig, 1920.

alleys which exclude or permit only with the greatest difficulty incorporation into the general fabric of our educational system (e.g., the preparation of teachers, girls' schools) : such is the first important idea in the organization of the common school based on indisputable principles of psychology and education. Associated with it are important social ideas; the same right to education and culture for all children, abolition of the class-school, bridging the gaps among the people by means of an education for social unity. On the basis of psychology, educational theory, and sociology alone there emerges the notion of the common school which can be developed naturally and organically. It is gratifying to see with what relative rapidity it has been able to lead to a reorganization of the Prussian school system, which with the clearness and simplicity that places the stamp of common sense on all great reforms, has without violence incorporated the historical school types in one organic system.

This common school should not and cannot be organized as a "super-denominational" common school, admitting all children without reference to their religious affiliations. The religious structure of our people which the centuries have developed cannot be set aside by organization. It would be the negation of German spiritual life which is intimately permeated with religious ideas, to create an organization in which an artificial super-denominational religion is bestowed on the school as a cultural possession. Nor should the common school claim to be coeducational on absolute principles. Male and female dispositions show such striking traits of difference and the curve of development of boys and girls deviate so far from each other that sex differences must be taken into consideration at least at the beginning of puberty and the common school should not be adopted in the sense of a unity that is external and schematic.

The common school should under no circumstances become a school patterned on a plan that is identical or uniform for all. It must always recognize the limits set for every organization; it must not draw to itself what defies compulsion, but must confine itself to the task of combining into one whole existing types of schools, whose worth, significance, and need have been proved, together with new types to be created, and to weld these into an articulate whole corresponding to the educational and social ideas already discussed.

This common school is also the one required in the Constitution of the German Republic (Article 146):

The public school system is to be built up organically. On the basis of a foundation school *(Grundschule)* common to all there will rise the middle and higher schools. For this structure the variety of life's callings, for the admission of a pupil into any particular school his ability and inclinations, not the economic or social status or the religious beliefs of his parents are to be the determining factors.

Prussia has met this requirement with a cautious and considered organization of the common school. She traced back the demand for the common school to its inherent principle and will continue along this line. It must be admitted, however, that even here not everything could be carried to its fulfillment. Demands and wishes, justifiable in themselves, had to be postponed on account of the economic conditions. Whoever reads this book will realize that every part of the Prussian school system is governed by this single principle or organization. The abolition of preparatory schools *(Vorschulen)*, the gradual closing of normal schools and institutions preparatory to them, the establishment of the new types of secondary schools *(Aufbauschulen)*, the reform of secondary education for boys and girls, adult schools, the reform of higher education—all this is to be comprehended under the motto of the common school: "One people, one school." It must, however, be asserted with emphasis that only the soundness of the Prussian educational system before the War made it possible to incorporate all existing types of schools in this system. Here, too, progress has been by evolution, not by revolution. Important as this organization of the common school is, it is not the last nor the most important. It by no means provides as yet for cultural unity which must always be before us as the ultimate goal. It may through institutions, however skillfully organized, secure a certain uniformity, yet it will not restrain individual schools from endangering cultural unity through conflicting ideals of education, nor prevent religious, moral, political, and national antagonisms, that disrupt our people, from operating in the common school. This transitional situation, the child of circumstances, need not throw the common school into disrepute, for in the last analysis it too was begotten of the valuable idea of a cultural synthesis.

Despite everything over and above the unified organization, it is important that an advance be made to unity of education, to unity of cultural consciousness, to national solidarity, and here, too, as in the case of organization, the demand must be for unity and not for uniformity. A system of educational administration in Prussia that disregarded Prussia's historical mission, would thereby endanger the foundations of Prussia's political existence, would be disregarding that sober clarity of the political consciousness of Prussia.

The common school as an educational principle is infinitely more important than the common school conceived only from the point of view of organization. The common school should be the school that brings unity to our people. It must set itself the task of bringing about such uniformity in the general education of our people as is possible in our cultural conditions: it must bridge the gaps that have developed alarmingly in our people, and the great differences between the educated and the uneducated, employers and employees, the wealthy and the disinherited of fortune. It should build the bridges to the large number of Germans outside the borders of our country, who are bound to us by the same language and the same culture. Accordingly, instruction in schools of all kinds, from the foundation-school to the university, must center around a core of German subject matter. This German subject matter should develop unity in our whole educational system. If in this way the cultural subjects in the whole range of instruction acquire the central position, so long desired, and if the German content is assured under all circumstances, the unity of our educational system is better served than if an artificial organization is carried into effect in all details.

If Prussia in carrying out this idea is conscious of the peculiar tasks that it has to perform for Germany and German culture in developing an independent cultural policy, this does not denote any narrowness. Prussia must develop a specific cultural policy even though her particular tasks are quite definite and strictly limited.

This is the contribution of Prussia to the common culture of Germany, that the state and culture develop in mutual association with each other. Prussia, to maintain her existence, has been compelled to pursue a cultural policy, from the point of view of the interest of the state. This has provided for her educational policy the organic growth, the necessary influence, and the statesmanlike vision which have enabled her to assume the leadership in the educational affairs of Germany. Within Prussia, naturally not without conflict and friction, the antagonisms between East and West, between state and local areas, between Protestantism and Catholicism, between the interests of the state and autonomy, between industry and agriculture, have always been reconciled in such a way that continued development along the diagonal of the parallelogram of forces was possible. A federal educational policy of a similar kind is not yet possible, because the same antagonisms within the Empire have not yet been reconciled in the same way. The opposition between the states and localities is still too strong. Just at this moment the centralization of all German educational policy is still utopian, since the unrest in politics, the increased mistrust, the conflict between the states would hinder organic development. For this very reason a division of Prussia into cultural provinces would be a national misfortune, because disruption into detached and isolated sections would be inevitable and there would develop within Prussia herself a divorce between the idea of a state and cultural consciousness. Hence from the standpoint of cultural policy we have the greatest interest in a strong Prussia, in which cultural and state consciousness have always been combined, in a strong Prussia, which has always pursued a German cultural policy in the best sense. Thus, and only thus, will the cultural mission of Prussia become quite clear—to create unity in national education in the state of Germany that is the greatest and richest in educational antagonisms. Accordingly, the aim of our universal education in elementary, middle, and secondary schools and even in our universities is training for German nationalism, as was urged by Fichte a century ago.

Of most serious importance, pregnant with consequences, the problem of religious instruction ranks above all else. It has never been clearer than in our own day that the spiritual revival of a people must have its source in religious forces if it is to grow wholly out of the depths of popular spirit. We live, far more than would appear on superficial observation, at a time of great religious crises and, at the same time, of deep religious living. Even the challenge to dominant religions is often stimulated by religious motives and it is obvious that new religious forces are attempting to work themselves out in the religious activities of many sections both within and without the church and even outside of Christianity. The passionate fight for the school has grown out of sectarian motives. Separation of church and state, the right of all groups to schools of their own beliefs, the renewed entrenchment of the strong clerical parties as a result of the new situation in ecclesiastical politics, all these factors combine to complicate the situation in educational politics. The state cannot dispense with these religious forces; they create the highest feelings of duty and responsibility, the strongest impulses for moral conduct, the motives that are indispensable for associated living, without which the state cannot exist but which of itself it cannot create. It must allow the religious forces to work themselves out wherever they manifest themselves. Wherever in addition schools of a particular complexion are demanded, they cannot be refused, whether they style themselves denominational or secular or community schools. But wherever a community does not insist on a denominational or secular school, it is to the interest of the cultural unity of our people to hope that the old interdenominational school (*Simultanschule*) will be retained as a school representing general Christian consciousness. All these schools should be granted the freedom guaranteed by the Constitution to the fullest limit and it is obvious that the Prussian Ministry of Education will grant autonomy to those schools that dispense with religious forces in education and instruction, in so far as they are sectarian, that is, to the so-called secular schools. Each of the various school types should enjoy its freedom without which true life cannot prosper. The state, however, must unconditionally be watchful over one thing, that in all of these schools none of the cultural possessions that are of value to the nation shall suffer; hence the state must reserve to itself the right to supervision in the fullest sense. It must be on its guard that no ominous tendencies of sectarian or anti-sectarian education, or of religious or anti-religious life, disturb the peace of the schools and conjure up an educational conflict of immeasurable consequences. It must work in a conciliatory spirit, and must deal with narrowness in one place as with extravagance in another; it must always keep the school as an institution of the state in that great cultural association on which depends everything that desires to live.

The conflict around the denominational schools strongly inflamed in the days of the Revolution is almost silenced. A saving formula has not yet been discovered by means of which the application of secular points of view in the domain of school organization should be regulated by a federal law. The denominational school, however, is firmly entrenched. Article 146, Section 2, of the Constitution required that in the elementary school attention be given to religious denominations and secular beliefs. This consideration is best guaranteed in denominational schools, especially in those cases where they have grown up historically. For the instinctive and more naïve intelligence which predominates in the elementary school continuity of denominational, spiritual impressions furnishes a source of strength with which the state cannot dispense in its educative tasks. The state must only be on its guard that in these schools the German cultural content also retains its central position. Under no circumstances should the denominational school lead to narrowness. In parts of Prussia in which the interdenominational school is customary, and which after it has existed for a long time becomes more or less denominational, the education authority will in no way affect it.

So far as the secondary school is concerned the Constitution only required consideration for those of dissenting beliefs but imposed upon it the heavy task of furnishing a general German education. For this reason the Ministry, as it had done for the last fifty years, rejects the establishment of denominational secondary schools, insisting always on the principle that it is a political necessity that in the secondary schools those to whom will fall leadership among the people should not be segregated along sectarian lines when they have reached their religious majority. For these we must insist that they obtain such an insight into the differentiation in our historical culture as will give them a historical appreciation of the variety of points of view in the population. The Protestant must recognize the tremendous power vested in Catholicism and the Catholic must realize that the cultural influences originating in Protestantism have moulded our modern spirit.  Hence a universal German culture which cannot be reduced to a common religious denominator must be common to both.

With the religious quickening of the education of the young is closely associated the moral strengthening of our youth.  Before the War serious educators were of the opinion that overwhelmingly intellectual education had neglected character formation, that we did not understand how to exercise a strong and lasting influence on the will and emotions of the rising generation through instruction and education.  The War and the Revolution with their terrible consequences, the economic distress, the shattering of the deepest moral values, the shameless lust for pleasure, the wild frenzy of speculation, the abandonment of many moral restraints in political life, have endangered the spiritual integrity of our youth.  There remains to-day not a single moral ideal that is not questioned, not a single immoral transaction that is not justified on some new ethical principle.

The recognition of this danger to the morals of our youth and the knowledge that this constitutes the greatest problem for education are to-day the common property of all interested in moral training, and in spite of the chaos in the theory of moral training, it is a welcome sign that the formation of character, education for humanity, and the realization of the ideas of a sound social theory of education are seriously accepted as the most important task before the school.  Here again the state cannot reconcile the conflicts of ethical beliefs; it cannot impose on any educator or on any pupil a particular ideal of humanity as universally valid.  As in the case of religious instruction, the historical and traditional conditions of our state must here be taken into account.  The state must, however, insist that the work of the school revolve around practical experiences of life, development of personality, and social education.  For this purpose it can prepare the way and set up objectives through teacher-training, through organization of the school system, through courses of study and school regulations.  The influence of creative personalities can be enlisted for education; support can be found for experimental schools of a particular type, or professorships established in the sciences pertinent to moral training; above all the vital powers of self-education that

are themselves operative in the youth can be rendered effective
for school life. In the curriculum and suggestions, new possibilities of influence and increased responsibilities in reconciling
freedom and authority, the individual and society, can be pointed
out to the teachers. The state can urge the teachers ever and
again to permeate every subject and every method with moral
objectives; it can here set up special objectives for each subject
and at the same time utilize for character-formation whatever
resources it may afford. But it is essential, none the less, that
those moral forces that have been handed on in the conventions
and customs, in the tradition and life of the people, shall be
protected and fostered. Care must be taken that the forces of
moral health that still slumber in the villages and small towns
are not destroyed by the destructive spirit of the metropolis, and
the strength of German morality that is still latent in the home
and countryside, in the speech and manners of the people, should
not be underestimated on account of abstract theories. This
idea in particular was in the mind of the Prussian educational
ministry when it established the *Aufbauschule* and the *Deutsche
Oberschule,* and the fundamental principles of the circular on
these schools (February 18, 1922), which incorporate this tendency, cannot be lightly ignored. These principles apply equally
to the other higher schools, which we also wish to be inspired
with the spirit of German idealism. It is in the higher schools
that whatever has been and still is vital in the moral idealism
of our people emerges into the consciousness of the older pupil,
so that the great ethical teachers of Germany are first studied
without prejudice to subsequent self-determination in the field
of morals, that Schiller and Kant, Goethe and Fichte finally
attain their due position in our education.

One special section of moral instruction is the education for
civic consciousness, political education. The educator must
recognize the fearful seriousness of the situation, for never
was the civic consciousness in our people, not naturally given to
politics, more menaced than to-day, and that more particularly
among especially outstanding sections of the people and the
youth. Reverence for ancient holy symbols, distortions and exaggerations of the popular conscience, German loyalty to the old
dynasty, century-old monarchical traditions, fighting instincts
and desire for vengeance stimulated by humiliation, glorifica-

tion of the past, depreciation of the present, placing on the new state the responsibility for all distress, for all social revolution, and for the shattered hopes of the future—in all this stirs the soul of many of our young against the new form of the state and by an easy step frequently against the state itself. On the other hand, the young in their thinking and feeling negate the state and replace it with new social ideals, international ideologies, utopian dreams of a new humanity, and life in a super-state. All these notions are presented by agitators to the young without any restriction and are frequently abused for purposes not recognized by them. The young must finally realize that the state and the form of the state are somewhat different things, that the state is more than the form which determines its character from time to time. The young must come to recognize the state as the living organism which has been handed down from the dim past by our ancestors from generation to generation through the centuries, that we must preserve it as the great trust from the past with its problems for the present and the future. Therefore its form must not be despised, for such contempt strikes at the state itself; the air that our young must breathe becomes rarefied. Positive service for the state must be the ultimate goal of political education. Opponents must be won over by conviction; little must be expected from compulsory or restrictive measures of an external character,—not even in school. Pupils have never been influenced for any length of time in a particular direction desired by the school by rules or threats of punishments. What applies to frequenting saloons and smoking applies equally to participation in politics or party affiliations. Forbidden fruits are attractive. Free men are created by intercourse that is engaged in with independent decision. The vitality of the state depends far more on the vision of it in the soul of the citizen than on coercion or threats. If the state wishes to survive, it must woo the conscience and emotions of the citizens. Otherwise the civic sense declines into superficial expediency which in times of stress turns against the state as it is, or the state degenerates into a police system whose demands are looked on as unmerited tyranny, or into a class organization which serves the interests only of one section of the people.

That political consciousness is something more than emotion, however high it may be keyed, that a clear recognition of the meaning of the state and the will to serve it are to be valued more highly than an orgy of patriotic emotions, that the state is rather a moral community to which other groups, cultural or otherwise, subordinate themselves to promote its worthy ends and their own existence, these facts have become an account of our history unfortunately as obviously intelligible to us Germans as to the English, French, and Americans. Our weakness has always been a cause of surprise to the foreigner. Let us abandon these errors and let us learn from other nations, who have also lived through a chequered history and have also seen in the hour of agony their power in ruins, that it is not sentimental whining but only a steeled will for political existence that has saved them and again raised them up. And here is another lesson that we should learn from others, that without reservation we place at the service of the state the forces that are found in our glorious past. In spite of the Revolution, we must therefore bring our young in living contact with our people's past and imbue their souls with the history of the German nation, the great national teachers of old and the personalities of our great rulers and statesmen. Training of the civic consciousness is thus the most pressing problem of the day. It does not suffice, however, to shelter our youth from ideas that are unfriendly or hostile to the state, nor to develop a knowledge of civics with the help of the Constitution; much rather must a demand be made for a training in civic idealism based on a thorough knowledge of history and the exaltation of the German state to an ideal in which a genuine feeling of patriotism and intensely deep sympathies for humanity are intertwined. A state that is firmly rooted in itself, that is secure through the strength of its institutions and the repute of its power can well tolerate the dangers of centrifugal tendencies, which may, indeed, even increase its vitality. The German Republic must to-day demand the dominance of the idea of the state, and this idea must accordingly in education become a principle that pervades all branches of the system, for only as a political people will we survive as a cultural nation.

Only unreserved devotion to the state can be the objective of civic instruction. A special subject, however, cannot serve these aims, but rather the permeation of the whole of school life and of all school activities with the civic conscience. If it is accepted

that not the sentiment of obedience or subordination to authority, but free devotion, sense of responsibility and independence
must be the goals of civic education, that civic idealism should
at the same time be the expression of the most worthwhile personality and the deepest cultural consciousness, that responsible
individuals alone should be the true citizens of the new German
Republic, then education finds here too quite special motives.
All materials and methods of instruction must hereafter stand
the test whether they succeed in developing this responsible free
activity, the creative powers that are essential, and the ideal objectives that motivate it.  In this connection, great changes in our
educational ideals are under way which find expression in instruction through self-activity, training through current events,
esthetic education, realistic education, creative education, and
other systems more frequently obscure, vacillating, and ambigu-
ous.  All these catchwords, however, do in fact relate to problems
which have their roots in our history.  That these problems are
more often confused rather than clarified by one-sided, radical,
even grotesque formulæ should not absolve the administrative authorities of the duty of taking them seriously and instituting
experiments by which alone it can be proved what in this movement is strong and vital, what sketchy and dreamy.  Many
innovations have already been tested.  The significance of art,
drawing, and music, not merely as a means of penetrating into
our national culture but also of releasing free creative powers,
has received widespread recognition with remarkable rapidity.
To-day the principle of self-activity with its educative, sociological, and moral significance is scarcely questioned; indeed, it has
together with the ideas that are implicit in it already revolution-
ized the objectives of school work in particular.

All these new ideas, forces, and tendencies are eager to establish themselves by might and main.  The administrative authorities which have been frequently attacked by school reformers
for their slowness and reactionary spirit can and must follow
here step by step.  It may be said that they have already undertaken too many tasks at one time; perhaps it is not without
reason that a reform of reforming has been demanded; possibly
it has been forgotten in some places that a new generation of
teachers, equipped to handle these ideas, must grow up. Nowhere
are impatience and impetuosity more harmful than in education,

which for its work needs quiet above all things. So the Prussian Ministry will throw itself open to both charges, reaction and impetuosity, while it advances cautiously and experimentally.

In the following pages a simple and businesslike report is presented of what Prussia has actually accomplished in forwarding the organization of the common school by the employment of the real spirit of the ideas developed on this subject. Several critics have up to the present scarcely taken the time to make an actual study of the objects of their criticism. Frequently it was not possible to learn from decrees and circulars what the actual situation in Prussian educational reform is. So extensive were they that one often overlooked the spiritual tie which in spite of the apparent diversity in the innovations bound the whole into a well-planned unity. This view of the real situation was also frequently obscured by the great confusion that was caused by polemics and agitation. This applies also quite definitely to the discussions on the reform of secondary education which have not always been free from political passion. Much is still in a state of flux and nothing in the following chapters contains the last word. We are still in the formative stage of a new era. Whether promising buds and blossoms will unfold into leaves and plants, whether the fruit will mature, depends on three conditions: First, that we make peace with our former enemies who are our antagonists and even now fear our culture; secondly, whether we succeed in enlisting the moral forces which are latent in their rich bloom in our youth, in the service of reconstructing our state; and, finally, that there is always available for the great tasks of education and instruction a supply of men and women with such personality as teachers that they joyfully give to our young the best and finest that is in them.

# CHAPTER III

## THE ESTABLISHMENT OF THE COMMON SCHOOL IN PRUSSIA

### I.  THE GRUNDSCHULE [1]

The establishment and development of the common school (*Einheitsschule*) contemplated in principle in Article 146 of the Federal Constitution have not been effected either by federal or state law up to the present time.  In anticipation of a federal law that should regulate all the questions involved there has already been created, by the law concerning the *Grundschule* [1] and abolition of the *Vorschule* of April 28, 1920, the four-year *Grundschule* as the common primary school for all children. According to this law the first four years of the elementary school are to be organized as the common preparatory school for all, on which the system of intermediate and higher education is to be built.

The same conditions apply to the *Grundschule* as are applied under the Constitution to the elementary school in general,— those entitled to education have the right under Article 146, Section 2, to demand denominational, mixed,[2] or non-sectarian schools; but—and this was the safeguarding clause adopted in the Constitution—the legal situation remains unchanged under

---

[1] It would seem preferable to retain the term *Grundschule* in order to avoid misunderstandings that may arise from a translation.  ''Foundation'' school, while a translation, does not adequately express the idea of the *Grundschule*, nor does the term ''common school,'' which is more nearly equivalent to the idea inherent in the term *Einheitsschule*.  The *Vorschule* was a preparatory school, paralleling the first four years of the elementary school but charging fees and in some cases introducing the elements of secondary subjects.  The chief objections to it were (1) that it was a class school, and (2) that its pupils were given the preference in admission to the secondary schools.

[2] *Simultanschule*, i.e., a school attended by children of different denominations, but given the religious instruction of their respective denominations by special teachers.

Article 174 until the issue of the Federal Education Law. The whole range of these problems, which belong to the most debated and most difficult problems in educational legislation, is to be solved by a special Federal Education Law. Such a proposal is at present before the Federal Parliament but hitherto no unanimity has been reached on the subject, and it appears to be questionable whether the present Parliament can find a solution for these difficulties. In Prussia this condition of suspense has had consequences that have caused the Ministry of Education serious difficulties. Publicly, in parent and teacher organizations, an appeal is made to the Constitution, which in Article 146 guarantees secular schools and in Article 149, Section 2, leaves the imparting of religious instruction to the wishes of the teachers and participation in religious subjects to the wishes of those who have the right to decide on the religious education of the child. Accordingly, a teacher who refuses to give religious instruction, and a pupil, if he is religiously of age, who himself declines to participate in it or is withdrawn from it by those who have the right to guide his education, cannot be compelled on the one hand to give or on the other hand to attend religious instruction. To this is added the fact that Article 148, Section 2, contains certain regulations under which in general instruction the convictions of opponents must be respected. Since, however, instruction other than religious instruction can affect the freedom of conscience according to the claims of all who represent such a point of view, they also demand separate instruction in these subjects as well and see in the prescription of Article 174 of the Constitution, which leaves the legal situation as it is until the promulgation of a Federal Education Law, an intolerable interference with the liberty of conscience guaranteed by the Constitution which owing to the intolerably unsettled conditions in Prussia led to a temporary solution three years ago in agreement with the Imperial Minister of the Interior. This solution aims to assemble such children as do not desire to participate in religious instruction in special classes without religion. These classes are to be taught by such teachers who on their side claim the right to be exempt from giving religious instruction under Article 149, Section 2. This solution of course cannot be said to be ideal; it is but a transition measure until some decision about a Federal Education Law is reached.

Although there are many whom it has not satisfied and in whom
it still arouses widespread antagonism, it has had its good points.
The friends of the denominational school have frequently declared that this settlement on the basis of an agreement to differ
has been welcomed by them and they completely accept the
solution that children who do not wish to participate in religious
instruction should also receive their instruction in other subjects
in separate classes.   This would furnish a guarantee that their
children would receive both their religious and general education
in denominational schools without running into the intolerable
obstacles of Article 148, Section 2, which requires that the convictions of dissenters must be respected.   Unless a decision is
soon reached on the Federal Education Law, this temporary
solution must be placed on an assured legal basis.   This can
only be effected by an emergency law which the Federal Parliament must necessarily pass quickly after repeated requests from
Prussia and which would put an end to the unpleasant conflict
which ever and again, now here, now there, starts a conflagration
like sparks from a fire.

In accordance with the law the four classes of the *Grundschule* do not constitute an independent school type.   They are,
while fully performing their own appropriate tasks, parts of an
eight-year elementary school.   At the same time, however, they
have to furnish the necessary preparation for direct entrance
into the middle and secondary schools.   For this reason the law
abolishes all public or private schools existing to give special
preparation for admission to middle and secondary schools—the
existing public preparatory schools (*Vorschulen*) to close immediately or gradually so that they disappear entirely not later
than by the beginning of 1924-25, the private preparatory schools
to close with the reservation that on account of economic distress
to those concerned or special local circumstances the final disappearance be postponed to the beginning of the school year
1929-30.   Private education for individual children or for the
children of several families in common must only be permitted
in special and exceptional cases to take the place of attendance
at the *Grundschule*.   The requirements of this law do not apply
to the education and instruction of children who are blind, deaf
and dumb, deaf, defective of speech, mentally defective, sickly,
morally defective, or crippled.

The Federal Ministry of the Interior on July 18, 1921, issued *Suggestions on the Aim and Organization of the Grundschule (Richtlinien über Zielbestimmung und Innere Gestaltung der Grundschule)*,[3] in which it was expressly stated that:

This separation of pupils in the *Grundschule* for the purpose of preparing particular groups of children for admission to the secondary schools must not be permitted. The completion of the *Grundschule* in less than four years would be contrary to Section 1 of the *Reichsgrundschulgesetz* and is also to be avoided for economic reasons. Admission to the middle or secondary school is without exception to be permitted only after the completion of compulsory attendance at the *Grundschule* for four years.

In conference with the Federal Ministry of the Interior it was frequently repeated that several states had already approved these *Suggestions* and that Prussia alone was dilatory. After some negotiations Prussia also gave her approval to the *Suggestions* of the Federal Ministry of the Interior of July 18, 1921.

It was frequently pointed out in public generally and in Parliament that Württemberg had adopted another system. Up to a certain point this is correct. In April, 1922, before approving the *Suggestions,* Württemberg had issued a regulation permitting some differentiation in the *Grundschule,* namely, the transfer of pupils to the middle and secondary schools after three years. Subsequently, however, Württemberg also accepted the *Suggestions,* so that the *Suggestions* issued by the Ministry of the Interior with the consent of all the states are binding on all the states, have been published in the Federal Gazette (*Reichsministerialblatt*), and have accordingly binding force on Prussia as well.

The task of putting the law of the *Grundschule* into operation accordingly fell on the Prussian Ministry of Science, Art, and Popular Education (*Ministerium für Wissenschaft, Kunst und Volksbildung*), which has frequently and emphatically declared that Prussia would recognize as its task and duty the loyal enforcement of the *Grundschule* law.

In answer to the attacks that have recently been repeated it must be stated that the Ministry has fulfilled its duty. First, the Circular of April 13, 1921, explained the *Reichsschulgesetz,* and issued detailed directions for the gradual closing of the

[3] See Part II.

preparatory schools, for making the arrangements for teachers in these schools, and for the private preparatory schools and classes and their teachers. This Circular was further supplemented by the Decree of May 9, 1922, in which it was provided that during the transition period up to the beginning of the school year 1924-25 admission to the middle and secondary schools should not be conditioned on the completion of four years in the *Grundschule,* but that after the beginning of the school year 1924-25 pupils should only be admitted to a middle or secondary school after four years of school attendance.

Since numerous violations of the law were noticed in the first two years, renewed conferences took place in the Federal Education Committee which resulted in a common agreement in all the states. In Prussia this agreement was incorporated in the Circular of March 31, 1923, in which the operation of the law of the *Grundschule* was further clarified on a number of doubtful points. The most important regulations of this Circular are here quoted verbatim:

1. The law of the *Grundschule* became effective on May 21, 1920—after the beginning of the school year 1920-21; its requirements are accordingly first to be applied to children who are of school age at the beginning of the school year 1921-22. Children who are of school age at Easter, 1921, and those who have attended private preparatory schools or classes must, therefore, become eligible for the first time for admission to a public or private middle or secondary school only on the completion of four years of compulsory attendance at a *Grundschule* that is, after Easter, 1925.

2. It is a breach of the Federal Law, under which four years of compulsory attendance at the *Grundschule* is established, to organize within the public *Grundschule* so-called accelerated classes or to make other arrangements aiming to facilitate the transfer of pupils to a higher or intermediate school at Easter, 1924, after three years of attendance only. Such arrangements are not to be permitted.

3. The same regulations, that they are not to be admitted to a secondary or middle school until the completion of four years following the commencement of the age of compulsory school attendance, apply also to children who receive their education under special arrangements,—groups, private instruction, family schools, etc.—attendance at which is permitted as an exception under Section 4 of the Law of the *Grundschule* in any place of attendance at the *Grundschule,* or who are in any other way handicapped in their school attend-

ance. It must again be pointed out that it is the duty of the school administrators to test accurately whether children are to be regarded as incapable of attending public schools.

4. Private preparatory schools have not only to adapt their curriculum to that of the *Grundschule* but also to establish special classes for the fourth year of compulsory attendance at the *Grundschule*. The Federal Law of the *Grundschule* does not define the number of pupils to be admitted to this class, but it must certainly not exceed the average in preparatory school classes.

Lively criticism, repeatedly expressed also in the discussions on the educational budget in the Prussian legislature, has been raised against the regulations of this decree as well as against the enforcement of the four-year compulsory attendance in the *Grundschule,* particularly among the parents, those whose children have hitherto attended the preparatory school, as well as among sections of the teachers, especially among the classicists. This criticism is based particularly on the claim that a deficiency would result from the abolition of the preparatory schools which must be carried out by Easter, 1924. Since the pupils who would be dismissed from these schools would first be admitted to the secondary schools in 1925, the entering classes in these institutions would be in the main left unfilled at Easter, 1924, and become overcrowded in the following year. A condition of low numbers in one year and overcrowding in the next, it is claimed not without justification, would become increasingly noticeable and be found undesirable in the secondary schools during the succeeding eight years until the graduation of these two classes. It is accordingly desired for 1924 that transitional provisions be adopted permitting gifted and mature children to enter the lowest class of the secondary institutions at Easter, 1924, after three preparatory years.

These proposals were adopted both by the Prussian Diet and by the Federal Parliament. Just as the resolution of the Prussian Diet of June 7, 1923, so the almost unanimous resolution of the Thirtieth Committee of the Federal Parliament of December 8, 1923, demanded transitional regulations in accordance with the decree. In parliamentary as well as in governmental circles it was clear that the carrying out of these resolutions must lead to a certain contradiction with the regulations of the *Grundschulgesetz* and the *Suggestions* of the Federal Ministry of the Interior of July 18, 1921.  On the other hand, it was not forgotten that the real question was to remove some technical gap in the organization of the *Grundschulgesetz*, which, to ignore, would put an end to the idea of the foundation school. After agreement with the Federal Ministry of the Interior the Prussian Ministry decided by its Decree [4] of December 28, 1923, that from the beginning of the school year 1924-25 specially gifted children who had reached the age of compulsory school attendance at Easter, 1921, should again be admitted to the lowest class of secondary and middle schools.  At the same time it was stated with full clearness and definiteness that this regulation "was an emergency measure for the single occasion without the possibility of repetition."

This, it must be strongly emphasized, seemed all the more necessary since the critics have continued to object against the strict enforcement of the four-year compulsory attendance at a *Grundschule* in general.  These objections are based partly on educational, partly on economic considerations: too long retention of the mature and gifted pupils in the *Grundschule*, the danger of retarding their mental development, the extension of the total period of education to thirteen years, a factor which in these difficult times would render it impossible for many parents, especially in the middle classes, to permit their children to complete the secondary school, and which might ultimately increase the danger of reducing the length of the course in the secondary schools from nine to eight years.  A modification of the law of the *Grundschule* is demanded with the aim of introducing differentiation on the basis of which gifted and mature pupils could be admitted to the secondary schools after three years in the *Grundschule*.

The counter-position is mainly of a constitutional character. Laws and political understandings, so long as they are in force and have not been modified, must conscientiously be enforced in accordance with their spirit.  Particularly does the greatest of the federal states have the duty of observing this principle when federal regulations are involved.  It must not set the other states a bad example in this connection, as would indeed be the case if Prussia made holes in the federal law of the *Grundschule*. The advocates of differentiation according to ability involving

⁴ *Erlass vom 28. 12. 1923—U II 1512.1.   Zentralblatt*, 1924, p. 10.

a reduction in the attendance at the *Grundschule* themselves admit that their proposals imply the return of the preparatory school in a disguised form. Instead of preparation that looks exclusively to transfer to the secondary schools after three years, and that is even more directed to the formal and abstract, the four-year *Grundschule*—and here we take up the genuine objection of educational theory—has quite a different aim. Its particular object, quite differently and with greater depth and comprehensiveness than were hitherto possible in the elementary school, is to provide an all-sided intellectual training by developing and maturing by means carefully adapted to the psychology of the pupils. Because of its increased demands for independent acquisition of the materials of instruction, this process can, only at the risk of injurious forcing, be compressed into the shorter period of but three years. Finally, not even the warmest friends of differentiation can dismiss the fact that social prejudices also militate against the common *Grundschule*. Of course, it cannot be denied that children from a comfortable home, rich in intellectual interests, come to the elementary schools with a better preparation, and that in many cases there is more effective coöperation with the educational task of the school. On the other hand, there may be listed the experiences from districts that rank high educationally, as for example Westphalia, where the preparatory school was unknown and was not missed, and where an appreciation was acquired of what it means in the training of succeeding generations for the service of the commonwealths to have all children attending the common public school.

It is also not without interest to compare the recent demands for a reduction of the attendance required at the *Grundschule*, with the position adopted by all parties in the National Assembly when the Federal Educational Law was discussed. All parties at that time declared themselves in favor of the four-year "social" *Grundschule* for all grades of our people; the representative of the most extreme right wing directed a request to his followers that they should try to appreciate the reasons for the introduction of such a school, a foundation school for all classes of society and to do all in their power to win the good will of all sections in the nation for these ideas.

If in wide sections of our German Fatherland, he continued, in the South Germany and in Saxony, as well as in Westphalia, the common public school has long replaced the preparatory school, then must we in other parts of the country make a new test to see to what extent it is possible to send one's own child to the common school, and thereby, even though many risks may be involved, at any rate fill him with a feeling of common, shared citizenship, which can be of great significance to our German people.

Everything has thus been done in Prussia to put the law of the *Grundschule* into operation. Still more significant are the provisions for the internal organization of the *Grundschule*. Above all, reference must be made to the Decree of March 16, 1921, which circulated the *Suggestions for the Making of Courses of Study for the Grundschule (Richtlinien zur Aufstellung von Lehrpläne für die Grundschule)*. These *Suggestions* now take the place of the corresponding regulations for the first four years in the *General Ordinance on the Organization, Purpose, and Aim of the Prussian Elementary School of October 15, 1872.*

The general introductory sentences are here quoted verbatim to indicate the spirit of these *Suggestions:*

The purpose of the *Grundschule* as the common school for all children in their first four school years is to give the pupils a training in fundamentals on which may be based and continued the instruction of the four succeeding years of the elementary, as well as of the middle and secondary schools. This school must, therefore, arouse and train all the intellectual and physical forces in the children and equip them with those skills and that knowledge which, as the foundation for every type of further education, constitute an indispensable requirement.

In all parts of the instruction in the *Grundschule,* the principle must be made effective that information and skills are not merely acquired from without, but that everything that children learn must be experienced within and be achieved independently. Hence all instruction must carefully foster the relations to the home environment of the children and be linked up with the intellectual attainments already acquired by them before entrance to the school, even to the extent of taking the peculiar dialect of the pupils into account. The self-activity of the pupils, in their play, in the observation of processes in nature and life, particularly during walks and excursions, in manual activities such as work in plasticene and clay, colored drawings, cutting-out, is to be utilized to its full extent for purposes of instruction.

The subjects of study in the *Grundschule* are religion, local information,[a] German, arithmetic, drawing, singing, gymnastics, and needlework for girls in the third and fourth years.

A strict distribution of subjects by specific periods is not prescribed for the instruction of beginners; instead, the work is rather to be integrated, the change from one subject to another being made without any compulsion. The core of the integrated instruction (*Gesamtunterricht*) is the observational work based on the pupils' environment, round which are incorporated the fundamental exercises in speech and reading, drawing in color, writing, arithmetic, and singing. The first conversations and lessons on religious and moral questions can also be introduced in the same connection. This vital integrated curriculum, which requires constant coöperation between teacher and pupils, should be made available for beginners in a school with few grades. Provided external circumstances such as the necessity of the young accompanying the other pupils to school, or part-time attendance, do not prevent it, the time-schedule must be so arranged that at least four hours a week are set aside for the newly admitted pupils during which the teacher devotes himself wholly to them without the presence of the other classes. During the first few weeks, the instruction of new pupils in such schools should definitely be limited to these hours, in so far as participation in physical games, work in drawing or similar occupations are not in question. The time over which this integrated instruction should be extended, the selection of material from the different subjects, and its distribution by classes or years are questions to be settled in the courses of study of each locality or district. In making out the courses, appropriate consideration must be given to the peculiar characteristics of the sexes, particularly to the needs of girls' education.

The selection of materials of instruction should, in the first place, be determined by the capacity and the psychological needs of the pupils, and, in the second, by their significance for life. Premature or excessive work, especially home lessons, must be strictly avoided. The amount of material to be employed will in each case have to be differentiated by the organization of the school. A fully graded school, with a class for each year, will contain a greater amount in the course of study and greater variety in each subject than the school with few grades which is compelled to combine the pupils of several or all years in one class. The objectives set up in the following suggestions must, however, be attained completely in all schools.

---

[a] *Heimatkunde*, literally "knowledge of the home," includes all the information that is available within the child's immediate environment.

It is obvious from these introductory statements, which are further corroborated by the detailed recommendations on the single subjects, that these *Suggestions* should be greeted as an important educational advance. This advance lies in the fact that the course of study is not prescribed in detail to each school or each teacher, but that only direction-signs are suggested, that a framework is recommended only to be filled up with a rich content through the work of each teacher. In this way, the teacher finds greater scope for freedom and independence and can give full play to his own peculiar gifts and those of the pupils. At the same time, the fullest facilities are afforded for the elaboration of courses of study adapted to the special needs of each school in a district or locality. From the earnest zeal of the teaching body and their lively ambition for further professional training, it should be expected that they will make a rightful use of this freedom and independence in the sense of joyful and responsible coöperation. The *Suggestions* are not the emanations of a bureaucracy, but have been conceived in closest sympathy with the everyday work of the school and with the coöperation of the teaching body itself, which was given an opportunity by the county authorities of passing an opinion on the first draft. It is thus well established that the fundamental principles of the *Suggestions* have met with approval.

The contribution of the *Suggestions* to the educational theory of the time has already been tested in the reforms of the whole teaching body. As is declared by their spiritual father, Oberregierungsrat Pretzel in *Theorie und Praxis der Arbeitsschule,* "they are not intended to go ahead and point the way of development, but rather to follow it. Nothing more can be said than that they should set up what the whole body or, at any rate, a large majority of the teachers have on the basis of experience and thought recognized as sound. They aim to place the official stamp on the results of the development that has taken place in recent years in the field of instruction, and to leave the door open to further development." Because this is their purpose, the *Suggestions* are in no sense *directions (Bestimmungen)*; they mention no penalties; they do not lay down fixed immovable barriers; they only point the way. Hence it is not surprising that such phrases as "so far as practical," "so far as possible," "in the main," and so on frequently occur. It would be a serious misconception to regard this as a sign of weakness or vacillation, as has been done by some critics.

Freedom and variety, these are the two words that best express the most important principle of the *Suggestions*. So far as the other educational principles on which they are based and by which they were inspired are concerned, in the selection of materials of instruction emphasis is specially placed on this, that the determining forces are the right of the child, his intelligence, and the psychological stage of his development. In this way, the *Suggestions* have hit upon a sound principle for the *Grundschule* and have provided a sound basis for every kind of further education. Side by side with this, special notice must be given to the strong emphasis on the home and local environment as a principle of instruction which is urged throughout the *Suggestions*. Finally, reference must be made to the serious attention given in the *Suggestions* to the sound idea of the "activity principle" (*Arbeitsunterricht*) as a method of instruction in contrast to the practice of earlier days, which, perhaps, with some exaggeration, has been criticized as a bookish method (*Lernschule*). The "activity principle" implies a practice by which the pupils under the guidance of the teacher acquire the observations, ideas, knowledge, and skills in the materials of instruction by their own activity. This method is to a great degree calculated to impart joy in study, to develop the intellectual powers, to stimulate the emotions, and to strengthen character, while in manual work it trains the muscular sense and technical ability of the pupil.

It is unnecessary to enter into any details here on the recommendation on each subject or on the time-schedule; it should, however, be mentioned that by the Decree of March 16, 1921, the number of hours prescribed for religious instruction is not the same for Protestant as for Catholic children. This led to very great unrest in many sections of the Protestant population and gave rise to questions in the Prussian Parliament; considerable difficulties have also arisen in schools attended by children of both denominations. Since in other ways it was also shown that the total number of hours for Catholic pupils was too high in the second, third, and fourth years, the decree was modified by the Circular of January 18, 1923, by which the number of periods for religious instruction was made the same for both denominations, namely, three hours a week in the first year, and four hours in the second, third, and fourth years.

With the publication of the *Suggestions* for the *Grundschule*, a significant step in the inner organization of the common foundation of the common school has been taken. Now it is necessary to allow the *Grundschule*, which has only just begun to develop and realize itself, to work without interference and to watch the operation and results of its method of instruction and practice. Not until then will a sound basis have been found for deciding the question of the duration of the course in the *Grundschule*. A four-year course in the *Grundschule* following the new *Suggestions* is something essentially different from the first four years of the public elementary school; hence, the objections to the four-year course in the *Grundschule* have so far only a theoretical basis. It would have been more to the point to raise these objections before the law of the *Grundschule* was passed in the Federal Parliament. Now it can only be earnestly wished that the four-year *Grundschule* should first be worked out. Without this practical experiment, a final verdict cannot be reached. From the teachers of the *Grundschule* it will be expected that by loyal work in the spirit of the *Suggestions* and by their skillful instruction the four-year *Grundschule* will be able to meet the criticism of parents and the demands of the middle and secondary schools for which it serves as a foundation.

## II.   THE UPPER GRADES OF THE ELEMENTARY SCHOOL

According to the Constitution, all other types of schools are organically built up on the *Grundschule*, the common foundation of the whole of our common school system. The immediate and direct continuation of the *Grundschule* is the elementary school proper or, since the *Grundschule* is also to be regarded as a general elementary school, the upper grades of the elementary school. These include pupils from ten to fourteen, and constitute the closing school period for all children who at the end of their fourteenth year enter vocational life and continue their further education in general only in the vocational continuation schools. Even in the most critical days of the agitation for reforms, no serious objection was raised against this organization of the elementary school. This institution is to remain what it has been hitherto and what it has in particular become in the last decade—the most important school in our whole educational system for giving a foundation in knowledge and skill, and serving as the decisive educational influence for the great majority of our people. About ninety per cent of our German people pass through the elementary school only. Even if the varied opportunities offered in the organization of the common school reduce this percentage somewhat in the future, the elementary school will still continue to be the school of our people to which the state must devote attention commensurate with its importance.

Two demands present themselves here. First, it is essential that adequate external provisions be made for its responsible task of instruction and education. Under all circumstances by modern and sanitary arrangement and equipment, the suspicion must be removed that our elementary schools are schools for the poor. For the ninety per cent of the children of the people, air and light, a friendly, cheerful, and artistically furnished school must be demanded insistently. For the elementary schools are not only the centers for serious work, but also a place for joy. Shining eyes should receive impressions of beauty and freedom which, with a contented spirit, become a blessing through life.

Successful work in the elementary school is, however, jeopardized if the size of classes is too large. With classes of sixty, seventy, eighty and more pupils, which according to the figures published by the Prussian Statistical Bureau are still to be found in Prussia,[6] the task of teaching and education means torture not for the teachers alone. With the best will and ability, the teacher cannot produce the necessary results. This situation presents serious problems to both state and communities. The sad economic situation and the financial distress are heaping up insurmountable obstacles to their early solution, and the realization of many hopes must be postponed to a distant future. But even in these hard times, neither the state nor the communities should relax their care for better external equipment of the elementary school. It should be stated that in spite of the serious lack of funds the Prussian state and to no less a degree the equally poverty-stricken communities have been conscious of this duty and have raised considerable sums for the purpose

---

[6] *Preussisches Statistiches Landesamt, Statistik des preussischen Schulwesens* (as of November 25, 1821), in *Das Schulwesen in Preussen* (Berlin, 1924).

under discussion. Reference need only be made to the Decrees of May 24 [7] and September 16, 1922 [8], on the abolition of over-crowded schools and classes, and to the considerable increase in funds which have been provided in the latest budget as grants in aid to necessitous school districts for school buildings and the creation of new teaching positions. As long as Prussia still has resources, the most serious attention must be devoted to this charge.

A subject of special concern to the Prussian administrative authorities has for a long time been the better equipment of the elementary schools with materials of observation and apparatus suited to the needs of modern instruction. Here, too, we are confronted with an almost insoluble problem, and it is incumbent on us to be modest in our requirements and to limit ourselves for the time being to meeting the most urgent demands. Even this measure will only be made possible through all kinds of makeshifts for the preparation and elaboration of which an important and satisfying share falls to the initiative and coöperation of the teaching body. The support of parents and considerable assistance from publishers are also essential. Hints and suggestions for such makeshifts have been issued by the Ministry of Science, Art, and Popular Education in numerous decrees, which were collected in the Decree of June 25, 1924,[9] on *Teaching Apparatus in Elementary Schools.* The *General Regulation on the Organization, Scope and Aim of the Prussian Elementary School,* of October 15, 1872,[10] contains a list of the essential and desirable apparatus for this type of school. This list is considerably extended in the Decree of June 25, 1924, already mentioned, to correspond to the remarkable progress in the manufacture of teaching apparatus and the increased demand for instruction purposes. At the same time, the difficult question of cost is discussed in detail. The decree provides that in those school districts in which the necessary teaching apparatus is not yet fully provided, a plan be devised for their supply over a series of years. The decree, following the idea of instruction through activity, also points out that the coöperative work of

[7] *Erlass vom 24. 5. 1922—U III E 4384. Zentralblatt,* p. 278.
[8] *Erlass vom 16. 9. 1922—U III E 4383 II. Zentralblatt,* p. 431.
[9] *Erlass vom 25. 6. 1924—U III 13129. Zentralblatt,* p. 202.
[10] *Erlass vom 15. 10. 1872—B 2311. Zentralblatt,* p. 585.

teachers and pupils be enlisted as far as possible for the maintenance, repair, and often the manufacture of apparatus. Finally,
those districts in which there is need are encouraged to set up
advisory councils for the purchase and supply of equipment.

Important as the external equipment of the elementary school
is, its internal development, that is, the best possible organization on the educational side, is of infinitely greater importance.
Here the results of research and the progress in the principles
of elementary education must be considered, since in the last
few years and decades they have made contributions of extraordinary value through the enthusiastic coöperation of the elementary school teachers. This progress it is essential to incorporate in the course of study and methods of instruction of the
elementary school, and here in recent times a very significant
progressive step has been taken.

On October 15, 1922, the *Suggestions for the Organization of
Courses of Study for the Four Upper Years of the Elementary
School* [11] were published and made the basis for the future work
of the elementary school. This decree appeared on the fiftieth
anniversary of those *General Regulations* of Minister Falk
which were greeted by the teaching body as a most progressive
measure and which did in fact later become epoch-making for
the development of the elementary school. But they, too, have
had their day. Under them the teacher made a valuable contribution to education and instruction in the past fifty years.
This very contribution, however, made in the intervening period
in the classroom, in the psychological laboratories, and in speech
and writing, went beyond those *Regulations,* which have proved
themselves in many parts outworn, and stimulated a demand
for a reform.

The *Suggestions for the Four Upper Years of the Elementary
School* are the direct continuation of the *Suggestions for the
Making of Courses of Study for the Grundschule,* and are based
essentially on the same educational principles and views that
were adopted there. This will be recognized from the introductory section which deals with the general principles, and which is
here quoted verbatim:

[11] *Erlass vom 15. 10. 1922—U III A 2060. Zentralblatt,* 1923, p. 171.

The four upper years of the elementary school constitute the closing school period for those children who on the conclusion of the compulsory attendance period will enter vocational life and continue their further education mainly in vocational schools. It follows, therefore, that the courses of study must take greater cognizance than the *Grundschule* of the needs of life. Here, too, however, the educational needs of the pupils' age-range and the task of constantly and continuously promoting the general development of the pupils, particularly on the side of the emotions and will, must be decisive. The further task of the upper classes of the elementary school, of giving the necessary training to enable particularly gifted pupils to pass into the *Aufbauschule*, does not conflict with the acceptance of this point of view.

Just as in the *Grundschule*, so in the upper grades, instruction must be based on the self-activity, both intellectual and physical, of the pupils. The coöperation of the pupils should not, in the main, consist in the absorption of the curriculum-content, but the results of instruction are to be acquired under the guidance of the teachers by means of observation, experiment, judgment, research, and independent reading.

The manual activity of the pupils should be utilized as extensively as possible. Opportunities for this are offered by the preparation of plans, drawing, teaching and study apparatus (particularly for geometry, geography, and nature study), the arrangement of collections, the devising of experiments in the field of nature study, the care of animals in the terrarium, aquarium, insectarium, the care of flowers and gardening, as well as instruction in needlework and domestic science.

Books, too, must be extensively resorted to by the pupils as sources of information. To this end only such books are appropriate as give a living treatment of their subjects with illustrations and detail. Works of this kind should be provided in school libraries which are, therefore, essential for all schools, and especially for the small ones with few classes.

School excursions, instituted primarily to promote physical training, furnish opportunity for observing the life of plants and animals, the soil and climate, phenomena in the sky, conditions of communication and industry, as well as practice in estimating distances and in simple graphical representation (sketching). By these means they contribute to the extension of intellectual training. Shorter walks undertaken for special teaching objectives, visits to agricultural and industrial plants may be arranged in addition as need arises.

The subjects of instruction are religion (or moral instruction[11] as

---

[11] *Lebenskunde*, literally ''life information,'' is here translated as ''moral instruction''; it is the subject that may be substituted for those who claim exemption from religious instruction.

the case may be), German, history and civics, geography, nature study, arithmetic, drawing, singing, gymnastics, and needlework for girls: in addition, if the necessary equipment is available, manual work for boys, and domestic science for girls.

The *Suggestions* offered herewith indicate and define in general the content to be covered. Selection and distribution in detail are matters for the courses of study which are to be drafted for each school and in the arrangement of which the principle of local needs must be observed. The amount of material to be selected varies with the type of school, but in all schools great care must be taken that the content included in the course of study is not dealt with superficially, but offers scope for genuine intellectual activity. Schools with few classes will, in order to be able to provide a richer selection of content, make use in their arrangement of courses alternating by years.

The objectives of each subject of the curriculum determine the direction of the work even in the *Grundschule,* the general purposes of which compel it to lay a foundation for every type of education that is to follow.

The general aim underlying these *Suggestions* is not, therefore, to develop new ideas, to propose new aims, and through official regulations to point out new methods of instruction, but rather to follow intelligently the progressive movement and development of ideas which are elaborated and tested in the school by the teachers themselves.

The new official regulations are not speculations of a bold reformer, nor do they have the character of compulsory requirements; they are the results of the methodical work of the teaching body in the last decades and accordingly only constitute the collection and cumulation of their own educational activity. The supreme guiding principle of education is thus "Freedom and Variety," by which not only the further organization of the courses of study is again left to the activity of the teaching personnel, but their appropriate expansion is made possible and actually suggested. There is no standard course of study for Tilsit and Trier, for Flensburg and Beuthen, or one that can be suitable for schools with one, two, three, or more classes. Every district, even every school will and should work according to a course that is made by the teachers themselves and takes into consideration the character and conditions peculiar to this school; and further within the school itself each teacher should enjoy freedom. The course of study should only define general objectives for him instead of binding him down to tasks by the week or month, to be followed slavishly. But this great idea of freedom, which waves like a banner over these *Suggestions*, should not only imply release from compulsion, but responsibility as well. It should not lead to a confusion between freedom and license or lower the intellectual level of work in the school. Rather should it lead to the expectation of the highest of joyful, responsible, and loyal activity from the teachers upon whom falls the task of giving content, life and reality to the *Suggestions* in each course of study.

The guiding principle for the selection and arrangement of the content is the "development and training of the mental and physical powers of the pupils"; in other words, as in the *Suggestions* for the *Grundschule*, the educational need of the child itself is the determining factor. Adopting the principle, "make the child the starting point," the *Suggestions* are not only in accord with the demands of modern psychology, but on the side of method they also indicate the correct way for the teacher's work, which permits and insists that the character of the individual child be considered more than hitherto. Since the pupils of the elementary school must enter life and then receive no further formal education beyond the excellent vocational training in the continuation school, it is essential that these principles be supplemented more carefully than in the *Grundschule* by meeting the demands of practical, and particularly, of political life.

Further, the environmental principle, the close association of all the work of the school with the world of the home and life about the home, indicates the correct method of selecting and handling subject matter. The child has his roots in the home environment; accordingly, the school also derives its greatest strength from this source and must associate the task of education and instruction as closely as possible with the home. The factor of home information should above all be utilized in teaching geography, history, nature study, and German, with strong emphasis on dialect and customs; but it can and should be made more fruitful than before in all other subjects of instruction.

Finally, these *Suggestions* should be considered in relation to the idea of the activity school. Active coöperation of the pupils in attaining the results of instruction, and in the unfolding and development of the individual powers of each is here the matter for consideration. Hence the pupil should not merely learn, but he should be trained how to study by himself, and thereby acquire the most valuable foundation and most effective stimulus in life to further independent study later. Naturally this applies equally to manual training and skills.

Nothing more could be attempted here than through an emphasis on the guiding principles to indicate the spirit in which the *Suggestions* have been drafted and in which tasks planned by them should be carried out. Reference may be made only to two points. The *Suggestions* are written wholly with the eight-grade elementary school as the internal organization in view. There is naturally no implication here that such an organization is preferable to some other Prussian elementary schools or that it is to be borne in mind at all, yet it is of the greatest importance that the educational and cultural ideal of an eight-grade system should apply equally to the school with one class as to the school with many classes. The same task is set before all types of schools, irrespective of the number of classes—''Deepening of popular culture, increased and vital participation of all grades of the people in the activities of the community and of the state.'' This task can of course only be accomplished if the teachers find real pleasure in carrying out the aim of the *Suggestions.* May the same progress be made from this point on as from the days of the *Regulations* (October 3, 1854) through the *General Regulations* (October 15, 1872), to the *Suggestions* (October 15, 1922).[13]

In conclusion one important supplement to the *Suggestions* of October 15, 1922, should be mentioned. It is found in the Decree of May, 1923, on the *Organization and Use of the Reader.*[14] The modification and extension of the principles still in force under the Decree of February 28, 1902,[15] were necessitated by the changed economic, social and political conditions of the present and the progress in the methods of teaching German. This decree is in every way in harmony with the spirit of the *Suggestions;* here, too, only what has already been achieved is adopted. After recalling the principles laid down

[13] For the time-schedule of the Elementary School, see Part II.
[14] *Erlass vom 24. 5. 1923—U III A 19.1. Zentralblatt,* p. 257.
[15] *Erlass vom 28. 2. 1902—U III A 3165. Zentralblatt,* p. 326.

in the Decree of February 28, 1902, it emphasizes decisively that the reader must above all serve the purpose of literary and esthetic training and that it will in this way accomplish the moral educative aim which permeates it as well as instruction in general.  Hence the requirement in the decree that the reader contain only matter of literary value instead of fragments that with their manifold variety confuse the youthful heads and fail to develop pleasure in suitable German literature.  Behind the requirements of this decree there stands out clear and well defined the common-sense educational principle, which has at times been allowed to be forgotten, that the reader, considered in relation to education in general, is not an end in itself but should in the main prepare the way of the young to German literature.  From this there naturally follows the further requirement of the decree that the reader should be supplemented by a complete work and that in the upper grades of the elementary school a complete work may be substituted for the reader.

In this way the supremacy of the reader is restricted and free scope is given for works of literary value; on the other hand, there is avoided, to the disappointment of reformers who would go further, the complete abandonment of the reader, on which higher literary demands are to be made in the future.  A sound compromise between the old that has survived and the new that is full of promise may thus have been made.

Within the *Grundschule* and the elementary schools special auxiliary arrangements are necessary to make better provision than is possible in the ordinary school for pupils of low ability, for normal pupils retarded on account of sickness or other reasons, and for pupils defective in hearing or speech.  On this point the independent auxiliary elementary schools for physically or mentally abnormal pupils should be mentioned in particular.  In this field, too, the administrative authorities have taken over a rich inheritance from pre-War days.  The years immediately preceding the War saw a brilliant development in the system of auxiliary schools.  New schools of this type sprang up in many school districts; by the provision of courses for training teachers of auxiliary schools and through the examina-

tion regulations of October 1, 1913,[16] the foundation was laid
for the fruitful development of these institutions. The War
brought this development to a standstill, and the succeeding
economic distress imposed many restrictions on the lively interest of communities and the state in this field as well. Still, in
recent years there were numerous indications of new progress.
The auxiliary schools profited considerably from the newly
awakened life in all branches of educational activity; especially
significant was the revival, facilitated by the appropriation of
state funds, of courses for auxiliary teachers, the attendance at
which showed a gratifying increase. It was in conformity with
the high appreciation always shown by the Ministry for auxiliary
schools that in the Decree of March 1, 1924,[17] for the reduction
of personnel urged on educational authorities concerned the
duty of showing special consideration for auxiliary schools, and
requested them to undertake restrictions in this field only if
they could be imposed without endangering the real value of
existing arrangements. These recommendations, so far as can
be seen, were everywhere taken into consideration. According
to the *Statistics of the Prussian School System* already mentioned, there were on November 25, 1921, in the whole of Prussia
441 auxiliary schools with 41,592 pupils (76 percent of the total)
and 2126 teachers. It is to be hoped that, when the still
prevailing economic difficulties are overcome, these institutions,
of such remarkable value from the educational as well as social
point of view, will continue their gratifying development.

Just as the auxiliary schools, the independent institutions for
work with abnormal pupils, so the special arrangements provided
in the regular elementary schools for pupils of low ability and
for specially gifted pupils are of great value. To these must be
added, although still limited in number, the courses and classes
for speech defects. In all these fields there are promises of
satisfactory development. Unfortunately almost everything must
for the present be left to the initiative and ability of the large
towns and communities, in which alone the question of providing these and similar arrangements arises. The same applies
to kindergartens for pupils of the pre-school age, to open-air
schools, and other special schools associated with the elementary

[16] *Erlass vom 1. 10. 1913—U III A 1295. Zentralblatt*, p. 799.
[17] *Erlass vom 1. 3. 1924—U III E 4393.1. Zentralblatt*, p. 81.

schools, which have assumed greater significance at the present time for the maintenance of our national vigor and for the special educational problems affecting those whose health is impaired.  The state must unfortunately, for the time being, limit itself here, too, to giving encouragement and, so far as possible, providing financial assistance.

### III.  THE MIDDLE SCHOOL

The middle school was in the days of the Revolution and is still, perhaps, the most vigorously contested point in the general organization of the common school.  The fight for the complete elimination of the middle school was conducted by a large section of the elementary school teachers themselves.  Just as the *Vorschule* was attacked as a class institution, and its abandonment demanded for social reasons, so attacks were made also on the middle school.  It was charged that it attracted a large number of able pupils and teachers with which a good elementary school could not dispense, and, above all, that its existence was adequate proof that the state had neither recognized nor performed its duty to the elementary school.  The demand was made at the time and is still repeated to-day with much insistence that the upper classes of the elementary school should be raised to the level of the middle school and that accelerated classes be established as need arises for gifted pupils in the last classes.  Even those who have recognized the general standard of the middle school as necessary for the large masses of the people, demand that the middle school should not be retained as a special type of institution, but should be established parallel with the elementary school, open to specially gifted pupils who have already distinguished themselves by outstanding work in the *Grundschule*.

However justifiable the demand for raising the standards of popular education is,—the *Suggestions* of October 15, 1922, show indeed to what extent the Ministry of Education has realized these ideas,—the demand for the abolition of the middle school is on the other hand wrong, for its position and significance in the general scheme of the common school is only too often misunderstood.  That the independent middle school is essential and warranted is obvious without further discussion from the variety of the requirements of modern life.  The need of meeting these is not yet one that can be discussed. Whoever holds that the purpose of the common school does not lie merely in establishing uniformity, but in the possibility of providing for diverse abilities, will recognize the need as well as he who refuses to leave the assignment of pupils to a particular school type wholly in the hands of the teacher but insists immediately on the deciding voice of parents in the schooling of their children.

What was the origin of the middle school? The development of manual work, art industry, commerce and manufacture has required in the last decade better training of boys and girls for these vocations. At the same time, with the development of the whole system of state and local administrative machinery, there began to make itself felt the need of more appropriate preparation for intermediate positions in these services. However well organized, the elementary school, on account of many difficulties under which it continues to labor as a general compulsory school, could only meet these needs to a small extent. In the higher schools the aims are predominantly academic training, so that these institutions also were not in a position to maintain an adequate supply of trained candidates for these positions. Hence arose the necessity of more deliberately creating a type of school between the elementary and the secondary, which on the one hand would give a training beyond the level of the elementary school, however well developed, but on the other would definitely be distinguished from the secondary schools in the selection and treatment of the curriculum by adapting instruction to the needs of practical careers. This end is served by the middle school which was already established as a special type of school by the *General Regulations* of 1872.[18] By the Decree of February 3, 1910,[19] the school was further developed and was given a course of study excellent on account of its flexibility and adaptability. This is still the basis of its work and enables it to meet in quite an exceptional way the educational needs of the middle classes. The maintenance of this middle school is perhaps more than ever in the interest of the survival of the middle classes which, because of the disappearance of the one-year military privilege, should show a greater preference for educating their children in this school.

[18] *Erlass vom 5. 10. 1872—B 2312. Zentralblatt*, p. 598.
[19] *Erlass vom 3. 2. 1910—U III C 170. Zentralblatt*, p. 343.

The middle school, whether for boys or for girls, is thus side by side with the elementary school the first extension upwards of the four-year *Grundschule*. It graduates its pupils in a six-year course and best fulfills its position between the elementary and secondary school if it abstains from too zealous identification and resemblance to the academic character of the secondary school, while placing great emphasis in the upper classes on preparation for practical careers, and then branches out into differentiated courses according to the requirements of different localities and vocational types. In the industrial towns the emphasis will fall on technical training; in commercial towns on commercial training; in small towns with an agricultural environment, these needs will be taken into consideration. For the rest the middle school, because of the elasticity of the course of study, can be adapted to the direction suggested by the bent of the pupils, the vocational prospects, and the local needs. The training in one foreign language is limited to the one objective— the practical mastery of the language in speech and especially for correspondence with reference to the requirements of the different vocations.

One unconditional demand is made from these institutions, that they have a final examination which insures for them that position which they undoubtedly deserve in the confidence of the parents and the public at large. This question is being carefully considered in connection with the discussions that are now taking place on the "intermediate certificate" (*mittlere Reife*). It is to be hoped that the negotiations that are being conducted between the states under federal direction will shortly be brought to an end.

The transition from these middle schools will be most appropriately made to the intermediate and higher professional schools. That provision is made for the possibility of transferring all pupils whose ability and bent demand the continuation of their training in a secondary school, follows naturally from its position in the common school system.

To meet the views which regard the middle school as alien to the continuity of the common school and against the attempts to abolish it under any circumstances, it must again be insisted that the standards of the elementary school are not so high nor can they be raised to such a level as to be in a position to perform the function of the middle school. This does not exclude the possibility in smaller towns, where an independent middle school cannot be provided, of adding so-called advanced classes which in these places can undertake a part of the work of the middle school. It would, however, be a retrograde step, fraught with danger, to abolish everywhere the flourishing middle schools which besides enjoy the special esteem of the parents concerned, and to assign to the elementary school tasks which it is not in a position to perform, partly because of its general purpose and present status.

More recently the further expansion of the middle school beyond its present scope, particularly with reference to its relations with technical and intermediate professional schools, has been professed, and frequent requests have been made that the Ministry should issue courses of study and suggestions. This question is now being discussed, but a reform on a large scale is not required on this point. What is needed now is a modification of the course of study. This work is now being done and includes adaptation to the course of study of the *Grundschule*, still stricter application to practical requirements, and raising of the standards, so that the greater maturity thus attained by the middle school pupils will secure the "intermediate certificate" for them on graduation.[20]

To the middle school as understood by the law of June 11, 1894,[21] belong also the so-called *Rektoratschulen* (*Lateinschulen, Bürgerschulen,* etc.). These are in the main feeders for secondary schools and enjoy great popularity in different parts of the country. Their aim is chiefly to prepare pupils of the social classes under consideration to pass without considerable loss of time into higher schools, while continuing to enjoy the training and care of their homes as long as possible. From the educational, economic, and social point of view, they are accordingly of great significance. Where, however, their work completely follows that of the higher schools, they serve the actual needs of the real middle classes only in a limited way. The middle school can perform this function better. It would accordingly

---

[20] For time-schedules of the different middle schools, see Part II. These are the schedules adopted in 1910, *Erlass vom 3. Feb., 1910—U III C 170. Zentralblatt,* p. 343. The new schedules are not yet quite completed.

[21] *Gesetz vom 11. 6. 1894. Preussische Gesetzesammlung,* p. 109.

be desirable if such schools provided the necessary educational facilities for wider sections of the population by adopting the plans of the middle school.   In the interests of efficiency the Ministry must direct its particular attention to this question in the near future.

# CHAPTER IV

## PREPARATION OF TEACHERS

On the question of teacher preparation a decisive step was taken on October 7, 1924, when the Prussian Ministry of State at the request of the Ministry of Education resolved that elementary school teachers should for the future receive their general academic training in secondary schools up to the period of graduation. Thus has been solved for Prussia the most important point in one of the great educational problems of the German people which has exercised governments and parliaments of the Republic and the states for the last six years and filled those who are interested in education with anxiety. No matter now how the professional preparation that follows the general academic training may be organized in detail, the important question whether teacher preparation is to be given within the confined limits of a special professional school and thus to be isolated to its detriment from the broad stream of German culture, is settled for Prussia by this significant ministerial resolution and this decision will exercise a compelling influence on the organization of the professional side of teacher preparation.

The charges that have been brought for years against Prussia on this question are well known. Prussia, as the "leading state," has been assigned a special mission on the question of preparation of teachers and has appeared extraordinarily "reactionary" to many people because she adopted a waiting policy. But sane judgment must recognize it as a service on Prussia's part that, although she is the largest part of the Republic, she refrained from opposing a uniform regulation of teacher preparation in Germany under constitutional, and therefore federal-wide, provisions, so long as a possibility of such regulation existed and the interests of her own school system still permitted such delay. The position of the Prussian government was so much the more justified because the appropriate federal department, after some hesitation, due to the extraordinary difficulties of the question, repeatedly endeavored to regulate teacher preparation by federal law.  The final result was frankly the further disagreement on the part of the states in dealing with the question; Saxony and Thuringia have already decided on separate action and the Federal Cabinet on account of serious reasons of domestic and foreign politics has been compelled ''for the time being'' to give up a regulation of the question by federal law.  The Federal Government finally adopted a definite position in the Third Tax Ordinance of February 14, 1924, [1] when it was decided that school and educational questions be left to the states for independent regulation and action.  Shortly after the Prussian education authority submitted its proposals for the reorganization of teacher preparation in Prussia to the Ministry of State and at the conclusion of the necessary discussion by the government the resolution of October 7, 1924, already mentioned, was adopted.  A decision on the professional preparation of teachers was still postponed, but it was and still is clear that a solution must be found in the near future.  The speedy settlement of such a far-reaching problem was naturally only possible because the ultimate refusal to regulate teacher preparation by federal law had always to be reckoned with.

Prussia was thus restrained for a long time by considerations of the constitutional authority of the Republic; only on one point was she compelled to take independent action and that was on the question of closing the preparatory institutions (*Präparandenanstalten*).  The tremendous oversupply of candidates for whom there would be no positions or occupations prohibited a constant increase of unemployed teachers, by admitting students to the preparatory institutions.  Once these institutions were closed their reopening could no longer be considered, even if the supply of teachers had permitted the admission of new candidates for training.  On this question there was unanimity in the Prussian government and among all educators that the system of preparatory training must be abandoned once and for all, no matter what system of teaching preparation might be adopted.  Accordingly the closing of state preparatory institutions was decided upon by the Decree of April 26, 1921, [2] and

---

[1] *Reichsgesetzblatt*, p. 74, paragraph 42.
[2] *Erlass vom 26. 4. 1921—U III 6576.*

of preparatory institutions attached to normal schools by the Decree of March 22, 1922. [3] But without the preparatory institutions the normal schools were left without a foundation, so that the disappearance of the normal schools as such will become inevitable, even though a new system of teacher preparation were not yet established. The result of all these measures is that in 1926 the last of the normal school students will be graduated, while new candidates for positions, and these only in limited numbers, cannot be given employment until 1928. It is not impossible that the question of supply may cause certain difficulties for some years, however great the present oversupply may be; but it has been and still is unanimously agreed that the preparatory institutions could not in 1920 be continued further without change, and that in 1922 and 1923 new preparatory classes or entering classes in the six-year normal schools could not be established. The difficulties of supply can be overcome; widesweeping and significant changes in organization are never undertaken without transitional disturbances and limitations.

The organization of the professional side of teacher-preparation still awaits official decision. The plans of the educational authority on this subject are in general known; it looks for a two-year training in special pedagogical institutes on a university level. The duration of this course may at first sight seem open to criticism, but it must not be forgotten that only a professional training is under consideration, and not academic preparation of the kind obtained in the universities by secondary school teachers. A two-year professional course for teachers means almost a doubling of the time hitherto devoted to professional subjects in the normal schools. Further, these two years will be continued and completed by a carefully regulated training of young teachers in service during their "temporary appointments."

The future preparation of teachers thus represents a significant improvement over former conditions if considered from the point of view of time alone. The two years' training will naturally require a strictly planned course of studies. But there is no reason for complaint. Not only for professional ends but also for the intellectual training of young teachers is it not far

[3] *Erlass vom 22. 3. 1922—U III 710.*

better that the necessary and essential professional equipment of the young teacher be pursued with complete devotion and thoroughness instead of distracting the intellectual powers and interests over a wide range of subjects? Free, independent work in fields specially adapted to the needs and abilities of the individual is not restricted by such compulsory requirements but is in fact facilitated. The education authority will, of course, do everything in its power to encourage young students to work freely on subjects of their choice. The two-year course in itself implies abandonment of university training, for a two-year university course is a contradiction in terms; in addition, there enter other limitations which are almost insuperable. A teacher-preparation course which covers about ten subjects and which must prepare about five thousand candidates annually has no place in our universities. Reference has been made to the large number of higher institutions of learning; but the pedagogical institutes cannot be combined with agricultural, veterinary, commercial, and art institutions.

The universities themselves, indeed, take up a different position on the question of assuming the task of preparing teachers, but are unanimously of the opinion that they must not undertake the theoretical and practical training in methods of teaching the individual subjects. Training in special methods is, however, a very essential part in the preparation of teachers. It is true that they have been considered as part of the "Introduction to Professional Practice" and have accordingly been assigned to "Practical Institutes"; this is but an attempt to safeguard the principle that the academic side of training should be given by the universities. The theory of special subjects is, however, equally a science like "General Pedagogy," and if this subject, adapted to the many subjects of the elementary school and to thousands of candidates for elementary school service, is not taught in the universities, it becomes clear that the universities could not undertake completely the theoretical preparation of teachers.

If for a number of reasons the preparation of teachers must accordingly be given in pedagogical institutes, isolation can undoubtedly be seen in the plan. The Ministry is charged with being responsible for this new "training in isolation," and reference is made to the Federal Constitution which in Article

143, Section 2, provides that the preparation of teachers should be regulated on the principles "that apply to higher education in general." It is, however, obvious from the nature of the case that a form of training whose content and aim are wholly determined by professional interests must be distinguished from courses for other professions. Secondary school teachers also receive their professional preparation, not in universities, but in secondary schools. If the charge of training in isolation was brought against the system of teacher-preparation that hitherto prevailed, it was justified on the ground that separation for vocational purposes began too early. One objection at any rate should not be brought against the preparation of teachers in universities, and that is that the academic training of teachers should not be placed on the same level either in character or in standard as the work pursued in the university, that here, as it were, there should be a lowering of the requirements, because other aims in teacher preparation are more important. But the Ministry is firmly convinced that any system of teacher preparation is wrong which fails to develop strong personalities in teachers, and further that every educational effort remains in the last analysis futile which does not include every part of the aim of education, which fails to realize every educational value, including those that are outside of and lie beyond the intellect. From this starting-point, very significant suggestions will be issued for the inner life and general organization of pedagogical institutes. Both of these must be strong and sound, promoted and cultivated by men and women whose whole lives are rooted in work with the young, who know and live the life of the elementary school, who have the finest appreciation of its finest needs, who enter on their task with love and reverence. With this as the aim of the Prussian education authority, there can then be no doubt that if the academic training of the teachers is not thoroughly grounded, if the new institutions should cultivate perhaps a false, superficial type of intellectualism, then it would be better to leave the reform of teacher preparation alone. It is obvious that pedagogical "intellectualism" must be overcome; but it was the lack of academic knowledge that permitted this intellectualism to dominate, and it is academic scholarship that points to the decisive significance of the teacher's personality for success in the task of education, and, on the other hand, indicates the interdependence of all educational aims and values. Hence the training of the pedagogical institutes should be organized with these interconnections as a starting-point. The theoretical training of the young teachers in the professional subjects should be pursued with all earnestness and thoroughness; it should be, if not in direction, yet certainly in quality, of a university level. This would in particular be the standard for the selection of teachers. During the period of transition there will be many obstacles to overcome on this point, but a generation of teachers is growing who measure up to the magnitude of the task, and who with appropriate academic training and with fine pedagogical skill combine everything that we regard as essential in the education of teachers besides intensive practical training, cultivation of personal life, social spirit, spirit of devotion to youth and service for youth, and in the narrow sphere of professional preparation, the pursuit of art and physical training. Everything will depend on a consciously planned organization of the powers that we regard as essential for the education of the young. The pedagogical institutes will develop something quite new, a life of society for society, a gathering and assembly of young men inspired with enthusiasm for their profession, who must learn as early as possible how difficult a profession is for all who pursue it earnestly and conscientiously. This earnestness and this recognition must be taken into consideration in the development and organization, the existing limitations and restrictions must certainly be removed with determination, and care must certainly be taken that no new errors and eccentricities arise, that the new really becomes better than the old.

The question of "denominational" teacher preparation has recently given rise to lively discussions. The right of the denominations in education is, after all that has been said earlier (see pp. 14 ff.) on the subject, incontestable and is hardly denied by those who reject religious education for themselves. The question here is whether sectarian and secular lines should be drawn in the training of teachers. The Ministry has found the solution to this question dictated not by politics but by the Constitution and statute. If we are to have in the future schools which in accordance with the Constitution and statute are sometimes differentiated on denominational and secular lines, and

sometimes bring together teachers and pupils of every denominational and every secular point of view, and if it is practically
impossible, for reasons of organization and finance, to prepare
teachers for these different types of schools in the same institutions, then segregation in their preparation is unavoidable. The
Ministry deserves neither praise nor blame on this account; the
course adopted has been imposed on it. That an educational
theory which has its foundation in a definite point of view is not
on that account unscientific should be denied by no one who is
familiar with the character of this subject. Similarly it is quite
intelligible without further proof that what is necessary for
pedagogical institutes is not on that account applicable to universities and technical institutions.

The plans of the Ministry for the reorganization of teacher
preparation have met with widespread approval not only in
parliamentary groups, but also among the education authorities
of other states in Germany. But criticisms have been raised
against these plans in spite of the moderation and care with
which they were drafted, and little would be gained to consider
such criticisms lightly. Yet the question involved in the reform
of the preparation of teachers is not to satisfy class demands, as
is maintained by superficial critics, but to raise the level of
elementary education and consequently of popular culture, and
the question whether the plans of the administration can serve
this purpose is surely serious enough.

In the main the criticisms deal with three points: Whether
the poverty-stricken state can bear the cost of the new system
for long, whether this form of teacher-preparation may be expected to secure the necessary supply of recruits, and whether
in particular it is suited to the character and special functions
of service in the elementary school.

The first question can after careful calculation be answered
briefly thus: that the means to be provided by the state for the
establishment and maintenance of the six-year normal schools
are quite adequate for the creation of the required number of
*Aufbauschulen* and pedagogical institutes, and later to cover the
cost also of a moderate improvement of teachers' salaries in so
far as this seems justified by the changed system of preparation.
This being the case, the education authority was able without
reservation to meet the determination of the Ministry of State

that no new charges be imposed on the state by the new system. The favorable result is due on the whole to the fact that the maintenance of the large number of normal schools was relatively expensive, while the new plans involve considerable savings on account of the acceptance of existing secondary schools for the general academic training of teachers, and on account of the centralization of the professional preparation in higher institutes, which at the same time make more appropriate methods of instruction possible.

The problem of supply of recruits is generally determined by the view that for a secondary school graduate the choice of university is, as it were, natural, and that the young candidates for the teaching profession, once they have passed the final examination "would sacrifice two years more" in order to enter an academic profession. As a matter of fact, the situation is in reality quite different. Forty per cent of secondary school graduates already enter practical careers, and it cannot be doubted that many of the young people who for one reason or another deny themselves university study would readily decide to select the teaching profession if they can obtain an assured position in it earlier than in a commercial or official career. It must be admitted that the number of students who, now and in the future, first decide on the teaching profession at the close of their school course, is not adequate to meet the need; much more pertinent is the question whether approximately the same number of students who hitherto entered the preparatory institutions and normal schools, will in the future attend the secondary schools, the regular or the *Aufbauschulen,* with the intention of entering the teaching profession by way of secondary school graduation and the pedagogical institute. This question must be answered in the affirmative, if the widespread leaning among the youth of the people toward the teaching profession continues in the future and the cost of preparation is not higher than before the War. The great majority, about eighty per cent, of future candidates will then attend a school at home or in the immediate neighborhood up to their nineteenth year. So far as the regular secondary schools are concerned, these will almost all be affected by the proposed reduction of fees, and even the pupils in the *Aufbauschulen* can up to almost seventy-three per cent, according to available information, remain at home to the end of their school course. In contrast with this, about the same percentage of candidates (at least seventy-five per cent) formerly attended an institution away from home from fourteen to twenty, an inevitable result of the professional school system, and if one-third of these were admitted to the boarding houses of the normal school during the second half of their training period, the expenses of board were still higher than the cost of maintenance at home. At the close of the normal school period, there followed usually the fairly expensive period of military service, so that appointments took place as a rule on the completion of the twenty-first year; while in the future the period from nineteen to twenty-one will be occupied with attendance at a pedagogical institute. In general attendance at a pedagogical institute away from home will be expected of future teacher candidates, but the cost of both years will be considerably reduced, according to the plans of the administration, by the award of the usual privileges,—remission of tuition fees, and grants of subsidies. These privileges are not intended to attract unsuitable elements, but to facilitate the preparation of able men and women from the less well-to-do classes for service in the elementary school. The state will never be able to abandon the grant of such privileges for candidates for the elementary school service, if it wishes to maintain the elementary school and service in this school in intimate connection with wide sections of our people. If all these conditions which are here merely sketched in outline are appreciated, the significant fact emerges that the homes from which the supply of teachers has come hitherto will continue in the future to be in the position to send their boys and girls into the teaching profession. It may then be that in individual cases a change in plans may be made before or after the final school examination, as happens often enough, and that a graduate may in spite of previous plans decide in favor of the teaching profession. But the opinion frequently heard, that a great many graduates will give up their intention of becoming elementary school teachers in order to take "two years more" and enter a profession with full academic standing, is erroneous, for in reality it means an addition on the average of six or seven years if the time up to remunerative appointment is included.

It is obvious that young people who wish to devote themselves to the teaching profession must take appointments in rural schools into account. Is there any likelihood that one who feels a real calling for this profession will allow himself to be deterred by this? Is it less worthy and satisfactory to coöperate in the essential and moral training of our rural youth? Several other considerations may be adduced on this question of service in the country. The determining factor will surely be personal inclination, just as this is decisive in other callings. Where this inclination, this personal joy and devotion exist, there a young teacher will be ready to accept service in a village school; where this is lacking, the state will dispense with such teachers without sorrow even in the city school. The Ministry has frequently pointed out in the founding of *Aufbauschulen* that above all it is important to get hold of the local forces of the open country and to prepare them for service in the reconstruction of all our people. It had in mind particularly the forces in the country that are of significance as the future educators of our rural youth. It is convinced that it is from these classes of society that there will come teachers for the rural school who admirably meet all the requirements that must be met by the future rural school teachers. We know what we owe to the rural school and its maintenance; its needs will be considered to the fullest extent in the plans to be published for the pedagogical institutes.

The question whether training in secondary schools and institutes of a university level is suitable for future elementary school teachers is determined by the requirements imposed by the elementary school on its teachers now and in the future. Profound changes have taken place in educational theory, which in their fundamental spirit are of permanent significance and whose compelling influences can be checked by no school. It is on the whole incomprehensible that any other theory will be pursued in the elementary school than that taught by science and adopted by other schools. This newer theory cannot be put into practice without a considerable amount of independence and maturity of educational judgment, and these conditions can only be satisfied by a course of training which after graduation from the secondary school finds its culmination and completion in instruction of a university character. It obviously follows that the new preparation must include everything that the teacher needs. This applies to knowledge of content subjects and skill in the artistic-technical subjects; it applies to educational theory as well as to practice in teaching. On all these points there is no justification for the worries that have arisen. Through appropriate utilization of educational possibilities in the secondary schools and equally appropriate organization of the pedagogical institutes care will be taken that the future teacher lacks none of the equipment that he needs for his task. In many things the former normal schools well indicated the right way; in the last decades their standards and contributions have risen as high as possible, and have already pointed beyond themselves to a new organization with higher aims. In the last analysis, in spite of all signs to the contrary, the question is not to break with the past, but to continue the evolution with other means and other methods.

For a long time it appeared as though the choice before the government was to leave the preparation of teachers in its traditional forms, or to risk the practical interests with new forms. The Prussian Ministry considers that it must be regarded as a fortunate dispensation that at a time of economic need a way has been found which guarantees the most suitable preparation for our elementary school teachers without imposing new burdens on state or parents, or endangering the supply of teachers needed by the elementary schools. The Ministry undertook with full confidence the solution of this difficult problem; it hopes that the method adopted by it is sound, that it will provide the elementary school with teachers who in the finest sense of the word will be educators of the people, teachers and educators of youth, leaders of the people.

# CHAPTER V

## SECONDARY EDUCATION

### I. REFORM OF EXISTING SECONDARY SCHOOLS FOR BOYS

The educational ideals of the secondary schools were particularly the subjects of heated controversy during the critical days of the Revolution. Even during the War serious defects in the secondary school system had already been frankly recognized.[1] After the disaster those who sincerely desired to help the secondary schools of the future by open criticism and significant proposals for reform were joined by others in the days of the political change who loudly characterized the traditional secondary schools as the fundamental root of our troubles and professed to see the cause of the unfortunate outcome of the War in the false training by which the nation was miseducated in the secondary schools. Hard words were heard in the Prussian Parliament to the effect that, just as the Prussian elementary school teacher had been the victor at Königgratz, so the World War was lost through the German secondary school teacher. More serious than these criticisms which emanated from politicians and agitators and to which the Ministry paid no attention, was the criticism of those who wished to create a new foundation for popular education by a reorganization of the whole school system.

Serious objections had already been raised even in the trenches against the particularism of the secondary school system, and a demand was made for the greatest degree of uniformity and simplicity in form and organization. This was the meeting-point of wishes which had already been loudly expressed before the War, especially at the large conferences of elementary school teachers, and which demanded the common school as the basis of a completely new organization of the German school system,

[1] Norrenberg, P., *Die deutsche Schule nach dem Weltkriege* (Leipzig, 1916).

61

which barely left room for the existing types of secondary
schools.  The proponents (of whom Tews is the best representative) started out with a six-year foundation school *(Grundschule)* upon which were to be built a three-year middle school
followed by a three-year upper school, with the result that only
this three-year superstructure remained as a secondary school
in the accepted sense of the term.  The majority of opinion that
demanded this common German school system was relatively
strong.  Behind Tews there stood many thousands of elementary
school teachers who supported this scheme.  These demands,
therefore, implied the strongest possible lower and middle
foundation as the basis for a training for the learned professions
only then to be broadly differentiated.  The fundamental idea
of this reform, in addition to the social demand, was a certain
automatic selection of gifted pupils through and beyond the
elementary school.  Some recognized the conception of the new
school most clearly realized in the common school and a man
like Harnack at the Federal Educational Conference expressed
his sympathy for this idea as most significant and profound,
but rejected it in view of the needs of our widely ramified cultural
life, particularly on account of its obvious depreciation of the
conditions underlying successful scientific life and research.
This plan was doomed to failure; even at the Federal Educational Conference it was not accepted, and it is greatly to the
credit of Tews that as representative of the elementary school
teachers he agreed, with the representatives of the secondary
school teachers, on a compromise that demanded the four-year
*Grundschule* and permitted the development of a widely differentiated system of secondary institutions on this basis.  As
a consequence the idea of the ''German school,'' for which Tews
stood all his life, lost its force.  The idea of the differentiated
common school was victorious over purely schematic proposals.  The propaganda for Tews' common school ideas was
silenced.

No less sharp was the fight at the time of the political change
which was waged by the so-called *Entschiedene Schulreformer*
against the existing secondary schools, and has not yet died
down.  Their numbers have perhaps declined; but the handful
of those who are contending for the type of school advocated
by them is closely knit together.  At the Federal Educational

Conference they were represented by Karsen and Oestreich. The center of their attack made with the bitterest criticism is conducted against the traditional secondary schools. They have been, it is alleged, only schools of a dead tradition, of the most unreal rationalism. Living wholly in the past, they developed formal understanding as a means for individual adjustment to the world. Analysis, specialization, characterize the work of the secondary schools; nowhere is access provided to unending problems of the world around us. Division and separation constitute their peculiar features; separation and division were the results attained by their existence and work. The secondary school system presents a true picture of the age of inner lack of freedom and subject specialization. Such were and still are the charges. In their plan the *Entschiedene Schulreformer* demand the School of Experience, the School of Production,[2] which alone furnishes the positive powers of life that seeks and creates types. Its task is, they claim, to free and to organize for experiencing. This life which manifests itself in a different form in each individual while continuing always to be one and the same life, surrounding all existence, all men, must be released, must be organized for experiencing. This result, however, cannot be attained through general ideas, through a consecrated scheme, through practical demands imposed by the culture of the moment, but only out of the heart of life itself. "It is not the external that has to form man, but man is to be placed in a position to express himself, no matter what form he gives to the external." Following their method—the school is a coöperative group for work and life—as well as their organization—the pupils are divided in accordance with their bent and inclination into work-groups—this school of experience implies the complete abandonment of the old secondary school types and their arrangement of years and types. By a radical breach with the past they wish to create something completely new and take care that in creating this new system they have teachers and people who reject the old ideas. This is a utopia which was rejected by the Federal Educational Conference by a large majority. Experiments along the lines of these ideas may well be undertaken, and are perhaps to be welcomed, but for the development

[2] *Erlebnisschule, Produktionsschule.*

of our educational system such ideas cannot be taken as suggestive.

While the proposals of Tews and Karsen implied a revolution in secondary education which found no response among the real experts, the conflict between other reform plans, which were extensively proposed, had to be taken more seriously. The proposals of Karl Reinhardt[3] commanded great attention because they emanated from a man who has for long enjoyed a prominent position in the field of secondary education and has, as presiding councillor in the Prussian Ministry for many years, acquired an insight into the organization of secondary education such as no other man has enjoyed. Starting from the principle of the twofold requirement, the one looking chiefly to the practical and artistic, the other to the theoretical side, Reinhardt proposed a stronger development of the middle school as organized under the Regulations of February 3, 1910, on the basis of the four-year *Grundschule*, side by side with the extended upper grades of the elementary school. On the one side, this institution should be open to all pupils on completion of the *Grundschule* whose ability on the practical and artistic side justified further training beyond the elementary school; such pupils should be prepared for successful attendance in professional schools. On the other side, the middle school should serve as the preparatory school for all who should later attend a six-year secondary school *(Oberrealschule, Gymnasium, Realgymnasium)* from their twelfth to their eighteenth years in accordance with their ability. The duration of instruction in the middle school for future pupils of the secondary schools should be two years, so that all who would later enter a secondary school would attend the elementary school for four years and the middle school for two years, and finish with six years of secondary education. Intimately connected though this idea is at first sight with the idea of the common school, it is still open to serious criticism.

The middle school from the point of view of both aim and method is not an academic school in the same sense as the secondary schools. Able pupils, particularly if they enjoy assistance at home, can be prepared in it to pass into secondary schools, but this type of school cannot be the universal prepara-

[3] In *Neugestaltung des deutschen Schulwesens* (Leipzig, 1919).

tory school. It is obvious that the foundation course in a foreign language in the first class of the middle school must be organized quite differently than in the lowest class of the *Oberrealschule.* The same holds true of mathematics, natural sciences, German, history, and other subjects. The danger that the middle school would gradually adopt the methods of instruction of the secondary schools and that the aim of this type of school would disappear is so great that for the sake of the middle school and its significance a compromise must be rejected which at a time of political unrest seeks to build bridges in order to save the form of the common school.

Reinhardt's proposals again were not adopted as the basis for the reconstruction of the Prussian educational system. As early as the Federal Educational Conference, in which Reinhardt himself took no part, they were withdrawn both in the Second Committee[4] (School Organization), as well as at the plenary session.

At the same time, the Conference gave expression to the aim to which the Prussian Ministry had directed its attention from the beginning, that while recognizing the necessity of establishing an organic common school system with opportunities for forward progress and for transfer between all kinds, no change should be permitted to be introduced in the traditional aims of the different types of schools, in the methods, or in the duration of the course.

In spite of all criticism and attack, the Ministry held close to this point of view from the start, not without full consciousness of the fact that much must be improved within the secondary schools and drastic reforms must be introduced. At no time were the complaints louder than during and after the War that the natural cultural possessions did not enjoy in our secondary schools the position they merit, that our higher schools are too "foreign." Moreover, the War and the Revolution showed with startling clearness that between popular and higher education, between the elementary and the secondary school, between elementary and secondary school teachers there existed a cleavage which reached down into the depths of the people's life and community of culture and was constantly becoming wider.

[4] The Second Committee (School Organization) consisted of eighty-two members under the chairmanship of Dr. Jahnke of the Ministry of Education.

From another angle living contact with the present was found to be lacking in the secondary schools. No bridge appeared to exist between the ideal of the school and the everyday life of the people and youth. One spoke of a Chinese wall around the secondary schools. Others again charged that cultural fields of the greatest importance, like art, music, political theory, social organization, citizenship, economics, and many other subjects found no place in the secondary schools compared with the traditional school subjects. The proposal was therefore made that the old schools should be fundamentally changed or that provision be made for modern educational needs in new school types. The most serious criticism was that which pointed to the organization of subjects of instruction side by side or in opposition to each other, to the unmethodical variety of our schools, to the multiplicity of the unbalanced educational tendencies which lacked any central objective and which actually prevented intensive pursuit of subjects that characterize any particular type of school without actually giving a so-called general education. It is well from time to time to bear in mind this criticism of the secondary schools, even though expressed in harsh terms, in view of the objections brought against the reorganization of the school system by those who praise the good old days. We are quick to forget. Unfortunately, indeed, we forget too quickly that the recognition of the need of a reorganization of our school system has long since become a commonplace with all. The criticism which sounded a warning note was really serious.

For the sake of common educational ends these earnest critics proposed a common secondary school in which there is grouped around a core of cultural subjects specialized instruction adapted to individual capacities and vocational needs with as flexible organization as possible. In sharp contrast to these others proposed that the traditional types of schools should in fact be reinforced with their own peculiar characteristics and that the varied educational objectives that can no longer be met by one school should be satisfied through division of labor and differentiation. The Prussian Ministry neither could nor would adopt the first course, convinced as it was that the educational tendencies whose peculiar potentialities had been developed in the old school types still continue to-day and cannot be artificially suppressed. The educational values that are based on them urgently demanded their perpetuation. Reforms could therefore succeed only if conceived in conformity with their particular educational ideal and do not consist in identification with other school types. It would have been an irreparable loss for German cultural life if external pressure had led to the abolition of existing types of schools.

Accordingly, the reorganization of the system of secondary education, begun in 1924, is deliberately connected with the traditional school types, and continues—let it be emphasized—the further development of the characteristics of each type as introduced in 1901.

The Ministry before undertaking the reorganization had already introduced a new type of secondary school, the *Deutsche Oberschule* (see pp. 84 ff.), in which new educational content and tendencies were to be worked out. Furthermore, it was the intention of the Ministry that more scope should be given in the older schools to the new and important ideals in education. In the future old types of secondary schools will have in common a core of German or cultural subjects which, while more extensive in the *Deutsche Oberschule*, will nowhere have less than one-third of the time. This increase was already required to prevent a complete breakdown of the curriculum of the secondary schools as a result of the differentiation of objectives and becomes particularly significant in view of the new function that has been added in the meantime to the conditional purposes of the secondary school. For in the future, as was pointed out above, (pp. 50 ff.), the elementary school teachers for whom these subjects are of special importance in their later work will pass through the secondary school and remain until graduation. In a very real sense the secondary school thus assumes the central position in national education. They will be genuinely incorporated in the common school system more firmly than would have been possible merely by a scheme of organization.

It would have been simple in the external organization to incorporate in the school system the common foundation for the secondary schools established by Reinhardt and to adopt the general introduction of the Reform Plan. In this way it would have been possible to create a common foundation with one foreign language for the whole secondary school system so that the decision of the pupil on the choice of a particular type of institution would be postponed to the end of the seventh school year, or about the thirteenth or fourteenth year of his life. Sound reasons can be alleged for this common foundation. By the time a pupil is thirteen, provided the school and home are in close connection, an almost certain judgment can be reached on his ability. The guidance of a pupil of more mature age to a course in classical languages or mathematics and sciences or modern languages protects the school, the home, and the pupils against misjudgments which were often fraught with serious consequences. If in the three-year intermediate course *(Sexta* to *Quarta)* the capacities, diligence, will and inclination of a pupil are carefully observed, the observations can be used as an almost certain basis for guidance according to differences of ability and easily recognizable bent. Undoubtedly, the idea of the Reform Plan has such practical advantages that it can never be wholly abandoned from our educational system. On the other hand, there is no doubt that the first foreign language could only be a living language. On this point the idea of the Reform Plan, so attractive on the constructive side, must fall; the humanistic *Gymnasium* defies incorporation into this plan. The proposal to return to Latin as the first foreign language ignores the realities of life, and would sound the death knell of *Real* institutions. The fact, however, that such a proposal could be seriously made indicates the strength of the desire even to-day to utilize the peculiar power of this language from the start and to overcome the difficulties as early as possible in order to lay a sound foundation for later study of all languages. This must be the peculiar task of the *Gymnasium* which would be most injured by the one-sided introduction of the Reform Plan.

The advocates of the Plan have constantly emphasized that the form of the traditional *Gymnasium* and *Realgymnasium* can be retained, especially in larger cities, side by side with the Reform institutions. It is quite clear, however, that the *Gymnasium* would have suffered a serious loss and not merely in number of schools; more important would have been the loss to its peculiar character. The Prussian Ministry, after experiments with the *Realgymnasium*, has been driven by the reports made to the conviction that this type is not practicable as the regular form of the *Gymnasium*. Apart from the fact that the number of pupils who later elect Greek, which older pupils find difficult to learn on account of the wealth of forms, remains small everywhere, it has been shown that the *Reformgymnasium* requires specially favorable conditions to succeed. Where a specially trained faculty, enthusiastic for its difficult task, and a selected body of pupils are available, it has produced excellent results; and here its continuance in future should be possible. As a rule, however, the task of the *Gymnasium* requires for both Latin and Greek a course such as the old type of *Gymnasium* has hitherto provided. There is by no means the suggestion here that lower requirements should be imposed on the pupils. It should be confessed quite frankly that not a small number of the humanistic schools, which exist under unfavorable conditions, has been unable to maintain the traditional standards of the humanistic institutions. It is not necessary that the number of old *Gymnasia* remain as high as at present. Fewer *Gymnasia* of the older type, but in them more scholarly activity under teachers who possess a profound humanistic background, and with pupils who were formerly more carefully selected than is unfortunately often the case, such is the demand made by the Ministry as well as the warmest defenders of the humanistic *Gymnasium*. Not numbers but the spirit that prevails in these institutions should be determining. Accordingly, the Ministry has decided in its reform to retain the nine-year Latin and six-year Greek course of the old humanistic *Gymnasium*. For reasons that have been carefully weighed, it has rejected the attractive proposal to sacrifice something great and important for the sake of what appears superficially to be the idea of the common school. This action was taken in spite of the insistent demand from many sides for a common intermediate stage with a modern language as the general basis of secondary education.

Starting with these ideas, the reorganization which was begun in February, 1924, the *Memorandum of the Ministry*,[5] now generally available, has retained a double foundation for boys. Latin will be the first foreign language in the future in the *Gymnasium*, in which instruction in a modern language may be substituted in the middle stage, and in the *Realgymnasium*. The work of the first three classes is common to both. The *Re-*

[5] *Denkschrift des Ministeriums* (Weidmannsche Buchhandlung, Berlin, 1924).

*formrealgymnasium,* the *Oberrealschule,* and the *Deutsche Ober-schule* begin with a modern language.[6]  Within this system there is a common foundation for three years, which for the first two types is extended to five years.  The transfer to and from the *Deutsche Oberschule* after five years is still relatively slight. For girls, with whom the classical course still has a modest place, the need of a double foundation did not exist for this reason. Hence the *Studienanstalten* follow the Reform Plan, since the pupils, without exception, because of their combination with the *Lyzeum,* begin with one of the modern languages.[7]

With this scheme, it was necessary to work out clearly the character of the existing school types.  The development of our secondary education, besides the multiplicity of uncorrelated educational ideals, has resulted in a piling up of subject matter which resulted in exercising too strong and compelling a claim on the youth in school and in preparation for school.  Hence, practically all educators insistently demanded a reduction in the number of weekly periods in the secondary schools to about thirty a week, bearing in mind the danger of overpressure and the necessity of mental relaxation of the young through physical culture of all kinds and in particular through excursions and athletics.  So much greater stress was placed on the need of periods of relaxation by the needs of the times due to under-nourishment that the administration could not ignore it.  Prac-tically every party in the Prussian Diet had sponsored this de-mand in 1923.  Its adoption was possible only if the secondary institutions of every type again retired, not without some painful sacrifice, within the field that represents their specific educa-tional ideal.  The further reform of secondary education has accordingly been undertaken also from this point of view, and the Ministry had already issued time-schedules at the beginning of 1924 which after mature consideration reduced the length of instruction in all secondary schools except the *Aufbauschule* to an average of thirty periods a week.[8]

Every thoughtful person recognizes that this result cannot be attained by mere curtailment of this or that subject.  In each

---

[6] By *Erlass vom 10. 2. 1923, U II 157.  Zentralblatt,* p. 88, the choice between French and English has been made optional.

[7] See charts on pp. 174-75 and Part II showing the organization of secondary schools for boys and girls.

[8] *Erlass vom 13. 3. 1924—U II 295.  Zentralblatt,* p. 122.

of the existing types of school the test had to be made whether its attainment was prevented by a multiplicity of subjects which was piled up like a barrier.  A dominant aim was most easily recognizable in the *Gymnasium* and in the *Deutsche Oberschule*. Accordingly, it was simplest to take away from both whatever had no specific educational value for attaining the designated objective.  Reconstruction was more difficult in the *Oberrealschule* and above all in the *Realgymnasium* in which in the course of their evolution the latest aim had been subjected to more or less serious modifications.

The whole organization of the *Deutsche Oberschule* (see pp. 84 ff.) was from the start based on the possibility of a reduction of the class periods.  The fundamental principles of the reform were already formulated when it was created, so that the adjustment was easiest in this case.

In the *Gymnasium,* in which in addition to the subjects that furnish the core of all school types both ancient languages must naturally furnish the characteristic educational elements, a few difficulties arose because those who are concerned about its perpetuation have opposed a clear definition of aim.  They made no attempt to deny even in theory that the humanistic *Gymnasium* had in the last decades assumed a series of subjects which prevented the carrying out of their educational ideal that "the path to German education lies through ancient culture."  In the opinion of the Prussian authorities the central feature could most successfully have been saved for the course which leads through ancient languages into the life of ancient culture by requiring in addition only one modern language to be studied in somewhat diminished scope and yet not merely for practical purposes alone, and by providing the further necessary curtailment in mathematics.  It was considered, however, that it must be anticipated in practice that this type of *Gymnasium,* maintained for years past in Bavaria, could not hold its own in competition with other secondary schools.  The Ministry, after some hesitancy, took this position, which at the same time does not argue profound faith in the strength of this educational aim, into consideration only to the extent that it did not affect the peculiar character of the *Gymnasium*.  It decided, therefore, to assign a larger place to the modern language than was originally planned and to curtail mathematics only to a slight extent. Consequently a reduction had to be made in the time for Latin. The administration regrets the sacrifice, but believes that the character of the *Gymnasium* is not affected thereby. The abolition of translation into Latin as a requirement for graduation means a genuine reduction of the load on Latin instruction. In any case this but represents the logical evolution of a movement which began with the disappearance of the Latin essay. The question whether both classical languages are assigned a coördinate place is answered forever by the time-schedule; Latin, as the first language taken up, continues to be the foundation for language study and maintains its prominence in both the lower and the middle stages in the total periods assigned to it. In the upper stage Latin will in most schools take a secondary place to Greek. The increased flexibility which should be introduced everywhere from now on in place of the former rigid course of study will not prevent the possibility of laying greater stress on Latin where the need arises.

The *Oberrealschule* has, in course of time, adopted more and more the mathematical-scientific group of subjects as its special feature. The reform has proceeded on the plan of reducing somewhat the emphasis on the two foreign languages, while strongly stressing the educational values of mathematics and natural sciences. This is in harmony with the aim of this type of school, as it becomes more fully developed, that in place of one of the customary modern languages another, whose need is determined by local conditions, may be substituted; the administration has in mind Spanish, Russian, Polish, and Danish.

For the *Realgymnasium* the chief emphasis must be on French and English, which serve as an introduction to the life and civilization of both the leading nations which whether side by side with or in opposition to us have determined the development of Europe. To emphasize the distinctive national characteristics, whatever our political relations may be, is at present a task for German education. It may be questioned to what extent Latin is necessary for this task. This language is obviously an excellent foundation for the study of language and cannot entirely be dispensed with either by the side of or, better, before the study of French in particular. The culture of the three Western European nations has its roots in that period of European history which was not so strictly differentiated and which linguistically was dominated by the Latin.  But if the principle of a limitation of content is to be taken seriously, it is impossible in the *Realgymnasium* to pursue all these subjects with equal intensity.  Further, mathematics and natural sciences have contributed important features to the type of culture which should be the basis of this school.  It is, therefore, justifiable on the face of things to give these subjects wider scope than in the *Gymnasium*.  This holds true even if the thesis is rejected that this is not demanded by the tradition of the *Realgymnasium*.  In no type of school can the principles underlying the reorganization be so little linked up with its past development as in the *Realgymnasium,* which was characterized by the formless multiplicity which the reorganization wishes to abolish.  It was essential, therefore, to give this type of school a character which has already been more markedly developed in all others.  The administration has been convinced that the mathematical-scientific subjects must be given greater consideration.  The question of Latin became the more difficult. In the *Realgymnasium,* which is indispensable side by side with the *Gymnasium* and which also begins with Latin, this language is so deeply rooted in the common foundation of the first three years that no other course is open than to use it as the keystone of the whole structure.  Care must naturally be taken that the Latin course in the *Realgymnasium* does not lean too far over in the direction of the *Gymnasium*.  It must be incorporated into the aims of this school, which are quite different and to the attainment of which it can undoubtedly make a real contribution because the fruits of its work, begun in the earliest stages, are allowed to mature.  In the *Reformrealgymnasium* the situation is quite different.  Begun several years later, Latin cannot because of its difficulty become the chief factor in the educational task of the school.  It would be more appropriate if the language were here given quite a different status and French and English were in practice made the chief language subjects.  Their position in the *Realgymnasium* is, it must be admitted, least affected by Latin, and it requires careful attention in the practice of the next few years to maintain a proper balance and to avoid the mistakes of the old *Realgymnasium*.

These are the methods pursued in the reorganization of the system of secondary education.  Intimately connected by a common core of German or cultural subjects, with special stress on classical, modern language, mathematical, scientific, or specifically German subject matter, there are four ways for acquiring knowledge of and familiarity with our many-sided German culture. The educational needs of our youth are to be met not by eliminating but by developing the special characteristics of each type of school. But for the very reason that such distinctively developed systems of education are under consideration, particular importance must be attached to the discussion of the question whether it is possible or desirable to introduce flexibility into our somewhat rigid secondary schools and to give some attention to the idea of differentiated abilities by permitting a freer organization of instruction in the last years where suitable conditions exist. The rigidity of the diverse types of schools had already been criticized as a defect long before the War and attempts were made to meet the needs of different ability by introducing alternative subjects, especially in the *Gymnasium* (English in place of Greek from the fourth year on), and later by the method of compensatory marking in the final examination. Occasion to carry this idea further has been furnished by the frequently expressed wish that new subjects recognized as worth while be incorporated in the course of study and that opportunity be provided for the further and deeper study of subjects already included. To this was added another more important educational idea of developing the initiative of the student in a larger field selected by himself, and of training him in research methods of work before entrance to the university by specialization in a smaller number of subjects and by the preparation of larger theses as the outcome of free activity. The natural corollary would have been to lower the standards correspondingly in other subjects. This suggestion of freedom of election was to a large extent adopted by the Prussian administration in its Decree of January 24, 1922.[9]

Four possibilities were provided by this decree of meeting the ideas of adapting the school to differentiated abilities, of training for greater self-activity, and of approximating the research methods of the university. This could be done either by organizing groups in each class or through the provision of a core curriculum around which the free elective subjects are grouped, or

---

[9] *Erlass vom 24. I. 1922—U II 1507.  Zentralblatt, p. 38.*

through voluntary study groups.   Finally, in those schools in which two types of schools with different objectives are combined into a double institution, the decree made it possible for pupils to transfer from one type to the other.   The experiments introduced on the basis of these possibilities have already in their early stages given rise to certain criticisms.   In some institutions, for example, in which the periods for the minor subjects were considerably reduced, the amount of work required in the major subjects[10] was in no way increased.   Further, it was observed that pupils often chose their subjects not on the basis of objective standards but according to the popularity, for example, or the severity of the teacher.   Fashions can play a serious part here and it must be remembered that it is not always the ablest or most stimulating teacher who is the most popular, but frequently the one who makes least demands.   Other misunderstandings may easily arise, and have already arisen, if the real character of an institution disappears completely on account of the system of electives, and if instead of variety a regrettable dissipation of energy is permitted and pupils are overburdened with a variety of subjects that lead to confusion and superficiality.   The desire to avoid serious hard work and to taste immediately of all fruits of knowledge must not be fostered by the authorities.   With every wish to consider individual differences, variety in our system of schools must not be carried to excess.   It was the purpose of another decree issued on February 14, 1923,[11] to direct attention anew to the point of view expressed in the decree of January 24, 1922.   This decree aimed to check the exaggerations and one-sidedness that had sprung up in a number of experiments that were wrongly conceived and wrongly carried out.

This question has assumed another complexion since the reorganization of secondary education was begun.   One of the key questions to be answered was whether to retain the rigid types of schools which were inherited from the last century and whose particular characteristics it was one of the tasks of the reform of 1901 to develop further.   Their abolition in favor of

[10] The major subjects are those that give a school its special character, e.g., classics, or modern languages, or mathematics and sciences, as the case may be.

[11] *Erlass vom 14. 2. 1923—U II 125.   Zentralblatt*, p. 116.

an elastic unitary school was advised by many who though not numerous were very prominent and regarded themselves as the advocates of an opportune advance, apart from the fact that at the time of the reorganization the condition of Prussia precluded experiments whose cost would have meant an intolerable burden on the state and local bodies for the purposes of secondary education.

The experiences with the freer organization instituted in many places in accordance with the Decree of January 24, 1922, have already given rise to the considerations mentioned above. They have in fact justified the administration in deciding on the retention of the existing types of schools. This was also the conclusion reached in the Federal Educational Conference, and the Ministry in establishing the new *Deutsche Oberschule* by the side of the old types had already announced that it intended in agreement with this conference of leading experts to advance by the process of evolution rather than of revolution. The acceptance of the idea of selected content instead of the phantom of ''general culture'' has compelled it to develop the different types of schools in accordance with its characteristic cultural aim. Hence, there remains little scope for a freer organization with the range previously mentioned. The constitution of each individual school implies a limitation of the earlier standard course of study whose operation was the basis of the Decrees of January 24, 1922, and February 14, 1923. That parents have always attached great importance to it is indicated by the fact that of the various secondary schools of Prussia only four per cent made use of the freedom granted. The new system has, however, taken over from the sound ideas in those experiments one which is adapted to ensure real specialization in the highest classes of all schools. An opportunity is offered to the gifted and specially interested pupils not to avoid by election what is not suited to the apparently one-sided but in reality less gifted pupil, but rather to add what serves to deepen and supplement the work required by the school. In spite of the financial difficulties of the state, all nine-year institutions are allowed to assign freely a few periods over and above the regular periods for the organization of study groups, especially in the last year. That this number is limited to six periods is due not merely to financial considerations. At the beginning of a reorganization where the aim is to relieve pupils from the multiplicity of subjects in the secondary schools, it would in fact be dangerous to offer too great an opportunity to be used in opposition to this fundamental idea.

In addition there remains the possibility of instituting elective courses, outside of the regular curriculum, in subjects not already included here. There has been no change in the justness of this scheme. Thus Hebrew is a possible subject in the *Gymnasium*, Latin in the *Oberrealschule*. The only difference is that the moderate cost for each be separately provided. This is the only sacrifice which, though not easily made, is still permissible, that the courses in secondary schools must be organized to meet the needs of the time. No one hopes more sincerely than the Prussian Ministry that this measure due to stress should be of short duration.

When a decision of these questions has been reached for the regular schools along the lines suggested, it will not be impossible to approve experimental types of schools without narrow-mindedness. The Ministry does not here have in mind so much the *Reformgymnasium*, which has already passed beyond the experimental state and proved its value under special circumstances, even though it has not been accepted as the regular form for the *Gymnasium*. The continuance of such successful institutions of this kind has already been approved in quite a number of cases. But beyond this, opportunity should be afforded for other experiments, including the development of the possibilities that now exist for the freer organization of upper classes,—experiments which may furnish lessons for the secondary school in general. In the case of many large schools, which were predominantly concerned with the freer organization of the upper classes, the old system of bifurcation can be retained by developing one part of the school in accordance with the plan of another school type.

The Ministry has also adhered strictly even after the issue of the Law of the *Grundschule* to the nine-year duration of secondary schools for all pupils who wish to enter a secondary school on completing four years of attendance at the *Grundschule*. On the special conditions of the *Aufbauschule*, which is based on seven years of elementary education and whose character may be recognized in the classes established since April,

1922, a report is given in another place (see pp. 89 ff.). If the school career of pupils who make normal progress through school (4 plus 9 or 7 plus 6 *(Aufbauschule)* years) is thus extended by one year, this fact cannot be used as an argument against the three-year course. More than half of all pupils have entered the secondary school hitherto only after four years of attendance at the elementary school. Far more than fifty per cent of all pupils have not completed the secondary school in nine years but have required a longer period. It is to be hoped that with a sound development of the *Grundschule* the number of so-called repeaters will be reduced. The fact that for the moment determined the Ministry in its decision to retain the nine-year course for the regular secondary schools was that the fourth year of the *Grundschule* in no way attempts the subjects of the first year of the secondary school and that the *Grundschule* should not be compelled to undertake a task that is alien to it. The relatively small number of pupils that pass from it to the secondary school should not force considerations on it that are opposed to its inner law. If the secondary school course were reduced to eight years, instruction in the appropriate foreign language would be shorter by a full year. One year of development in the secondary schools would be eliminated and this year, as has often been pointed out, would not be at the beginning but at the very end of the course. At the very time when the total number of weekly class periods has been reduced, it is quite clear that it would be extremely dangerous at this juncture to enter on an experiment of shortening the whole length of the course in a secondary school by a year. According to the unanimous opinion of the whole section for secondary education in the Prussian Ministry a reduction of the length of the course from nine to eight years would do incalculable damage to the cultural level of our people. There will certainly be cause later for gratitude to the Ministry for its resolute and determined action in retaining the nine-year course in the face of pressure from influential bodies and organizations, which proposed to shorten the length of the course by a year at the very time when the regulation for reduction of personnel came into force. The firm resolution of Prussia has already borne fruit; Hamburg, which had prescribed an eight-year course for its secondary schools shortly after the Revolution, has repealed this regulation and restored the nine-year course.

Serious disputes have always arisen on changes in organization of the school system. A proposal that is regarded by one as far-fetched and revolutionary is rejected by another as a reactionary step. Thus everything that is here suggested and left unchanged must stand a crossfire from those who hate the old school and from those who most resolutely defend the "good old system" for which the War and the Revolution have no lesson and no problem to suggest, even in the field of secondary education. But more important than all changes in organization is, in the opinion of the administration, the aim of developing the system of education and instruction in accordance with the ideas presented in the second chapter of this book. Here we are, it is to be hoped, in the way to establishing the school wholly to the end of training each individual as master of a strong cultural attitude and of strong moral ideas, to the end of promoting cultural unity and community of spirit in the whole population, to the end of educating to political consciousness, which should inspire the younger generation with burning enthusiasm for the political unity of our people. With these points in mind the Ministry in the reorganization of secondary education has attached greater value to the reform of the inner life and method of work in the secondary school than to organization and time-schedules on which public discussion has overwhelmingly centered. If it has in fact been warned by persons who must command consideration not to lose sight of the sober everyday work of the school in the midst of great educational ideas—"ideas have their dangers"—it is justified in its answers that it is because we appreciate this everyday work that we hold the ideal up before it.

The defects that have appeared in the inner life of secondary schools are presented in detail in the *Memorandum on the Reorganization*,[12] to which attention should be explicitly directed. The sources of the weakness that should be mentioned are variety and multiplicity of subjects which arise from the ideal of a "general education," an ideal borrowed by the other types of schools from the *Gymnasium* of Johannes Schulze, and the

[12] *Denkschrift zur Neuordnung.*

method of work which through a too logical development of the heuristic method with its play of question and answer failed to develop satisfactorily the self-activity of the pupils. If we add further that this work of the secondary school concerned itself almost exclusively with imparting content to the mind and often ignored the other aspects of developing personality, it can be understood that the function of education was too frequently left in the background. The result was that the secondary school was in danger of sacrificing its position as the central point in the life of the youth and of becoming a power which was felt to be alien but of which the best had somehow to be made. The real falsity that rose in the relation of the school not only to the pupil but to his home has often enough been the subject of complaint. The authorities hope through the new courses of study that are being prepared and will soon be completed to point out ways that lead to a higher end. The drafts of courses of study or of parts of courses, some seven hundred and fifty in round numbers, presented to the Ministry by the teaching body, have given convincing proof that the administration was justified at the beginning of the reorganization in stating how closely it associated itself in its work with the desires of the best among the teaching personnel. Gaudig was of the opinion that free intellectual self-activity of pupils should establish itself as a method in the elementary school first. But it was in fact clear in the draft proposals that the secondary school had long ago begun to turn to a method of instruction which employs continually independent self-activity of the pupil in place of the passive absorption of knowledge, however skillfully used. The new courses of study will apply these fundamental ideas to instruction, naturally taking into account the various stages of development of the pupils. They will have to draw the necessary conclusions for the administration of written tasks in class as well as for homework. This was one of the weakest points in secondary education. The reform will mean an improvement of school life. It will also be of importance from this point of view if new courses of study seriously consider the principle of inner concentration which has long been proposed. Without exaggeration, for an idea, no matter how sensible, can be reduced to absurdity by exaggeration, they will not be satisfied with the more or less occasional coöperation of separate subject departments. They will rather have to suggest methods that lead to a kind of integrated instruction which grows out of the distribution of the scope of the subjects. Reciprocity between the subjects and the departments that constitute the majors, and the general subjects of each type of school is a preliminary condition.

Not only will the new courses of study have to offer enrichment and depth to the pupil to save him from the lack of connection between subjects which are piled up side by side with each other, but the teacher should be granted freedom from the narrowness of definitely prescribed tasks, freedom to do independent work within the scope, of course, of coöperative study groups among the teachers. Above all things the danger must be avoided of allowing the work of individual institutions to become so differentiated that a transfer from one school to another is made intolerably difficult. It was thought desirable to issue the warning that precision and thoroughness might be surrendered as the basis for the work of every secondary school. This reorganization does not aim at any pampering of the pupils. On the contrary, the administration hopes to raise the standards, which will be made possible by more rational methods of work and consideration of the contributions of child psychology.

The reform of secondary education, which takes all these points of view into consideration, will neither wish nor be able to lose sight of the necessity of reorganizing the leaving examination. The regulation for this examination now in effect is in harmony neither with the ideas of method nor with the new organization of instruction especially in the last few years. If to this is added the alternation and regrouping of subjects as suggested earlier, it is obvious that the examination which is to decide the readiness of the pupil for life and for the university must be organized differently from what it is at present. The impression must also be avoided that in testing this readiness the problem is merely one of certifying to examinable knowledge. The leaving certificate should indicate that the young man who enters on life and devotes himself to a career or goes to the university, is prepared, that is, has the ability, to acquire knowledge for himself and to develop judgment and power through organized knowledge. This is worth far more than the possession of subject matter acquired quite extrinsically and examinable information artificially crammed. Similarly the consequences of the reorganization of secondary education will demand a reorganization of the method of preparing secondary school teachers, a question dealt with in detail in another chapter.

For the inner life of the school, which through all these measures should be markedly changed, serious preparation whose significance cannot be ignored had been made in earlier years. Reference should here be made to the attempt to meet a problem which with its superficiality and deceit has for long been a cross for the secondary school, that is, the participation of pupils in societies within the schools themselves (Decree of December 12, 1922).[13] On the one hand, traditional restraint which has always conduced to violations of school regulations; on the other, obscure, not quite comprehensible, prescriptions which unfortunately brought our school system into politics, both must be resolutely abandoned by the administration. The responsibility for membership of pupils in organizations of all kinds must be placed on the home, and responsibility should be assumed only for pupil organizations existing within the school itself. At the same time in the decree to which reference was made, the responsibility was most earnestly impressed on the school for the all-round education of the youth. What the school surrendered were only formal rights; therefore it had to assume a far greater and stronger moral responsibility for the youth entrusted to its care. The Decree concludes with the words:

If the school itself by establishing and promoting pupil organizations gives sympathetic attention to the youthful need for free, self-determined coöperation, if it develops all its life activities in the spirit of genuine coöperation in life and work, organizes class and school communities in the sense of true comradeship, if education and instruction are permeated with civic ideas, a more than equivalent substitute will be found for many formal requirements. The school will insure the effectiveness of its work most successfully if the teachers take greater pains than ever before to meet the pupils sympathetically instead of applying to them adult standards which are often strange to them.

[13] *Erlass vom 23. 12. 1922—U II 1404. Zentralblatt*, 1923, p. 19.

This responsibility is surely of more serious import than the purely formal rights of old which the school could not hope to exercise.

To a far greater extent than ever before, the administration has been concerned to spread the sound idea of self-government in schools of all kinds. However limited the extent to which ideas of school communities, pupil committees, pupil councils, which swept the school immediately after the Revolution (Decree of November 27, 1918 [14]), could be forcibly carried out anywhere, it is impossible to ignore the sound principle that lies in training for genuine corporate life and responsibility in freedom. The regulations for directors and teachers in secondary schools issued on December 12, 1910, have already recommended the introduction of representatives in the upper and middle classes. Starting from this point after school communities had been most decidedly rejected, the pupils themselves fostered the development in succeeding years. This development has not yet stopped and it is to be hoped that it contributed to the promotion of ever-growing sympathetic relations between pupils and teachers. Where school communities still continue to-day, especially in smaller institutions, they have abandoned everything which, like playing at Parliaments at a time of political excitement, appeared to be worth striving for even to the young. What has remained is that as a rule there is coöperation and a new feeling of shared responsibility in the life of the school and the community.

Welcome also was the renewed and very striking desire in the troublous times to introduce another relationship between school and home by the creation of parents' councils. The basic decree which goes back to October 1, 1916,[15] was issued shortly before the Revolution and was signed by the Minister of Education at that time, Dr. Schmidt. Originally it was intended only for the state secondary schools. By the Decree of November 5, 1919,[16] the arrangement was extended to all Prussian schools. This plan has also had its growing pains. But where limits

[14] *Erlass vom 11. 27. 1918—U II 1967, 1968. Zentralblatt*, p. 710.
[15] *Erlass vom 1. 10. 1918—U II 294. Zentralblatt*, p. 634.
[16] *Erlass vom 5. 11. 1919—U II 1769. Zentralblatt*, p. 662. See also Varrentrapp, *Elternbeirat und Elternbeiratswahlen, Weidmannsche Taschenausgabe*, Vol. I, 2nd ed., 1924.

were not exceeded on the one side or on the other, it has in all cases proved its worth, and has contributed genuinely and in welcome measure to the creation of an atmosphere of confidence between the school and the home and the promotion of an appreciation of the functions of the school. It is indeed the most valuable part of the scheme of parents' councils and parents' evenings that parents come into direct and real contact with the teachers and the school, which before they frequently only knew from tales and certificates of their children. Respect and understanding for the amount of responsibility imposed on the teacher and educator, personal appreciation of the men and women to whom they entrust their dearest, unreserved frankness in the common discussion of educational needs and educational problems on the side of the parents, for the school the opportunity of insight in quite a new way into the needs of family life, into the problems of fathers and mothers, these are the results which can be noted only with satisfaction.

## II. DIE DEUTSCHE OBERSCHULE

As was mentioned earlier, the *Deutsche Oberschule* has since April, 1922, been established as a new type of school by the side of the existing types of Prussian secondary schools. The need for its establishment, as it arose out of the educational tendencies of the last decades and the experiences of the War and Revolution, is described in a special *Memorandum of the Prussian Ministry of Education*.[17] Reference should be made to this pamphlet on which the distinguished collaborator, Ministerial-Councillor Richter, has written a valuable monograph in his *Deutsche Aufbau- und Oberschule*.[18] The scheme for the organization of this new school has been available since Easter, 1924, and the courses of study have been in force since then. There is introduced here a completely new type of school which aims to give a general education adequate for scientific study in German universities based on the resources of German culture. It has found enthusiastic friends who are working vigorously on its development; it has, however, also met with opposition not only among those who rejected any new type of school whatsoever but also among the most thoroughgoing advocates of the

---

[17] *Denkschrift der preussichen Unterrichtsverwaltung.*
[18] Richert, H., *Die Deutsche Aufbau- und Oberschule* (Leipzig, 1922).

very important educational ideas for which this new school stands.

The demand has been made, for example, that this new type of secondary school should be a purely modern school with a content based wholly on present conditions and with a curriculum directed to the needs of our present culture and promoting the education of men of to-day. The administration rejected these demands because while the present as the starting-point in education must be the dominating principle in all schools, no deductions can be derived from this with reference to the content of education. It would be madness to suppose that only subjects taken from present conditions can promote the needs of the present in education. Higher education of all kinds must be historical with an emphasis on present needs. Thus all secondary schools should serve the present, not even excluding the old humanistic *Gymnasium;* only on this condition can the existence of a secondary school be justified. It must be a center of historical training. In this sense, and only in this sense, should the *Deutsche Oberschule* be a modern school.

From another direction objection has been raised against the idea of establishing a new and independent type of school because with an extensive development of election it would be quite possible for other secondary schools to satisfy the educational demands which are to be met by the *Deutsche Oberschule* so that the reasons for its existence as a separate institution would disappear. A statement of this kind argues complete ignorance of the character of the *Deutsche Oberschule.* Its peculiar educational function can only be performed in the closest possible connection with the task achieved by the elementary school, if it is to educate individuals of a particular stamp. The diversified experiments with the elective system in the last year of the secondary school cannot be accepted as a substitute for a self-contained educational organism like a school planned in principle to be independent. In such discussions the time-schedule as the determining element for a type of school plays a part that has in no way been established. School types with almost identical time-schedules can be quite different in curriculum and content. The *Oberrealschule* and *Oberschule,* which are often interchanged like twins, are in fact of quite different character. Unquestionably the different aims of different types of schools should only represent differences of emphasis, the expression of variety in uniformity within a large, identical sphere of education. It would be an equally unjust and unfounded charge that any secondary school has hitherto wholly neglected a national culture. It would, however, equally be an illusion to believe that any secondary school can give equal attention to all national cultures. Every division of labor implies here some sacrifice.

In answer to all these objections there should once and for all be a clear statement of the aims which the administration had before it in establishing the *Deutsche Oberschule.* The *Deutsche Oberschule* places in the center of its educational tasks the cultural subjects which it brings together into an organic whole. Its founders start with the conviction that the educative forces contained in these subjects, enjoying the central position assigned to them, provide an education which is so valuable that it can no longer be neglected. Just as the central subjects in other school types are equally indispensable for German culture, so the *Oberschule* cannot neglect these subjects, while the other schools have on their side never ignored the educational value of cultural subjects. This must be clearly emphasized, since in the conflict around this new type of school these obvious facts have been forgotten on both sides. It is, of course, an exaggeration to claim that it is only in the *Oberschule* that a really German personality can be developed, that only there would true German culture be pursued.

It would, however, be equally naïve from the viewpoints of history and philosophy to maintain that the *Oberschule* will create a new German cultural ideal from within itself. Such ideals have indeed been formulated for it. This or that epoch in the German past has been proclaimed as the classical cultural period of the real Germany, forgetting that such ideals are only an expression of contemporary desire for culture which sees its ideals in the past. A secondary school professing genuine cultural aims must rather strike deep roots into the cultural epochs that have actually influenced the culture of the present. All romantic idealization of distinct epochs in the past depart from reality. All attempts to exclude dependence on foreign cultural forces are from the point of view of race psychology ineffective so long as these influences are not superseded by a re-creation of the cultural consciousness of all Germans. The educational ideal of the *Oberschule* must be justified by the history of the intellect. Its founders have readily admitted that they are disciples of Dilthey, that they have learned from him to look on German intellectual history in association with the history of the origin of the modern European spirit and to recognize the epoch of German idealism as the last great classical "formative period of the German spirit." From this alone, they realize, can an understanding of the present be attained, and in this are rooted the future ideals for the development of the German spirit. German intellectual history is so interwoven with that of antiquity, Christianity, and European intellectual life, that a deep understanding of the German spirit at the stage that it has reached is possible only by incorporating these historical relations into the cultural study of the *Oberschule.*

The peculiar character of this school lies in this—that it incorporates into the whole of its cultural course all living expressions of the German spirit, that it not only assigns a central position in its work to German history and German literature, but also recognizes the creative arts, music, philosophy, religion, law, economics, customs and dialect as essential educative materials for the German man of letters. As a consequence the purely esthetic educational ideal has deliberately been pushed into the background and the subjects of study have been arranged into a new order of values; or, to express it better, out of the juxtaposition of different subjects integrated instruction has been developed, which no longer pays any attention to what was known as an order of values.

This integrated instruction only superficially appears to be an expansion of subject matter which has been criticized as encyclopedic. The educational idea of the *Oberschule* implies in fact the necessary standards for the limitation of content. All schools are governed by the fundamental principle that the particular culture, whether national or foreign, that they teach can only be transmitted in a general survey, as a preliminary orientation. The cultural sketch that is here designated should always be compared to a map in a school atlas. Individual pictures of different sections, characteristic developments, representative aspects will at the same time facilitate an appreciation

of the picture as a whole. These pictures of German cultural
life will be particularly impressive because the pupil already
has emotional susceptibilities which even the mature student
of foreign cultures only rarely brings to his work. Cultural instruction is especially well adapted to utilize methods of experience and activity based on child and race psychology, if
complete freedom is granted in the selection of cultural material
that is characteristic for the pupils and the country concerned.
It was accordingly one of the chief concerns in drafting the
*Suggestions for a Course of Study in the Oberschule* to develop
clearly the standards for selection, since nothing is more opposed to mere memoriter acquisition and purely passive attitude on the part of the pupil than material drawn from his
own cultural world that sets in motion imagination, feeling,
and will.

For much of this material it will be necessary to work out
suitable and appropriate methods, which will only be discovered
if it develops out of the class itself and the coöperative activity
of the specialist teachers. Integrated cultural instruction, if it
is to result in the general picture outlined above, requires intelligent coöperation of all specialist teachers of a class and the
complete elimination of all narrowness of the specialist from
which class instruction suffers so frequently to-day. This new
attitude will only be attained by a teaching body that takes a
whole-hearted interest in the educational function of the *Oberschule*. It is a pleasure to state that after violent conflicts
among the friends of the *Deutsche Oberschule* agreement appears
to have been reached on these fundamental questions.

The only question that continues to be the subject of serious
discussion is that of foreign language instruction, on which the
various states in Germany have gone their own way. While it
is nowhere denied that a foreign language and culture should
be extensively pursued, because German language and culture
can develop a rich and conscious clarity of its peculiar character by contrast with a foreign picture, the admission of a
second foreign language has aroused impassioned protest, as if
the educational idea of the *Oberschule* would be completely
falsified and ruined thereby. For the Prussian authority this
question was from the start only one of utility. When the
advocates of one foreign language were willing to admit a sec-

ond only as an elective, they admitted involuntarily that at least a portion of the pupils attain the objective of the school even with two foreign languages. The Prussian Ministry was determined to grant to the new school all privileges already enjoyed by other secondary schools. Under no circumstances should the new school be burdened at the outset by the discouraging struggle for privileges. Since, however, the supporters of the *Oberschule* among university teachers regarded two foreign languages as indispensable for university study, it was decided that the second language, even though somewhat on the margin, should be included among the obligatory subjects.

On account of the cultural relations with England and France, English or French was selected as the first foreign language. The position assigned to the second language made it possible to take into account the educational needs of various sections of the country and to admit in addition to Latin all those languages that are desired by the population.

The new school will have to fight its way through under difficult and embarrassing circumstances. The impoverished state was unable to place in its cradle as birthday gifts equipment that is desirable (e.g., for manual instruction, training in use of instruments). For a long time there will be a lack of textbooks and other supplementary materials. Many inquire with concern where there will be found teachers fully equipped for the new tasks. It is pointed out with justice that important problems are hereby assigned to the university whose solution demands a special organization of its work. But a school that has been born of a great idea will succeed in spite of everything, slowly of course, and of course not without setbacks and annoyances, perhaps even in its contacts with the other types of schools. But the educational idea underlying the *Deutsche Oberschule* will not again be lost unless the sources of our German culture are themselves obstructed and exhausted.

### III. DIE AUFBAUSCHULE

The establishment of a secondary school, giving a six-year course on the basis of seven years of elementary education and granting university entrance and other privileges of the same kind as those of other secondary schools, was inevitably required to be included within the framework of the common school.

On the one side, the common school consists of an organic system with possibilities of advancement, transfer and cross-connections between schools of all types; on the other, the demand for advancement to the secondary school after the completion of elementary education is a demand supported by logic and justice at the same time. The school life of pupils who pass from the elementary school to the *Aufbauschule* in the common school system should not be longer than that of pupils attending the other secondary schools. The curtailment of the elementary school by one year and the six-year type of secondary schools were natural corollaries of this. The idea of making secondary education accessible to pupils practically on the completion of the elementary school course could not meet with serious opposition if only for social reasons. All experts were unanimous at once that only really gifted elementary school pupils could after six years be prepared for admission to the university, even if the standards of the elementary school were given some considerable weight. On the basis of its long experience the administration was convinced that there should be no pressure on the average pupil in the nine-year course of the secondary school; it could not, therefore, believe that average pupils could reach the standard of university entrance in six years.

For these reasons it was not considered desirable to establish *Aufbauschulen* in larger cities, through fear that purely financial reasons might lead to the creation of the new type of school with the result that the burden would in the end fall on those pupils who would be graduated by the accelerated plan.

Attention was accordingly directed to the small towns as appropriate for the *Aufbauschule,* a view supported by very serious questions of educational politics. The *Memorandum* of the Ministry [19] shows with remarkable lucidity that the advancement of pupils in villages and small towns has hitherto been limited and restricted. At a time when all intellectual forces in Germany must be set in motion for her reconstruction, it seemed intolerable to allow these gifted children to suffer in the future under such unfavorable educational conditions. Such

[19] See Part II.

schools in the country appeared necessary not merely for the
sake of these children, but, and here was a decisive influence,
it was clearly recognized that the advancement of the young
into the higher professions must bring a restoration to whole-
someness for our German culture.  Criticism, as it has been impressed on contemporary thought especially through the writings of Lamprecht, Simmel, Tönnies, Sombart, and earlier of
Lagarde, was directed against the large town spirit of our
modern culture and gave evidence that this spirit would ruin
the national and social foundation of our whole popular culture.  With these considerations it seemed necessary not to tear
the village and small town children away too early from the
invigorating and healthy protection of their homes and hand
them over prematurely to the culture of the large towns which
is especially dangerous for them.  Thus the *Aufbauschule* in the
country and small town came to occupy the center of interest.

This interest was considerably increased by the abolition of
the preparatory institutions and normal schools.  In spite of
all criticism of these institutions for preparing teachers, which
because they are professional schools with a fully developed professional training could not be incorporated in the common
school system, it must in justice be recognized that they performed an important and significant service in the very sphere
in which the *Aufbauschule* should be effective.  An unbridge-
able gap would have arisen in our German educational system
if either nothing at all or isolated secondary schools of the traditional type had taken their place.  The secondary training
given in a six-year course to gifted elementary school pupils has
already afforded proof that secondary education can be attained
in a six-year course.  Experience had in fact shown incon-
testably that many elementary school pupils were almost prepared for admission to the university in the normal school
course.

The idea thus presented itself of transforming the condemned
normal schools into *Aufbauschulen*.  The educational influences
which were hitherto specially adapted to elementary school
teachers and which gave the country school teacher a particularly valuable attitude towards the national forms of human
life that he had to develop should for the future be made productive for other higher professions.  Among the first are in-

cluded, of course, such professions as can work successfully
with the same attitude in villages and small towns—pastor,
country doctor, judge, etc.; but there are also others which it
is hoped may be entered in the large cities by men who bring
thither a handful of the sacred soil, a bit of the homeland
with them.

The Ministry has repeatedly and clearly stated that elementary
school teachers must enter secondary schools of all types, if this
profession, so important for our development, is to have a sympathetic understanding with all cultural classes of our people.
That the *Aufbauschule* would be the preferred preparatory
school for the teaching profession was the hope of all who
would retain the national forces represented in a particular
degree in the teaching profession.

These considerations must lead to important decisions on the
question as to the type of school on which the *Aufbauschule*
is to be modeled. From the point of view of its organization the
six-year *Aufbauschule* can be regulated after all the prevailing
types of schools. The *Aufbauschule* that the Ministry had to
have in mind pointed undoubtedly to the *Deutsche Oberschule*
in which are combined into a living unity those educational
influences that can be strengthened for a higher education
directly on the basis of German culture. The *Oberschule* aims
to be the ideal popular school. It aims without a breach with
the education of the elementary school to advance the pupils in
organic growth and with the same materials to the full height
of a national education. It thus has without doubt characteristics identical with the normal school. Everything that the
elementary school pupil brings with him into the *Aufbauschule*
is here further developed. Again the *Oberschule,* which in its
curriculum advances from the home to the fatherland and
thence to humanity, is the school which more than other schools
must adapt itself to the peculiar character of each German district, if it is to attain its goal.

The *Oberrealschule,* closely related to the *Oberschule,* also
came up for consideration for the *Aufbauschule.* For this
school, too, the ambitious gifted pupils drawn from the village
and small town populations possess particularly favorable
preparation. Where these pupils will later turn to commerce,

industry or even agriculture, the *Oberrealschule* will be the type to be selected.

That a humanistic *Gymnasium* can attain its aim in a six-year *Aufbauschule* may be maintained only if this *Gymnasium* with definite limitations on the antiquities is freed from other tasks assigned to the nine-year *Gymnasium*. Practical experiments alone can determine the establishment of such an *Aufbauschule* on the lines of a *Gymnasium* where a need exists.

An *Aufbauschule* along the lines of the *Realgymnasium* enters least into consideration, for this school still shows a multiplicity of subjects which both on the linguistic and the mathematical-scientific sides imposes serious demands that cannot easily be met in a six-year course.

The experiences that have hitherto been had with *Aufbau* classes on the lines of the *Deutsche Oberschule* and the *Ober-realschule* already indicate that this practical course in school politics is sound. In any case the *Aufbauschule* will develop successfully only if it remains steadfastly true to its character as a school for gifted pupils, and if the administration remains resolutely opposed to all attempts to found this school on other considerations. It must be fully understood that concern has been expressed among secondary school teachers that it may be possible through the stress of the day to eliminate the nine-year secondary school by indirection through the *Aufbauschule* and that in places where *Aufbauschule* and secondary schools of the traditional type exist the shorter and cheaper course in the former might depopulate the nine-year institutions. The authorities, because they recognize this danger, will be able to avert it by the appropriate selection of locations for the *Auf-bauschulen*, through pressure on these to maintain the requisite standards, through suitable organization of secondary education in general. The request of the secondary school body not to establish any *Aufbauschulen* at all in larger towns, the Ministry could not grant. If in any city sufficient pupils are available and ready to advance from the elementary to a secondary school, no education authority should leave such educational needs unsatisfied. Pupils of average ability will remain away from these schools. Parents and local administrative bodies will soon realize that only a minority of boys and girls can in six years [20] be brought up to the standard of admission to the university.

At the moment there are state *Aufbau* classes in seventy places; of these the classes in fifty-three places will as from April 1, 1925, be recognized as "higher institutions (*Aufbauschulen*) in process of development." Further, there are five *Aufbauschulen* for boys and for girls associated with city secondary schools. In addition there is one *Aufbauschule* for girls connected with a private secondary school.

### IV. SECONDARY SCHOOLS FOR GIRLS

The incorporation of the education of girls into the general system has developed relatively slowly. The administration has for a long time hesitated to accept even the general recognition that the girls have the same right, the same claim to education as the boys. The *Reorganization of the Educational System for Girls*,[21] issued in 1908, represents indeed a considerable advance over the efforts of the nineties and some tentative experiments, but it left important demands unsatisfied.

The Regulations of 1908 introduced the *Lyzeum* at that time as the usual school for girls, an institution similar to the *Realschule* and comprising a seven-year course above the preparatory stage. On the fourth class of the *Lyzeum* (seventh school year) a *Studienanstalt* along the lines of the *Realgymnasial* or *Gymnasial* reform school could be built up, and from the third class the *Studienanstalt* of the type of the *Oberrealschule* could branch off. These three *Studienanstalten* resembled but did not slavishly copy the corresponding institutions for boys; so far as privileges were concerned they were identical. The *Oberlyzeum*, however, which came into being as an advanced normal school or a practical arts school for women, had no parallel. The latter had at first to contend with great difficulties and seemed unable to arrive at a stable position, until the Regulations [22] of 1917 opened up for it new possibilities of development. The *Oberlyzeum* of the academic type, on the other hand, spread rapidly. There soon developed a widespread effort to

---

[20] For the time-schedules of the *Aufbauschule*, see Part II.

[21] *Neuordnung des Madchenschulwesens; Erlass vom 18. 8. 1908—U III D 6561. Zentralblatt*, p. 692.

[22] *Erlass vom 31. 12. 1917—U II W 405 II. Zentralblatt*, 1918, p. 276.

divorce it of its character as a professional school and to turn it into a school for general culture at least in the last three classes. Up to 1913 the movement succeeded only in securing for the holders of the teachers' certificates the right to matriculate in the faculty of philosophy; graduates of the *Oberlyzeum* were required to take a supplementary examination to enjoy the same status as graduates of a complete secondary school—a solution which could not be considered as wholly satisfactory. Further study of the problems of secondary education of girls continued in a state of flux but was unfortunately checked by the War.

Then followed the Revolution. New problems in full measure pressed for solution in the whole political field. The question of the education of women did not appear to be so urgent, and compared with the great organizations strongly interested in the reform of the whole educational system the leading groups in the women's movement among the public at large appeared for the moment to be exhausted when the council of the people's representatives in its proclamation of November 12, 1918, to the German people granted women the right to vote, which was later embodied into Article 22 of the Federal Constitution. Thereby a struggle was settled, in which even the most convinced supporters of women's rights had scarcely dared to dream that the prize of victory would so quickly and so easily fall into their laps.

Few, however, realized the number of new and difficult problems that were set up by this measure. With the right that the new state granted at this time to the German women, it had to associate the duty of striving with combined strength that all their abilities should be utilized for the tasks that now confronted them. Had the ballot aimed only at drawing the strong reserve of the female sex into elections in order to make one party victorious over the other, this would have resulted in debasing woman into a tool in the political struggle. But if the new rights imposed on women the serious moral duty of devoting their peculiar qualities to political life in order to coöperate creatively at a time of sorest need in the upbuilding of Germany, then new aims were set up for the education of the coming generation of women. On the one hand, there must be the task of giving a better training than hitherto to the German housewife, the German woman, the German educator; on the other hand, to direct the capacity and intelligence of women to the wide range of practical occupations and to win as active collaborators in the political community millions of able personalities hitherto not employed, often neglected through social prejudices. Preceding generations left very much undone in the education of rising womanhood, not to mention at all preparation for professional activity outside the home and in the service of the state; women were only called into council hesitantly on questions that affected the destiny of their sex. Even at the Federal Education Conference the situation could arise that women were assigned a regrettably subordinate place in the active coöperation in the development of the educational system. At the plenary session on June 19, Helene Lange protested seriously that the Federal Conference had not assigned to women a representation corresponding to the significance of prevailing questions in the reports of the full assembly; she urged that "an irrevocable opportunity had been lost to win the support of the male colleagues in boys' schools of all types, in which the influence of the male is decisive for the conviction represented by us, that the influence of women should be decisive in the training and education of girls if they are to attain their aim of rendering the intellectual and productive ability of women useful for the whole community."

The warning of the bold protagonist for an appropriate organization of the education of girls was unfortunately passed over almost without a hearing. The large problems of school development, the question of teacher preparation and the methodical organization of each school subject, the participation of parents and parents' councils in the equipment of the school, and others too often dominated the public discussion to make it possible to bring the question of girls' education to a conclusion. The strong contradiction between the proposals, which no one felt sufficiently confident to carry out, made the situation difficult. The tendency to reject entirely special arrangements of a scholastic nature for women and to set up in the school system an exact parallel to the provision for boys was opposed to another tendency which demanded an organization in accordance with the special intellectual and spiritual nature of girls.

In 1921 Prussia resolutely took hold of the problem. The

August conference was summoned at which a large number of men and women devoted two days to a consideration of the reorganization of education of girls, fifteen years after the June Conference of 1906 which was expected to solve the problem of women's education under the chairmanship of Althoff. The Conference, convened and opened by Minister Becker and presided over by Ministerial-Director Jahnke, was required to clarify the contradictory views and give expression to the resolution of the Ministry to find a solution for the varied problems of the present by practical work. It was significant that shortly before this the position as councilor on girls' education in the Ministry had been entrusted to a woman.

The central point of the discussion concerned the question whether the *Lyzeum* and *Oberlyzeum* should be retained or modified. On this one group supported the old demand that the *Lyzeum* be converted into a *Realschule*, while the other group would have preferred to see it changed to the *Deutsche Oberschule*. In any case the defects of the existing school type again became obvious and valuable suggestions were offered for its future organization.

After this conference, which had also been occupied with the *Deutsche Oberschule* and coeducation of boys and girls, the reform was successfully carried through by quick, steady work in the Ministry. When the education budget came up for discussion in 1921 and 1922 the political parties in the Committee of the Whole were given an opportunity to express their opinions in detail on existing questions; in December, 1922, the main outlines of the reform were ready; the Ministry of the State approved it in March, 1923; and on March 21 it was possible to issue a general decree [23] on the subject.

The main object of the reform was to develop and enrich the education of the rising generation of women, for which the Regulations of 1908 had only introduced a temporary solution; at the same time it was intended to incorporate the secondary schools for girls with the common school system. It was desirable to free the greater part of the education of girls from a certain isolation, and to ensure for girls in general the same educational opportunities, including access to the universities,

[23] *Erlass vom 21. 3. 1923—U II W 486. Zentralblatt*, p. 147.

as had been enjoyed by boys for a long time. It would have been a mistake to approach the reform entirely from the standpoint that every girl in a secondary school should be prepared to become a university student. Just as the Prussian Ministry in no sense regards the secondary schools for boys as preparatory institutions for the learned professions and considers "graduation" as something quite different from "maturity for university education," so it refused to undertake the reform of girls' education with an erroneous leaning towards intellectualism.

The needs of an organization of girls' education would not have been met simply by a compulsory transfer of the types of secondary schools for boys. Not only will the development of their peculiar intellectual characteristics be better promoted by enlisting the influence of women in the training of growing girls, but the desire to organize girls' education in accordance with its own laws and to give it a special form different from that for boys is readily understood. The *Oberrealschule* with its strong emphasis on mathematics and sciences, the humanistic *Gymnasium* with its aim of enriching education through the antiquities, the *Realgymnasium* as the modern *Gymnasium* sacrificing Greek to necessity in order to find more room in its curriculum for modern languages, mathematics and sciences, the *Deutsche Oberschule* with its strong emphasis on German humanities and its reference of all subjects to German as the core of integrated instruction, all these have proved themselves useful means for a self-contained system of education for girls. They need not, however, be the only ones. The *Lyzeum* and the *Oberlyzeum* of 1908 have already proved that these types are entirely suited to the feminine genius with its peculiar gift for linguistic-historical subjects and for religious and ethical emotions. All that they needed was to be developed in such a way that they can be regarded as of equal standing in all respects with the other secondary schools.

Two provisions were needed for this. In the first place the Ministry was compelled, on the basis of experiences with the so-called Kottbus plan [24] to guarantee, when the course of study

[24] The so-called Kottbus Plan of 9, 1, 20 (*Erlass vom 9. 1. 20—U II W 15 1977 I und II*) represented a serious solution under stress which has caused the administration considerable difficulties. The administration gave permission in one case (Kottbus) and as an experiment to transform the three

was issued, that the institutions adopting it also granted a certificate that would in fact be accepted for admission by the universities. An experiment over a longer period, which would have kept these institutions in suspense, might have rendered the whole reform illusory. A certain amount of leaning toward the hitherto recognized school types was therefore essential. The curriculum of the *Lyzeum* of 1908 closely resembles that of the *Realschule D 1* of 1901. Hitherto, however, this type has not been extended in boys' schools beyond the sixth year as far as university entrance standards. It was only the free organization of the course in the upper classes (Decree of January 24, 1922) that made it possible to introduce side by side with the mathematical-scientific emphasis another in which the language subjects are the main features. This type seemed to be the appropriate one for development as the normal type for girls' schools. By the introduction of a fourth period for arithmetic and mathematics, long desired, by the improvement of the history course which has been urgently needed, through philosophical enrichment of instruction in the upper classes, a type of school could be created which without objection justified recognition as an institution reaching the standards for admission to the universities.

Further, the demand must be made that the faculties of these institutions be composed in such a way as to meet the higher standards. So far as preparation of teachers is concerned the same regulations must accordingly apply to girls' schools as to schools for boys, and it must be required that all academic instruction from the fourth class on, and in the preceding classes at least half of the academic instruction, be entrusted to university trained teachers.

These two conditions (expansion and enrichment of the curriculum and more university trained teachers) are all the more

upper classes of the *Oberlyzeum* of 1908 into a three-class *Oberrealschule-Studienanstalt*. In these classes the two hours a week for educational theory were to be dropped and the work in mathematics and sciences or foreign languages or German and history were to be increased thereby. Before the information could be obtained on the effects of this, the experiment became general, although it soon appeared that the *Lyzeum*, as formerly organized, was unable to give a foundation for this superstructure. Accordingly the experiment was not sanctioned further by *Erlass vom 10. 1. 1922*—(*U II W 3210, Zentralblatt*, p. 106) and *Erlass vom 13. 4. 1922*—(*U II W 938*).

necessary because of the change from the former ten-year school
for girls (seven years of *Lyzeum* and three years of *Oberlyzeum*)
to the nine-year school (*Oberlyzeum*) because the course has
been shortened by one year in favor of the *Grundschule*. Without fulfillment of these conditions this type of school could not
have obtained recognition as a fully privileged school taking
girls up to the standard of admission to the university. This
measure, however, was necessary not so much to increase the
flow of girls to the universities but rather to facilitate thereby
their entrance into practical careers. Experience shows daily
that young persons of both sexes advance more readily in industry and commerce and many other branches of wage-earning
careers if they can give evidence of a completed school education. The change can be quickly accomplished in the majority
of institutions and will be simplified by certain transitional
measures so that in a short time the first graduates will come
out of these institutions.

To-day the reorganization of the school system for girls as
here outlined is termed the ''small reform,'' for since the beginning of 1924 it has been incorporated in the reorganization of
the Prussian school system. Although the *Memorandum on the
Reform of Our Secondary School System* deals only briefly with
the problems of girls' education, it would be a mistake to deduce
from this that they should be regarded as of less significance
than problems of boys' education. The contrary is intended.
The ideas that are directive in the change of our school system
should also be developed fully in the education of girls. The
special functions of each school type will be described in the
courses of study that will shortly be published.

In the meantime the question that will help to relieve parents
has also been clarified, that is, whether the new types will be
recognized as preparatory institutions to universities in the
other states. The situation at present is as follows: The graduation certificates of the *Oberlyzeum* and *Oberrealschule* are accepted for admission to the universities of some states. The
certificate of the ''new'' *Oberlyzeum* [25] is for the time being
refused recognition only in Bavaria. On the *Deutsche Oberschule* negotiations are being conducted between the govern-

[25] See Part II.

ments, while for a transitional period up to 1931 recognition is assured for the certificates of such *Oberlyzeum* as are in process of transformation into *Deutsche Oberschulen;* Bavaria alone has withheld her approval also on this point.

The "old" *Oberlyzeen,* that is, the few that have continued according to the Regulations of 1908, will in a few years have disappeared, since the regulations on the preparation of teachers resulting from the resolution of the Ministry of the State on October 7, 1924, prohibit their further continuance. It is to be hoped, however, that the new *Oberlyzeum,* with its own appropriate time-schedule, will win an honorable position as a distinct type as a result of its strongly specialized character.

In the discussion on the future secondary school for girls the question of the duration of the course was warmly contested. While the principals and teachers of the *Lyzeum* and *Oberlyzeum* strongly advocated the ten-year course for the complete institution, by far the largest majority of women teachers and parents stood energetically for the position that the earlier situation be restored when no distinction was made known between duration of courses for the two sexes. So there developed the realization, to which the Ministry did not lend its support, that after the legal introduction of the four-year *Grundschule* a school course of four and ten (fourteen) years means a burden on girls which must be injurious for them. All reasons, urged also by medical councils, for the retention for girls of the ten-year course (or seven years in the *Lyzeum*) which, after all, was first introduced in 1908, were most seriously weighed, and it is unreasonable for the advocates of the ten-year course to maintain that the demands of quite a small group of women for purely mechanical equivalence gained the victory in the Prussian Ministry. The real reason for the measure is obvious. After the four-year attendance at the *Grundschule* was legally established and the weakness of a three-year preparation for the secondary school which had become the rule for girls had been removed, the really artificial extension of six years in the *Lyzeum* and nine years in the *Oberlyzeum* to seven and ten years respectively could again be abandoned immediately. The whole length of the school period, which formerly was three plus ten (thirteen years) remains the same except that the total is differently distributed into four and nine years.

If in opposition to these reasons, frequently adduced, the friends of the ten-year course point to the unavoidable and necessary protection of young girls, particularly at the time of sexual maturity, it should not be forgotten that protection should equally be demanded for boys at the time of puberty. And yet an extension of the school period for boys from nine to ten years is hardly demanded seriously. This question can in fact not be solved by an extension of the school period; with greater resolution than hitherto it must be attacked by successful campaigning against overburdening of all our youth. On this there is required the same attention for both sexes on the part of the authorities and the whole teaching body. Under any circumstances, the number of hours per week must be reduced to a tolerable load, and the efforts for educational reform which aim at intelligent, individual treatment of the growing boy and girl must become the possession of all. Then will be silenced the complaints which continue to be made on the reduction of the course in girls' secondary schools from ten to nine years.

Since boys and girls have thus to spend the same amount of time until graduation from school, there can be no question that the course for girls is made identical with that for boys by the sacrifice of a year; rather is it the case that the education of boys has been made of the same duration as that of girls through the operation of the *Grundschule* law. While the education of boys formerly lasted three plus nine (twelve years), to-day its length is, like that of girls, four plus nine (thirteen) years. This extension will bear good fruit, just as soon as the number of periods per week is reduced to a teachable load.

One word in this connection on the question of coeducation of boys and girls, keenly advocated by many in the days when the school system was being reorganized. The Ministry was seriously opposed to this demand, for reasons based on developmental psychology and educational sociology. The course of development of the growing boy is quite different from that of the growing girl. To bring them together for common education and instruction would at a time of sexual and intellectual maturing inevitably mean the subordination of one side to the detriment of the other. Further, just in those years in which education in the case of girls must be associated with quite different complexes of emotion and ideas than in the case of boys, and in which there is quite a differently constituted yearning for social living, neither side would receive its due. If the common school is preëminently a school for differentiation, it is difficult to see why in this most important and scarcely uninvestigated field uniformity should suddenly be proposed.

Coeducation, or rather, coinstruction, as a makeshift is in a different position. Everywhere where intellectually gifted girls, especially in small towns, have no opportunity to attend an *Oberlyzeum* or *Studienanstalt* leading to the university, provision should be made to admit them as individuals to the secondary schools for boys. Such a measure is demanded by social considerations for all who would otherwise be excluded from advanced education. The Prussian Ministry has in several decrees [26] issued uniform regulations on the question of admission to boys' secondary schools. Experimentation with this so-called limited coeducation is not yet completed. Extremely favorable results on one side, a few not quite so good on the other, encourage the hope that the method entered upon is the right one, particularly when some serious tendencies of fashion have spent themselves.

The lower and middle parts of the newly created nine-year *Oberlyzeum*, the six-year *Lyzeum* (VI to U II), will, when conditions for the composition of the teaching staff to be imposed on the complete institution are met, confer the privilege of granting to a pupil after successfully passing through U II admission to O II in an *Oberlyzeum* on the basis of a promotion certificate. The *Lyzeum* thus stands in the same relation to the *Oberlyzeum* as the *Realschule* to the *Oberrealschule*.

Experience has shown that the majority of girls complete their schooling at the close of their tenth school year, and the efforts neither of groups of women interested in the reform nor of the administration are directed toward bringing all girls up to the standards of university entrance. Hence for those girls who have no ambitions of this kind but have a particular inclination to practical subjects a way must be found of giving them an opportunity to develop their powers in accordance with their abilities. Provision will be made in U II of the complete institution or of the *Lyzeum* to distribute the pupils, so that one group,

[26] *Erlass vom 3. 7. 1922—U II 695. Zentralblatt,* p. 337; and *Erlass vom 24. 4. 1923—U II 481.*

which we may call the academic, continues its studies according to the plan pursued up to that point, while the other, practically inclined, receives limited instruction in foreign languages and increased instruction instead in technical subjects. By a special course of study in mathematics and history an effort will be made to prepare the pupils for direct entrance into a course of vocational training, while an increase of three hours in religious instruction will again exert strong influence on the girls at the very end of the school career.[27] The class as a whole will find its completion in the *Frauenschule*.

Since the problem of the reorganization of the whole of our educational system is concerned with a change which should not be hasty but which should develop slowly, quietly and steadily, there is no reason to require all existing *Lyzeen* at once to adopt the new regulations hurriedly. Of course, the time-schedule must be the same everywhere, but the new requirements for the composition of the faculty cannot immediately be met everywhere. It is surely of no small importance for the further development of our system to discover experimentally what deviations will occur in the results attained in an institution with a full academic faculty and in others with a mixed staff consisting of teachers trained in normal schools and in universities. These institutions, however, cannot be given the privilege of granting a certificate admitting pupils to O II of an *Oberlyzeum*. It will probably not be difficult for girls coming from these institutions to pass an entrance examination for O II of the *Oberlyzeum*. The *Lyzeum* is not prohibited from adding another class beyond U II in place of the lowest class that has been lost to the *Grundschule* and organizing it as a *Frauenschule* or as an academic graduating class. Each institution will be granted fullest liberty of organization.

Only the new courses of study, which are about to be completed, will show how the new type of school should be provided with new content. Just as the inner connection between different branches of the girls' schools was formerly more strongly emphasized than in the boys' schools, so the reorganization of the education for girls, as introduced by the Decree of March

[27] In the *Suggestions* of March 21, 1923, a somewhat different course was planned for U II B. In this form, however, the class seemed to possess little attraction; hence the changes in the time-schedule.

21, 1923, presents the clearest articulation in the whole of our educational system. After the common four-year *Grundschule* for all, girls will continue their education either in the four-year elementary school, or in the six-year middle school, or in the *Lyzeum*. Following the intermediate course (classes VI to IV), common to all secondary schools, according to the reorganization of 1924, in which a modern language will be studied—the Decree of February 10, 1923,[28] also leaves it open whether this first modern language shall be French or English—the pupils are divided according to their ability. The following choices are open to girls after their seventh school year: They may either continue directly the course already begun and graduate in three years from the *Lyzeum* or in six years from the *Oberlyzeum,* or they may transfer to the *Studienanstalt* with three courses, *Gymnasium, Realgymnasium,* or *Deutsche Oberschule,* and graduate in six years. The *Studienanstalt* of the type of the *Oberrealschule,* which formerly branched off from U III of the *Lyzeum,* is in future to follow U II, so that pupils may graduate in three years. The resulting picture is that classes VI-IV of the *Oberlyzeum* or *Lyzeum* provide an excellent intermediate structure for the whole system of girls' education on which are directly based the *Deutsche Oberschule, Gymnasium, Realgymnasium,* the *Oberlyzeum,* with the *Oberrealschule* as a branch. Transfer to these institutions involves no byways. The common intermediate course of the secondary schools for girls will be attended by all whose ability and attainment warrant it. Still the financial difficulties of the state and the necessity facing all families of putting their children into practical careers as early as possible as wage-earning members of the home, will often render the practical development of the ideas of the common school, which is now an actuality, illusory. The *Deutsche Oberschule* is placed side by side with the *Oberlyzeum* because the provision of the cultural subjects appropriate to this school should be regarded as specially valuable for the training of German women.[29]

[28] *Erlass vom 10. 2. 1923—U II 157. Zentralblatt,* p. 88.
[29] For the time-schedules of the regular schools for girls, see appropriate section in Part II.

# CHAPTER VI

## ART HIGH SCHOOLS AND FINE ARTS IN THE SCHOOLS

Fundamental distinctions in matters of education are to-day of fateful significance to our nation. For the last and noblest capital left to us lies in the hands of our youth as discoverers, inventors, as investigators and creators. To discover creative power wherever it may be stirring, to let it develop and contribute to the work of the whole nation, this general cultural problem will be also solved anew in the fields of art education.

The new state, as heir of the past, succeeded in the field of creative art to the long-established and developed system of art academies.[1] From different points of view both the experts and the public have for some time pressed for a reform of the systems of art training. Aims, methods of work in the art academies, the general ideal indulging their educational theory, all these had of necessity to be carefully sifted after the War in accordance with the changed attitude of the time toward art and with the changed conditions. New ideas which here influenced the Prussian Ministry of Science, Art and Popular Education are collected in the proposals of Ministerial Councillor Waetzoldt: *Gedanken zur Kunstschulreform*.[2]

The following were the chief aims for reform to which the Ministry at the suggestion of Waetzoldt directed particular attention: incorporation of the system of art training into the economic system, the association of this system with the artistic and spiritual movements of the day, the restoration of the craft basis for art, and the combination of fine and applied arts. These

---

[1] Within the purview of the Prussian Ministry of Science, Art and Popular Education there belong: the High School for Creative Arts with the academic studio, the Educational Institute of the Arts and Crafts Museum, both in Berlin, the Art Academies in Dusseldorf, Cassel, Königsberg, the Academy for Art and Art Industry in Breslau, and the Art School in Berlin.

[2] Waetzoldt, W., *Gedanken zur Kunstschulreform* (Quelle und Meyer, Leipzig, 1921).

aims can be attained without disturbing the approved and established institutions, without creating new and doubtful types, and without affecting the training of an extensive supply of craftsmen and artisans. This, as is well known, is the task of the Ministry of Industry and Commerce, which has charge of trade and industrial art schools.

The Ministry was from the start convinced that the reform of art education should not be divorced from the scope of the general reform of education, but rather that it should be incorporated in the organic development of the German educational system. The special professional training, the creative callings, should in the future be built up on the basis of a training in sense of form, ability to observe, and feeling for material acquired in the general schools and imparted to all sections of the population. In the education of the child the concrete objective world must receive greater emphasis than heretofore side by side with the ideational intellectual side. Beyond this the powers of observation and creation that exist in the child must be aroused and cultivated—the young must be brought by self-activity and contact with art objects to a personal spiritual attitude to creative art.

The methods of drawing instruction reorganized in the school reform [3] of 1900 had already attempted to work in this direction for a number of years. Efforts to raise drawing instruction to the position of an art subject of the same value as the academic subjects did not receive official recognition and support until the issue of the new courses of study and the reform of the training of drawing teachers. According to the *Suggestions* even the elementary school is assigned the task of ''allowing the creative power of the child to develop through independent activity,'' and is to-day the foundation for inner appreciation of the works of art. The course of study for the *Deutsche Oberschule* pointed in the same direction but with higher aims, while the artistic task of the drawing lesson is still more strongly emphasized in new courses about to be published for several higher institutions. In accordance with these ideas the drawing teacher is not merely to be the guide of the young in art; rather he should, in co-operation with the representatives of German, music, physical

[3] *Erlass vom 3. 4. 1902—U IV 3147 II. Zentralblatt,* p. 349.

training, endeavor to inspire the whole school with the artistic spirit and make it a model center for the arts of expression. In order to facilitate the fulfillment of this great task steps have been taken to guarantee a more comprehensive and sounder training in art and educational theory. Hitherto this training has been given in special departments, separated from the others in the art high schools, and lower standards of ability in art were set up for those entering these departments than for the art students. By a Decree [4] of November 11, 1920, it has been decided that prospective art teachers must show the same ability in art as prospective artists and that they should be trained not in separate departments but side by side with the art students. Following on this preparatory measure the *Regulations for the Examination of Fine Art Teachers in Secondary Schools* [5] could be issued on May 22, 1922. Starting with the idea that the methods of the art teacher rest upon his own attitude upon the questions and problems in his field and that his point of view must cover the educational ideals in art and its relations to intellectual life in general, the regulations require eligibility for admission to the university, thorough training in art—which also includes the field of manual work, and preparation in psychology and education directed to the aims of art education. Compliance with these requirements insures the candidate a position equivalent to that of the academic teachers and confers on instruction in drawing and art the same recognition as is given to the academic subjects. The significance merited by this subject as an important method for the development of personality is indicated in the time-schedules,[6] which require the introduction of this subject in all fully organized secondary schools from the first to the last classes. It is also indicated in the Decree [7] of July 1, 1920, which provides that drawing is to be taken into account in considering the standing of pupils for purposes of promotion and graduation.

To arouse the sense for the concrete-objective and to guide the natural creative impulse of children in the direction of purposeful and appreciative creative activity is the particular task

[4] *Erlass vom 11. 11. 1920—U IV 8073 II.*
[5] *Erlass vom 22. 5. 1922—U IV 10758 II. Zentralblatt, p. 257.*
[6] See Part II.
[7] *Erlass vom 1. 7. 1920—U II 22. Zentralblatt, p. 593.*

of manual instruction.  It has admittedly taken a long time before the recognition of the significance of this branch and of the educative value of handwork in particular dawned.  Even to-day, in spite of Article 148 of the Federal Constitution which requires activity instruction (*Arbeitsunterricht*) as a subject of the curriculum, there is not lacking opposition, which combined with external obstacles holds up the introduction of manual work in the schools.  Some progress has been achieved in so far as manual instruction has been included in the *Suggestions* for elementary schools and in the courses for the *Deutsche Ober-schule, Aufbauschule,* and U II b of the *Oberlyzeum;* it was already included in the middle school.  The general economic stress which prevented the establishment of regular school work-shops proved a boon in that it led to the enlistment of the co-operation of pupils in meeting the material needs of the school, while it aroused among parents understanding for manual work and stimulated them to give assistance.  This concrete applica-tion of manual instruction was materially promoted by the Decree [8] of April 9, 1921.  Reports from school authorities who refer to the subject not only indicate the wide expansion of self-help in the schools, but also furnish a valuable survey of the extent of practical tasks which could be carried out in service of school instruction as well as to meet their own needs.[9]  Un-fortunately there is a dearth in not a few places of teachers sufficiently trained in manual work and art to guide the pupils in practical work and to develop their creative ability.  To remove this deficiency and to enlist academic teachers by the side of art teachers in the service of manual instruction, the Ministry in the *Regulations for the Examination of Teachers of Art* [10] of May 22, 1922, made manual activity a compulsory major subject, approved by the Decree [11] of November 10, 1923, the same subject as a minor in the examination for academic teachers, and on May 24, 1924, issued a special *Regulation for the Examination of Manual Instructors.*[12]  Further, manual instruction in its main branches, with the necessary equipment,

[8] *Erlass vom 9. 4. 1921—U III A 5661. Zentralblatt,* p. 197.
[9] A comprehensive report will be published in the *Jahrbuch des Zentral-instituts für Erziehung und Unterricht.*
[10] *Erlass vom 22. 5. 1922—U IV 10758 II. Zentralblatt,* p. 257.
[11] *Erlass vom 10. 11. 1923—U II 16974. Zentralblatt,* p. 379.
[12] *Erlass vom 24. 5. 1924—U III A 719. Zentralblatt,* p. 179.

was introduced for the first time in the art academies at Cassel and Königsberg, and the establishment of municipal institutions for training teachers of manual work was promoted in Hildesheim, Düsseldorf, and Cologne. State support for current expenses is also given to the three last-named institutions. It is thus to be hoped that in spite of the temporary disfavor manual instruction will be further developed and that it will also promote in increasing measure the artistic education of the young.

The reform of art education is associated with general educational questions in still another sense. The inner organization of schools of art will in the future be materially affected by the general adoption of the new educational ideal which is characterized by the will to truth, increased pleasure in responsibility, and warm community feelings. The strict discipline of the workshop, without which serious workmanship is impossible, is balanced on the road to the master schools that crown the whole system by a gradually increasing participation in management on the part of the learner and a greater measure of self-determination which is implicit in true "academic freedom."

With these fundamental principles as a starting-point a reform of the Prussian art high schools has been carried out since 1921. In view of the fact that the financial conditions of the state at a time of decisive changes were of themselves obstacles, the section of the Ministry responsible for the supervision of art affairs was compelled to accept certain restrictions in its program. The traditional system of a schematic organization of the academies in classes which had to be passed in a definite order was replaced by a more flexible plan which permitted the young artists after being admitted freer choice of their course and teachers (Decree [13] of February 10, 1923). For admission of students to the Prussian art high schools preparation in manual work as well as evidence of artistic skill and training in drawing are required on principle.

In order to give the faculties in academies more participation than hitherto in the internal affairs of the institutions, their coöperation in the appointment of new members has been provided for in the same way as has been the practice traditionally in the universities.[14]

[13] *Erlass vom 10. 2. 1923—U IV 2658.1. Zentralblatt*, p. 134.
[14] *Erlass vom 8. 9. 1923—U IV 1978.*

The provision of art training in schools for manual instruction, the alternation between classes and workshops, the possibility of moving from one field to another in the high school according to the stage of individual capacity, the introduction of a composite art notion into education through the close association of institutions and classes for free and applied art, this *requirement* of many-sided training on the one hand and freedom on the other to follow according to individual capacities a course of art and craft education from the study of manual work right up to the master studios or to complete it with a well-rounded professional training—these are the chief characteristics of the reforms so far introduced. They are also the principles on which was based the Decree of September 8, 1924, or the *Regulations for the Combined State Schools for Pure and Applied Art* at Charlottenburg. The Combined State Schools for Pure and Applied Art arose as a result of the combination in organization and buildings of the Industrial Art Museum and the former High Schools for Creative Arts. In scope, reorganization, and existing constitution these schools represent a new type of art high school. Its organization appeared in the Course of Study issued in the winter semester of 1924-25.

At the head of each of the three divisions there is a divisional chief selected from the faculty, while seven elected representatives of the faculty constitute a teachers' council that assists the director of the whole institution. The director is also assisted by a governing body of which officials of the Ministries concerned and representatives of art societies, arts and crafts, and individual arts are members. That these ideas carried into practice with the approval of the Prussian Diet represent a general tendency of the day is indicated by the lively interest shown not only by the art administrators of German states but also by the attention with which the work of the Prussian art administration in the field of school reform is followed in foreign countries.

Three fundamental values are to be retained or to be achieved in the reform of art schools. In the forefront stands the creative art of young men working on a common task in close association with outstanding creative personalities, with "masters." Secondly, there is the educative value of the spiritual, which must not be confused with the intellectual. Finally, all creative work must be inspired by the advantage that comes from productive work in contrast to the blight of mere planning for which there is no demand. It must be admitted that we realize throughout the dangers to which the art school of the future will be exposed, the dangers of dilettanteism, of pseudo-craftsmanship, of fashion, of the drilling of students in artistic style. But these dangers can be successfully met since they are foreseen.

On details of the reform there is room for argument. Some things will not be carried out according to plan; for others conditions of an administrative nature must first be slowly prepared. Material needs will be met by persistence, ambition, and professional spirit. Success will not at once attend every phase, and various solutions will be found in different localities. This is all to the good, for the finest plan for reform remains lifeless as an artificial head, if it be not supplied with the blood of resolution inspired by race and country.

In the cultivation of and training in music important problems have been attacked and effort made toward their solution. As the war years drew to an end and so many intellectual interests were revived, the significance of music, the least rationalistic of all arts, increased and gained in real strength not only in the life of the individual but more widely in communities, societies of youths at school, at home, and in clubs. This is to be greeted with the heartiest welcome, for it is the spiritual development of our people that should be promoted by all means. Accordingly, the Prussian Ministry devoted careful attention to this contemporary movement which is clearly reflected in public life in order to smooth the road for the most important movements by appropriate measures.

The conviction is rapidly being established that the cult of music can only succeed if the musical instincts that are living in the people are aroused and fostered with every care. It is not only the concerts and operas that are daily offered in our cities that set the standard for the musical culture of the German people. Only when every sound and song, in church and school, house and club, town and country are given respectful attention, will it be clear how infinitely deep and living is the love of all musical expression in our people. Hence the state is endeavoring to apply the modest resources available for the promotion of art also to the general problems of musical education in order to satisfy the immediate needs of the people. The countless musical societies, clubs, and organizations constitute a strong foundation for the development of musical interests. This broad basis furnishes a guarantee that, in spite of external need and pressure which are our lot, the roots of German music remain sound and strong.

The reform of musical education is based on this fundamental idea. In a *Memorandum for the General Cultivation of Music at School and Among the People,* written by Professor Kestenberg and presented to the Diet on April 25, 1923, the links between life and school, between art and the people are developed in detail in order to define the field for the future organization of German music.

The problem of first importance was to secure professional training in music, which had suffered seriously during the War and to insure anew the status of German institutions for musical education. In the master schools for musical composition appointments were given to the leading personalities like Hans Pfitzner and Ferruccio Busoni, who are setting their marks on the creative work of to-day; these with George Schumann, who is also an active master in classes, represent the characteristic tendencies of our time. On the death of Busoni the Ministry is compelled to search for a master worthy to succeed the creator of a "new classicism."

The State High School for Music in Berlin is experiencing a new lease of life, since the positions unfilled until now have been given to authorities well known in the public musical life of our day. A new impetus was given to the Operatic School which graduates its students almost without exception as practiced stage singers. In an Operatic Chorus with a huge attendance, the future operatic choruses are trained. A large High School Choir is doing exemplary work in the performance of masterpieces from the whole range of choral literature. The State Cathedral Choir recently incorporated in the High School is also of great significance for the introduction of students to classical church music. Through the collection of records and instruments and through general lecture courses the students receive rich inspiration. A Preparatory Orchestral School established in conjunction with German Musical Association is intended to meet so far as present means permit the increasingly noticeable lack of suitable material for our orchestras that stand in the forefront of art.

While the High School for Music aims to train for opera and concert, chorus and orchestra, the Academy for Church and School Music cultivates sacred and school music. The principles underlying the reform of the Academy lie in the new tasks of education which assign considerably greater significance than in the last decades in the general school program to instruction in music for the purpose of arousing creative powers. On the occasion of the centennial celebration of the Institute for Church Music on June 6, 1922, the Institute was given the title of Academy for Church and School Music, the organization and scope were extended, the attendance increased, women were admitted as students, and additional space was placed at its disposal in the Charlottenburg Palace. Further, a music school for the young was attached to the Academy, in which gifted children receive free instruction in singing and instrumental work and means are provided for the students for training in methods.

The new course of study of the Academy is closely associated with the *Regulations for Examination for Fine Arts Teachers in Secondary Schools*.[15] Through these examinations the way is opened for the teacher of music to become a *Studienrat* and the representatives of fine arts subjects are placed in a position of equality with academic teachers, since their preliminary preparation requires study in a higher institution or university. Candidates may prepare for this examination either in state or in state-recognized institutions. The city administrations in Cologne and Frankfort are planning in coöperation with the Ministry the establishment of institutions which are to be given the same recognition as state institutions. In addition to the Institutes for Church Music, which are affiliated with the universities of Breslau and Königsberg, there will thus be available shortly in Prussia six musical institutions, either state or state-recognized, that can prepare fine arts teachers. Immediately after the appearance of the *Memorandum on the Reorganization of Secondary Education* the position of music in secondary schools was discussed in detail in a fundamental Decree [16] of

[15] *Erlass vom 22. 5. 1922—U IV 10758 II 1. Zentralblatt*, p. 257.
[16] *Erlass vom 14. 4. 1924—U II 456. Zentralblatt*, p. 135. See also

April 14, 1924. While this Decree could only describe the future position of music, the new *Course of Study in Music* which became effective in secondary schools at Easter, 1925, indicates in a practical way what the tasks and aims of music instruction are in the new organization of secondary schools. The revision of the course in elementary and middle schools, and the erection of a new building for music instruction in the future pedagogical academy are still required to provide a broad and effective foundation for the plan of reform in music.

The promotion of the German folk song stands foremost among all these movements. Choral societies that show a special interest in the folk song have in recent years received particular attention from the Ministry. On the occasion of the great Music Festival, held at Hanover in August, 1924, a decree devoted to the encouragement of choral singing was issued. The publication of provincial song books by the Prussian Folk Song Committee to promote the folk song locally, the institution of continuation courses for choir leaders in Berlin and in the provincial capitals, the issue of souvenir records on the occasion of the fiftieth, seventy-fifth, and hundredth anniversaries of famous choral societies, all these evidences have been received with interest and pleasure among those concerned.

For some time no complaints have been heard about abuses in the field of private instruction. Long before the War measures were prepared to institute a certain amount of supervision over conservatories and musical clubs as well as over individual teachers, for musical education at home, which determines our musical culture, stands or falls with the private teacher. The importance of this educational problem led to an introductory decree in May, 1922, which established supervision over the whole field in its different types and variations by requiring all private institutions and teachers to be registered in official records.

As a result it is now possible to take up the task of reorganizing private musical instruction and to introduce state regulation. The most important task will be to protect the public against damage from unqualified teachers. The difficulties in finding qualified music teachers are particularly great, since it is hard

Horstmann, H., *Die Reform des Musikunterrichts an den höheren Lehranstalten Preussens* (Weidmannsche Taschenausgaben, No. 8, Berlin, 1924). Also Part II in this volume.

for an individual to decide on the artistic and pedagogical competence of a teacher in this field, while advertisements are not usually reliable sources of information. Through the introduction of an optional examination, success in which confers the right to call one's self a piano, violin or singing teacher by state examination, through strict enforcement of the regulations for obtaining an official license to teach, an effort will be made to meet the frequent complaints from those concerned in general and professionally.

Not so long ago any coöperation of the state in the wide field of musical culture was rejected as undesirable interference in the free realm of art; to-day there is developing among wide circles of the population an increasing demand for strong universal state guidance and encouragement of esthetic education.

For the German people music is an important part of its strength; in it the people find life and meaning; of all the arts music is the closest to their spiritual emotions. The state honors itself, if it succeeds in securing the common participation of the whole of our people in our irreplaceable musical heritage and in smoothing the path for a new and more fortunate generation of active teachers and students of music. That a specially important function is to be performed by the school in this work, now that normal schools which were so important for musical instruction have disappeared, is increasingly recognized. The Prussian Ministry is conscious that in everything that it plans and does it will serve to uplift the life of the people if it succeeds in developing fully the strong spiritual influences that are embodied in music and above all in German song.

# CHAPTER VII

## ADULT EDUCATION

An entirely new series of problems was undertaken by the Prussian Ministry of Science, Art and Popular Education when it determined after the Revolution to become a Ministry of Popular Education in the broadest sense of the term. This meant that it must turn its attention to the system of folk high schools which pressed for organization and development during the War, largely as a consequence of experiences during the War. To believe that the folk high school can be dismissed as a temporary fad is to ignore its significance. The folk high school may perhaps have made a somewhat stormy appearance, but preparation for it had already been made for some time past. A study of the development of the work of German popular education during the last few decades reveals that the folk high school is not some momentary phenomenon which sprang up without resources and for the first time during the Revolution; rather does it enter on a new stage of development which reaches back to the middle of the last century and which in the best and fullest sense aims at the coöperation of all the people in a uniform German popular culture.

Historically speaking, the folk high school is the third phase of the system of the free popular culture in Germany. From the middle of the nineteenth century the Evangelical and Catholic churches created in the Evangelical Workers' Associations (1848) and the Catholic Journeymen's Associations (1849), like the Associations of St. Charles Borromaeus (1844), organizations which became and still are important factors in German education with a denominational character. This first sectarian phase in the folk high school movement was followed by the separate group of liberal social democratic cultural societies which arose after 1870, aiming to be like other groups the bearers and transmitters of a philosophy of the world and of life. After 1871 there began the period of "neutral" popular culture which,

117

starting from the conception of an objective science, thought that it was possible to keep out all questions of politics, religion, and philosophy of life from its undertaking to transmit science. From the point of view of method this group offered in the main individual lectures, the subjects of which were diverse and varied, to large audiences. "Culture" was here identified with the acquisition of as comprehensive an amount of knowledge as possible.

During the course of the War attention was directed from various quarters to the ideas of the Danish, Swedish, and English systems of adult education. A few German folk high schools had already sprung up before 1914 in Schleswig-Holstein. The Village Church Conference held at Marburg in the summer of 1916 was devoted entirely to the idea of the folk high schools and it spread widely among groups interested in the work of denominational adult education. After the War the folk high school acquired a sudden popularity in circles which had hitherto remained aloof from the free folk high school movement and which recognized in it a sort of panacea against disaster. Although in many cases all intrinsic and in part external conditions were lacking, there were everywhere established on a wholesale scale folk high schools, which naturally could not survive the hard test of the succeeding years and which were in any case doomed to failure. The old organizations for adult education, in so far as they adopted the idea of the folk high school, have entered on a new stage in their development. German Popular, Lutheran, Catholic, Socialist folk high schools have sprung up and in spite of the extremely threatening financial situation still exist. By the side of these a place is sought by the "neutral" folk high schools. In general the situation is as follows: the folk high schools everywhere constitute the center around which the sphere of adult education revolves.

The Prussian Ministry of Science, Art and Popular Education has regarded it as its duty not merely to promote the idea of the folk high school but in particular to safeguard it against the danger of superficiality which threatened occasionally in the early days. This was done through the publication with the help of the Ministry of the journal, *Die Arbeitsgemeinschaft* [1]

[1] Combined since January 1, 1924, with the existing *Archiv für Erwachsenenbildung* (*Verlag der Arbeitsgemeinschaft*, Berlin).

through decrees (see the official documents *Zur Volkshochschul-frage* issued by the Ministry [2]), and in particular through courses of a week or two weeks, held in provinces in Prussia for the directors of folk high schools, at which the theoretical and practical problems of the folk high school were discussed. Up to the present eighteen such courses have been held. The principle of the working community *(Arbeitsgemeinschaft)*, which consists at most of thirty members of all occupations and every kind of political and religious creed and remains together under the same teacher for common study over several years, was naturally represented here with the result that the idea of the working community was recognized throughout Germany and Austria. This formal principle was accompanied by another point of view. The purpose of the folk high schools is not merely transmitting knowledge; the working community of the folk high school only affirms its real object if it gives its members an opportunity to win for themselves personal possession of important spiritual goods, irrational command of rational knowledge. A center for such work, which offers each individual an opportunity to deepen not only his knowledge but his whole outlook on the world and his inner spiritual attitude, to strengthen him in honest struggle with different points of view, it should, in spite of some objection to the name, be called folk high school, because the so-called educated man needs it as much as the working man. In con-trast to the widespread opinion that the folk high school is in the first place intended for the workers, the Ministry has always adopted the view that the folk high school is of significance for all classes of the population.

For this reason there has originated the conclusion—a view frequently heard to-day everywhere, even in Parliament and press—that the folk high school has not carried out what was expected of it. The folk high school is an institution not merely for the working class, though primarily intended for it, but also for wide sections of the middle class, an institution for which there is no substitute and which is for that reason retained at all costs. Of those who attend the folk high schools one-third to two-thirds belong to the working class, depending on the com-position of the population and the extent to which the school

[2] Quelle und Meyer, Leipzig, 1919.

meets the intellectual needs of the workers. The other members consisted here as everywhere of employees, officials and teachers, merchants, handworkers and housewives. According to available reports there is foundation for the view that the folk high school movement has been run to death. That with the thousands of schools provided in 1919-20, which lacked all the requisite conditions, a reaction must inevitably set in, was to be expected and was anticipated in a Decree of March 26, 1920. To-day only a fraction of the institutions that were called into being remain. Events have shown that only those folk high schools have the chance to survive that have grasped the idea underlying them in its full meaning and have organized their work accordingly. Where this has happened, the most surprising success has been met with even in the country, as experience shows. The folk high school, of course, stands and falls with the personality of the teacher. Hence the most pressing task in this field is in the near future to attract and train competent teachers.

In addition to city folk high schools which in the main carry on their work in evening courses, there is a second type, the residential folk high school. In Prussia there are at present the following residential folk high schools: at Bethel near Bielefeld, Hermannsburg on the Luneburg Heath, Richerode near Jesberg in Hesse, Karlshof in East Prussia—all four on an Evangelical basis; at Gudensberg near Cassel, and Springe on the Deister, both conducted from the Free German Young-Socialist point of view. Of particular significance are the residential folk high schools near the frontiers. In Schleswig-Holstein there are such schools at Leck, Lurden, Mohrkirch-Osterholz, and Rendsburg; in the Rhineland at Orsoy near Mörs; in upper Silesia a school is being established at Neisse-Neuland. While the members of the ordinary folk high schools range in age from twenty-five to forty, the residential schools are generally attended by younger people from eighteen to twenty-one. Naturally in the residential folk high schools, the idea of mutual instruction can predominate. In general these schools are attended by young women in summer and by young men in winter. The course is based on local history, literature and religion.

From another point of view the system of adult education with its residential and day folk high schools, with its free preparatory training of all kinds, has quite a special significance.  It will not be forgotten that Denmark to a great extent owes the result of the referendum in the border regions to the folk high school.  It is Denmark too that has had for a long time in its northern folk high schools educational centers from which has emanated an extraordinarily vigorous cultural movement.  From here it permeated and won the country.  For our threatened frontiers in the East opposite Poland, in the North in Schleswig, as well as in the West in the territory occupied by foreign troops, it will be necessary to conduct a policy of education through systematic penetration with folk high schools of all kinds.  So long as we have faith in our strength, we intend to prove our faith.  Failure should not discourage us, but should give us new strength to do better where we recognize mistakes. Above all we must ever win more men and women who are ready to shoulder this task joyfully and with profound idealism.

# CHAPTER VIII

## UNIVERSITIES AND TECHNICAL HIGH SCHOOLS

In the well-known Ministerial Decree intended by the Ministry of Haenisch to present to the public a reliable discussion between the Prussian universities and the government on the reorganization of higher education, it is stated in the introduction that immediately after the Revolution voices were heard in all parts of Germany demanding a reform of higher education as a prerequisite to intellectual reconstruction. In fact, demands and reform plans which were already discussed in smaller circles before the War were now pushed forward more strenuously with more far-reaching criticism because two facts became known to the masses after the crash; first, the recognition that the universities had toward the end of the nineteenth century won a greater significance for national life by the broader expansion of their scope and by their direct effect on the most widespread classes of the population, and second, the realization that "the really decisive influences of the day were no longer tied to the universities." The inner conflict between the democratization of our education and the aristocratic character of the universities became clear.

The universities, which must be organized in accordance with their immanent idea, are naturally slower than other institutions in following the changes of the times. Hence it might appear that, in spite of all external brilliance, they have lost any real contact with the decisive influences of the generation. Those who failed to understand the problem which lies in the nature of the case or demanded an immediate change on the part of the universities to meet the new tasks of the day, gave passionate and violent expression to the feeling of disillusionment at their failure; no less emphatically they demand an immediate reform of the universities, root and branch, by which all problems of external organization, internal structure and research and teaching function, the student body and student life should be solved.

It was a fortunate circumstance that the Ministry had in State Secretary Becker a man who as a university teacher and administrator possessed an insight into the whole complex of questions from the most varied angles and attacked the task of reform within the limits set by the situation itself.

The decree which originated from his pen stated with absolute definiteness that the spirit of science must not be affected by administrative measures, that scientific progress is the product of creative personalities, that the development of science must be wholly from within. The limits thus set by the state being clearly reorganized it was of greatest significance that the leading statesman in higher education could, in spite of criticism in the universities, give utterance in his book *Gedanken zur Hochschulreform* [1] to the comforting statement that "At the core our universities are sound." The Ministry could not, however, close its eyes to the view that it should not at the same time suggest a systematic program for the tasks to be solved outside of their limits but that it should rather provide the basis for a discussion so that the conflicting forces and tendencies should through an interchange of views reach the solution of the problems. Greater historical institutions, which like the universities have their roots sunk deep in the past, cannot be changed by programs, however carefully they may be prepared in accordance with a logic which in theory is unimpeachable. Consequently neither the criticism of the public nor the attack of the parties concerned could influence the Ministry on the direction or the rate of the reform. By those not directly concerned the clear line of this reform is to-day recognized.

Just as the whole reform policy of the Ministry takes its direction from the idea of the common school, so the incorporation of the universities in the system of the common school became an administrative measure to be solved immediately. In fact no alteration of the internal status of the university was thereby either necessary or indeed desirable, if the university was to be changed in some other way in its innermost character in accordance with the law peculiar to science and with that alone. If it is possible to open in the common school

---

[1] Becker, C. H., *Gedanken zur Hochschulreform* (Quelle und Meyer, Leipzig, 1919). Cf. also the recent book by the same author, *Vom Wesen der Deutschen Universität* (Quelle und Meyer, Leipzig, 1925).

system a free path to the university for those of ability, then
the way should not and ought not to be only through the recognized secondary schools. The numbers here in question will
always be small. Yet the demand for education on the part of
the German people, the almost immeasurable variety of educational efforts in all classes, the permeation of professional and
vocational schools with tendencies to academic education, the
advance from vocational work to theoretical group of problems,
all these ever and increasingly demand an organic connection
with the universities and opportunities for advancement up to
the completion of academic training. Here the Ministry had to
strengthen its position against opposition from the universities.
If it was no longer permissible for the universities to prescribe
regulations for the secondary schools, the Ministry could certainly not allow an artificial barrier in front of those who, overcoming greater obstacles, wished to make a path for themselves
to the universities. These are in fact individuals of the greatest
and most original abilities, men who bring new ideas and creative powers into the higher professions and at the same time
help to bridge the gaps that separate our people and so break
down the development of a system of caste. The universities
will not wish to withdraw from the task, which is certainly not
light, of training in academic work students prepared in different ways and differently constituted. Besides the principles of
organization it also will be necessary to organize preparatory
courses to facilitate transition and progress. To keep one's
work in harmony with the university standards that should not
be lowered will actually serve as a higher discipline for the
academic individual for the selection of really promising talent.

But the demand for many new roads to the university was not
fulfilled with the incorporation of the university in the common
school system. It imparts to the common school the spirit of
the German cultural ideal and as a consequence unity of content.
This most profound yearning for education of the age can only
be satisfied in its full sense by the university. What Becker has
said in his first chapter on the training of our thought and feeling for the general and universal, on the necessity of synthesis
as an ideal which means intellectually a new way of thinking
and morally a new attitude, is undoubtedly the death-knell of
cultural criticism of the last decades and has received in the

last great work [2] of Troeltsch scientific foundation that is thoroughly sound. This point is also quite clear, that the problem of a cultural synthesis itself has been completely left out of consideration in many aspects of modern science. The reasons for this lie in high pressure development of science itself, in the supremacy, in the extension of material needs, and in the consequent division of labor and specialization. It is a superficial way of thinking to desire for the sake of a cultural synthesis and of rational education to set up barriers to research. And yet there is justice in the statement of the Decree of May 17, 1919, that our universities not only serve scientific research and teaching but are also centers of training for the greatest variety of public officials and for liberal professions. Perhaps it should have been stated more clearly in this decree that these educational problems, "dependent on time and circumstances and therefore changeable," have grown out of science and for its sake are philosophical problems to be solved in order that the universities be not asked to undertake tasks foreign to, but tasks peculiar to their character. The absence of synthesis has thus revenged itself at the same time on science as well as on the professional classes trained by it. Everywhere where the life of the professional man compelled him to step outside the limits of his special subject, he naturally fell into dilettanteism, which spread in politics, sociology, and general outlook and showed that superficiality, that unpolitical attitude and sociological naïveté from which the whole German education obviously suffered.

Even though this development of science be regarded as historically unavoidable, and the cultural synthesis that is demanded be considered as a problem that has been suggested but is no longer or not now possible of solution, the will to a synthesis and therefore to a new attitude toward this task is the call of the hour for science. Science should no longer persist in the old isolation; it must not formally reject the problems posed by life and not least by professional life, unless it wishes intellectual life in Germany to split into compartments and become sterile. The university is not in fact merely an institution for research; in the best sense it is an educational institution.

[2] Troeltsch, Ernst, *Der Historismus und seine Probleme*, J. C. B. Mohr, (Paul Siebeck), Tübingen, 1923.

Scientific research must accordingly in the last analysis be incorporated in a system of values which should not remain aloof from the ethos of the people; and this in the end continues to be more dependent on decisions of the will and on acts of faith. The incorporation of the university into the general system of education is therefore an attempt to set before higher education anew the tasks which it has neglected so that the professional man trained and educated by it may be at once a citizen and a German in the full sense of the word. The universities, it is justly claimed, must be informed with the same educational ideals as the other schools. The cultural possessions already enjoyed by other schools must be here taken hold of, established and worked over in their full meaning. What one possesses by nature, another will acquire scientifically by the sweat of his brow in order to make the highest measure of education his own as "a kind of second nature." This is the cultural unity that we need. When all teachers in elementary or secondary schools or in the universities in the service of the same educational task work for German youth and the German people, each one equally responsible to the nation, we will succeed in advancing from cultural to national unity.

All this, however, is only possible if the universities and technical high schools are readily open to the reform ideas from the point of view of education and organization. Much in these institutions appeared too crude and stiff not merely in the disturbed days of the Revolution. This was true in particular of the prevailing administration in universities. For this reason the Prussian Ministry, in its discussion of university reform, placed organization in the forefront. Next it took hold enthusiastically of the question of educational reform, even though up to the present owing to the difficult situations only gradual success could be expected, and devoted all its attention to the development of the student body.

Prussia has on principle retained as a condition for admission to the state universities graduation from a full nine-year secondary school. No other course is possible if the high position enjoyed academically by our university system is not to be lowered. The state has not, however, stood idly by but has opened the way for university study under certain conditions for especially gifted and competent students who of necessity had some other preparatory education. Only the future can show whether these extensions of the admission basis are fully justified and whether the conditions and guarantees that are associated with them protect the universities against the admission of unqualified students.

By Regulations issued on September 19, 1924, *University Studies for Elementary Teachers*,[3] an opportunity to study in the universities was opened up to teachers temporarily until the problem of teacher training is finally solved. The Regulations anticipate three courses: Either the study of education and philosophy without a previous supplementary examination and of course without any further privileges; or a study of the mental and natural sciences for the purpose of acquiring qualifications for teaching in a secondary school after a supplementary examination; or, finally, study also of the other subjects after passing the abbreviated examination for admission, varying with the particular subject. The last method has not satisfied the elementary school teachers, who rather expected that this abbreviated examination would be accepted as generally valid for all professional subjects. The Ministry, however, did not have it in its power to grant these wishes, since its authority only covers admission to study for the examinations for the secondary school teaching profession. For admission to state examinations in other subjects other authorities are responsible and up to the present these have been unable to decide to reorganize the abbreviated examination as equivalent to the regular secondary school leaving examinations. It must be admitted that this situation is unsatisfactory. The university is accordingly endeavoring, in agreement with the other states that have universities, to reach a general recognition of the abbreviated examination as a qualification for entrance.

In addition to these opportunities of access to the university, intended mainly for elementary school teachers, the Ministry has also opened up other roads to higher education. Thus in order to secure uniform regulation of admission to matriculation and graduation in the economic and social science faculties of Frankfort and Cologne for those who have not graduated from a nine-year secondary school, a substitute examination [4]

[3] *Erlass vom 19. 9. 1919—U I, 1977. Zentralblatt,* p. 580.
[4] *Erlass vom 1. 8. 1922—U I 21021. Zentralblatt,* pp. 417-19.

was introduced in 1922 in general cultural subjects, which on the basis of experience in the interval was reorganized in 1924 (Decree [5] of August 12, 1924) and expanded with reference to regulations for admission and academic awards. Candidates who have completed the seventh year of a secondary school and have graduated from a higher school of commerce or have passed a commercial or similar professional examination in a university with at least the mark of "good" are admitted to this examination. Success in the substitute examination confers in the field of industrial management and with certain limitations in political economy all the rights otherwise associated with the regular graduation certificate of a secondary school.

Similar arrangements are being made for inexperienced agriculturists. In agreement with the Ministry of Agriculture, Domains and Forests, a substitute examination for agriculturists is being organized, which in the same way will provide for the professional and general principles in the study of agriculture.

In this connection a reorganization of the regulation for admission to technical high schools which has been warmly welcomed is of special significance. In order to furnish especially gifted graduates from technical trade schools the opportunity of academic training and to open a free path for talent in all ranks of society to positions of leadership in the technical field, an ordinance [6] was issued on July 7, 1922, which makes academic study possible for these graduates by passing a supplementary examination.

More recently two decrees have made access to university study possible to particularly gifted students without the secondary school leaving certificate. The prerequisite is that candidates by their whole personality and intellectual abilities offer a certain guarantee that they can pursue academic instruction in the subjects of their choice and that they will after their necessary study make some distinguished contribution either in their old or in some new profession. Besides reaching a definite standard in general knowledge a sound foundation in the field selected is absolutely essential. As special evidence of character and ability, proof should be forthcoming that the candidates have performed already services of recognized merit in the occupa-

[5] *Erlass vom 12. 8. 1924—U I, 1260.*
[6] *Erlass vom 7. 7. 1922—U II 2787. Zentralblatt, p. 353.*

tion that they have followed. The question can thus arise only in very exceptional cases; above all, this opportunity is not in tended to meet desires in general for a change in occupation. Those who in the course of their development were in a position to gain admission to the universities by the usual methods, such as school leaving or supplementary examinations, etc., must be left out of account. Twenty-five is to be accepted as the lower age limit and forty as the upper. The request for admission to the university must not come from the candidate himself but from competent persons who are familiar with the requirements and character of academic study and know the candidate from his accomplishments up to date. Applications will be considered by a special examining office and, if suitable, will be referred to an examining committee. This body decides the requests on the quality of one or more written essays of the candidate, prepared under supervision, and on the basis of a personal interview. Admission is granted only to one definite subject or a definite group of closely allied subjects. With this restriction the candidate is admitted to study in Prussian universities as a fully matriculated student.

Finally, according to the regulations of 1914 for students, officials and those engaged in gainful occupations were not allowed to be admitted as regular students even if they held the school-leaving certificates, but were admitted as auditors only. The semesters thus spent by them could not be counted as regular study for purposes of examinations. In view of the changed circumstances the Ministry determined to remove those restrictions by the Decree [7] of October 19, 1923. To meet the danger that the group concerned would begin to study after the regulation was fully removed, without arranging for an adequate amount of time necessary for full devotion to study, quite definite conditions have been provided which were necessary in the interests of the students themselves.

In all these regulations there stands out clearly the desire of the Ministry to facilitate access to the universities and technical high schools for persons ambitious and able, without yielding to demands whose acceptance would mean danger for the academic life of the universities and for the high cultural level of our people.

[7] *Erlass vom 19. 11. 1923—U I 2725.*

For the inner life of the universities the change in their administrative organization is of decisive importance. The change was embodied in the decree issued by the Prussian Ministry on March 20, 1923,[8] on *Principles for the Reorganization of the Constitution of Prussian Universities.* According to these principles the constitution of each university was forthwith drafted in a new form, consideration being given to purely historical or local peculiarities. With this decree that part of the reform of the universities will have been completed which State Secretary Becker in his day introduced in the Prussian Ministry through strenuous personal devotion. The fundamental notion, which met with complete approval on many occasions in the Prussian Diet, has been made clear for purposes of enactment.

The striking characteristic in the reorganization of the university organization is the reform in the relations of individuals and groups active in the academic community to the official agencies of the corporation. These agencies, faculty and senate, were, in accordance with the old constitution, built up on the basis of representation of the traditional branches of instruction and research for which professorships were systematically provided in the budget. In this way the full professors, actually shouldered the self-administration in the universities, while the other grades of instructors (associates, special, and private docents) did not enjoy the representation corresponding to their professional and individual significance. Further, it happened that the representation of a subject by an associate professor frequently did not depend on the fact that the subject or person concerned was of less significance, but on financial or other extraordinary conditions which required that the situation should be satisfied by the regular appointment of an associate professor instead of a full professor who might have been more appropriate. Hence, even from the point of view of a subject, representation through the full professors no longer corresponded in fact to the status of the science.

The Ministry, even before the issue of the *Principles,* had nominated existing associate professors to titular full professors

[8] *Erlass vom 20. 3. 1923. Grundsätze einer Neuordnung der Preussischen Universitätsverfassung.*

and made them members of the faculties with all rights.  This was an extension of the practice previously followed by nominating titular professors, although there were few actual exceptions and a reservation of a special rule for the University of Berlin. In this way it was intended to change the regular associate professorships into full professorships on the budget; the financial difficulties of the state, however, tended to check the full operation of this measure after a start had been made.  Side by side with the former officially appointed associate professors there arose a new classification of special professorships not officially appointed to which private docents are nominated, provided that they have proved themselves in teaching and research and have the qualifications expected from incumbents of academic chairs.  On their nomination they acquire simultaneously the higher status due to them in recognition of their academic importance.  The nomination of superannuated private docents and associate professors to honorary professorships has been abolished.  Henceforth only non-academic persons whose assistance in teaching and research is necessary to meet a need are nominated to honorary professorships.

The reform of the constitution provides that besides the full professors representatives of other grades, elected by their group, should belong to the faculty and that they, as representatives of their graduating students, should enjoy the same rights as full professors.  In the narrower and broader senate this group has a status in accordance with the regulations of the faculties, while the broader faculty includes the whole body of the professoriate besides the full professors.

The reform introduces in the institutions arrangements which had already developed by the side of the old regulations and have proved desirable.  These include coöperative committees of the faculties for the conduct of matters affecting several faculties, committees coöperating with students which should consist of representatives of the docents and students of a faculty, intended to raise discussions on questions of instruction and to invite the students for consultations on professional problems which particularly interest them.  The promotion of physical exercise is made a statutory function of the universities by the constitution and the student body is created a constitutional member of the university.  The title "University Judge," whose judicial functions in the sphere of the university have long been subordinated to the task of advising on legal problems, is changed to "University Councillor." A new disciplinary law for students is in the process of preparation.

The range of the duties of the university curators has been considerably expanded with the increase in the whole field of administration and the burden on the department concerned in the Ministry presses for more extensive decentralization. For this purpose success has attended the practice of changing the existing part-time positions as university curators into full-time positions.

In the course of the reform of the university constitution some opposition has appeared from the very start up to its complete introduction which is still under way. The reform has throughout been conducted by the Ministry as a reform with and not against the universities. This conviction has been constantly confirmed, and even in quarters that at first regarded somewhat skeptically the readiness of the university to introduce reforms it has been recognized that preparation for the groundwork on which self-government of the universities rests is not a sign of weakness but a strengthening of the determination to retain the positions of the universities as guardians of teaching and research, if they are to fulfill their high mission.

The reconstruction of the general organization in higher education was also carried out in the technical high schools, whose strong resemblance to the universities was further reënforced by placing the professors in both types of institutions on the same salary levels and allowing both to share the privilege of emeritus rank. Further, the organization of faculties and deanships [9] was applied to the technical high schools by combining into faculties the subject departments in accordance with community of interests. There were thus established faculties for general sciences, building (including architecture and building engineering), mechanical engineering (including engine construction, electrotechnics and, in Berlin, ships and naval engineering), and (with the exception of Hannover) technology (including chemistry, metallurgy and mining).

Further, by the Decree of June 30, 1921,[10] there was estab-

---

[9] *Erlass vom 15. 6. 22—U I T 1225.*
[10] *Erlass vom 30. 6. 21—U I T 1652.*

lished in the technical high schools a new type of institution in the form of external institutes entrusted with the duty of promoting for the whole field of technology and economics all such undertakings pertaining to the technical and economic arts and sciences which did not fall within the scope of the faculties but whose accomplishment seems desirable for the general interests. In particular there are conducted in these external institutes lectures and courses for practicing engineers, while leaders from the field are invited to give lectures to promote the vital relations between academic activity and practice.

With educational reform, the second part of the program of university reform, considerable progress has also been made. Some questions have not yet been attacked; these include the reorganization of the psychological and natural science studies in the faculty of philosophy, because here the reorganization of secondary education is not yet complete. Other questions that appeared to be settled have had to be referred back, as, for example, the reform of legal study, where it was proposed to permit greater emphasis on political economy in both the course of study and examination regulations and to attach greater weight than hitherto to the proper study of case law. Without the addition of another year of study success in this course could not be expected, even though such an extension would provide an opportunity to give further training for young lawyers in case law. The Ministry of Justice raised such strong objections to an extension of the course by a single semester on account of the economic situation that the reform had to be limited to an emphasis on economic subjects in the bar examinations. The forthcoming reform of the system of promotions in the legal profession will furnish an opportunity to consider the needs that have been recognized in this field.

The regulation of the political science course, on the other hand, has been completed by the establishment of the examination for the diploma in political economy and the extension of the course leading to the *Dr. Rer. Pol.* from six to eight semesters.[11] The former is intended to meet practical needs and requires after six semesters evidence of knowledge of political economy and law given before a commission consisting of pro-

[11] *Erlass vom 26. 2. 1923—U I 353.*

fessors and others from the practical fields. The doctorate in political science is intended for holders of the diploma in political economy who besides being qualified for their profession, as tested by the examination, desire to produce proof of thorough academic training. The decision enabling probationers in law and the civil service, like those holding the diploma in political economy, to take the examination for the *Dr. Rer. Pol.* after a further study of two semesters makes it possible to bring economics and law into the necessary relations, corresponding to the needs of economic theory.

The reform of the medical course planned by the university authorities in coöperation with authorities in other German states had of necessity to be postponed like the reform of the legal course on account of the economic condition of the students which in itself prevented an extension of the course by a semester. It was intended to pay considerably greater attention to the new professional subjects that have sprung up in the last decades. The examination regulations that are being considered contemplate, though within limited scope on account of the short course, the greatest possible consideration of these subjects.

To raise the standards in academic instruction in agriculture and forestry the courses in both subjects were by agreement with the Ministry of Agriculture extended to six semesters. Connected with this the privilege of proceeding to degrees has been granted to the agricultural and forestry universities after the latter was reorganized under rectors instead of under directors.

The Ministry of Education was associated with the Ministry of Commerce, which is primarily concerned in the reform of the commercial course, since the universities of Frankfort and Cologne continue the work in commerce as successors of the former schools of commerce. The creation of economic and social science faculties provided the best possibilities for purposes of organization. The discussions on the reform of the commercial courses were recently brought to a conclusion. Here, too, the development of commercial science as a science of management and practical needs have been taken into account. The study of science of management has been organized in a six-semester course, the examination regulations have been modified, and the new examinations for diplomas for business men and teachers of commerce have, in view of admission to the doctorate in political science, approximated to the examinations for the diploma in political economy. In some quarters a further demand is made for the privilege of granting degrees in high schools of commerce. This demand rests, in the opinion of the Ministry, on the misconception of the academic functions of high schools of commerce and the limitation to which they as professional schools are exposed without intimate connection with a larger academic corporation. On the other hand, there is full readiness and more recently the possibility of supplementing the regulations for degrees in the universities to meet these justifiable wishes by facilitating the transfer from the high school of commerce to the universities for the purposes of obtaining a degree.

To meet the efforts that have been under way for several years instruction in the technical high schools has been given freer character to enable each student to devote himself to those subjects to which he is attracted by bent and ability. The weekly periods of the courses recommended to but not required from the students have been reduced as much as possible to leave time for general and specific elective subjects. The examination regulations were completely changed. A uniform examination regulation has been introduced which allows the student entirely free choice in the grouping of subjects in which he desires to be examined, naturally on condition that the faculty may require proof that the selection assures evidence of a well-rounded course. The examination provides further for recognized groupings of subjects for each professional specialty which leave room for broad election in the major examination. The requirement of practical work was also introduced for architecture and building construction. In special cases time spent in practical work within certain limits may be counted for the course after the preliminary examination.

The change in the examination regulations for teaching in secondary schools made it possible for teachers in the mathematics–natural-science group in secondary schools to receive their complete training in technical high schools.

Special importance was attached in the reform plan of the Prussian Ministry to the economic training of workers which at first showed very promising signs. The stress of the time fell heavily on this new movement, which for the moment must count on serious material sacrifices.

The necessity of training adult workers in economics arose through the development of industry. Coöperation as industrial councillors and in groups for self-government imposed after the Revolution on the leaders in trades unions new tasks for which the Ministry established a new form of education. On May 2, 1921, the Academy of Labor was thus established in association with the University of Frankfort-a-M. The Academy is attended by the industrial organizations of workers, employees, and civil servants. Various tendencies are represented. Scholarships are awarded to participants by the municipal authorities. The representatives of the industrial organizations are also members of the committee of management and take part in determining the course of study, which covers problems in politics, economics, sociology, law of workers, all important for organization leaders. Instruction is given during the day and the course lasts nine months. Besides three, sometimes two, full-time docents, the faculty consists of docents in the University of Frankfort-a-M and specialists who are invited from outside for special lectures. The cost of maintenance is met by state and federal sources. The unions bear the cost of maintenance and the fees of the participants. During the inflation period the unions were not in a position to meet these expenses, but their interest in these educational provisions is so great that the organization of the courses is assured for the future.

In addition to the Academy of Labor, whose particular characteristic was continuity of semester work, short-term courses were also instituted. The arrangements are also made by the unions representing various tendencies; the courses cover especially problems of practical economic politics, science of management, private management and political economy. Such courses have been offered at the University of Münster, the University of Halle, the Technical High School at Hannover, and the Technical High School at Aachen. Arising out of the local composition of the members and the special preparation of the docents concerned characteristic differences have arisen in these courses: At the University of Münster special emphasis is placed on the economic questions of the Rhenish-Westphalian industry; at the University of Halle consideration is given to the economic conditions of the industry of central Germany; at the Technical High School at Hannover seminars are conducted in political economy. In coöperation with the Ministry of Commerce two vocational educational weeks were organized at the University of Münster to consider the educational problems involved in workers' education in economics in relation to the conduct of vocational education.

To discuss the further internal development of the universities through the creation of new chairs would be beyond the scope of the present work. It is only necessary to refer to the fact that the Prussian Ministry continues to be vitally concerned in meeting new demands of science and practical needs as far as possible. Restricted as it has been by the financial condition of the state, it has yet been able to maintain progress.

The financial straits of the time are not only marked in the restricted support of the institutions. The supply of new blood in the academic world is under the existing financial conditions exposed to the greatest danger. The distress of many private docents is well known. The greatest difficulty arises here because the docents are not officials. It would not be in keeping with the principle of free competition, on which the recruiting of a dignified supply of academic material rests, to incorporate the private docents into a definite official system. As possible means of relief there are suggested the increase of positions as assistants, the distribution of teaching commissions and the offer of maintenance grants. In this way a successful attempt has been made to check the apparently ceaseless stream away from the academic career. Even though the teaching commissions and maintenance grants do not offer a full income, they often give courage to continue in the profession. Yet the danger is great. If failure attends the effort to maintain a supply of academic material which was in any case decimated by the War, and to attract new forces, then all our universities are menaced. The Prussian state must not surrender the duty of intervening here with greater and ever increasing aid.

The need of coöperation between the different states has made itself more strongly felt in the universities than ever before the War. On the one hand, it was desired with all the variety to give expression to the idea of unity in the field of culture; on the other hand, the strength looked for was found in co-operation as against the one-sided efforts of this or that state. In the same way as the university authorities are in constant touch with each other on fundamental problems of higher education, and a satisfactory organ for coöperation exists in the regular meetings of university representatives in the so-called university conference, so the German universities have combined in the *Verband der Deutschen Hochschulen* (Association of German Universities) to represent their common interests.

The individual student bodies of German universities, which in the Prussian universities have received state recognition and the grant of a special institution and the right to levy compulsory contributions for their purposes, have combined in the *Deutsche Studentenschaft* (German Student Union) into an organization which, in contrast to the Association of German Universities which is restricted to universities in the German Republic, includes also the student bodies of German-Austria and Sudetic-Germany. In the development up to the present obstacles have arisen to check the peaceful activity of the German Student Union because of the fact that the individual bodies are compulsory organizations enjoying rights and duties from the state and the German Student Union is a free society; while the member societies outside of the German Republic are organized on quite a different principle from the individual German student societies. It is hoped that the existing points of difference will be satisfactorily settled in the further development particularly of the law affecting Austrian students.

Up to the present time it has been possible to maintain the high status of German science in the German universities and high schools. To balance the loss of Danzig in consequence of the Treaty of Versailles, there has been added the University of Cologne, founded through the devotion and willingness of the city of Cologne and above all through the initiative of Oberburgermeister Adenauer. His memorandum of December 20, 1918, turned on the necessity of establishing a center for intellectual life in the threatened West; the separatist movement in the Rhineland could most effectively be met in this way. Accordingly, the city of Cologne proposed that the Prussian Ministry should develop the organizations for higher education in Cologne (the High School of Commerce, the High School for Communal and Social Administration, the Academy for Practical Medicine, and the Research Institutes) into a university. In spite of important objections bearing particularly on the questions whether the Rhineland could support another university, the Ministry decided to approve the plan of the city of Cologne. The agreement with the city was concluded on May 27 and 29, 1919. In accordance with this, the university will be supported financially by the city, although by its constitution it is a creation of the state and thus enjoys the same privileges as the other universities. The university has in its development fulfilled all expectations and with its 4,000 students in the summer semester of 1924 has become the second university in Prussia from the point of view of numbers.

Although already established in 1914, the full development of the youngest university but one in Prussia, that of Frankfort-a-Main, really belongs to the year following the War. As an endowed university it is in constitution quite similar to the University of Cologne and served in fact as the model for the latter. Characteristic of both and established from the first is the predominant importance of economics, which finds its external expression in the two faculties for the economic and social sciences.

The organization of the University of Münster by the addition of a medical faculty is not yet completed. The preliminary conditions for this is the completion of the extensive buildings for the necessary clinics and institutes. Despite the serious financial situation building operations were continued during the post-War years and carried so far that their completion and the consequent commencement of a full medical course are expected early in 1925.

An addition to the faculties for medical training is promised in the reorganization in 1923 of the former Academy for Practical Medicine in Düsseldorf into a medical academy. To the Academy for Practical Medicine was assigned on its foundation the function of giving further training in medical science to practicing doctors. The overcrowding of the medical faculties after the War made it appear to be desirable to grant the Academy a share in the work of the universities. Further, doctors and students of dentistry studied there after passing a preliminary examination. By resolution of the Council of the Republic a medical and dental examination commission was created at the Academy. The good results attained in the institution here, particularly on account of the excellently equipped clinics, made it possible to give the Academy a permanent share in medical training and to develop the Academy from an institute for training in service into a research and teaching institution. Some objections were raised against this plan energetically pressed by the city of Düsseldorf and the Academy, because the separation of single faculties from the *universitas litterarum* involves the danger of developing a professional school which is foreign to the German conception of training for an academic profession. Without having the character of a detached faculty and therefore surrendering the right to give degrees and academic rank, the Academy has received an academic constitution and the right to train students of medicine and dentistry after the preliminary examination up to the final examination. Like the other universities the Academy is by virtue of its constitution a creation of the state, even though it is supported financially in the same way as the University of Cologne.

It has been possible, in spite of the financial situation, to make progress with the development of the Technical High School at Breslau. Through the budget of 1923 a mining department, for which there was special need in Silesia, was created. The addition of a faculty for building construction, to include architecture and structural engineering, had to be postponed for financial reasons.

To meet the distress which affected scholarly production particularly, the German universities, academies and other scientific organizations united in 1923 under the leadership of the Minister of Education, Dr. Schmidt-Ott, into the *Notgemeinschaft der deutschen Wissenschaft*. Besides considerable funds which poured into the Society from commercial and industrial circles, the Republic placed at its disposal funds necessary to carry out the program. By filling up gaps in the scientific libraries, through grants for printing scientific publications, through the provision of means for research in scientific work, through subsidies to several important scientific undertakings, the Society contributed materially to facilitating the progress of scientific production. It also assisted in making valuable connections abroad and securing thence aid for German science. Coöperating with the Society there are a number of foundations that serve the same purposes, such as the Justus-Liebig Society of the German Chemical industry, and the foundation of the Japanese Hoshi, both for chemical research, the Rockefeller Committee for Medical Sciences, and the Electro-physical Committee, whose funds were provided from American sources.

The German Student Society also organized student aid societies in order to meet the threatening economic need. Its central office is the *Wirtschaftshilfe der Deutschen Studentenschaft* in Dresden of which the aid societies of the individual student bodies in the universities are members. Associated with it is the loan fund of the German Student Society with branch offices in each university. The operations of the aid societies include principally aid for students in need, the securing and assigning of part-time jobs, the organization of institutions to reduce the cost of living, such as dining clubs (*mensæ*), workshops, salesrooms, lodgings, and so on. The provision of student aid, such as the loan fund, rests on the efficient coöperation of students, professors, representatives of governments, commerce, banks, industry and agriculture. Promoted originally by the Quakers, and then through the International Union of Christian Student Societies, student aid has continued to receive valuable assistance from foreign countries through grants of money, food, and gifts of all kinds. The Republic as well as the states has given material assistance to these arrangements for self-help.

While the scholarship funds could not, on account of the financial condition of the state, be granted in sums corresponding to the depreciation of the money, it was possible during the worst years of inflation to use the special fees paid by foreign students for purposes of student welfare and to employ these resources for the support of organizations for student aid and the grant of free meals and scholarships. After the tax on foreign students was withdrawn, it was found possible to increase quite materially the funds available for student aid. The distress of the students was taken into account in that the university fees were for a long time only slightly increased and that on account of the fixing of fees from the beginning of the summer semester, 1924, at the pre-war level, special contributions could be made to provide free tuition. Up to twenty per cent of all students could be entirely exempted from fees.

Finally, in this connection reference must be made to the Kaiser Wilhelm Institutes. The Kaiser Wilhelm Society for the Promotion of Science, which is incorporated in the state organization of science, and which since its origin has been under the direction of Adolf von Harnack, has been in need of assisttance from the Republic and the state in order to continue the great research institutes at Dahlem previously supported by their own funds. It has also been possible, in coöperation with industry, to bring into existence a number of research institutes, the support of which is borne by the industries concerned. Thus there has been established since the War the Silesian Institute for Research in Coal at Breslau, the Kaiser Wilhelm Institute for Research in Metals, which has recently been combined with the State Testing Office at Lichterfelde, the Kaiser Wilhelm Institute for the Chemistry of Fibres at Dahlem, and the Institute for Biochemistry associated with the Kaiser Wilhelm Institute for Experimental Therapy. At Dresden there has been founded the Kaiser Wilhelm Institute for Leather Research.

From the *thoughts* on University reform the Prussian Ministry has advanced to action, not by exaggerated efforts at reform which readily sacrifices what has grown organically, been tested and proved, but by the calm elaboration of matured ideas. Only one idea governs the Prussian Ministry, to maintain and develop our universities, libraries, and institutes in such a way that they fulfill the highest duties that fall to their lot in these difficult times through mutual coöperation with the complete spiritual life of Germany. In our days one gladly points to the event a hundred years ago when Prussia in the hour of her greatest need founded the University of Berlin. As a reminder to the Prussian of to-day the action of his forefathers always stands before his soul, and everything that Prussia has done for universities and high schools has been done with the consciousness that our future rests first and foremost on their maintenance and development.

# CHAPTER IX

## PHYSICAL TRAINING AND EDUCATION IN THE SCHOOL

The principle, *mens sana in corpore sano,* has served as a guide to the Prussian Ministry and has determined it to devote attention to physical training in all types of schools. After the disastrous result of the War which compelled Germany to abandon compulsory military service and deprived the country of the most effective means for maintaining the health and strength of the people, the demand for this assumed a significance that was surprising. In addition to free gymnastics and games the duty fell to all schools to conserve the health of our youth and to strive more vigorously and more systematically than ever before for the physical invigoration of the sons and daughters of our people. This duty was particularly important in view of the dangerous health situation among large sections of the population that are still suffering to-day owing to poor housing and frequently inadequate nutrition.

The Prussian Ministry has long shown its appreciation of the value of gymnastics and has expressed it by formally recognizing physical exercise as a necessary and indispensable part of education and incorporating it in the number of educative materials for the people. This view was confirmed more strongly than ever after the War by the movement which emanated from the youth itself and originated not only in an unconscious urge for self-preservation but in an unmistakable desire for reconstruction and yearning for a simple, more natural form of life and for purity in the field of physical culture. The Wanderbird and Youth Movements and the participation of large sections of our youth in the movements for gymnastics and sports of our day are not wholly and exclusively explained by these reasons, but they cannot be ignored.

In order to open the way for these demands for an improved health program and for the greater emphasis on physical training

143

within the scope of the general educational system, the Ministry has in the last few years issued a number of significant measures. First, there was created on October 1, 1922, a special department in the Ministry in which the promotion of physical training in all Prussian educational institutions is concentrated in one place and all efforts within the Ministry which are directed toward physical training are entered. The strategic position of Ministerial Councillor was offered to the former director of the state physical training institution at Spandau. This had already been preceded by the organization of a professional advisory council for physical training and education which meets for sessions at the Ministry whenever needed.

Of the fundamental decrees and regulations which deal with the promotion and organization of physical education in universities and schools the most important may here be cited.

The first regulations [1] were devoted, above all, to efforts toward rendering possible and encouraging the revival and equipment of the centers, gymnasiums, and playgrounds, which had been closed and damaged as a result of war activities, and the provision of new facilities. Further, the Ministry was concerned to increase the number of teachers of physical education who had lost their ablest representatives in the War. To fill these gaps the physical training institution at Spandau took up its work again, and courses were renewed once more at the universities and other places. In view of the important duties of future teachers of physical education and in response to the emphatic suggestions and wishes from the professional groups, the training was lengthened and made more intensive. The period of training at the institution at Spandau, styled by the Decree of September 28, 1921,[2] the *Preussische Hochschule für Leibesübungen,* was extended from seven to twelve months, and the same provision was made for all the other courses. By the Decree of March 31, 1922,[3] the two semester academic courses at

---

[1] See the *Denkschrift des Ministeriums für Wissenschaft, Kunst und Volksbildung, vom 7 Juli 1921—U III B 11291.1-,* which gives a survey of the development of school gymnastics in Prussia and presents in detail the Principles of the Federal Conference on Physical Education. The most important regulations and decrees have been collected by Dr. Schütz in Numbers 4 and 5 of the *Weidmannsche Taschenausgaben,* Berlin, 1925.

[2] *Erlass vom 31. 3. 1922—U III B 11713. Zentralblatt,* p. 397.

[3] *Erlass vom 31. 3. 1922—U III B 10711. Zentralblatt,* p. 178.

the universities were extended to four semesters, but without any material increase in the number of periods for lectures and practical work.  In the interest of physical training in the elementary schools, especially in rural districts, numerous shorter introductory courses were established and largely attended by teachers, while the high school at Spandau invited annually supervisory officials, principals, and teachers of all schools to the urgently needed introductory and continuation courses.

Of fundamental significance were the regulations of the Ministry which aimed to extend the scope and appreciation of physical education in the schools.  By the Decree of March 29, 1920,[4] regular weekly play afternoons and monthly excursions were prescribed for all schools, while the pursuit of healthful sport, like swimming and rowing, skating and skiing, were encouraged to supplement gymnastics and games.  The Ministry still retains the days for games and excursions whose educational value cannot be esteemed highly enough.  In some places they do not find much favor with parents, who look only on the shady side without properly appreciating their value.  But the greater the joy with which teachers take up this task, the more quickly prejudices will disappear, which in this, as in so many other aspects of school life, often give way too slowly.

Unfortunately an excessive number of exemptions from physical exercises had to be taken into account in the past.  The requirement[5] of a certificate from a school or practicing physician luckily resulted in a great reduction of the number of exemptions.  Upon principals, teachers, and supervisory officials was imposed the duty of carefully promoting physical training on the basis of its heightened significance as an essential part of education.  The greater appreciation of physical education in school was further emphasized by the decision that the physical training teacher should become a voting member of the committee for the leaving examination; that physical training be regarded as compensatory for promotions and the leaving examination; at the same time a special leaving examination in physical training was introduced by the Decree of October 4, 1921.[6]  The inclusion in the budget of a number of positions of

---

[4] *Erlass vom 29. 3. 1920—U III B 6543.  Zentralblatt*, p. 297.
[5] *Erlass vom 24. 1. 1920—U III B 7827/19.  Zentralblatt*, p. 202.
[6] *Erlass vom 4. 11. 1921—U III B 11353.  Zentralblatt*, p. 399.

*Oberlehrer* of physical training *(Oberturnlehrer)* also deserves to be noted in this connection.

The scope of physical instruction in Prussian schools is to-day indicated by the fact that in the courses of study of the elementary and middle schools, with the exception of the lower stage and of the fifth year, three hours a week are provided for the subject in all classes. To this must be added the weekly afternoons for games and the monthly excursions. In the secondary schools the reform introduced a change to the extent that in addition to the monthly excursions four hours were required for physical training—two for actual gymnastics and two for games, which are compulsory for teachers as well as pupils.[7] This regulation does not meet the wishes or the demands of those who with real enthusiasm stand for the introduction of a daily hour of physical instruction in the school program. The Ministry gave careful attention to this question and reached the view that the realization of these wishes could in the first place not be secured and must be held back for the future for the reason that the external conditions with adequate gymnasiums, playgrounds, and teachers are lacking. Beyond this, however, the Ministry is of the opinion that the introduction of a full half-holiday, following the reform of secondary education, has provided so much scope for physical activity that sensible free athletics and excursions can be carried on to a much greater extent than formerly. The effects of this voluntary activity should be awaited. If necessary there will always be time later to introduce supplementary measures. Perhaps the complaint will then be that athletic activity is excessive rather than inadequate.

The Ministry has in recent years also given special attention to the promotion of physical training in the universities and high schools. The most important measure for this end was the appointment of full-time gymnastic and athletic directors in all institutions for higher education, whose duty is to arrange and direct the practical work of the students. Since this work has been taken up, the number of students taking regular physical exercises has shown a satisfactory increase. For the students who still stand aloof, the Decree of August 18, 1924,[8] which requires from applicants for state examinations evidence of

[7] *Erlass vom 24. 6. 1924—U VI 788. Zentralblatt*, p. 200.
[8] *Erlass vom 18. 8. 1924—U VI 1169.*

regular participation in physical exercise in the first two semesters of study, has served as a strong stimulus. For teachers in secondary schools special regulations which are now being prepared are to be issued. As regards practical work by students beyond the requirements, account must be taken of the fact that scientific research and teaching activity in the universities are gradually showing a stronger tendency in this new direction and are receiving special consideration in the faculties of philosophy and medicine, and may perhaps lead to the creation of special institutes for physical training.

The practice of physical training in all types of schools, from the elementary school to the university, will be developed in a systematic plan by the Ministry. It is well understood, however, that with the active development to-day enjoyed by gymnastics, games, and athletics, and the many contradictory points of view in the various tendencies, the agreement that is desired on the main questions will only be reached gradually. In the meantime the Ministry is proceeding consciously on the path determined by the well-being of youth and the people as a whole. In this connection two regulations in particular acquire significance. The one brings nearer the realization of the idea that no healthy German child shall leave the school without having learned to swim, through the introduction of compulsory instruction where the conditions for it exist. (Decree of May 3, 1924.) [9] On the other side, the Ministry in a Decree of September, 1924,[10] by reviving orthopedic gymnastics in schools directs its special interest to the large number of pupils who, on account of physical weakness and curvature of the spine, require special care and remedial aid.

Among the many questions in the field of physical education that are to-day occupying the attention of professional bodies that of physical training for girls has recently assumed a more important position. The discussions on the selection and reform of the practical course have led to the demand from many sides that physical training for girls must more than formerly take the sex characteristics into account for the older groups and that the introduction of rhythmic-gymnastic exercises represent a real advance from this point of view. The Prussian Ministry has

[9] *Erlass vom 3. 5. 1924—U VI 2765. Zentralblatt*, p. 166.
[10] *Erlass vom 29. 9. 1924—U VI 1102. Zentralblatt*, p. 264.

followed the development of the question up to the present with care and has required and permitted practical experiments at the Prussian High School for Physical Education at Spandau. The results up to the present do not point to a fundamental reorganization of physical training for girls. Where, however, teachers are available who have given thorough study to the method of rhythmic gymnastics and have taken recognized courses, a limited use of rhythmic-gymnastic exercises in physical instruction can be permitted in the same way as provision already exists in music instruction in secondary schools for girls.

# CHAPTER X

## GERMAN TEACHERS AND THEIR CALLING AS EDUCATORS

If the saying, "One people, one school, one teaching profession," is understood in the sense that teachers for all schools should enjoy a completely uniform training and that their employment should be assured in schools of all types, and if it is thought that the unity of the teaching profession would thereby be secured, the ideas are based on entirely false premises. To carry out such a demand would mean a levelling down which would be accompanied by the most serious injuries to our whole cultural life. The elementary school requires an entirely different type of training for its teachers from the secondary schools, and the universities still another. We must adhere to the ideas of the common school clearly developed earlier, its implications must be thoroughly grasped; only in this way will the conception of the common school convince us of itself that we require for the most varied types of the "differentiated common school" teachers with varied types of training and that this varied preparation as a consequence involves distinctions in external organization of the teachers in different schools.

If, however, we understand by the saying, "One people, one school, one teaching profession," that we must all recognize an obligation to the people under the influence of the great idea which is to unite us all in a bond of unity; if we understand by this the requirement that teachers of all kinds should be prepared for one thing,—to devote themselves wholly and sacrifice all their strength to the young in the common and unified call of education, then the demand has quite a different significance. Everyone who has the welfare of the people at heart will agree with this. The notion of the common school as a cultural principle, that the instruction of every kind from the *Grundschule* to the university should be grouped around the culture subjects, permits the emergence of that profound inner solidarity of teachers

149

in all school types as servants of the great idea which is a sign of a great unified profession.

This does not exclude the necessity of a varied system of preparing teachers. The plan proposed for training teachers for elementary and secondary schools was described above (pp. 50 ff.). The Ministry brought severe criticism down on itself because it could not decide to introduce university training for elementary school teachers. References were made to states in Germany that provide such training for their teachers. Prussia, however, has thoroughly sound reasons for disregarding this type of preparation. It was not only practical considerations that the future supply of teachers might easily fail, but the determining influence in Prussia was primarily the idea that the general preparation of future elementary school teachers should be required as strictly as possible in a secondary school, but that a pure academic training in the spirit of research, such as is offered by the universities, must be rejected as unsuited for the elementary school. Indeed, preparation of future elementary school teachers in the universities would divert them from their real calling and would seriously menace the real character of the elementary school. The aim would be directed too much at intellectual training instead of at an objective that we desire above all else in the teaching profession: strong, whole-hearted devotion to the great functions of instruction and education. On a foundation of general academic preparation received in one of the four secondary schools, the Pedagogical Academy should complete the practical training of the future teacher along lines borrowed from university methods. The training in method and theory should be given here, and here he should above all grow as a teaching personality into the living community of future educators.

The Prussian Ministry requires that teachers of all kinds should be in the first place educators and that the school itself should be more than a mere transmitter of knowledge and practical ability. It should be an educational institution in the spirit of Pestalozzi, of Fichte and Süvern.[1] If we wish above all to educate our youth to become German men and women and to take their place in the community and serve the state as moral

[1] Kaestner, P., *Kraft und Geist unserer deutschen Volksschule* (Quelle und Meyer, Leipzig, 1923).

personalities, the function of the *teacher as an educator* must be emphasized, and the way to realize these aims must be opened up. For this reason we need enthusiastic men and women who devote themselves to the profession as teacher and educator because of an inner vocation, and we demand from the state the provision of opportunities for the fullest development of the capacities of teachers, and especially future elementary school teachers. Such teachers should be prepared by a thorough training in a secondary school to harmonious personalities and then prepared in their pedagogical training mainly for their future calling as educators. But beyond this we require from the young teacher when he has entered upon his work serious further study in the field of child observation, child psychology, adolescence, general theory and principles of education and method in all subjects as these have been set in motion in a gratifying way in Prussia by the officially recognized coöperative study groups.[2] The training of teachers in service has through these groups developed in many places in Prussia into a large coöperative enterprise. It has struck out new paths that have been welcomed by the Ministry, which cherishes the hope that the teaching profession will in the future give proof in the second teachers' examination of sound methods of work and of knowledge required through coöperative activity.

The Ministry has noted with serious concern the ever-increasing distress of unemployed teachers. As a consequence of the unfortunate Treaty of Versailles a large number of teachers have returned to the homeland from the surrendered territories. Our gratitude to these men and women who served their country successfully in her hour of need has of course made their re-employment our obligation, yet it is to be regretted that the unhappy result of the War prevents the absorption of all teachers into the system. These young teachers must, however, if they are to be retained in their high calling as teachers and educators be kept in close contact with school work. This object is served particularly by a Decree issued in December, 1924,[3]

[2] Suggestions for Coöperative Study Groups of *30. 11. 1920—U III C 1125, I and II, Zentralblatt,* 1921, p. 19; *Ergänzungserlass vom 23. 4. 1921— U III C 1125/20 IV, Zentralblatt,* p. 224; *Ergänzungserlass vom 23. 9. 1922—U III C 88.*

[3] *Erlass vom 11. 12. 1924—U III C 5149. Zentralblatt,* 1925, p. 6.

which makes considerable resources available to assist young teachers in their further study. The Prussian Ministry looks with concern on the distress of the young teachers and profoundly regrets that the financial condition of the state ties its hands when it would gladly manifest greater activity. But it retains its confidence in the idealism of our teaching body that will not lose courage because of the pressure of times and will not surrender its love for the school and for the young. The present situation certainly requires long-suffering patience from the young teachers. The hour will soon strike when the elementary school will need them; the school will call, and men and women ready to serve the young with devotion will answer it.

That the teachers shall engage in their work with inner freedom unrestricted by bureaucratic fetters or the pressure of authority, the Ministry has expressed itself freely in a series of fundamental decrees. The Decree [4] issued in 1919 for elementary school teachers and particularly the organization of extensive corporate school management in the districts of Wiesbaden, Düsseldorf, and Hannover had necessarily to be restricted somewhat by the Decree of October 30, 1923, yet the principle of corporate responsibility of all members of the faculty for the school and its work must not be sacrificed. The Ministry desires that every teacher show a constant interest in the common task in order that the feeling of responsibility be strengthened and the community spirit be kept alive. This does not mean that in the last analysis the real responsibility for his school and its spirit does not fall on the principal who at all times must enjoy the right of informing himself on the condition of his school.

For the teachers in our secondary schools of all kinds the Ministry can naturally not dispense with a complete academic training at the universities. The teacher in secondary schools has the task on the one hand of training the members of the learned professions and on the other hand of instructing and educating young men who should leave the school with a well-rounded education for life. But this function he can perform with success only if his own knowledge and power are rooted in scientific methods of research. The examination for secondary school teachers must first and last demand evidence that the

---

[4] *Erlass vom 20. 9. 1919—U III B 2271. Zentralblatt,* p. 615.

future teachers have undergone a serious academic training; that they can think and reflect scientifically for themselves and that they command a fund of knowledge that is indispensable for instruction in academic subjects.  Ways must further be discovered by which future secondary school teachers reach their full development as teachers and educators.  This cannot be postponed to the two years of practical training which follow the academic studies after the academic examination has been passed.  The charge is not altogether unfounded that intending secondary school teachers have hitherto not been properly trained in the ideals of their profession at the universities; during the academic studies there was frequently lacking the real emphasis: training for the work with youth which should serve through life.  The professional ideal was too often the ideal of the scholar rather than the ideal of the educator, an ideal based, of course, on a serious academic training.

Special attention will have to be given to this problem in the reform of the university courses which will be taken up immediately after the reform of secondary education is completed.  For example, the special subject preparation of the future secondary school teachers at least should be organized on the principles of the activity instruction.  More practical work, more seminars, so that here, too, serious efforts be made to substitute productive methods for receptive methods.  Further, particular care will have to be devoted to associating professional preparation and the development of teaching capacities with academic training of the candidates for secondary school positions.  Hence more weight than ever must be attached in the universities to systematic theory of education, and within this subject to the psychology of adolescence to which must be assigned the central position in our theory.[5]

Of the organization and reform of secondary education, the statement made above in the discussion of the reform of the *Grundschule* and the elementary school holds true here also, that educational projects and reforms lead nowhere if the plans, ideas and proposals are not built on the living personality of the teacher prepared to meet the highest demands of instruction and education.  It will be the first duty of the state to see that

[5] Spranger, E., *Psychologie des Jugendalters* (Quelle und Meyer, Leipzig, 1924).

for these new and serious tasks now planned in the reform a generation of teachers be produced that has enjoyed a pedagogical training by which the secondary school teacher of the future has matured through serious work to a true teacher and educator.  The Regulations for Candidates [6] which came into effect on April 1, 1924, has already given expression to the desire of the Ministry to select future candidates especially on the basis of their suitability for the profession as teachers and educators.  This idea will become established even though the demand is raised in many quarters for the retention of the single principle of seniority.  The school has the right to insist that only the really capable be appointed to the responsible position of teachers and educators.

The state must see to it that every possibility be afforded for fully developing the qualities of future educators.  The regulation for practical training of July 31, 1917 [7] had, it is true, already introduced considerable improvement, but its operation in practice was too often neglected behind beautiful theories.  It is, therefore, a step in advance that simultaneously with the issue of the regulations for candidates the pedagogical examination has been made uniform in the provinces.  It is, however, only an impetus to a complete reorganization of the course of studies and training in the sense described above.  Only considerations of the importance of these problems and the realization of their difficulties have prevented the Ministry from attacking this complex of questions at the same time as the school reform.  To mention only one such problem, it will have to be discovered whether it is possible during the university period, perhaps even immediately in connection with the secondary school leaving-examination, to give the future teacher an opportunity to participate in instruction and thereby try out for himself his suitability as a teacher and educator betimes and to be in constant sympathy with the selected profession.  The born teacher will disclose himself here and be easily recognized as such.  But the man who thus early stumbles on difficulties which show him to be unsuited as a teacher of youth, will, while there is time, find for himself an occupation better suited to him and to the

---

[6] *Die Ordnung der Anwärter für das Lehramt an höheren Schulen in Preussen vom 24. 4. 1924—U II 2902.  Zentralblatt, p. 152.*

[7] *Erlass vom 31. 7. 1917—U II 1197.  Zentralblatt, p. 612.*

community.  The almost completely specialist training hitherto
given in the universities will thereby be supplemented in a significant way.  Further consideration must be given to discover
to what extent such training is suitable for the demands of the
new situation and how the final examination can at the same
time be organized so as to be an effective factor of selection.

Practical preparation following the state examination must
accordingly be placed in the hands of prominent schoolmen who,
while devoting themselves to the training of the future teacher
and educator, attach decisive importance to the connection
with scientific life.[8]  Whoever has satisfied in two examinations
the by no means inconsiderable requirements and has during
his practical training shown himself a promising teacher, will
be called to serve the secondary school.  The state needs in
order to carry out the highest functions of the school highly
qualified teaching personalities who are not only transmitters
of subject matter but educators in the truest sense of the word.
Only through living sympathy with youth and by self-sacrific-
ing work for youth can we develop a generation of teachers and
educators to save us in our struggle for the maintenance of our
lofty national possessions.

So far as life in the secondary school and coöperation among
members of the faculties are concerned, what has been said
above applies: the school can only be served with complete success by men and women who coöperate in the great task of
education in a spirit of inner freedom and responsibility.  This
is not contradicted by the refusal of the Ministry to sanction
the widespread demands for faculty control.  In the secondary
schools, if anywhere, with their strongly developed system of
specialists a mind is needed that is in touch with every phase,
that guides and with a full sense of responsibility truly leads.
There is urgent need, particularly in view of the freer organization of curricula in the individual instructions, of men and
women in sufficient numbers, who place their stamp on the
schools like the great principals of old.  This may well happen
without the restriction of bureaucratic bonds and without strong

[8] See Jahnke, R., *Handbuch für höhere Schulen zur Einführung in ihr
Wesen und ihre Aufgaben; Ziele und Wege des Unterrichts;* also *Werden
und Wirken, Gedanken über Geist und Aufgaben des Lehramtes* (Quelle
und Meyer, Leipzig, 1915, 1919).

authoritative pressure from outside. With this in view the Ministry undertook a revision of the *Service Regulations for Directors and Teachers in the Secondary Schools for Boys*,[9] of December 12, 1910, and proposes the issue of a new regulation which more strongly than hitherto emphasizes the responsibility of every member of the faculty and the single-minded coöperation of the whole teaching body as the central point in the life of a school. *The Regulation for Conferences in Secondary Schools*,[10] issued in July, 1922, is the beginning of this revision. As soon as the work on the reform of secondary schools is completed, the Ministry will take up the further revision of the service regulations.

[9] *Dienstanweisung für die Direktoren und Lehrer an den höheren Lehranstalten für die männliche Jugend. Erlass vom 12. 2. 1910—U II 2470, Zentralblatt, p. 887.*

[10] *Erlass vom 3. 7. 1922—U II 274. Zentralblatt, p. 335.*

# CHAPTER XI

## THE *ZENTRALINSTITUT FÜR ERZIEHUNG UND UNTERRICHT IN BERLIN*

In order to repair the damage by which the school and education in general were affected through the War and the consequent conditions, and to take up again and carry forward the broken threads of development, the voluntary and willing coöperation of the teaching profession was needed in considerable measure. It was on that account of great value that the Ministry had the assistance of an Institute, which, without any official standing, coöperates with school authorities and teachers of all its branches, promotes the understanding of new questions of education and instruction, and encourages to a considerable degree the efforts of teachers for further training. The Institute at one of the most critical moments in the educational history of Prussia, when a new era required the reorganization of the educational system, promoted the further training of teachers with most enthusiastic and devoted coöperation on their part, and not only assured for the school its still surviving inner strength but brought new strength into many fields. This Institute is the *Zentralinstitut für Erziehung und Unterricht in Berlin.*

Founded through the Jubilee Endowment for Education and Instruction established by the Prussian Ministry of Education in 1914, the *Zentralinstitut* entered on its activities as a bibliographical information and research center for the whole field of education and instruction. Outside of Prussia, most of the German states, the Central Government, the German and Prussian City Conferences and the large teachers' associations are supporters of the endowment which is maintained and administered by the Institute. Prussia is greatly in its debt especially since its administration was placed in the hands of Ludwig Pallat. Prussia, in her efforts in all fields of education, has received

157

from this source lively encouragement and the strongest support. Important problems of education have been studied here
by scholars and men of practical experience; much has been
analyzed here to the very core and through serious coöperative
work the application of ideas attractive in theory have been
tested in practice.

The Institute is divided into five divisions: Pedagogical Division, Exhibition Division, Art Division, Foreign Division, and
Pictures. The *Staatliche Auskunftsstelle für Schulwesen in
Berlin* serves as an information bureau and, like the *Preussische
Hauptstelle für den naturwissenschaftlichen Unterricht,* is
associated with the *Zentralinstitut* into the *Pädagogische
Arbeitsgemeinschaft.* The Institute is united into another co-
operative group with the *Staatliche Stelle für Naturdenkmal-
pflege in Preussen,* and is also closely associated with the *Gesell-
schaft für deutsche Erziehung und Schulgeschichte* and the
*Deutscher Archiv für Jugendwohlfahrt.* In the Institute itself
there is a series of teachers' coöperative study groups for different branches of teaching.

How vital the activity, for example, of the Pedagogical Division was during the difficult years following the War and how
vigorously the reform work of the Ministry was assisted may be
indicated by a brief summary of the arrangements of this division. Twenty-seven general education weeks were held in five
years, of which two were in Berlin, eighteen in Prussian cities,
three in cities outside of Prussia, and four in foreign countries.
Besides these general "weeks" numerous courses were organized
as for secondary school assistants, for demobilized soldiers, for
beginning teachers, for leaders and members of coöperative
study groups among elementary school teachers, courses on
vocational guidance, a course on homemade equipment, another
on sex education, others on practical work in drawing, handwork, etc.

A considerable number of such activities were devoted to
free intellectual work in the school, pupil initiative, and activity
instruction. In no less than fifty-one cities in all parts of Prussia work was done on the theory and practice of the activity
school through lectures, demonstrations, and discussions with
teachers. These undertakings everywhere attract extraordinarily
large audiences, in many cases of more than one thousand per-

sons. Of a book published by the Institute on *Theorie und Praxis der Arbeitsschule*,[1] 36,000 copies were distributed. No less active was the Institute in developing an intelligent understanding of *Heimatkunde* (Local Studies). Ten courses on local studies in ten different cities were in the last four years supplemented by thirty-two local study excursions, of which a considerable number had to be repeated two and even three times on account of the demand. The participants in these activities represented a varied diversity of teachers, men and women, from every corner of Germany, from every type of school, who devoted themselves under the guidance of specialists to coöperative enjoyment of German nature and German folk songs and to the study of the monuments and treasures of German history and art in East Prussia or Silesia, Franconia or Lower Bavaria, on the Rhine and in Suabia, in the Hanse towns and in the Mark, in Dantzig or in Vienna. A highly important and valuable advantage of these travel and study groups was that the members of the different sections of Germany learned to know and appreciate one another and that the diversely organized educational activities in the different states were brought into touch with each other. In still another field of education courses were given on education for citizenship. After a Conference of Leaders was first held in Berlin, the proceedings of which were published in the excellent book *Staatsbürgerliche Erziehung*, *Staatsbürgerliche Wochen* (Citizenship Weeks) were held in about thirty different cities. That, in spite of the tension locally, no political disturbances of any kind occurred at any of these courses is an argument that it is possible to treat this difficult problem quite objectively and at the same time to arouse respect for the views of the opposition. In the last few years there has been added to the coöperative work of local studies and citizenship training the study of adolescence. The first course held in Berlin was followed by three more in other cities.

A special group of undertakings was intended to clarify the views on the characteristics of individual school types and their aims. A beginning was made with a tour of German *Landerziehungsheime*, which was followed by a series of lectures to afford the representatives of the reform movements opportuni-

[1] Published by the Institute.

ties to present their views to the public as well as to the supporters of the older types of schools on neutral ground. Thus there were held a *Realschule* Week, and a *Lyzeum* Week, while preparations are being made for a *Gymnasium* Week, *Realgymnasium* Week, a Middle School Week, and a *Landerziehungsheim* Conference. The proceedings of the Real School Conference are reprinted in the book, *Die Realschule*.[2] The volumes on the other types of schools will be issued in the same series. A strongly attended conference on the rural school also deserves mention in this connection. Not counting the lecture courses in Berlin with their fifteen to twenty lectures, the number of activities of the Pedagogical Division alone amounted to more than one hundred and fifty in the last five years.

In addition to these important undertakings those of the other divisions must be considered. The Exhibition Division not only maintains the permanent exhibition of teaching apparatus at the headquarters of the *Zentralinstitut,* but arranges new special exhibitions from time to time and sends exhibitions on tour both in and out of the country. By means of changing exhibitions of carefully selected and especially novel teaching apparatus and equipment, by means of displays of new textbooks, pupils' illustrated compositions and drawings from different cities in Germany and abroad, and finally through the presentation of pupils' work of the most varied kind as samples of the self-activity of children, in part prepared for the school itself, the Division helps to show what teaching aids are available for the school and the intellectual tendencies that are operating in education. It thus helps to point out directions in which the development is moving of itself or in which it can be guided. Changing exhibitions of suitable clothing for children, of picture books and toys are not despised. Everything is intended to lead to the educational enlightenment of parents and schools. Lectures and short courses were generally associated with such undertakings; often indeed they were designated as "schools for parents." Combined with the Exhibition Division are libraries of handbooks and textbooks in the different school subjects and a Pedagogical Book Display which was opened recently and to which most important educational publishers

[2] Quelle und Meyer, Leipzig, 1924,

regularly contribute their new publications.  All services are available to everybody without charge.  They mean a strong enrichment of educational studies and researches of the Institute, a happy mastery and understanding of problems of education and the possibility of a rapid and almost comprehensive survey of the educational tendencies of the present.

Contact with foreign educational systems is maintained by the Foreign Division in particular.  Close connections are maintained, especially with Germans in the borderlands and abroad, by furnishing information on the conditions of German education and instruction, by giving advice and assistance in the purchase of German teaching materials and by the exhibitions of such materials in many different countries, and by guiding foreigners, especially those of German stock, on educational tours and visits to German schools.  It conducts Foreigners' Weeks, attended by visitors from the Baltic States, Roumania and Bulgaria, Germany, Austria, and Czechoslovakia, as well as from England, Sweden, Norway, etc., who wish to study German culture and especially the newer German education at the source.

The Fine Arts Division gives its attention to the extensive and promising field of esthetic education in and outside of the school, a field that is greatly in need of study and development. School Music Weeks in Berlin, Cologne, and Breslau, conferences on Æsthetic Physical Training in Berlin, others on youth and the stage in Frankfort-a-M., have shown in a most impressive way to teachers and others engaged in education the tendencies under way at present, the probable lines of development to be followed, and the problems that require definite study and solution.  The permanent influences of the conferences are assured in the books that have appeared on the different topics: *Musik und Schule*,[3] *Künstlerische Körperschulung*,[4] *Jugend und Bühne*.[5]

The moving picture and radio, both of which are exercising and can exercise a strong influence on education in and out of school, have rendered a careful and objective observation and study by the *Zentralinstitut* urgently desirable.  An organiza-

[3] Quelle und Meyer, Leipzig, 1923.
[4] Ferd. Hirt, Breslau, 1923.
[5] Ferd. Hirt, Breslau, 1924.

tion for the approval and examination of pictures and films of
such tremendous value for purposes of popular education became necessary.  This Picture Division of the *Zentralinstitut*
has not only to examine pictures of educational and educative
value and to issue official certificates on their usability, but it
also encourages methodical impartial testing of these in the
schools.  For this purpose it conducts "picture weeks" to illustrate the difference between still and moving pictures, the
organization of performances and the rental of pictures and
films by means of lectures, demonstration lessons and exhibitions,
and gives information of every kind with the help of charts and
lists, catalogues and personal association with firms and moving
picture directors as well as by means of relevant literature.
Such Picture Weeks have been held in Berlin, Munich, Stutt-
gart, Essen, Hamburg, Jena, Gleiwitz, and the introduction of
the picture into the school has been extensively promoted.

To introduce the radio there were discussed at a conference in
Berlin the two questions, what the school must know of the
radio and what service it can render to make it useful for education and instruction.  A widespread organization for the training of teachers in service through the radio is in process of
development.

The superficial account of the scope and variety of the activity
of the *Zentralinstitut* is impressive enough, but does not do
justice to the real value of its services.  To obtain an idea of
the many directions and how thoroughly problems have been
attacked either spontaneously or on suggestions from other
quarters the best course is to examine the extensive series of
publications that have thus far appeared.  The *Jahrbuch des
Zentralinstituts* [6] presents in the report of activities a useful
survey of the actual development of the Institute as well as
some insight into the spirit with which some of the tasks have
been undertaken and carried out; it also contains valuable comprehensive discussions of problems occupying the attention of the
educational world.  The *Pädagogische Zentralblatt* [7] gives current information on educational development at home and
abroad.  The reports contained therein on undertakings before
the *Zentralinstitut*, especially on the radio lectures, will from

[6] E. S. Mittler und Sohn, Berlin, 1919-1922.
[7] Julius Beltz, Langensalza,

the beginning of 1925 be distributed to schools in Germany and to German schools abroad in a separate journal. As a further new undertaking the *Pädagogische Literaturnachweis*,[8] giving a survey of the literature on child welfare, has recently come into existence.

Of individual publications, issued in pamphlet or book form, which may be regarded as syllabi of the courses and conferences held by the *Zentralinstitut*, or which serve or have served partly as advance pioneer work, there should be mentioned in addition to those already cited:

*Deutsche Abende; Technische Abende; Geschichtliche Abende; Geographische Abende; Soziologische Abende* (Mittler und Sohn, Berlin, 1916-1920); *Biologische Schularbeit* (Quelle und Meyer, Leipzig, 1916); *Einführung in die Sexualpädagogik* (Mittler und Sohn, Berlin, 1921); *Die Deutsche Schulreform* (Quelle und Meyer, Leipzig, 1919); *Die Reichsschulkonferenz in ihren Ergebnissen* (Quelle und Meyer, 1919); Gaudig, *Freie Geistige Schularbeit in Theorie und Praxis* (Ferd. Hirt, Breslau, 1922); *Beiträge zur Berufsberatung* (Mittler und Sohn, 1919 and 1921); *Handbuch für das Berufs-und Fachschulwesen* (Quelle und Meyer, Leipzig, 1923); *Lehrmittelführer für allgemein bildende Schulen* (Julius Beltz, Langensalza, 1924); *Schule und Leben* (Mittler und Sohn, Berlin, 1922-1924); *Bild und Schule;* Gunther und Lampe, *Erläuterungen zur Prüfungsordnung für technische Leiter von Licht-bildvorführungen an Schulen und in der Jugendpflege* (Ferd. Hirt, Breslau, 1924). There are in preparation: *Das Oberlyzeum* (Quelle und Meyer, Leipzig); *Die Volksschule auf dem Lande* (Ferd. Hirt, Breslau); *Die Arbeitsgemeinschaften für Fortbildung der Volksschul-lehrer* (Julius Beltz, Langensalza); *Jugendkunde und Schule* (Julius Beltz, Langensalza); *Neue Pädagogik des Auslandes,* (Julius Beltz, Langensalza); *Rundfunk und Schule* (Julius Beltz, Langensalza).

A retrospect over the activity of the *Zentralinstitut* for practically ten years and in particular over its services under most trying conditions following the War justifies the conclusion that the Institute has contributed its share to the reconstruction of the Prussian educational and school system, and that active coöperation has been established between the Prussian Ministry of Education and the Institute. Moreover, it can also be satisfactorily established that in accordance with its original purpose it has become a central meeting place where teachers of all types of schools have met with each other and with university teachers, with school officials, with parents, and with the friends of the school, for educational work with an objective purpose, and

[8] Published by the *Zentralinstitut*, 1924.

where it is to be hoped they will continue to meet in a community spirit that bridges all differences of rank and opinions.

The Ministry cannot dispense with the aid and coöperation of the *Zentralinstitut* and hopes that this unique center for educational research and experiment and for statistical assistance of the greatest value will continue to develop with greater resources. The more complete the organization of the *Zentralinstitut*, the more assured the guarantee that it will become the intellectual center for educational activity of all Germany; here will meet the threads from all the states of Germany; here will be the place for coöperative work; here variety in unity will be made possible in a harmonious fashion; here all states will contribute to the great task of education for German cultural unity. Prussia is aware of this; it contributes its share willingly to the attainment of this goal; it will receive and give with willing hands, grateful for every stimulus, particularly in the difficult years of the reconstruction of its educational system.

# CHAPTER XII

## CONCLUSION

The survey of the organization of the Prussian educational system since the Revolution, as presented in broad outline in the preceding pages, will have proved that the Prussian Ministry on the question of the organization of the common school did not succumb to the danger of a purely mechanical reform of the educational system on a completely new principle. The good tradition of the Prussian educational system served as a protection against that. Consideration could not be given to a completely new, and as many demanded, as simple as possible, foundation with a structure rising above it. The aim of the reform plan could only include timely modification, reorganization, and combination of diverse methods of education, retaining whatever of the existing system had stood the test. Appendages that have grown up here and there in the course of time without any inner connection with the main plan, must be eliminated or incorporated in the whole, connecting links must be created, and separate parts which frequently existed side by side without any connections must be reduced to an organized system. Unity with every kind of variety in the educational possibilities must be the great dominating idea of the whole scheme. The real meaning of the common school is incorrectly understood by those who see in it only a place to bring about identity and uniformity. On the contrary, to maintain the greatest variety of educational possibilities and to make them accessible to everybody in such a way that individuals of every capacity and bent can find the path to the highest type of training and education suitable for and at all attainable by them, this is one of the great tasks to be accomplished now and in the future. More important, however, than all this must be the idea of internal unity, of cultural unity, which will weld the whole people in all its parts into one great single whole.

Many things will be missed in these pages.  Of method and principles of teaching, which derive their strongest features from the new and inspiring ideas of activity instruction, of the methods of education for citizenship, which should develop a strong civic consciousness by means of all the subjects of instruction, of important innovations in the field of school administration, only hints have been given here and there.  Had all these topics been considered in detail, the scope of the present work would not have sufficed.  The important object was to present the development of the Prussian school system in such broad outline that all friends of the German educational system could realize clearly what has already been achieved, and that the foundations on which the further development can be built are now definitely laid.  An important section is also lacking on the whole system of vocational and trade education in itself and in its relations to the elementary and middle schools and the universities, an account of which would have completed the picture of the common school.  That an account has not here been presented is not merely because conditions in this field are particularly in a state of flux.  Vocational and trade education are under supervision of the Ministries of Commerce and Agriculture.  Hence a discussion of this field would not have been possible without encroaching on ideas and plans whose preparation and introduction do not belong within the scope of the Ministry of Education.  It is for this reason that a significant work on the Prussian system of vocational and trade education [1] has been prepared by Geh. Regierungarat Dr. Kühne, the specialist in the Prussian Ministry of Commerce, a work which presents an exhaustive account of the organization and development of the system of continuation schools, trade schools, and free vocational education.  The diverse educational routes that lead from the elementary and middle schools through the trade schools are excellently treated in this volume.  It indicates how the great variety of educational routes in the field of secondary education is balanced by a still more diversified array of educational possibilities for the ambitious adolescent from the elementary school. This work, excellently suited to be a book of reference, may then be noted as a necessary supplement to the present volume.

[1] Kühne, A., *Handbuch für das Berufs- und Fachschulwesen* (Quelle und Meyer, Leipzig, 1922).

When the first edition of the present book was completed about a year ago the author along with the general public and thousands of teachers was affected by the shock of the distressing measure for the extensive reduction of personnel. The Federal Government was compelled to introduce it, and Prussia to follow, and with all the other states to yield to the necessity of retrenching in the field of education by eliminating positions. In February, 1924, the Prussian Ordinance for Reducing Personal Expenses in the Public Administration became statutory. [2] A year ago only hopes could be expressed and appeals made to confidence and intelligence, expressions contained in the author's address at Halle on February 27, 1924, and treated in detail in his pamphlet, *Abbau oder Aufbau unseres Bildungswesens.* [3]

To-day this demobilization is actually a thing of the past, after burdening the school and educational system for a year like a nightmare. To-day, however presumptuous it may sound to some, it can honestly and frankly be claimed that the school has successfully been preserved from the danger which threatened to overwhelm it. To-day it may be said that there can be no word of "reduction of schools," or "reduction of culture," or "reduction of spirit." The objections raised against "starving the school," "destruction of the school," "annihilation of the school" have been an honest expression of concern for the maintenance of our culture. The Prussian Ministry was under an obligation to see that the reduction of personnel expenses did not lead to ruin. By undertaking changes in organization it opposed to the risk of destruction the great positive ideas of reconstruction.

Of course these words may seem unintelligible to many and the author is aware that he is exposing himself to the danger of the charge of lack of sympathy for the distress that befell a large number of teachers of all grades. He knows the fate of those that were dismissed and feels for these men and women who, suddenly separated from a profession that has become dear to them, suffering serious economic injury and embittered, not understanding the state, fight for their rights or silently retire. But the question here is not of individuals but of the school as

[2] *Gesetzsammlung*, p. 73. The regulations on personnel reduction in the Prussian school system have been collected by Ministerial Councillor Lande in Pamphlet No. 10 of the *Weidmannsche Taschenausgabe* (Berlin, 1924).

[3] Quelle und Meyer, Leipzig, 1924.

a whole. The school has withstood the personnel reduction without a scar, and that may be a consolation to many who in their retirement made a sacrifice for the common ideal and who truly love the school.

It must be insisted that in spite of all financial distress, there has not been a reduction in the number of schools. A few elementary schools, being schools attended by ten or fewer children, have been closed, but many new ones have been established where new settlements required them. A few intermediate schools could not be maintained, but the loss was more than compensated for by placing on the municipal budget private schools that were financially going to ruin. Three city secondary schools were combined with others, but on the other hand thirteen new public secondary schools have been established since October 1, 1923, and eighteen incomplete institutions were developed into full schools. The universities have been maintained undiminished and the state art institutes continue unchanged. The demands for retrenchment that could not be escaped by the educational system have been met by measures to reduce expenses but the whole organization of the educational system has been tided over without loss.

The reduction in personnel in the educational system was made possible by measures of organization whereby the differences in the separate branches of our educational system were taken into consideration in carrying out the reduction. It must be recalled that for some time the elementary schools have been affected by the fall in the birth-rate and that before the actual personnel reduction a natural, unsystematic reduction had already begun, the brunt of which fell on beginning teachers since teachers already in service could not be dismissed. On the other hand, the secondary schools, perhaps as a direct result of the lower birth-rate, enjoyed at the same time a surprising and possibly not altogether harmless increase in enrollment.

This is perhaps enough to explain the differences mentioned. A reduction in personnel had necessarily to take place in the elementary schools on account of the lower birth-rate and inevitably led to savings in teaching positions for the state and school districts. An advantage could, however, be gained thereby that should not be underestimated: By limiting the size of classes in the *Grundschule* to fifty, a maximum has for the first time been introduced in the elementary schools. The other administrative measure was a regulation of the teaching load of elementary school teachers. If the one to three class schools, where from the nature of the case a reduction was scarcely possible, are left out of account, the personnel reductions thus facilitated, amounted to 6.9 per cent, including the numerous positions previously left vacant, and may rise slightly higher because the movement has not yet reached its full limits. The situation is similar in intermediate education.

In the universities and technical high schools restrictions in personnel, as the character of the institutions demanded, were as a rule not made on a wholesale scale but as cases arose. The secondary schools, however, found themselves in the most serious situation; here where there was no natural decline in numbers, which could serve as a starting-point, it was above all important to place some limitation on mechanical reduction of staff. The closing of schools with small attendance, especially in small towns, readily presented itself; such a measure would have been contrary to the idea of the system of secondary education, and would undoubtedly have led to a considerable lowering of the educational standards of the country, particularly in the sparsely settled and culturally backward sections in the East. This was, therefore, also met. In the search for administrative solutions that would leave the development of secondary education unaffected and would spare the secondary schools, the only possibility that could be suggested appeared to be a considerable increase in the established teaching load. It was a matter of a great satisfaction to keep this increase, on account of which grave concern arose among large bodies of teachers, within limits that corresponded to the functions and character of secondary education.

And yet these dangers could only be avoided by acting quickly and adopting the ideas discussed earlier, that is, the old proposal that went back to the thirties of the last century, of reducing the number of compulsory weekly periods for pupils. Originating in educational insight, recognized by the whole professional body, this measure had already been prepared in advance, with the result, since a purely mechanical scheme of eliminating periods was impossible, that secondary education was reformed, as treated in detail in an earlier chapter.

It thus became possible by a moderate increase of the teaching load and reduction in the number of weekly periods to plan for a saving of 11 per cent in the positions of secondary school principals and teachers. The personnel reduction in secondary education may now be regarded as completed. This statement should banish all concern on this point.

These brief references to personnel reduction and its consequences may suffice here. The distressing attacks on the positions of so many teachers, the profound disturbance of the quiet work in the schools, unavoidable mistakes and injustices in individual cases, the impossibility of absolute justice—this and many other factors render a retrospect no easy task. But this ungrateful and widely attacked task, which had to be performed and for which the author here expresses his gratitude to the provincial authorities who labored devotedly and impartially often beyond their strength, the Prussian educational system was carried over the greatest danger to which it has been exposed for many years. What has already been accomplished and described in detail in the preceding pages, should, if one may say so, furnish adequate proof that the Prussian Ministry fully appreciated the seriousness of the hour. That a restriction in the number of teachers had to be undertaken was to it a matter of regret. Reasons of state demanded such action, but such reasons need not discourage our people and to-day, as a year ago, the Ministry turns, with a full sense of the responsibility that the destiny of our people has placed upon it, to professional representatives, to all organizations, and to the public with the request not to withhold their understanding and patience from these reasons. We must understand how to make a virtue out of the need of our day, and devote ourselves wholly to replacing what has been taken from us in material resources by spiritual means and the common pooling of all our moral strength. Now, for the first time, we face the terrible effects of the pitiless Treaty of Versailles. We must show how much unyielding strength resides in our people. To safeguard it and to cultivate it must be our greatest task. The task of destiny! Full of strength and more than ever before we must resort to the spiritual powers that lie dormant in our people. Even now that need should release all powers to work for the restoration of our poor German country. The school and the whole of our German educational system will in this process have to meet the most difficult test.  They will meet them if each individual who strives in the school for the moral and spiritual regeneration of our people joyfully places himself and his all, the best and finest that is in him, at the service of the state.

# APPENDIX

## EXPLANATORY FIGURES FOR THE ACCOMPANYING CHARTS
### I. GENERAL SURVEY

1. Public *Volksschulen* .................... 5,461,594 boys and girls
2. Middle Schools ....................... 316,309 boys and girls
3. Secondary Schools
   Boys ............................. 298,447
   Girls ............................. 197,885
4. Art Academies ....................... 432 boys    129 girls
   Art Schools .......................... 311 boys    253 girls
   State Music Schools .................. 312 boys    200 girls
5. Universities .......................... 33,723 men   3,906 women
6. Technical Universities (*Technische Hoch-schulen*) ............................ 8,894 men    47 women

### II. SECONDARY SCHOOL FOR BOYS [1]

| | SCHOOLS | | PUPILS | | | |
|---|---|---|---|---|---|---|
| | 1914 | 1924 | 1914 | Per Cent | 1924 | Per Cent |
| *Gymnasium* ........... | 333 | 295 | 101,052 | 40.2 | 89,582 | 30.4 |
| *Progymnasium* ........ | 22 | 15 | 3,140 | 1.2 | 1,708 | 0.6 |
| *Realgymnasium* ....... | 99 | 128 | 32,092 | 12.8 | 39,955 | 13.6 |
| *Realprogymnasium* .... | 34 | 35 | 4,558 | 1.8 | 4,858 | 1.6 |
| *Oberrealschule* ........ | 108 | 134 | 44,988 | 17.9 | 64,654 | 22.0 |
| *Realschule* ........... | 192 | 189 | 35,297 | 14.0 | 40,515 | 13.8 |
| *Reformgymnasium* ..... | 15 | 21 | 3,929 | 1.6 | 5,824 | 2.0 |
| *Reformrealgymnasium* .. | 78 | 124 | 24,139 | 9.6 | 44,270 | 15.0 |
| *Reformrealprogymnasium* | 17 | 13 | 2,378 | 0.9 | 2,414 | 0.8 |
| *Deutsche Oberschule* [2] .. | ... | 4 | ... | ... | 662 | 0.2 |
| Total .............. | 898 | 958 | 251,573 | 100.0 | 294,442 | 100.0 |

[1] See the excellent collection of statistics in *Jahresberichte der höheren Lehranstalten in Preussen*, prepared by the *Staatliche Auskunftstelle für Schülerwesen*, Dr. M. Kullnick, Freytag, Leipzig.

[2] In addition to these since 1922 are 73 *Aufbauschulen* in development, which are following in general the program of the *Deutsche Oberschule* and have an enrollment of 4,005 pupils.

Double schools, such as a *Gymnasium* organized with a *Realgymnasium*, are counted in each category.

The losses by the treaty of peace amounted to 65 secondary schools; 27 *Gymnasien*, 5 *Progymnasien*, 10 *Realgymnasien*, 3 *Realprogymnasien*, 6 *Oberrealschulen*, and 14 *Realschulen*, including the *reform* schools. Since that time 25 schools have been added, 1 *Progymnasium*, 2 *Realgymnasien*, 10 *Realprogymnasien*, 3 *Oberrealschulen*, 9 *Realschulen*. Outside of the losses by the peace treaty and the increase in the numbers from 1914 to 1924, the changes which have appeared are due to modifications of school types.

**LEGEND**

△ TRANSFER TO SECONDARY SCHOOLS WITHOUT LATIN AFTER EXAMINATION

S AUFBAUSCHULE CAN BE ORGANIZED WITH THE OBJECTIVE OF THE DEUTSCHE OBERSCHULE AND THE OBERREALSCHULE

○ COMMON MIDDLE SECTIONS UP TO AND INCLUDING OBERTERTIA

× THREE-CLASS REFORM MIDDLE SECTION (SEXTA TO QUARTA) WITH ONE MODERN FOREIGN LANGUAGE

+ THREE-CLASS REFORM MIDDLE SECTION (SEXTA TO QUARTA) WITH LATIN

UNIVERSITIES AND OTHER HIGHER INSTITUTIONS

ADULT EDUCATION
FREE EDUCATIONAL SYSTEM

TRANSFER FOR SPECIALLY GIFTED

TRADE AND VOCATIONAL COMPULSORY CONTINUATION SCHOOLS

VOLKSSCHULE UPPER GRADES

VOLKSSCHULE GRUNDSCHULE

| SCHOOL YEAR | REALPRO-GYMNASIUM | REALGYMNASIUM | PRO-GYMNASIUM | GYMNASIUM | REALSCHULE | OBERREALSCHULE | REFORM REALGYMNASIUM | DEUTSCHE OBERSCHULE | AUFBAUSCHULE | MITTELSCHULE |
|---|---|---|---|---|---|---|---|---|---|---|
| 13 | + | + | + | + | | | | | | |
| 12 | + | + | + | + | | | | | | |
| 11 | + | + | + | + | × | × | × | × | | |
| 10 | + | + | + | + | × | × | × | × | | |
| 9 | + | + | + | + | × | × | × | × | ○ | |
| 8 | + | + | + | + | × | × | × | × | S | △ |
| 7 | | | | | | | | | | 7 |
| 6 | | | | | | | | | | 6 |
| 5 | | | | | | | | | | 5 |
| 4 | | | | | | | | | | |
| 3 | | | | | | | | | | |
| 2 | | | | | | | | | | |
| 1 | | | | | | | | | | |

ORGANIZATION OF THE SCHOOL SYSTEM FOR BOYS

LEGEND

△ TRANSFER TO SECONDARY SCHOOLS WITHOUT LATIN AFTER EXAMINATION

S AUFBAUSCHULE CAN BE ORGANIZED WITH THE OBJECTIVE OF THE DEUTSCHE OBERSCHULE AND THE OBERREALSCHULE

X THREE-CLASS MIDDLE SECTION WITH ONE MODERN FOREIGN LANGUAGE

O ON THE LYZEUM ARE BUILT UP (a) FRAUENSCHULE (b) TECHNICAL NORMAL SCHOOLS. IN ADDITION A 7TH FINISHING CLASS MAY BE BUILT UPON THE LIZEUM

* THE CLASSES OBERSEKUNDA TO OBERPRIMA OF THE OBERLYZEUM CAN BE ORGANIZED ACCORDING TO THE PROGRAM OF THE OBERREALSCHULE

SCHOOL YEAR: 13, 12, 11, 10, 9, 8, 7, 6, 5, 4, 3, 2, 1

ADULT EDUCATION FREE EDUCATIONAL SYSTEM

UNIVERSITIES AND OTHER HIGHER INSTITUTIONS

TRANSFER FOR SPECIALLY GIFTED

TRADE AND VOCATIONAL COMPULSORY CONTINUATION SCHOOLS

GYMNASIALE STUDIENANSTALT

REALGYMNASIALE STUDIENANSTALT

OBERLYZEUM

LYZEUM

DEUTSCHE OBERSCHULE

AUFBAUSCHULE

MITTELSCHULE

VOLKSSCHULE UPPER GRADES

VOLKSSCHULE GRUNDSCHULE

ORGANIZATION OF THE SCHOOL SYSTEM FOR GIRLS

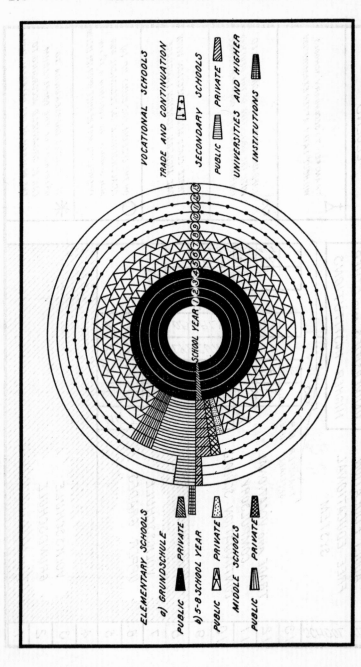

DISTRIBUTION OF THE PUPILS BY YEARS IN THE DIFFERENT TYPES OF SCHOOLS

# PART II

COURSES OF STUDY, SUGGESTIONS AND
REGULATIONS

# Section I

## Suggestions of the Prussian Ministry for Science, Art, and Popular Education for the Courses of Study of the Volksschulen

### I

## CONSTITUTIONAL BASIS OF THE ELEMENTARY SCHOOL [1]

### Fundamental Rights and Duties of German Citizens [2]

#### Section 4: Education and Schools

*Art. 142.* Art, science, and instruction in them are free.[3] The State guarantees their protection and participates in their promotion.[4]

*Art. 143.* The education of youth shall be provided for through public institutions.[5] The *Reich,* the states, and the municipalities shall coöperate in their organization.

Training of teachers shall be uniformly regulated for the *Reich* according to principles which apply generally to higher education.[6]

Teachers in public schools shall have the rights and duties of state officials.[7]

[1] From the *German Federal Constitution of August 11, 1919.*

[2] The translation of the constitutional sections is from McBain and Rogers, *The New Constitutions of Europe* (Doubleday, Page & Co., New York, 1923).

[3] This fundamental principle is the mandatory law for the promotion of justice and for administration. However, academic freedom in the sense of a free profession is limited by Articles 144 and 147, and by the Federal Foundation School Law of April 28, 1920.

[4] See Article 150, paragraph 2.

[5] This holds not only for instructional but also for other cultural and educational institutions.

[6] This requirement does not apply to teachers in technical and continuation schools. A federal law is necessary for its enforcement. The details of its enforcement are left to the various states.

[7] The Federal Constitution has not adhered to the decision of the

179

*Art. 144.*  The entire school system shall be under the supervision of the state; the latter may permit the municipalities to participate therein.[8] Supervision of schools shall be carried on by technically trained officials who are mainly occupied with this duty.[9]

*Art. 145.*  Compulsory education shall be universal.[10]  This purpose shall be served primarily by the elementary school with at least eight school years,[11] followed by the continuation school up to the completion of the eighteenth year.  Instruction and

Federal Supreme Court which declares teachers in and of themselves to be direct officials of the state.  The question as to the official character of the teachers remains open and is left for decision by the states.  In Bavaria, Mecklenburg-Schwerin, Hesse, Anhalt, Thuringia, and the Hansa states, teachers are direct officials of the state.

[8] School inspection includes: (1) inspection of private schools; (2) administration of those external affairs of the schools which fall under the control of the communities; (3) administration of the internal affairs of the school in which the communities can take part as representatives of the state.

*Extract from the Prussian Law* Concerning the Supervision of the Instructional and Educational System of March 11, 1872:

§ 1.  As a result of the abolition of all contradictory regulations in the several parts of the country, the supervision of all public and private instructional and educational institutions is under the authority of the state.  Accordingly, all officials and authorities entrusted with this supervision act on behalf of the state.

§ 2.  The appointment of local and district school inspectors and the delimitation of their inspectional districts rest  solely with the state.  The commission given by the state to inspectors of the elementary school, in so far as they administer the office as a supplementary or honorary office, is revocable at any time.  All contrary regulations are abolished.

§ 3.  The participation in school supervision assigned to communities or their agents remains undisturbed by this law.

Local school inspection in Prussia is abolished by the law of July 7, 1919, beginning with October 1, 1919.

[9] Herewith part-time and ecclesiastical school inspection are abolished. Still, this function may be delegated; for example, duties of state school inspection may be transferred to local school officers—city school superintendents.

Private schools existing for purposes outside the province of the public school system are also placed under state supervision—language, music, and infant schools.

[10] General compulsory attendance is a civic duty of those responsible for children's education—not of children under legal age.

[11] See Article 147, Federal Constitution.  The federal government hereby changed from instructional compulsion over to school compulsion.  See paragraphs 1 and 4 of the Fundamental School Law.

school supplies shall be free in elementary and continuation schools.[12]

*Art. 146.* The public school system shall be organically constructed.[13] The middle and secondary school system shall be developed on the basis of a *Grundschule* [14] common to all. This development shall be governed by the varying requirements of vocations; and the admission of a child to a particular school shall be governed by his ability and aptitude and not by his economic and social position [15] or the religious belief of his parents.

Nevertheless, within the municipalities, upon the request of those persons having the right to education, elementary schools of their own religious belief or of their *Weltanschauung* shall be established, provided that an organized school system in the sense of Paragraph 1 is not thereby interfered with. The wishes of those persons having the right to education shall be considered so far as possible.[16] Detailed regulations shall be prescribed by state legislation on the basis of a federal law.[17]

To enable those in poor circumstances to attend secondary and higher schools, the *Reich*, the states, and the municipalities shall provide public funds, especially educational allowances, for the

[12] Levying of tuition fees on non-resident children is not affected by this article.

*Decree of the Prussian Ministry for Science, Art and Popular Education,* May 7, 1921—U III A III4L. The regulation in Article 145 of the Federal Constitution by which instructional materials in elementary and continuation schools are to be free, will only have the force of law, when an enforcement act therefor is passed. The enactment of this law is the duty of the federal government. Until then the existing law will remain in force, to the effect that the provision of the necessary instructional materials devolves upon those responsible for the child's education, and in case of their inability, those responsible for the maintenance of the school must provide the necessary means.

[13] This article contains no directly applicable law, but suggestions for the organization of the public school system. "Organic" development implies bridges from one school type to another.

[14] See the Foundation School Law of April 28, 1920.

[15] In this way the transition from the individual to the social principle of education is attained.

[16] See Article 120, Federal Constitution: The education of the coming generations for physical, spiritual, and social ability is the highest duty and the natural right of parents over whose activity the state keeps watch.

[17] See Article 174, Federal Constitution: Until the decree of the federal law provided for in Article 146, paragraph 2, present legal status remains unchanged.

parents of children who are considered qualified for further education in middle and secondary schools until the completion of such education.[18]

*Art. 147.* Private schools as a substitute for public schools shall require the approval of the state and shall be subject to laws of the states. Such approval shall be granted if the standard of the private schools in their curricula and equipment, as well as in professional training of their teachers, does not fall below that of public schools, and if no discrimination against pupils on account of the economic standing of their parents is fostered. Such approval shall be denied if the economic and legal status of the teachers is not sufficiently safeguarded.

Private elementary schools [19] shall be established only if, for a minority of those persons having a right to education whose wishes must be taken into consideration according to Article 146, Paragraph 2, there is in the municipality no public elementary school of their religious belief or of their *Weltanschauung*, or if the educational administration recognizes in it a special pedagogical interest.[20]

Private preparatory schools are abolished.[21]

The existing laws shall continue in force for private schools which do not serve as substitutes for public schools.[22]

*Art. 148.* In all schools effort shall be made to develop moral education, public-mindedness, and personal and vocational efficiency in the spirit of the German national character and of international conciliation.[23]

---

[18] Educational, not only school assistance, i.e., scholarships, and the like.

[19] All schools neither organized nor maintained by the state or by a self-governing body are considered private schools.

[20] The regulations of Article 145, Federal Constitution, concerning free instruction and free instructional materials hold true also for private schools. Special pedagogical interest may also be considered as present, if the private school is connected for educational purposes with an institution of general welfare.

[21] See Federal Foundation School Law of April 28, 1920, section 2, paragraph 2.

[22] Accordingly statutory regulations and the regulation of the Federal Council of August 2, 1917, concerning private industrial and commercial technical instruction, remain in force. All private schools exist under the Law for Workmen's Councils of February 4, 1920.

[23] "Above all, German educational material shall be sought out of German cultural sources."—Representative Weiss in the National Assembly.

Instruction in public schools shall take care not to offend the sensibilities of those of contrary opinions.

Civic education and manual training shall be part of the curricula of the schools.[24] Every pupil shall at the end of his obligatory schooling receive a copy of the constitution.[25]

The *Reich,* the states, and the municipalities shall foster popular education, including people's universities.

*Art. 149.* Religious instruction shall be part of the regular school curriculum with the exception of non-sectarian (secular) schools.[26] Such instruction [27] shall be given in harmony with the fundamental principles of the religious association concerned without prejudice to the right of supervision by the state (*Staat*).[28]

[24] See the *Richtlinien* for the *Courses of Study of the Prussian Elementary School.*

[25] Edict of the Prussian Minister for Science, Art and Popular Education of March 12, 1921—U III A 368. (*Erlass des preuss. Minister für Wissenschaft, Kunst and Volksbildung, 12. 3. 1921—U III A 368.*)

According to a notice from the Federal Minister of the Interior it will not be feasible to give to pupils copies of the Federal Constitution printed at the expense of the Federal Government before the completion of attendance upon the *Volkschule.* He has no objection if copies are distributed before final departure from school to those pupils who continue their education after the completion of the general compulsory attendance period. Since, however, the chief purpose of the regulation in Article 148 lies in the fact that leaving pupils shall possess copies for civil life, the time of giving them out shall be postponed as late as possible. For the purpose of introducing the children of the *Volksschule* to the principles of the Federal Constitution, it must suffice, bearing their youth in mind, that teachers acquaint the pupils with the essential content. Still I have no objection if copies are loaned to pupils in some periods of instruction during the last weeks of school with directions that they take the greatest possible care of the books.

[26] Compulsory only for the course of study, but not for teachers or pupils.

[27] Statute law determines who shall give instruction in religion, but beyond that this instruction is under the supervision of the state.

[28] According to Ministerial Regulations of February 2, 1876, and January 1, 1880, the following fundamental principles are valid for imparting and conducting regular religious instruction in *Volksschulen:*

1. Regular school instruction in religion is given in the *Volksschule* under its supervision by those bodies assigned thereto by the state.

2. This instruction is chiefly the duty of teachers assigned to the school, who have proven their ability for this work in the prescribed examination.

3. Where previously it was the practice to so divide the regular religious instruction between the appointed teacher and the pastor or his regular representative (vicar, chaplain) that the former take over the Biblical history, the latter the catechism, this practice may be continued on condition that the minister, in consideration of his relation in

Teachers shall give religious instruction and conduct church ceremonies only upon declaration of their willingness to do so;

the state, is not objectionable to the school inspection authority, and loyally complies with all administrative measures thereof, especially with reference to textbooks, apportionment of subject matter of instruction in the various classes, discipline, and prompt observance of class periods.

4. In localities with mixed denominational population in which a teacher of the other confession is not living, all the religious instruction of the latter confession, where this was formerly the custom, may be assigned also to the clergy under the conditions mentioned in paragraph 3.

5. The school inspection authority decides concerning differences with reference to religious instruction between the clergy and the teacher.

6. In cases where there is no legally certified teacher, the county government decides to whom this instruction shall be assigned.

7. No single pastor has the right naturally to claim the direction of instruction in religion. However, as a rule, and so long as ecclesiastical authorities do not appoint another official thereto, the legally appointed local pastor is to be considered the official appointed for directing religious instruction. But the local pastor, as well as any other cleric appointed by the ecclesiastical authorities for the conduct of the religious instruction, may exercise this duty so long as by his conduct he does not endanger those purposes which the state pursues with the education of the youth through the *Volksschule.*

8. When a case arises, it will be the duty of the state inspection authority to inform the minister that he may no longer be permitted to conduct the religious instruction. This decision is at the same time to be brought to the attention of the ecclesiastical authorities, with the suggestion that they name to the state inspection authority another candidate. If the state inspection authority raises no objection against the latter, he is admitted to the direction of religious instruction.

9. The pastor or other minister recognized as the official of the religious organization concerned is authorized to visit the regular school instruction in religion in the hours set apart therefor, and to assure himself by questions and, so far as is necessary, by occasional participation in the instruction, whether the instruction is being given thoroughly and adequately by the teacher, and what progress the pupils have made in it; further to correct the teacher from the point of view of subject matter (of course, not in the presence of the children); to bring to the attention of the state inspection authorities wishes or complaints concerning the religious instruction and finally at the leaving examination, where such takes place, after this previous examination, to determine a grade in religion.

10. By the regulations designated in paragraph 9 no change is made in the right of inspection, which the state exercises through its officials, in accordance with the law of March 3, 1872 (see Article 144, Federal Constitution, note 1), over the entire instruction in every *Volksschule,* and also over the sectarian religious instruction in the *Volksschulen.* Accordingly, these officials have the right to attend the instruction mentioned. They must see that it is imparted in the periods set aside in the course of study and according to the standard of the general regulations issued by the school inspection authorities. But the material content of religious instruction may be interfered with by the state school

participation in religious instruction and in church celebrations and acts shall depend upon a declaration of willingness by those who control the religious education of the child.[29]

inspection authorities only in so far as it may contain nothing which runs contrary to civil and political duties.

11. Regular school instruction must not be disturbed unreasonably by the ecclesiastical confession and communion instruction. (See Ministerial Edict of October 11, 1920, concerning the place of the confirmation hours.)

12. The use of the school house may be denied only by the school inspection authorities for the religious instruction mentioned in 11, when either the school instruction suffers impairment through such use, or, when a minister, excluded from the management or imparting of the regular religious instruction, arouses the well-founded suspicion that he is using the religious instruction in order to give regular school instruction.

According to the Ministerial Edict of October 11, 1920, the confirmation and communion instruction is to be given in Prussia chiefly upon school-free afternoons (outside of Wednesday and Saturday). If it is not possible for the clergy to use this time there shall be left open therefor: either the last hour twice a week, which must not be preceded by more than four school periods, or in the case of great distances (over 2½ km.), the last two hours on two week days. Only with the permission of the Minister and for special reasons is a whole day to be left open. Church instruction extending over more than a year is to be given outside the regular school time.

[29] The enforcement of this requirement is the function of the states. The federal government holds the principle that, in the schools in which religion is an ordinary subject of instruction, the question is not one of volunteering for it but of claiming exemption. This conception corresponds also to the point of view of the Prussian educational administration and of the National Assembly. The edict of the Ministry of Science and Art and Popular Education, of January 19, 1921 (U III A 2407) demands that the right of free declaration of intention in this matter be in no way restricted by formal regulations. The only requirement is that the written or oral declaration is without any doubt that of the person concerned and is a clear expression of his intention. The Ministerial Edict of March 29, 1921 (U III A 572) also determines that the written declaration of parents may also be handed in by any third person, and also by the chairmen of parents' councils.

See also Article 135, Federal Constitution: All inhabitants of the Republic enjoy full freedom of belief and conscience. The undisturbed exercise of religion is guaranteed by the constitution and exists under the state's protection. General state laws on this point are unchanged.

From the Federal Law concerning the religious education of children of June 21, 1921 (*Reichsgesetzblatt*, 1921, p. 38):

§ 1. The voluntary agreement of parents determines the religious education of the child as far as the right and duty of caring for the person of the child belong to them. This agreement is revocable at any time and is annulled by the death of one parent.

§ 2. If such an agreement does not exist or ceases to exist, then the

Theological faculties in institutions of higher learning shall be maintained.

*Art. 150.* Artistic, historical, and national monuments as well as landscapes enjoy the protection and care of the state (*Staat*).

It shall be the duty of the *Reich* to prevent the removal of German artistic treasures to foreign countries.

regulations of the Civil Code concerning the right and duty of caring for the person of the child also apply to its religious education. However, while a marriage is in force it can be decided by neither parent without the consent of the other that the child shall be trained in another faith than the common faith at the time of marriage or in another faith than hitherto, or that the child shall be excused from religious instruction. If this consent is not given, then the mediation or decision of the Court of Wards may be called in. The aims of education are regulatory for the decision in so far as a violation in the sense of paragraph 1666 of the Civil Code does not arise. Before a decision is made the parents as well as relatives and the teachers of the child, if necessary, are to be heard if this can be done without too great delay or immoderate expense. Article 1847, paragraph 2, Civil Code, finds corresponding application. The child is to be heard if it is ten years old.

§ 3. If the right and duty of caring for the person of the child devolves upon the father or the mother besides a guardian or trustee appointed for the child, then in case of difference of opinion concerning the determination of the religious faith in which the child shall be educated, the opinion of the father or of the mother has preference unless the privilege of religious education on the basis of section 1666, Civil Code, is denied the father or mother. If the care for the child's person belongs solely to the guardian or trustee, then he must decide concerning the religious education of the child. In addition thereto he needs the approval of the Court of Wards. Before this approval the parents and, if necessary, also the relatives and teachers of the child are to be heard if this is possible without too great delay or immoderate expense. Article 1847, paragraph 2, Civil Code, finds corresponding application. Neither the guardian nor the trustee may alter the decision concerning the religious education of the child thus secured. Likewise the child is to be heard if it is ten years old.

§ 4. Agreements concerning the religious education of a child are without civil validity.

§ 5. After the completion of the fourteenth year the child is qualified to make the decision as to which religious faith he will belong. If the child has completed his twelfth year, then he may not be educated against his will in another faith than that in which he was educated previously.

§ 6. The foregoing regulations are correspondingly applicable to the education of children in a view of life not conformable to their faith.

§ 10. If both parents are dead when this law goes into effect and if it can be proved that they were agreed concerning the child's education in a certain faith, then the guardian may determine that his ward be educated in this faith. He needs in addition to this the approval of the Court of Wards.

## II

## LAW CONCERNING THE *GRUNDSCHULE* AND THE ABOLITION OF PREPARATORY SCHOOLS [30]

*April 28, 1920*

The German Constitutional National Assembly passed the following federal law, which, with the approval of the Federal Council, is published herewith.

### I

The *Volksschule* is to be organized in its first four years as the *Grundschule* (foundation school) [31] for all, upon which the middle and secondary school systems shall also be built. The regulations of Articles 146, Paragraph 2, and 174,[32] of the Constitution of the German Republic are likewise valid for the *Grundschule*.

These *Grundschule* classes (or sections) [33] shall guarantee, along with a complete preservation of their principal task as part of the *Volksschule*, also satisfactory preparation for direct entrance into either a middle or a secondary school. This regulation does not apply to classes in the auxiliary schools.

Central school authorities of individual states can make provision for special cases [34] so that still more classes of a *Volksschule* can be organized as classes of the *Grundschule*.

### II

The existing public preparatory schools (*Vorschulen*) or preparatory classes are to be abolished immediately. Instead of an

[30] *Gesetz, betreffend die Grundschule und Aufhebung der Vorschulen, vom 28. April, 1920, Reichsgesetzblatt—S. 851.*

[31] The foundation school (*Grundschule*) is not a special type of school, but only a designation for the lowest classes of the *Volksschule*, and, of course, of every *Volksschule*, both the denominational and the secular school.

[32] See Article 146, Imperial Constitution, note 5.

[33] The designation ''section'' applied to the ungraded schools in which the instruction for the several years is not given in separate classes.

[34] Special cases arise, for example, when a single school shows a large percentage of non-German speaking children, or when there is a question of a worthwhile educational experiment. Still such exceptions must not be prejudicial to the unity striven for in the organization of the German school system.

187

immediate and complete abolition, gradual dissolution can take place in the following manner:

That from the beginning of the school year 1920-21, or, where this is not feasible, at the latest at the beginning of the school year 1921-22, the lowest class will no longer be organized, and that the final closure of the school must be completed at the latest by the beginning of the school year 1924-25.[35]

The same regulations apply to private preparatory schools or classes, yet the complete dissolution may be postponed until the beginning of the school year 1929-30, in cases where an immediate dissolution or sudden abandonment would work material economic hardships upon teachers or proprietors, and where it is inadvisable for local reasons.[36] If postponement is permitted, care must be taken that the total pupil enrollment does not exceed the previous enrollment.

If through the dissolution or gradual abandonment material economic hardships fall upon teachers or proprietors,[37] indemnity is to be provided out of public funds, or compensation is to be provided through other public means.[38]

In the sense of these regulations, paragraphs 1 and 2, those classes in the middle and secondary schools shall be considered as preparatory classes which are attended by children in the first three years of the compulsory attendance period, as well as independently existing school classes which serve for preparation for entrance into a middle or secondary school. In general, either for individual school types or for individual schools, the

---

[35] *Erlass des preussischen Ministeriums für Wissenschaft und Kunst und Volksbildung*, April 13, 1921. The dissolution of the preparatory school classes is to continue yearly without interruption. When a class is dropped, non-promoted children must leave the school; they are to be transferred to the *Volksschule* if they cannot find admission to another preparatory school class of the same grade. Only those who reach school age after the beginning of the school year 1921 and those then attending a public school are obligated to the full four-year attendance on the *Grundschule*.

[36] *Aus den Richtlinien des Reichsministeriums des Innern*, February 25, 1921. Pupils of private preparatory schools can transfer to higher schools only after four years in classes of the *Grundschule*. *Erlass vom 13. 4. 1921*. The decision as to whether this condition exists rests with the individual states. Necessity of postponement must be proven each year.

[37] Public funds of the federal government cannot be given, when the need can be avoided through granting of a postponement.

[38] Such measures may be as follows: Taking over private teachers and directors into the public school service, or into other suitable occupations outside the school service.

class which is designed for a further compulsory school year
can be declared a preparatory school class in the sense of this
regulation for purposes of dissolution.

### III

If, in consequence of the dissolution or abandonment of the
public preparatory schools or preparatory classes, regular, full-
time teachers (of either sex) are no longer needed in their former
positions, these teachers can be transferred, even against their
wishes, to public elementary schools or middle or secondary
schools, without detriment, however, to their salary claims.

*Erlass des preussischen Ministeriums für Wissenschaft, Kunst und
Volksbildung,* April 13, 1921: Through this regulation the instruction
of Article 87 of the Prussian Disciplinary Law of July 27, 1852, for
non-judicial officials, is so changed that the new position does not need
to be accompanied with like rank and salary as the former position,
but it is sufficient if a possible loss in salary is compensated in another
manner.

So long as teachers becoming unemployed owing to the abandonment
of these schools cannot be provided for otherwise, they will continue
to receive their salaries from their former employers in the same
manner, as if they were still employed in their teaching positions.
They are obligated during this time to take over without pay employment assigned them at another place: for example, substitute work
or work in the school administration service.

### IV

Private instruction for individual children or private group-
instruction for children of several families, who unite for the
purpose, can be permitted in place of attendance upon the
*Grundschule* in exceptional cases only.

Exceptions can be based upon an extraordinarily dangerous
condition of the child's health, upon unusual distances from
school, and upon similar pressing circumstances.

An endangered condition of health does not of itself carry
with it the privilege of private instruction. Generally there will
arise the question of postponing instruction. In this case compulsory attendance upon the *Grundschule* will be correspondingly extended upward.

In Prussia the conditions for family or private instruction, as
well as for their teachers, are defined by law in the State Minis-

terial Instruction of December 31, 1839. While sharp demarcation between a private school and a family school is possible only in individual cases, still the following general differences are to be recognized: In a private school, its proprietor (a teacher or a corporation) is supporter of the organization, while in the family school, it is the family. Accordingly, in the first case the director of the school passes upon the enrollment of pupils, while in the second case the family, and not the teacher appointed by it. The family school usually instructs a smaller number of children in a manner that corresponds to the nature of home instruction; the private school, generally a larger number of pupils, according to the manner of school instruction.

Private and family instruction as supplementary to public instruction is limited by the foregoing law only to the extent that the supplementary private instruction may not cut short the four years' compulsory attendance at the *Grundschule*. See Article 147, Federal Constitution.

### v

The provisions of this law do not apply to the instruction and education of children who are blind, deaf and dumb, hard of hearing, defective in speech, weak-minded, chronically sick, morally dangerous, or crippled, nor to the institutions set aside for the instruction and education of these children. See Section 1, paragraph 2, sentence 2.

These schools and institutions mentioned are also freed from the obligation of organizing their lower classes as a *Grundschule*, if perchance they fall under Section 2 of this law.

# III

## GUIDING PRINCIPLES FOR DETERMINATION OF THE AIM AND FOR THE INNER ORGANIZATION OF THE *GRUNDSCHULE* [39]

These suggestions are to be regarded as a stimulus to the uniform organization of the *Grundschule*. In other respects, however, with regard to the inner organization of the *Grundschule*, to its problems of method and curriculum the states maintain their full freedom and independence.

1. The *Grundschule* common for all children is not a special type of school. It is rather a part of the *Volksschule* and comprises its first four years, which form at the same time the foundation division of all middle and secondary school groups.

2. The first four years of school have their own goal and a unified sphere of activity. Their goal is the gradual unfolding of the child's abilities out of the instinct for play and movement toward a normal desire for work which manifests itself inside the school community. Its unified sphere of activity is receptive and formative comprehension of the child's physical and spiritual environment with special consideration of the cultivation of the child's linguistic expression and well-planned training of eye and hand through his own activity as well as through observation of nature, work, and work shops. Besides, physical education is to be cultivated especially through games, gymnastics, excursions, and, according to season and age, through swimming, sledding, skating, and other physical activity.

3. This aim of the *Grundschule* demands also the conscious familiarization with the mother tongue and its treasures in poetry and language for children; that is, reading, writing, and singing; further, the comprehension of spatial forms, rhythm, and number, especially that which may be developed out of practical activity with things, and by means of drawing, modeling, and cutting.

[39] *Erlass vom Reichsministerium des Innern, 18. Juli, 1921: Richtlinien über Zielbestimmung und Innere Gestaltung der Grundschule.*

4. So there results an integrated instruction (*Gesamtunterricht*) as a foundation structure which gradually develops into a concrete study based upon local environment along with and through expressional activities, language instruction, arithmetic, singing, drawing, physical training, and manual work.

Through the determination of aim out of the child's development and with an adjustment between it and the demands of culture, the *Grundschule* creates out of its own being the foundation of all further education, including also the secondary school, without thereby being burdened with the task foreign to its nature, of being a preparatory school for foreign language instruction.

# IV

## SUGGESTIONS FOR THE CONSTRUCTION OF COURSES OF STUDY FOR THE *GRUNDSCHULE* [40]

*Berlin, March 16, 1921*

The following guiding principles for the construction of courses of study for the *Grundschule* replace the corresponding regulations bearing upon the first four years of school as given in the *General Order Concerning the Organization, Aim, and Work of the Prussian Volksschule* of October 15, 1872, and which are hereby set aside. It is immediately required that the courses of study for the *Volksschule* and the practice schools at the normal schools be reorganized according to these principles and that the instruction in the school be imparted according to the spirit therein set forth. In the construction of the courses of study for individual schools opportunity for coöperation in its widest sense must be granted the teaching staff.

(Signed) *Minister of Science, Art*
*and Popular Education*
HAENISCH

*To the Provincial School Boards and County Governments*

### GENERAL

The *Grundschule*, as the common school for all children in the first four years of school, has the task of giving to the children who attend it a basic training on which not only the *Volksschule* in its last four years can be built, but also the middle and secondary schools with their more extended instruction. Therefore, it must awaken and train all the spiritual and physical forces of the children and equip them with those knowledges and skills which, as ground work for every type of further instruction, are absolutely essential.

In the whole instruction of the *Grundschule* the fundamental principle to be enforced is not merely that facts and abilities

[40] *Erlass vom 16. 3. 1921—U III A. 404.1. Zentralblatt, p. 185. Richt-linien zur Aufstellung von Lehrplänen für die Grundschule,*

193

are to be superficially acquired, but that all which a child learns must be inwardly experienced and independently acquired. For this reason all instruction must carefully cultivate the relationships to the home environment of the children and tie them up with the spiritual possessions which they have already acquired before they entered school, even their right to their local idioms being admitted. Self-activity, of course, must be richly used for the purposes of instruction, in play and in observations of nature and life processes; for example, on school excursions and trips, and in the execution of manual activities, such as modeling in plasticene or clay, laying of sticks, freehand drawing, and cutting.

The subjects of instruction in the *Grundschule* are religion, local informational studies (*Heimatkunde*), German, arithmetic, drawing, singing, physical training, and sewing for girls in the third and fourth school years.

A sharp demarcation between subjects according to definite hours is not to be prescribed for beginning instruction; rather an integrated instruction is to be permitted in which the various subjects interchange freely. As a central point in this integrated instruction stands observational instruction based upon a concrete study of the local community in which the fundamental exercises in speech and reading, in drawing, writing, arithmetic and singing, integrate themselves. Indeed, the first conversations and discussions in religion and morals can be tied up with this integrated instruction. In order also to make available to beginners in the smaller or ungraded schools this vital integrated instruction, which calls for a constant coöperation of teacher and pupils, the program of hours of these schools, where circumstances do not absolutely forbid,—i.e., necessity of older and younger children going and coming together, or half-day instruction,—should be so organized that at least four hours weekly be added in order that the teacher, in the absence of the other classes, may devote himself entirely to the beginners. In the first weeks of the school year the instruction for beginners in such schools will be definitely limited to these hours, except in so far as participation in games and occupation with drawing and such like is involved.[41] Not only is the amount of time to

[41] Ministerial decree, June 24, 1921. The question as to how far the integrated instruction is to extend in the *Grundschule* is left to the deter-

be occupied by this integrated instruction left for determination through the courses of study for individual localities and districts, but also are the choice of materials in the various subjects and their distribution as to classes and years. In the construction of the courses the differences between the sexes, namely the special needs of girls' education, must be reckoned with.

Choice of materials of instruction is determined first of all by the child's ability to comprehend and the intellectual demands of his period of growth; in the second place by its meaning for life. All prematureness and overloading, for example, through home tasks, is to be strictly avoided. The standard of materials to be covered will have to be decided differently according to the organization of the school. The fully developed school, in which every year's work has its own class, will show in its course of study a higher standard and a greater amount of individual facts than the less graded school which is compelled to unite the work of several or of all the years into one class. The instructional objectives set up here are to be attained in general in all schools.

### EVANGELICAL RELIGIOUS INSTRUCTION

The instruction begins with free conversations which link up with the religious concepts which the children already have, and with Christian customs, usages, and organizations. In the winter of the first school year, in connection with Christian festivals, stories selected from the New Testament appropriate to the understanding of children are told by the teacher and are reproduced by the children in free, childlike form of expression. Three half-hours weekly are to be used in this way. In the second school year, the instruction is given in two hours, or four half-hours; in the third and fourth years, in three hours weekly.[42]

Bible stories from the Old and New Testaments suitable to the mental development furnish the material. The treatment

mination of the individual courses of study. Consideration, therefore, in the application of this regulation—namely, that in ungraded schools, teachers must devote at least four hours weekly exclusively to beginners while the other sections of the school are absent,—can be given to local conditions and to wishes of teachers. In any case this regulation holds good for the entire first school year unless its enforcement cannot be carried out for urgent reasons which are set forth in these regulations.

[42] Changed by *Min. Erlass vom 18. 1. 23*, see time-table on page 202.

consists in the telling of these stories by the teacher, which method can be enlarged or replaced by a development or dramatized lesson, in free reproduction by the children, in the development of the religious and moral truths inherent in the stories and the application of these truths to the lives of the children. Suitable memoriter materials, as Bible verses, sentences from the catechism, prayers, stanzas from church songs, are connected freely with the Bible stories; church songs and verse from songs can also be treated in connection with Christian festivals. Burdening of the memory, especially through home work, must be avoided. The introduction of a textbook for use by the children is discouraged in the first three years of school.

CATHOLIC RELIGIOUS INSTRUCTION

The Catholic religious instruction is intended to train the children for the fulfillment, in accordance with their age, of their moral and religious obligations, and to introduce and accustom them to the practice of their religious and moral duties through word and example, and especially to ensure for them an understanding of and participation in the religious practices of the church, in the celebration of the Holy Mass and in reception of the Holy Sacraments, as the Church prescribes. The amount of religious information imparted is determined and limited in accordance therewith.

The religious instruction in the first school year is connected with the religious ideas which the children have gained at home, and with instructions incidentally acquired, which it seeks to clarify and extend. Thereupon follows, if possible, in connection with the days and feasts of the church calendar, the treatment of corresponding Biblical stories. These are told by the teacher with dramatic intensity, but still without violence to historical accuracy; then they are discussed with the children and reproduced by them freely.

For the correct conception of these New Testament lessons, it goes without saying that they are to be preceded by the first stories from the Old Testament concerning the creation of the world, the angels and men, the fall of man, the promise of the Redeemer. At suitable places in the course of the instruction the children are trained in the performance of the most important prayers for Catholic children.

In the second year of school, Biblical material (previously studied) from the Old and New Testament is suitably increased. An objectively developed narration of Bible events precedes the oral presentation of the stories in the childlike form found in the Small School Bible. The reproduction is free but gradually approaches the simple and childlike form of expression of the Small School Bible, which even in this school year is not placed in the hands of children. The passages most important for the religious-moral life of the child of this age are developed from Bible stories which have been adapted to his understanding, and are made directly applicable. The phrasing of these passages, which must present the Catholic doctrine as a whole, is determined by the Shorter Catechism.

In the third and fourth school years, the instruction is based on the Small School Bible and the Shorter Catechism, which are in the hands of the children. Selection of the material takes into consideration that the children are now receiving the religious foundation and early preparation for the reception of the Holy Sacraments of the Atonement and Communion. The entire content of the Catechism and of the Bible stories, so far as it affects this section of the school, is treated in a two-year course. A purely memoriter acquisition of the material of instruction must be avoided.

On the objective side of religious instruction, in connection with the subject matter studied during the several years, the children are acquainted with the local church and organization, with the sacred service, especially Holy Mass, with the prayers and religious usages in the church and at home, and with the lives of various saints. Here also a beginning should be made in inculcating in the children, through precept and example, good behavior in church and school, at home and on the street.

#### MORAL INSTRUCTION

If in schools that do not offer instruction in religion (non-denominational, secular schools), or in other schools (for such children as do not take part in religious instruction) moral instruction or instruction in ethics (*Lebenskunde*) is introduced, suitable narrative materials shall receive chief emphasis.

HEIMATKUNDE (COMMUNITY STUDY)

Observational instruction dealing with local environment takes
its materials during the first two school years from the child's
world of experience.  Home, yard, and garden, schoolhouse and
school yard, street and market, fields, meadow, and forest, life
at home and at school, work at home, in the shop, in the factory,
on the farm, in the vineyard, all, as the community presents
them for observation, form the subject matter of this work.  This
instruction is enriched by story telling and dramatization of
fairy tales—also the newer literary fairy tales, fables, and
similar stories,—as well as by singing and reciting of folk and
children's rhymes and older and more modern children's songs.
Modeling, freehand and descriptive drawing, and cutting-out
serve as media of expression in addition to oral speech.

Community study is treated from the third year on as preparation for later instruction in geography, nature study, and history.  From the observation of the daily and yearly course of
the sun and the changes of the moon, the elementary principles
of astronomy are learned, while, in a similar manner, the fundamental principles of geography are developed through the
observation of local earth relationships and water forms; further, the foundation of map reading is laid through modeling of
earth forms on the sandtable and by plane surface drawings of
local regions.  Observations of animals and plants lead to an
understanding of their structure and life and the relationships
existing between the two.  Study and reproduction of local
myths and traditions prepare for the study of history.

In the fully organized schools geography of the local province
is incorporated in the course of study for the second half of the
fourth school year, and the narration and treatment of the
myths of this enlarged environment and a discussion of particular occurrences of note from its history are treated in connection
with this work in so far as it is adapted to the comprehension of
children of this age.  Likewise, the schools with fewer classes
must make provision, within the limits of their entire course of
study, for the treatment of this material in suitable form.  The
historical phase may assume a less important position with
reference to the geographical phase of the subjects.

The following is taken from Ministerial Regulation of June 6, 1920, concerning instruction outside the schoolroom:

For community study in its widest sense, i.e., for local observation studies of the first school year, and likewise for the acquisition of the fundamental experiences in the fields of geography and community study, of different branches of natural science instruction, and for certain portions of geometry, observations, experiments by teachers and by pupils, taking of measurements, and similar activities outside the schoolroom are of material importance, and, if the instruction is to shape itself in a fruitful way, are not to be dispensed with. Also in other periods of instruction, from time to time, lessons given outside the schoolroom are especially realistic and become hours of vital experience. For this reason, not only are the excursions which are conducted in all schools for recreational purposes encouraged where possible, but also teachers are encouraged to give various lessons in the school yard, in the school garden, or in any other suitable place in the open, even in the woods, if the location of the school makes it possible.

### GERMAN LANGUAGE

Instruction in German includes, besides the general linguistic training, in which it is supported by the entire instruction of the school, the development of the skills of reading and writing, introduction to literature according to the ages of the children, the acquisition of the fundamental principles of grammar, the mastery of spelling up to a certain degree of accuracy, and the first attempts and exercises in written expression.

Regulations restricting the development and form of the beginning instruction in reading and writing are not provided. Wide freedom is left for efforts to find new methods in these fields, so far as it is compatible with the needs and unity of instruction in the individual school or schools of the locality. The requirement, however, must be satisfied that the children, when they have passed through the first four years of the *Grundschule,* are able to read simple passages fluently with correct pronunciation and accent, and have acquired in writing German and Latin script such accuracy and skill as to render unnecessary further instruction in writing in special periods after the fourth year. In reading the children are acquainted with literary selections in prose and poetry which are suitable for them, chosen from the treasures of German literature. A limited number of poems should be memorized. Home work of this sort is not to be permitted. A fine presentation of the poems memorized is to be attempted, but this must not deteriorate into affectation. Faultless and clear enunciation and expressive speech must also be carefully nurtured so far as possible through technically suitable exercises.

With reference to language and grammar, it must always be kept in mind that, in general, correct use and understanding of written language are gradually acquired through a variety of oral and written exercises, and that this branch of language instruction can be fruitful only when it permeates the whole instruction of the school and also exists in living connection with the life of the pupils. Acquisition of the fundamental skills in syntax and etymology necessary for further language instruction must be given in connection with exercises in correct speech and writing, and begins regularly in the third school year for the first time. By the end of the *Grundschule,* with reference to this point, some accuracy in the determination of the parts of a simple sentence and of the most important parts of speech is required, and also in distinguishing and in forming the inflections of nouns, adjectives, and verbs, and in the use of the correct cases after the most frequently used prepositions. Foreign language terminology is not to be used.

Exercises in spelling cover the writing of phonetic words, of words with the *Umlaut,* and indication of long and short vowels, capitalization of nouns, and the use of punctuation marks. Likewise, this phase of instruction is treated in close connection not only with the other language instruction, but also with subject-matter instruction.

Exercises in written expression consist in the preparation of short compositions in which the children freely incorporate materials out of their world of experience and imagination.

In the choice of subject-matter of these compositions, the greatest amount of freedom is to prevail. Likewise, the selection of suitable titles by the pupils themselves is desirable. The entry of such exercises into a special composition book is not required before the fourth school year. Besides these free written exercises, note taking is cultivated.

### ARITHMETIC

As to the objective of arithmetic instruction, by the end of the *Grundschule* period, there must be accuracy in the four fundamental operations with whole numbers, acquaintance with most commonly used coins, measures and weights, and their calculation, as well as a knowledge of the fractions which occur most frequently in daily life. Distribution of this material may be organized according to the difficulty of the calculations involved rather than according to the number groups now in common use—1 to 10, 1 to 20, 1 to 100, 1 to 1000, any numbers—so that, for example, in the first school year the easier calculations in the number space from 1 to 100 may be taken up; in the second year, the more difficult cases in this group and also the easier calculations in the number space from 100 to 1000; and in the third year, the more difficult combinations up to 1000. Consideration is constantly given to the connection of arithmetic with the other subjects of instruction and with the life of the children. Oral exercises involving more than three-place figures should be avoided. Introduction to written processes should be taken up generally in the fourth year.

### DRAWING

Instruction in drawing is prepared for through descriptive drawing, which is taught in connection with the local community studies (*Heimatkunde*) of the first two school years. Real drawing instruction begins in the third school year and is chiefly drawing from memory. This method continues in the fourth year. Selection of objects to be drawn takes into consideration life in nature, games, activities, festivals in the different seasons of the year, and also the content courses of instruction—local community studies, in so far as the latter offers worthwhile exercises for representation. In classes for girls, also, those objects especially are to be drawn upon which are used and prepared in sewing classes. Besides drawing from memory, decorative drawing is also taught in connection with it.

### MUSIC

Until further notice, music instruction is to remain as is described in the regulations for the course of study of January 10, 1914.[43]

[43] See page 220.

## PHYSICAL TRAINING

Games, free exercises, marching and apparatus work are given according to the official regulations for physical education instruction for boys' and girls' schools.

## SEWING

This instruction begins in the third school year with an introduction to the preparation of those objects which children use in play, and develops further into the ability to crochet and knit and to do simple sewing.

*Min. Erlass vom 21. 4. 1923—U III A 444:* In sewing not more than thirty girls are to be taught in one class.

## TIME-SCHEDULE

The following time-schedule is intended for the fully developed school in which every year's work forms its own class. In schools which have fewer classes, the number of hours must be made to conform to conditions. The figures in parentheses hold for classes with girls only.

| SUBJECT | SCHOOL YEAR | | | |
|---|---|---|---|---|
| | 1 * | 2 | 3 | 4 |
| Religion ** | .. * | 4 | 4 | 4 |
| Community Observation Instruction.. | .. * | { 9 | { 10 | { 11(10) |
| German | .. * | | | |
| Writing | .. * | 2 | 2 | 2 |
| Arithmetic | .. * | 4 | 4 | 4 |
| Drawing | .. * | .. | 2(1) | 2 |
| Singing | .. * | 1 | 2(1) | 2 |
| Physical Training | .. * | 2 | 2 | 3(2) |
| Sewing | .. * | .. | (2) | (2) |
| Total Number of Hours | 18 | 22 | 26 | 28 |

* Integrated instruction (*Gesamtunterricht*).
** See page 195 for original number of hours in religion.

In the first school year three hours are used for religious instruction. The religious observational instruction is to be given during the hours set aside for religion.

*Min. Erlass vom 23. 3. 1923—U III A 503:* Usually the children are to be taught by the same teacher, at least during the first two years of the *Grundschule,* and also during the last two years.

# V

## SUGGESTIONS FOR THE ORGANIZATION OF THE COURSES OF STUDY FOR THE UPPER FOUR YEARS OF THE *VOLKSSCHULE* [44]

*Berlin, October 15, 1922*

The accompanying suggestions for the organization of the courses of study for the upper years of the *Volksschule* go into effect to-day, in place of the corresponding regulations for these last school years, as given in the *General Regulations Concerning the Organization, Aim, and Objectives of the Prussian Volksschule* of October 15, 1872.

Regulations of the decree of March 16, 1921, are to be applied in the spirit of the accompanying suggestions. I anticipate the publication about April 1, 1924, of a summarizing report concerning operation of the regulation in paragraph 1. Transcripts of the courses of study are not subjoined to this report. Copies for the Seminar directors, normal school directors, and district school secretaries are herewith inclosed.

(Signed) *Minister of Science, Art, and Popular Education*

BOELITZ

### GENERAL

The upper four years of the *Volksschule* constitute the finishing school for those children who, after completion of the compulsory school period, will enter practical life and will receive their further schooling chiefly in vocational schools. Consequently, it follows that the courses of study must take into consideration the needs of life more than those of the *Grundschule*. However, here, too, must the educational need of this age and the objective of the constant and symmetrical development of the child's whole being, especially with reference to his emotion and will, be the deciding factors. Consideration of

[44] *Erlass vom 15. 10. 1922—U III A 2060. Richtlinien zur Aufstellung von Lehrplänen für die oberen Jahrgänge der Volksschule.*

203

these points of view does not conflict with the additional problem of the upper school classes, that of providing the education necessary for the transfer into the *Aufbauschule* for specially gifted children.

As in the *Grundschule,* so also must the instruction in the upper school years be based upon the self-activity of the pupils, the intellectual as well as the physical. The coöperation of the pupils must not consist chiefly in the absorption of knowledge, but the objectives of instruction are to be worked out under the guidance of the teacher through observation, experiment, investigation, independent reading, and verification.

Manual activities of pupils are to be employed in the widest possible range. The preparation of sketches, drawings, instructional materials—especially for geometry, geography, and nature study—offers opportunity for this type of work, as well as do the organization of collections, the study of experiments in the field of natural science, the care of animals in terrariums, aquariums, insectariums, the culture of flowers, school gardening, and also instruction in sewing and home economics.

Books are also used by the pupils as sources of materials to a very wide extent. Only such books, however, are suitable for this purpose which treat their subject matter objectively and which go into details in a lifelike way. Primarily, such books are to be provided through the pupil libraries. Libraries of this sort are necessary, therefore, for all schools, and particularly for the small, ungraded ones.

School excursions, which serve primarily the work in physical education, offer opportunity for the observation of plant and animal life, of earth and weather conditions, the heavens, conditions of business and labor, as well as for exercise in judging of distances, and in simple sketching, and thus contribute to the broadening of intellectual development. Shorter excursions, which are undertaken for definite instructional purposes, and visits to agricultural and industrial activities are added according to need.

*Note.*—Guiding Principles of the Federal School Committee on School and Home, April 27-29, 1922.

1. For cultural, educational and social reasons, greatest consideration and care are given to home education *(Heimatbildung)* both inside and outside the school.

2. In order to conform more than formerly with the educational ideal of the *Heimatschule,* all instruction is to be organized on the fundamental principle of the study of the local community, and a sufficiently large number of hours must be assigned as well to local studies.

3. The technique of the *Heimatschule*—instruction in the open, school gardens, gardening, excursions, and observations—is to be built up both in the city and in the country with every possible agency, according to the special conditions and needs. A book dealing with the home and a map of the local community must be found in the hand of every school child. The acquisition of pictures of the local community in every form—landscapes, models, photographs, films, etc. —shall be encouraged according to funds available. The future books for both teachers and pupils to be organized on the basis of the home.

4. Attention must be given to this point of view in the matter of the teachers and school officials. The training of the teacher must keep definitely in mind everything that has to do with local studies. Teachers are to be made acquainted with home study and investigation through scientific means. Group studies, excursions and trips dealing with the home, as well as the publication of valuable literature pertaining to the *Heimatschule,* shall be promoted to the greatest possible extent.

5. The organization of rural and youth welfare movements—vacation camps, vacations in the country for school youth, exchange of pupils between city and country, regulation of railroad rates for pupil and school excursions—serve directly the interests of *Heimatschule.*

6. Education concerning the home shall be furthered also by educational organizations outside the school—public libraries, museums, people's universities, and popular educational organizations. Efforts for the protection of nature and the home are to be vigorously encouraged.

7. It is the duty of county governments to realize the *Heimatschule* in its widest sense and to the greatest degree. In all districts libraries dealing with the local community are to be organized, in every locality a local information bureau, and in every university provision for investigation with reference to the study of the home.

The subjects of instruction are religion (or moral instruction), German, history and civics, geography, natural science, arithmetic, geometry, drawing, music, physical training, and sewing for girls, and in addition, when provision can be made, manual training for boys and home economics for girls. The guiding principles given below determine and limit in general the materials that are to be treated.  The choice and distribution in particular are matters for the courses of study to be drafted for the individual school, in the organization of which the principle of basing instruction upon life in the community must be respected.  The amount of materials to be chosen varies with the kind of school.  In all schools, however, care must be given that the materials prescribed in the curriculum are not superficially treated, but may be really worked through from an intellectual point of view.  Schools of few classes, in order to be able to secure a richer selection of materials, may organize their work on the basis of alternating year courses.

The objectives set up for the several subjects of instruction also determine the direction of the work in the *Grundschule,* whose general objectives oblige it to lay the foundation for every type of subsequent education.

### EVANGELICAL RELIGIOUS INSTRUCTION

The aim of Evangelical religious instruction is, through the awakening and cultivation of the religious tendencies of the child, to contribute to the building up of his whole religious and moral personality, and to afford him the fundamentals for leading an Evangelical Christian life within the community.  In particular it is its task to present and explain the nature and truth of Christianity according to a conception of reformers in a manner corresponding to the pupils' stage of development.

Its content is the Gospel, which, after its preparation on the basis of Old Testament piety, has found in the New Testament its fundamental statement and its quickening expression in the development of the Christian Church to the present time.  The personality of Jesus holds the central place in all of the religious instruction.

In the organization of material, divided courses running side by side—Biblical history, catechism, hymnology—should be avoided if possible.  It is preferable to organize a course of study in which the instructive and poetical materials—catechisms, Biblical phrases, and numerous sections from the Bible suitable at this point, and church songs—arrange themselves freely in the presentation of their historical development.  The arrangement of the catechism can be by paragraphs or so taken up that its treatment follows in connection with the history of the Reformation. But, by the last-named method of organization, thoroughness of the development of the materials of the catechism must not suffer. There is not, however, the slightest objection to treating the catechism in connected and complete form in the next to the last or last school year. Where Luther's shorter catechism is used, the fourth and fifth articles are assigned to religious instruction; the text and explanation of the first two and the text of the third articles are to be learned. In the determination of the other materials of instruction, the point of view adopted should be that only those portions are to be selected which have proved themselves in the spiritual life of the community and which are suited to the development of Christian personality at the present time. With reference to Biblical phrases, the choice of those to be learned should be limited to a not too large selection of the most important ones. The children are to be acquainted primarily with the longer instructional and poetic parts of the Bible through reading—Psalms, selections from the prophetic books and from the epistles of the New Testament. Church songs are likewise correlated with materials historically related and with Christian festivals. The study of church songs is not limited to those which are to be memorized.

In the choice of historical materials, care is to be taken primarily that the children become acquainted with and familiar with religious personalities. There are treated: the Old Testament history, limited to the most important essentials, with emphasis on the work of the Prophets, the life of Jesus, Apostolic history, and periods from later history of the Christian Church, particularly that of the home, the district, and the life and the organization of the Evangelical Church of the present day. Restrictive regulations for the distribution of these materials to particular years are avoided.

### CATHOLIC RELIGIOUS INSTRUCTION

The aim of the religious instruction of the upper four years is to bring the religious and moral development of the children to such maturity that they are capable at the time of leaving school and inclined and willing to fulfill their religious and moral duties as living members of the church according to the doctrine and pattern of Jesus Christ.

Four hours a week are available for the pursuit of this objective.

The content of religious instruction comprises the fields of Catholic catechism, Biblical history, church history, and church service. These four fields, according to their nature, stand in living organic connection with one another, and must in no case in the religious instruction itself be separated.

The children have in their hands as a textbook the larger catechism, the school Bible, the diocesan prayer-book, and hymnal.

The spirit of the entire religious instruction of this section of the school must be the doctrine of the Catholic Church as it is expressed in the catechism prescribed.

The entire content of the catechism, as well as of the shorter school Bible, is so divided in the first three of the upper four years that the Second Article and the Old Testament—with the exception of the stories coming in rather loose connection with sacred history—fall in the fifth school year; in the sixth school year the first article and the New Testament—from the beginning of the public teaching of Jesus to the Apostolic history; in the seventh school year the Third Article and Apostolic history, together with a comprehensive review of the Old Testament according to definite points of view important for comprehension of sacred Christian history and an understanding of some of the more important periods and characters from church history.

It is of material importance that in all years of the school, review of the doctrine and ethics be taken care of so that a conclusion to the moral and religious instruction may be reached for children who will leave school before they reach the highest class. The eighth school year affords in two chief fields of instruction a summarizing conclusion, as well as direct preparation for entrance into practical life.

The summarizing treatment of the most important instructional divisions of the catechism has primarily the practical purpose of preparing and educating the pupils about to leave school for the difficulties facing them in life.

The treatment of all materials of instruction must shape itself so concretely, interestingly, and solidly, that the pupils will not only comprehend the thought content of the individual religious principles and accept their truth and authority with a joyous conviction of faith, but also be inspired with their beauty and sublimity, as well as with the Christian life values embodied in them, and above all be led in a practical way to lasting religious and moral conduct according to the fundamental principles of life that may be formed out of them.

The instruction in Biblical history has for its function, in the eighth school year, the transmission of an inspiring and comprehensive picture of the life and work of Jesus. In addition thereto, in case the advancement of the class permits it, some stories and sections from the apostolic letters and other parts of the Holy Scripture, which are particularly important for those pupils about to leave school, can also be inserted and treated in a manner corresponding to the advanced spiritual development of the children, and with practical applications to life.

The instruction in church history must place such persons and events in the foreground of consideration that are characteristic and typical for certain periods of time and fields of activity. Wherever it is possible, connection herewith is to be established with the history of the home. In particularly favorable school conditions an attempt is made to bring the children to an understanding, corresponding to their educational development, of the historical connections existing among the various periods that have been treated.

The liturgical instruction has for its function the expansion and intensification of the instruction acquired in the *Grundschule* by putting the children in more intimate relation to the life of the Church and to win them over for life in the spirit of the Church.

The treatment of the evangelical pericopes is chiefly a question of providing the children, through an awakening of the all-important comprehension and a sympathetic elaboration of the chief thought and truth which are connected with the respective church festival, with the ability and willingness for profitable attention to the sermon on Sundays and holy days, as well as an understanding and hearty participation in the common church service, with ceremonies which elevate thought and spirit. Since the pericopes from the Epistles are too difficult in general for this stage of the child's development, they are excluded from instruction in the *Volksschule*. Only very isolated lessons from the Epistles which contain the thought of the respective festival can be taken up during the instructional period. The instruction concerning the external organization and the inner meaning of the Holy Mass, as well as the explanation of the prayers and hymns which occur at the celebration of the Holy Mass and at other sacred worship must enable and accustom the children to unite in spirit with the priest at the altar and together with him make the Holy Sacrament.

Accordingly, it becomes the duty of the teacher of religion to prepare the church hymns well for the subsequent sacred worship. The church hymnology must, through industrious application in the entire religious instruction, be made so familiar to the children that they may use it easily as prayer.

The children are to be prepared briefly but impressively each time for the common reception of the Holy Sacraments.

Next, after divine grace, the influence of the teacher's whole personality is of decisive importance for the success of the instruction. Hence, it is essential that the good and winning example of a teacher with a strong and pious personality be added to convincing instruction.

### GERMAN

Instruction in German shall bring the pupils to an understanding of the German language, awaken their feeling for speech, cultivate the free and natural use of the spoken and written word, and arouse pleasure in German literature.

The general directions with reference to the instruction in the German language which were given in the *Suggestions for the Organization of the Courses of Study for the Grundschule* hold true here also. The following are to receive special attention:

The reading book will serve as means for the introduction to literature, and besides it, or in place of it, suitable single classics or collections of poems. Not only are selections from prose and poetry to be read, but also selections, valuable in form and content, from history, civics, economics, natural science, geography, and other fields of knowledge. These selections also may be read in the instructional periods set aside for the subjects mentioned. The individual classics are to be chosen in a similar way. In addition to reading in class, home reading is to be widely cultivated and employed for the purposes of instruction. The number of poems to be learned by heart which are required of all students is to be limited. However, pupils are to be encouraged in the voluntary memorization of poetry. It is more worthwhile that they are made acquainted in this way with a greater number of poems and secure pleasure in them, than that they learn a few more by heart. The statement in the regulations for the *Grundschule* concerning the recitation of poetry holds true here.

Frequent written and oral exercises for the attainment of accuracy in correct speech are to be continued in all classes. The instruction in forms of speech, along with the development and intensification of the materials treated in the *Grundschule*, extends to the declensions, use of the cases, a knowledge of the most important parts of speech, the tenses and conjugations of the verb, and grammar in connection with punctuation. These lessons are to be limited to that which is absolutely necessary for the correct use of speech.

Introduction to the study of meanings and changes of words, is to be carefully developed, not only in the German period, but also in connection with other subjects. Further, some understanding of the fact that the language is developing rapidly is to be awakened. At the same time a comparison with dialect forms is necessary, and must also be considered fully on other occasions in language instruction.

Effort is to be made through all of the written work of the pupil to secure accuracy in spelling. At the same time attention is primarily to be directed toward protecting the pupil against errors in writing. Dictation particularly will best serve this purpose if it is looked upon usually as an exercise in correct writing and only seldom as model work. The drill on rules in spelling is to be limited as much as possible. No weight is to be given to subtleties as they appear, particularly in capitalization, and in the writing of words of similar sound, and also in the writing of foreign words (which as far as possible must not be used at all in instruction, but must be definitely counteracted). The dictionary is also to be used by the pupils as a means both of avoiding mistakes and for fixing correct spelling.

The pupils are accordingly to be continually encouraged in the early use of the dictionary.

The number of free compositions by the pupils is not to be placed too high. For the last three years, twelve each year might serve as a rule. Besides these compositions short written exercises are to be prepared regularly in class. The instructions applying to this work in the *Suggestions for the Classes of the Grundschule* derive increased significance for the four upper classes of the *Volksschule*. Pupils are trained also in letter-writing, as well as in the preparing of business letters and the filling out of forms. Readiness and skill in writing are to be promoted chiefly in this way so that attention in all written exercises is directed to a clear, simple script and good arrangement on the paper. Mere exercises in writing are to be limited to essentials. Regular periods in the week are not to be added for this work; the exercises as needed may be taken up in the periods set aside for German instruction; all pupils are not to be compelled to attain similarity in form and in position of letters, but rather is freedom to be given to individuality in handwriting as it develops.

### HISTORY AND CIVICS

This instruction has for its objectives familiarizing the pupils with the chief facts in the development of the German people and the German state, and at the same time creating for them the bases for understanding the present period and the present state, and to awaken in them a consciousness of mutual responsibility for the people and the state as a whole, as well as a love for people and fatherland.

The highest law of history instruction must be to come as near as possible to historical truth. The history of the German people (including border and foreign Germany) organizes its material according to its different phases as a representation of the development of the political, social, economic, and spiritual life of the German race. Wars are chiefly to be evaluated by their causes and results.

It cannot be the objective of the elementary school instruction to give the child a complete view of historical development. It is rather a question of presenting concretely and vividly decisive events and steps in development, in the form of single well-rounded illustrations. The mere portrayal of conditions is as far as possible to be avoided, but rather everything should be translated into actions and events. Where it is possible, important historical personages and personalities of the home are to be placed at the center of consideration. As a beginning, or for purposes of clarification, source materials are to be drawn upon for definite purposes. The older Brandenburg-Prussian history is not to be treated separately, but is to be handled within the limits of German history. From the time of the Great Elector on, Brandenburg-Prussian history comes to the front. The history of other peoples is to be considered in so far as German history has been decisively influenced through it.

Civics,—that is, an introduction suitable to the understanding of this stage of development into the political, economic, and social conditions,—is to be studied from the beginning in connection with history instruction as well as with other subjects. At the same time, comparison is to be made with the present. The portrayal of present political conditions, organized in as detailed and as concrete a form as possible, constitutes the conclusion of the instruction. The constitutions of the federal government and of the Prussian state should be treated in this instruction.

*Note.*—These are suggestions for the coöperation of the schools and universities for the protection of the Republic. They were combined in the common decree of Ministers of Education on July 19, 1922. The coöperation of the school in the internal establishment of the Republic includes measures for civic education and discipline:

I. Departments of education have before them the following tasks in the fields of civic education:

1. In history textbooks the political educational tendency was formerly education of the youth for a monarchical form of state. It is necessary to create history textbooks which—with strict preservation of historical truth—cause those facts and situations to stand out more strongly that are adapted to awaken and develop that independent consciousness of responsibility of the citizen of a republic for his place in the state and society. For the presentation of the history of recent years, there must be prepared, with official approval, documentary foundation in brief form.

Pupils' libraries are to be subjected to an examination from similar points of view.

2. Civic instruction according to Article 148 of the Federal Constitu-

tion, so far as it has not yet occurred, must be introduced regularly into the curriculum of all schools. Useful textbooks are to be prepared with the coöperation of departments of education.

3. The courses of study for the various types of schools, so far as they still represent in material and method the tendencies named in paragraph 1, must be adapted to the new objectives of civic education, and be placed from the point of view of method on the foundation of community education through the principle of self-activity.

4. In the training of teachers, sufficient room is to be given to the scientific and pedagogical objectives of civic education through a re-organization of the courses of study of teacher-training institutions. At the universities the arrangements necessary for the civic education of academic students are to be provided. Necessary arrangements are to be provided for the further education of teachers in service for civic and history instruction, so far as is possible in connection with teachers' associations.

5. For the *advancement and facilitation* of regulations which are to be put in force by the educational administrations of the various states, a committee will be formed in the Federal Ministry of the Interior from representatives of school authorities of various states, historians, political economists, and teachers, which will support, advise, and encourage the modification and creation of textbooks and instruction materials, and advise in the organization of courses.

II. The administration of these regulations presupposes a teaching staff in all schools, and particularly in the universities, who are conscious of their responsible task, as educators of youth, and of the duties of an official in the Republic and state in like degree. The principle that holds true in all states for the laws which govern officials, that the official must conduct the duty assigned to him conscientiously, and according to the constitution and law, and must show through his conduct, both in and out of office, that he is worthy of the respect which his calling demands, places upon the teacher very special duties. It is not sufficient in execution of his official duties that he avoid every disparagement of existing government or of the constitutional governments of the Republic or states, but he has also to train the youth for coöperation in the Republic, to educate them to a mutual responsibility for the welfare of the state and to awaken and cultivate a political consciousness.

It is the duty of the supervisors of the school to support the teachers in the execution of this task with their whole authority and to interfere vigorously on the occasion of any violation. That influencing of pupils in a partisan sense is not in harmony with the spirit of civic education, as in general the avoidance of partisan politics in the schools, goes without saying. For this purpose, it is necessary that the pupils remain out of organizations whose purposes run counter to civic objectives of the school. The school authorities, therefore, will give increased attention to the club life of the students, and particularly will have to take suitable steps for the prevention of such organizations. Similarly, the external features of the school, decoration of the classroom, the organization of school holidays, must conform to the demands of the new state.

The schools, according to consideration of their particular conditions, will undertake the distribution of this material. A distribution by which the same phases of the material are treated several times is to be avoided. Besides the concluding civics instruction, special and summarized considerations of development of single phases of the economic and social life, such as agriculture, handwork and technology, commerce and business, middle, agricultural, laboring classes, are assigned to the last year. Local history, too, which must come in for treatment as much as possible in all classes, finds here its summary and conclusion.

### GEOGRAPHY

Geography instruction seeks to promote acquaintance with the home, a more intimate knowledge of Germany, a general acquaintance with foreign countries and parts of the earth, and an understanding of the position of the earth in the universe.

The instruction in the last school years, building upon the ground work laid in the *Grundschule*, besides the geography of the fatherland, must also cover the study of the other countries of Europe and other parts of the world. Predominantly those countries in which Germans live and work and with which Germany maintains important relations are to be treated in this study. The consideration of these countries according to their geological structure and their natural relationships forms the foundation of this study. The climatic, economic, and colonization conditions are to be presented in relation to the former. Extensive use is to be made of sketching on the board by the teacher, as well as drawing and modeling by the pupils. For objective comparison, local conditions must be drawn upon constantly. Excursions and trips in the local community are therefore indispensable for the study of the fatherland and the treatment of foreign countries. In astronomy, the starting-point will always be from the phenomena which the home offers and to the observation of which the children are to be introduced. The illustration by means of apparatus has here the purpose only of explaining and clarifying the knowledge gained through observation. The children are to be acquainted with the most important stars and constellations. At the same time opportunity will offer itself to point out to them the wonders of the firmament. It is of special value, particularly in the rural schools, to emphasize regular observation of the weather and to give an introduction to knowledge of weather maps. The distribution of materials through the various school years is left here, too, to the individual schools. Still, it is desirable to distribute astronomy over all years and take up again in the concluding part of the course the region of the home and the fatherland, particularly with reference to their economic conditions and their position in world commerce. At the same time connections with other subjects, especially with civics and natural history instruction, are to be established. The thought of the protection of the home is also to be brought before the child in the concluding study of home community.

### NATURAL SCIENCE

In natural science instruction the children are to be led to observe and to judge objects, life, and processes in nature so that they may acquire pleasure in nature and achieve a modest degree of understanding and knowledge of nature, and be enabled to make use of this information in life. Materials selected from botany, zoölogy, physiology, physics, and chemistry, in connection with geology, form the content of this instruction. The particular materials are to be chosen according to local conditions and needs. Particularly in rural places must the schools take into consideration extensively the demands which the pursuit of agriculture makes on those who in the future will be active in it, while in schools in large cities technical and industrial points of view come to the front. Here also the instruction must pay attention to the importance, organization, and chief forms of agricultural production. Consideration must be given to the cultivation of flowers, breeding of small animals, and similar educationally valuable home activities in all schools to a reasonable degree. Where home economics instruction for girls and manual training for boys are introduced, natural science instruction must maintain the closest possible relation with them. The emphasis does not lie in botany and zoölogy, in classification and description, but in observation of life phenomena and their causal connection with the structure of plants and animals, and in the applications to agricultural use and to the economic importance of nature's productions. Preparation of school gardens, the care of animals in aquariums, terrariums and insectariums by the children can further effectively the purposes of instruction. Drawing and modeling are to be used freely for the development of the power of observation. Reproduction from memory, particularly on the blackboard, is especially to be cultivated. While care must be taken that the instruction awakens an appreciative understanding for all life in nature, it will serve at the same time as aid for the protection of animals and plants, to the advancement of which it will create opportunities in other subjects outside of this instruction.

In physiology the chief aim is to be directed toward understanding the processes of life and work of the human body and its hygiene. Specifically, thought must be given to the explanation at this time concerning regulations for public health (as for example, vaccination against smallpox, prevention of tuberculosis), and to the injury which is done through the use of narcotics, especially the misuse of alcohol. In girls' schools where it seems possible, important questions of the care of the sick and of infants will come up for discussion in connection with physiology. Instruction in care of sick and of infants can also be treated. The care of infants can always be treated in a special course.

The starting-point in natural science is always from life phenomena. School experiments which so far as possible may be undertaken by the pupils themselves will serve to clarify those things which have been observed in reality. Experiments are not to be attempted which are set up only for the sake of a certain type of comprehensiveness.

Close and manifold correlations should be established wherever possible among the several branches of natural science instruction. There is also no objection if the course of study combines the materials appearing in one or two years' work. The distribution of materials to the various years will be guided by the special needs of the schools and their immediate environment.

## ARITHMETIC

Arithmetic instruction is to develop the number sense of the pupils and to lead them to understand the conditions of life from a mathematical point of view and to enable them to solve independently and accurately arithmetical problems which arise therefrom.

Calculation with compound denominate numbers, together with common and decimal fractions, makes up the material of the upper years' work. It includes also the application of arithmetical skill to problems of daily life and particularly to the so-called business methods, which must be taken up to a suitable degree beginning with the fifth year. Problems are to be given wherever possible so that the pupils will be compelled through their own thinking to determine which arithmetical process is to be applied. Further, the pupils are to be encouraged to make up problems of their own, and to use therein price lists, results of their own measurements and weighing, as well as of the official census, time-tables, and the like. Likewise the estimation of the result is to be practiced before and after exact calculation. The topics for the several classes and divisions should be so limited that in every arithmetic hour sufficient time remains for regular drill exercises. Group problems which have no importance at all for life, for example written addition of long columns of compound and denominate numbers not of decimal value, calculation of time in interest problems, complicated problems in fractions, as well as fractions with large denominations, are to be limited as far as possible or entirely eliminated. In the solution of problems not only is a definite method, the normal method, permissible, but efforts should be made that the pupils discover independently as many different methods as possible. In the written calculation of examples from business arithmetic, as in the vocational school, processes used by the merchants and industrial workers and farmers should be considered. Wherever possible, mere calculation by rule should be avoided. It is best to make no use at all of arithmetical procedures which favor this process.

### GEOMETRY

Geometrical concepts of the pupils are to be developed through geometry instruction, and the ability is to be developed in them to understand, represent, and calculate the geometrically quantitative facts which come up in life.

Fundamental exercises in the comprehension and representation of regular areas and solids, the principles of lines and angles, the calculation of solids and areas, form the materials of instruction for the one-class schools, for other schools of few classes, and for the girls' sections of the fully graded schools. The material is increased for the boys' section of the fully graded schools by the addition of the principles of congruency and equality, comparison of areas, proportion and similarity, or a part of these fields.

Instruction begins with objective consideration of geometrical forms, which is to be clarified and intensified by varied representations and manual activity wherever possible by the pupils themselves (modeling, drawing, folding, cutting, combining, weighing, and calculating). The starting-point is to be taken from objects of daily experience by the pupils. In proofs, the process of measurement and rotation (rearrangement, transposition, and rotation) is to be preferred as contrasted with a proof through mere steps in reasoning (Euclidian method). The application of the latter form can be entirely abandoned.

Distribution of the material is to be organized according to special conditions.

### DRAWING

Drawing instruction, supplemented by writing, sketching, modeling, handwork, and the like, is to enable the pupils to use form and color as means of expression and explanation.

Freehand drawing instruction has the peculiar objective of developing the creative ability of the child through his own activity and cultivating his power of imagination and representation. This instruction proceeds definitely from free drawing and painting, which furnish the child a mode of expression for his inner life and his relation to the external world (imaginative and memory work). In connection therewith exercises are to be taken up in cutting and drawing of objects from the observational experience of the pupils (from nature as well as from memory), in cutting and filling in of surfaces with color, in blackboard drawing and decorative writing. The instruction of the teacher must adapt itself to the child's manner of artistic expression, which is constantly to be observed, and to the child's feeling for form and color. At the proper place also the study of works of art is to be encouraged.

Mechanical drawing instruction is to develop the power of spatial representation and to lead to the understanding of working drawings. Its goal with reference to manual training is skill in the use of the centimeter measure, compass, T-square, triangle, and where possible, also, the drawing pen. The exercises should aim at the geometric representation of simple objects from the environment of the pupil, especially such as are taken from the field of manual training, etc. It begins with the measuring of simple flat objects, proceeds to drawing similar objects according to a given scale, and then takes up the representation of solids.

Linear drawing is to be studied in the drawing periods in all four classes, in connection with the free-hand drawing. In the two upper classes twenty hours a year, which are to be given in consecutive weeks if possible, will be devoted to it.

### MUSIC

Music instruction pursues the objective of awakening joy in singing and in song, and especially in the German folk song, of leading up to an understanding or feeling for fine tone qualities, and preparing, through training of the voice and ear, the pupils for participation in singing in later life. The course of study for music instruction of January 10, 1914, which remains in force until further notice, contains the details concerning the choice and distribution of material, as well as the instructional procedure.

*Note.*—The course of study of January 10, 1914, for singing instruction in the *Volksschule:*

### General Aim of Instruction

Music instruction has for its purpose the awakening of the desire for singing and, in general, the arousing of pleasure in German folk songs and also in classical music; of furthering the development of the spirit and of training the voice and musical appreciation; of drilling effectively a wealth of valuable spiritual and secular songs; and of preparing the children for activity in singing in religious and community life.

## REMARKS ON METHOD

The central point of singing instruction lies in the songs which are to be sung by the children,—beautifully, with understanding, and without hesitation.

In addition thereto, certain exercises are necessary, which are to be employed in as close connection with the songs as possible.

There are exercises in the following topics: breathing, voice building, notes, rhythm, notation exercises, listening, and dynamics.

Attention is to be given in the breathing exercises to deep inhalation (combined falling of the diaphragm and abdominal breathing), holding of the breath, and long, regular exhalation.

Exercises for the acquisition of a fine tone (tone building exercises) are to be taken up at the beginning of every singing period. Particularly are soft blending of the voice and the smooth tone of the voice to be cultivated. Head-tones are to be built up, and a balancing of the register is to be sought for. Extremely loud singing is to be avoided under all circumstances. In order to protect the youthful voice organs the range of the voice is not to be exceeded. The range of voice up and down is to be extended gradually and carefully. It is desirable that the teacher determine once or twice a year, through an examination of the range, the voice development of his pupils. In order to protect the voice from fatigue, a change in every singing period must occur with individual, group, and class singing.

Children who are at the age of voice changing may be excused from singing, but not from music instruction. Singing and voice exercises which are to be prepared for through language exercises must strive for a pure pronunciation of the vowels free from dialect and for a phonetically correct formation of the consonants. Attention is at the same time to be given to free movement of the lips and correct position of the tongue, as well as to a free movement of the lower jaw. The notation exercises are to be taken up in methodical order and with exclusive use of the notes. The notation begins first in C major,—but the singing begins at a pitch corresponding to the voices of the children,—and also with German names for notes and with suitable German syllables, but which must not be for permanent designation to definite pitches or scales, and with words and rhymes and short phrases corresponding to the child's experience. (The exclusive or predominant use of the syllable "la" is to be avoided in the interest of tone building.)

The feeling for time on the part of the children is to be developed, and the rhythm of the songs is to be prepared for through special rhythmic exercises. At the same time, it is of importance that the children also keep time. Notation and rhythmic exercises are associated with exercises in listening. It is recommended to have that which is heard written down and simple musical dictations prepared.

As soon as the children have been brought to a sufficient understanding of the notes, the songs may no longer be drilled mechanically by ear. The uncomprehending imitation of a melody which has been played or sung by or with the teacher is forbidden. Still, in singing instruction the singing of the teacher will always be of great importance, especially when it is a question of fine tone, right breathing and phrasing, and good diction.

In all grades, one-part singing and leading of songs by the children are to be encouraged.

In the two- or more-part singing of the folk songs, the melody is to be learned by all the children and is to be sung at a pitch which is suitable to the average voice range of the music class. Folk songs are to be sung primarily in one or two voices; chorals, as a rule, in only one voice. Before singing a song, the content is to be brought to the understanding and feeling of the children through a short explanation of the setting in order that it may be sung with more intimate participation. However, the simple, unaffected diction must not suffer, especially in the case of folk songs. Attention is also to be given to correct breathing so that both the text and the melody are thoughtfully divided.

The treatment and memorization of songs with difficult text belong to the German and religious instruction.

In every school there should be selected a list of songs for the individual classes, wherein the church feasts and the seasons are to receive consideration. The entire number of required secular songs and chorals should not exceed thirty a year. These songs are to be sung entirely and independently by the children. Besides the songs in the prescribed list, still other songs are to be sung whose choice is left to the teacher; but here also the folk song must stand in the foreground. The practice material set for each class is to be repeated in the following classes; similarly, those church and folk songs which have lasting value for later life. Chorals must be practiced with reference to text and melody as required by the church authorities.

In the correlation of music with physical training, care must be taken for health reasons, especially in closed rooms. A systematically arranged songbook is necessary in the hand of the pupil. Songbooks without notes are not allowed. The employment of suitable instructional material is recommended for class instruction.

## Subject Matter for One- and Two-class Volksschulen

### LOWER SECTION,—FIRST AND SECOND SCHOOL YEAR

Singing by ear, whereby conscious singing is gradually prepared for; simple exercises in tone and sound building, conception of tones as to number, length, pitch, and strength; simple rhythmic exercises in connection with counting, tapping, and marching; some game songs, and also children's and church songs.

### MIDDLE AND UPPER SECTIONS,—THIRD TO EIGHTH SCHOOL YEAR

Tone and sound building exercises; singing by notes, notation exercises in scales C, G, and F major and in the minor; rhythmic exercises in the most commonly used measures, listening exercises, the most important signs of execution; two-part singing, if the necessary voice material is available; folk and church songs; and liturgical singing for Evangelical schools.

## Subject Matter for Volksschulen with Three Ascending Classes

### LOWER SECTION

Material as in the *Volksschule* with one or two classes.

### MIDDLE SECTION

Exercises in tone and sound building; singing by note; tonic, rhythmic, and listening exercises in C, G, and F major; the most important signs of execution; introduction into two-part singing; folk and church songs.

### UPPER SECTION

Tone and sound exercises; tonic, rhythmic and listening exercises in D, B, F major and in the minor; folk and church songs; and liturgical singing for Evangelical schools; in particularly favorable school conditions, A and E sharp majors may also be studied, as well as three-part singing.

## Subject Matter for Volksschulen with Four to Eight Ascending Classes

### LOWER SECTION

1. First school year: Material as in the lower section of the *Volksschule* with three ascending classes.

2. Second and third school year: Tone and sound exercises; singing by note, which begins in the second school year; C major; the scale; the trial on the first step with its inversions and permutations; the whole, the half, quarter and eighth notes, and similar rests; the

dotted half note; 2-4, 3-4, and 4-4 time; unaccented syllable; notation, rhythmic, and listening exercises; play, children's, folk, and church songs.

### MIDDLE SECTION

Tone and sound building exercises; C major; triads on the fourth and fifth step with their inversions and permutations; combining of chief triads; appreciation and indication of intervals; structure of major scales; distinguishing and singing of whole and half steps in tones; G and F major; the chief triads and their combinations; tones above and below the scale; dotted fourth and eighth note; sixteenth note and rest; 3-8 and 6-8 time; notation, rhythmic, and listening exercises; two-part singing; most important signs of execution; folk and church songs.

### UPPER SECTION

Tone and sound building exercises; D, B, A and E sharp major; the minor scale; the chief triads and their combinations; the fifth step (the dominant seventh chord); notation, rhythmic, and listening exercises; three-part singing; folk and church songs; and some popular and classical singing; liturgical singing for Evangelical schools.

### PHYSICAL TRAINING

Physical training is to advance the whole bodily development, and especially to strengthen the health and accustom the pupils to good position, breathing, and care of the body, as well as strength, skill, and courage. [45]

The material of instruction is to be chosen according to the official manual corresponding to special conditions, and is to be distributed over the various years according to ability to do the exercises. Generally exercise is to be performed in the open. Special value is to be attached to games, popular exercises, and

---

[45] From the Ministerial Edict, January 24, 1920:

Exemption from physical training instruction is given only for a period, at the most for half a year, and in general not from physical instruction entirely, but only from those exercises not suitable for the pupil at that time. A doctor's certificate is not necessary in cases in which the need of temporary abstention from definite exercises is easily recognized, as, for example, in the case of external injuries. The directors of the school must take care that the pupils during this time in which they are not taking part in regular gymnasium exercises are employed to a reasonable extent, as far as possible, with easier exercises, games, activities in the open air, suitable to their condition of health, or with gardening and the like. Complete exemption, not merely from the regular exercises but from every type of physical exercises, is to be granted only on the basis of an official or medical certificate.

excursions in the sense of the ministerial regulation of March 29, 1920, while bathing and swimming and winter sports, such as tobogganing, snow shoeing and skating, are to be cultivated according to opportunity. [46]

## NEEDLEWORK

Instruction in needlework will enable the girls themselves to prepare, as need arises, useful articles with needle and scissors,

[46] Ministerial Regulation of March 29, 1920:

In a great number of institutions of all kinds, there exists already the arrangement that besides the regular hours for physical training, a half-holiday is introduced each week on which boys and girls in a regular way can devote themselves to free activity in healthful bodily exercises, such as hiking, games, winter sports, swimming, or rowing.

I herewith direct that this arrangement, from April 1st of this year on, be extended to all elementary and middle schools, to normal schools for men and women, as well as to all secondary institutions of instruction for boys and girls, in so far as the local conditions may permit. Consideration, wherever possible, is to be given in this work to the wishes of the youth concerning the type of exercises to be undertaken by them, depending upon the time of year and local conditions.

Beginning with the sixth year, a whole day out of the instructional time is to be devoted to physical training excursions, on the average of one every four weeks where conditions do not make it impossible. These excursions are to arouse a free and happy disposition and wanderlust, to develop a conscious power of seeing and hearing, to assure joy in nature, in the home, and in comradeship, and to bestow endurance. In addition to this, it should lead, for example, while at rest, to discrimination of objects at a distance, to judging of distance, to orientation in the countryside, and to judgment of the latter. In connection with this, simple sketches of the countryside drawn in the open can render worthwhile service to geography instruction.

Opportune and joyful singing of physical training and tramping songs increases the pleasure and the endurance of the participants. Similarly field games in the form of paper chases and the like can serve this purpose.

Boys and girls are to be accustomed to respect the rules of health which hold true for hiking; particularly is the use of alcohol and tobacco to be avoided. Necessary attention to well-directed care of the feet is to be given.

On account of the differences in endurance of boys and girls, hiking is to be done by classes, as a rule.

The preservation of order is lightened by dividing the hikers into groups, for which a suitable pupil is appointed as the group leader.

I trust that all members of the teaching staff will feel themselves responsible not merely for the spiritual and moral, but also for the physical welfare of the youth entrusted to them, and in the execution of the foregoing regulations which serve to restore and preserve the public health, are ready to coöperate, each according to his ability.

Particularly are class teachers obligated to support the physical training teachers in this work.

also to alter and repair them, and to train their taste for that which is pleasing and serviceable as well as their sense of form and color, and to awaken in them joy in useful work.

These exercises include sewing (where provisions are made, also machine sewing), knitting, darning, and embroidery. The instruction is to be given as class instruction. Repair work (mending and darning) is specially to be emphasized. In the course of the instruction, and especially at the beginning of a piece of new work, the girls are to be instructed concerning the origin and manufacture of the materials to be used and of the tools employed.

As a condition for attaining these objectives not more than thirty girls at a time are to be instructed in sewing.

Instruction in needlework will seek close connection with instruction in drawing. It will supplement the instruction in the care of children, in that it teaches and practices the making of children's clothing.

### MANUAL TRAINING

Manual training has in general to serve not only for the education of the pupil in the sense of the regulation of April 29, 1921, but also for the needs of the school. Where this can be carried on in wide scope, it begins with instruction in light woodwork, continues to instruction in pasteboard, and then to instruction in bookbinding, metal work, and bench work.

*Note.*—Ministerial Regulation, April 4, 1921, concerning manual training in the schools:

If manual training is to fulfill its educational purpose, it must not approach the school as something foreign, but must grow naturally out of the needs and objectives of the school itself. For a long time, it has been thought of almost entirely in connection with the problems which result from instruction; but the external affairs of school organization and the common activities of the pupils, in excursions, play, and art, contain a rich number of problems that the youth will gladly take over and perform unselfishly as they perform such tasks in the home. Particularly may the student body, together with a mutual responsibility on the part of teachers and parents, be entrusted with the economic affairs of the school, which up to this time have been cared for exclusively by the state and community. Tasks of this kind are: Care of the schoolhouse, its surroundings; the making and repairing and care of teaching and instructional materials; care of playground

apparatus; decoration of the school; and other tasks of this kind.
These tasks, however, will not run along in addition to the former
school tasks. They are rather, so far as possible, to be incorporated
in the entire work of the school, and used for their educational value.
If it is possible to so enliven the spirit of the pupils for such new
tasks that they cheerfully take them over as a duty, so also is their
civic education developed along these lines in an entirely natural
way.

Such an extension of school activity is only possible when all those
concerned work together with one spirit, and when it succeeds in
making the manufacturing establishments which are near the school
incline toward the provision of the materials, tools, and technical advice.
It must, therefore, be the duty of school authorities, school principals
and teachers, together with the more mature pupils, their parents, and
friends of the school, to consider how this self-help, demanded by our
necessity, can be formed and executed in the spirit of the work-
school. In particular, many different methods will be utilized, each
according to the given conditions. To find the latter, it is recommended
that the preceding suggestions be discussed in conferences of the
provincial and county school authorities, school councils and governments, as well as in conferences of school superintendents, principals
and teachers, parents' councils, and school communities, and at other
suitable opportunities, especially during parents' evenings. Attempts
which may be voluntarily undertaken at suitable institutions are to be
promoted as vigorously as possible.

Instruction in light woodwork shall enable the pupils to make
simple toys and small articles of use from planed wood, or
perhaps from cigar-box wood, or from boxwood planed thin.

The instruction in cardboard work will place its chief emphasis
upon the construction of small articles for the pupils' own use,
or for school purposes. It can also assist in the maintenance of
books. The pupils are to be led to construct paper covers themselves (pasting paper).

The instruction in bench work is to enable the pupils to
prepare with saw and plane from rough boards simple articles
for home and school use.

Every object is to be sketched by the pupil independently in
the simplest possible form. The sketch is to be worked out as a
working drawing in natural dimensions.

The pupils are to get to the point in metal work instruction
of constructing simple projects in wire and sheet metal, which

come up occasionally in every home, or which can serve instructional purposes. The pupils can finally learn to make small useful and artistic objects from copper and brass.

The instruction in bookbinding has for its purpose service to the school itself, through repairing or even binding for the time their own books or those belonging to the school. This work limits itself to simple bindings; imitations of wood, leather, etc., are not permissible as material.

Where conditions seem to make it desirable, the techniques mentioned above can be replaced by others (original home projects, such as weaving with willow and reed, hand weaving, brooming, etc.)

In the course of instruction, the pupils are to be informed concerning the working materials, their source and manufacture, and also concerning the tools.

### HOUSEHOLD ECONOMICS INSTRUCTION

Instruction in home economics has for its function imparting some fundamental knowledge of home economics and a modest amount of practical skill to growing girls. In connection therewith this instruction will cultivate the homemaking attitude of the girls.

This instruction has as classroom work, in the spirit of the activity school principle, the function of educating the girls to thoughtful, independent work. Activity and instruction are to be united as closely as possible. Most intimate relationships are to be established with other subjects, especially with arithmetic, natural science, and civics.

The course includes cooking in connection with nutrition and housework. Where it is possible, the school garden also is to be employed in the service of home economics instruction.

The materials of instruction are to be chosen according to special conditions. The season of the year and the market are to be taken into consideration as far as possible. The girls are to be trained for sensible buying and for the keeping of household accounts. They are to be enabled to prepare simple, nourishing, and tasteful dishes. In connection therewith opportunity is to be provided for practice in the use and cleansing of the most usual household articles, and in performing the most common household duties. Particularly, also, is heating to be studied, and in connection therewith instruction in the economical and practical use of fuel is to be given. The study of articles of food is to be closely connected with practical work. Reckonings of time and price are absolutely essential to the training of thinking in domestic economy. In the extension of the instruction to infant care, domestic economy instruction teaches and practices the preparation of food for babies and small children.

### PROGRAM OF STUDIES

| SUBJECT | BOYS' SCHOOL | | | | GIRLS' SCHOOL | | | |
|---|---|---|---|---|---|---|---|---|
| | 5 | 6 | 7 | 8 | 5 | 6 | 7 | 8 |
| Religion .......... | 4 | 4 | 4 | 4 | 4 | 4 | 4 | 4 |
| German .......... | 8 | 7 | 6–7 | 6–7 | 7–8 | 7 | 6–7 | 6–7 |
| History and Civics.. | 2 | 2 | 2 | 3 | 2 | 2 | 2 | 3 |
| Geography ........ | 2 | 2 | 2 | 2 | 2 | 2 | 2 | 2 |
| Natural Science ... | 2 | 3–4 | 4 | 3 | 2 | 2–3 | 3 | 3 |
| Arithmetic ⎱ ....... Geometry ⎰ | 4–5 | 5–6 | 5–6 | 5–6 | 3–4 | 4 | 4 | 3 |
| Drawing .......... | 2 | 2 | 2 | 2 | 2 | 2 | 2 | 2 |
| Singing .......... | 2 | 2 | 2 | 2 | 2 | 2 | 2 | 2 |
| Physical Training .. | 2–3 | 3 | 3 | 3 | 2 | 3 | 3 | 3 |
| Manual Training .. | 2 | 2 | 2 | 2 | ... | ... | ... | ... |
| Sewing .......... | ... | ... | ... | ... | 2 | 2–3 | 2–3 | 2–3 |
| Total .......... | 28–30 | 30–32 | 30–32 | 30–32 | 28–30 | 30-32 | 30–32 | 30–32 |

*Note.*—Where home economics instruction is introduced for girls, two of the four hours set aside for this work are to be obtained by reducing the time for other subjects.

In boys' schools, where manual training is given, the weekly number of hours may not exceed thirty in the fifth school year, and, in the others, not more than thirty-two.

I

## THE REGULATION OF JUNE 1, 1925

The far-reaching reorganization of our political, intellectual, economic, and social life, which has taken place in the last decade, has confronted our whole school system, and particularly the middle school, with new and difficult problems.

The middle school was not able within the limits of the Regulations of February 3, 1910, to adapt itself to problems, successful as the work has been, which it otherwise has been able to perform upon the basis of these regulations.

The following new "Regulations Concerning the Middle Schools in Prussia" are to remove this deficiency. They adhere to the proven bases of the previous regulations, point out new and timely selections of educational values and methods of work, and seek to assure the middle school the place rightfully belonging to it in the living organism of our school system.

I charge the county governments—county or the provincial school board—to take the steps necessary for the enforcement of the new regulations as soon as possible. Herein the following is to be observed:

1. The new regulations are in force from to-day for classes VI and V. They go into effect with the beginning of the school year 1926-1927 for class IV.

2. In classes IV to I or III to I, by means of the organization of suitable provisional courses in 1925-26 and 1926-27, the gradual growth into the educational aims and objectives provided in the new regulations is to be striven for. In this matter careful attention is to be given that any overburdening of the pupils be avoided.

3. From the beginning of the school year 1927-28 the new

regulations are to be the standard for the educational aims, instructional objectives, and methods of work for all classes of the middle school.

4. The special programs to be developed at the individual schools upon the basis of the new regulations are to be ready for classes VI and V by October 1 of this year, for class V by January 1, 1926, for classes III to I by January 1, 1927. They require the approval of the county government—or of the Provincial School Board.

The organization of the programs for the transition period is not involved.

I trust that the county government or Provincial School Board, mindful of the high importance which is to be granted the middle schools in educational, social, and economic respects, will further these schools as far as resources permit. The special care of the county governments must be directed to seeing that the reorganization of the middle school system takes place without friction through their effective assistance in setting up the transitional and final objectives.

I reserve the privilege of demanding at a given time the curricula of individual schools.

The existing regulations still apply to the recognition of a school as a fully developed middle school.

Special regulations will be issued with reference to the problem of privileges and the duties of the administrative officers (board of governors).

New regulations with reference to religion and music in the middle schools will be issued in the course of the present year.

*Berlin, June 1, 1925*
BECKER.

# II

# INTRODUCTION

The development in the fields of manual activity, industrial art, commerce and industry, agriculture and forestry demands increased preparation of the boys and girls for these vocational branches. In connection therewith, there is need also of a suitable type of preparation for many sorts of intermediate positions in the administrative service of the state or municipalities, as well as in the larger industrial and commercial enterprises.

The *Volksschule*, even in its most highly developed form, is able to serve these needs to a limited extent only on account of the manifold difficulties under which it operates as a general compulsory school. In the secondary school the objectives are directed primarily to academic purposes, so that it also is not able to satisfy these needs in a satisfactory fashion.

Accordingly, there arises the need of a school standing between the *Volksschule* and the secondary schools, which, unhindered by the duties devolving upon it as a general school, enables its pupils also to satisfy the increased demands of later vocations of life. Such a school is the six-class middle school, which is built upon the *Grundschule*.

The efficiency of this type of school does not have for its ultimate justification the greater maturity of the pupils resulting from a two-year longer period in school. The importance of the years which fall in the most important period of youthful development cannot easily be overestimated, for the intellectual development as well as for the moral growth and strength of the pupils. The effect of the longer instructional period will be essentially increased by the smaller number of the classes, by richer provision of instructional materials, and chiefly by home conditions generally more favorable for school work.

In many smaller places attempts have been made to satisfy the need for a school going beyond the objectives of the *Volksschule*, by establishing city and private *Rektoratschulen*, higher schools,

Latin schools, and the like. These schools fulfill the purpose largely of preparing their pupils for later transfer into a secondary school without any appreciable loss of time and thereby permit them to enjoy as long as possible the education and the care of the home. In educational, economic, and social respects such schools are of great importance. However, since they work exclusively along the lines of the higher schools for which they prepare, they serve in general only to a limited degree the needs of wider classes of society. They might serve the purpose better by adopting the middle school organization. Through a corresponding codification of the school program and by the introduction of section instruction in individual subjects of the secondary schools—for example, foreign languages—the middle school is able to prepare also for the secondary school, without neglecting its real function.

# III

## GENERAL REGULATIONS

### I.  ORGANIZATION OF THE MIDDLE SCHOOL

1. The fully developed middle school is based upon the *Grund-schule* and comprises six superimposed year courses, usually in six separate classes.

2. Admission to the lowest class, especially as to the minimum age necessary for entrance into this class, is determined by the corresponding regulations applying at the time to the secondary schools.

3. The supplementary classes attached to the *Volksschulen* can attain the objectives of the fully developed middle school, if they correspond to it in organization, curricula, and organization of faculty.

4. A tuition fee is charged in the middle school, the amount of which must be approved by the county government.

In order not to allow the training which the middle school desires to give to be solely dependent upon the economic conditions of the parents, in every middle school a reasonable number of scholarships is to be offered for such needy children as distinguish themselves by industry and ability.

5. The highest number of boys and girls in the various classes of the middle school is regulated by the regulation applying *at the time* thereto.

6. If the number of pupils is small, two years' work with the approval of the county government may be combined in one class.  Then, however, care is to be taken with reference to a reasonable reduction of the maximum number otherwise admitted to classes of this section.

7. The middle school organizations will chiefly be organized separately for boys and for girls.

Where the necessary number of boys or girls is not available in order to form middle schools or sequences of classes separately for boys and girls, it is permissible to combine them.

Likewise in middle schools in which the sexes are primarily divided, boys and girls may be taught together in individual classes, when the number of boys and girls of the individual year's courses is not sufficient for the organization of divided boys' and girls' classes.

8. Accordingly, it is permissible with a small number of pupils to organize middle schools with only three classes of which each two successive grades are combined.

## II. TEACHERS

1. Instruction in academic subjects shall be given only by teachers who have secured the certificate to teach in the middle schools, or who have passed the examination to teach in the secondary schools.

2. Men and women teachers of music, drawing, physical training, sewing, gardening, home economics, and manual training, if the number of hours is sufficient to employ teachers full time in one or more of these subjects belonging closely together, shall have given evidence of special preparation for and passed examinations in these subjects, in so far as such examinations are arranged therefor on the part of the state.

3. Women teachers will teach primarily in the classes for girls. In mixed classes men and women teachers will work side by side. No fundamental objections exist against using women teachers in boys' classes.

## III. CURRICULA

1. The number of hours, including the elective instruction, is to be limited to six recitation hours daily. The undivided day is the rule.

2. In the middle school, which is not responsible for preparation for secondary schools, required instruction is given in one foreign language. Boys and girls whose general conduct and achievement give promise of further regular progress, may be granted the opportunity of pursuing on an elective basis a second foreign language, specifically English beginning with class III, and other modern foreign languages beginning with class IV.

3. In the arithmetic instruction of the upper classes bookkeeping is considered to the extent set forth in the following

curricula. In the middle schools which prepare for commerce and trade, special hours in bookkeeping are to be introduced.

4. In all middle schools home economics instruction is to be organized for girls; and manual training, and so far as possible gardening also—for boys and girls. The instruction in these subjects is usually elective; however, upon the decision of the competent local school authorities participation in home economics and manual training can be made obligatory.

5. Participation in shorthand for which time is to be provided in the programs of all middle schools, is elective. Instruction in typewriting is given on the elective basis for the finishing classes which work according to Plan II or Plan IV.

6. In order to avoid any overburdening of the boys and girls, the maximum number of hours of instruction weekly, including elective instruction, is fixed at 32 for boys and girls of classes VI and V, at 34 for those of classes IV and III, and at 36 for those of classes II and I.

7. Through fixing a minimum and maximum standard of hours for the language, the mathematics, the natural science subjects, and drawing, some leeway is to be allowed each individual school in adapting the program to its special needs in order to intensify the training in those subjects which are especially important for later vocations.

8. The arrangement of the maximum number of hours is to serve less to extend the fields of subject-matter which are treated than to serve their thorough mastery. In every reduction of the number of hours the subject-matter is to be limited to such an extent that the necessary thorough mastery is assured under all circumstances.

9. For adaptation of both sexes to conditions of existence which are becoming ever more complex, as great flexibility as possible is to be given in classes III to I of the middle school. Economic necessity is, however, to be regarded carefully in the organization of these classes. For all forms of the school, the work of three lowest years is to be organized as much alike as possible.

10. Even if the upper sections of the middle schools in a locality are organized with different curricula, the pupils who have attained the maturity for the upper section may transfer with-

out further examination to the schools especially designed to prepare for their future life vocation.

### 1.  PLAN I:  GENERAL CURRICULUM FOR BOYS

| No. | SUBJECTS | NUMBER OF HOURS IN CLASS | | | | | | |
|---|---|---|---|---|---|---|---|---|
| | | VI | V | IV | III | II | I | Total |
| 1. | Religion * | 2 | 2 | 2 | 2 | 2 | 2 | 12 |
| 2. | German | 6 | 5 | 5 | 5 | 5 | 5 | 31 |
| 3. | History | | 2 | 2 | 2 | 2 | 3 | 11 |
| 4. | Geography | 2 | 2 | 2 | 2 | 2 | 2 | 12 |
| 5. | First Foreign Language. | 6 | 4–5 | 4–5 | 3–5 | 3–5 | 3–5 | 23–31 |
| 6. | Second Foreign Language | | | (3–5) | (3–5) | (3–5) | (3–5) | 12–20 |
| 7. | Arith. (Bk'g), Geometry | 4 | 4–5 | 4–5 | 5–6 | 5–6 | 5–6 | 27–32 |
| 8. | Natural Sciences | 2 | 2–3 | 2–3 | 3–4 | 3–4 | 3–4 | 15–20 |
| 9. | Drawing | 2 | 2 | 2 | 2 | 2 | 2 | 12 |
| 10. | Manual Training | (2) | (2) | (2) | (2) | (2) | (2) | (12) |
| 11. | Gardening | | | | (1–2) | (1–2) | (1–2) | (3–6) |
| 12. | Music | 2 | 2 | 2 | 1 | 1 | 1 | 9 |
| 13. | Physical Training ** | 3 | 3 | 3 | 3 | 3 | 3 | 18 |
| 14. | Shorthand | | | | | (1) | (1) | (2) |
| | Maximum Number of Hours of Required Work | 29 | 30 | 30 | 32 | 32 | 32 | 185 |

The number of hours in the subjects grouped with a brace { may be divided in other ways.  The hours in elective instruction are designated by parentheses ().

* See *Erlass vom 10. Januar 1917—U III D 2089.1.*
** To the three hours for physical training are added in all classes the play afternoons and the monthly excursion day which are required.

In large communities with several middle schools for boys or in large middle schools with several divisions of classes for boys, it is recommended that the various type curricula, according to measure of necessity, be organized purposely for individual middle schools or divisions.

Where such an arrangement is not possible, the middle school will use the general curriculum—Plan I—which keeps the various needs equally in mind.  However, that does not keep one of the special curriculum types from being chosen, in places with very pressing needs, for the only middle school or the only division for boys.

In case a marked need for preparation for certain special vocational branches, as agriculture, navigation, mining, becomes apparent, provision therefor can be made within the limits of the program of the upper section.  Care is to be taken, however, that

## 2. PLAN II: CURRICULUM FOR BOYS WITH SPECIAL REFERENCE TO THEIR LATER CALLING

| No. | SUBJECT | VI-IV as in Plan I (Common Course) | WITH REFERENCE TO A VOCATION IN | | | | | | | |
| --- | --- | --- | --- | --- | --- | --- | --- | --- | --- | --- |
| | | | COMMERCE AND TRADE | | | | INDUSTRY | | | |
| | | | III | II | I | Total | III | II | I | Total |
| 1. | Religion * | 6 | 2 | 2 | 2 | 12 | 2 | 2 | 2 | 12 |
| 2. | German * | 16 | 5–6 | 5–6 | 5–6 | 31–34 | 5–6 | 5–6 | 5–6 | 31–34 |
| 3. | History | 4 | 2 | 2 | 2–3 | 10–11 | 3 | 2 | 2–3 | 10–11 |
| 4. | Geography | 6 | 2 | 2 | 2 | 12 | 3 | 2 | 2 | 12 |
| 5. | First Foreign Language | 14–16 | 5–6 | 5–6 | 5–6 | 29–34 | 3–4 | 3–4 | 3–4 | 23–28 |
| 6. | Second Foreign Language | (3–5) | (3–5) | (3–5) | (3–5) | (12–20) | (2–3) | (2–3) | (2–3) | (9–14) |
| 7. | Arith. (B'k'g), Geometry | 12–14 | 5–6 | 5–6 | 5–6 | 27–32 | 6–7 | 6–7 | 6–7 | 30–35 |
| 8. | Natural Sciences | 6–8 | 2–3 | 2–3 | 2–3 | 12–17 | 4–5 | 4–5 | 4–5 | 18–23 |
| 9. | Drawing | 6 | 2 | 2 | 2 | 12 | 3–4 | 3–4 | 3–4 | 15–18 |
| 10. | Manual Training | (6) | | | | (6) | (3) | (3) | (3) | (15) |
| 11. | Gardening | | 1 | 1 | 1 | 9 | (1–2) | (1–2) | (1–2) | (3–6) |
| 12. | Music | 6 | 3 | 3 | 3 | 18 | 1 | 1 | 1 | 9 |
| 13. | Physical Training ** | 9 | (1) | (1) | (2) | (4) | 3 | 3 | 3 | 18 |
| 14. | Shorthand & Typewriting | | | | | | | | | |
| | Maximum Number of Hours of Required Work | 89 | 32 | 32 | 32 | 185 | 32 | 32 | 32 | 185 |

So long as the maximum number of hours is not exceeded, the program of the upper section can be modified with reference to later commercial or industrial vocations.

* ** See notes on Plan I.

### 3. PLAN III: GENERAL CURRICULUM FOR GIRLS

| No. | Subject | Number of Hours in Class | | | | | | |
|---|---|---|---|---|---|---|---|---|
| | | VI | V | IV | III | II | I | Total |
| 1. | Religion * | 2 | 2 | 2 | 2 | 2 | 2 | 12 |
| 2. | German | }6 | 5 | 5 | 5 | 5 | 5 | 31 |
| 3. | History | | 2 | 2 | 2 | 2 | 2 | 10 |
| 4. | Geography | 2 | 2 | 2 | 2 | 2 | 2 | 12 |
| 5. | First Foreign Language | 6 | 4–5 | 4–5 | 3–5 | 3–5 | 3–5 | 23–31 |
| 6. | Second Foreign Language | | | (3–5) | (3–5) | (3–5) | (3–5) | (12–20) |
| 7. | Arith. (B'k'g), Geometry | 3 | 3–4 | 3–4 | 4–5 | 4–5 | 4–5 | 21–26 |
| 8. | Natural Sciences | 2 | 2 | 2–3 | 2–3 | 2–3 | 2–3 | 12–16 |
| 9. | Drawing | 2 | 2 | 2 | 2 | 2 | 2 | 12 |
| 10. | Manual Training | | | | (1) | (1) | (1) | (3) |
| 11. | Gardening | | | | (1–2) | (1–2) | (1–2) | (3–6) |
| 12. | Sewing | 2 | 2 | 2 | 2 | 2 | 2 | 12 |
| 13. | Domestic Economy | | | | | (3–4) | (3–4) | (6–8) |
| 14. | Music | 2 | 2 | 2 | 2 | 2 | 2 | 12 |
| 15. | Physical Training ** | 3 | 3 | 3 | 3 | 3 | 3 | 18 |
| 16. | Shorthand | | | | | (1) | (1) | (2) |
| | Maximum Number of Hours of Required Work | 30 | 30 | 31 | 31 | 31 | 31 | 184 |

### 4. PLAN IV: CURRICULUM FOR GIRLS WITH SPECIAL REFERENCE TO FUTURE VOCATION

| No. | Subject | VI-IV as in Plan I (Common Course) | With Reference to a Vocation in | | | | Domestic Economy and Social Welfare | |
| | | | Trade and Commerce | | | | | |
| | | | III | II | I | Total | III-II | I |
|---|---|---|---|---|---|---|---|---|
| 1. | Religion * | 6 | 2 | 2 | 2 | 12 | As by Plan III | 2–3 |
| 2. | German | 16 | 5–6 | 5–6 | 5–6 | 31–33 | | 4–5 |
| 3. | History | 4 | 2 | 2 | 2 | 10 | | 2 |
| 4. | Geography | 6 | 2 | 2 | 2 | 12 | | 1 |
| 5. | First Foreign Language | 14–16 | 5–6 | 5–6 | 5–6 | 29–34 | | 3 |
| 6. | Second Foreign Language | (3–5) | (3–5) | (3–5) | (3–5) | (12–20) | | (3) |
| 7. | Arith. (B'k'g), Geometry | 9–11 | 4–5 | 4–5 | 4–5 | 21–26 | | 2–3 |
| 8. | Natural Sciences | 6–7 | 2–3 | 2–3 | 2–3 | 12–16 | | 2 |
| 9. | Drawing | 6 | 2 | 2 | 2 | 12 | | 1 |
| 10. | Manual Training | | | | | | | |
| 11. | Gardening | | | | | | | |
| 12. | Domestic Science | 6 | 3 | 2 | 2 | 12 | | 1–2 |
| 13. | Domestic Economy | | | | | | | 4 |
| 14. | Hygiene (Care of Sick and Infants) | | | | | | | 4 |
| 15. | Music | 6 | 2 | 2 | 2 | 12 | | 2 |
| 16. | Physical Training ** | 9 | 3 | 3 | 3 | 18 | | 1 |
| 17. | Shorthand and Typewriting | | (1) | (1) | (2) | (4) | | 2 |
| | Maximum Number of Hours of Required Work | 91 | 32 | 32 | 32 | 187 | | 32 |

* ** See notes on Plan I.

the line existing between the functions of the middle schools and the technical schools in question at the time is not overstepped.

Plan III follows the curriculum of the boys' schools in so far as the small number of hours occasioned by the girls' weaker physical structure and instruction in domestic art and domestic science do not make changes necessary, especially in Classes III to I. In other respects, what was said with reference to Plan I applies here.

Plan IV is adapted to the need for special preparation of girls for definite vocations. So far as needs in other directions make themselves apparent, the curriculum can be modified with respect thereto with the approval of the county government.

The organization of a curriculum for the preparation of girls for home economics and social vocations corresponds more and more to a need which is making itself felt. Particularly, let it be observed that the subjects formerly elective—home economics, manual training, and gardening—are required here, and that in other respects, with the dropping out of geometry, all of the instruction is to be adapted to the special purpose of the class. Detailed regulations are given on page 297.

With reference to the organization of special middle schools

5. PLAN V: FOR MIDDLE SCHOOLS WHICH PREPARE ALSO FOR SECONDARY SCHOOLS

| No. | SUBJECT | VI-IV as in Plan I (Common Course) | NUMBER OF HOURS IN CLASS | | | |
|---|---|---|---|---|---|---|
| | | | III | II | I | Total |
| 1. | Religion * | 6 | 2 | 2 | 2 | 12 |
| 2. | German | 16 | 3–5 | 3–5 | 3–5 | 25–31 |
| 3. | History | 4 | 2–3 | 2–3 | 2–3 | 10–13 |
| 4. | Geography | 6 | 2 | 2 | 2 | 12 |
| 5. | First Foreign Language | 14–16 | 3–5 | 3–5 | 3–5 | 23–31 |
| 6. | Second Foreign Language | 3–5 | 3–5 | 3–5 | 3–5 | 12–20 |
| 7. | Mathematics | 12–14 | 4–6 | 4–6 | 4–6 | 24–32 |
| 8. | Natural Science | 6–8 | 3–4 | 3–4 | 4–5 | 16–21 |
| 9. | Drawing | 6 | 2 | 2 | 2 | 12 |
| 10. | Music | 6 | 1 | 1 | 1 | 9 |
| 11. | Physical Training ** | 9 | 3 | 3 | 3 | 18 |
| 12. | Sewing for Girls | 6 | 2 | 2 | 2 | 12 |
| | Maximum Number of Hours of Required Work | 89 | 34 | 36 | 36 | 195 |

* ** See notes on Plan I.

for girls, what was said for special middle schools for boys applies here (Plan II).

As has already been pointed out in A, in smaller places the responsibility often rests upon the middle schools not only of reaching the educational objective peculiar to them, but also of preparing pupils for the secondary schools for both sexes.

There come into consideration, here, primarily the secondary schools with whose curricula the curriculum of the middle school shows so much kinship that it can be made exactly like them without the character of the middle school materially suffering. These are the *Oberrealschule*, the *Deutsche Oberschule*, and *Oberlyzeum* in fundamental form, and in form of the *Aufbauschule*.

The middle school can also prepare for the *Reformrealgymnasium* and the *Studienanstalt* with the curriculum of the *Reformrealgymnasium*. For the pupils thus concerned, group instruction in Latin is to be provided at the proper place, and the necessary time is to be secured by a partial exemption of the participants from technical instruction, and occasionally, also, by a reduction of the time set aside for German, mathematics, and natural sciences. Exemption from physical training is not permissible.[1]

[1] See *Erlass vom 31. März 1925—U II 777. i.* (*Zentralblatt f. U. V. p. 113*).

# IV

## COURSES IN THE INDIVIDUAL SUBJECTS

### Notes on Method

The instruction in the middle school is chiefly departmental. Now, as before, the earnest attention of the middle school must be directed to seeing that the pupils have time and opportunity to go deep into the particular subjects, to grasp their character and structure with increasing intellectual power to an ever-increasing degree and thus to gain accurate knowledge and power. In addition, it must be seen that by this departmentalization of instruction there is not impaired the chief purpose of the middle school, a purpose which rests upon every general cultural school regardless of its special function: that is, training the youth that their capacities develop, that their wills become active and persistent toward working for their own improvement and serving society with devoted consecration. Therefore, regard for the following principles for the entire work of the middle school is indispensable.

1. It goes without saying that the instruction must be built upon the pupils' own activity, intellectual as well as physical, and that the results of instruction must be worked out under the guidance of the teacher by means of observation, experiment, judgment, and independent reading. Beyond this the teacher must carefully see to it that the inclinations and tendencies of the individual, and the types of ideas, thought, and imagination peculiar to him are given the widest consideration, furthered and utilized in an instructional manner.

Primarily, the point of view must be held that the topic of instruction must be placed before the pupil first for attentive, persistent consideration, for quiet comprehension, for meditative enjoyment, and for deeper spiritual experience. If an explanation is to be added, it should take place (wherever the necessary conditions are available) in the form of free instructional conversation in which the pupils are not only to take part either listening or answering, but also, as far as possible, as interested participants eager for information. The instructional outcome should develop thus as the result of a common activity to which each has contributed according to the measure of his ability, and which, therefore, signifies for the individual an enrichment not only in an intellectual but also in a moral way.

There is no doubt that such a method of instruction frequently meets with difficulties, and not least in the school years in which the increasing demands of instruction combine with all sorts of spiritual restrictions of the years of adolescence.

The teacher takes this into consideration in that, among other things, he does not draw the limits of instruction too sharply but, in connection with what is commonly considered or treated as "school knowledge," he permits questioning and prompts discussions which through life itself come to live in the pupils and exert a vital influence upon them. It goes without saying that anything which is interrupting or distracting in its nature must be carefully and definitely eliminated.

Such discussions, in most cases, arouse the pupils to independent efforts the importance of which again lies in both an intellectual and a moral direction. Therefore, from the lowest class up, time is to be allowed for them, and indeed most time when the consciousness of growing strength presses forward to a greater self-activity. Herein inclination and endowment are to receive as great consideration as possible. Besides the recitation of poems which they have themselves chosen and which need not always be taken from the school text, come the reports on reading, the new method of solution of mathematical problems, the physical and chemical experiments, the observation of manifold processes in nature, and the finished product in the technical and artistic subjects.

The gain which develops from such voluntary work for the active pupil and also for the whole class does not depend ultimately upon the sort of grade which is given for every piece of work. While emphasizing thoroughness the teacher will ever have to take care, in addition to the determination of the actual value, not to overlook the amount of painstaking effort which has been expended.

2. The self-activity of the pupils will find its greatest assistance in the organization of the curriculum as well as of the

instruction around the home and present-day problems. Corresponding to the variety of forms of German life in the various districts, special local curricula will be organized differently. Especially in the last class much time is to be afforded the intensive study of the home, the discussions of problems of life to-day, in so far as they generally relate to the school. Beyond this, all of the instruction must be correlated with the home and the present time. This is so, not alone because the knowledge of what is near at hand leads to that which is far away, not because the picture of the great country and wider reaches of the earth reflects the history and the geographical and linguistic relationships of the home, not because all historical knowledge must proceed from the present and in the end lead back to it, but because the elements of culture, which the pupils bring with them from home and from life surging around them, are strongly and emotionally colored, and through their effect on the whole content of the middle school course are called upon to serve to a great degree its chief purpose as a general cultural school.

3. The middle school will come nearer to fulfilling this function the more unified the training which it transmits. Delving into detail, as it develops from the specialization of the instruction, does not militate against this unity. Engrossment in detail provides alone the comprehension of the finest and most intimate relationships existing among the various subject matter fields. Only the process must not rest with mere comprehension. It is indispensable that the instruction links up the related materials of instruction and so equips the pupils that they are able to derive clear, broad concepts through a many-sided consideration and especially that they are able to lay the foundation for moral concepts of life.

Such connections are especially important among the so-called culturally educative subjects. It is undesirable that the study of the historical development of the German people pass over the eloquent testimony which is still presented to-day by the dialects and literary monuments from earlier centuries, and not least by the appearance of the German countryside. It is undesirable again that the instruction concerned with the discussion of literary creations fail to rediscover the emotional and thought content of the literature in the creations of the pictorial arts, and, thus deepened, cause them to live anew.

The following courses of study carry these demands in various directions. Beyond the curricular requirements which must give far-reaching consideration to the inclinations and special endowments of the teachers, the instruction must endeavor to link together related material as possibility permits. Above all, it is important to liberate the range of the technical-artistic subjects from their former isolated position and to place them at the service of the cultural subjects. The foreign language instruction, whose general cultural value must in no way exhaust itself in formal training, should also be associated with these subjects. However, the study of German nationality will find rich and fruitful development in the study of foreign peoples, especially those who are our neighbors. It scarcely requires proof that the mathematics-natural science subjects, where possible, must also be related to each other and to the other subject matter groups, and thus be made serviceable to the unified purpose of instruction in the spirit of its chief functions.

In all this, moderation is to control and the limits must not be forgotten which are already set for the middle school with reference to the age and intellectual maturity of the pupils. Especially does it seem unnecessary and not at all desirable that the whole instructional work covering wide periods of time be subordinated from the beginning according to definite principles whose determination can ensue not without caprice. There exists then the danger that the instruction become one-sided and lose itself only for the sake of the subject in details of minor importance. It is better to postpone the development of such principles to the time in the last class when comprehensive reviews take place.

4. The foregoing suggestions can only be carried out if the teachers of a school, in constant coöperation, remain clear concerning the progress and purpose of its instructional activity. As it is the business of the conferences, especially class and subject-matter conferences, to work out a detailed course of study which corresponds to the special conditions in the schools, so it will be the duty of every individual teacher, in the execution of this course, to do his part of the whole work with understanding

and in constant sympathy with his colleagues with whom he comes in contact in his work.

### Ia. Evangelical Religion

Modification of the former course is postponed.

### Ib. Catholic Religion

Modification of the former course is postponed.

### II. German

*Aim*

Understanding of written and spoken German. Skill in grammatical, clear, and natural expression of thought. Acquaintance with the structure of the language and its vocabulary. Insight into its historical development and its chief dialects and idioms.

Familiarity with the valuable works of German literature for the purpose of awakening joy in its beauty as well as love for it and the fatherland.

#### A. LITERATURE

### VI

*Program*

Easier epic and lyric poems, also in local dialect. Especially folk and literary tales, children and animal stories, stories of adventure, fairy tales in ballad form, riddles and children's round songs. Prose selections of literary value and adapted to the comprehension of the class which deal with the local environment and its life.

In preparation for history instruction, tales from local and national myths and history.

### V

German folk and national lyric and epic poetry, carefully adapted to the understanding of this age group. Especially German myths, legends, ballads, songs, rhymes, proverbs, and riddles. Prose selections as in VI, pertaining to the German Fatherland and also, in connection with history, to the mythology and history of Greece and Rome.

### IV

German heroic myths in popular prose romance, epic, ballad and song, also in the poetry of modern times. Medieval materials from the older—New High German translation—and the newer poetry. Prose selections as in VI and V in connection with the subject matter instruction of the class.

## III

The seventeenth and eighteenth centuries as reflected in German poetry; also modern and current verse. In connection with the discussion of the intellectual history of the close of the eighteenth and the beginning of the nineteenth centuries: Poems, and lighter dramas, of the classical and romantic period, including the poets of the War of Liberation. The biographies of some of the prominent poets are to be developed so far as a suitable appreciation of their poetic individuality is to be attained on the basis of what has been read. Prose selections as before.

## II

Dramas, novels, and short stories primarily from the nineteenth century and most recent times, in connection with history; summarizing survey of the chief periods of German literature upon the basis of what has been read, and with strict limitation to the essential. Local poetry, also poetry in dialect. Prose selections as before.

*Method*

For the selection of reading material the curriculum purposely provides wide latitude. Thus the possibility is afforded to consider special needs to a suitable extent. A reading course is to be set up each year for every school, which requires the approval of the county government, in so far as it contains materials which are not taken from the reading book adopted for the school.

Everything is to be eliminated that cannot be designated as of undoubted literary value.

The wealth of our people in most valuable reading materials is so great that this requirement must be rigidly adhered to. It is also to be observed with reference to the prose selections from the fields of history, geography and natural science, which, in this sense, must not only satisfy the scientific requirements, but the literary as well.

The choice of reading materials must also take into consideration the stage of intellectual and spiritual development of the pupils at any given age. Especially must there be taken into careful consideration the more strikingly marked differences between boys and girls that emerge as their intellect develops. This applies primarily to the choice of the longer poems to be selected for the upper classes. In mixed classes which can scarcely dispense with common reading material in class instruction, the differences between the sexes must receive attention in the selection of their private reading. Finally, in these grades those poems are usually to be preferred which portray in lively form German manhood and womanhood in times of stress.

This appears necessary, because, from contact with German literature, there must grow the most valuable enrichment of what is contributed to a knowledge of German nationalism in the earlier and modern times by other instruction in cultural history. The course of study indicates the conclusions that follow for the selection of reading materials in general. In particular, those poems, of course, are to be studied which, apart from other demands, contain comprehensive and vivid portrayals of German nationality.

In addition, local and even dialectical poetry is to be used with especial care. It finds its place along with the lighter poetry in class VI, is studied by pupils, so far as suitable material is found, in all sections, and is concluded and summarized in class I. The path from poetry in local dialect leads to other dialectical poetry, with whose chief representatives the instruction will have to concern itself.

The introduction to German literature and especially to German poetry must aim above all to inculcate interest in the noblest reading matter so that it becomes a lasting need among the pupils. The greatest care must be taken that the poetry itself exercises a direct influence on the pupils. "Every reading lesson should be for the pupils an hour of joy in a personal experience."

The treatment of lyrical poetry, selected chiefly for sentiment, rhythm, and sound, will find, accordingly, its high point in perfect delivery by the teacher and its culmination in as good a reproduction as possible by the pupils. It is entirely in harmony with the spirit of this instruction, and it is therefore urgently desired that pictorial art and music be called upon in order to deepen its effect, particularly if directly connected with the presentation of the poem. Besides the requirements of the instruction, the inclination and endowment of the teachers will of course have to be a decisive factor in this matter.

Usually the spoken word, be it the model presentation or be it expressive reading, is indispensable also for the most thorough assimilation of the values inherent in epic poetry, of either the metrical or the free type. Here, too, the pictorial arts and music can be of valuable service where favorable conditions are at hand. But just as in the case of dramatic poetry discussion can in general not be dispensed with. Its chief purpose consists in increasing the effect of the poem upon the emotions of the pupils. A too extensive analysis of the content stands absolutely in the way of this and is to be avoided. Pleasurable penetration into the poetic content is to be striven for, the direction of which is determined by the character of the poetry; and not by a scheme drawn up in accordance with general artistic principles.

Especial care is to be paid to the introduction to dramatic poetry. The school is able only to a relatively small degree to secure from it direct and effective results. Reading with rôles assigned, which should always be carefully prepared, and occasional dramatizations by the pupils can bring good results. Attendance at good public performances of works which have importance for the school is to be encouraged as far as possible.

From the intensive study of the poetic content of the single poem there arises gradually and without any forcing the appreciation of poetic forms and artistic methods. It presupposes an increased intellectual maturity and is, therefore, usually not to be attempted before class IV. From the arrangement of reading materials for the individual classes there arises naturally an increase in the requirements in this respect. At least the pupils of the last class must attain the capacity for conscious æsthetic enjoyment.

In the interest of æsthetic education, it is also essential that in every class a few especially noteworthy poems are learned by the pupils. They are to be designated in the detailed course of study. In addition, there is the voluntary work for which as great freedom as possible is to be afforded.

Reading in class will be supplemented by reading at home, partly as part of the regular home work, partly as free home reading (private reading). The latter, too, in so far as the conditions themselves permit, is to be utilized for instructional purposes. It is essentially furthered by specially organized pupil-libraries, which must be provided in every school and, if possible, arranged by classes.

The reading book is usually the basis for class reading in the lower section—classes VI and V. In classes IV to I the individual classic comes more and more to the foreground. The use of the reading book cannot be given up entirely even in these classes.

### B. ETYMOLOGY AND SYNTAX

*Program*

### VI

The parts of a simple sentence; easier forms of attributes, complements and adverbial adjuncts.

Kinds of words. Inflection, strong and weak forms; exercises in the regular conjugation of verbs; strong and weak conjugations; exercises in the use of prepositions; word formation by combining individual words of the language. Simplest word formation by means of prefixes and suffixes.

### V

The expanded simple sentence. Sentences with several coordinate clauses. The complex sentence in its simplest form. Difficult forms of inflection and conjugation. Word formation by means of suffixes and prefixes.

### IV

The complex sentence. Combination and structure of sentences. Exercises in the use of conjunctions.

### III

The more difficult forms of complex sentences. Sentence contractions. Irregularities and variations in language usage.

The change of meaning in connection with the local dialect in its cultural-historical aspects. Formation of word families with constant attention to the original and derived meaning of the words, and also to the other phases of the change of meaning.

### II AND I

Repetition and fixation of principles of syntax already stated, by continued exercises, especially with more difficult materials. Borrowed and foreign words in relation to cultural development. Summary of the significance of the change of meanings. Beginning with the local dialect, survey of the chief German dialects; in connection therewith insight into the historical development of the German language.

## Method

All of the instruction in the middle school must emphasize strict discipline in the use of language. Grammar—etymology and syntax—and the exercises in written and oral expression, associated closely with grammar and with the other instruction, must lead the pupils primarily to a consciously correct use of the language in speech and in writing.

For this purpose, a part of the time set aside for German is to be taken. Its extent depends upon the need of the age-group and the special needs of the school. In classes VI to IV technical language study is to be essentially completed. The task of occasional review and application is left chiefly to classes III to I. The following types are to be considered especially: analysis of the difficult complex-compound sentences, determination of the parts of speech and word forms; fixing of irregularities in inflections and in word formation (assimilation); characteristics of language usage in local and neighboring districts as well as of individual poets and writers; criticism of ungrammatical expressions in newspaper, book, and business German.

It goes without saying that the language facts should be considered, if possible, in connection with living units of speech.

Persistently and continually, from the lower class up, everything is to be taken into consideration that according to experience causes the pupils difficulties in speech and writing. Herein variations of dialect are to be observed and from time to time should be listed, if they exercise an influence on the pupils.

In all classes the association of German with foreign language instruction—even in a purely linguistic sense—must not be neglected. Character of tone, accent of word and sentence, vocabulary, inflection, and sentence-structure offer numerous points of contact. Herein the chief part of the work falls to the foreign language instruction; however, the German, too, must not neglect opportune allusions which will deepen the feeling for language.

Between the German and foreign language instruction common technical grammatical expressions are to be agreed upon.

In all instruction, however, only such foreign words may be permitted which are still entirely in general use or which can only be replaced by suitable German words with difficulty.

Special attention is to be paid to etymology. Of course, all of the instruction must assist in organizing and enriching vocabulary, in increasing the comprehension of words and their constituent parts, and in effecting a recognition of the active development of the German language in the past and in the present. The special task falls to instruction in German, and particularly in vocabulary, of bringing together the material worked out and found here and there, and, so far as possible, of arranging it about concrete materials.

From the lowest class on the pupils are to be directed to the fundamental, objective meanings of words. The increasing power of the pupils permits the requirements in this respect to be gradually increased. Especially from the study of medieval history and of poetry from older and modern periods the occasion arises continually of going to the source of borrowed words, figurative expressions and metaphors, and proverbial phrases.

Attentive observation of dialects, especially of the locality, also offers rich returns. The pupils should be continually urged to investigate the local dialect with reference to its tone quality, its vocabulary, the turns of speech and proverbs characteristic of it. It is desirable that the material gained by the pupils in group activity be written up and then made useful to them even after school days are over.

The comparison of the local dialect with the spoken and written New High German makes possible very easily a new insight into the historical development of the German language. There can be no question of making this development, even in its chief outlines, the subject of instructional activity in the middle school. It suffices if the pupils learn to see the language as something living, an idea living still to-day in unbroken development. The change of meaning, the foreign word, the borrowed word give in this respect valuable suggestions. The comparison of the tone character of the Old and Middle High German with the New High German will be able then to serve as fully sufficient supplementary work. Also here, limitation is necessary to especially outstanding types, for whose choice the local dialect frequently offers the best basis. Some examples of Old High German and Middle High German literature—always with good translations—can be offered to the pupils, but only for the purpose of permitting them to see very generally the difference between the earlier and the present language. As a rule detailed linguistic considerations should be avoided.

### C. WRITTEN AND ORAL EXERCISES

*Program*

### VI

1. Spelling. Large and small letters. Long and short vowels without special marks. Homonyms.
2. Exercises in written and oral expression. Presentation of children's own experiences, chiefly in narrative form. In addition, simple reports on readings.

### V

1. Difficult words whose spelling can be acquired only by practice. Easy foreign words.
2. Compositions as in class VI. In addition, easy letters.

### IV

1. Foreign words difficult to translate or still in general use. Review exercises from all types of spelling, especially those which are determined by rules.
2. Compositions based upon children's own observations and experiences, in the form of reports, with increased demands for exactness of observation and clearness in judgment. Letters.

### III

Compositions in connection with personal observations and experiences, reading, and materials from all school work. As forms of composition in addition to the narration and the report, description and delineation are to be employed.

### II AND I

Compositions as before with gradually increased requirements as to content and form. Letters and business correspondence from real conditions familiar to the pupils.

*Remarks on Method*

In all written work a clear, neat handwriting and good arrangement upon the paper are to be required. In cases of ne-

cessity special writing exercises are to be undertaken in the
time set aside for German.

1. Instruction in spelling is completed in class IV. In the
upper classes dictations are written and reviews are set only in
so far as these exercises prove to be necessary.

As the basis for the instruction in spelling the pamphlet,
"Official Rules and Word List," is to be used.

The actual need at hand determines the extent of the material
to be studied. Exhaustive treatment of all possible cases, especially of the exceptions, is not the function of this instruction.

Punctuation is to be treated in close connection with syntax.

In addition to correct pronunciation, systematically graded
exercises in spelling from memory and dictation are to be used
chiefly in this subject. Drill on rules should be limited as far
as possible. The pupils are to be introduced carefully and continually stimulated to the use of a good dictionary.

2. In classes VI to IV every three weeks, and in classes III
to I every four weeks, a rather long written composition should
be prepared. Attention should be given in all classes to the fact
that these compositions are to be kept within reasonable limits.

Life going on about the child offers primarily the material for
writing as well as for reading and the content subjects. The increasing intellectual maturity of the pupil makes possible also
here the gradual increase in the requirements. In the upper
classes, especially in the last class, more and more opportunity
should be given the pupils to present and justify their personal
opinions, including the æsthetic aspect.

The special purposes of the middle school demand, in this subject, a reasonable consideration of the form of letters and
business correspondence.

The individuality of the pupil in organization and composition is to be carefully cultivated. Free choice of topics is to
be permitted here and there, beginning with the lowest class.

All topics which go beyond the development of the pupils
must be rigidly avoided, since they would lead only to empty
forms of speech and unchildlike consideration and judgment.

The composition is to be lively, logical, clear, brief, and simple.
Weight is to be attached to clear and intelligent arrangement of
material from the lowest class on. Beginning, perhaps, with

class III an outline is usually to be developed for the composition.

Preparation for written composition cannot be entirely dispensed with in class VI to IV. It must limit itself solely to the collection and arrangement of ideas which the pupils already have, and naturally, in this case, is dispensed with if there is a question of the free development of the personal experiences of the pupils.

In addition to these compositions, short, regular written exercises are to be prepared in connection with the school work and with the pupils' own individual world. Here, too, the different forms of writing are to be used as in the regular composition work.

Special care is to be devoted to free oral compositions which the pupil is to be urged to do regularly in all subjects from the lowest class up. These are primarily to enable the pupils more and more to present their thoughts before teacher and classmates without fear, thoughtfully, tersely, clearly, and with good expression.

The material for these oral compositions is to be taken, as given in the curriculum, essentially from the same fields as furnish the basis for the written composition. However, the essential difference which exists between written and oral compositions must not be overlooked in this respect.

The pupil reciting must feel that he is offering something of his own, little known to the other children or not at all, or not in the form chosen by him for presentation. Therefore, in the choice of topics much freedom, limited only by the interests of the pupils, should ordinarily be allowed. Inclination and endowment mean much here too, and are to be taken into consideration to a corresponding degree.

The purpose of these oral compositions may only be gained if strict language discipline is practiced in all classes and the pupils are required from the lowest class up to organize independently the material worked out in class and to present it in connected form.

Special functions also devolve upon German instruction at this point. Exercises in expressive reading, and in the recitation of poems, offer opportunity for technical language perfection, especially if they are accompanied by regular training in speech and voice. Teachers of music and German must co-operate on these points.

Special preparation of the oral composition work or declamation is entirely unnecessary. Preparation of notes on what is going to be said is not to be required. On the other hand, the pupils should be stimulated early to the use of "cues" and should be informed as to difference between the composition arrangement and the outline of a speech.

## III. HISTORY

*Aim*

Knowledge of the development of the German people as well as of external influences which were of importance in its development. Understanding of the political, economic, and social conditions of the present. Awakening and development of love of the fatherland and of civic attitude.

*Program*

### VI

Stories from local and national mythology and history in the German instruction prepare for history, instruction in which appears first in class V.

### V

Sketches from Greek and Roman myths and history.

### IV

German history to the end of the Middle Ages.

### III

German history from the end of the Middle Ages to the end of the War of Liberation.

### II

German history from the end of the War of Liberation to the present.

### I

Survey of the development of the German people politically, socially, and economically.

*Method*

An especially important position is assigned to history in the list of those subjects which are called upon primarily to fulfill the chief educational task of the middle school. Because of this position the obligation devolves upon it, even beyond the requirements of the course of study, of remaining in constant and close contact with these subjects and in common with them of bringing the pupils to a vital comprehension of the development and nature of the German people. Still further, it must take especial care to refrain definitely from everything which might disturb the steady progress of the educational activity of the school. Denominational questions are to be treated with especial tact. Nor is there a place in the history instruction for the discussion of partisan political questions.

The history stories in class VI are primarily to awaken the pupils' historical sense and arouse the desire for extending and deepening their knowledge. The choice of stories demands, therefore, careful examination. In this the relation to the local community is to be especially kept in mind.

The instruction provided for in class V in ancient history will limit itself to that which is within the reach of the understanding and the interests of the pupils of this age. The study by the pupils of the state, economy, and culture of the ancient peoples can be carried only to a moderate extent. Occasional references in German instruction—ancient materials in German poetry—and the comparison of ancient life with German life present and past reserved for the last class, will supplement this later.

The course of the historical treatment will be determined essentially by the political history. Cultural history is to be bound up with it most closely, and in such a way that the connection will be recognized as clearly as possible. Only the essential, only that which is developmental in nature, can be considered. The purely military aspect is everywhere subordinated. In general, only such wars will be thoroughly studied as have been of decisive importance for the German people.

From the time of the Great Elector on, the Brandenburg-Prussian history assumes the dominant rôle. Approximately from the same time the history of neighboring peoples, especially those whose language and culture are the subject matter of middle school instruction, are taken up for political consideration. Particular attention is to be devoted to the fate of those German peoples who in the course of history have separated from the Imperial Federation,

Attention is always to be given to the close connection of the history of our people with the history of the community and the local racial branch. In the last class, local history—in connection with local poetry and local geography—is to be surveyed. In addition, opportunity often presents itself to discuss prehistoric conditions in the home community.

Names and dates are to be carefully chosen and—limited to a minimum—thoroughly drilled upon. From class IV on, definite reviews of materials learned in earlier classes are to be arranged in the local courses of study.

Approximately up to class III the instruction groups historical events and conditions of somewhat extensive periods of time around units of life and culture. Continuing from this point, the pupils are to be stimulated to trace larger related movements and to comprehend leading tendencies in politics, intellectual life, and cause and effect in economic and social development. Thus the foundation is laid for the work of the last class, which must concern itself essentially with the development of such related ideas.

Instruction in history in other ways also offers great opportunity for the self-activity of the pupils in the sense indicated in the "Notes on Method." All sorts of possibilities in this field develop from the study of local historical monuments, from the use of available instructional aids, from visiting museums, and not least from home reading of suitable literature. It will be possible, here and there in the upper classes, to leave the development of the units of life and culture chiefly to the independent activity of the pupils, in which activity not only the individual contributions of especially gifted children, but also the work of pupil-groups, must find expression. This procedure, of course, can be applied only when there are available the necessary instructional aids including besides historical source material scientific and impartial accounts suited to the capacity of the pupils.

The greatest importance, too, is to be assigned, on the other hand, to the presentation by the teacher which steers the pupils through all sorts of difficult questions and which exercises an influence upon their emotions.

Special hours should not be set aside in the course for civics. It is rather to be most closely associated with the history instruction. From class IV on the attention of the pupils is to be directed to what is characteristic in the political, economic, and social forms of the various periods. Complicated development of ideas and dry expositions of all sorts that are often found in history textbooks are to be avoided. It is rather solely a question, at least in the beginning, of comprehending individual phenomena in their reciprocal effects and from the life of the times. The continued study of history, especially with the possibility which is to be carefully taken advantage of, of comparing the earlier events with the more recent, leads gradually to a definite determination of the ideas chiefly involved in an understanding of political, economic, and social relationships. For the last class there arises the problem of understanding the present as the result of significant evolution over many centuries, and of recognizing the duties resulting therefrom for the individual. [1]

In girls' classes the social and legal position of woman in the various periods of historical development are to be more minutely discussed. The consideration of the rights and duties of the woman in present-day life constitutes the culmination of the work.

## IV. GEOGRAPHY

*Aim*

Thorough knowledge of the fatherland with reference to its natural formation, the relation between its character and its inhabitants, and its political organization. More intimate acquaintance with Europe and more general familiarity with the other continents. Some knowledge of the structure and the formation of the earth, of the gases covering the earth, and of the position of the earth as a heavenly body.

*Program*

## VI

In connection with the review study of the local landscape: The North German districts; more detailed introduction to a knowledge of the relief, map, and globe; observation of the apparent daily path of the sun, also of the apparent daily path and the chief phases of the moon.

[1] See also *Richtlinien für die Mitwirkung der Schulen und Hochschulen zum Schutze der Republik* (*19. Juli 1922*).

## V

The South German districts. The Alps and Carpathian countries. Summarizing review of the German Empire with a study of the districts withdrawn by the Treaty of Versailles.

River basins, divides, natural and historical boundaries.

Observation of the sky on suitable days. The sun's meridian; its ascending and descending course. Average daily and monthly temperature, its increase and decrease. Weather observations. Time of rising and setting of the moon and its chief phases. Position of the chief phases at certain hours.

## IV

European countries, outside of Germany, with especial emphasis upon the states neighboring Germany.

Glaciers, primary formations, sedimentary rocks, importance of the altitude for temperature and plant growth.

Observations of the sun's altitude as in class V; in addition, observation of points of rising and setting of the sun. Some striking constellations of stars and their apparent movement.

## III

Foreign continents with emphasis upon the regions more important for Germany, especially the former German colonies.

Coastal forms, the land-forming power of water. Air and sea currents, ebb and flow. Parallels and meridians, zones. Distribution of plants and animals. Human races.

Review and summary of subject matter in astronomy previously studied. Further observations of constellations and their apparent movement.

## II

More intensive study of Germany with especial reference to the home community.

Summary of the fundamental facts of general geography.

Relation of the apparent movements of the earth observed in classes VI to III to movement on its axis, axial position, and yearly revolution. Explanation of the phases of the moon from its relative position to the earth and sun. Course of the moon. Eclipses of the sun and the moon.

## I

In connection with history and civics, the foundations of the economic life of Germany; its trade with other countries and continents. German colonial activity. The countries of origin of raw materials and export countries important for Germany. Border and foreign Germany, especially in its importance for the nation and business. Discussion of questions of political economy in connection with commercial arithmetic.

## Method

The subject matter in geography is organized as far as possible around natural land units; within these units physical geography and political geography are to be most closely correlated.

General geography, astronomical geography, and economics will find their place in all grades to a limited extent and in a natural manner. Economics is the point of emphasis in the geography instruction of the last class.

By means of their relation to the home, an insight into the geographical character of foreign countries grows out of a comprehensive knowledge of home surroundings. The local district receives its final and more thorough study in class II. In this connection questions concerning the protection of the home are also to be discussed.

The self-activity of the pupils is to be called into play to the greatest extent in all classes.

The observation of real things on excursions and small trips, especially the survey of the chief points in the home community from some elevated position, and the observation of the heavens and of the weather, as the most important and impressive means of instruction, should be utilized generously by the teacher himself and by the pupils under his direction. The pupils should write brief accounts of these observations and of the results noted.

In addition pictorial and concrete instructional aids offer opportunity for many-sided activity. Pictures, maps and globes are to be used in all lessons. Map reading, actually finding the directions from a map (surveyor's map and official map of Germany) and correct understanding of the drawing traced for the enlargement of the map, find especially frequent use from the lowest class up. Frequently opportunity is offered of presenting the result of common activity in graphic representations.

With more maturity pupils are to be required to coördinate independently the individual geographic facts and phenomena in their inner relationships, to develop the fundamental geographic principles from suitable facts, and finally, too, to combine the individual facts into greater wholes from objective points of view.

Memoriter material is to be chosen carefully and must be limited to the most essential and thoroughly drilled upon. Figures are to be dealt with in round numbers; comparative figures should be frequently used.

Drawing and modeling by the pupils are used primarily for fixing the map in mind and for review. They must be limited to reproductions of the simplest kinds.

As far as possible there should be maintained in all classes a close connection between geography and the other subjects of instruction. Especially must geography assist materially in attaining the objectives sought in German and in history. References on this matter are to be found at appropriate points in this outline. On the other hand, instruction in geography is richly assisted by the work in German, history, and natural science instruction. Literature, myth, and history, which are associated with certain districts and places, are to be used to a reasonable extent.

## V. FOREIGN LANGUAGE

*Aim*

Accuracy in defined grammatical knowledge and ability to understand correctly the spoken foreign language, and also ability to read somewhat easy literature independently. Some skill in oral and written expression.

Defined knowledge of the foreign people, of their history and country, and their spiritual and material culture.

The special local conditions and needs are to be decisive in the choice of the foreign languages, especially in the choice of the required foreign language.

The following courses are designed for the required instruction (first foreign language). The reorganization of these courses for the elective instruction (second foreign language) must take into consideration that only pupils take part in it of whose steady progress there is no doubt and who are already trained in a foreign language.

*Program*

## VI

Regular study of the sounds. Oral exercises in connection with objects and occurrences of daily life, pictures, and selections in the reading book. Reading of connected language materials. Memorizing shorter prose selections, poems, riddles, and singing of short songs.

Acquisition of a small vocabulary. Regular grammatical forms. Chief rules of syntax, so far as they are necessary in understanding simple sentences.

Copying and rewriting of textual materials treated. Short dictations.

## V

Speech and reading exercises with increasing requirements for fluent and correct pronunciation and for the content of subject matter treated. Extension of the vocabulary.

Review and enlargement of regular accidence. Chief facts of syntax.

Written reproduction and rewriting of that which has been read or spoken. Dictations. Translations from the foreign language and vice versa.

## IV

Oral and reading exercises as in class V. Extension of the vocabulary by composition of words from etymological and technical points of view. The most important irregular verbs. Chief rules of syntax.

## III

Exercises for the pupils in speaking on more difficult topics. Reading of easy modern English texts. Extension of the vocabulary by composition of words as in class IV. The irregular verbs. Constant review and conclusion of accidence. Chief rules of syntax.

Dictations, compositions, translations, and simple letters.

## II

The oral exercises are continued. Further reading of modern English authors. Extension of the vocabulary. Acquisition of a number of commonly used figures of speech. Continuation of syntax. Summarizing and supplementary review of grammar.

Free compositions. Dictations, including subject matter with which the pupil is not yet familiar. Translations. Written reproduction of what has been read or experienced. Business letters.

## I

Oral exercises as in the earlier classes, in which the land and people of England are chiefly considered. Reading of more modern authors, including also materials from economic life and especially such that have to do with the later practical vocations of the pupils.

Enlargement of the stock of phrases and words. Grammatical reviews as in class II, with especial study of those parts of grammar which, on the basis of experience, are known to cause pupils difficulty. Important synonyms.

Written exercises as in earlier classes. Free written exercises of simple character. Special training in letter-writing and also in commercial correspondence.

### B. FRENCH

For the written and oral exercises the same regulations apply as for English. In the following paragraphs, therefore, only the objectives of the grammatical instruction are indicated.

## VI

The verbs in *er, avoir* and *être*. Grammar of nouns with the articles of gender; adjectives and numerals. The most important pronouns. Fundamental rules of syntax; for example, position of words.

## V

The pronoun and the most common and easiest prepositions and conjunctions. The verbs in *ir* and *re*. Frequent exercises with regular verbs, including interrogative and negative forms. The reflexive verb.

## IV

Irregularities in declinable words; the most common irregular verbs.

## III

Less common irregular verbs. Position of words. The most necessary facts concerning the use of tenses and modes, especially the subjunctive.

## II

The most important facts about the infinitive, the participle, the gerund, the article, the adjective, and the pronouns. The common prepositions. The rules which have been learned in all stages of the instruction concerning the syllabification of words and punctuation are summarized and reviewed.

## I

Review of the grammar in connection with reading and special reference to those parts of grammar which, according to experience, give the pupils difficulty. Increase in the stock of words and phrases. Synonyms.

### C. OTHER FOREIGN LANGUAGES

If another modern language is studied as an elective in place of English or French, special courses of study are to be organized and submitted for official approval.

*Method*

1. The gradation of the course arises in this curriculum essentially from the arrangement of the grammatical material. This does not mean that a rather preferential position in the instruction is allotted to grammar. Rather, the living language of speech and writing occupies the middle position in the instruction, and with it all exercises, and especially those in the grammar and phonetics, are to be most closely correlated. The language of instruction from the lowest class up should be the foreign language itself and should take a secondary position in the grammar work only.

2. The greatest care is to be given in all classes to the acquisition of a good pronunciation. The pronunciation is to be watched over and constantly corrected, a task in which the pupils should be made to coöperate more and more. Choral recitation and singing should be used freely and the requirements in accuracy, fluency, and accent should be raised according to circumstances. Attention is always to be called to the difference between letter and sound, and between speech image and speech sound.

3. Oral exercises are to be carried on from the very beginning, first in simplest form, and then in all classes and periods, increasing not only in view of a widening field of subject matter but also on account of increased demands for fluency and connected thought. Personal experiences may be discussed, which means naturally whatever can be comprehended as it presents itself to the pupils at home, on the playground, in

school, or on the street. Further, the following topics may be treated, depending upon the type of pupil: business, industry, handwork, housekeeping, food, routes of commerce and trade, harbors, post, telegraph and railroad connections, mechanical activities, manufacturing in metals, wood, and the like. Also the life of the foreign people receives attention. Primarily an effort must be made to acquaint the pupils with the character of the foreign people, and with the noteworthy characteristics of their home and public life. So far as possible, in all this work, concrete observational material is to be employed. Pictures, maps, and other instructional aids serve only as substitutes. Further, the special exercises can be correlated with the reading material. In other words, these exercises must not sink to a spiritless question and answer performance. From the beginning class on, an effort is to be made that the conversation between teacher and pupils take on life and warmth through the pupils' questions and interest. In addition to this, the connected composition is to be carefully used as early as possible. The form of these oral exercises must consider the characteristic need of each school. A definite method is to be set for them in the detailed course of study.

In judging work done, pronunciation and ability in speech are to be assigned reasonable value.

4. In addition to the oral exercises, reading and translation form a chief means in learning the foreign language. At first this is based upon the textbook; later upon a reader. Still later, school authors are used, and, in the upper classes, those of technical content. In this selection that field is to be emphasized which is of the greatest importance for the pupil's later vocation. Furthermore, the reading is to be so selected that through it insight into the foreign people and into the culture of the country in question is gained. Prose receives chief emphasis, and gradually story is separated from description. Language exercises, grammatical and otherwise, must never push the reading itself back into a subordinate position. In all sections fluent, lively, and well accented reading of the foreign language text is to be striven for along with the study of word and sentence tone. Special attention is to be devoted to a good German translation. The peculiarity of the linguistic expres-

sion of every foreign idiom is to be brought to the attention of the pupils.

Short prose selections and poems in limited number are to be learned by heart and recited in an expressive but natural manner; a variety of songs, whose melodies can be learned in the music period, are to be sung.

5. The assimilation and the fixation of the necessary vocabulary and stock of phrases are connected with the oral and reading exercises. Vocabularies arranged according to sense are useful in addition to collections of related words made by the pupils.

6. In grammar instruction must be limited to the most important facts, in order that the pupils may be brought to a mastery of the essentials. Seldom used irregularities of form and sentence structure are to be learned from the dictionary. Unimportant material from accidence and syntax must be left to be explained as they appear in the readings. Wherever possible, the connection of foreign language forms with corresponding forms in the mother tongue—English, Low German—is to be kept in mind. Rules are to be developed inductively, first in individual forms or sentences, later in typical examples in the reading. By means of summary and review they become the pupils' own possession, ready for easy use.

Grammatical analysis is to be used extensively.

7. The written exercises serve, in addition to the reading and oral exercises, primarily to enable the pupils to use the language with reasonable freedom. They promote the mastery of grammatical knowledge. Copying, writing from memory, and dictation are their earliest forms. In addition to these there are the rewriting of short stories which have been presented, and of letters, from grammatical points of view—changes of time and person. In this case it is to be understood that violence is not done the language. In addition there are translations. In the upper classes free written exercises, especially letters of a vocational character, are prepared.

When in these upper classes a smaller number of hours are available for foreign language instruction, the range of the material will have to be reduced. Accuracy and skill must not suffer by a reduction of the number of hours.

## VI. Mathematics

*General Aim*

Ability to understand quantitative relations in facts and processes in nature and in life; to comprehend number facts and spatial concepts in accordance with their inherent relations, and also to calculate, draw, and represent them concretely. Habituation in obtaining clear ideas of facts with the aid of number and diagram and applying mathematical thinking usefully in practical life.

### A. ARITHMETIC

*Aim*

Accuracy and skill in calculation, especially in mental calculation with whole and fractional numbers in application to the conditions of everyday life.

Acquaintance with the fundamental processes in algebra.

*Program*

### VI

Fixation of written calculation in the large numbers with constant increase in skill and in mental calculation, especially in the number range, 1 to 1000. The German coins, measures, and weights. Application of the decimal system of notation. Exercises with the compound denominate numbers and application to exercises in proportion. Preparation for work with fractions.

### V

Common fractions. Many problems in proportion from daily life. Reading decimals; simple decimal calculation.

### IV

Decimal fractions, also in combination with common fractions. Compound proportion in more difficult problems of daily life, especially in percentage. Introduction to calculation with algebraic numbers. Evaluation of literal expressions by substitution of definite numbers.

### III

Percentage—calculation of weight, profit and loss, discount, and interest.

The four fundamental processes with absolute and relative whole and fractional numbers. Graphic representation. Continuation of the exercises in calculation of values of literal expressions. Application to simple and involved equations of the first degree in constant connection with everyday arithmetic.

## II

Percentage in application to more difficult problems of daily life, commercial methods of calculation—interest, discount, partnership, and alligation.

Proportion. Equations of the first degree with one or two unknowns. Consideration of problems of geometrical content. The function idea and the graphical representation of the function. Graphic solutions of equations of the first degree. Powers and roots.

## I

Calculations by compound interest and insurance tables. Money and money transactions. Savings bank. Bank. Stock exchange. Checks. Exchange. Securities. Negotiable paper. Calculation of current accounts. In connection with arithmetic, introduction to industrial and commercial bookkeeping. Logarithms. Equations of the second degree in one unknown, arithmetic and geometric progressions. Compound interest. Graphs.

*Note:* In girls' classes algebraic calculation is carried as far as the solution and application of equations of the first degree in one or more unknowns. In this application work in everyday methods of calculation and problems of the household receive chief emphasis. Introduction to household bookkeeping is taken over by class II. Industrial and commercial bookkeeping is reserved for class I.

### B. GEOMETRY

*Aim*

Knowledge of those principles in plane and solid geometry which are important in practical life. Ability to apply them in problems of construction and calculation. The development of the fundamental practical knowledge into a definite, clear unit, and also training in abstract reasoning and proof. Application of the results which have been determined to practical problems, especially those of industry.

*Program*

## V

Introduction to the fundamental principles of space perception wherein space is to be considered primarily as the vehicle of planimetric space relationship. Spatial dimensions, surfaces, points, lines, and points in space. Plane figures as surfaces of solids and as independent figures, in which the ideas of angles, parallelism and symmetry are brought to the attention. Continued exercises in drawing figures with ruler and

compass and in measuring them with ruler and protractor.
Further measurements of objects in the vicinity and exercises
in estimation of distances and angles. Simple problems in the
calculation of surface and volume, together with the calculation
of the relationship of weight and volume.

## IV

Principles of degrees and angles. Most important principles
of the triangle and the fundamental geometrical constructions.

## III

Principles of the parallelogram and the trapezium. The fundamental principles of the circle. Consideration of the change
of the total character of figures by the change in the dimensions
of individual parts. Constructions with analytic hypotheses
and proof.

## II

Similarity of surface and calculation of surfaces of figures
with irregular edges. Square root. Proportion of areas and
similarity of plane figures. Measurement and surveying, with
a plane table, of areas and inaccessible lines and altitudes. Approximate calculation of surfaces bounded by irregular lines.

## I

Trigonometric functions. Principles of sine and cosine.
Trigonometric calculation of right angled and acute angled
triangles by means of tables of natural functions and of logarithms of the trigonometric functions. The most important facts
concerning the position of lines and planes in space. Calculation of the length of edges, surfaces, and contents, as well as
the parallel perspective drawing of the simpler stereometric
figures. Cube root.

*Note:* In girls' classes geometry limits itself to the most necessary facts
of space perception,—solids, surfaces, lines, points, angles, parallelism, symmetry, proportion, similarity, and congruency. Only the most important
principles of the triangle, quadrangle, and circle, as well as the most necessary facts of the measurement of surfaces and solids, come in for treatment
in objective method of proof along with the application of geometric
formulae.

### Method

In the whole field of mathematics everything is to be avoided
which is not found useful for further application in instruction
and in life.

In all classes especial stress is to be laid upon practical application of the facts developed. Only those problems are to be used which are taken from practical life, or which clarify concrete images and, therefore, have concrete value, and which can be easily explained to the children. Meaningless technical relationships and involved problems are to be eliminated. Insight into number and space relationships must be attained in all cases upon a concrete basis gained by the pupils' own observation, together with as great an activity on the part of the pupils as possible.

In all classes the pupils are to be stimulated, before solving a problem, to make calculations, estimates, comparisons, and graphic plans if possible. By means of numerous examples after solutions are completed, by means of discussions of the possibilities of solutions, and of the number and kind of solutions coming in for possible consideration, the pupils are to be accustomed to strict self-criticism. In all stages of the instruction opportunity is to be given the pupils regularly for a completely independent solution of problems, even of such as are taken from fields not yet treated. Utilization of the freer methods of solution and of the so-called short cuts is to be permitted as a principle. They are to be stimulated to independent formulation of problems.

The instruction in all classes calls for regular reviews of the fundamental portions of the previous work and preparation for that which is to be next studied. The whole of the mathematics instruction is, regardless of its other purposes, to serve for the clarification of concrete relationships, and to develop a deep appreciation of reality in vital connection with the other subjects of instruction, which is to be indicated more exactly in the special local courses of study.

In arithmetic instruction the beginning is to be made first of all with oral calculation with smaller numbers, and progress is to be made toward written calculation with gradually larger numbers. Calculation with very large numbers is to be avoided, especially in fractions with large denominators. In the number range 1 to 100, and in a limited degree also in the number range up to 1000, a complete mastery of all number relationships is to be sought, even for oral calculation. The children in the upper section are to be acquainted with the practices in business and industry which, in general, differ from those in ordinary use. The so-called Austrian method of subtraction may be studied at a suitable time.

The importance of calculation with algebraic numbers lies in the fact that it permits calculation with concrete numbers as an application of general rules to a special case and thus helps the attainment of a larger view and greater skill.

In all sections of the school, geometry must develop space perception by measurement, estimation, calculation, drawing, construction of plane figures and solids, and consider its application to those fields of life subject to mathematical formulation. The parallel perspective drawings are to be executed, if possible, to a given scale and with given foreshortening and displacement.

Motion, parallel displacement, superposition, rotation, are to be widely employed. Only on the basis of clear images thus attained are the explanations of ideas and fundamental principles and propositions to be developed. The further step of abstract perception, especially of analytic deduction and its corresponding proof, is to be increased gradually with constant regard for the intellectual maturity of the pupils at that time. The self-activity of the pupils must not be affected by preliminary and subsequent proofs or by means of other inappropriate aids.

Height, surface, and diagonals of the room are determined before measurements of areas and altitudes in the open are undertaken.

### VII. Natural Science

#### A. NATURAL HISTORY

*Aim*

Knowledge and understanding of the structure and of the most important forms of plant, animal, and human life, as well as of the manifold relationships of their modes of life to one another and to man. Knowledge of the chief groups of the animal and plant kingdoms, as well as of the minerals most important for man. Ability to recognize the importance of nature for national economic life and later to continue one's interest in the natural science field by means of personal observation and popular literature, and to study and utilize nature with intelligence and to take pleasure in it.

*Program*

## VI

Spring and growth. Water forms. In the field and meadow.
Fall and decay. Winter guests in the school yard. In house
and yard.

*Note:* For the study of individual forms those plants are to
be chosen which, on account of structure and blossom, attract
the attention of animals, chiefly birds and mammals.

## V

The garden. Indigenous reptiles. Amphibia. Fish. Human
body. Essential constituents of local soils and minerals important for man.

## IV

Leaf-bearing trees. Fields and meadows. Asparagus beds.
Vineyards and other cultivated fields, depending upon local
conditions. Mollusks of the home community. Vertebrates, especially important foreign types. Comparative study of the
organs, organ systems, animals, and animal groups from the
vertebrate kingdom.

## III

Pine and fir trees. Brooks. Water plants. Large and small
crabs. Insects. Spiders. Foreign cultivated plants. Minerals
as food for plants and animals. Health springs. Drinking
water. Simple exercises in the classification of plants.

## II

Brooks, stagnant pools, and ponds. Ferns, mosses, mushrooms, lichens of the local forests. Bacteria and parasites.
Plants and animals of primeval times. The part of plants and
animals in the building of the earth and stone—amber, humus,
peat, ground coal, anthracite coal, and chalk. Most important
stones and the stone-forming minerals. Continued easy exercises in the classification of plants.

## I

Plant diseases. Distribution of animals and plants. Exercises in classification of plants. The human body. General
comparative study of structure and life of organisms. Characteristic phenomena in nature in the vicinity.

Protection of nature and the home. Prehistoric man and his
world.

*Method*

The wealth of material in natural history demands in its treatment limitation to that which is typical and essential. Only the most important objects of nature and the most important processees of life of plants and animals and their relationships to one another and to man are to be considered. The following come into consideration:

    *a.*   Materials which are near the child either physically or intellectually.

    *b.*   Materials which are distinctive as being characteristic of nature and culture in the local community.

    *c.*   Materials which bear a typical character and which admit of independent work on the part of the pupil.

    *d.*   In connection with the historical and geographical instruction, materials which are of general importance from the point of view of political economy.

The indispensable condition for thorough instruction in biology is a fundamental stock of accurate knowledge of the facts in nature and of objective data.

The fundamental stock must be worked out by the pupils through their own learning and experience, and then mastered and constantly increased. This is most surely attained by instruction in the open, in the school garden, in the park, and near the stream; through the use of the excursion days for biological observation, through the children's own observation at home, along streams and lakes, near water, and in field and forest. In this work special attention is to be paid to avoid damage and to protect unusual plants, in accordance with official regulations. The objectives are also attained by the installation and maintenance of vivariums, by visits to collections and museums, by the use of the microscope and physiological apparatus which must be present in every school.

Habituation in correct observation,—in general, careful development of the power of observation in all sections of the school,—is one of the most important tasks of the natural science instruction.

The subject and the starting point of the work are primarily the natural objects or phenomena, not pictures of them. Anatomical and physiological exercises of the simpler sort supplement the instruction in all classes. Botany is studied not only in summer and zoölogy not only in winter, but the time for study of animals and plants is determined rather by the possibility of observation of their essential life processes.

Knowledge of the plant system is not the goal of middle school instruction. However, by means of concrete examples it appears essential in the course of the instruction to work out the concepts of variety, genus, family, order, class, and species; and in this way to enable the pupils to systematize and thus to simplify the classification of plants and animals.

In studying minerals only that will be stressed which arises from objective observation. The study of their composition and decomposition has its place in chemistry.

The study of the structure of the human body treats anatomical detail only so far as it is necessary for the comprehension of the function of the organs of the body. The chief purpose of this branch of study is the introduction to a correct mode of living, especially as to the avoidance of pleasure-giving narcotics.

According to local conditions, attention is to be paid to gardening, floriculture, agriculture, and horticulture. The ideas which the children have acquired at home in connection with these occupations are to be used to the fullest advantage.

The self-activity of the pupils is to be stimulated everywhere. In this respect the following come in for consideration: Keeping of carefully prepared observational notes, preparation of sketches, drawings, cutting out and modeling of natural forms, construction of aids for instructional and collection purposes, organization of simple collections, development of school museums, activity in the organization of vivariums, garden work in the school garden.

### B. CHEMISTRY AND PHYSICS

*Aim*

Knowledge of the more important physical and chemical phenomena and laws, especially of those which have significance for home, industrial, and commercial life, as well as for climate and weather. Introduction to the manner in which they are employed for cultural purposes in the fields named.

## IV

The essentials of the mechanics of solid, liquid, and gaseous bodies. Heat in connection with the observations of daily life. The simplest facts of weather.

## III

The principles of sound. Magnetism and frictional electricity.

The fundamental principles of inorganic chemistry. Chemistry in its application in the prominent industries of the community.

## II

Principles of light. The electric current, with the exception of induction.

Continuation of inorganic chemistry with constant consideration of its application in local economic life.

Minerals which are used in industry and technology. The most important rocks of the earth's crust in organic connection with nature study and geography.

## I

Important parts of mechanics. Induction and radiation.

Easier phenomena from organic chemistry and dietetics with constant consideration of the local industries.

The distribution of the materials in these four classes may be made so that individual fields important for a later vocation may be treated preferably or exclusively in class I,—for example, technology and chemistry of the kitchen. Within each class, according to the number of hours, physics and chemistry can be taught together or in sequence.

The girls' middle school, in the selection of materials to be studied, aims primarily to give the girls a knowledge and understanding of the physical and chemical processes which confront them continually in their work at home, in the garden and kitchen. The instruction in physical science finds its practical application in the home economics instruction.

*Method*

The experience which has been gained primarily by observation in daily life serves as the basis of this instruction. Experiments are admissible as substitutes or as supplements. All apparatus which is used in these experiments must be as simple as possible.

The pupils are to be encouraged to pay attention to and make regular observations of natural processes lying within the province of their perception. They must learn to see correctly the phenomena appearing in their environment, to distinguish the essential from the non-essential, and to express correctly that which they have clearly understood.

It is desirable to require them to construct rather simple physical apparatus and to perform rather easy experiments, and to set up equipment suitable therefor in the physics laboratory. In any case the pupils should, so far as the instructional material permits, at least make sketches of the physical apparatus.

The pupils should be encouraged to make regular observations of atmospheric temperature and pressure, humidity, precipitation, and direction of wind. The results of the observations should be recorded. In this way a better understanding of the weather chart and of the weather report of the region in question is attained.

So far as possible, easy physical and chemical lessons for the purpose of understanding life phenomena in the plant and animal world are appropriately given in the simplest form, in the preceding course in biology. The minerals which have already been studied in this course are treated more fully in chemistry.

In all classes the importance of chemistry and physics for the family household, local and national economic life, and cultural development should be clearly worked out. Their influence upon the world's civilization is emphasized at the proper place.

## VIII. DRAWING

*Aim*

Drawing instruction associated with writing, manual activity, sewing, and art study is to enable the pupils to express external impressions and consciously arranged observations by means of the construction of figures in two and three dimensions, and to awaken and develop the feeling for form and color.

According as the objectives of drawing instruction demand a conception and execution that are free, personal, or conditioned

by a purpose and material, is the distinction to be made between
freehand and mechanical drawing.

*Program*

## VI TO IV

*Freehand Drawing.* Free composition of impressions and
experiences from the environment and imaginative world of
the child through drawing, painting, cutting, pasting, modeling, weaving, and the like. Exercises in simple decorative
writing—old style—and in black and white and colored plane
surface work. In due time, according to the intellectual growth
of the pupils and the occasions which arise in free composition,
transition to conscious observation and to reproduction of
natural objects from memory.

*Mechanical Drawing.* In the construction of toys and simple,
useful articles from paper, cardboard, cloth, and the like, an introduction to the use of rule, tape measure, and compass.

*Art Appreciation.* For enrichment and intensification of
pupils' work, use of pictures, drawings, simple local architectural types, and trade products.

## III TO I

### (A) PLAN I—GENERAL COURSE FOR BOYS

*Freehand Drawing.* Free compositions of impressions and
experiences from the widened experience of the pupil, without,
however, the requirement of imaginative creation if an inclination thereto is no longer present. More emphasis upon observation and direct as well as memoriter reproduction of objects in
nature. Exercises in black and white and color representation
of solids and surfaces. Continuation of exercises in decorative
script, Carolingian and Gothic, and in space arrangement.

*Mechanical Drawing.* Projective representation of simple
solids: prism, cube, pyramid, cylinder, sphere, and combinations
of these forms; representation of simple articles to a given scale,
if possible, in connection with manual training.

*Art Appreciation.* In connection with the exercises in spatial
representation: Study of forms of architecture as examples of
spatial forms conditioned by purpose and materials, dwelling
houses, castles, churches, cloisters, schoolhouses, railway stations, factories. Study of outstanding works especially of German painting, graphic and plastic art.

### (B) PLAN II—WITH REFERENCE TO THE LATER INDUSTRIAL VOCA-
TIONS

*Freehand Drawing.* Free composition of impressions and
experiences from the widened range of the pupils' experience,

without, however, the requirement of imaginative creation, if an inclination thereto is no longer present. More emphasis upon observation and direct as well as memoriter reproduction of objects in nature. Exercises in black and white and color reproduction of solids and surfaces. Continuation of exercises in decorative script, Carolingian and Gothic,—and in space distribution and arrangement. Easy problems for definite purposes, together with simple printing, for example, invitations, programs, resolutions, copybook and book covers, bookmarks, and the like.

*Mechanical Drawing.* Projection of simple solids: Prism, cube, pyramid, sphere, and combinations of these forms, and drawing of simple articles, apparatus, containers, parts of buildings—columns, pillars, roofs, doors, windows, cornices, and the like—along with a study of local architectural types and craft products. Sketching of simple objects and making working designs in connection with manual training.

*Art Study.* In connection with the exercises in spatial representation: Study of buildings as examples of spatial treatment conditioned by purpose and materials—dwelling houses, castles, churches, cloisters, schools, railway stations, factories, and the like. Also in connection with the exercises in representation: Study of works of art and industry, which show how the periods with a fixed feeling for style have modified dwelling rooms, house furniture, clothing, writing and printing, industrial and trade marks. Study of outstanding works, especially of German painting and graphic and plastic art.

#### (c) PLAN III—GENERAL COURSE FOR GIRLS

This course is the same as for the boys' schools; in mechanical drawing, however, the problems for the projective representation of simple solids and utensils are to be reduced in favor of problems from needlework.

#### (d) PLAN IV—WITH REFERENCE TO THE LATER INDUSTRIAL VOCATIONS

The necessary changes of the course given in (c) are to be taken in connection with Plan (b) so far as consideration of the later industrial vocations of girls is involved.

### Method

*Freehand Drawing.* Since the graphic method of expression of the child develops naturally, in general, according to definite principles, but differently in individuals, the drawing instruction must adapt itself to the age and characteristics of the individual. The drawing instructor must, therefore, give the pupils abundant opportunity in free exercises, developed from the imagination, to show their personal manner of expression and the degree of their ability. He must keep hands off when interest for certain methods of representation, subjects, and means of expression begin to stir, and adapt his help and instruction to the need in the case, whether it be of an individual pupil, a group of pupils, or a whole class. Accordingly, he must not set for all time certain exercises for certain classes. Yet he must be intent, in connection with the free exercises, on enriching the pupils' imaginative life by means of studies of reality and especially by reproduction from memory; he must be intent on developing the pupils' feelings for organic form and their manual skill. Purely external imitation and mechanical drill of definite forms and techniques must be avoided.

The practice materials, in so far as they do not arise in the free exercises, are to be taken from the range of the pupils' experience, to which, of course, the other subjects of instruction belong.

The educative function of the instruction consists in the habituation to an independent, purposeful method of work.

*Mechanical Drawing.*   In addition to freehand drawing, mechanical drawing is to be pursued in all classes. It is to develop the spatial imagination and prepare for an understanding of working drawings. Its industrial function is skill in the use of rule, tape, compass, T-square, triangle, and drawing pen. The pupils in class VI are already acquainted with the use of the rule and the tape. The representation of objects is based upon insight, gained by direct observation, into the relationships which exist between the purpose, the material, and the form of the object. The problems are developed first freehand and, so far as possible, from memory. In many cases sketches are sufficient if the purpose of the problem is thus attained.

The practice materials are taken from the pupils' range of experience, just as in the case of freehand drawing. In the choice of objects to be drawn, first instruction should be planned to correspond to the stage of development; then later, talent for hand work and technology are to receive consideration.

Copies or printed charts must not be used.

STUDY OF WORKS OF ART

The pupils are to learn to observe by a careful study of works of art. They are, therefore, not taught by words, but are led to reproduce independently, from memory, in words or by imitation what they have seen. Above all things, in the choice of material, examples of architecture and art in the school and its vicinity, collections and products of good handwork which are dominated by a definite feeling of style are studied. Where any opportunity offers, simple architectural forms and craft products of the community are to be taken up, whether it is in freehand, projection, or a combination of both. The connection, especially with religion, history, and German instruction, is established so far as it is done without being forced.

## IX. MANUAL TRAINING

### A. BOYS

*General Instructional Aim*

Manual training is creative handwork. It serves not only the physical, mental, and moral development of the children, but also the needs of the school (see *Erlass* of April 9, 1921) especially by the preparation and preservation of teaching materials. As branches of work, wood, cardboard, and metal work are chiefly considered.

*Special Aims*

The following distribution of the instructional activities to the various classes is not compulsory. The instructional activities can be arranged in another order and distributed over several years. Where it is possible, different types of work can also be carried on side by side.

### VI

The instruction includes weaving and light wood work. Its purpose is to enable the pupils to make toys, playground apparatus, and small utensils with the simplest tools.

### V

The light wood work is continued and extended to somewhat more difficult problems. The forms of the objects shall be very simple and the sketches must be limited to the straight line, right and obtuse angle, the circle or the arc.

## IV

The work is in cardboard. The pupils are to be trained to make small useful articles out of cardboard and to cover them with decorative paper which they have made themselves. The work is limited to simple forms. Sketches with acute or sharp angles should be avoided. The more advanced pupils can be given the elements of bookbinding. This work is restricted to simple bindings. Imitations of wood, leather, and the like are not to be used as material.

## III

The instruction in cardboard and bookbinding is continued. In some cases, instead of this, joinery can be begun. The instruction in joinery is to enable the pupils after previous construction of the ordinary wood joints—dove-tail, etc.—to make simple useful articles with saw and plane and, of course, in general from the rough boards. The finished work can be oiled or stained.

## II

Joinery corresponding to the work in class III. The problems can be made harder; still the range of the individual pieces of work must not exceed a certain manageable size. Pupils who are particularly adapted to this work can continue with bookbinding instead of joinery.

## I

The work extends to metal work. It is to enable the pupil to execute the simple problems in wire and sheet metal which arise occasionally in every home and can serve the purposes of the instruction. The pupils shall also, where possible, make small articles out of brass and copper.

### B. FOR GIRLS

The general program is the same as for boys, only more emphasis is laid upon the point that the home-building capacities of the girls be developed. This can take place through the development of the following fields of activity.

### SPECIAL INSTRUCTIONAL PROBLEMS

## III

Preparation of toys out of cheap material; preparation of social games, magic lanterns, and the like according to pupils' own ideas. Simple hand weaving on a board or frame. Weaving with a weaver's reed or with a Swedish weaving plate.

## II

Easy wood work,—fret-saw work in planed wood; for example, sewing box, doll furniture, and key plates.

## I

Carton and cardboard work; for example, making daily schedules, inventory lists, picture frames; repairing books; preparation of maps, lanterns for festival decorations, and decorative paper.

### Method

Building upon the child's actual instinct for activity, manual training instruction leads the pupils to work with different sorts of material independently and purposefully, and to express their own individuality in the work. It makes the hand skilled and sure, sharpens the eye, refines the taste, develops a feeling for form and space relationship and for the value of the simple and the real. The urge inherent in the nature of manual creation, to overcome obstacles and to do true and accurate work, trains the understanding and the will, and at the same time the social sense, if the work is carried on cooperatively by a class or pupil group.

The manual training teacher must adapt the instruction to the age and the individual characteristics of his pupils. He must not, therefore, simply take over any method, not even the best one according to his own opinion, and bind himself once and for all to one definite course. He must rather, even as he must accustom the pupils to an independent, purposeful activity, set for himself his own objectives as they develop out of the pupils' stages of development, the technical necessities, and the nature of the handwork. He must seek to attain these objectives, through adaptation to the methods of work and advancement of the pupils as well as through skillful employment of their personal inclinations.

The pupils, as soon as they are beyond the pure detail work, sketch independently in the simplest form possible every new object that is to be made, and in some instances model it. In time they must come to the point when they are able to produce a working drawing in natural size and to read simple working drawings. (See the "Course of Study for Drawing," under Mechanical Drawing.) Further, care is to be taken that pupils are clear as to the type of execution of a piece of work before beginning it, that they choose the materials and tools correctly, and also that they calculate the length of time and the cost. At suitable times, therefore, the materials, along with their source, production, characteristics, nature, purpose, and method of treatment, manufacture and preservation, and price are discussed. Also, at an opportune time in this connection, the earlier stages of development of the tools and of the industry are made concrete by means of word and picture.

In this way the manual training, without being forced, is correlated with the other subjects of instruction, especially with history, geography, mathematics, and natural science.

Strict attention is to be given to economical use of material, careful treatment of tools, order and cleanliness. Dirty and carelessly prepared exercises are to be rejected by the teacher.

Manual training instruction is always given in consecutive hours.

In girls' schools the manual training is placed in charge of a woman well-trained in this field. Where no certificated manual training instructress is available, a certificated children's nurse or leader of the adolescent youth should be employed.

### X. Gardening

Work in gardening covers the planting of a simple house garden, the improvement of its soil, work in the vegetable and flower garden, the orchard, their care and use, and the struggle against injurious plants or animals.

All instruction should provide the pupils with practical work as the best type of instruction. Theoretical instruction, limited to the very essentials, should be based on the work of the pupils.

### XI. Sewing

*Aim*

The girls are to be trained to make with the needle simple, useful garments, upon their own initiative and in good technical, tasteful fashion; also to mend garments suitably. Through training the sense of color and of form, as well as by careful instruction concerning materials, appreciation and understanding of genuine work are cultivated and the girls are trained to be consumers of sound judgment. The instruction should awaken joy in work and train for order, cleanliness, economy, and industry.

*Program*

## VI

Crocheting; for example, covers, caps, and jackets. Sewing with delicate material, making, for example, aprons, working-bags, and buttonholes.

## V

Patching and darning. Hemstitching; for example, doilies, handkerchiefs. Knitting socks, half hose, and footing stockings.

## IV

Repairing of articles of clothing. Sewing a garment; for example, corset, petticoat, gymnasium bloomers, blouse. Introduction to finer work in technique already learned; for example, hemstitching, crocheting, and cross-stitching.

## III

Lettering and embroidery. Machine sewing: the machine and its care. Simple articles, pillowcase, petticoat, smock, apron, head towel.

## II AND I

Continuation of machine sewing. Application to ornamentation, of techniques acquired,—shirt, drawers, combination, petticoat, blouse, and dress. Suitable techniques as review; for example, handbag, girdle, purse, children's clothes.

*Method*

The instruction is class instruction. Supplementary exercises within the limits of the class work may be given to girls adapted thereto.

The instruction develops the insight of the girls first, and subordinates form and execution to the principle of utility. The greatest possible freedom is allowed the girls in the choice of material, pattern, and ornamentation. Before purchasing, the girls receive instruction with reference to the material to be used. The material should be simple, good, useful, and tasteful.

Every article is to be made by the pupils themselves. Patterns are to be made, if possible, by fitting. To every article only that technique will be applied which is necessary for its preparation. The ornamentation should be modest and in good taste. It should conform to the purpose, material, and form of the article to be made.

In connection with the drawing instruction in the upper classes, the history of clothing is to be discussed from time to time and the prevailing tendency in style is to be critically judged with the help of the fashion magazines.

The greatest attention is to be given to mending, thereby accustoming the children to the idea that their clothing should always be in good repair. Approximately from class IV on the girls are to be required to do mending at home, which they are to submit occasionally to the teacher.

Not more than twenty-five girls shall belong to one class in sewing. In machine sewing one machine is necessary for every three or four girls. Besides, the following instructional materials are essential to the work: one sewing frame with support, large wooden knitting needles, a large wooden crocheting needle, a thick roving in two colors, stiff muslin, several frames with extensions for the various techniques, samples of yarn, cloth, wool, dyes.

## XII. HOME ECONOMICS

*Aim*

The home economics instruction is to acquaint the girls with the work of the home and to introduce them to its sensible and appropriate administration. The pupils are to learn to observe the work and to be able to see their way through the problems of the home independently and to solve them with the least expense of time, energy, and money. This instruction should train them in care and foresight, in faithfulness in small things, in order, cleanliness, and economy.

*Program*

The instruction must treat the following fields:

1. Nutrition—principles of nutrition and cooking: Need of nourishment, food, raw materials, foodstuffs, types of albumin, fats, carbohydrates, mineral matter, vitamins, and water. Pres-

ervation of foods by cooking; their nutritive value; preparation of food, dressings and seasonings, delicacies, food for invalids and infants.

2. The Home—study of the material of the home and house work: Care of the home with special reference to the kitchen and the care of its equipment. Home decoration, including care of flowers, table covers, heating and lighting, hearth, fuels and their use, washing and care of the laundry.

*Method*

The instruction begins with the simplest activity and correlates most closely with the work.

Each food is to be tested for its food value and its preservation by cooking. Herein the principles of cooking must be discovered by the girls themselves and assembled in a convenient notebook. These principles of cooking are applied to the preparation of food and make recipes, in general, superfluous. Attention is called occasionally to the advantages and the disadvantages of the use of a cook book. In a similar manner the method of cleaning and caring for furniture and utensils is to be derived from the nature and treatment of the raw materials involved.

In connection with geography and natural science the close relationship between home economics and political economy is to be gone into at every opportunity and the feeling of responsibility toward the people as a whole is to be strengthened from this angle. Among other things, arithmetical problems from economics, which make the results of careful housekeeping concrete, serve this purpose also.

Attention is to be directed to the advantages of careful buying. Where it is possible, the buying is done by the pupils themselves. Occasional buying in groups and visits to markets and stores are to be recommended. In a division of the work with that in bookkeeping, pupils are introduced to the calculation and accounting of household money.

The greatest emphasis is placed upon well-planned distribution and careful execution of all activities. Correct setting of the table, even for everyday purposes, is to be cultivated. Training in order and cleanliness should consider also working clothes, which should be suitable, simple, and neat.

The arrangement of the school kitchen should afford room

for from twenty to twenty-five working places and should include all equipment, furniture, and apparatus indispensable to the introduction to a well-ordered household. Modern conveniences which save time and energy should be considered at suitable times. In their provision, however, necessary considerations of the conditions of the families of the pupils must not be neglected.

## XIII. Hygiene

### (SEE CLASS FOR MOTHERS)

*Aim*

Somewhat detailed knowledge of the structure of the organs of the human body, introduction to the care of the body, both in health and in sickness, with special attention to that of women and infants,—hygiene for women and care of infants.

*Program*

The following topics are treated:

1. The human body: Structure of the human body, its organs and their functions. Growth and waste of the body.

2. General hygiene: Influence of external living conditions upon health—air, light, water, clothing, dwelling, food, work, and recreation. Public health.

3. Care of infants and small children: Nutrition, care of the body, clothing, nursery, games, plays, and toys.

4. Nursing: Cause and prevention of disease, sick-room observation and care of the sick, execution of the physician's orders, protection against infection, first aid.

*Method*

Discussion of the human body in connection with general hygiene forms the basis of the instruction. It is not treated, however, as a preliminary course. In every topic, rather, the details which are related in any way to the small child or to the female human body are to be correlated immediately; similarly with the discussions on the hygiene, injury, and disease of the organs that are studied.

Infant care and the most important rules of nursing are studied again in connected form in the last term.

Problems and reports from the girls' fields of experience, in so far as they can be connected with the aim of the instruction, are taken up; tact and interest in the health and welfare of the girls can be made to aid in the instruction. However, it is not to be forgotten that the instruction in hygiene is not intended to take the place of a physician.

The course in hygiene should so far as possible be kept in close connection with the other subjects of instruction, especially with physical training, which supplements in many respects the instruction in hygiene through practical application. The discussion of the proper kinds of clothing leads to sewing, the discussion of nutrition to home economics, and the elements of public health work to civics.

The following articles are desirable as aids to instruction: doll with children's clothes, first-aid kit, a bottle, and blackboards.

## XIV. BOOKKEEPING

Special periods of instruction in bookkeeping beyond those to be developed in Plans II and IV—with reference to commerce and trade—are not given. The arithmetic periods in class I are to be used in connection with bookkeeping.

*Aim*

Ability to keep orderly and carefully account of the receipts and expenditures of the household, as well as of a simple, small business establishment; to invest any savings advantageously; and in special cases, to secure greater amounts of money corresponding to the purpose in view,—thus the awakening of the sense of order and economy.

*Program*

Exercises in the orderly accounting of household and industrial receipts and expenditures. Instruction concerning: social welfare laws and the local social welfare organizations; types of insurance and savings institutions; investment and cost of saving; cash payments; credit—its advantages and disadvantages.

In the classes developed according to Plans II and IV, the requirements of the instruction are to be increased to a corresponding degree.

*Method*

Portions of the subject matter to be treated here have already been discussed under other subjects, especially arithmetic, German, and history. They are summarized and supplemented.

All of the instruction is tied up with definite organizations of practical life which are known to the children, with special consideration of local conditions. The practical work receives chief emphasis in this subject.

## XV. Music

The publication of the new regulations is reserved.

## XVI. Physical Training [1]

*Aim*

Promotion of health, the whole physical development and efficiency by regular strengthening of the vital organs, nerves, and muscles. Habituation to good posture and to a light natural movement. Introduction to care of the body and endurance. Training for independence and self-control, courage and endurance, order and obedience, public spirit and mutual helpfulness.

The instruction must be so imparted that the regular pursuit of physical exercises extends even beyond the period of compulsory school attendance and becomes a pleasurable habit and a normal popular practice.

*Program*

## VI TO IV

### TEN TO TWELVE YEARS OF AGE

I. Exercises of the Body.

1. Exercises in walking of all types, also with singing and with instrumental music. Marching, walking on the toes, hopping and limping, walking with knees high, goose-step, straddle walk, walking on balance bar.

2. Training in running for systematic practice of racing. 50 to 75 meter dash, distance running up to 2,000 meters, relay races.

3. Exercises for posture and correction,—types of the freest sort from life and school.

    *a.* Imitation of animals' movements: Running like dogs, cats, horses; walking like bears; hopping like frogs and flying like birds.

    *b.* Working movements: Chopping wood, sawing, mowing,

---

[1] The following plan refers to physical training for boys. There is now a plan to issue special regulations for physical training for girls. Until further notice the regulations of the *Manual for Physical Training for Girls, 1916,* remain in force.

bell-ringing, swinging the arms, rolling a wheelbarrow, crawling exercises with riders, rowing, tag, pirouette, and the like.

c. Simple regular exercises in relaxation, expansion, stretching, especially for the purpose of making the trunk pliant and strong and for correcting faults in posture, in standing, sitting, kneeling, and lying. Body bending and twisting, full-knee bending, body rotating with neck, arm, and leg exercises. Simple exercises in balancing,—balancing exercises, standing on one leg and with the use of the balancing bar. Posture exercises on horizontal and parallel bars; swimming movements on land.

II. Performance Activities.

1. Jumping and throwing: Broad jump 1.4 meters to 4.2 meters; running high jump, 60 meters to 125 meters; various types of jumping over fixed obstacles.

Throwing a baseball 12 to 40 meters; throwing at a mark; exercises in catching and batting the ball.

(For running see the regulations on exercises of the body.)

2. Exercises for strength, courage, and skill with apparatus: Climbing races on poles; climbing on ladders.

Horizontal bar: Exercises: Hanging exercises. Swinging on the knee up the horizontal bar. Turning on the knees backward. Pulling up to the bar. Rotation backward.

Parallel bars: Different types of sitting. Change of position. Vault. Rear vault.

Horse: Straddle vaults.

3. Floor exercises: Falling and getting up. Sitting and rising with a partner. Somersault forward and backward. Short hand stands at the wall. Pushing and pulling games. Tug-of-war. Cat-and-mouse. Obstacle race. Obstacle crawl.

III. Games.

Simple running and ball games of the elementary school: Old Bear. People's ball. Hunters' ball. Wander ball. Baseball with simplified rules.

## III TO I

### THIRTEEN TO FIFTEEN YEARS OF AGE

I. Exercises of the Body.

1. Exercises in walking as in the lower section.

2. Running and running exercises with increase of requirements. Short dashes up to 100 meters in 13 to 17 seconds. Starting exercises from the crouching position. Distance running up to 3,000 meters, from 12 to 15 minutes. Relay races. Cross-country races.

3. Posture exercises as in the lower section. Light body bending. Also sideward and backward with the upper portion of the body. Body turning. Leaning rest exercises. Instep exercises. Walking with the use of balancing poles and ladders. Exercises on stall bars.

II. Performance Activities.

1. Jumping and throwing: Running broad jump, 2.20 meters to 2.50 meters. Running jump .75 meter to 1.35 meters. Baseball throwing, 20 to 60 meters; throwing at a mark. Hammer throwing—1 to 1.5 kilograms, 14 to 36 meters. Shot putting— 2.5 kilograms, 4 to 7.5 meters; 5 kilograms, 3.5 to 7.5 meters. (For running see regulations on exercises of the body.)

2. Exercises for strength, courage, and skill on apparatus. Climbing and hanging on poles and ropes.

Horizontal bar: Rotation and knee grind from swinging to hanging position; sitting rotation, hanging by knees and pulling up to sitting position with weight on arms; pulling knees up to bar and turning around; vault from side, back vault, kneeling on bar, straddling from stand and hanging positions.

Parallel bars: Straddle, scissors, vault, rear vault, side vault, screw. Rolling from straddle to straddle. Shoulder stand from sitting position. Lying position, arm bending and stretching. Running and swinging vaults. Hand stand.

Horse: Mixed jumps.

Rings: Swinging with half turn. Swinging with elbows bent.

3. Floor exercises: Exercises with partner; hand stand with support; comic exercises; preliminary exercises for wrestling.

III. Games.

Games for the lower sections: Prisoner's base, baseball, handball, football.

### HIKING

Regularly in all classes; at first a half-day excursion and from the 12th year on whole-day excursions on the monthly hiking days. Observation exercises for the sharpening of the senses, map reading, cross-country games, cultivation of tramping and national songs. Distance walked must not be too great. On a whole-day excursion, 12 to 18 kilometers are sufficient for classes VI to IV and 18 to 24 kilometers for classes III to I.

### SWIMMING

In a physical training period and on afternoons set aside for play in general where opportunity is present for it. For the fulfillment of this requirement, no healthy child is to leave the school without having learned to swim—preparatory dry swimming exercises from the sixth class on. Swimming exercises in class III or IV. In classes III to I the different types of swimming. Simple dives. Introduction to life saving and first aid.

Skating, snow-shoeing, and tobogganing, especially on play afternoons.

Orthopedic exercises, where arrangements are made therefor; participation required by pupils selected by the school physician.

*Method*

1. In all classes three hours of physical training per week are available for compulsory physical training besides required play on an afternoon, on which there are no lessons. In addition there is an excursion day each month.

2. Physical training instruction can fulfill its special health and educational functions when it is given according to a unified plan. This holds true for the gymnasium periods as well as for the conduct of the play afternoons. The choice and sequence of the exercises, from a sensible attitude toward youthful nature, must be adapted to the physical, mental, and moral development of the different ages of the children, and are determined by the need of exercise and the aims and means of education. It is not the purpose of physical training instruction that the class learn as many exercises as possible, but that the individual pupil be advanced in health, vigor, and elasticity, efficiency, independence, courage, and endurance to a degree that can be attained by him.

3. In the program for activity and exercise, which each school must set up for itself, it is recommended to assign to each individual class a definite basic amount of material which is fundamental and required. The activities proposed above are merely offered as suggestions. Specifically, because of the difference of district and local conditions as well as on account of the physical make-up of the children, a certain degree of freedom and flexibility in the selection of material is necessary and desirable.

4. The numerous and many-sided exercises which are applicable to physical training may be arranged into three groups according to their importance for the physical and intellectual development of the pupils. In the "Exercises of the Body" are

grouped those types of exercises which are particularly advantageous for the building up of the body and the constitution and which are suitable to bring about good posture, deep and efficient breathing, and a light, elastic step; thus the walking, running, and posture exercises are of service in the widest sense. In the second group, "Activity Performances," belong exercises in jumping and throwing, the so-called "floor exercises," wrestling, and exercises on the apparatus. All of these assist to a certain degree in training for skill, endurance, courage, alertness, and self-control. "The Games" from the simple running and ball games of the lower sections to the competitive games of the upper classes form a third group.

5. The method of instruction must correspond to the particular age-groups and their development, but at the same time must take into consideration also the different types of exercise. While in the *Grundschule* play predominated, or the exercises were put in a form which appealed to the personal interest of the child, from the tenth year on the pressure for many-sided activities and the insistent need of activity are determining; at the same time introduction to regulated practice and habituation to discipline and order are necessary. In accordance with this principle, this section demands the development of a lively, rigid physical training course carried on in groups. This applies also for the stage of later childhood which comprises boys from approximately twelve to fifteen years and represents the period of development of the second great growth in height in which the heart and lungs have an equal and essential part. In both sections the pupils, even the weaker ones, are always to experience joy in success in the exercises and in the increase in their ability and efficiency.

6. Formal types of exercise are, in general, carried on as class exercises. The word of command is solely to regulate a rapid execution of the drill, but never to disturb the rhythm of the pupil who is exercising.

Natural exercises must not be broken up too much into their constituent parts. Mistakes are lessened by a limitation of the extent of the movement, and avoided by practice auxiliary exercises. The introduction to movements which conserve the strength and which are performed according to the natural laws of movement is an important task of the teacher in all sections. Where the activity itself does not call forth the natural and interested participation of the pupils, intellectual appeals—reasons and statement of its value and purpose—will increase the slackened interest and promote understanding, thus giving a new impulse to the exercise.

7. In order to make allowance for the need of independence of pupils and for the differences in their performances, occasional voluntary gymnastic exercises should be added in organized fashion in classes VI to IV. These are organized also in classes III to I in greater number and in freer form according to the demands of "activity instruction."

8. Only if the physical training teacher works with inner enjoyment and pleasure as a comrade of his pupils and at the same time as their leader, will he achieve educative results. He will be able, especially if he endeavors by his own example, to make clear to the pupils, most impressively and most naturally, in the gymnasium, in play, and on excursions, the need of a regular care and inurement of the body, the necessity of an intelligent mode of life and the importance of abstinence from alcohol and tobacco.

9. Every physical training period must be utilized to the greatest extent. It is to be lively, richly stimulating, and of wide variety. The selection and arrangement of the exercises must take place from the point of view that in every physical training period a complete and thorough work-out of all pupils is assured.

10. The exercise period begins with a stimulating exercise for the purpose of a quick transfer from the seatwork and study of the previous hours to the physical activity and relaxation of the pupils; with a short run or, in the lower classes, imitative movements, or with a short singing march.

To the rigid character of the body exercises of every period belong posture exercises of the modern type. They correspond, with limitations, to an ebb and flow of physiological demands and youthful nature, more than would a manifold series of postures and movements, and are admirably suited to render the whole body, especially the trunk, strong and pliant, and to counteract faults in posture. Usually about six exercises are combined to form an exercise group and are to be repeated eight to sixteen times, each according to its difficulty and the age of the pupils. In order to afford those exercising the possibility of executing the movements in suitable rhythm, it is recommended that not every individual repetition be executed with counting. In a trained class, if the exercise has been demonstrated and explained, the exercise is carried on freely until the teacher gives the command to stop.

On account of their importance for the development of the heart and lungs, running exercises also belong to the regular work of every physical training period which is carried on in the open air. They, like the other popular games, are to be cultivated regularly and primarily in the more favorable seasons, but also in the winter if the weather permits.

Exercises for skill on apparatus are carried on in all classes as group exercises. Herein the pupils are to be employed as continuously as possible, but an effort is to be made that the pupils learn to execute the simpler exercises with the right expenditure of energy, with complete control of the body, and in good posture.

While the simpler games, especially in the lower classes, make a happy ending of the physical training period, the large group and competitive games represent the chief part of the play afternoons. In addition, suitable posture exercises may also be undertaken on play afternoons, and wherever possible, running, jumping, and throwing exercises.

In all exercises especial attention is to be given to breathing.

11. Fundamentally, physical training is to be carried on in the open. If the gymnasium must be used, careful attention must be given to ventilation and cleanliness.

12. Clothing for physical exercises is to be light and suitable and should adapt itself otherwise to the various seasons of the year.

13. Regular measurements, continued from year to year, whose results are made known, furnish great stimulation to the children to increase their records by conscientious practice. They also furnish the teacher a safe judgment concerning the physical development and ability of the individual children and provide him the standard for the condition and progress of his class.

14. Competitive games and contests are an important educative aid. The participation of the pupils is usually to be

limited to the very common summer festival (meet) and possibly
to a meet under public auspices, as the National Junior Field
Meet. The school meets should never dispense with gymnastic
exercises.

## XVII. CLASS IN MOTHERCRAFT

### SEE PLAN IV

*Aim*

The class in mothercraft is to train the girls for reasonable participation and creative coöperation in the organization of family
life upon a sound, German cultural basis, in that it trains the
home-making and home-caring powers of the girls, introduces
the girls through participation to practical activity and through
concrete instruction to the work of the housewife and mother.
It awakens in them the feeling that every woman is called to
do her part in a constructive scheme of political economy.

*Program*

Not only the instruction in needlework and home economics,
which is to be given more intensively, as well as the hygiene appearing for the first time, but the whole work of the class, regardless of the general purposes to be fulfilled by it, is to be
placed at the service of the aim indicated above. In this matter,
the closest possible connection of the various fields of work is to
be adhered to very carefully. The selection of the material has
to be considered in the following fields especially:

Religion: Religious life, social and charitable problems and
organizations.

German: The German family as an agent of culture. German woman's life and work; fairy tales and folk lore.

History-Civics: Cross-sections from cultural history of
family life and home economics; introduction to the duties of
woman, woman's rights in the public life, with special reference
to the work in the community.

Geography: The part of woman in German economic life.

Arithmetic and home economics bookkeeping: Accounting of
the household receipts and expenditures; number as an economic
unit; insurance and tax system; credit and savings.

Music: Children's round and folk songs.

Physical training in connection with hygiene: Intensive study of the training and care of the body, running games and folk dances.

Gardening: Planting and care of a vegetable and flower garden for the needs of the household.

The class in mothercraft is not to supplant the school for housewives. The latter will receive its special problems and aims as a superstructure upon the middle school, especially upon the class in mothercraft. Wherever it is possible, it is to be furthered as a valuable type of school which is still in the stage of development.

## SECTION III

## SUGGESTIONS FOR THE COURSES OF STUDY OF THE SECONDARY SCHOOLS OF PRUSSIA

### I

### INTRODUCTORY REGULATION

*Min. Erl. vom 6 April, 1925*

The Prussian Ministry of State has given its approval on the basis of the decision of April 4, 1925, to the *Suggestions for the Curricula of the Secondary Schools of Prussia.* At this time I am having copies of the *Suggestions* forwarded to the Provincial School Boards. From Easter on these *Suggestions* come into operation for the instructional activity of all secondary schools in Prussia. The programs announced in the Regulations of October 31, 1924, remain in force. Special regulations have been issued with reference to the programs of the *Reformgymnasium*, the *Reformrealgymnasium* with Latin from *Untertertia* on, and the *Oberlyzeum* of the *Reformrealgymnasium* type.

It is the duty of the school faculties within the current school year to organize, according to a temporary plan of work, the school's activity in accordance with the sense of these *Suggestions* and to distribute the instructional material in such a way that adjustment to the new teaching objectives will be accomplished, if possible, by Easter, 1926. In the course of the year 1925-26 the faculties are to work out the courses of study for individual schools as required by the *Suggestions* and submit them for approval to the Provincial School Boards by February 1, 1926. The *Dezernenten* of the individual institutions are to consider it their most important task to advise with the faculties in this work. The most important problems of curriculum construction should also be taken up for discussion at conferences of directors. Real progress will be achieved in this task by means of local or district teachers' "activity groups" (*Arbeits-*

*gemeinschaften*) organized by the different groups of teachers in the secondary schools. The Provincial School Boards likewise will encourage the exchange of school curricula, and so far as possible will make the work done at one school available for many schools. By June 1, 1926, I anticipate a report dealing with curriculum-making which will include some especially successful courses of study. By June 1, 1927, the Provincial School Boards will make extensive reports on the experience that has been gained up to that time in putting this reform into effect.

I make the following special notations:

1. As electives, the subjects which are in the curricula of 1901 and 1908 are to be approved primarily. Thus in the *Gymnasium,* Hebrew and the second modern foreign language, and also in the especially approved *Reformgymnasium,* drawing from the *Untersekunda* on; in the *Realgymnasium* and in the *Oberrealschulen* mechanical drawing; in the *Oberrealschulen* and in the *Oberlyzeen* from *Obersekunda* on Latin; in the *Lyzeum* sewing in the *Untersekunda.* The number of hours heretofore available must not be exceeded in this matter. The regulations of the Order of February 16, 1925, with reference to Hebrew instruction in the *Gymnasium* and Latin in the *Oberrealschule,* dealing with the use of any remaining periods for this elective work, apply correspondingly to mechanical drawing instruction in the *Realgymnasien* and the *Oberrealschulen* and to instruction in sewing. Whenever elective work in still other subjects is to be offered beyond that previously customary, my approval is to be secured. The courses of study for this elective instruction are to be worked out in the curricula of the schools. The principles of method of these *Suggestions* have corresponding application.

2. With reference to the instrumental music instruction, manual training, and gardening the regulations of the Ministerial Decree of March 13, 1924, paragraph 4, apply to all secondary schools.

3. Since the negotiations with the ecclesiastical authorities of the Prussian National Church have not yet been concluded, I refrain from any changes in the courses of study for the Evangelical religious instruction.

4. In reply to the fears frequently expressed that the ac-

tivity groups in philosophy might lead to the destruction of
the pupils' religious view and their outlook upon life, I make
it the earnest duty of the teachers in the sense of the *Notes on
Method,* pages 326 ff., always to keep in mind that the unity of
education in the religious-moral field must not be disturbed by
the school, and that in view of the spiritual condition of our
people, it cannot be the function of the public school to transmit to the pupils any definite philosophy of life.   The right
of the home and of the larger groups to which the pupil belongs
the school must respect in all fields and thus protect the pupil
against difficult inner struggles.

5. The *Fundamental Introductory Remarks,* the *General
Suggestions* and the *Notes on Method* on the individual subjects, apply equally to the *Deutsche Oberschulen* and the *Aufbauschulen,* as well as do the objectives in music, sewing, and
physical training.   Otherwise the *Suggestions for a Curriculum
for the Deutsche Oberschulen and the Aufbauschulen,* March 13,
1924, remain effective.   Through the flexibility of the regulations
of these *Suggestions,* the organization of a common lower section
of the *Deutsche Oberschule,* the *Oberrealschule,* the *Reformrealgymnasium* and the *Oberlyzeum* in classes *Sexta* to *Quarta* will
be easy to organize.   With reference to the reduction in number
of hours in the natural sciences in the *Deutsche Oberschule,* the
distribution of hours from *Untersekunda* on is to be arranged
as follows:

U II, Physics, first semester, 2 hours.
U II, Chemistry, both semesters, 2 hours.
U II, Biology, second semester, 2 hours.
O II, Physics and Chemistry, each, 2 hours.
U I and O I, Physics during the whole year, 2 hours each.
   Biology, first semester, each year, 2 hours.
   Chemistry, second semester, each year, 2 hours.

The programs of the *Deutsche Oberschulen* must take this
arangement of hours into consideration when the course of
study is drawn up.

# II

## DECREES DEALING WITH THE CURRICULA

### 1. ELECTIVE INSTRUCTION [1]

In the introduction of the new time-tables the elective instruction in Hebrew is especially to be taken adavantage of.

There are, however, no objections to be raised against using any of the remaining hours which are available for elective instruction, wherein especial regard is to be paid to Hebrew in the *Gymnasium* and to Latin in the *Oberrealschule* and the *Oberlyzeum,* since these subjects are of importance for vocational preparation.

### 2. PROGRAM OF THE REFORMGYMNASIUM [2]

The program of the *Reformgymnasium,* which has been aspecially authorized, is from *Sexta* to *Quarta* (VI to IV) that of the *Reformrealgymnasium,* from *Untertertia* on that of the *Gymnasial-Studienanstalt.*

The special music instruction approved from *Untertertia* on disappears. The hours thus set free, in counterbalancing the larger demands for total hours in the lower section, are to be distributed in *Obersekunda* as follows: German receives one (1) additional hour a week in *Obersekunda,* and in *Untertertia* (U III) to *Untersekunda* (U II) each, one (1) more hour a week is given to Latin, which drops one (1) hour each week in *Oberprima.*

Thus results the following program of the *Reformgymnasium.*

[1] *Min. Erlass vom 16. Februar 1925—U II 191.*
[2] *Min. Erlass vom 14. Marz 1925—U II 400.1.*

## PROGRAM OF THE REFORMGYMNASIUM

| SUBJECTS | VI to IV as in the *Reform-realgymnasium* and *Oberrealschule* | U III | O III | U II | O II | U I | O I | TOTAL |
|---|---|---|---|---|---|---|---|---|
| Religion | 6 | 2 | 2 | 2 | 2 | 2 | 2 | 18 |
| German | 16 | 4 | 4 | 3 | 4 | 3 | 3 | 37 |
| Latin | .. | 8 | 8 | 7 | 6 | 6 | 5 | 40 |
| Greek | .. | .. | .. | 8 | 8 | 8 | 8 | 32 |
| Modern Foreign Language | 18 | 3 | 3 | 2 | 2 | 2 | 2 | 32 |
| History | 4 | 2 | 2 | 2 | 2 | 2 | 3 | 17 |
| Geography | 6 | 1 | 1 | 1 | 1 | 1 | 1 | 12 |
| Mathematics | 13 | 4 | 4 | 3 | 3 | 3 | 3 | 33 |
| Natural Sciences | 6 | 2 | 2 | 2 | 2 | 2 | 2 | 18 |
| Drawing | 6 | 2 | 2 | .. | .. | .. | .. | 10 |
| Singing | 4 | .. | .. | .. | .. | .. | .. | 4 |
| Total | 79 | 28 | 28 | 30 | 30 | 29 | 29 | 253 |

To these are to be added the same hours as in the other regular schools for boys.

## 3. THE REFORMREALGYMNASIUM WITH LATIN FROM UNTERTERTIA ON AND THE OBERLYZEUM OF THE REFORMREAL-GYMNASIUM TYPE [3]

Upon request I will approve in exceptional cases the following variations from the programs of my decree of October 31, 1924:

1. See my decree of March 14, 1925, concerning the programs of the *Reformgymnasium* which have been especially authorized.

2. In the *Reformrealgymnasium*, according to the following regulations, Latin can be begun in U III. It receives, then, the number of hours provided for the normal type of school in the second foreign language, the latter that of the Latin. Only in *Untertertia* does French surrender an hour to Latin.

Before the presentation of requests for approval of the special form of the *Reformrealgymnasium*, the Provincial School Boards will be required to determine and carefully express in their reports whether this deviation from the regular sequence of languages actually accords with the special educational needs. In schools which must reckon with a rather heavy elimination from *Untersekunda*, it will generally be more to the purpose for the pupils who are willing to be content with the certificate

[3] *Min. Erlass vom 31. März 1925, U II 777. 1.*

for *Obersekunda* to have studied a modern foreign language for three years. Likewise it is of greatest importance for preparatory schools (six-year types) which send their pupils to a full (nine-year) school that this transfer should not ensue until *Untersekunda*. Through the normal form of the *Reformrealgymnasium,* access to *Untersekunda* of schools with the language-history basis, as well as the transfer to the *Oberrealschule* organized upon the mathematics-natural-science basis, will be opened up to boys and girls from middle schools, from so-called *Rektoratschulen,* and also in many cases from *Lyzeen.* This opportunity probably disappears if Latin is introduced in *Untertertia.* However, consideration for such transfer is more important than the wishes of the individual school, whether they are expressed by the faculty or are represented by the parents' council. Again, the modern foreign language with which the *Reformrealgymnasium* in question begins is not without importance. In general, from instruction begun in *Untersekunda* it is in English alone that results may be expected that promote the educational purpose of this modern language type of school. Fundamentally, therefore, the prerequisite of beginning Latin in *Untertertia* is that French will be studied as the first foreign language.

The educational purpose of this *Reformrealgymnasium* is just the same as that of the regular type. To this point in the organization of the curricula of the schools careful attention must be paid in determining the standard and in distributing the subject matter in Latin as well as in English. Latin instruction in both *Tertien* cannot be combined with that of a *Reformrealgymnasial* division which may be in the school.

3. In addition to the *Realgymnasial Studienanstalt* in the sense of B 5 of the programs of October 31, 1924,[4] I also authorize in girls' schools the curriculum of the *Reformrealgymnasium* as given in A II 1. However, it can only be so introduced that classes VI to O III correspond essentially to those of the *Oberlyzeum.* Music must be organized as in the boys' schools.

Applications are to be supported from the points of view set forth in paragraph 2 and laid before me for decision. This form can come in question only for full (nine-year) schools

⁴ See page 312.

and only then when for special reasons value is placed upon the more intensive study of Latin in the four upper classes.

4. In the *Oberlyzeum* (B 2 and B 3 of the programs of October 31, 1924) opportunity will be given for the study of Latin as an elective.

# III

## TIME-SCHEDULES FOR SECONDARY SCHOOLS

### A. FUNDAMENTAL SCHOOLS FOR BOYS

#### I. Institutions with Latin as Fundamental Foreign Language

##### 1. GYMNASIUM

| SUBJECT | No. of Hours in Class | | | | | | | | | |
|---|---|---|---|---|---|---|---|---|---|---|
| | VI | V | IV | U III | O III | U II | O II | U I | O I | Total |
| Religion ........ | 2 | 2 | 2 | 2 | 2 | 2 | 2 | 2 | 2 | 18 |
| German ........ | 5 | 4 | 3 | 3 | 3 | 3 | 4 | 3 | 3 | 31 |
| Latin .......... | 7 | 7 | 7 | 6 | 6 | 5 | 5 | 5 | 5 ⎫ | 53 |
| Greek .......... | .. | .. | .. | 6 | 6 | 6 | 6 | 6 | 6 ⎭ | 36 |
| Modern Foreign Language .... | .. | .. | 3 | 2 | 2 | 2 | 2 | 2 | 2 | 15 |
| History and Civics | .. | 1 | 2 | 2 | 2 | 3 | 3 | 3 | 3 | 19 |
| Geography ...... | 2 | 2 | 2 | 1 | 1 | 1 | 1 | 1 | 1 | 12 |
| Mathematics .... | 4 | 4 | 4 | 3 | 3 | 4 | 3 ⎱ | 4 ⎱ | 4 ⎱ | 33 |
| Natural Sciences. | 2 | 2 | 2 | 2 | 2 | 2 | 2 ⎰ | 2 ⎰ | 2 ⎰ | 18 |
| Drawing ....... | 2 | 2 | 2 | 2 | 2 | 1[1] | 1[1] | 1[1] | 1[1] | 14 |
| Music .......... | 2 | 2 | .. | .. | .. | .. | .. | .. | .. | 4 |
| Total ........ | 26 | 26 | 27 | 29 | 29 | 29 | 29 | 29 | 29 | 253 |

In the *Gymnasium*, with reference to optional instruction, the week-hours which have hitherto been used for Greek in U III to U II are assigned so as to give 2 hours each year to the modern foreign language already begun in IV and 4 hours to the second modern foreign language.

[1] Two hours every two weeks.

306

## 2. REALGYMNASIUM

| SUBJECT | VI-IV as in *Gymnasium* (common foundation) | NUMBER OF HOURS IN CLASS | | | | | | |
|---|---|---|---|---|---|---|---|---|
| | | U III | O III | U II | O II | U I | O I | Total |
| Religion | 6 | 2 | 2 | 2 | 2 | 2 | 2 | 18 |
| German | 12 | 3 | 3 | 3 | 4 | 3 | 3 | 31 |
| Latin | 21 | 4 | 4 | 3 | 3 | 3 | 3 | 41 [1] |
| First Modern Foreign Language | 3 | 4 | 4 | 4 | 4[3] | 4[3] | 4[3] | 27[24] [2] |
| Second Modern Foreign Language | .. | 4 | 4 | 3 | 3 | 3[4] | 3[4] | 20[23] [2] |
| History (Civics) | 3 | 2 | 3 | 3 | 3 | 3 | 3 | 20 |
| Geography | 6 | 2 | 1 | 1 | 1 | 1 | 1 | 13 |
| Mathematics | 12 | 4 | 4 | 4 | 4 | 4 | 4 | 36 |
| Natural Sciences | 6 | 2 | 2 | 4 | 3 | 4 | 4 | 25 |
| Drawing | 6 | 2 | 2 | 2 | 2 | 2 | 2 | 18 |
| Music | 4 | .. | .. | .. | .. | .. | .. | 4 |
| Total | 79 | 29 | 29 | 29 | 29 | 29 | 29 | 253 |

[1] In a *Realgymnasium*, which is not connected with a *Gymnasium*, Latin receives 6 hours in IV, the first modern foreign language 4 hours, so that total hours for Latin will be 40, and for the first modern foreign language, 28 (25).
[2] The figures in brackets apply, when English is the first modern language.

## II. Institutions with a Modern Foreign Language as Fundamental Language

### 1. REFORMREALGYMNASIUM

| SUBJECT | No. of Hours in Class | | | | | | | | | |
|---|---|---|---|---|---|---|---|---|---|---|
| | VI | V | IV | U III | O III | U II | O II | U I | O I | Total |
| Religion | 2 | 2 | 2 | 2 | 2 | 2 | 2 | 2 | 2 | 78 |
| German | 6 | 5 | 5 | 3 | 3 | 3 | 4 | 3 | 3 | 35 |
| Latin | .. | .. | .. | .. | .. | 4 | 4 | 4 | 4 | 16 |
| First Modern Foreign Language | 6 | 6 | 6 | 5 | 5 | 4 | 4[3] | 4[3] | 4[3] | 44[41][1] |
| Second Modern Foreign Language | .. | .. | .. | 5 | 5 | 4 | 3[4] | 3[4] | 3[4] | 23[26][1] |
| History (Civics) | .. | 1 | 3 | 3 ⎱ | 3 ⎱ | 3 | 3 | 3 | 3 | 22 |
| Geography | 2 | 2 | 2 | 2 ⎰ | 1 ⎰ | 1 | 1 | 1 | 1 | 13 |
| Mathematics | 4 | 4 | 5 | 4 | 4 | 4 ⎱ | 4 ⎱ | 4 ⎱ | 4 ⎱ | 37 |
| Natural Sciences | 2 | 2 | 2 | 2 | 3 | 3 ⎰ | 3 ⎰ | 3 ⎰ | 3 ⎰ | 23 |
| Drawing | 2 | 2 | 2 | 2 | 2 | 2 | 2 | 2 | 2 | 18 |
| Music | 2 | 2 | .. | .. | .. | .. | .. | .. | .. | 4 |
| Total | 26 | 26 | 27 | 28 | 29 | 30 | 30 | 29 | 29 | 253 |

[1] The figures set in brackets apply when English is the first modern language.

### 2. OBERREALSCHULE

| SUBJECT | No. of Hours in Class | | | | | |
|---|---|---|---|---|---|---|
| | U I-O III as in Reformrealgymnasium [2] (common foundation) | U II | O II | U I | O I | Total |
| Religion | 10 | 2 | 2 | 2 | 2 | 18 |
| German | 22 | 3 | 4 | 4 | 4 | 37 |
| First Modern Foreign Language | 28 | 3 | 3 | 3 | 3 | 40 |
| Second Modern Foreign Language | 10 | 3 | 3 | 3 | 3 | 22 |
| History (Civics) | 10 | 3 | 3 | 3 | 3 | 22 |
| Geography | 9 | 2 | 1 | 1 | 1 | 14 |
| Mathematics | 21 | 5+1[1] | 5+1[1] | 5 | 5 | 43 |
| Natural Science | 11 | 6 | 6 | 6 | 6 | 35 |
| Drawing | 10 | 2 | 2 | 2 | 2 | 18 |
| Music | 4 | .. | .. | .. | .. | 4 |
| Total | 135 | 30 | 30 | 29 | 29 | 253 |

[1] One hour each in U II and O II is devoted to descriptive geometry.
[2] Realschulen can increase German and a modern foreign language each 1 hour, and decrease mathematics and natural sciences each 1 hour.

### 3. DEUTSCHE OBERSCHULE

| SUBJECT | VI-IV as in *Reform-realgymnasium* and *Ober-realschule* | U III | O III | U II | O II | U I | O I | Total |
|---|---|---|---|---|---|---|---|---|
| | NUMBER OF HOURS IN CLASS | | | | | | | |
| Religion | 6 | 2 | 2 | 2 | 2 | 2 | 2 | 18 |
| German | 16 | 5 | 5 | 5 | 5 | 4 | 4 | 44 |
| History (Civics) | 4 | 3 | 3 | 2+1 | 4 | 3+1 | 3+1 | 25 |
| Geography | 6 | 2 | 2 | 2 | 2 | 2 | 2 | 18 |
| Mathematics | 13 | 4 | 4 | 4 | 4 | 4 | 4 | 37 |
| Natural Science | 6 | 4 | 4 | 4 | 4 | 4 | 4 | 30 |
| First Foreign Language | 18 | 6 | 6 | 4 | 4[3] | 4[3] | 4[3] | 46[43] [1] |
| Second Foreign Language | .. | .. | .. | 4 | 3[4] | 3[4] | 3[4] | 13[16] [1] |
| Drawing | 6 | 2 | 2 | 2 | 2 | 2 | 2 | 18 |
| Music | 4 | .. | .. | .. | .. | .. | .. | 4 |
| Total | 79 | 28 | 28 | 30 | 30 | 29 | 29 | 253 |

[1] The figures set in brackets apply when the second foreign language is Latin or French.

---

To the preceding programs under A I-II, four hours of physical training are added for each class from VI to O I. Two of these hours are commonly to be used in gymnastics, and two hours in action games out-of-doors (on afternoons when there is no school). The pupils are equally required to pursue both types of physical training. In so far as the action games cannot be carried on out-of-doors during the colder seasons of the year, the hours set aside for them are to be utilized in gymnastics or in other suitable methods of physical training. For the administration of this regulation enough sections in gymnastics and play are to be formed so that instructional provision of twenty-four hours a week results in a fully developed school.[1]

For example:

```
7 sections in gymnastics, 2 hours each........... 14 hours
5 sections in play,       2 hours each........... 10 hours
                                                  ——
    Total ...................................     24 hours
IV-O I, Music ...................................  4 hours
    For "free activity groups" of the upper section[2].. 6 hours
                                                  ——
    Total ...................................     34 hours
```

[1] In a partially developed school 16 hours a week; for example, 5 sections in gymnastic and 3 sections in play,—total 16 hours.
[2] This is not offered in a partially developed school, so that instructional provision of 166 hours a week results.

## B. FUNDAMENTAL SCHOOLS FOR GIRLS

### 1. LYZEUM

| SUBJECT | NUMBER OF HOURS IN CLASS | | | | | | | |
|---|---|---|---|---|---|---|---|---|
| | VI | V | IV | U III | O III | U II | Total | U IIb |
| Religion ........... | 2 | 2 | 2 | 2 | 2 | 2 | 12 | 3 |
| German ........... | 5 | 5 | 5 | 4 | 4 | 4 | 27 | 4 |
| First Modern Foreign Language ... | 6 | 5 | 5 | 4 | 3 | 4 | 27 | 2 |
| Second Modern Foreign Language ... | .. | .. | .. | 4 | 4 | 4 | 12 | 2 |
| History (Civics) ... | .. | 1 | 3 | 2 | 2 | 3 | 11 | 3 |
| Geography ........ | 2 | 2 | 2 | 2 | 2 | 2 | 12 | 2 |
| Mathematics ....... | 4 | 4 | 4 | 4 | 4 | 4 | 24 | 3 |
| Natural Science .... | 2 | 2 | 2 | 2 | 3 | 3 | 14 | 3 |
| Drawing .......... | 2 | 2 | 2 | 2 | 2 | 2 | 12 | 2[2] |
| Music ............ | 2 | 2 | 1[1] | 1 | 1 | 1 | 8 | 2[2] |
| Total .......... | 25 | 25 | 26 | 27 | 27 | 29 | 159 | 26 |

To the program of studies are added:

In each class from VI to O III, 2 hours sewing, U IIb,
4 hours sewing.[2] Total............................ 10(14) hours

In each class from VI to U II, 4 hours physical training (see A). Total.............................. 16

26(30) hours

[1] Combining of classes is permitted from IV on, except that the total number of hours must not be lessened.
[2] The 8 hours set aside for sewing, drawing, and music can be distributed differently in U IIb.

### 2. OBERLYZEUM

| SUBJECT | NUMBER OF HOURS IN CLASS | | | |
|---|---|---|---|---|
| | *Lyzeum* VI to U II | O II | U I | O I | Total |
| Religion ..................... | 12 | 2 | 3 | 3 | 20 |
| German ..................... | 27 | 4 | 4 | 4 | 39 |
| First Modern Foreign Language. | 27 | 4 | 4 | 4 | 39 |
| Second Modern Foreign Language | 12 | 4 | 4 | 4 | 24 |
| History (Civics) .............. | 11 | 3 | 3 | 3 | 20 |
| Geography .................. | 12 | 2 | 2 | 2 | 18 |
| Mathematics ................ | 24 | 4 | 4 | 4 | 36 |
| Natural Science ............. | 14 | 3 | 3 | 3 | 23 |
| Drawing .................... | 12 | 2 | 2 | 2 | 18 |
| Music ...................... | 8 | | 2 | | 10 |
| Total ..................... | 159 | 28 | 29 | 29 | 247 |

+ 2

### 3. Oberlyzeum Similar to Oberrealschule

| SUBJECT | NUMBER OF HOURS IN CLASS | | | | |
|---|---|---|---|---|---|
| | Lyzeum VI to U II | O II | U I | O I | Total |
| Religion ...................... | 12 | 2 | 2 | 2 | 18 |
| German ...................... | 27 | 4 | 4 | 4 | 39 |
| First Modern Foreign Language. | 27 | 3 | 3 | 3 | 36 |
| Second Modern Foreign Language | 12 | 3 | 3 | 3 | 21 |
| History (Civics) .............. | 11 | 3 | 3 | 3 | 20 |
| Geography .................... | 12 | 2 | 2 | 2 | 18 |
| Mathematics .................. | 24 | 5 | 5 | 5 | 39 |
| Natural Science .............. | 14 | 4 | 5 | 5 | 28 |
| Drawing ...................... | 12 | 2 | 2 | 2 | 18 |
| Music ........................ | 8 | 2 | | | 10 |
| Total ..................... | 159 | 28 | 29 | 29 | 247 |
| | | +2 | | | |

### 4. Deutsche Oberschule

| SUBJECT | NUMBER OF HOURS IN CLASS | | | | | | | |
|---|---|---|---|---|---|---|---|---|
| | Lyzeum VI to I V | U III | O III | U II | O II | U I | O I | Total |
| Religion ........ | 6 | 2 | 2 | 2 | 2 | 2 | 2 | 18 |
| German ......... | 15 | 5 | 5 | 5 | 5 | 4 | 4 | 43 |
| First Foreign Language ........ | 16 | 5 | 5 | 3 | 4[3] | 4[3] | 4[3] | 41[38] [1] |
| Second Foreign Language ..... | .. | .. | .. | 4 | 3[4] | 3[4] | 3[4] | 13[16] [1] |
| History (Civics) . | 4 | 3 | 3 | 2+1 | 4 | 3+1 | 3+1 | 25 |
| Geography ...... | 6 | 2 | 2 | 2 | 2 | 2 | 2 | 18 |
| Mathematics .... | 12 | 4 | 4 | 3 | 4 | 4 | 4 | 35 |
| Natural Science .. | 6 | 4 | 4 | 4 | 4 | 4 | 4 | 30 |
| Drawing ........ | 6 | 2 | 2 | 2 | 2 | 2 | 2 | 18 |
| Music .......... | 5 | 1 | 1 | 1 | 2 | | | 10 |
| Total ......... | 76 | 28 | 28 | 29 | 30 | 29 | 29 | 251 |
| | | | | | +2 | | | |

[1] The figures in the brackets apply when the second foreign language is Latin or French. See note on A 113

## 5. Realgymnasiale Studienanstalt

| SUBJECT | Ly-zeum VI to IV | U III | O III | U II | O II | U I | O I | Total |
|---|---|---|---|---|---|---|---|---|
| Religion .......... | 6 | 2 | 2 | 2 | 2 | 2 | 2 | 18 |
| German ........... | 15 | 4 | 4 | 3 | 4 | 3 | 3 | 36 |
| Latin ............. | .. | 6 | 6 | 4 | 4 | 4 | 4 | 28 |
| First Modern Foreign Language ... | 16 | 4 | 4 | 3 | 3 | 3 | 3 | 36 |
| Second Modern Foreign Language ... | .. | .. | .. | 4 | 4 | 4 | 4 | 16 |
| History (Civics) ... | 4 | 2 | 2 | 3 | 3 | 3 | 3 | 20 |
| Geography ........ | 6 | 1 | 1 | 1 | 1 | 1 | 1 | 12 |
| Mathematics ...... | 12 | 4 | 4 | 4 | 4 | 4 | 4 | 36 |
| Natural Science .... | 6 | 2 | 2 | 2 | 3 | 3 | 3 | 21 |
| Drawing .......... | 6 | 2 | 2 | 2 | 2 | 2 | 2 | 18 |
| Music ............ | 5 | 1 | 1 | 1 | 2 | | | 10 |
| Total ........... | 76 | 28 | 28 | 29 | 30 | 29 | 29 | 251 |
| | | | | | +2 | | | |

The table above is headed by the span "NUMBER OF HOURS IN CLASS" over the columns from Ly-zeum VI to IV through O I.

## 6. Gymnasiale Studienanstalt

| SUBJECT | Ly-zeum VI to IV | U III | O III | U II | O II | U I | O I | Total |
|---|---|---|---|---|---|---|---|---|
| Religion .......... | 6 | 2 | 2 | 2 | 2 | 2 | 2 | 18 |
| German ........... | 15 | 4 | 4 | 3 | 3 | 3 | 3 | 35 |
| Latin ............. | .. | 7 | 7 | 6 | 6 | 6 | 6 | 38 |
| Greek ............. | .. | .. | .. | 8 | 8 | 8 | 8 | 32 |
| Modern Foreign Language ....... | 16 | 3 | 3 | 2 | 2 | 2 | 2 | 30 |
| History (Civics) ... | 4 | 2 | 2 | 2 | 2 | 2 | 3 | 17 |
| Geography ........ | 6 | 1 | 1 | 1 | 1 | 1 | 1 | 12 |
| Mathematics ....... | 12 | 4 | 4 | 3 | 3 | 3 | 3 | 32 |
| Natural Science .... | 6 | 2 | 2 | 2 | 2 | 2 | 2 | 18 |
| Drawing .......... | 6 | 2 | 2 | .. | .. | .. | .. | 10 |
| Music ............ | 5 | 1 | 1 | 2 | | | | 9 |
| Total No. of Hours | 76 | 28 | 28 | 29 | 29 | 29 | 30 | 251 |
| | | | | | +2 | | | |

The table above is headed by the span "NUMBER OF HOURS IN CLASS" over the columns from Ly-zeum VI to IV through O I.

To the programs of study, B 2 and 3, the following hours are added:

VI-O I, each 4 hours physical training (see under A)  Total.... 24 hours
    For "free activity groups" of the upper section, Total  6 hours
VI-O III, each 2 hours sewing  Total.... 10 hours

                                       Total.... 40 hours

To the programs of study B 4-6, the following hours are added:

VI-O I, each 4 hours physical training (see under A)  Total.... 24 hours
    For "free activity groups" of the upper section, Total  6 hours
VI-IV, each 2 hours sewing  Total....  6 hours

                                         Total.... 36 hours

## C. AUFBAUSCHULEN

### 1. WITH THE GOAL OF THE DEUTSCHE OBERSCHULE

| SUBJECT | NUMBER OF HOURS IN CLASS | | | | | | |
|---|---|---|---|---|---|---|---|
| | U III | O III | U II | O II | U I | O I | Total |
| Religion .............. | 2 | 2 | 2 | 2 | 2 | 2 | 12 |
| German .............. | 5 | 5 | 5 | 5 | 4 | 4 | 28 |
| History (Civics) ....... | 3 | 3 | 2+1 | 4 | 3+1 | 3+1 | 21 |
| Geography ............ | 2 | 2 | 2 | 2 | 2 | 2 | 12 |
| Mathematics ........... | 5 | 5 | 4 | 4 | 4 | 4 | 26 |
| Natural Sciences ....... | 4 | 4 | 4 | 5 | 5 | 5 | 27 |
| First foreign language [1]. | 7 | 7 | 5[4] | 4[3] | 4[3] | 4[3] | 31[27] |
| Second foreign language [1] | .. | .. | 4[5] | 3[4] | 3[4] | 3[4] | 13[17] |
| Drawing .............. | 2 | 2 | 2 | 2 | 2 | 2 | 12 |
| Total No. of Hours .. | 30 | 30 | 31 | 31 | 30 | 30 | 182 |

[1] Hours in brackets apply when French or Latin is second foreign language.

## 2. WITH THE GOAL OF THE OBERREALSCHULE

| SUBJECT | NUMBER OF HOURS IN CLASS | | | | | | |
|---|---|---|---|---|---|---|---|
| | U III | O III | U II | O II | U I | O I | Total |
| Religion .............. | 2 | 2 | 2 | 2 | 2 | 2 | 12 |
| German ............... | 4 | 4 | 4 | 4 | 4 | 4 | 24 |
| History (Civics) ....... | 3 | 3 | 2-1 | 3 | 3 | 3 | 18 |
| Geography ............ | 2 | 2 | 2 | 1 | 1 | 1 | 9 |
| Mathematics .......... | 6 | 6 | 5 | 5 | 5 | 5 | 32 |
| Natural Sciences ....... | 4 | 4 | 4 | 6 | 6 | 6 | 30 |
| First foreign language [1]. | 7 | 7 | 4 | 4 | 4[3] | 4[5] | 30[28] |
| Second foreign language [1] | .. | .. | 5 | 4 | 3[4] | 3[4] | 15[17] |
| Drawing .............. | 2 | 2 | 2 | 2 | 2 | 2 | 12 |
| Total No. of Hours .. | 30 | 30 | 31 | 31 | 30 | 30 | 182 |

[1] Hours in brackets apply when the second foreign language is French.

To these tables are to be added:—

U III-O I, each 4 hours physical training (see A)    Total.... 16 hours
U III-O I, Music ...........................    Total.... 16 hours
     Free activity group in upper section ....    Total.... 6 hours

                                                   Total.... 30 hours

## SUGGESTIONS FOR THE COURSES OF STUDY

1. The suggestions for the courses of study of the Prussian secondary schools are based on the memorandum of the Prussian Ministry of Science, Art, and Popular Education which dealt with the *New Regulation of the Prussian Secondary School System* (page 299). The task newly assigned to the secondary school, since the appearance of this memorandum, of giving preparatory education to the elementary school teachers, and also of taking over the responsibility for all popular education, had already been considered in the preparation of this memorandum.

2. The most important point of view for these suggestions is the organization of the secondary schools within the *Einheitsschule* and the preservation of German cultural unity in the diversity of the secondary school system. The subjects which impart German culture stand therefore as core subjects in all secondary schools. The central position of the core subjects assures the inner articulation of the secondary school with the *Volksschule* and of the secondary schools with one another.

3. The special purpose assigned to each type of school gives a special place to the subjects characteristic of it which define the peculiar objectives for its entire activity. These characteristic subjects perform this work in coöperation primarily with the core subjects, but at the same time in accordance with the peculiar claims of their objectives as academic subjects.

4. The educational and cultural work to be accomplished by the secondary schools makes an organic coördination of all subjects necessary, since education from the point of view of national consciousness, the state, sense of law, and community life, for community education in all fields of life and harmonious development of personality are only possible in a common educational activity reaching out over the individual subjects of instruction.

5. The *Arbeitsgemeinschaft* (activity group) of the teachers

required for this purpose, through consideration of the special cultural position of the community, of the characteristics of the people, and of the educational possibilities of the locality, will be able to place on the individual schools special stamp, which will be in keeping with the highly differentiated variety of life in Germany.

6. The courses of study to be drafted on the basis of these suggestions must be so flexibly organized that the choice of the instructional materials makes possible adaptation to the peculiar gifts of the teacher, to the direction of the various interests in the several years, and to the varying capacities of the pupils. In this way teaching objectives which have been postponed in one year may come into their own in another year; at the same time the danger of one-sidedness and formalism will be avoided.

7. The organization of the educational work on the basis of adolescent psychology demands in education and in instruction a constant consideration of the differences between the sexes and a consideration of the steps in their development and of their characteristic peculiarities. In the nine-year course of the secondary school, classes VI and V comprise the period of childhood (period of primary experience); IV to U II the age of boyhood and girlhood (period of intuitive knowledge), O II to O I the age of maturity (period of reflective thinking).

8. In all classes or levels the special gifts of the pupils are to be promoted and cultivated. Still it must not be overlooked that it is essential to meet justifiable demands in those subjects which cause the pupils difficulty if deficiencies and weaknesses which are present are to be overcome by energy and persistence. Premature surrender here is just as harmful as premature consideration of the demands of a particular vocation. For this reason the free activity periods are to be organized for the upper section only.

9. As organic parts of the German *Einheitsschule* the universities have the right to demand that the secondary schools send them suitable pupils for academic training. In the diversity of branches of study, however, the university entrance certificate to be issued by the secondary schools can refer only to the ability to do academic scientific work which has been acquired at these schools. Special knowledge going beyond this

in most cases must be afforded by the universities themselves on their own responsibility.

1. *Flexibility.* In order to assure the same stage of accomplishment in the different schools and in order to make possible the transfer from one school to another, the yearly objectives worked out in these *Suggestions* are compulsory. But in the choice of materials these *Suggestions* allow the courses of study of the schools a large degree of freedom. The attempt to master all of the subject matter, which has been presented in the *Suggestions* solely as guides in the year's work of the class concerned, would stand therefore in sharpest contradiction to the spirit of the entire instructional reform.

2. *Concentration.* The result of the instructional reform will quite essentially depend on whether it is possible in actual practice to modify the ever-recurring demand for concentration. The surrender of the idea of complete mastery of subject matter and of Schulze's conception of general training creates the external possibilities of such a realization. The educational unity of all schools in German culture affords the ideal goal for this unified instructional activity. The special task set for each type of school and the consequent grouping of subjects make, however, the objectives of this concentration characteristically different in every type of school. The stronger emphasis of the educational objective, the adoption as an aim of the harmonious development of personality, the demands of national, civic, and art education, and philosophical penetration affecting the several subjects require, in contrast to the former emphasis on subject matter, the coördination of the whole into an integrated instruction. The lack of relationship of the subjects, the excess of motives contending against one another, not only result in an overburdening of the pupils intellectually but also undermine the unity of the instructional purpose of the teaching staff.

The variety of the aims set up for the secondary school demands in every case pedagogical consideration as to how the principle of concentration can adapt itself to these different aims. In the whole objective of a class it will be necessary to fix the special work assigned to each individual subject and also set the time for its accomplishment.  Indeed, the work set aside for a single subject frequently needs assistance from other subjects; thus the development of high points and connections will be truly successful only if all subjects pertaining thereto will unite in a division and in a community of labor. The same holds true for the situation where the teachers as a working group desire to develop a definite, concrete "life cycle" into a well-rounded presentation.  Time must be arranged for one of the larger objectives assigned to a single subject in such a way that integrated instructional activity may be made possible, either by the teacher for a period of time using the hours which he has for the various other subjects for this one task, or by exchanging hours with other teachers.

While a number of subjects for the sake of their technical objectives will for the time being have to subordinate the consideration of concentration to the individual claims of the subject, the work to be accomplished in German *Kultur* by the different cultural subjects must always be considered as a unity. This unity in fact keeps everything in the school related which has existed together in the life of our people and which in its entirety makes up the spirit of an age.  In this manner, indeed, can the important epochs of our past be brought into view, and only if all subjects contribute to such a cross-section through the epochs involved (cross-section instruction).  In cases where great cross-sections of life, such as home, country, ancient world, are assigned to classes for their special educational problem, then all subjects as far as possible must serve this larger objective by tying up with this central purpose.  Where certain subjects cannot contribute to such a large project, they must try at least within their subject group to unify their work from a technical point of view.

Concentration during the year's work of a class must lead neither to the point where material related according to the natural organization of a single subject is separated nor to the point where the pupils through exhausting activity are surfeited with one and the same field of work.  In many cases, therefore, this integration will be taken up effectively only in the work of later classes by renewing once more earlier interests in the various subjects.  It would mean the mechanization of the principle of integration if one merely attempted to satisfy it by choosing the time for the treatment. The development of contrasts can also serve the integration of instruction.

The development of these ideas will be salutary for the secondary school, then, if the principle of integration is not overstrained; for an integrated instruction which puts an end to the individual claims of subjects is not in harmony with the objectives of the secondary school. The idea of integration has here its natural limits in the law of progress characteristic of each subject.

3. *Activity Instruction (Arbeitsunterricht)*. The instruction is fundamentally "activity instruction." It demands from the teacher that he, in the selection of material, never consider solely the transmission of knowledge as the purpose of his work, but that he be sure what powers of the pupil can be developed and increased by the school activity, especially independence of judgment, disposition, imagination, and will. The principle of "activity instruction" renders it necessary to organize the class activity into a community of activity of the pupils in a mutual give and take under the direction of the teacher. It is a question of giving this work a direction which is appropriate at once to the nature of the pupil and to the educational objective of the school. To bridge the natural gap between the acquisition of definite knowledge, without which higher intellectual activity is not possible, and the acquisition of the ability to do independent work, without which knowledge remains unproductive, is the earnest and great purpose of "activity instruction."

What forms of activity instruction are to be applied at times depends upon the nature of the material and the intellectual maturity of the pupil. However, in all class levels the pupil will have to acquire a purposeful technique of work. The selection of content may often depend on the suitability of the matter concerned for special methods of activity.

The success of the "activity instruction" will depend essentially upon the organization of the class activity in the division of labor and in coöperative work. The various home tasks assigned the individual pupils must serve the common purpose of the class. Reports on the progress of an instructional period, the discussion of which is a valuable form of review, have often proved fruitful in this sense.

As great provision as possible is to be afforded in activity instruction for questioning by the pupils for the purpose of clarification, intensification, and further discussion. Errors will then be avoided, if the pupils are enlightened about the object of the work which they have to do, since the joyous coöperation of the pupils is generally far increased, when the purpose and the meaning of the work demanded of them are explained, and if from time to time they are allowed to coöperate in the selection of materials and purposes. With the more mature pupils the whole educational activity carried on by them and for them is to be discussed from higher points of view.

The pupils' power of imagination and work will be especially developed if their characteristic gifts, for example, manual dexterity, imagination, inventive faculty, skill in expression and representation, are taken into account in their home work and in class instruction.

If the pupils as members of an "activity group" are trained in all parts of school to act independently and upon their own initiative, they will mature to the point of being able in the upper classes upon their own responsibility to apply methods of work to materials which they themselves have chosen. In this mastery of simpler scientific procedures they will at the same time produce proof of ability to enter the university.

4. *Home Work.* "Activity instruction" of itself will simplify and perfect the home work, for it will overcome the diversity of supervised tasks and the preponderance of pure memoriter work and will bring home work and school activity into a more intimate relationship. The reform of the home work is to increase the efficiency of the pupil and to avoid, as much as possible, the feeling of being overworked, which is not always due to the mere amount of work to be done.

The lack of interest so often connected with home work was occasioned formerly by its exaggerated value in the whole estimate of the child, especially when only the home work was counted as the basis for the certificate. The rating of the pupil even for the certificate will, indeed, have to be based upon all of his performances in instruction, which, to be sure, cannot be rendered in terms of marks in one period when the whole class is working together.

The teacher must consider training in method of doing home

work as an essential part of his instructional activity. Only in school can the technique of this activity be made the pupil's own, as, for example, the technique of learning by heart, of the preparation of foreign language reading materials, of the index, of collecting materials, of observation, and the correct use of auxiliary materials.

Further, the teacher will have to decide in which cases the school work is to take precedence over the home work, and the "group activity" precedence over the individual work of the pupil at home. The teacher must watch that the "class community" and the authority of the teacher increase the performance of work especially with young children; that, likewise real learning, practice, strengthening of bonds, review, often must be reserved for school work, while home work should provide opportunity for the development of the imagination, the power of association, and independent reflection.

Of course the sure acquisition of all grades of memoriter material essential to later instruction and to life is necessary; especially in this work is the power of retention in the period of childhood to be employed. The more that this memory work appears to the child as an activity of his own, undertaken of his own free will, so much the more will his feeling of responsibility grow. Through this free choice of memory material, for example, in German poetry, the joy of learning can be still more increased.

In the lower and middle sections a rigidly organized and executed activity instruction will so strain the powers of the youthful mind that only such home work should be assigned as is essential to instruction. Also, in the upper section the chief part of the work is to be done in school; however, here, and of course to an increasing degree, home work leading to independence must be demanded, the inner value of which can be discussed with the pupils themselves and in which consideration can be paid to a great degree to the interests and personal inclinations of the individual pupils.

The home work must grow out of the instruction and its results must be made valuable to the pupils by discussion before the whole class. Home work in which this is not possible, or the testing of which shortens the time of the instruction excessively, is to be avoided.

Special tasks set for individual pupils, which "activity instruction" makes necessary, will develop a feeling for the value of the work more easily than if the work is undertaken of their own free will. Only in this manner is a moral value possible for home work; to a certain degree this applies to such activities as are performed in the service of the community life of the school. In these activities also such talents of the pupils will come into their own, which, as manual dexterity and artistic talents, otherwise very easily were allowed to remain idle during school life.

5. *Written Class Exercises.* According to the necessities of "activity instruction," which correspond throughout to the ideas underlying the so-called Decree on Themes (*Extemporale-Erlass*) of October 21, 1911, the written class work must grow organically out of the instruction and must be related to the regular class exercises. In this manner the written class exercises lose essentially their character as examinations. Therefore, only such assignments should be made as an average pupil can really perform in the given time, but which, however, call for a certain independence. Then these exercises will no longer be an oppressive burden to the pupil but will bring him the pleasure of success. Minor written exercises in the class as preparation for the major class exercises are indispensable. Their perusal will often give the teacher better indications of the ability of the pupils than the infrequent, comprehensive exercises. The further special preparations and reviews, still somewhat necessary for the work in class, must in no case be assigned for home work; they are essentially to be taken up in class because they could easily lead to overloading.

Only occasionally will the written class exercises serve as examinations, and even then the mechanical addition of errors without reference to the effort put into the work must not alone be decisive in the judgment rendered.

An examination of the work, which estimates the presence or absence of effort, will frequently be preferable to a mathematical judgment arrived at by the customary marks. In the lower and middle classes this can generally be done quickly. However, the exercises of the more mature pupils will demand a more exhaustive examination which will, by its form, call the attention of the pupil to the importance of his work. In the reports where a pupil's written work is to be marked by way of exception this judgment must be based not only upon the few written exercises but must consider all of his written work.

As far as possible in the class exercises the same helps (texts, dictionaries, tables, and formulæ) should be at the disposal of the more mature pupils as those which they have been trained to use constantly in their home work.

If the teacher, in examining the notebooks, should see that he has overestimated the ability of his class, he will then need to set a new exercise of a more suitable nature and in general entirely reject the judgment based upon the first work.

6. *The "Free-Activity Groups" (Freie Arbeitsgemeinschaften)*. The hours set aside in the program for free-activity groups will serve for deepening and enlarging the educational work to be performed by the type of school in question. They are, therefore, not to be used for elective instruction or for subjects not taken care of in the curriculum. Nor must they be used to increase the weekly hours definitely prescribed for all in the course of study, since participation in them must be absolutely voluntary. The point of departure, therefore, in their organization is essentially to be found in the interests of the pupils. All subjects of instruction of the type of school in question can be considered in this connection. It will be the duty of the faculty to take care that within one school year as many subjects as possible are included in this free activity of groups. It is accordingly desirable that the hours available be redistributed at least every half-year. In this distribution the program of work fixed for the whole year will be appropriately considered. But in every case, on account of its importance an activity group of one hour a week throughout the whole year should be arranged for reading in philosophy except as the Provincial School Board believes that for administrative reasons this ought to be postponed for a period of time. The "activity groups" in philosophy will seek to establish special relationships to the courses characteristic of the individual types of schools.

The regular curricular-activity groups will frequently stimulate student societies (*Schülervereine*). They will indeed not make unnecessary in any way the voluntary work already being done by many teachers with groups of pupils.

7. *Teachers' "Activity Group."* The reorganization upon

the educational and instructional principles of the school reform makes necessary a teachers' "activity group," in which
the natural cleavage between the subject interests and concentration, between the individual right of strong personalities and
the educational necessities of the special type of school, must
be settled in the spirit of freedom and responsibility. On the
director in particular devolves the weighty and responsible task,
in the unification of the work of the school, of welding the
teachers together as parts of a whole and of giving free play to
their abilities. Only then will it be possible to organize the
special talents of the teachers in such a way that they give to
their school a characteristic individuality.

Beyond the common discussions in conferences in which the
whole faculty, the technical teachers, the representatives of the
subject groups, and the class teachers, each according to the
question under consideration, come together, unity must be assured by mutual visitation, through coöperative experimentation with methods of instruction, and through reference to
new publications. It is to be recommended that individual
teachers be entrusted over a period of time with making regular
reports on certain questions. Exchange of opinion with teachers
of other schools, including those of the *Volksschule*, middle
schools, and technical schools, will be especially effective for the
common task of promoting German educational unity.

One of the most important functions of the "activity group"
is the working out of the course of study of the school, for which
the experiences of the other schools can be turned to good account
by a system of exchanges. It is also a function of the teachers'
"activity group" to advise the pupils in their more important
undertakings and in the selection of their own free "activity
groups." Generally no pupil in *Prima* with more than four
hours beyond the regular curricular work may take part in
the free "activity groups" or in elective work. However, a
class conference has the right, according to the nature of the
case, to lessen the number of hours which shall be approved
for the individual pupil, and also to increase it in the case of
specially gifted pupils.

In the integration of the instruction, the "activity group"
of teachers of a class will have to arrive at an individual judgment of the pupils not only for the general marks for the

reports but also for a similar evaluation of such results as develop in the several subjects; for instance, the power of expression, sureness of style, artistic skill, logical judgment, power of observation, and the like. If these observations are determined for a single pupil and extend over the whole period of school life, they will round out the whole picture of the pupil and make possible a complete view of his development.

It is to be expected that difficulties will frequently arise in the administrative execution of required regulations, as, for example, in mutual visitation, in interchange of periods, in the remission of school work for the larger home exercises of the pupils, in fixing the date in which the more important class exercises are to be written. These difficulties can only be solved if the teachers have acquired by means of this "activity group" a sympathetic understanding among themselves.

# V

# NOTES ON METHODS FOR THE INDIVIDUAL SUBJECTS OF INSTRUCTION

## EVANGELICAL RELIGION

Evangelical religious instruction seeks to reveal to the pupils the truths of the Evangelical faith in their Biblical foundations, their reformed organization, and their historical development, and thus prepare them for life in their church community. Its highest purpose will always be to awaken and advance the religious life of the pupils. It will, however, also be conscious of the limits which are set for instruction, especially class instruction. Its most important means is a living conception of the great personalities, through whom the Christian religion, especially of the Evangelical faith, has developed its being, and an intensive appreciation of the historical periods in which the spirit of these personalities continued to live. True to traditions of German Protestantism religious instruction must be marked in a like degree by religious as by scientific earnestness. If it traces carefully the interrelations between religion and general culture, it will avoid the risk of dismissing religion as a cultural phenomenon. It seeks only to define the eternal at that place where it has revealed itself in time and space, and will always, specially in the consideration of the high points of religious life, aim to direct the attention of the pupils to the eternal background of all temporal matter. It will also show them how the Christian religion as a part of European culture has helped to develop ideals and how in the present it can give meaning to the general cultural as well as the vocational activity of the individual. The instruction will also seek to inculcate in the pupils respect for all real religious life, even when it appears in strange garments, or in the guise of passionate denial.

The purpose varies more at different age levels in religious instruction than in other subjects because attitudes toward religion are subject to far greater changes. In the lower section most of the children bring from home the still unbroken faith of childhood and devotion to church customs, and where this is no longer the case, as often in the large city, at least a feeling for the clear, impressive form of the Bible stories, in which the fundamental truths of the Christian religion are given them. The purpose of instruction here is to fill the children with joy in the characters and events of the Old Testament and with love for the personality of Jesus; and to equip them with a first appreciation of the religious life surrounding them and, by drilling upon the most important material, to enable them to conduct themselves as long as they live with assurance in points of church ritual.

In the middle section, the pupil, still without being attacked by actual doubts, is especially inflexible toward direct religious influence. Here, therefore, the school instruction must restrain itself, also out of consideration for the church confirmation instruction which is given at the same time. In addition to the Biblical materials there come into the foreground stories from church history which should be chosen so that they satisfy the capacity for enthusiasm of this age, the sense for the heroic, the joy in sharply characteristic types. For the girls, especially, women saints and heroines are to be selected. In *Untersekunda* for the pupils who are leaving, the most important problems of life are to be illuminated from the point of view of principles found in the New Testament. Earlier instruction dealing with the Holy Scripture and church forms should also be summarized and rounded out so that the pupils leaving are in the position to take part in time in the life of the community. Girls on leaving should in particular be familiarized with the important duties of the woman in the Evangelical community.

In the upper section the problem is to impart a thorough understanding of Christian truth and to adjust it to other spiritual forces that have formed the German culture of to-day, an adjustment which is all the more urgent since the general crisis of the adolescent years in the case of nearly all boys and of very many girls expresses itself in the form of doubt concerning traditional truth and the value of the traditional form of social life. Religious instruction in these years again encounters great interest, but also sharp mistrust, which can only be overcome by absolute honesty. Which of the theological positions within the Evangelical church the teacher of religion represents must be left to his conscience. In any event his instruction can only be convincing if the pupils feel that behind the words of the teacher there is a conviction which rests upon deeper bases than those which can be proved by reason. Since, aside from some definite believers or unbelievers, the large part of the pupils as a rule will consist of those seeking and doubting and since the conclusion of this crisis lies beyond the short years in school, so religious instruction must content itself with creating satisfactory conditions for the later individual religious decision. It would achieve this soonest if it made the pupils see that an earnest and honest adjustment with religion is an indispensable educational task for a human being. Whether this adjustment proceeds more from problems of attitude toward the world, or, as perhaps in girls' schools, more from the problems of life, depends upon the spiritual attitude of the class. If the teacher is permitted to lead the children not only into the antechamber of religion, but more deeply into sacred things, he will find this the highest reward of his work. The pupils should at all times have the assurance that the teacher of religion has a warm heart for them in all their needs. It is a duty of honor for the teacher to preserve the religious character of the devotional exercises of the school and to order them in such a way that teachers and mature pupils take part in them gladly and with spiritual profit.

Religious instruction is like all other instruction, "activity instruction." It is associated with that which has been unconsciously experienced, shows how to use sources, makes voluntary home activities of the pupils valuable for all by discussion in the class. Its form is chiefly conversational; at important points it also affords room for lectures by the teacher. The pupil is to work out for himself the heroes of religion by use of the Bible and church history sources, and out of contact with them to sense that which cannot be worked out. The teacher, important as is his personality, is only a means to this end. Free "activity groups" for delving into the important historical problems or burning life problems will be desired by many pupils in the upper section. If they are to be full of life, the pupils must be given the assurance that they may express themselves with absolute freedom. It is desirable that a definite source be used as the basis of the common work in order that exchange of opinion is not lost in the limitless.

Religious instruction works hand in hand with the other core subjects. Christianity as a historical religion can only be understood in connection with world history; the characteristically German type of Christianity is only intelligible in the range of the whole German spiritual life. Religious instruction should be in constant and close contact with instruction in art and music. Not infrequently it will be possible, especially in the lower and middle sections, to permit lessons in religion to end in singing a song or in joyous appreciation of a picture. In the upper section the religious instruction will show numerous instances of motifs which the Christian religion has furnished for music and painting, architecture and sculpture. It will strive in this to awaken in the pupils the feeling that art as well as religion springs from the utmost depths of the human soul and that under certain circumstances the inmost religious feeling of a period expresses itself in purest form in art— Gothic architecture, Bach's music. Above all, however, religious instruction will seek to arouse in the pupils the comprehension of the great spiritual work which the Christian religion has performed for mankind in the adjustment with reasoning consciousness. It will show how the Christian Church in the periods of living faith has always had the strength to make an adjustment with the important intellectual influences of the time with the same weapons. It will especially emphasize the point how during the German Reformation religion and science formed an alliance which had to be formed anew by each succeeding epoch in its own manner. Finally, it will show the pupils how, in the sense of this alliance, the Evangelical Church considers state and social regulations as ''good gifts of God'' and work in earthly existence as the most important means for the fulfillment of life hereafter; how from this point of view, in different forms, in Lutheran and Calvinistic countries, it has as a people's church penetrated the whole life of the people with the ennobling influences of religion and does so still to-day. Religious instruction will thus open up to the pupil an understanding for the fact that this interpenetration between religion and art gives a world of meaning to Protestantism, which extends far beyond the influence of its organized churches into the general spiritual life. It will, however, not neglect the quiet, corrective activity of the Church in this respect, and its importance for counterbalancing contradictory social principles.

Within the individual types of schools efforts will be made to link up instruction with the subject groups characteristic of them. So in the *Gymnasium* the importance of ancient philosophy or the development of Christian principles of faith and morality, the importance of Aristotle for the organization of the mediæval age, the connection of humanism with the Reformation, all will be discussed intensively. The modern language *Gymnasium* will emphasize particularly the European connections of the most important ecclesiastical and religious movements, for example, monasticism, scholasticism and mysticism, the Reformation, the Enlightenment, and the revival of religious life about the beginning of the nineteenth century. The *Oberrealschule* will concern itself particularly with the adjustment of the Christian religion with research in natural science at different periods, but chiefly, of course, in the present period. In every particular must instruction take the difference between the sexes into consideration. It must consider that, in the Christian Church, from the beginning women's piety, whose characteristic is an all-enduring love, was equal to that of men, whose fundamental feature is an all-daring faith; and it must make allowance for this inner difference between the two identical yet complementary types in choice and treatment of the subject matter.

It will always bring to the front both points of view; however, in boys' schools it will primarily represent Christianity as a militant and rousing force, deeply affecting the history of the world and giving rise to problems of secular philosophy, while in girls' schools it will be taught more as a soothing, balancing force which heals wounds and solves life's problems. Pronounced women Christian characters and significant organizations of women's charitable activities must be carefully evaluated in girls' schools.

The most important memory material, whose content should be of vital importance and artistically organized, must be continued to the conclusion of *Tertia* and then constantly repeated. From *Untersekunda* on there comes, in addition to this, chiefly voluntary learning of single passages from the Bible and other writings in which religious feeling is expressed in artistic form. Individual portions of the Catechism and individual Bible selections are to be connected as far as possible with Bible stories. Church songs, in which the text and melody are always to be learned together, are to be treated according to the same principles on which other literary masterpieces are taught. It is neither possible, nor necessary, to explain every detail to the pupils. The school is able only to provide a beginning and a preliminary understanding for religious truths. Thus by making this earnest and most impressive form in which these religious truths are clothed a permanent possession, the school creates the indispensable foundation for later deepening of this understanding by means of inner and external life experiences.

### CATHOLIC RELIGION

1. *General.* Catholic religious instruction has for its purpose the transmission to the pupils of the divine revelation intrusted to the Church in order to train them by this means to be pious, devout Christians. The foundation is the belief in the supernatural character of the Catholic religion and the conviction concerning the moral and religious forces of the Catholic Church as a teacher of truth and as the means of grace. Its purpose is the living connection between God and Christ, the Son of God, the introduction into the religious community in obedience toward ecclesiastical authority, participation in a life of grace by means of the sacrament and the liturgy, performance of Catholic principles of life in private, social, and public life.

Although the educational values of the Church are the same for all boys and girls and the unity of the religious training must be preserved as far as possible, yet regard must be paid to the individual types of schools in the choice and treatment of subject matter,—in the humanistic *Gymnasium* to the ancient culture, in the *Realgymnasium* to modern culture, in the *Oberrealschule* to the mathematics-natural science culture, and in the German *Oberschule* to German culture. The same applies to girls' schools each in accordance with its particular purpose.

The individuality of the sexes demands more attention than the peculiarity of the type of school, and not merely in personal influence, but also in the choice and treatment of the subject matter. If religious instruction is to be worth while for group activity and education, it must fit in with the characteristics of both young boys and girls, it must take into consideration their range of activities and their future vocations. Growing boys, in view of their calmer, more reasoning character, need an especially careful development of clear concepts of faith and a deeper foundation of their religious life. A vivid description of the leading religious personalities from the Church history must give content and direction to their vigorous aspiration and ability for enthusiasm for everything great. Constant introduction to an inner life of prayer and to an honest, definite expression of faith must equip them with humility and steadfastness in the battles of life. On the other hand, in the case of girls, their predominating tendency is to the concrete and the personal; their peculiar, aesthetic, ethical, and religious feeling and aspiration are not to be overlooked, but great value is to be attached to accurate thinking and steadfast purpose. The importance and functions of the woman for the family, state, and church are to be developed in all sections of the schools.

The vigorous organization of religious instruction is served by concentration of instruction as well by the correlation of its individual parts as by its correlation with the other subjects of instruction, so that the valuable relationships that exist between life and religion appear. In this case the coöperation of the pupils in accordance with the principles of "activity instruction" is to be sought to the greatest extent, beginning with the religious observation and instruction in *Sexta* and continuing up to free discussion of religious problems in *Prima*. Very frequently this should be tied up with real experiences of the children, taking the Bible story and the rich life of the Church as the starting point. Thus, this working over and working out in the class will lead of itself to the penetrating understanding of the truth and educate for life out of faith. With all respect for these sound principles of the "activity school" the nature, of course, of Catholic religious instruction as the mediator of a revealed faith must be assured and the danger of leading to *subjectivism* and *rationalism* avoided.[1]

---

[1] See the suggestions of the Bishops' Conference at Fulda on August 18, 1924, concerning the ideas of the "activity school" as applied to religious instruction.

The triple sectioning of the secondary school into lower, middle, and upper sections demands differences in the selection of subject matter and in its treatment. In the lower section, the teacher of religion teaches concretely the Word of God. The pupil accepts it willingly and with faith, memorizes the essentials and fixes good habits in moral, religious, and church life. In the middle section, the ethics corresponding to the needs of this stage of development are thoroughly discussed and grounded, the theology more comprehensively treated, and the richness of the life of grace more clearly revealed. In this, the pupils are led to work through and develop the material themselves and also to progress in their education toward Catholic thought and action. In the proper section the religious instruction has to do with the abstract conception of the Catholic doctrine, the development of general points of view and problems, the comparison with other views, the training of a religious-moral personality which firmly and reasonably stands in contrast to intellectual life of the times and in joyous living with Christ and the Church, striving toward eternity. The independence of the pupil is furthered by lectures from source material, by free discussion and stimulation to free moral conduct. The teacher of religion will thus stand in this section at the pupil's side particularly as his friend and guide.

2. *Individual Divisions of the Subject.* In accordance with foregoing fundamental directions, instruction in the separate divisions of religious instruction will be organized in somewhat the following manner. Instruction in catechism offers the elementary truths of religion, and naturally each according to its particular nature in concrete or developmental form. Since it is a question of fundamental truths, they are to be made the secure possession of the memory. More mature pupils can be trained to deliver in recitation rather small portions of the Catechism in connected form. Of course it is not sufficient to develop religious knowledge merely; the conscience must be thoroughly trained. Above all must the consciousness of his adoption be impressed upon the pupil, a fact which the first chapter of the creed proves, whose realization is presented by the second chapter of the commandments taught as ethics, and finally whose attainment the third chapter of means of grace demonstrates.

Doctrine in the upper section must not serve to transmit technical, theological knowledge. The material of faith of the church is represented in its truth and beauty, in its impressive majesty, and in its harmonious completeness. With constant consideration for the scientific intellectual struggle its trustworthiness is found and proved. The life values inherent in it are to be made more intelligible and fruitful.

The apologetic subject matter is incorporated in the whole make-up of the creed. The purpose here is not so much to prove religious convictions, as to strengthen convictions already held. In the dogma relating to the Church the corresponding apologetic questions will be incorporated. The Church is to be represented as the "pillars and foundations of truth," as the ever-living Christ, to associate oneself in whose community is considered a duty and a good deed. The discussion of the ecclesiastical doctrine of Christ's person and work will afford the pupil a clear picture of the struggle against belief in Christ; the attitude of our day toward faith in Christ must show itself clearly. The whole conception of Christ is to awaken in the pupil the acknowledgment: "For to me to live *is* Christ . . ." Phil. 1:21. The doctrines of God's nature and works combine with the apology for the belief in God and therein modern agnosticism will receive proper consideration.

Since the cultivation of character and morality is the most important purpose of religious instruction, it must, therefore, continue through all sections. Ethics as a special objective, however, is reserved for *Prima,* and it stands in closest community of opinion with all subjects. It touches most widely the instruction in German, so far as it has for its content the delineation of character and the development of moral personality. The instructor in religion sees and evaluates the ethical results of the more important philosophical systems and shows the ideal conception of Catholic morality: the union of the soul with God in acknowledgment and love, the fulfillment of His Holy Will in their lives, and the labor for the Kingdom of God and for the bringing to pass of His divinely willed purposes on Earth. Thus ethics becomes virtue. Family and state are confirmed as the outpouring of God's will. The notion of real tolerance and inner national unity with all elements of our people is zealously cultivated. Discussion in class of ethical questions and free activity groups are to be given plenty of scope and thus will afford preparation for both life and the university.

The history of God's kingdom upon earth is offered in the lower and middle sections in connection with the Bible story in stimulating narrative form. Embellishment may only be allowed upon the basis of genuine Biblical fact. Study of the Bible and Biblical geography will be linked at suitable opportunities with the treatment of the Bible history. Bible reading in moderate limits of time and material is to serve to arouse religious life. First of all a clear picture of the divine Saviour must rise before the pupils' eyes. Likewise other personalities both male and female advance to meet the religious, ethical feelings of the youth and bring about a school beyond compare. Introductory and critical questions are to be limited to a minimum. Less important portions can be assigned for home reading while the explanation, intensification, and appreciation will remain for class work. In particularly important sections, impressive reading in class after the explanation is of great value. The purpose of Bible reading is not to give many books but to lead to an independent reading of the Word of God by means of the correct reading of a few books. In addition to the German text of the New Testament the employment of the original text is important if it is possible. The verbatim acquisition of classical selections is recommended.

Church history introduces the youth to the internal and external development of the Gospel dispensation of Christ. In connection with the study of the home (*Heimatkunde*) the lower section becomes acquainted with the lives of saints from near-by localities. In treating biographies and cultural cross-sections in the middle classes, the range of view widens over the history of the whole church, in which the most important facts and figures must be drilled upon in preparation for the real instruction in Church history. The upper section summarizes by reviews and free recitations the most important events and ideas in the struggles and development of the Church both in cross-section and in developmental views. Still these facts are not presented for their own sake. It is valuable through them to arouse the capacity for enthusiasm and the heroic sense of the youth as well as to further their love and adherence to the

Church, whether it is that the fulfillment of prophecies is apparent in it, or its fruitful effect upon mankind in culture and morals is demonstrated, or its victorious self-assertion is proved. In the pupil the conviction must gradually mature that the divine Christ reveals Himself in the earthly power of the Church and that the joyous acceptance of ecclesiastical guidance and the willing submission to the purposes of the Church is nothing else than service to Christ Himself.

The Liturgy, which fundamentally represents common divine worship, is in the highest degree at the same time confession of faith and homage, symbol and mediation of divine favor. Therefore, the liturgical instruction is to lead the pupil to feel himself in communion with God as a member of a community struggling in battle and distress toward God, also approaching Him not only with petitions and requests, but above all, with care, and love, and gratitude. If he gives himself in such frame of mind to the spirit of the Liturgy, his soul will be found always more and more with the divine. These ideas control the pupil's life of prayer, as to content and form. In all classes the desire to pray must be renewed ever again. The acquisition and use of good prayers and songs in the middle and upper sections, also psalms and hymns of intrinsic value—will accompany the instruction in order to acquire forms for prayer that will last throughout life. In this work the seasons of the church year are to be carefully observed, since in general the Liturgy is to lead to life with Christ and the Saints. Especial value is to be placed upon an appropriate celebration and organization of the divine service at the school. For this reason, familiarity should be developed with the diocesan song and prayer book and later, where it is possible, also with the Roman Missal. The inner content of the sacrifice of the Mass is to be disclosed more thoroughly from grade to grade; likewise a thorough presentation of the historical-liturgical development of the *ordo missae* in the upper section will develop fruitfully personal participation in the Holy Sacrifice. If with this there goes hand in hand a fine cultivation of the liturgical eucharistic stimulus, the sacramental life of grace of the pupils will be developed and heightened in every way.

The liturgical discussions lead of themselves to an explanation of the noblest forms of religious music and art. On the whole, reference in all classes to the masterpieces of all ages and their creators must train the aesthetic sense in the service of religious life.

From section to section the young Christian thus develops more and more into a free, pious, morally strong personality who thinks and lives with the Christ and who labors apostolically. In this the teacher of religion is not only the teacher but also the responsible guide and adviser. Therefore he must distinguish himself by an exemplary religious life, through zeal for souls and scholarly training. He will try to understand ever more profoundly the spiritual character of the pupils in accordance with their age and sex and always seek to adapt himself more completely thereto. Supplementary means, such as a pupil's religious library, exercises, celebration of confirmation in the Church, will serve him well. He will further the Marian Congregations and the Youth Movement in its healthy, worthwhile forms, and win and assure the support of parents for the accomplishment of his purposes. Above all he will commend to God and His mercy, in prayer and sacrifice every day, the youth intrusted to him.

### GERMAN

In German instruction the pupils are to learn to read and write German, to feel, think, and live in German. They are to be trained to a sure command of their mother tongue and to a vital conception of the cultural values which arise from the language itself, from the literature and art, and from the resources of a living people. The prerequisite for the experience of these intellectual values is earnest, intellectual work. Hence, while German instruction must be carried on in a scientific spirit, it must not lose sight of its goal beyond the scientific,— namely, education for a spiritual goal, and courageous, joyous Germanism. In a special sense German instruction can be pleasant work because the pupil already brings with him the understanding of the mother tongue and of the people, as well as of the surrounding environment, the spiritual foundations and conditions for that which he desires to make his own intellectually.

1. *School Speech.* The language of the school is the High German colloquial speech which is customary in the cultural

circles of the particular district. Its dialectical turn is to be brought to the attention of the pupils. Obvious dialectical crudities are to be eliminated gradually through use and instruction. The language of the stage is the model for all dignified speech. It is not the function of the school to teach dialect. It will, however, be well to try to cultivate it in a place where an indigenous dialect is found, since it frequently enters in for linguistic discussions, encourages pupils who master it to use it occasionally in class, and draws these pupils togther into a little activity group for the cultivation of dialectical literature.

2. *Speech Training.* Speech training is necessary during the whole school experience. It begins with breathing, phonic, and free speech exercises which proceed as soon as possible from the purely physical to the physical-intellectual exercise. In *Sexta* and *Quinta* the foundation is laid, especially with the pupils who do not bring the correct habits with them from previous classes. In the later years the objective must be kept in mind in every form of speech of the pupils, and above all in speaking, reading, and declaiming. The developmental obstructions which threaten in the period of puberty, with the change of voice, must be avoided. In constant contact with music and foreign language instruction the pupil is brought to the point where he is conscious of his own voice and speech according to tone and peculiarity of expression. He should be led to a natural, living, purposeful, thoughtful manner of speech.

3. *Reading.* The art of thoughtful and expressive reading must be practiced early and continued in the highest classes, and, of course, in all subjects. Good reading has its own value, for it requires the pupil to pay attention to the outer and inner forms of speech, and through interpretation familiarizes him with the structure and means of expression of the sentence and larger linguistic forms. It is at the same time a valuable stimulus to comprehension and generally also the best proof thereof. Real skill in reading can only be attained if the teacher does not allow regular model reading to discourage the pupil, and when the pupil is not daunted by patient, careful rereading. Unprepared reading is only to be practiced on subject matter adapted thereto.

4. *Memoriter Learning.* Memoriter learning stands in close connection with reading. Good reading is one of the most im-

portant aids to memorization. Every poem that is to be learned
by heart, therefore, must be not only discussed and read aloud
in class, but also carefully re-read. For home work the teacher
will take pains to give the pupils the necessary assistance, especially in consideration of the memory-type to which they belong. Suitable time is to be allowed for the recitation, that the
sentiment of the poem may not be destroyed during the recitation. Natural expression in the recitation of the poem is to
be encouraged, reasonable individuality of the pupils is to be
respected, and inclination to the dramatic, the affected, the unc-
tuous is to be discouraged. A small list of poems to be memorized, both ballads and lyric songs, the latter in agreement with
the music teacher, should be arranged and thoroughly drilled,
and regularly reviewed. It is to be emphasized that whole
poems and not merely single stanzas are to be the permanent
possessions of the pupils. In addition to this the pupils should
be stimulated to memorize poems voluntarily and, in the upper
section, effective prose selections for style, and to repeat both
readily before the class.

5. *Oral Exercises.* Through oral exercises the pupil is to be
trained to the point of saying what he has to say correctly in
an orderly fashion, with expression, and without embarrassment.
An important means to that end is to promote the joy of children in story-telling, and to maintain and cultivate the natural
freshness of their expression, and their natural language of
gesture. This ease is destroyed if the pupil is interrupted and
corrected at each little linguistic or factual error or if he is
forced in contrast to other conversational speech to speak in
the so-called "whole sentences" only. The chief material of
the oral exercises in the lower section is the pupil's own experiences and reproduction of stories. Where the pupil only reports on material assigned to him, he is to be trained to strip
the thought of the subject of its form and to give it a new garb
from his own experience. In the middle section, in which especially the boys often hide their inner thoughts, pure subject
matter observations are to be recommended, and in the upper
section also short reports by pupils on self-selected subjects,
following preparation at home. In longer reports the pupils
are to be encouraged to be content with key words and to leave
the linguistic form for the moment, in order thus to mature

gradually into a completely free delivery. It is important that the pupil accustom himself to speak before the whole class and to look his audience in the face. To require a certain position of him is to train him to be unnatural. A discussion will usually follow the recitation which will keep in mind the proper form of recitation as well as the recitation of the poems. The judgment of the class is always to be called for first. By means of report for and against, or through free discussion of a definite question, the pupils are to be trained for ready criticism, but always in the considered forms of cultivated conversation. The teacher in these recitations, by example and by influence, will accustom the pupils to respect the intellectual efforts of their comrades, and in the discussions to strive for facts and for respect for the convictions of others. An important means in training pupils in this spirit is the preparation of notes dealing with such discussion, and on occasions also on lectures and individual class recitations.

6. *Written Exercises.* The written exercises are to train in clear organization, systematic arrangement of thought, and natural and forceful expression. At first, they are connected with the oral exercises, but in time branch off from them through the more careful structure and the sharper organization which the written presentation demands, since the aids of intonation and gesture are lacking. The imaginative essay, narrative, and report are to be followed by the descriptive essay. Pupils are to be trained to the observation of character details and to the mastery of the means of literary expression, especially to fine shades and tones of expression. Later the logically arranged treatment is added to these forms. Difficulties inherent in the matter must not, through exaggerated demands, be increased by stress on a minutely detailed classification and an exhaustive treatment of the material. There should be avoided subjects that are beyond the comprehension of the pupils as well as those that depend only on collection of materials or memory work. In class composition dealing with literary topics the book can be placed in the pupils' hands. The most important forms of the treatment must be made clear to the pupils. The comprehension for inner arrangement is to be practiced through suitable reading selections and by means of definite problems set up especially for this purpose. Certain freedom is to be allowed the

pupils in the choice of subjects for themes. Usually the teacher should set up a number of topics for selection. He will so proceed in the selection of these topics that nearly every ability will be taken care of. At times he can also allow the pupil to choose his own topic, subject to his approval. However, the pupils must, if they are to be trained for reality and for fitness in life, be confronted with a very definite common task in which no consideration is paid to special abilities or inclinations. Such assignments can frequently be taken out of the German instruction, and also from other branches of study, in case the German teacher has the necessary supervision of the field. In the development of the theme, independent organization, independent judgment, tendencies toward personal modes of expression, should be evaluated as points of excellence. In the middle section, the beginning of the adolescent years, accompanied by the desire for reading which often sets in, leads in the majority of children to a loss of the simplicity of childish expression and to a mode of expression in which their own and that of others are curiously confused. In the upper section, the outspoken subjectivity of the period of maturity will express itself in content in a marked state of inconsistency. The teacher who knows that these transitions are unavoidable will consider it his duty to lead the pupils with inner comprehension through these difficulties. In general, in the course of the year, about eight compositions should be written; in the majority of cases these should be class compositions for which a period of two or three hours on the average might suffice on occasions; however, more extensive developments, taking the whole forenoon, are permissible. Larger independent pieces of work of the pupil are to be encouraged in every way. They can take the place of one or of several home-compositions. Besides the composition, shorter written exercises, such as shorter observations, descriptions, portrayals of situations, characterizations, also subject matter classification and paraphrases are often worthy of commendation. They are to train particularly for accuracy and pertinence of expression.

In the lower section special spelling exercises are necessary. Here the starting point is that accuracy in spelling is based upon the close association of word- and meaning-images and that the certainty of the word-image depends upon the intimate penetration of the sensation of sound, sight, and movement. Every word, whose spelling is to be drilled for the first time, must, therefore, first be explained; then it must not only be carefully pronounced by the teacher and then by the pupils but also be written in script on the board and copied by the pupils. Rules shall only be given if they are simple and purposeful. Reasons are given in case they can be easily made clear to the pupil. Dictations serve for practice in what has been learned. Every dictation must be a connected whole, interesting to the pupil, and should omit all trivialities. Unusual words and subtle rules, such as those concerning capital and small letters, are not to be drilled upon; rather the pupils are to be introduced to the official rule and word list and to be held to its use in both home and school work. An excessive rating should not be assigned to his performance in spelling in the final estimate of a pupil's ability in German.

Correction of written work aims at advancing the pupil intellectually. It must look for what the writer had in mind, and point out his errors to him. Care must be taken that the pupil seriously follows these suggestions. Therein lies an essential prerequisite of his progress. In the working out of details the pupil should be led to find the correct form by his own reflection. Written corrections must be required only of errors in grammar and style. Typical errors, which appear in a number of papers, are discussed in class in common. In this the teacher avoids everything which will offend or discourage the pupils. Especially will he guard himself against exposing weak efforts or failures before the whole class; rather he will do everything in order to preserve in the pupil the joy of writing which so many in these years lose forever. He will praise what there is to praise, and recognize good and distinctive efforts as such. In the compositions it is particularly necessary that judgment be recorded not merely by a mark but also by some comment.

7. *Grammar*. Grammar seeks to arouse and fix in the pupil a clear concept of the meaning and the value of his mother tongue and a sound judgment about the correct and incorrect, about what is good and unsuitable in its use. German grammar must give the pupil the basic categories of the linguistic knowledge and thus on this foundation lay the basis for grammar instruction in the foreign languages. Only in the mother tongue does the pupil possess the natural feeling for language which

enables him to understand directly the facts and processes of language.  Only in the mother tongue is he able to trace behind the linguistic form the formative spiritual force which has created the form.  Only in the mother tongue can he experience the original imagery of human speech and in it realize the real creative force of the people.  Grammar in the secondary schools seeks, since the elements are already known to the pupil from the days of the *Grundschule,* to enable the pupil to create for himself an insight into the genius of the structure of the language. It proceeds from the sentence as the organic form in which all parts derive their meaning from their relation to the whole.  It makes clear linguistic phenomena in the light of psychological proofs; it draws attention to the relation of punctuation to the structure of the sentence or to the classification of the expression.  Uniform grammatical terminology is essential for every school.

In the upper and middle sections grammar expands on the one hand into history of the language and on the other hand into principles of style or rhetoric.  The historical consideration of language is already prepared for in the lower section by individual examples of change of sound and meaning, by reference to borrowed or foreign words, to older forms which are familiar to the pupil from literature, proverbs, dialectical and other popular expressions, but in such a manner, however, that the so-called irregularities will always appear as unused regular forms. Connected instruction dealing with the history of the language covers, from Rudolf Hildebrand's point of view, not only the change of the sounds, but also that of the forms, sentence structure, and word meaning.  It does not place the chief emphasis upon individual facts, but seeks in the more mature pupils to build up comprehension as to how the language as a social organism, as ever-changing as all life, has developed from the most ancient times to the present and how it has been the oldest and for every age the truest mirror of our race, its history, and its view of world affairs.  The importance of idioms, their relation to High German and to conversational speech is thereby clarified.  The pupils are to be introduced to the nature and purpose of the German dictionary.  The relation of original, borrowed, and foreign words is to be explained in the light of the history of culture.  It will be a pleasing task to estimate the rich and pictured treasures of the German language, especially those reflections of earlier cultural conditions which remain in so many words and phrases. Attention will be called on every occasion to the agreements and differences of the organizations of the German language in comparison with Latin, Greek, English, or French. In *Prima* what has been acquired will be summarized, and the pupils shown how the intellectual attitude of a nation likewise reflects itself in its language.

With the increasing maturity of the pupil, training in style gradually takes the place of grammatical instruction. The pupil is trained not to be satisfied with what is grammatically irreproachable, but from different possible modes of expression to select that which is rhetorically the best. In the work the teacher takes pains to open the pupils' eyes to the image-forming power of the language, how to sharpen the ear for the beauty of sound of the words and for the rhythm of the sentence and sentence structure. Exercises in the choice of the right word and word position, in the search for the most striking, and still linguistically pure expression, in the Germanization of foreign words (where it is not a question of substituting German for foreign words, but of expressing the thought in German), careful attention to popular and also especially to dialectical modifications will acquaint the pupil with the wealth of possibility in expression and gradually give him, too, a certain general sensitiveness for the difference of nuance in related words, and for the emotional content of the word. It will be possible relatively early to make clear the difference between an elevated and a simple manner of speech through sentence structure, word placement, and also the single word as a means of expression, and to show that polite expression is expression arising from a more intense sensitivity. In the upper section the teacher will try to increase the pupils' sense for the characteristic manner of writing of the outstanding masters of style and also for the peculiarities of style of whole periods and particular vocational groups, and show them thereby the unending plasticity of the language. Examples of poor style can also be used occasionally as a contrast if the pupils are trained to give attention to the psychological, sociological, and historical causes of these defects in style.

The methods of activity instruction are of especial importance in grammar and rhetoric. The pupils must learn to pick out the laws of the language from usage; by observation, analysis, interpretation, and remodeling of the current materials of speech they will be brought to a knowledge of the regular forms. Systematic organization results only at the end of rather long periods of time. Mechanical grammatical exercises, for example, inspection of forms, are to be avoided in the mother tongue. Only such home work is to be assigned as does not destroy for the pupil the joy of research and discovery.

8. *Literature.* The introduction into German literature shall fill the pupils with understanding and love for the characteristic creations of the German intellect in the field of literature, shall train them intellectually by penetration into the content and form of the great masterpieces and shall enrich them inwardly through life values residing in these works. The instruction will always be carried on with respect for a great work and its creator and will make the pupil realize that it is a primary purpose to discover for himself the fullest appreciation for intellectual creation to its fullest value. It will also encourage the pupil to make his own adjustment to the work. For only when both are combined can the knowledge of the content rise to experience of intrinsic worth, joy in the beautiful to conception of form, the natural admiration for genius to respect, the enthusiasm for the hero to courageous will, German feeling to German understanding. The literature to be treated in school extends from primitive national poetry, the fairy tale, and the myth up to the highest revelations of genius available to the pupil. The central point of this consideration in *Obersekunda* is the first golden era of German literature; in *Prima* falls the renaissance of Germanism in the idealism of our classicism and romanticism, in which the German mind drew together all the cultural forces playing upon it into a new and characteristic unity and thereby not only influenced the intellectual history of Germany and its cultural development until the present time, but also exercised a fruitful influence upon the whole spiritual life of Europe. The important works of the poetical realism of the nineteenth century, in which problems of the new development of German life take form, will demand their full recognition.

The choice in detail must heed the adolescent considerations

just as much as the central relationship of German to all subjects and the educational objectives of individual classes. Under
certain circumstances the same work may be treated twice;
it can in the middle section be read for the sake of its direct
effect as something that gives evidence of German nature and
heroic sentiment; the upper section can turn back to it in
order to conceive it consciously as an artistic production or, for
its deeper meaning, as a step in the development of the poet,
or as a monument of contemporary history. Thus, instruction in
*Prima* can only evaluate the whole effort of the classical period
satisfactorily if a part of the works are known to the pupils in
the earlier classes. In addition to the epic, lyric, and drama,
and according to the same principles, the prose of modern times
must be studied. Scientific prose is also to be introduced in
the consideration of particular eras, especially the modern era.
It serves not only to complete the picture of an age, but has,
just as modern prose has, in addition to its content value, special importance for the pupil as a model for the development
of his own style of writing.

The treatment of the literary selections must be carried on
with the conviction that every work of art has its own inner
nature; only from this point of view can it be understood and
only as a whole can it be experienced. One general method,
therefore, is not permissible. A lyrical poem in the lower section, for example, can either be read aloud by the teacher or
be taken up silently by the pupils, or an association may precede the presentation, which can be linked with the common
or special experiences of the pupils, with the seasons, festivals,
memorial days or birthdays. The only problem is that the
poem must become a living experience for the teacher and
through him for the pupils. Poems must not be dissected
by logical analysis, still less be misused for exercises in style.
Explanations of detail may only be given so far as they are
necessary for the comprehension of the whole. Special value is
to be attached to the fact that the pupils really make the poem
their own through expressive reading. The unexpressed, in
fact, goes over into the child's mind most certainly through
careful reading. With increasing maturity the pupil is to learn
to think of the poem as a personal experience or confession of
the author. Shorter epic-lyric poems (ballads) can be offered

under certain circumstances in connection with a discussion of some phase of the history or culture which has removed all subject matter difficulties from the situation. Even after the preparation and presentation, there can also still be given a projection of fully developed views, a clarification of thought along which the sentiment runs, an illumination of the characters. Finally, the ballads can be presented as a whole and the details can be worked out by the pupils independently under the teacher's guidance. The main notion is that the effect of the poem be felt as a whole. If, in the discussions, divisions must be made, they must follow only the inner organization, as in ballads at the change of scene, in lyric poetry at the change of thought or sentiment, and not merely the arrangement by verses. Works of the pictorial arts which contain a similar or related motive can be used for the purpose of intensifying the thought. A ballad should be sung if possible.

The drama should also be treated with the pupils as a complete work of art in the handling of which it should always be recognized that it comes to its full expression only on the stage. This is impossible if all the individual scenes are taken up in exhausting uniformity, if the technical structure is analyzed to its last detail, if an attempt is made to answer according to a fixed plan all the questions which the work might suggest, and to exhaust each sentence it contains.

The drama, as every work of art, can be understood only from within, from its vital focus. Proceeding from the motive, the problems, the chief character, the experience of the author, or the structure of the drama, the instruction can give the pupils penetrating insight and show how the whole grows out of this focus by means of the special resources that are available to the dramatic poet. The teacher must have freedom in selecting the principal points of view. He will try in various dramas to illustrate the several possible points of view. The teacher must give the pupils points of reference for the first complete reading at home which precedes each thorough study. The special assignments—the progress of the plot, the meaning of special scenes, the development of individual characters, the experience of the author, the relation to a source or the sources of materials, and the like—are distributed to the pupils individually or by a group according to the principles of division of and coöperation in activity. The results thus obtained are exchanged and discussed in class, and made fruitful so that finally the whole class, by working together, receives a total picture of the masterpiece. A summarizing discussion by the teacher is indispensable in this work, particularly in the evaluation of special high points and in the mastery of special difficulties. Especially important or impressive scenes can be read in class after careful preparation, while, on the other hand, mere unprepared reading by assigning rôles is not in harmony with the principles of art education. The teacher will gladly lend his advice or assistance for dramatic productions of the pupils on occasions of school or class celebrations. He will endeavor to acquaint the pupils for this purpose with the simplest rules of dramatic and stage art. Where there is opportunity, he will encourage them to attend the theatre, which alone can assure the full dramatic impression inherent in the work of art.

In addition to the lyric, epic, and drama, special attention is to be given to prose which has developed since the period of romanticism and classicism. For the illumination of the condition of the recent generations with reference to community and personal life this prose is more essential than the drama of the same period. Suitably chosen tales and simple short stories from *Untertertia* can serve as an introduction to a consideration of certain prose works. With increasing maturity the pupils will seek to understand the German short story in its tendency toward the psychological problems as well as to understand the German novel essentially as the adolescent literature. The conditioning of the work of art through the point of view of life held by the author and through his being rooted in the spirit of the time is likewise to be considered here carefully. What has been said about the drama applies to the treatment of the prose.

German instruction cannot overlook current writing, which, quite reasonably, exercises upon the mature youth an especially lively attraction. Even if the German teacher cannot treat current literature regularly, still he must remain in constant contact with it, and as opportunity affords must go into the works which arouse the pupils' interests both in the class and in individual discussion. He will seek to reveal to the pupils the nature of the newer influences, set forth their connection with the whole development, and by means of opportune examples clarify the worthwhile new production as well as the incongruities which unavoidably are attached to the effort for new forms of art. In part he will be able to connect this with questions and problems raised by the class, and in part he himself will point to personalities and works which are of importance in current German intellectual life. The German "activity groups" can also be made especially fruitful for treating current-day literature.

9. *History of Literature.* In the lower section the study of the history of literature does not come up for consideration. In the middle section a picture of literary art can be sketched from the works of those authors who have been read. Further, in the upper section the instruction deals with the high points and high lights of German literature in close connection with the other academic cultural subjects, especially with history and religion. The masterpiece will be primarily the beginning point. Proceeding from the individual classic, together with the addition of other sources which are to be treated by the pupils in individual and in group work, the instruction strives to build up in the pupils a picture of the author's experience and his importance. It strives to make them recognize his place in intellectual history, the effect on him of the general intellectual tendencies, his part in the development of German intellect, his relation to the whole of German nationality. The conception of poetic forms and their transformation, insight into the typical artistic means of literature and individual types in literature, the explanation of the fundamental ethical principles, as well as the recognition of cultural continuities will be disclosed from individual works and by comparative methods. The further the instruction proceeds, so much the more it will offer insights into larger connected wholes in addition to detailed accounts. What the pupil cannot work out for himself, the teacher must give.

Since the objectives of German instruction are so widely diversified that no teacher can be equally skilled in all, he must have a certain degree of freedom in the selection and treatment of the works studied. However, this freedom will find its limits in the importance of certain works and tendencies for the history of German intellect in general and for the relationship of the German intellect to that special cultural field which is characteristic for the type of institution in question.

Of special importance for German instruction is the private reading of the pupils. In addition to the reading necessary for "activity instruction," which will determine partly common and partly group assignments, the teacher will recommend to the pupil the reading of other works which can serve to widen and intensify the instruction. Beyond this, he will further promote free, independent reading on the part of the pupils in every way and will stimulate them to do so where it appears to be fitting. He will encourage activity groups and societies for literature in the schools, and promote their establishment where they do not yet exist. The most important aid to German instruction is a well-conducted, liberal school library. With its help, the pupil can, in the choice of his reading, best find his way with intelligent counsel but without supervision.

10. *Poetics.* Instruction with reference to the artistic forms of poetry really begins in the middle section. It begins with individual classics and acquaints the pupil with the most important types and means of expression in poetry. The composition of the greater poetical masterpieces is developed first in ballads and tales, and then in the drama and novel. In the upper section the instruction will attempt, again in connection with masterpieces studied intensively, to assure to the pupil a deeper insight into the legitimacy of the individual types of art. It will also strive to make him see that for the great poet each thought bears in itself its given form and that the apparently similar external forms transform themselves inwardly in the hands of different authors or in different ages. In the ballads and in many short tales, this permits of easy demonstration, thanks to the fact that they are easily grasped. Particularly will the teacher take pains to sharpen the feeling of the pupils for the difference between æsthetic value and æsthetic effect. To illustrate the point he will also employ, on occasion, works of lesser rank. In this way he will endeavor to train the pupil in foresight, caution, and consciousness in judgment. Especially must the pupil be taught to understand that standards are not applied to a poet which were only developed after him and perhaps only through him, or which belong to a form of expression formerly classic but no longer valid.

The characteristic laws of German poetry in contrast to the ancient and Romance poetry are discussed in the development of poetic forms, namely, during the seventeenth and eighteenth centuries. The most important facts from the history of the German theater are developed in connection with the drama of different periods along with the opera.

11. *Folklore.* Folklore in the lower and middle sections is intended to acquaint the pupil spiritually with the home and through it with the fatherland. Its basis is a vivid study of the home (*Heimatkunde*) derived not from books but from observation and experience. In the home community and by excursions into the narrower and wider vicinity it permits the pupil at once to grow into the community of race, as it has expressed itself in dialect, in popular poetry, in costume and in food, in special appreciation of certain plants and animals, in names, in forms of settlement and buildings, in customs and usages, in law, in practices for festivals and funerals, in all sorts of superstitions. It teaches him to observe, to collect facts, and to arrange and understand them; it directs him to evidences of the history which has taken place in the local vicinity.

Its field widens gradually from the home in a narrower sense to the fatherland; from tribal characteristics to nationality, always with the purpose of allowing the pupil to see and experience that which still lives in the nation. That which has only archæological interest does not belong in school instruction. The upper section provides comprehensive discussions concerning folk art. Proceeding from the study of German antiquity and from a study of the German race, in close connection with German cultural history, the instruction seeks to lead the pupil gradually to a psychological comprehension of German art, as it expresses itself in fairy tales, saga, myth, folk song, and more especially in the language itself, in law, custom, and usage. This instruction is based upon a reader dealing with a study of German culture or upon individual sources. Personal observation and local tradition, wherever possible, are to be turned to account. Frequently the individuality of the German can be made especially clear by comparison with that which is foreign. The highest purpose of folklore is to awaken in the pupils that feeling for the common racial unity which reveals itself in the variety of the individual tribes, that national unity which exists behind all change of sex or of life forms, and leaves behind it all differences in class and education.

12. *Art Appreciation.* The consideration of works of German pictorial art and the introduction to works of German music are indispensable for the comprehension of German character. German instruction can in general draw both into the field of its activity, only in close connection with drawing and music instruction, but upon occasion, and assuming that the teacher is able to do so, it will also take an interest in art appreciation and in discussing music. While in the lower and middle sections both limit themselves to individual consideration and serve for the enrichment of the instruction in literature and folklore, it will more often be possible in the upper section to make an epoch of German cultural history clear from the point of view of art. This applies besides to the early German period especially to the Roman, high Gothic, the baroque, the romantic. The unity of the creative national spirit must be felt intensively in such considerations. Art can also be utilized for pointing out the material exchange between German and foreign cultures or for clarifying certain characteristics of the German nature which express themselves especially in the modification of cultural values taken from foreign peoples. Group visitations of art collections are to be recommended.

Folklore likewise can be of service in art appreciation. It makes the pupils upon excursions attentive to the beauty of natural architecture in its connection with the landscapes, and opens to them the artistic values contained in the products of local handicrafts. It might still be possible for many schools, to which no museum is available, to establish a small collection of local art.

13. *Philosophic Summarization.* Philosophic treatment is a necessary objective for German instruction. German instruction, correctly treated, leads in all its parts to philosophical questions on the most varied subjects. Through the introduction into the structure of the language and of literary works, it develops in the pupil the elements of logic and general psychology. By delving into the poetical and clearly developed characters it furnishes an important preparation for the comprehension of the psychological types. Through discussions concerning the artistic forms of poetry it leads toward some funda-

mental ideas and problems. However, it also knows how to point out to the pupils the problems of the great literary works as general problems of life and of attitude toward the world, which can really be grasped only on the basis of philosophical consideration; and it will introduce them thus to ethics, and, to be sure, directly to the most important ethical questions. Finally, German will show them how every great work of art gives a world picture, how every great poet represents a world point of view, and by the development of this metaphysical background will give the pupils an insight into the diversity of possible world views. The individual epochs in the history of philosophy and German instruction have especial relations. Particularly the classical period of German idealism and the development following it require tracing the cultural presuppositions and the returns of the great poets and poems.

14. *Civic Education.* Folklore already seeks to animate civics instruction by love of home and by the feeling of unity with all racial companions. Reading, however, has an important task in the development of this community of feeling in so far as in the choice of its material it considers works which permit the pupil in an artistic manner to realize that he is becoming acquainted with the inner and outer needs of those classes with which in life he has no direct connection. Likewise poetry too can aid essentially in the development of a national consciousness by the choice of such works as treat the frequently tragic problems that spring out of the relation of the individual to the group. The great number of these problems in German literature will lead the pupils to the recognition of the great importance of the state, as well as to the point of view that in the individual delineation of German nature there lie certain inner opposing forces of development of a fixed attitude toward the state. Older legal sources, which show the characteristic strength as well as the limits of the original German feeling toward law, can be used in this sense in the upper section. German instruction seeks further, in view of the interlacing of German cultural development with other European culture, to elevate the German feeling of nationality to a true and well-disciplined national consciousness, which is conscious of its own nature as of its limitations, believes in itself, remains true to itself, without despising that which is foreign. Finally, German

instruction will make the pupil understand that the great poets, removed from all struggle of class, race, or creed, belong to the whole people, even those parts which to-day live outside the borders of the German state, and that the German poems, as the language in which they are written, are a sure and common possession of all Germans.

15. *Concentration.* In view of the close mutual relationship which German instruction has to all subjects, particular care is to be taken in the distribution of subject matter that the inherent claims of German are preserved.

A careful demarcation which will take into consideration the problems of the various schools is especially necessary with reference to religion and history. Many topics must be divided between history and German. Various forms of social organization, as the guilds of the Meistersinger, and various sources of law, as the Saxon and Swabian Codes, can be taken over by the work in German, since their importance lies more in their intellectual character than in their historical and political effect. On the other hand, the instruction in history can treat various literary events and tendencies which are predominantly of historical import, such as the political lyrics of the young German movement. In cases where the same topics appear in history and in literature, the history is supposed to evaluate them for their political, social, and economic importance, while the German will consider them more from the point of view of their artistic form and of their importance for the development of German intellectual life, and will especially dwell upon those passages where transcendent values rear themselves from the stream of time. In coöperation with the religious instruction the work in German will seek to point out the German influence which can be felt in all religious movements and tendencies in German countries as well as the religious trend in the great changes in German intellectual life. With the geography course, German will show all of Germanism to be one great spiritual unity which reaches far out over the present boundaries of the nation. It will point out the German influence in foreign civilizations, it will promote relationships with Germans living abroad and will make clear the difficult struggles that they have had to wage for the preservation of their intellectual individuality. German together with geography awakens an appreciation of the natural conditioning factors of German intellectual life in general, of the varied literary development of the various German races, of the permanence of racial characteristics as they are recognizable in the literature and as they are reflected in the various dialects, and also an appreciation of the special forms of German character in the various districts.

In the various types of schools German primarily seeks correlations with the subjects which are characteristic of the school. Thus in the *Gymnasium* the influence which the classical period in its revival has exerted upon German intellectual life is to be emphasized especially. However, at the same time the individuality of the German mind, which expresses itself in the assimilation, reworking, and reorganization of classical culture, is to be emphasized also. In the modern language *Gymnasium,* German will treat especially the influences of Roman culture and the ancient church and later the influences of English and French culture upon the intellectual life of Germany, and will treat also the adjustment of the German mind to these forces. In both cases the teacher is to emphasize the ability of the German mind to assimilate and independently reorganize that which has been acquired from other countries. However, he must not conceal that there have been periods of slavish imitation. The reaction of German idealism upon the whole of European culture must be intensively treated. In the *Oberrealschule* German will dwell upon the importance of mathematical and natural science subjects for various thinkers and poets and upon the many motives and problems which have been furnished literature by natural science and later also by technology. German will, however, emphasize also the importance of the purely intellectual movements for the exact sciences. More important and more fruitful still is the contribution which the subject matter groups, characteristic of the various types of schools, can on their part make to the problems of German instruction.

16. *Free Activity Groups.* The activity groups in German offer rich possibilities for strengthening and enriching the instruction. They are of particular importance in schools for which only a comparatively small number of hours are available for German. They can afford wide consideration for the special interests and desires of the pupils. Either various authors who do not occupy a prominent place in class work and

especially those who are of importance for the district in question can be studied; or literary motifs or various tendencies in literary development may be pursued. Fundamental ethical principles can be explained, and under certain circumstances the pupils may be introduced to the method of literary criticism and philological study. The various literary tendencies of modern times can be evaluated in their connection with the general intellectual movements and with the corresponding tendencies in foreign countries. Similarly, examples of literatures, such as the Nordic and Russian literatures, which cannot be considered in the regular instruction owing to the general cultural objective, may be treated in these "free activity groups."

### ACTIVITY GROUPS IN PHILOSOPHY

The activity groups in philosophy serve to strengthen, through suitable reading, the interests aroused in philosophy through the other subjects. These groups can therefore be organically incorporated with all corresponding subjects; however, they will adjust themselves to the special educational function of the type of school in question. It is their function at the same time to equip the gradually maturing pupils, by reading the important philosophies, with the ability to work out independently an understanding of philosophical works.

The reading in philosophy aims fundamentally at no systematic knowledge, nor technical philosophical knowledge, nor solutions of final problems of life, but rather at an insight into the work and method of philosophy, and into the method of thinking of great philosophers in the struggle with their problems. It is the purpose of philosophy to make fruitful, and thus strengthen, the logical, psychological, and metaphysical points of view gained in other subjects in order to understand the purely philosophical reading.

The compulsion of common inquiry into the sharp and incisive formation of an idea, into the compelling force of rationalization, into the depth and extent of the foundations of a system of thought of an important philosopher will always clarify the elementary character of such philosophical reading and will form an important educational counterbalance for the youthful thinking, which tends to radical and premature conclusions.

Especially fruitful will be such works as bring out the

importance of a philosopher for the creative periods of civilization, and thus lead to a more thorough comprehension of the age in question.

## HISTORY AND CIVICS

1. *Aim.* History closely correlated with the other subjects, primarily the other core subjects, should contribute to thoroughly acquainting the youth with his own community, German nationality, and the state. It strives to lead to a comprehension of the present in the light of the past and thus to enable the maturing youth to take a critical attitude with reference to the political problems which he will meet in life; it aims to arouse readiness to act and a feeling of political responsibility through the realization that only decisive vigorous action attains results in history.

The knowledge of the past serves for the transmission of scientifically determined facts. It is not, however, a question of absolute completeness of knowledge, but rather that the effective forces in historical life be recognized by means of the development of important and decisive points. The historical sense is to be trained and the vision of the pupil so sharpened that the pupil can understand historical events in the light of the character of the times. The mere learning of many details for the sake of knowledge alone must never be an end in itself.

Primarily history instruction will treat of the history, character, and place of the German people. Its political, social, and economic institutions and the whole richness of its culture must be brought so naturally to the pupil that the will for its preservation and development will be aroused, and be based upon historical insight. The relation of German history to world history must be revealed.

Vivid personalities as intellectual and spiritual leaders, statesmen, inventors, discoverers, heroes of faith, leaders in social movements, on account of their especially educative influence, are to be cited as examples of sacrifice and devotion. The contrast of different attitudes toward life must not lessen the respect for the person of the opponent. Not only are the political and religious views of divergent groups to be discussed without hatred, but it is precisely one of the chief functions of history to cultivate an appreciation of other points of view, and thereby a spirit of tolerance.

2. *Selection of Subject Matter.* While in the middle section German history dominates the work, in the upper section it must be consciously woven in with world history, with the interdependence of great nations with one another with reference to accomplishment, claims, and obligations. Here according to the educational objectives of the various types of schools and for the sake of understanding the present-day situation, this or that portion of the history of other nations will also be thoroughly studied. The youth are to recognize herein the great deeds of other peoples as well and learn to appreciate them. Understanding and sympathy for the importance of Germanism in the surrendered territories and in foreign countries, and for the fate of German Austria must also be awakened.

From the subject matter only that will be chosen which has been of historical importance. The discussion of tendencies in evolution and the elaboration of crucial turning points need not be postponed to the upper section.

At suitable points the pupils should be made vividly conscious of the richly emotional, even tragic interdependence with which the fundamental relations of human associations constantly change. The omnipresent active polar forces, such as the individual and the state or society, might and right, authority and freedom, ruling and ruled group as caste or class, one's own and the foreign nation, are to be made clear in their opposing character and in their interconnectedness.

There is no exclusive antagonism between political, economic, and cultural history. For this reason, even if the state is to be portrayed as the most powerful form of civilization, the organic unity of the political, intellectual, social, and economic forces is to be constantly emphasized. The study of law is to be especially stressed with two objects in mind: insight into the development, the organization, and the relation of our legal system to other historical forces, and respect for existing law. In the introduction this work is to be associated with remains of old legal customs and of legal language. The individuality of the Germanic attitude toward law as distinguished from the Roman must be made clear to the pupil. The work is to be shortened especially in the study of dynasties, diplomatic con-

flicts, and struggles of succession. Only absolutely necessary
facts dealing with the history of wars will be given, the chief
among which are the character, the political causes, and results
of a campaign. Only the changes in tactics and strategy which
are really important for world history, as found illustrated in
various outstanding battles, are to be brought up for consideration. Attention should be paid to the desire of youth for
hero worship by placing before the pupils portrayals of heroic
personal and national life.

3. *Memoriter Material.* Drill upon definite factual knowledge
and not too large a list of dates is necessary. In this way the
history work in the middle section prepares for that of the
upper section. It is, however, never to be thought that the
memoriter material in the middle section must be an end in
itself.

4. *Treatment of Material.* In the developmental stage of simple experience, classes VI and V, stories are to be related in the
German hour which deal with events that have taken place in
the immediate or more remote vicinity and are to be given in
portrayals full of phantasy, color, and movement. The children
must see the events in fine detail and in vivid pictorial form.
They must never have their appetites dulled with didactic summaries and surveys. The children can, however, themselves relate in class what they have assimilated at home from the reader
or other suitable accounts and short historical narratives.

In the period of objective comprehension, classes IV to U II,
deed and personality still stand in the foreground for study.
Political and social conditions will also, therefore, so far as is
possible, be treated in close connection with the influence of
heroic personalities or groups. Historical notions are to be developed through the preparation and association of striking and
characteristic features, in the explanation and realistic treatment of which observations are to be included which the pupils
can make in their own vicinity and upon excursions.

Training in independent activities, which are to be utilized in
class work, will already have been begun in the middle section.
Frequently the pupil will work over by himself at home the factual material which his history textbook contains or which has
been given him in the form of source material. To sources in
the school sense of the word, in addition to original sources,

belong also biographies, travel, but not in too fragmentary form, poems, short stories, novels and dramas of cultural value, and portions from important historical works. These materials are to be carefully selected as to form and content for the particular age group. The teacher gives points of view according to which the materials are to be utilized. That which the individual has seen occasionally or which the class on visits to the museum and upon excursions has observed of historical value in sculpture, in monuments, in the market place, on houses, and along the streets and in whole communities, must also be used as *source material*. If the material necessary in the reincarnation of a personality, in the illumination of a historical problem, or in the portrayal of an event has been collected in such a manner, then work upon it can be commenced in class. Either its treatment and formulation can be carried on in typical class procedure, or several pupils may give reports, if possible, on the same theme but from different sources, or an advanced pupil may discuss it. A general discussion can be connected with this procedure in any case. In every case the teacher must insist on rigorous thinking. In this section of the school the teacher must also take over the discussion in the more difficult development of an important or decisive point or in the transition to the next high point in the work, or in rounding out an epoch or in concluding the characterization of an important personality.

In the stage of thoughtful penetration of historical material and of the regular training of the historical sense, the compelling and retarding forces and the changeable complications and limitations of all fields of human history are to be brought up for consideration. The pupils assemble, as in the middle section, the raw material for work in the class from the history textbook and from sources suitable to their intellectual maturity. These materials are then used again in the class as subject matter for group activity. Likewise in the upper section the self-activity of the pupils takes most of the direction from the teacher in that he indicates certain points of view in the light of which the problem is to be solved independently. Discussion by the teacher will be necessary here in exceptional cases only. At suitable places, the pupils of *Sekunda* and *Prima* learn how a situation is critically determined from original reports and where the limits of certainty of historical knowledge

lie.  The activity instruction has reached a vital objective when
the more mature pupil acquires this certainty in an increasing
degree, and is no longer delivered defenseless and without standards of judgment to every political opinion of the day.

5. *Civic Education and History.*  The objective of civic education is to create and strengthen an active attitude toward
politics, patriotism, and public-mindedness, and upon the basis
of a clear comprehension of the conditions, character, and constitution of our state to develop with reference to its institutions, a feeling of personal responsibility and sense of duty.
The prerequisite to the fulfillment of these tasks is that the
whole life of the school be shot through with public spirit and
that all partisan politics be kept out of the school's affairs.
Civic education must awaken and cultivate the feeling of law
in the young man and provide a clear picture of the structure
and characteristics of our legal and social institutions.

The study of the state must lead to the view that interests of
the individual and of the group are indissolubly bound up with
the whole, that the state is more than family and vocation, more
than a community of interest or purpose, and finally that the
highest consummation and most valuable fruition of a capable
people is humanity.

Supported at all points by the whole curriculum, history with
special problems promotes the study of citizenship.  In general,
the principles of history instruction apply in the selection and
treatment of the subject matter, namely, not overloading with a
mass of detailed facts but coöperatively developing longitu-
dinal- and cross-sections in history, delving into developmental
tendencies and sequences and into principles and methods of
thought.

The interest in civic problems will already have been cultivated in the lower and middle sections.  In order to fill the civic
concepts of life and thought for the youth and to make such
concepts comprehensive, the beginning point must be within the
the pupil's range of experience, and the experiences in the
class and pupil organizations must be made use of in laying
the foundations of civic training.  Such experiences include the
manner and method of organizing groups among the pupils, the
election of representatives and members of councils, the need
of a meeting, the simple forms in which the common will ex-

presses itself and creates its institutions, and the observations the pupils make on the street and in public life. One should allow the pupils to make reports upon the regular and honorary activity of the citizen and use their reports as an introduction to the study of sociology, of community life, and of the judicial system. Excursions through public institutions and organizations, through commercial and private wholesale and retail businesses, and glimpses into the workshop of an artisan can be made to serve the development of a sense for facts and of social consciousness. The teacher must avoid as far as possible giving schematic, abstract sketches and didactic, systematic surveys of civic materials. Again such problems as are to be studied only by more mature pupils, as national and foreign political economy, social organization of various peoples, tax systems and types of distribution of income, the principles of the penal and civil codes, important political and political-economic theories, self-determination of peoples, international law and international leagues, are most successfully treated where they have been made real in a historical setting. Occasional reviews of various portions of the work and summaries of a definite part of the field in civics are desirable even in the middle section.

In vocational guidance opportunity must be taken again to explain explicitly the relation of the individual and his work to community and national life.

In girls' schools attention should be given in the selection of subject matter in civics to the nature of girls, to the method of thought characteristic of them, and to the special problems of the woman in the home.

6. *Philosophical Treatment.* Education by means of historical study proceeds from historical and philosophical postulations which the mature pupil will first sense intuitively, but which should further be brought to his attention in the present crisis in political life if they are to be of meaning to him in later life.

The reflective penetration of historical problems demands therefore consideration of fundamental philosophical questions, especially in cases where ideas, views of life, and ideals as compelling forces determine the course of events. Metaphysical and logical statements of problems are necessary if the pupil is to understand the intellectual forces operating in each historical situation and is to recognize the historical categories which are fundamental in every historical appreciation of the past. Thus, for example, an appreciation of the essential difference between the concept of *law* in natural science and *law* in history is an insight fruitful for both fields of study. Similarly the explanation and the proof of the fundamental notions, as applied in history, which have to do with general human institutions, are the basic prerequisites for the appreciation of every historical situation. Not less important for historical training are the most significant historical-philosophical theories which are absolutely indispensable in understanding great historians. The knowledge of the philosophy of history must make clear to the pupil finally that it is decisions of the will which determine historical action and historical responsibility. The turning from that which was to that which is to be, which gives history instruction its value, can proceed only in this way.

It goes without saying that instruction in history can thus effect philosophic reflection only if it coöperates with those other subjects which aim at historical training. History instruction, therefore, can treat such problems only if wisely limited and with avoidance of exhaustive treatment and in rather close connection with other instruction. More important than an excess of knowledge is the inner experience of philosophical problems found in history in characteristic individual cases and in such problems as move the pupils profoundly. Insights thus acquired can occasionally be recapitulated by means of a survey of the development of a problem. The employment of worthwhile works in the philosophy of history and their study in the free activity groups will be of value in this respect. The views of the teacher with regard to the philosophy of history will here, as in every subject, find expression. The final educational objective of all instruction in history, "belief in eternal, transcendent values in history, in spiritual objectives, which alone give meaning to every form of human activity, and the clarification of freedom as the highest expression of humanity" must give direction in history instruction to all philosophical study.

7. *Concentration.* All subjects seek to give training in history.

Therefore, in order that all of the work in history may be a unit, close connection between history and the other subject groups is necessary. The instruction in history on its own behalf must leave some essential topic of its own field to other subjects. It must also in part adapt itself to the different educational objectives of the various schools. On the other hand, history instruction must never permit the task of developing an understanding of the state, business, and society, which it alone can fulfill, to be interfered with by its relations to the other cultural subjects.

Particularly close will be the connection in the "activity groups" between history and the other core subjects on account of their inner relationships. Likewise instruction in every foreign language will furnish valuable assistance in training in history, because we can understand a foreign national spirit only if we delve deep into the mother tongue of that country. Some historical problems can be developed only out of the foreign languages. Some topics furnished by these subjects can be utilized by the work in history in order that the picture of any people as painted by history or of a historical movement may be given more vivid form and the interrelation of events as presented may be developed more clearly and thoroughly. In the *Gymnasium* the classical language instruction in conjunction with the work in history has the special problem of introducing the development of a historical situation from the sources.

Physics and chemistry offer the possibility of treating more intimately problems of modern technology; arithmetic and mathematics in general will aid somewhat in the explanation of the banking and stock exchange systems as well as be of assistance in statistics.

Finally, the contacts between history and geography are very numerous. By an extensive distribution of work between these two subjects, historical situations are considered upon the basis of the forces active in the locality which condition them; the relation between civilization and nature is disclosed, and appreciation is increased for natural laws as determining factors in the location of settlements, and in the origin, expansion, and decline of states. Geography will also relieve history of worthwhile preparatory work in that it will portray the struggle for rivers, passes, seas, sources of raw materials and regions of export, commercial routes and channels of trade throughout the world, and history will thus devote its attention to colonial history and the history of exploration. In this connection also it considers the relation between natural, political, ethnographic, and language boundaries, investigates the importance of means of exchange for the existence of great nations, and describes the characteristics of agricultural and industrial regions, their mutual dependence even out beyond the national boundaries. This will be accomplished by working out these ever-narrowing interrelationships through a progressive division of work in modern civilization.

8. *Art Appreciation.* In the whole picture of civilization, art, architecture, sculpture, and music cannot be omitted in the development of the high points of history. Art study within the history course, therefore, in conjunction primarily with German, religion, drawing and foreign languages, and by means of small but characteristic examples, emphasizes the individuality and the change of artistic expression, of life motives and concepts of various ages. Of course, the work will find its starting point in the architectural and artistic monuments of the more immediate community.

History by use of art study can very clearly objectify the cultural relationships existing among great nations.

Drawing instruction primarily will lead to deeper insight into the formal structure and formal value of the art work and into the laws of development of style.

9. *Free Activity Groups.* The "free activity groups" in history organize their work in many ways with respect to materials and methods of work. They can continue and strengthen all problems of instruction in history and bring in also important fields of study which were merely touched upon or entirely passed over. In the selection of subject matter, the type of school, the trend of interests among the pupils, and the special field of work of the teacher must be considered chiefly. Further the district and its educational conditions, primarily in neighboring communities, will provide worthwhile points of stimulation. Study of the local community and local history, back to prehistoric times can, by means of observations, collections, and source reading, afford insight into historical

method.  Reading of foreign language sources or important historical accounts will likewise afford an appreciation of the tools and methods of historical research.  The discussion of various questions and problems from the philosophy of history can also be carried further in these activity groups.

### GEOGRAPHY

1. *Aim.*  Instruction in geography in coöperation with the other subjects is to awaken and cultivate in the pupils love of the native soil, the home and the fatherland, to contribute to an understanding of German civilization both past and present, and to help to train the pupil for German citizenship.

It is to furnish the knowledge of the physical composition of the earth's surface with reference to its form and its topographical divisions, according to position, climate, types of soil, water forms, plant life, and distribution of animal life and their mutual interdependence.

It is to teach the physical distribution of mankind divided according to races and peoples, stages and forms of economic development, as well as political institutions, together with humanity's dependence upon the position and the natural resources of its environment.

It is to make known the condition of the soil in civilized countries as the result of human effort and to create thus a measure of the work of the nations of the earth and particularly of one's own country.

It is to share in supplying knowledge of the position of the world in the universe in conjunction with mathematics and physics.

It is to show that the map is the most important geographical means of expression and to enable the pupil to read maps with understanding and use them upon excursions.

Finally, instruction in geography should train the pupils to use their eyes with understanding when observing their environment.

2. *Selection of Subject Matter.*  The selection of subject matter must be guided by the intellectual maturity of the pupil, the educative value of the subject matter, and its adaptability to certain methods of work.  Further, the educational objectives of the type of school and the whole educational purpose

of the class must be taken into consideration. Finally, the subject matter must be selected with respect to its value for German civilization. For these reasons a limitation of subject matter is urgently necessary.

For the development of the emotions and of the imagination in the lower section, vivid pictures of typical districts are to be painted which at first are to be taken entirely from the immediate vicinity for the sake of securely establishing basic geographical concepts. The ability for easy retention, characteristic of this stage of development, makes possible the permanent inculcation of topographic facts. The training of the judgment, however, must begin with the discovery of very simple causal relationships as early as the lower section.

The instruction in the middle section should contribute to the training of the will through thorough mastering of practical knowledge and accounts of the cultural contributions of the nations, and by portrayal of great personalities who devoted their lives to investigation. Excursions in the open afford, particularly in this section of the school, the first steps in intelligent observation.

The selection of subject matter in the upper section is determined by the necessity of training the pupils to reach accurate judgments concerning the relationships of the phenomena treated in general geography. The facts of general geography, which in the lower classes are taught only very occasionally in the study of the lands, are welded together here into composite pictures and furnish the *Primaner* the absolutely essential breadth of view. By study of the problems of cultural and political geography, an understanding with reference to the limits of private and public activity is attained, and with it, a just appreciation of all human effort.

3. *Local Community Study.* The pursuit of local community study is a natural duty of the geography teacher. Even in the lower section the cultural foundations of life in the locality can be derived from geographical conditions. Introduction to basic geographical concepts and to understanding the map must come in close connection with the local environment. The surveyor's chart of the community and enlargements therefrom can be used in this connection to advantage. From the middle section on, each pupil must learn to know the political maps of

the community and to use them out in the open. The relief map of the home district belongs to the collection of materials of every school. Its construction on the sand table is to be recommended. Statistics of the more immediate and more remote home districts comprise material which is to be thoroughly memorized. Foreign countries and their characteristic features will become much more real to the pupils by means of frequent comparisons with local conditions. Insight into the natural conditions of life in foreign countries will keep the youthful mind from uncritically preferring foreign to home conditions. The obligation of caring for and protecting the home must be made clear to every pupil. Acquaintance with the chief natural points of interest of the home is sought.

The study of the local community carried on in geography must extend to the study of the fatherland. It must not happen that a German pupil is better informed concerning a foreign country than his own country.

4. *Civic Education.* In civic education geography has a task to perform similar to the special task of history in this field. It must lay the broad natural foundations of the state which determine the type and activities of its citizens. Clear notions of the size and position of one's own country and of foreign countries and of the relations existing between geographical formation and political organization will make more clear to the pupil how narrowly each state is bound by the geographical environment in which it has developed. Only in this way can the pupil clearly comprehend that races in their political life are determined by entirely real, earthbound interests.

In addition to a study of the land of a state, the people must become the subject of civic instruction. Problems such as emigration, density of population, domestic and foreign colonization, land reform, growth of large cities, depopulation of rural areas, offer rich opportunities for intensive study of the subject matter from a civic point of view. The insight thus won into the manifold interdependence of all citizens will arouse in the pupil the feeling of the homogeneity of all members of the nation and of the responsibility of each individual and of the state to each other. In the comparison with other races, the work will duly evaluate the accomplishments of the pupil's own race, and thus train him in fairness toward his fellow countrymen. By means of unbiased consideration of their customs and accomplishments, the pupil must also acquire tolerance toward foreign peoples.

The discussion of economic-geographical relationships will reveal the state as an economic entity. Herein it is of special importance that the pupil come to understand the great importance of economic conditions for international tendencies of the present time.

But geography will take over not only definite fields of civic instruction but also a part of the civic education. Geography has many opportunities in the everyday instruction in class and upon excursions of arousing the spirit of coöperation and public-mindedness. On the longer excursions the love of country and race will grow through intimate contact with the soil and people. Definite problems upon geography trips can also serve in training the pupils as guides and can call forth the feeling and joy of responsibility.

5. *Activity Instruction.* Carrying on activity instruction will give, on account of the intellectual and manual activity of the pupils, joy and freshness to geography which are decisive to the success of the work.

In addition to a lively urge toward activity, the pupil of the lower section is characterized by great receptivity which permits him to approach the work in geography with the greatest sympathy. The zeal of the pupils to relate the many impressions which they bring with them from their immediate environment, from walks and trips, and their frequently rich treasure of local myths must be made fruitful for this instruction. Full advantage must be taken of observational materials in this section. The manual activities of the pupils will furnish further means of illustration,—models in cardboard, wood, and sand; models of locks, dams, dikes, houses, settlements, and mountain forms of the local community. As early as the lower section exercises will lead to intelligent use of the map. The introduction to map reading is to be carried on in close connection with a study of the immediate environment through the use of models, relief maps, and aerial photographs. In the elements of map reading, the development of locational relationship should point out the importance of the atlas as one of the most valuable instructional aids. In this work, if possible, all pupils should have the same atlas. The use of a richly illustrated geographic reader is permitted if worked out upon the principle of pupil activity. In home work it can be used for looking up answers to definite problems. Simple exercises in map reading are also adapted to home work.

In the middle section further possibilities are available for activity instruction. The work leads the pupil into foreign lands, whose features, though lying outside of his range of experience, must be made as clear to him as possible. In this matter imagination and ability to put images together will guide the pupil to clear, concrete knowledge, and also enable him to work out causal relations between climate, soil, plant world, colonization, business and trade.

Activity instruction demands working over the material in class. Of course there will be occasional opportunities for division of labor and organization of working groups, and individual pupils may be assigned rather large special problems which will serve to advance the whole work of the class. More and more the experiences which are acquired upon excursions and trips can be used in class work. Outstanding natural phenomena—storms, earthquakes, forest fires—important discoveries and journeys of exploration furnish upon occasion starting points for the pupils' activities.

Greater value is attached in this section to map reading exercises which are to lead now to the thorough study of the map content. They will furnish opportunity for estimation, measurement, graphic representation, modeling in sand and plastiline; for use of pictures, aërial photographs and stereoscopic views and lantern slides; for comparison of maps on different scales and different origin in time; for comparison of map and photograph and map and relief. Particularly important is the surveyor's map, the rich content of which must be exhausted. In this connection problems such as map coloring, enlarging of small sections, drawing profiles, and representation by relief can be assigned. Further problems will treat the types of colonization and the peculiarities of their location, the history of commercial routes, the transformation of forests into fields, the change in the course of rivers, the rise of industries. In addition the pupil can be acquainted with the geological map. Simple models and experiments will assist in an easier comprehension of geological phenomena.

The use of the textbook must not lead to mere transference of knowledge and a receptive attitude on the part of the pupil. The textbook must serve rather to educate for self-activity and self-reliance. Its pictures, tables, maps, and graphs should be frequently used in home work and to a reasonable extent made use of in class.

Methods based upon the principle of activity of the pupil must determine the character of the instruction also in the upper section. As occasionally in the middle section, in the upper classes the materials collected by individual pupils or groups are arranged and organized in coöperative activity and worked over further in answering definite problems. If occasionally the teacher, in a few words, supplies the model or pattern of a geographical sketch, he furnishes the pupils by this means an example for their own spontaneous accounts in which they are to venture upon geographical problems of the most varied types. Occasionally the pupils may measure their intellectual strength on the pro and con of the theories, and on the basis of suitable examples gain insight into scientific geographical work. Geography instruction is to guide the pupil gradually to form independent judgments on geographical questions and enable him to understand and evaluate the development of the peoples of the earth.

Drawing is of great importance in activity work in geography. At first, hand sketches by the teacher will serve for working out maps, sketches which have for their purpose not only drill upon locational relations but emphasis upon definite facts from the multitude of facts on the wall map or in the atlas. The pupil must also be required to do similar sketches, in which he is not to copy mechanically but is to solve definite problems upon the basis of thought. Mere copying from the atlas is to be avoided. The drawing of profiles, diagrams, and graphs of all sorts is desirable in all sections of the school. Extensive geographical drawings must, however, not be set to be done entirely at home. Voluntary drawings by the pupils are to be studied in class with reference to their content and used for instructional purposes. The posting of especially successful work in the classrooms or in the halls of the school serves to fix more thoroughly what has been presented, and increases also the desire to do voluntary work. Sketching is to be recommended upon excursions. Thus there can be used as subjects the local landscape in summer and winter, the silhouette of the locality, natural phenomena—floods, landslides, effects of wind storms—natural and architectural projects of interest, types of landscape, types of vegetation, perhaps also types of houses, costumes, and implements and utensils of the house and fields. Preference should be given to modeling before sketching; especially should practice in modeling in sand be undertaken for the purpose of acquiring correct concepts of natural regions.

Geography instruction out of doors should be given frequently. Exercises in orientation can be undertaken in the school grounds, as can also observations of the apparent path of the sun, exercises in measurements with simple instruments, and exercises in modeling in the sand pile. From the observatory goniometrical measurements and meteorological and astronomical observations can be made.

The pupil is to be acquainted with nature to a wide degree. Geography excursions can be organized from the lower section on with profit. They sharpen the powers of observation and train in their thoughtful use. Of course that which has been observed must be used for class work. Occasional visitations widen the range of the pupils' imagery. Such visits include visits to industrial plants, business organizations—post, railway, packing plants, and harbors—visits to agricultural activities, establishments for providing the public with food, power, water and light, and visits to characteristic parts of the city. In connection with such visitations, many problems of social and economic nature are treated in class. Visitations such as those to museums and expositions must be carefully prepared for and supervised if they are to secure the desired result for the pupil's advancement.

Rather extended geography exercises will be of value in all sections. They will serve in developing fundamental geographical principles by means of observation of detail, and aid in comprehending the contour of the country and in appraising the work of our people upon their native soil. Tramping with the use of the map must be widely employed.

Exercises in the open, such as sketches of routes, preparation of easy outline maps, and experiments on the banks of river and lake to determine speed of water and the current of the stream, may be arranged for these excursions. One should acquaint the pupils with the keeping of trip-records and should round out the longer trips by enriching trip-reports with photographs or drawings and with profiles or sketches. Trip-records and reports will be the richer in content the more one permits the organization of groups and division of labor upon these excursions. Also, as far as possible, upon these excursions the pupils should learn the various districts of their country, mountains and coastland, moor and forest, village and city, industrial and agricultural sections, and the variety of German races with reference to customs and usages. These school excursions should help the pupils to solve geography problems independently upon their own excursion maps.

6. *Free Activity Groups.* The ''free activity groups'' of the upper section serve to go deeper into the various especially important problems in geography. They take into consideration the inclinations and abilities of the pupils and the educational purpose of the type of school, as well as give attention to the principle of *concentration.* On the basis of excerpts from geographical literature the pupils can immerse themselves in scientific problems and round out their civic education by means of reports upon daily events or reading in the commercial section of the press. The pupils discuss international and geographical-political problems but must not discuss, for example, questions in historical geology or problems concerning the creation of the world. Visitations in more immediate districts will be a further problem for the activity groups in geography and will aid in going deeper into problems in sociology and political economy.

Map study exercises can also lead to a more thorough knowledge of the various districts of the fatherland. They can be organized as measuring exercises in the open, using simple measuring apparatus which has been made by the pupils themselves. They can investigate the difference between photographic and cartographic representations, and study the surveyor's maps and the map of the German nation from points of view of morphology, geology, population, and trade. Such exercises may also be serviceable in local informational research and can be used as supplements to a text dealing with local information studies (*Heimatkunde*). The crowning feature of all geography group activity should be trips of several days through Germany. Their great importance for integration of instruction makes them especially valuable.

7. *Concentration.* A special function in the realization of the idea of concentration devolves upon geography in all types of schools. In consequence of its peculiar nature it can, as no other subject, make the connection between natural science and cultural subjects.

In all schools, however, geography must work in close sympathy with the other core subjects. Geography will assist the work in religion by pointing out the geographical foundations of many religious-historical movements. It will also discuss the routes of expansion of religions and their distribution upon the earth. Ethical and important life problems can be explained upon the basis of geographical illustrations. German instruction will derive value from geography reading, such as reports of journeys and descriptions of countries, just as German will assist geography by means of oral and written treatment of geographical subject matter, whether from ethnology or from economic geography. On account of the close connection between the earth and human life, an intelligent coöperation between history and geography is necessary. In manifold ways historical events depend upon geographical foundations and, of course, without their treatment cannot be understood. Thus geography will provide the understanding of the earth's decisive influence upon historical facts, conditions, and developments. In the interest of all of the training in history, geography will have to keep in mind that not all important races are treated in the history instruction.

Since a variety of relationships links geography with mathematics and the natural sciences, a division of work among these subjects is absolutely necessary. Geography will aid arithmetic by estimation, measurement, and calculation by scale. It advances the work of mathematics, in that it utilizes widely the illustration afforded by mathematics of numerical quantities by means of lines and areas, and also presents statistical material graphically and derives averages. On the other hand, the exact treatment of the principles of map projection and astronomical geography falls to mathematics. In physics the principles of natural science will be discussed in relation to natural phenomena, such as climate, tides, and the earth's magnetism. In conjunction with chemistry geography treats the origin of ore, salt, and coal deposits, of mineral springs, and of types of rocks and soils. It shows, in connection with this subject, the dependence of the plant and animal world upon soil and climate, the relation of life organisms to political economy; it treats the importance of foreign cultivated plants and gives a survey of the evolution of life in the course of the earth's history.

Geography as a core subject has an extraordinarily important function in the pupil's whole education by pointing out the natural relationships of all life, of the individual as well as of the community, and by furnishing a knowledge of the races and rounding out the cosmic picture. By a study of political life, and by deep insight into people and country, it serves in coöperation with the other core subjects to unify all of education. In this matter it will be able to consider the special character of the various types of schools.

In the classical *Gymnasium* geography points out, in connection with ancient history, the geographical foundations of the activities of ancient peoples which have been of great cultural value down to the present and indicates the geographical forces which aided in their extension. Geography illumines natural laws and phenomena on the basis of the geographic-political problems of ancient times and of classical economic geography. The geographical treatment of these things will be especially profitable if it is made serviceable in understanding political conditions of to-day.

In the *Realgymnasium* geography, in coöperation with the other courses characteristic of this type of school, must show the origin of the modern spirit. By means of intensive geographical treatment of Atlantic Europe, the study of race psychology and geographic-political questions, geography will work out an appreciation for the civilizations of western Europe particularly, and estimate their value for Germanism throughout the world.

The *Real* institutions, by means of the knowledge secured in mathematics and natural science, will be able to carry the pupils further in an understanding of the causal relationship of the earth's phenomena and will emphasize the practical importance of number as one of the fundamental factors of modern inter-national economy. Geographical problems of economy, technology, and trade can be treated with especial thoroughness.

### FOREIGN LANGUAGE INSTRUCTION

1. All language instruction must take its beginning from the child's world of observation, experience, and interest. In drill upon new words, the aid of the eye, ear and speech must be equally employed.

2. The method of all instruction in grammar is inductive. The principle is to be worked out from the abundance of language facts and experiences. So-called exceptions are to be shown, so far as possible, to be products of another regular development.

3. All language instruction must be based upon grammatical facts already acquired and must link up with linguistic knowledge already at hand—such as is found in the mother tongue or in a foreign language previously acquired. The fundamentals of an understanding of language facts in general must be acquired in the mother tongue itself.

4. Technical terms in grammar must be uniform at least in every school for the different languages, the same thing must be designated by the same name, and the same phenomena must be explained in the same way; for example, the gerund and historical perfect in Latin and French. The general use of Latin terminology is to be recommended for the common forms, such as substantive, verb, perfect.

5. In grammar instruction the usual method of studying isolated facts is supplemented by a method which tends to summarize the facts; for example, in Greek, general use of the objective; in Latin, similar formation of the perfect in the different conjugations; in French, uniform laws for the formation of the various verbs of the modern and archaic conjugations; in English, the different relationships as expressed by the various prepositions.

6. The reading must acquaint the pupils only with such words as are valuable in themselves; however, in its selection, the intellectual maturity and individuality of the class must

be the deciding factor. Emphasis is always to be placed upon intelligent reading of the foreign language text. Beyond this, the aim of the reading must be to feel the effect of the artistic structure and content of the whole work, and to work out the style, the technique of the author, and the individuality of his personality in the light of his times.

## ANCIENT LANGUAGES

*Introductory Remarks.* The general function of the course in ancient languages is the education of the youth by means of the formative resources which are contained in ancient intellectual and cultural life, especially in the ancient languages and literary creations.

The following detailed aims of classical language instruction cannot possibly all be equally well treated by the same teacher; rather, and quite naturally, the one or the other will be a decisive factor in attaining these aims. That they are here given equal treatment is due not only to the form of presentation, but is necessary because one aim of this course is essentially to bring about a certain harmony between them. Although the following statements apply primarily to the *Gymnasium*, they are applicable to the *Realgymnasium*, so far as the situation permits.

1. *Grammar.* Instruction in the ancient languages must aim at the pupils' conceiving the dead language as something living, and, by means of constant comparison with methods and forms of expression in the mother tongue, must seek to gain a clearer comprehension of the latter. Oral exercises in Latin and Greek are also necessary for this purpose. The use of grammatical-technical expressions must never kill the feeling for the vital nature of the language. From the first the pupils must be led to seek similarities and differences in the forms of expressions of Greek and Latin and make comparisons with German and also with other languages known, and to direct their attention to the vocabulary, the nomenclature, the word placement and sentence structure, and the like, within the various languages. Of course, the mother tongue alone will develop the organization of the grammatical knowledge itself. It is of especial importance to establish clearly the intimate relation between our mother tongue and the classical languages by means

of a study of the language wealth taken from these tongues as it appears in foreign, borrowed, and translated words. It should be the highest aim, beyond the mere study of details, to acquire a feeling for the characteristic genius of each language and thereby to refine the feeling for style in general and strengthen the feeling of responsibility for one's own style.

The results of the study of the psychology of language, particularly in the field of syntax, can be utilized widely in language instruction, as will also facts of historical philology if they lighten the learning and fixation of the foreign tongue, or bring about a larger relationship which is clear and convincing to the youth. This will be possible in Greek to a greater degree than in Latin. The principles of school grammar must never contradict the recognized principles of philology. The subject matter in grammar, particularly in Latin, with the greatly reduced number of hours, needs a thorough examination: More sharply than before distinction must be made between language facts which on their occasional appearance must be drilled upon or handled through a vocabulary and those facts which must be recognized and practiced as principles of the language. Memorizing of the so-called phrases as preparation for written exercises must be left off. The thorough mastery of knowledge thus acquired must, however, be absolutely demanded of the *Gymnasium* and the *Realgymnasium* if they are really to reach their objectives.

In pronunciation naturally only a weak approximation to the original is to be attained and complete uniformity cannot be achieved for the greatest variety of reasons. However, the following rules of pronunciation already proved to be practical are to be enforced except that the instruction must not thereby become unduly burdensome.

I. In Latin: 1. *c* as *k;* 2. *r,* if possible, without difficulty, as sounded on the end of the tongue; 3. initial *s,* mute; 4. *t* always as closed consonant, thus also before *i* as *t;* 5. attention to length of quantities so far as they are scientifically determined; attention also to double consonants and vowels in open and closed short and long syllables, for example, *sum-mus, fĕ-re, fĕr, re, lēctus.* In reading of poetry, the final vowel and the final vowel + *m* before the initial vowel are not to be entirely silent. This is accomplished by fusion of the vowels; II. Greek,

1. *al* as the ει in the pronunciation used on the stage (*Leib*); ει as ε with subsequent sound of *i* (ei); 2. η as *ä; ζ* as *d* with a vocal *s* (ds); 4. ϱ, if possible without difficulty as sounded on the tip of the tongue; 5. initial σ mute.  6. Attention paid to quantities, also single and double consonants; for example, νό-μος, ὄμ-μα and the length of ᾱ, ῑ, ῡ.

In dictating the Greek text the teacher will take pains to lighten the work of understanding the text by a still more correct pronunciation. It may be reserved to a later time to attain further objectives in this respect. In Greek no great weight needs to be laid upon writing the accent marks. If the pupils understand the rules of emphasis, they may be excused from placing accent marks, aside from exceptional cases, such as παιδεῦσαι, παιδεύσαι, παίδευσαι. The necessity of learning the accent at the same time that the word is learned is not affected, although the teacher must sometime explain fully the nature of the Greek accent in contrast to the German.

Instruction begins with the sentence. From this beginning words and fundamental forms are explained; then they are to be arranged and practiced in grammatical and thought units. Industrious drill upon the recognition and structure of forms and a sure mastery of a very definite vocabulary is the absolute prerequisite for fluent translation and successful reading. The vocabulary itself is best acquired in a way that from the beginning, in addition to the fundamental meaning of the foreign word, some important transferred meanings are acquired, though, of course, they are not necessarily to be acquired at the same time. These words must always be linked up with words which the pupils already know, such as borrowed words, foreign words, and words previously acquired in foreign languages. Continual use of the blackboard in practice upon words and word-forms is necessary, and the use of good wall charts for making concrete ideas hitherto unknown and for enlivening instruction is recommended. Up into the higher classes systematic arrangement of acquired words according to linguistic relationship and content, and also reviews of earlier vocabularies, are necessary. If hearing these vocabularies in class is necessary, this can often be done by the pupils themselves. So long as exercises are written in the foreign language, questions must be asked in the foreign language and the native tongue, even if only in the form of random tests, because the psychological processes of translation from and into a language are essentially different. If translations only from the foreign language are prepared, then the vocabularies are to be learned and recited only from the foreign language, as is always done in reading Homer.

Translation into the foreign language serves the purpose of making the pupils facile and sure with a definite grammatical fact or rule. In addition to this the teacher himself, sometimes with the aid of the pupils, would best make very easy sentences which illustrate this fact and serve as a supplement to the illustrative examples given in the school grammar. The other purpose, also a purpose to be considered in the lower section, is that of making clear the characteristic differences between the German and the foreign language; for example, the preference in German for the active voice as contrasted with the equal use of both forms in Latin; the wide use of abstract and nominal expressions in German as contrasted with the concrete and verbal in Latin. At the same time the aim is to effect the change in manner of thinking in a phrase, clause, sentence, or in a whole chain of thoughts as it is put into the foreign tongue, a task which falls primarily upon Latin in the *Gymnasium*. In order to bring about equal participation of all pupils, the work of translation, outside of sentence exercises, is best carried on in oral group work. Longer periods can also be utilized in this oral group work, along with use of the blackboard. In the lower section the German exercise book is to serve for review at home of sentences which have already been translated. Later it can be used to advantage also at home and in school for translating individual selections adequately prepared for in class. It is to be very generally required that the German selections for translation correspond to the present stage of ability and intellectual maturity of the pupils, are always to be done in good German and not in "translation German," and are always to afford a concrete, thoughtful, valuable content and present connected thoughts. What he translates must never be a matter of indifference to the pupil. From the very beginning there are added to the real translations supplementary exercises to the Latin sentences given, answers to questions, retelling of stories told by another person, transposition of stories into conversational form, short repetitions of stories, concise briefs of content, and other such language exercises.

2. *Written Class Exercises.* The number of written exercises, which as far as O III usually grow out of the practice exercise, is determined by the teacher's "activity group."

In general, it is of greater educational value to require short, easy written exercises of the pupils and to mark them more strictly than it is to discourage them with too difficult assignments or to permit them to do careless, bungling work. In particular, translation from a foreign language is so difficult an art that a pupil can test his ability well even on easy reading. In all types of these exercises, aside from those which are performed in the elementary stages of the work, it is much more valuable to develop and fix the ability really to comprehend and express an idea either in one's own or in a foreign tongue than to test the exact present knowledge of definite words or individual rules. It is just for this reason, then, that assistance from the teacher, when occasion arises or at the request of an individual pupil, is to be readily justified.

The principles developed on page 376 are to apply to the written exercises as long as there are translations into the foreign language. Specifically, every piece of work must contain a thought and must not represent a collection of grammatical difficulties. The highest goal of this translation work in Latin in the *Gymnasium* should be the translation of a very easy, short selection of German narrative prose. Grammatical transposition and amplification of given Latin selections, as well as reproduction of stories of the simpler type, are added to the real translations. The more one is able to train the pupil to independence in this field so much the greater will be his joy in the work. Translations from the foreign language serve also to supplement class reading, and it is for this end that a closer connection between the two will be sought. The use of a lexicon approved by the teacher is also permitted. The text, whether in German or in the foreign language, is to be dictated or given in hectographed or printed form.

3. *Reading.* Only such works are to be read as are valuable in themselves. In the organization of the reading the predominant thought in general should be that transcendent values are incorporated in the greatest works of the Hellenic mind,

while Rome means to us the representation of a great people, the adaptation of borrowed spiritual values into nationally characteristic form, and a universal historical mission of world importance, as well as one of the essential foundations of European culture. The choice of authors, however, must be subordinated throughout to the fundamental principle of the particular type of school. Latin instruction in the *Realgymnasium*, for example, will be organized on an essentially different basis from that of the *Gymnasium*. Still, however, a general compulsory principle cannot be set up for a particular type of school; for the individuality and ability of the teacher and that of the class must be taken into consideration in this choice within the limits, however, of the writers to be indicated later. It is, moreover, an unconditional requirement that at the beginning of the year the principles which are to control in the year's reading are determined in a conference with the other subject matter teachers of the class and the selection which is to be made is indicated and explained before the class. In this matter attention is to be given to the wishes of the pupils in order to secure diversity. However, in order to avoid disconnectedness in the instruction, simultaneous, continuous reading of poetry and prose in the same subject is to be absolutely avoided.

The reading itself is to be so organized that, until the upper classes, "activity instruction" in class, not home preparation, is to bear the chief burden. Impromptu translation can be carried on in various ways. One comes most quickly to reading by a literal translation, practiced possibly from youth up, of a sentence either read or spoken before the class, upon which translation there follows free reproduction, in good German, of the thought contained. Thorough knowledge of vocabulary and practice in recognition of individual forms is the prerequisite for this work. Construing of a sentence beginning with the verb and analysis of a whole phrase, which really is possible only if the whole sentence is already understood, are to be limited to individual cases which are especially adapted to developing the logical abilities of the pupil. The teacher will read a selection to the more mature pupils, later assign it also to be read as a whole, and after the explanation of unknown words and more difficult inflections, require them to translate it. The common determination of a final translation, a matter of course in the lower section and the rule in the middle section, is often unnecessary later. The material worked out in school must, as a rule, first be given for review. However, if the style of the author has become easy for the pupils, their careful reading or reproduction of the thought sequence renders more valuable service than the so-called retranslation. If the teacher summarizes the results of the group activity in a model translation, this is never to be assigned for literal rendering. Similarly the systematic assignment in regular sequence of a piece to be retranslated or translated first by the teacher is to be absolutely avoided.

Only after the upper section has been reached is home preparation accompanied by any real success, and then only after the introduction to the use of the lexicon. Toward the end of school course, however, a certain independence of performance must be required in this field which can especially enliven the course of reading, in that various translation exercises can be assigned to different pupils even in the class instruction itself. Every pupil must read privately in the last year a small special edition of a classical text, in the choice and performance of which the teacher is to counsel him. Where study days are introduced, these can be employed for this purpose.

The aim of the reading must always be to bring about a rounded picture of what has been read, a total impression of the author's personality, and to place vividly in mind the characteristic linguistic form, the rhythm, the intellectual content, and the artistic structure of the work. Excerpts from literature which do not make this possible are to be avoided. The further aim of the course should be to bring the work and its creator into a larger cultural unity and to point out their effect upon our intellectual life.

Thoughtful reading of a foreign text, to attain artistic delivery of poetical selections, is one of the chief objectives of classical reading; the young students can, indeed, carry this to a remarkable degree of perfection in performance. The continuous reproduction of connected portions of epic poetry by various pupils or the reading of a whole dramatic poem with rôles assigned to different pupils will form the most effective conclusion of such reading.

In this reproduction the German stress accent cannot be

well abandoned since the rhythmic relations for the German ear would not otherwise appear pronounced. This auxiliary accent must never be so strong that it destroys the quantity relationships upon which it chiefly depends. The pupils must be able to read in the Greek: hexameter, pentameter, trimeter of tragedy, trochaic tetrameter, anapestic types. From the Melian portions of tragedy only the recitation of songs to a very limited degree is generally attainable, wherein the designation of the individual colons is unnecessary. Able classes will try out their ability in delivery on the choral songs. Likewise *Demosthenes* should, at least in some portions, be recited just as is the poetry. In Latin, reading of hexameter, pentameter, and other meters is to be required as well the strophes of *Horace,* without there being need in this work of placing great value upon the designation of individual verses or strophes with grammatical terminology.

From the lower section on, only quotations, verses, poems, and prose selections the permanent possession of which is of value to the pupil are to be memorized. In this matter, scope can be allowed the selections of the individual pupil; however, each school will make up a short special list of essentials to be learned.

Good German translations can be widely used as auxiliary materials. They serve to supplement what has been read in the original by establishing connections which otherwise might not be clear, and serve also for the development of reading in general. The problem of *original* or *translation* is to be thoroughly discussed once with each pupil generation. A comparison with the original text and several available translations will afford deep insight into the nature of their own and of the foreign language and make clear the irreplaceable, inherent value of the original.

4. *Art Appreciation.* The reading will be supplemented by the study of works in the creative arts. To be sure, only those trained therein would dare to use them in their instruction. The employment of worthwhile pictures and books from the collections of the school, the teacher, or the pupils, and, wherever possible, repeated visits to museums and excavations are to be recommended in this connection. For the introduction to an appreciation of classical creative art in the *Gymnasium,*

the examples of Greek vase painting are admirably suited because they give the youth something concrete and easily understandable. The works of Roman craft and architecture have corresponding application in the *Realgymnasium*.

If the drawing and the art instruction are to lead to deeper penetration into the formal phases of art, then there devolves upon the Greek and Latin instruction the problem of presenting the work of the plastic arts in addition to that of the rhetorical arts as the expression characteristic of the period and thus as much to deepen the appreciation of its special character as to make clear the characteristic nature of the foreign art as such. Thus the knowledge of cultural interrelationships and obedience to natural laws of intellectual development can at least be begun. The other problem, that of causing the present value of the work to be appreciated and the ethical and aesthetic meaning significantly grasped, is not, to be sure, to be separated from this.

It is also essential for the pupil of the *Gymnasium* to develop a notion of the importance of Greek music, not only on account of its directly commanding position within Greek culture, and its inestimable value for national unity, education, and drama, but primarily because of the fundamental attitude of the Greeks toward music, which expresses itself in their emphasis upon its ethical and educative significance and which, indeed, is beginning to become ours. The reading of tragedy and Plato forces us directly to a discussion of these problems.

5. *Philosophical Study.* The ancient language instruction offers a very outstanding opportunity for philosophical study and for discussion of philosophical problems. Indeed, language instruction cannot pass over the problem of the importance and validity of rules of logic within the language, and the attempt, which is always to be made, to indicate syntactical phenomena from the point of view of its psychological foundations, will give meaning to the pupil's own personal intellectual life and that of the race.

The chief part of the work, however, falls to the reading. Indeed, instruction in philosophy is first to expand the picture already attained of ancient civilization, and second, chiefly in the Greek, to acquaint the pupil with the original problems of philosophy and their vital influence down even into our own

intellectual life.  According to the personal aptitude and genius
of the teacher, the one or the other objective will assume the
more prominent place.  In any case the formerly much used
plan of laying weight upon attitudes which are of little value
for intellectual training is to be discontinued, as, for example,
the various pre-Socratic theories of the elements.  The discussion must always begin with the reading of the sources, never
with a lecture by the teacher.

If the doctrines of ancient philosophers are studied in connection with Greek and Roman civilization, its special function is to present the characteristic interlacing of philosophical
theory with the political life, with the literature, and with the
art of that epoch.  It should be shown, for example, how the
awakening of the true philosophical problem of the sixth and
fifth centuries is connected with the development of personality
generally, as is illustrated by the lyric poetry, the drama, or
the plastic arts, even though in various degrees and ways.  Again
it should be pointed out how the period of enlightenment in the
second half of the fifth century is most intimately related to the
political revolution and how Plato's theory of the state is most
closely connected with the political necessity of the age.

The purely philosophical approach can thus develop the mind
of the youth in a most remarkable manner, and train it for
independent thought; so that the youth is once more led along
the way, as it were, which the only original European philosophy
has gone, mounting with deeper logic from childlike beginnings
quickly to the most difficult problems.  The same result can be
reached by thorough investigation of some special problem or of
the theory of any single personality.  In fact, intensive study of
the works of Plato alone can result in affording this general
training of the mind.

Among the many great fields of ancient philosophy and the
numerous great individual personalities, the following are of
special importance for instruction in school:

a. As preparation for the reading of Plato in general: Among
the pre-Socratic theories those of substance and matter, of
mind and formative principle; those of the notions of genesis
and being, of unity and plurality, of perception and thinking;
Parmenides and Heraclitus, the personalities which essentially
represent the two original types of philosophic thought.

*b.* In connection with reading of the *Gorgias:* the epoch of the enlightenment and the theories of the sophists with reference to the relation between nature and law, nature and morality, nature and the state, nature and religion.

*c.* In association with the *Apology,* the Socratic dialogues, *Phaedo,* Socrates, the dialectician, but preëminently the moralist, who stands and is the great exemplar of complete unity between theory and life.

*d.* In the reading of the *Meno, Phaedo,* the *Symposium,* or the *Republic:* Plato's discovery of the *à priori,* his theory of the relation between the physical world and the world of values with love as their connecting link, his theory of the ideal state, to which Aristotle's ethical and political theories form an especially educative and valuable supplement.

*e.* In reading Cicero, Seneca, Marcus Aurelius, and Epictetus: the two typical, antithetical systems of morality, the Epicurean and Stoic.

How much of this can be treated in the instruction itself and how much in the "activity group" in philosophy will depend primarily upon the aptitude of the class for philosophy.

6. *Civic Education.* The reading of Greek and Roman historians, statesmen, poets, and philosophers leads necessarily to a discussion of political ideas, problems of political life in the field of domestic and foreign politics, economic questions, the question of the relation of the individual to the community, of the duties of the individual to his fellow men in general. Emphasis will be laid upon the point that, of the notions by which humanity to-day seeks to mold political life, almost all spring from the ideas of the ancients or are shaped by their manner of thinking. If it is possible to give the greater relationships here instead of isolated facts, to sketch by means of examples within a year or portion of a year a picture of the nature of Attic states and their civilization under Pericles or of the Roman empire under Augustus, or if it is possible to present the problem of the ideal state as given by Plato, Aristotle, or Polybius (in connection with the reader of Wilamowitz), still greater would be the value of the instruction. Premature comparison of present-day political and economic conditions with those of ancient times, the teacher will seek to counteract; much rather will he endeavor truly to clarify the mind by

working out similarities and differences. But beyond this instruction, the course must set up ideals and create types, cause men to speak whose patriotism is an illuminating example, cause ages to be relived whose unity of spirit was of remarkable strength and resolution, as compared with others in which differences led to misery and decline. In the same way the narrowness of the pre-Hellenic conception of the state as well as the unsocial organization of ancient society must be made clear. The peculiar relation of the Roman to his state deserves especial consideration. But it is also important to recall that leading German minds have more than once been strengthened in times of political necessity by the inspiring loftiness of an ancient ideal.

7. *Concentration.* Since Latin and Greek are the characteristic subjects of the *Gymnasium,* the other subjects must seek connections with them as the beginning point, in that within their individual fields they should indicate that the foundations of science and of all individual sciences were laid by the Greeks and have come to us through the mediation of the Romans, that many other relationships exist between European and ancient civilizations, that also in artistic fields their accomplishments and views are of greatest value for the present age. The highest aim for the entire instruction in literature, creative arts, music, and gymnastics can be to make the youth sensitive to the beautiful as interpreted by Plato and to show them their obligation and path to the regulation of their own lives. Mathematics will in the same way strive toward this goal of a truly humanistic training. Upon German and history will fall the special task of developing the constantly renewed influence of the ancient world—be it liberating or restrictive—upon the intellectual and cultural history of the German people; and upon the German instruction the task of pointing out its incomparable importances for the golden age of German literature from Lessing to Hölderlin and even beyond to our present day.

But the classical language instruction must also from its own standpoint enter into mutual activity with the other subjects and will at other times have to play a supporting rôle. Especially must it take over important problems from the instruction in ancient history, furnish material, supplement and deepen in *Prima* earlier presentations, and especially in *Obersekunda* through the selections for reading assist in the study of older German and of medieval history and literature. If, however, in the Greek instruction of *Prima* itself, for example, Goethe's *Achilleis* or the *Helena*-act and the classical *Walpürgisnacht* from Faust II, or Hölderlin's *Archipelagus* are discussed, the very intimate relations between ancient and German intellectual life must be made especially clear to the pupils.

In the *Realgymnasium* the close relation between the Latin and the French instruction must not only serve as evidence of the development of the Romance language but must also assist in explaining the nature of the Romance civilization as such. The relationship with the German and the history instruction must primarily make clearer the influence of the Latin-Romance element upon the intellectual and cultural history of Germany and work out this relationship itself more sharply by contrasting Romance and German characteristics. Between English and Latin there appear manifold relationships in the fields of language, literature, and politics.

8. *Free Activity Groups.* Classical language "activity groups" are to solve special problems for the gifted and especially interested pupils, problems which serve to extend and intensify class instruction. They must not serve in any way to develop a group of specialists; but here, too, the attention must ever be directed toward the essential and those things which aid in general culture. Materials and methods of work are manifold. The Latin language instruction might attempt here with those interested the more difficult translations into the foreign tongue. Primarily, however, a freely developed extended reading of the Greek and Latin, even late Latin, poetry and prose, will afford worth while enrichment. Out of these "activity groups" to a still greater degree than from class instruction will grow longer home exercises in German which can serve as a substitute for compositions prepared at home.

### MODERN LANGUAGES

*Introduction.* Modern language instruction in the secondary schools seeks through literature to introduce the pupils to the cultural and intellectual life of foreign nations upon the basis of an all-round, thorough knowledge of the language.

The introduction to the foreign intellectual world should seek no mere acquaintance with isolated cultural facts and situations; it is rather a question of teaching how to understand life as it affects the whole of a foreign civilization, especially in its language and literature, and of making it useful for the pupil's spiritual training. Especially should the pupil be led to a thorough knowledge of the genius of his own race through a comparison of the foreign character with the German. This problem expresses itself characteristically in the various types of schools, according to their specific educational objectives.

The pupil is to be so far advanced in the use of the language that he is able to express orally and in writing, in a manner in keeping with his age, simple subject matter or thought connections with which he is familiar.

The general aim set up here for modern language instruction must control in a situation where according to the program of instruction a smaller number of hours is assigned to a foreign language.

*Principles of Method*

1. *Pronunciation.* As the acquisition of good pronunciation is the chief care in the early instruction of a foreign language, so its development remains an essential problem in all classes. The aim will be to give the speech organs of the pupils complete adjustment for the foreign language, as nearly as possible approximating that of the foreigners. If once this foundation of the sounds especially characteristic of the foreign language is attained (the vowels in French, and in English *l, r,* and the dental consonants in addition), it will be easy to get the other individual sounds. Peculiarities of the local dialects of pupils serviceable for pronunciation are to be watched for especially, as the North German *l* and *r* for English, as well as those which interfere, as the confusion of mute and voice consonants. Just as important as acquaintance with the correct pronunciation of the individual sounds and sound combinations is the acquisition of the sentence modulation characteristic of the foreign tongue, which is also of extraordinary importance as a syntactical device. Only untiring illustrative speech on the part of the teacher (who must from time to time train his own ear by visits to foreign countries and by means of phonograph records) and carefully supervised speech imitation by the pupils, can

lead to satisfactory results in this respect. The teacher must endeavor in this instruction to recognize any special difficulties in the case of each individual pupil and try to eliminate them. The oral exercises in elementary phonetic instruction are always to proceed from observation, to be accompanied by action if possible, and in general to be as lively as possible. In the first few weeks of language instruction, the phonetic point of view must predominate under all circumstances. However, phonetics must be only a means in the instruction. It is left to the judgment of the instructor as to how far he will employ in the beginning a special phonetic script. In any event, the same phonetic script must be used in all language instruction of the same institution, the best being that of the *Association Phonétique*.

2. *Oral Exercises*. The oral exercises are to train the pupil in a free use of the foreign language. Since in this work the fresh enthusiasm of the pupil is of decisive importance, the grammatical controls must be practiced to such degree and in such form as will not endanger the real purpose of these exercises. The pupils are to ask and answer questions among themselves as occasion permits and thus arrive at a constantly increasing independence in work. However, the teacher must not forget that he is the chief source of all the skill of the pupils and the chief model for their pronunciation in learning a foreign language. In keeping with the principle that knowledge of the word and meaning must go hand in hand, the oral exercises take their starting point from observations of the simplest objects, the immediate environment, and the incidents of daily life in school and home.

The sections of the reader are to be read only after they have become the pupil's possession by means of oral exercises. Later the oral exercises are correlated with the reading for the most part, without, however, becoming a mere repetition of what has been read. The oral exercises in connection with the reading or dependent upon it must be of assistance in all classes in the activity group work of the various subjects, since they take in the fields of local environmental studies, geography, history, technology, and the like, which at times stand in the foreground.

3. *Grammar*. The grammar instruction should not, as has frequently been the case, give rules for translation, but should clarify the inner character of foreign language phenomena. In this

work the comparison with the mother tongue and with other foreign languages, as well as psychological and historical explanations, must be called into play as opportunity is afforded and according to the pupil's stage of development.

Grammatical knowledge is fundamentally inductive and, so far as possible, should be worked out on the basis of concrete language materials already acquired. Instruction in the various languages must be connected in such a way that the knowledge gained in one language can be made useful for other languages taken up later. The essentially important facts which appear in all languages (word placement, verbal nouns, mood and tense) are to be so thoroughly treated on their first appearance in any one language that it will suffice in the other languages to call attention to the peculiarities of their use. Thus becomes possible an organization of all language instruction which guarantees uniform knowledge and saves valuable time. The uniform method of study must find its expression in a uniform terminology for the subject, which is to be fixed or constant for every individual institution at least. On account of the difficulty of the subject it is impossible to give the grammatical instruction other than in the mother tongue. Technical expressions from the modern foreign languages are necessary so far as they do not designate a phenomenon characteristic of a special language. The regular grammar work has to treat only that which is essential and that which is really living in the language. In the beginning stages of the instruction in connection with the observational material of the language and with the coöperation of the pupils, the most necessary and simple grammatical statements are to be made; still these must be in a form which has a scientific basis to preclude their being rejected later as incorrect. Thus it is important that the difference between element of meaning and element of relationship be clear from the beginning. Syntactical peculiarities of the foreign language are to be made the pupil's possession in the lower section on the basis of imitation. In the higher section it is necessary to understand in an increasingly more thorough and connected manner the rules of language development. The observational materials in language necessary for this purpose are to be brought together from reading materials already worked out and from the linguistic possessions already at hand. So far as possible this is to be done by dividing the work among groups of pupils. The statement of rules, the association with what has already been learned, the derivation of conclusions, the explanation of difficulties and apparent contradictions, take place in lively "activity groups" made up of the teacher and the pupils. The latter must learn that phenomena which superficially are conceived as irregularities or as exceptions to a rule indicate that this rule is not yet sufficiently well understood or indicate the result of another development just as regular. (*Viens* compared with *venons, meurs* compared with *mourons, lève* compared with *levons,* are just as regular as *parle* compared with *parlons.*) The power of analogy in language must be brought to the pupil's attention early. The illustration of a rule through the similarity of the coexistent (*read: sets* similiar *to books:* friends; *loved: ended,* similar to *things: foxes* or *horses*) can also be supplemented, where the pupil's knowledge permits, by insight into the law of consequents (phenomena of French etymology and syntax in relation to the Latin, and of the English in relation to the German). Occasionally it can also be pointed out how language usage is regulated by arbitrary determination and the natural connection concealed. (The present participle in French by intervention of the Academy.) At the end of the discussions on grammar and out of the fullness of similar phenomena, the principle must stand clearly developed before the pupil's mind. The search and construction of illustrative examples may again be carried on through group work.

Any consideration which takes the individual fact in grammar out of its natural setting is to be avoided. It is advisable, for example, to take up the French verbs in such a way that the most common verbs could be drilled upon in the present stem forms at the same time, corresponding to the customary method of instruction in the lower section, where the descriptive method of elementary instruction chiefly requires the present form. In further cross-sections through the whole conjugation there follow, then, in connection with the various individual forms which have already become familiar in poems and stories learned, the forms of the historic perfect, the imperfect subjunctive, the perfect participle, and, finally, the future, in groups related by the laws of language. If the conjugation is to be grasped in its comprehensive regularity, summarizing longitudinal sections, that is, sequential organization of the forms of the individual verbs must fix what has been learned. In the study of the French subjunctive the different meanings of the moods are to be worked out first and so far as possible are to be brought to higher units; then for the first time the cases may be summarized where the subjunctive is used in principal, subject or object, adverbial or adjective clauses. In the study of the preposition, it is best to begin with the types of relationships which are expressed by the various prepositions; then upon this basis the various possible methods of procedure may not be wholly kept apart from one another, but that they must naturally interact goes without saying.

In the upper section the treatment of grammar must be considered from different points of view than in the middle section. Here the incisive characteristics of the nature of the foreign language are observed and the facts from the various fields brought up to the same level. In addition, language history and the comparative study of the several languages are recommended to encourage the pupils to make their own observations in connection with their reading.

4. *Oral and Written Exercises.* In these exercises it is to be assumed as a fundamental principle that a language is acquired only by a progressively freer use of linguistic attainments previously acquired from models of perfection. Thus, the first exercises consist, among other things, of dictations, answering simple questions, paradigms, sentence conjugation, completion of sentences, and inversions. As the observational material, the pupil's immediate and more remote environment, pictures, experiences, and occurrences must first be treated orally in the class instruction before the corresponding sections of the reading book are used, so also should the written exercises connected therewith be prepared first orally. Since these exercises are to become progressively freer and more independent, the pupils will undertake all types of composition in connection with the reading material,—reproduction of stories from the German and foreign languages, portrayal of their own experiences, and letters. The problems increase in extent and difficulty in the upper section, where particularly the practice in understanding and retaining rather long connected spoken passages in the foreign language must also not be neglected. Translations from

the German must be related to the language ability already developed by the pupils. A practice book for this purpose is not possible because of the great amount of modern language reading material. These exercises, therefore, are to be taken up in class, use being made of the blackboard and the pupils' notebooks. By gradually increasing the difficulty, the teacher himself can read rather long connected passages to the pupils, and, beginning with the central thought and adding the other elements in logical fashion, can translate these passages with the students into the foreign language. In this manner the pupil arrives at a really fluent, idiomatic reproduction of the sentence whole instead of a halting translation after the fashion of the practice book. As capsheaf, then, of this type of exercise in the upper section, the free translation of a pure German text can be attempted from the German reading material available to the pupil.

Memorization of foreign language selections is very necessary for the development of language feeling and, therefore, at times is to be recommended in the lower section. However, the reproduction of memorized material should, if possible, be combined with a change, even though small, in language form, for example in tense and person, and should gradually lead to free reproduction. The principle of coöperative work can very often be made fruitful, for example, in preparation of dialogues.

The number of written class exercises, which as a rule up to the *Obertertia* grow out of the practice exercises, is determined by the teachers' "activity group."

5. *Vocabulary.* Memorization of single words before they have appeared in vital situations in speech and have been practiced upon is, of course, without purpose, because relatively seldom are two expressions in different languages exactly equivalent. Vocabularies, then, are to be assigned for drill only after the material has been worked through and, of course, in such a manner that the pupils will also be trained thereby for independent work by classifying the words according to form and meaning. Special gifts of the individual pupils are to be considered as far as possible. The extension of the pupils' vocabulary must be pursued systematically in various directions. At regular intervals, perhaps every month, their knowledge is to be tested, and in every year's work the objectives for the de-

velopment of the vocabulary are to be fixed, keeping carefully in mind the vocabulary already acquired.

6. *Reading*. Reading is the central point of emphasis of the modern language instruction. The connected reading of entire works or independent portions thereof is to begin as early as possible; in the case of the fundamental language, in the third or fourth year, and in the case of the second language, at the latest in the second year. The guiding principle in the selection of reading material, besides the requirement of higher worth in form, is the introduction to the various fields and epochs of the foreign intellectual life in the special direction required by the special type of school. However, proper consideration is always to be paid to the pupils' stage of development in order that they may be intimately acquainted with the works studied. This point of view applies equally to the question of the extent of recent literature that may be employed in the course. More important than many-sided stimulation is it to inspire the youthful mind, and this can in general be effected better by masterpieces of proven worth than through works for which the necessary perspective of distance is still lacking. In order to facilitate correlation with other subjects and to open up to the students as manifold cultural materials as possible, from the middle section upwards a collection of poems is to be employed, only for supplementary purposes in relation to the connected reading, of course; and, at least in the upper section, a collection of rather long prose selections, organized around certain particular points of view.

In the earliest years an appreciation of the reading material is to be developed in the class period. The association of the new with material previously read affords for home work the most varied type of exercise, assigned to individual pupils according to their inclination and ability, so that what has been read in one class period can be reproduced in the following class hour by various pupils in entirely different ways. After the pupils are accustomed in class to careful preparation, home preparation can be done more and more on the basis of division of the reading work, and the reading of a selection will more often form the conclusion of a discussion in the foreign language leading to it. Naturally, since a thoughtful reading presupposes an exact acquaintance with the reading material, working through the material must precede the actual reading.

The discussion of questions in foreign cultural and intellectual life is also to be based as far as possible upon home preparation in which the work is distributed among the pupils. This includes summaries of materials previously read, reading of assigned portions from foreign authors, and German works which have not been studied. It is a fundamental aim that the foreign language be used as much as possible in connection with the work in reading; however, this must not be employed at the expense of clearness and thorough intellectual appreciation. Particularly out of consideration for pronunciation and language feeling, frequent comparison between mother tongue and the foreign language is to be avoided. In the upper section the evaluation of the artistic form and of the spirit therein expressed must form the climax of the discussion. The relation of the individual work to the author's entire production, his position in his period, and the importance of his works for intellectual history are also to be developed. Thoughtful, expressive reading discloses values which are not obtained through any translation or explanation, and it is therefore to be especially cultivated by teacher and pupil. In general, it must be one of the most essential functions of the foreign language reading to permit the works studied to be understood and experienced as works of art in the French or English language. The translation of individual passages into good German, which permits the stylistic character of the foreign tongue to be seen in especially sharp contrast with that of the mother tongue, must be worked out in class or assigned frequently in all sections. Written exercises of this type are an excellent means for developing German style. Artistic German translations can be utilized to supplement and round out cross-sections in literature, as well as to disclose more intimately the meaning of what has been read.

In the discussion of problems of poetry the pupils are to be shown the relation between the artist's means and his desire for expression. For example, they are to be shown how the inner rhythm of his discourse vitalizes the scheme of the chosen meter. Similarly, they must get some insight into the relationships existing between theory of versification and the general character of the language.

In every class some important poems and occasionally suitable prose selections must be made the pupils' permanent possession by memorization and frequent repetition. This selection, especially in the upper section, can be left in part to the individual pupils.

The pupils' individual reading in the foreign language, at least in the last years in school, can be vitalized by assigning to each according to his inclination and ability a work—naturally, one not too comprehensive—which he will report upon in the foreign tongue in special periods set aside in the general plan of instruction. The reading of a newspaper or a magazine is recommended in the upper section.

7. *Philosophical Treatment.* To be sure, the grammatical study which penetrates into the nature of linguistic phenomena, as well as the comparative study, is an exercise in philosophical thought in which the psychological and the logical considerations are concerned to a like degree. A philosophical language study can inquire, beyond the various laws and phenomena, concerning the inner impelling forces of linguistic life. Philosophical discussions of all sorts attach themselves to every worthwhile piece of reading. There is no lack of philosophical writers in French and English literature who can be read with profit by the pupils of the upper section. The particularly pragmatic character of English thought can be made just as fruitful for the pupils' training as can the French power of abstraction. Finally, the evaluation of the fundamental characteristics and the significant features of the foreign intellectual life, in contrast to corresponding factors in German thought, imposes upon this philosophically intensive study a task that is not easy but has its compensations.

8. *Art Appreciation.* The observation of works of art becomes a valuable aid in supplementing corresponding reading as an introduction of the pupils to the total character of an important epoch in French and Anglo-Saxon cultural life, as of the French Middle Ages, the age of Louis XIV, the French intellectual development in the eighteenth and nineteenth centuries, and the Victorian age. If the pupils are shown that a similar development arose in the painting, sculpture, and music of a people, and that a change in the political and social conditions runs parallel, this will generally give him an appreciation of the principles controlling intellectual development. In this manner

not only the cultural epochs of an individual people become clear but also do the relations of the various cultural fields in mutual giving and taking, and, finally, the incisive characteristics of the foreign type, but always in comparison with their own.

9. *Civic Education.* Civic education through modern languages will be associated primarily with the reading of works and essays that have historical or political content, but it will be also an important method of approach in the evaluation of social and political organization in foreign lands, and of important social and political movements as well as of outstanding personages.

10. *Concentration.* The following are named as examples of problems which modern language instruction can take the lead in or help in solving in coöperative work with the other subjects: Germanic nationality (principles of the English constitution and social order, Germanic elements in the French and English languages, and similar problems). Germanic folk poetry (English ballads). Humor and feeling (Dickens). Fundamental forms of artistic composition (Shakespeare and French classicism). Germanic and Romance sense of form (English and French lyric). Fundamental forms of political and historical thought (French and English statesmen and historians). Fundamental forms of philosophic attitude (English and French philosophers). Forms of artistic and social culture (French poetry of the ages of Louis XIV to Louis XVI). Nordic renaissance (Shakespeare). Romantic spirit (English and French writers, but not merely of romanticism in its narrower sense). Relation between literary and cultural development (French lyric in the nineteenth century). Means of poetical composition (English and French poetry). Phases in the decline of intellectual life (French and English literary history as a whole). Problems of contemporary economics, technology, and social order (French and English and American writers of the present day).

In the *Realgymnasial* schools, where the modern languages form the characteristic subject groups and together with the core subjects are responsible for the educational unity of the school to an especial degree, connections must be made reaching out from them in all directions and in well-considered relationships, in order that the pupil may acquire a vivid picture of the forces which have stood in mutual interchange with German culture and which together with it have formed the intellectual being of Europe to-day. As English, as an essentially Germanic language, together with German, directs attention to the related Nordic peoples, and much in English literature is adapted to deepen the German feeling of life, so also will the French in close connection with Latin furnish the supplementary counterpart. This objective, of course, must not bring the modern language instruction in the *Realgymnasium* into a one-sided dependence upon the other subjects, not even upon history.

Again, the emphasis upon the present which is demanded in the *Oberrealschule* is not to be understood to mean that the great values of the past are to be pushed into the background; and the connection with natural science and technology must be sought more in the intellectual than in the material.

In the *Gymnasium,* where French is the modern language, the instruction will emphasize especially the Latin element which has been operative in its effect from classical times down and which also appears clearly in modern literature; while English as the modern foreign language in the *Gymnasium* will be connected especially closely with the study of Germanism.

Since the study of the same topics in the various subjects naturally cannot be taken up all at the same time, the modern language instruction will be in relation to the instructional problems of the other subjects, partly preparatory, partly parallel, and partly retrospective.

11. *Free Activity Groups.* Many of the problems indicated here can be pursued further in the free activity groups. For these groups the intellectual development of the pupil and the organic connection with the whole of instruction must be the directing points of view. To a certain degree, however, consideration can also be given to the special interests of the pupils, for example, through showing a preference for contemporary literature and the discussion of problems of the day in connection with editorials found in newspapers.

### ELECTIVE LANGUAGE INSTRUCTION

The principles laid down for modern language instruction in French and English find corresponding application to the other modern foreign languages, both in the restricted elective instruction in the *Oberschule* and the *Aufbauschule*, and in other elective instruction. The organization of detailed courses of study must for the time being be reserved for the individual institutions.

## MATHEMATICS

*General Aim.* Accuracy and skill in calculation with finite numbers, especially in oral arithmetic and in the application of these attainments to daily life. Training in the correct conception of values of quantities. Development and assimilation of accurate mathematical knowledge which leads to the point of view that mathematics is an ordered science which can be built up out of its own fundamental principles. Attainment of the ability to recognize form, dimension, number, and principle in objects and phenomena of the environment, and also to apply this acquired knowledge independently. Especially, the development of the power of spatial comprehension and skill in mathematical conception of the mutual dependence of variable quantities. Training in logical procedure and proof, and definite knowledge of the philosophical value of mathematical processes and the importance of mathematics for intellectual history.

*Remarks on Method*

I. *General Principles.* 1. Definite mathematical knowledge, resting upon clear understanding, is to be attained by constant adaptation to the pupils' capacity of perception and through their intellectual coöperation, according to the principle of activity instruction. This is attained by rejecting thoughtless memorizing of explanations, principles, and rules, and by completely eliminating memorization of proofs. The subject matter is to be viewed from the standpoint that only such principles and processes as have value for their inner relationships and for their practical application are to be utilized in the instruction. Memoriter material is to be limited to that which is absolutely essential, but this is to be fixed by continual repetition.

2. Mathematical knowledge is to be developed into power by means of solutions of exercises and problems. The exercises are not to be limited to drill upon the subject matter, but shall attach importance to searching out geometric and algebraic principles and to readiness in reasoning and proof; gradually they

should lead to intellectual independence in the treatment of mathematical questions, even in the solution of more difficult connected problems.

3. Applied problems shall be taken from real life and shall lead to results of practical value. Through a study of the other subjects of instruction and of the pupil's environment, the applications are to be made worth while with respect to concrete instruction, especially that which deals with the phenomena of economic life. Skill in actual calculation must not be lost in this process. In these applications the very closest connections are to be sought with the study of the local community.

4. The pupil is to be led early, by means of a simple calculation or graphic sketch, before the exact calculation of his problem, to give an estimate of the answer to be expected. He must form a judgment concerning the problems of solubility and the number and type of solutions, and, finally, he must test the correctness of the result found.

5. The insight, already attained in the middle section, into the limits of the estimation of the exactitude of such calculations, which are connected with measurements, will be developed in the upper classes in all suitable cases into an estimation of the degree of exactness attained in the final results.

6. The greatest value is to be laid in all classes upon care in language expression and practice in clear, comprehensive presentation.

7. The history of mathematics is to be thoroughly considered in this work, both in the development of the subject matter and in the assignment of problems. Its connection with the general cultural development is to be emphasized wherever possible. The pupils of the upper classes are to be stimulated to read writers important in the history of mathematics.

8. The mathematical terminology follows the proposals for the unification of mathematical terminology of the German Committee for Mathematical and Natural Science Instruction.

II. *Arithmetic.* 1. The arithmetic instruction, in addition to training in the calculation of numbers, is primarily to further the understanding of the importance of number values. Oral and written calculation is to be practiced generally throughout algebraic and geometric instruction. Special emphasis is to be placed in all classes upon calculation without pencil.

2. Exercises in short methods of calculation, especially from *Quarta* on, are best connected with measurements which afford the opportunity of showing that exaggerated exactness is meaningless.

3. Even in the arithmetic instruction in the lowest classes the employment of lines and surfaces to make quantitative relationships concrete is to be taken advantage of as far as possible. Approximately from *Quinta* on, one will permit the geometric representation of number series to follow the representation of the individual quantities. Great weight is to be placed upon the comprehension of the practical importance of such illustrations; they lead later on to the graphical representation of empirical functions, which then forms further the starting point for the graphical treatment of analytic functions.

4. The informational instruction necessary in preparation for everyday methods of calculation and for problems from economic life must not smother the real arithmetic and must hold itself within the range of experience that may be attained by the pupil.

III. *Algebra, Calculus, and Analytics.* 1. The arithmetic instruction in the lowest classes summarizes the simple rules of calculation by means of algebraic formulas. Algebra begins with the derivation of tables from formulas by means of insertion of number values. The fundamental principles of algebra are treated as a summary of the knowledge acquired in arithmetic instruction. The fundamental operations are practiced as far as possible in connection with the study of equations of the first degree, and similarly the principles of proportion.

2. The function idea, which is to be placed at the central point of instruction, is introduced at first objectively in order that it may be gradually conceived more sharply and in the upper section be treated in general form. The introduction to the fundamentals of graphic representation begins as early as *Untertertia* with practical examples. The most important characteristics of empirical functions are connected herewith in a purely objective treatment: continuity, variation, area. In order to attain a clear differentiation of the concepts *unknown* and *equation* from the concepts *variable* and *function,* the graphic representation in the right-angled coördinate system must be treated only after the equations of the first degree with several unknowns. In all sections, but especially in the middle classes,

attention is to be called to the fact that in the employment of graphic representations, pictorial reproduction is not an end in itself but only a means of surveying the course of a function. In addition to this the other means, the table, is to be fully evaluated in its importance.

3. Through the introduction of infinitesimal methods the pupils receive a knowledge of the most important tool of mathematics. Here the instruction must seek a middle path between justified requirements for mathematical rigidity and regard for practical needs, and it will have to employ freely the auxiliary means of geometric representation.

IV. *Geometry.* 1. A preparatory study, proceeding from the consideration of simple bodies, trains the power of observation, develops the power of geometric abstraction, trains for the correct description of geometric forms, and gives the pupils practice in estimation, measurement, construction of models, and in the first use of rule and compass.

2. This instruction provides insight into the systematic organization of geometry and leads from geometrical knowledge to geometrical understanding in that it proceeds from an empirical foundation to a logical, deductive method of study, and thus trains the pupils to the need of proof.

3. Even in the lower section, the mobility of plane and spatial forms is to be freely used and the influence of variation of individual parts of a figure upon the dimensions of the others is to be determined. Especially to be studied further are axial and central symmetry, rotation, displacement, and superposition of geometric forms.

4. Through the employment of suitable observational types from reality, and also in plane geometry, the connection with spatial relationships is to be vividly maintained.

5. In order to attain concreteness, attention is to be given to the correct and careful execution of figures, and to the use of crosshatching and color. Models are recommended as auxiliary means of development of power of spatial observation but must not hinder this development, since the power of spatial observation must grow gradually into the power of spatial conception.

6. Geometrical knowledge, especially in assigning problems, is to be brought into vital relationship with its application.

7. The geometrical constructions to be carried on in close connection with this course demand, in addition to rule and compass, the tools of mechanical drawing, especially the T square and drawing triangle. Approximate constructions are to be studied, and occasionally intensive work is to be done with reference to unfavorable relations of position. In the so-called analysis primary attention is to be given to thought procedures through which one arrives at the solution. Qualified pupils are to be encouraged to make critical comparisons of the various methods of construction. All artificial constructions from unusual phases of the subject are to be avoided.

8. Goniometry and trigonometry limit themselves to the simplest goniometric formulas and the fundamental principles of the plane and spherical triangle. After the introduction of the goniometric functions, calculation with their values according to the process of short decimal calculation is to be thoroughly practiced.

9. The introduction to solid geometry, which was carried at first on a purely objective basis, is studied now both graphically and arithmetically at the same time, and then goes over gradually to a regular, scientific method of instruction, which along with limitation to the most important principles, clothes the fundamental ideas and principles in concrete form.

10. Indeed, from the lowest classes up, geometrical drawing in close connection with the instruction makes clear to the pupil geometric facts, indicates their practical application, and makes him gradually more conscious of the close connections between spatial observation, spatial conception, and spatial representation. The perpendicular projection on a single plane is very simple and therefore purposeful for elementary instruction.

11. Measurements are to be practiced from the beginning. In this connection the exactness of measurements will be increased gradually by the use of more refined means, until finally an idea is obtained of the extraordinary difficulty involved in the exact execution of geodetic and astronomical measurements.

12. The necessity of preserving clearness concerning the purpose and meaning of work in mathematics arouses in the pupil the desire for a concluding survey of work in the elementary mathematics which has been studied, to which a view into its further development can be tied. The importance of mathe-

matics as a science and its influence upon life and life conceptions should be discussed.

V. *Concentration.* Between mathematics and the other subjects the establishment of as many interrelationships as possible should be sought. The close connections between the logical side of mathematics and the grammatical side of languages offer, even as does the necessity of the explanation of the technical words, the possibility of coöperative activity and mutual support. Spatial observation and the principles of projection can be used in the study of art. Classical and modern language courses can also include mathematical materials.

Mathematics should not only address itself to the pupil's power of judgment but should also quicken interest in the origin of mathematical content. Facts from the history of mathematics which are meaningful for the great general problem of human development furnish, together with the biographical element, important material for mathematics instruction. The mathematician can supplement the cultural history of the historian. So far as possible, the association of the problem of mathematics with historical postulation is recommended. In this matter ancient history will demonstrate itself to be very valuable for the *Gymnasium.* Occasionally the entire historical development of an important individual problem should be worked out.

Civic studies, too, must be considered in the mathematics instruction. Problems from the affairs of community and state, from commerce and trade, afford occasion in arithmetic for factual instruction. Agriculture and public food questions, use and manufacture of wares, and labor conditions furnish material for graphic representation in the middle section. Real problems in the upper section can be taken from the money system and computation of insurance.

Mathematics stands in closest relationship to all the natural sciences. The instruction must show that the accuracy of insight in natural sciences increases with the mathematical control over natural laws.

The fundamental conceptions of geographic representation are geometric in nature. Mathematical geography, astronomy, and geodesy are assigned to mathematics. The mathematics materials taken from these fields are also to be used for the cultivation of the "home idea."

Mathematics must devote a considerable portion of its time to drawing. The relations of the plastic arts to geometry and the importance of perspective as the basis of painting are to be explained by means of suitable examples during the mathematics instruction.

Logic and metaphysics find, too, their place in mathematics. The psychological foundations of mathematical thought should also be touched upon by this instruction. Individual problems, such as number and spatial concepts, are studied from a philosophical point of view wherever possible.

Handwork is to be so organized for mathematics that pupils themselves are taught to construct models of solids from pasteboard, after sketching the drawing plans necessary for the purpose. The models necessary for the development of geometrical thinking can be pasted together from prepared modeling paper. Skill in metal work and woodwork can be used in such a way that pupils can construct apparatus to make stereometric principles concrete.

VI. *Free Activity Groups.* Pupils in various classes can combine to form free "activity groups" for work in certain phases of mathematics which are units in themselves, without increasing the objectives of the school tasks.

The works of mathematical writers, as well as monographs, calculation and mathematical instruments, acturial mathematics, economic problems, and the like, can be recommended here to the pupils. The teacher occupies the position of an adviser in the activity of such working groups.

### NATURAL SCIENCE INSTRUCTION

### Introductory Remarks

The whole aim to be accomplished by all the natural science subjects makes imperative a narrow union of these subjects into a kind of integrated natural science instruction. In this connection, it will be one of the chief problems of the institutional programs of study to define the specific task devolving upon each separate subject. The effort toward unification should not be permitted, however, to lead to the rupture of important continuity within a subject in order to secure transitions to the other subjects. The interrelation of all branches of the natural sciences in the curriculum presupposes a mutual consideration in the distribution of subject matter. Should biology, for example, be given in the upper classes, the treatment of the physical and chemical fundamentals necessary for the understanding of life's processes would have to precede this instruction. Mineralogy and geology belong to the same section in school with paleontology. The final course built up through the hypotheses of cosmogony and the doctrine of evolution should be reached through simultaneous instruction. The natural sciences, in general, should give an insight into the related laws of all natural phenomena and into the significance of all natural processes for life.

It is easy to relate natural science to linguistic subjects through occasional class presentation of some works of outstanding scientists in their original text or to excerpt therefrom significant passages to be explained. The explanation of the technical terms makes it necessary to refer to foreign languages.

All the natural science subjects are adapted in a high degree to the stimulation of the historical sense. We recommend in the case of various problems the tracing of the erroneous and winding paths in the original progress of important discoveries. It is of high cultural value for the youth to hear of the frequently tragic lives of great students of nature. Through pointing out the connection between the natural sciences and the history of general culture, the cultural-scientific significance of the natural sciences will be made clear.

In relation to geography the following are examples of common materials: Alps and Alpine vegetation, general physical geography and weathering, climatology and meteorology, Erzgebirge and the deposits of silver, nickel, cobalt, tin, iron. All natural sciences find material for observation in the home community.

Wherever natural science instruction makes its appeal to the eye of the pupil, drawing is an important aid to understanding.

No natural science instruction can pass over the discussion of the more recent developments in technology. The description of important technical appliances is often connected with questions of deep interest to the pupils.

The methods of all the natural sciences offer occasion for epistemological, logical, and metaphysical considerations. The possibility of introducing philosophy into the instruction merits extensive utilization in this connection.

The construction of homemade appliances for physical and chemical experiments by the pupils presupposes the ability to prepare the proper laboratory materials, and thus establishes relations with manual training. The training of the hand by modeling contains significant educational value.

For the free activity group, reading of selected works of distinguished naturalists in all the fields of the natural sciences offers a rich field of activity. Moreover, such fields of subject matter as electrical engineering and colloidal chemistry, which extend beyond the confines of physical and chemical school instruction, can be treated in the group activity organization under the guidance of the teacher of the special subject.

### PHYSICS

*General Aim of Instruction.* Knowledge of the important physical phenomena, their laws, and the methods by which one arrives at these laws. Insight into a comprehensive view of nature and into the fundamental theories essential to a physical conception of the world. Acquaintance with such technical applications of physics as are significant in daily life or in their bearings on political economy.

*Remarks on Method*

1. Physics instruction proceeding from the observation of natural phenomena rests as much as possible upon the exercises and individual experiments of the students or upon observations in the immediate vicinity. The students should formulate the technique of physics investigations on the basis of their own reflections. The experiment, which at all levels remains the focal point of instruction, forms the point of departure in the inductive procedure and the conclusion to be arrived at in the deductive procedure.

2. The selection of the materials of instruction, especially necessary in the case of physics, should take into consideration in the course to be prepared only the simpler natural phenomena which have significance for a knowledge of the environment. In the upper classes, the same fields of subject matter can be treated more briefly if the students receive a

theoretically rounded picture of the remaining divisions of physical knowledge.

More important than the assimilation of a large number of individual physical facts, is a fundamental insight, based on self-activity, into the processes of research in physics.

3. The application of mathematics to physics instruction is only a means of enabling one to recognize the relationships among phenomena. Above all there should be avoided such misleading deductions as lead to artificial results through a roundabout way of infinitesimal processes without possessing the convincing strength of mathematical development. Where the mathematical resources at command are not adequate for strict deduction, owing to the inadequacy of the mathematical preparation, the results of calculation must suffice.

4. At all levels of instruction, the students should secure a clear conception of the dimensions of such physical magnitudes as have significant meaning for the assigned experiments or considerations.

5. The historical method of study plays an important rôle in physics instruction. Not only does it place the mathematical and natural sciences in a very desirable and closer relationship to the other subjects of instruction, but the historical discussion is often best adapted to introduce the students to a comprehension of the whole field of subject matter and to bring about a deeper knowledge of the various problems and their historically intellectual meaning. The historical presentation can be used with profit in the activity instruction, where, through connection with the historical evolutionary process, the students can be led to their own discovery and invention of things long since known. The historical method of consideration is indispensable if the question is one of discussion of the big basic principles and their connection with world-stirring questions and problems. In order to increase the intellectual improvement of the pupils through the discussion of critical physical theories, one will have to go back from historical knowledge to the beginnings of philosophic knowledge and point out that these problems finally merge into metaphysics.

If the students, through the discussion of the historical genesis of the great physical hypotheses, secure an impression of the limitations placed upon our knowledge, it follows that they will have arrived at the conclusion that where prescientific comprehension already believes to have found truth, the great problems really begin.

6. Beyond showing the close relationships between physics and technical science, the extraordinarily great significance of the technical applications of physics for economic life and civilization should be brought to the consciousness of the student and an understanding of the intellectual and creative accomplishments of the engineer imparted to him. Instructional excursions can be made useful for this purpose also.

### CHEMISTRY

*General Aim.* Knowledge of the most important chemical phenomena, in so far as they are important for understanding the animate and inanimate world, for housekeeping, or for political economy. Acquaintance with the laws at the basis of these phenomena and insight into the theories which disclose an understanding of these laws. Knowledge of the most important minerals with respect to their technical, economic, and geological importance.

### Remarks on Method

1. Chemistry offers opportunity in all fields for the cultivation of observation by means of carefully planned experimentation. Modern illustrative materials serve in a supplementary way, especially those taken from technology. The general principles and laws are developed by combining individual facts into complete thought units.

2. The pupils' practical exercises are to be brought into very close connection with the class instruction and must never be used exclusively as exercises in analysis.

3. Mineralogy is to be afforded greater time in chemistry instruction. Minerals are treated in connection with chemical compounds. As natural chemical compounds or representatives of whole classes of compounds and as important raw materials, they can form the starting point for discussions in chemistry, or they can be studied in connection with the treatment of the elements contained in them. Their economic value is to be carefully evaluated.

4. The controlling point of view in the study of geology is

that the geological importance of minerals should find consideration in addition to the observation of the constantly changing nature of man's environment.

5. Crystallography, on account of its mathematical nature, can be assigned to mathematics as a stereometric exercise and can be made useful in geometrical drawing.

6. Stoichiometric calculations are permissible only in so far as they are able to support an appreciation of the quantitative course of chemical processes. Calculations which have no relation to experiments really performed have no place in chemistry.

7. Short studies in the history of chemistry allow the chief characteristics of its historical development to be recognized at suitable points and by means of individual examples they demonstrate the growth of an important discovery or the influence of a personality.

8. Instructional excursions show how experiments which are carried out in the laboratory in only a small way have led in technical trades to the enormous development of our chemical industry. Besides pointing out the importance of a close connection between science and technology, insight based upon observation into the great value of chemistry for trade, public health, and modern cultural development should be developed.

9. The instruction in chemistry is to be used for the study of the local community (*Heimatkunde*). In addition, the grouping of the instructional material from local industry around the experiences of the pupils can be recommended. Where it is possible the pupil is to learn the geological processes in the origin and history of the local soil. Especial weight is to be attached to the practical application of chemistry to daily life.

10. The exaggerated use of chemical formulas is to be avoided. It is recommended that the ionic method of writing formulas be employed. In suitable problems, the pupils are to be trained to distinguish facts of experience from hypotheses and theories, such as the atomic, molecular, and ionic theories.

11. The principle of selection of subject matter is to be carried out in chemistry by shortening or totally eliminating various phases of chemistry instruction. The course seeks, by avoiding minute detail, a deeper insight into the methods of chemical research; in the most important fields it sets the phases of the subject worked out in systematic relation to one another and in

connection with the related fields of the other natural sciences; and it brings about gradually an appreciation of the great inter-relationships of all natural processes.

BIOLOGY

*Aim.* Instruction in biology is to acquaint the pupil with the phenomena of animate nature and enable him to derive the principles which lie at their foundation. It trains him in systematic observation of the living world and develops him as far as possible in an all-round way by means of the methods characteristic of biology. It seeks to awaken in him love of nature and of the home and above all respect for all life.

Instruction in biology leads to knowledge of the structure and of the most important life processes of plants, animals, and man. It develops insight into the relationships between bodily structure and manner of life, and between life systems and environment. It presents the importance of biological principles for political economy. It also teaches the evolution of the various organisms and makes clear the principle of classification in the system and the natural kinships, along with the study of extinct forms. It explains the conditions upon which the dispersal of life systems over the earth's surface depends.

In connection with the other natural science subjects and mathematics, biology reveals that all phenomena are controlled by law, points out the natural relationship of man and human culture, and thus makes an essential contribution to the development of the pupil's character and will. These biological insights can be used effectively for the conduct of personal life, and not to a small degree, for civic conduct. Finally, study in natural philosophy upon the basis of biological postulations will stress the importance of biology in the development of culture.

*Selection of the Material.* The selection of material depends upon its educative value and its suitability for definite types of activity. Penetration into the individual phenomena of animate nature is only possible if there is sharp limitation of subject matter. The phenomena of the immediate environment are to be considered primarily in this selection of material. Likewise in the case of materials of equal educative value, their practical importance for man and human culture will determine the choice.

In the presentation of biological subject matter, the starting point is to be that joy in experience and observation is to dominate in the lower classes, and in the middle classes effort toward perfection and classification, and in the upper classes effort toward deeper insight into the phenomena of nature.

Every natural object is to be studied in the various stages of development important for its comprehension. Plants are to be studied, for example, not merely in the period of blossoming, and animals not merely in fully developed form. As a fundamental rule, division of the instruction in plant and animal biology into summer and winter courses should be avoided.

*Activity Instruction.* More than in any other subject the pupils bring to the study of biology their own observations and facts, experiences, and ideas derived from the environment. In so far as the activity instruction associates itself with these interests of the child and affords him that personal relationship with things of nature, it creates, even in the lower section, favorable preparatory conditions for most varied application of the activity method. Therefore, the teacher should always be aware that everything from the spoken word even to the so-called living model is only a substitute for nature, and that book knowledge easily produces a far-reaching alienation from nature. However, because education toward systematic observation and conscious investigation of reality is one of the most essential tasks in biology, instruction out of doors is here also of especial importance.

Numerous investigations and experiments are necessary from *Sexta* to *Prima* for the activity instruction which is carried on in the class. Experiments with living animals are permitted only when every semblance of cruelty is avoided. Investigation and experiment are to be carried on with the simplest instructional aids. In many cases keeping notes is necessary for both types of work.

Introduction to the classification of plants and animals belongs also in this instruction. Prepared in *Sexta* through the development of clear conceptions of form, carried further in *Quinta* to the organization of simple classification tables, the pupil is trained in *Quarta* to the independent use of a simple flora and fauna, or a simple classification table in his textbook.

Exercises in the school garden are especially valuable. In

these the guidance of the teacher is not to be dispensed with. In the pupils' garden the teacher has the opportunity under favorable circumstances of instructing all pupils of a class successfully at one time. The exercises which can be carried out by the pupils in the school gardens should belong to their daily duties, but they must also be related to the course. Activities with the aquaria and terraria should be supervised constantly by the teacher. The teacher must give special attention that in this work animals are not neglected or tortured.

Frequently, facts which are important biologically will be made known to the pupils through observation only. If the less easily observable types of life and natural phenomena are to be observed and investigated on an excursion, it is recommended that a smaller number of pupils be taken along because often this work can be thoroughly and successfully carried on only with a few. The instinct for collection in the youth should be properly directed and be utilized for instruction in school collections. In this matter no compulsion must be exercised upon the pupil to carry on investigations and experiments on his own account at home. It is the teacher's duty, however, to stimulate his pupils to make safe investigations and experiments. Continuous problems in observation undertaken by individual pupils will be of special value. The teacher must, indeed, with his own drawing as a model, train the pupils to reproduce appropriately in drawing what they have themselves observed. In this work, attention is to be paid to cleanliness in execution and lettering. To overload the drawing with minute details is impractical. Occasionally it is recommended to encourage the pupils to construct simple models. In the free activity groups of the upper section the pupils are to be required to make exact drawings as proof of accurate observations.

This activity instruction must further equip the pupils with the ability to reproduce correctly, both in oral and in written form, that which they have observed, and also to present clearly the course of an experiment. Extemporaneous reports by the pupils serve in the middle and upper classes to supplement the instruction.

In cases in which, on account of the lack of suitable natural objects, written descriptions and theoretical instruction on the part of the teacher, or pictures must be used as instructional aids, the inductive method is to be employed wherever possible. When using either wall pictures or stereopticon or stereoscopic views, the teacher must satisfy himself whether the pupil forms the correct concept of the picture as to content, form, scale, and color. Stereopticon pictures must not lead to the confusion of the pupil by a superfluity of conflicting impressions. For the same reason, moving pictures are only seldom to be used. They should be used generally only as short films for very definite and very limited representations if the projection machine is equipped so that the machine may be stopped. All of these means of practice have the disadvantage in contrast to the drawing that they do not come into being before the eye of the pupil.

*Heimatkunde.* The instruction is to be very closely associated in all sections of the school with the study of the German homeland, for which it is one of the essential tasks of the natural science instruction to awaken and cultivate appreciation and love. Instruction out of doors and regular excursions are especially valuable for this work. Herein, wherever possible, play must be given to the joyous instinct of activity in observation and collection.

Teachers must introduce the pupil to the knowledge of the natural and artificial life communities which are of greatest importance for his environment. Insight into the economic life of the home and community which depends upon organic nature is indispensable for an understanding of problems in political economy. In this connection, fishing, the chase, the open and close season are to be taken into consideration. Through this intimate acquaintance with nature in his environment, the pupil is to be led to a full conception of the idea of the protection of nature. Regard for natural monuments and memory of such as have passed away are to be kept alive in the pupil, in order that he may acquire a conception of the development of German landscape in the different epochs.

Exhibits in show cases and cabinets and local botanical gardens, local rooms and museums, serve to bring together the biological examples which are most important for the study of the community.

*Æsthetic and Ethical Problems.* More than many other subjects, biology contributes to the pupil's æsthetic and ethical growth. In addition to the ability for exact and accurate observation, the instruction in biology endeavors to develop the power of emotional conception of animate nature and to awaken in the pupil appreciation of color and form, of sounds and smells and enjoyment in their harmony and rhythm.

The special qualification of biology for the ethical training of the youth is in part, of course, due to the necessity of carrying out projects in the "activity instruction" which go far beyond the strength of a single individual. The work in the school garden, for example, demands, if it is carried through successfully, a high degree of coöperation. Biological experiments and observations demand patience as little else does. Methods of investigation of biology place the highest requirements upon the honesty of the individual both toward himself and others. The instruction in biology will sharpen in every way the pupil's feeling of responsibility. Instruction in hygiene in particular will furnish moral stimuli both for the pupil's personal life and conduct and for the work in public health. From this follows the necessity of treating in a tactful way upon suitable occasions during the course of the instruction the problems of sexual hygiene and their importance for the individual and general welfare. From a discussion of these serious questions, moral decisions are likely to develop; such also must grow out of the discussion of the harmful effects of many luxuries and forms of enjoyment. Certain biological topics require reference to the limitations of human knowledge, without, however, killing in the pupils the zeal for investigation.

*Concentration.* Instruction in biology obeys the principle of concentration primarily in that it takes over portions of the whole educational problem of the class. Various relationships are also to be established in all classes with the other subjects, especially with the following:

*Study of German Culture.* Biology instruction can serve to develop the imaginative life of the pupils by the use of animal stories and fables, by reference to popular names for animals and plants and to the importance of life systems in popular superstitions and folk-medicine, riddles, and proverbs, which often reveal the finest appreciation for the characteristics in animals and plants. Reading of descriptions of landscapes and biographies of plants and animals will involve the German as well as the biology instruction.

*Geography.* Biology affords geography many auxiliary concepts, such as types of soil, foreign cultivated plants, and animals characteristic of those countries, typical landscapes, climatic conditions underlying the plant and animal world, the part played by plants and animals in the formation of the earth's crust, and the like. In the study of plants and animals, attention is to be called to the relationship existing between geographical distribution of certain plants and animals to certain human civilizations, for example, oil and wine in the Mediterranean Sea district, date palms, horses and dromedaries in the Arabian Orient, rice in China, papyrus in ancient Egypt, reindeer in the Polar regions.

*History and Civics.* Important phases of our political economy are based upon biological foundations. So, also, are agriculture, forestry, water power, and great portions of our industry. What biology instruction teaches concerning cultivation of plants and animals and their utilization, what it teaches concerning the lack of room, competition, and adaptation within a life community, what it teaches concerning the consequent but undesired results of human enterprise with nature, and what it teaches concerning the unmethodical impoverishment of the soil —all these prepare for history instruction. If the plant and animal production of colonial countries is discussed in connection with their economic value, the necessity of German colonial possessions becomes clear. A deepened appreciation of the more mature pupil for the organization of a life community will teach him to recognize the state as such a community, and will point out to him the indissoluble unity of its members. If the pupil is accustomed to biological thinking, he will apply these biological truths to human life and seek to make them fruitful for his own personal and public life.

*Free Activity Groups.* The field of activity for these free groups includes experiments by the pupils, making of collections, excursions, and work with biological literature. Some topics for the biological "activity groups" should serve only for stimulation and recognition: Determination of the more difficult blooming plants and of cryptogams; investigation of plant-animal communities; investigation of the plankton of the local waters at different times of the year; culture and investigation of bacteria; plant diseases and their stimuli; comparative study of structure of plants in different soils.

## MUSIC

*General Aim.* Music is to develop the innate musical powers in the child; it is to develop feeling, imagination, and a desire and power of musical creation, and thus is to serve the whole training of personality as well as ethical education.

Training for unaccompanied singing forms the starting point of music instruction. In addition to this, instrumental music and singing with accompaniment are to be cultivated in all sections. Herein, musical instruction must keep in mind an essential goal—coöperation from the school in the building up of a type of music for the home and social life, and also assurance of a well-prepared oncoming generation for the choral societies.

In connection with the study of the vocal and instrumental works, the musical ability of the pupils is to be systematically and fully developed: Ear training, power of direct appreciation and reproduction of rhythm, muscular control in the tone production in scales and chords, and a feeling for the organic development of form.

On this basis, the ability is developed of consciously and thoroughly appreciating a melody in selections in one or more voices, and of awakening desire on the part of the pupil to create motives and melodies, thus making way for an active experiencing of the greater musical masterpieces.

Finally, music instruction is to enable the youth to appreciate the importance of music in the life of the individual and society, especially in our German civilization, and to understand that music is not the affair of an individual group but a source of elevation and joy for all classes of people.

## Remarks on Method

1. It must always be remembered that music has also a hygienic objective in singing. Therefore, provision must always be made in the classroom for fresh air. Breathing and voice exercises, in connection with exercises in dynamics and tone production, are to be undertaken at the beginning of the class period. Careful attention should be paid to erect but natural posture, and to deep breathing and long, regular exhalations, both in the

exercises and in the singing. Exercises with soft attack and
a low singing are to be cultivated especially. The development of the head-tones downward and an easy transfer between chest and head-tones are to be striven for. In tone production correlations are to be made with speech instruction
in German and the foreign languages. In dynamics the de-
crescendo is to be practiced more than the slow, steady crescendo.

Overstraining the voice must never take place. Only a
minimum in range and strength is to be allowed the boys'
voices which have just undergone the change. Individual and
group singing must constantly alternate in class instruction.
Voice examinations should be given at the beginning of each
semester in every class. The teacher should always keep himself as constantly informed as possible with reference to the
range, character, and change of voices.

2. Music instruction in the lower section must be combined
with what was done in the *Grundschule,* being fixed and enriched
by repetition.

The training in rhythm at the beginning is based upon the
pupils' own physical interpretation of the rhythmic processes.
Its continuation and extension beyond the lower section in connection with physical training is to be extended, especially in
schools for girls.

In ear-training and in the development of songs the teacher
is free, in connection with notation, to use not only the musical
alphabet, but also special tone designations as solmization, the
Eitz tone syllable method, tonic *do,* and other auxiliary means.

One of the tasks to be undertaken in the lower section is to
make the pupils acquainted with the major and minor systems.
Herein all mechanical memorization is to be avoided. The
pupils are not to learn even the scales by heart, but are so to
grasp the principle of scale formation and all that pertains to
keys, in the lower section, that later they also can form the
scales for every tone as basal tone and be able to read from
every signature and derive from every key those related to it.
The measures of the common and church music are to be studied
first in the middle or upper section, if occasion demands.

3. Music instruction from the lower section on places great
emphasis upon the development of ear-training, tone imagery,
and tone consciousness. The exercises necessary therefor should

be associated with the song being studied. The pupil is to attain the ability to comprehend melodies which he has heard sung or played, to reproduce the tone syllables and to write them down. In order to save time this writing can be done on the board with the class helping. The keeping of a neat music notebook on the part of the pupil is, however, indispensable.

4. The music teacher must always remember that accuracy in singing from the page and accuracy in writing from memory alone insure an intellectual appreciation of the musical content and thus are only conditions for real musicianship and musical appreciation. The various length of intervals within the scales, the various expression values of these intervals and of the same interval in its various combinations must be felt and permanently comprehended by the pupils. In this manner, also, the feeling for correct sequence and contrast in harmony is built up. Rhythm must not only appear to the pupils as a time relationship, but must also be felt by them as the expression of increasing or decreasing, free or restricted activity; thus, the relation of rhythmics to dynamics will also become clear. Similarly the teacher has not merely to satisfy himself with superficially correct differentiation and reproduction of various measures of time, but to make them clear as the different limits of characteristic developments in the dance, march, cradle song, and the like.

5. In the development of melody, again, sight singing, no matter how correct, is valueless if it merely consists of a succession of notes. In order to awaken the feeling of organic development of melody in the pupil, the teacher must make him sensitive to the simple motif as the forward impelling desire for musical expression. The gradual evolution of the song upon the blackboard could be a way of objectifying the organic evolution of form.

6. The surest means of training for an inner experiencing of the value of musical expression and of musical phenomena is stimulation of the imagination to more independent musical invention or creation. Even in connection with the most fundamental rhythmic exercises, the pupils must be required to do independent creation of rhythmic forms. The exercise in rhythmic, as in melodic, invention can be associated with manifestations from daily life, such as street criers, bird-notes, auto signals,

and so on. Careful attention is to be paid to quick and exact conception of that which has been heard. Nor must training in musical memory in this work be neglected. It is purposeful to associate musical invention with dictation in music. In this connection, attention will be given to exact insertion of signs of expression. By means of judging the attempts on the part of the pupils and through common discussion of suggestions for improvement, influence may be exercised upon the development of the power of musical judgment. Successful melodies can be sung and made the permanent possession of the class.

7. The choice of songs is to be adapted to the ability of the pupils. In addition to serious songs, as many as possible of bright, cheerful content should be practiced. Consideration is to be given to sectarian feeling in singing religious songs. It is very essential from the beginning to acquaint the pupils as widely as possible with the variety of emotional expression in the field of music and thus to enrich and deepen their own emotional experience. The teacher should give special attention as to which songs are memorized by the pupils of their own accord and which are well sung by them. These he should consider in future selections as the songs well adapted for educative purposes. The German folk song of the fifteenth and sixteenth centuries especially is to be used in the middle and upper sections; local songs and those in the local dialect are to be used in all sections. In the lower section songs are selected that make natural points of association, leading from the song over into simple forms of instrumental music, such as the march, dance, and variations.

8. Irrespective of all exercises which are carried on in connection with the development of singing, it is indispensable to proceed with the song itself with a degree of ease permitting a type of singing to mature which is accurate in tone, pure in quality, and which produces the melody with expression, but which makes it possible also for the pupils to assimilate the entire content of the poetical-musical work of art. Usually all stanzas are to be sung. Only in songs which have too great a number of stanzas is a selection permissible, and then the selection must always give a complete poetical unity. In addition to the singing of newly practiced songs, older songs are to be reviewed

constantly. A number of songs of varying content and character must in this way become so well known that the pupils will be able to sing them from memory with complete mastery of the music and text and will also have them in later life as a permanent possession. A list of songs suitable for this purpose is to be set up by the music teacher at the beginning of every school year for each grade and for each section.

9. The work on a song is usually not completed when the control of its textual and musical content is obtained. Often the original form of a melody is to be indicated, attention is to be called to the cultural level from which it sprang, or the personality of its author is to be made known to the children. The teacher should never permit to escape such opportunities for unforced associations with the history of civilization and music. Time should be allowed in increasing degree in the middle and upper sections for such associations according to the measure of the general development of the pupils.

10. The canon and singing accompanied by an instrument carrying the melody serves as preparatory work for choral singing, in addition to any other suitable special exercises. The teacher should see that the pupils are made conscious of and sensitive to the antagonistic effects of consonance and dissonance in their varied gradations before and during two-part singing. In addition to one-part singing, several-part singing is to be cultivated especially in the middle and upper sections. The independent development of a second part is to be encouraged.

In all several-part singing, beginning with the two-part singing in the lower section, it is important that the pupil not only sing his own part with lively imagination, but that he also experience the work which consists of several parts as a whole. For this purpose it is necessary to separate the singers of one voice occasionally into groups which sing and listen alternately; and permit them where possible to sing from the score unaccompanied.

11. A three- or four-voice school chorus should be organized from the musically gifted pupils of the middle and upper sections. Where conditions permit in secondary schools for boys, a four-voice chorus with soprano, alto, tenor and base. But it is always permitted to substitute a low alto for tenor. This organization of the chorus is generally offered in six-year sec-

ondary schools; in smaller schools one should be satisfied with a chorus consisting of soprano, alto, and baritone, if a four-voiced chorus cannot be organized.

A three- or four-voice girls' chorus should be organized in girls' schools.

12. In chorus practice the pupils should work out their parts independently. The instrument is permissible in order to clarify harmonies and chords and in trials to supplement voices which may be missing. Attention at this point is also to be given to the purely vocal phases of the work. If necessary, special exercises are to be inserted. Conscientious care is to be given to the entire musical and textual appreciation of what has been sung.

13. In the choice of material for choral singing, original compositions which are suited in the range of its parts for the school are always to be given preference over transcriptions.

Appreciation of the great masters of choral music in German such as Isaac, Senfl, Lasso, Gallus, Eccard, Hassler, Schütz, and Schein, but above all Bach and Handel must be awakened in the pupils through their active participation in the choral period and through suitable references by the teacher to problems of style and history. In addition to this the choral literature of the Viennese classicists, including Gluck, and the most important masters of the nineteenth century are to be considered. The old German folk song must receive as wide cultivation as possible in the course in the compositions of the older and newer masters.

14. In addition to the large chorus a volunteer selected chorus should be built up, if possible, from singers whose voices are the truest and best. This chorus can relieve the large chorus at school celebrations, parents' meetings, and weekly religious services. An extension of this group to teachers and friends of the school, and especially also the relatives of the pupils, is to be encouraged, just as is the participation of those who play string and wind instruments.

15. The so-called *Brummer* must take part in the music instruction in every way and are to be excluded from the singing only when continual misleading of the other pupils has developed. Their musical development is to be given special attention. In the middle and upper sections the teacher is permitted to group those pupils who do not have voices to-

gether with those whose voices are changing, in a special period for theoretical and historical instruction.

16. The cultivation of instrumental music and the introduction to its appreciation constitutes a regular part of the music instruction in all sections of the school.

The music teacher should seek to encourage gifted pupils to study instruments if conditions in their homes permit it. He should always seek to be informed concerning the advancement and skill of pupils in instrumental playing.

Where possible, the instrumental players of the middle and upper sections are to be formed into a definite instrumental group or pupil orchestra. Its task is to cultivate, especially, popular home music, to make possible singing with obligato instruments and with orchestral accompaniment and to have ready examples from literature for the characterization of musical forms, style, and epoch. While the introduction to the appreciation of instrumental means of expression and forms begins in the lower section in direct connection with the study of singing, a beginning is also to be made in the middle and upper sections in the appreciation of the larger forms, such as the fugue and sonata.

17. Occasional group attendance at concerts and the opera on the part of teachers and pupils is very desirable. In order to make this especially beneficial to the pupils it is permissible on the part of the teacher to devote several music periods in preparation for this.

18. Musical history instruction is to be given continuously in the middle and upper sections in direct connection with the subject matter treated in the class period, with solo and choral singing and instrumental work.

19. Music instruction by means of systematic coöperation with the other subjects strengthens the position of music in the life of the individual and also in the culture of the community. The teacher should take care, therefore, to associate the natural lines of connection with the various fields of instruction, and should consider them, of course, in the selection of the vocal and instrumental material, which is best made in mutual agreement with the representatives of the other subjects.

Religion and music have their roots in the irrational and the supernatural. The devotional character of music, which is characteristic of the choral and folk song and which is generally characteristic not only of the religious music but also of all serious secular music, must be appreciated and felt by the youth. The meaning of music in public worship in the Catholic Mass and the Protestant liturgy, especially of the period of Bach, is to be made clear to the pupils in connection with church history by means of musical demonstration. In connection with the history of the Israelitic people and with the presentation of the life of Jesus, appreciation is to be awakened for Handel as the typical Old Testament composer, and for Schütz and Bach as the chief composers of the New Testament music. The close relationship between German and music instruction, which is based on the relationship of language and music and on the original unity of word and method, needs an especially careful development. The textual development, memorization and repetition of the songs selected on the common agreement of the music and German teachers can be assigned to the German instructional periods. Music instruction should seek to supplement and support the latter so far as possible through singing and discussing compositions based on the poems there treated; in this way in particular it secures the opportunity of cultivating the artistic song. In the introduction to opera and musical drama such coöperation is similarly possible by division of work. Finally, it is desirable that the connections in the historical development of both fields should be made clear to the pupils in the upper section through outstanding examples.

The connection with Greek instruction is to be derived especially from the reading of Attic tragedy and of the Platonic dialogues. In connection with the Greek drama, the music teacher should seek to awaken a deeper appreciation for the purposes and the nature of the opera of the Renaissance, the choral opera of Gluck, Handel's dramatic oratorios, and Wagner's musical drama. The music teacher of every type of school through all organizations of his instruction should seek from the very beginning to make the pupils appreciate the Greek ethical conception of music which they will meet in reading Plato.

The music teacher by practicing English and French songs can assist the modern language instruction. From the reading in these languages, he can receive stimulation for the treatment of musical subject matter materials, for example, of the French national opera and English madrigal and virginal music. The development of the foreign language music text must be taken over by the language concerned.

The music teacher should endeavor to quicken the material studied in history, particularly through the musical development of individual cross-sections in the history of culture, such as, chivalry,—Minnesong; German middle class of the fifteenth century,—Locheimer's Book of Songs; military system of the sixteenth century,—soldier songs, and the like. The music teacher should seek to enliven the material of the history instruction by the cultivation of the historical folk song.

In connection with musical acoustics, it is desirable that the pupils of the upper section be acquainted with the basis of our whole tone system, and with the possibility and the actual existence of other systems.

Intimately connected with the physical training instruction through the rhythmic element in marching and dances, the music instruction should devote attention to the marching song used in the physical training instruction. The music teacher should support the physical training teacher continually in his efforts for good singing during the gymnasium period, which seeks to restrain all shouting and all exaggeration in designating the rhythm.

However, music instruction has not only to maintain in the school constant connection with the other fields of instruction, but it must also preserve the community building force of music in choral singing, in group instrumental work, in the weekly religious services and celebrations, and in parents' evening meetings. In order to do this, the instruction must make music the expression of an elevated emotional feeling and every single period with all the detail work an hour of joy.

20. The voluntary "free activity groups" of the upper section are also to promote musical development and the scientific intensification of musical appreciation. According to the need and the desires of the pupils, vocal or instrumental exercises in the fundamental training of the theory of composition, or comprehensive courses in the science of music can be provided. The music teacher must give especial attention to those pupils

who intend after securing the graduation certificate to devote themselves to the profession of the elementary school teacher.

21. The music teacher finds himself at the present time in a difficult position, especially in smaller schools for boys, in fulfilling the comprehensive tasks here assigned within a number of hours which is not yet sufficient, particularly in the middle and upper sections. These conditions compel him to crowd the exercises which serve the development of musical ability essentially into the narrow period of time of the first two school years. The danger arising from this condition of an all too great limitation of subject matter in singing is to be counteracted in all sections by the strictest concentration and economy of the instruction, and primarily by the organic connection of the practice material with the study of songs themselves. Care is to be taken that the practical singing of songs in the school does not suffer. The music teacher should be interested in furthering according to his ability voluntary groups of pupils for musical purposes outside of school hours, if possible also through his own coöperation and through securing the coöperation of other members of the teaching staff for the work.

DRAWING AND ART INSTRUCTION

The instruction in drawing and art has, in general, the problem of coöperating with the means appropriate to it as an artistic subject in the development of personality and the deepening of cultural appreciation. It develops in the child the abilities of observation and expression which are present, brings the youth into a close personal relationship to the creations of plastic art, awakens in them the feeling for form and the desire for expression through form. The educational objective of this instruction consists in accustoming the pupil to an independent, purposeful method of work.

Exercises in the formation of flat and solid figures and in the study of works of art serve as means in reaching this objective. Since the objectives of the drawing instruction demand a free, personal conception and expression, or one determined by purpose and material, distinction is to be made between free and mechanical drawing.

Instruction in freehand drawing is to enable the pupils to express through form and color external impressions, inner experiences, and consciously assigned observations. It is to further natural abilities for creative expression in their development in that it affords the pupils opportunity for manifold activity and offers the aids which they need for their unfolding.

From the fact that the graphic method of expression in children develops in general according to law, but differently in detail, there arises the necessity that the drawing instruction must adapt itself to the age and the peculiar nature of the individual. The drawing teacher must, therefore, provide the pupils with rich opportunities of demonstrating in their free work their personal, individual method of expression and the degree of their ability. He must wait until the interest for certain methods of representation, objects, and means of expression begins to stir, and adapt his assistance in instruction to the needs either of the individual pupil, of a group of pupils, or of a whole class. Therefore, he must not set once for all definite problems for definite classes. He must, however, be on the watch in connection with the free exercises to enrich the pupils' store of conceptions through studies from nature and works of art and especially through reproductions from memory. He must be mindful of developing pupils' feeling for organic form and increasing their manual skill. Pure superficial imitation and mechanical practice of definite forms and techniques are to be avoided.

The materials for practice, so far as they do not arise themselves from the free exercises, are to be taken from the pupils' range of experience, to which, of course, the other subjects of instruction likewise belong.

Mechanical drawing serves, as does the freehand drawing, the whole problem of drawing and art instruction. It is to be pursued as practical linear drawing and as such has the problem of enabling the pupil to produce projective representation of objects taken from handwork, technology, and architecture. It should acquaint him with the practical application of pictorial perspective and shadow construction. In addition to representation, the independent formation of simple objects is to be practiced. This instruction seeks correlation with the work in mathematics, physics, manual training, and sewing.

Graphic representation and the formation of solid figures are to be based upon insight obtained by direct observations into the relationships which exist among the purpose, material, and form of an object. Pupils should be required to derive that form of representation which has the greatest purpose with reference to the technical demands of the subject. The exercises are developed first in freehand and if possible from memory. In many cases sketches will suffice if the purposes of the exercises are attained.

The pupils are to be acquainted as early as possible with the tools necessary for exact representation, for example, the rule, tape measure, compass, and the like.

Materials for practice in freehand drawing are to be taken from the pupil's range of experience. In the choice of material, corresponding to the age, play is to be considered more at first, and later the inclination for the technical side, while, finally, the artistic interests of the pupils are to be considered.

*Study of Art.* The instruction in free, as in mechanical drawing, should take every opportunity of cultivating its close relationships to art in general and to plastic art in particular. While it thus primarily serves its own purposes, at the same time it brings the pupil into living relationship with works of art. In the "free activity group," with the whole of the cultural instruction, it draws primarily German art and, according to the type of school, the creations of other peoples into the realm of its activity. While the cultural subjects clarify the work of art more in its historical and content phases, the drawing teacher is to guide the pupils toward deeper understanding more with reference to the formal treatment of the work of art and the personal method of expression of the artist. He leads them to clarify and fix their observation of the character of art by reproduction from memory. Wherever possible, he utilizes original productions, especially such as come from the field of graphic art. He instructs the pupils concerning the most important graphic and reproduction techniques and teaches them to judge the value of free or mechanical reproduction of art in its relation to the original. He stimulates the pupils to independent collection of pictures, and advises them as to their care and preservation. An especially important and fruitful task for the drawing teacher is to lead the pupils to study examples of architecture and art and such collections as may be at hand in the locality or immediate community. In addition, examples of good craftsmanship dominated by sure feeling of style are to be studied. Where opportunity offers, forms of architecture and art and productions of handwork of the locality are to be taken up, whether such work is freehand, projective, or a combination of the two forms. The pupils are to be urged to leave kodak pictures, especially any of monuments which are apt to be destroyed, in the existing or proposed local archives of the school.

It is necessary also that the pupils get an idea of artistic interior decoration by means of practical exercises in the drawing room, in the classroom, or in other suitable rooms.

In order that all the ability gained in the drawing period may be applied, it is recommended that pupils be stimulated to artistic treatment of school festivals, games, dramatic productions, and the like and that such activites be carried on in groups.

The drawing teacher, however, is not the only leader in art for the youth. As a representative of the creative arts he must endeavor rather to fill the entire school with an artistic feeling in coöperation with the teachers of German, music, and physical training, and make the school a model center for the expressive arts.

### NEEDLEWORK

Instruction in needlework in common with the instruction in the other art subjects should awaken joy among the girls in creative activity, should train systematically their sense of form and color, should transmit to them fine understanding and feeling for the materials to be worked upon, and should enable them to create and preserve simple garments and useful articles. This instruction should seize upon points of interest which arise from all cultural subjects and occasionally make clear the history of costumes and certain technique by means of examples. It also encourages, of course, the use of such costumes as models, especially in dramatic productions. In particular it will take account of the products of local art to promote the study of the local community, and wherever possible it will stimulate the pupils themselves to experiment on the hand-loom or on small weaving machines.

In connection with biology and civics, instruction in needlework enables the girls to recognize more clearly the household and economic duties of the wife and to assist in their solution.  The girls are continually to be trained to evaluate materials as to quality and construction and to use such material to the best purpose possible.  They must learn to use their tools, especially the sewing machine, correctly and to take proper care of them.  They should also be educated through this work toward a feeling of responsibility, order, economy, foresight, and faithfulness in the smallest detail.  The conscious development of taste will exercise an ennobling influence upon their whole conduct of life.  Through insight into the difficulty of labor processes and into the interrelationship of individual processes in modern economic life and through realization of the length of time consumed by the work and an evaluation of the remuneration for the work, an economic and social appreciation can be awakened.  This instruction can be also employed in the service of charitable undertakings.

The course is to be so planned that the creative instincts of the girls shall receive due attention in all classes.  The problems must be suited in various classes to the age of the children and the techniques be chosen accordingly.  As a rule, regular preparation is necessary for the success of any piece of work.  The pupils must in every case clearly appreciate the origin, character, and value of the materials to be worked upon and the tools to be worked with.  Common problems in the calculation of the costs of production are to be assigned and girls are to be advised with reference to the purchase of the material.  As in the drawing instruction, so in this work the relation of purpose, form, and material must be made clear.  Wherever possible the pupils themselves must determine the form by their own thinking, enquiry, and trial, and under guidance improve it so far that a useful style results.  Frequently, especially in sewing wash materials, it will be convenient, by employing knowledge in arithmetic and mathematics, to instruct the pupils how to take correct measurements and how such measurements are used in the construction of a garment.  The employment of ready-made patterns is to be avoided, as the invention of form must proceed from the common activity of the whole class.  So also must the introduction into the technical phases of the work be treated as class instruction.  Preliminary exercises for the elementary steps must not be too involved.  The so-called practice patches are to be done away with, however. Technique as such is always a means, never an end in itself. In the decoration of articles which are prepared, care should be taken from the lowest class on, that it is adapted to the purpose, material, size, and form of the article to be decorated. Emphatic caution is given against an overemphasis upon fancy work in the direction of stenciled ornamentation. The latter should not go further than simple border decoration or easy embroidery which grows out of the nature of the material. Progress and ability in this field should show rather in a gradual refinement of material, color, and method of work. The feeling for color is to be systematically developed by many exercises, such as are ordinarily found in drawing instruction.

The varied gifts of the pupils can and should be taken into consideration also in the classroom instruction. Clever and fast-working girls must either develop their problem to a greater degree of perfection or be assigned to new, freer problems which, however, belong in the same field. The instructional periods, however, are in no way to be used to the end that the girls mechanically practice certain techniques which they prefer. The free exercises should be turned to good account by means of discussions connected with them for the purpose of furthering the entire work. At every opportunity the teacher will call upon the whole class to judge patterns, sketches, and pieces of work which are wholly or partially completed, in order to develop the girls' taste and to teach them to be able to make careful and sound criticism. In all classes exercises for keeping old clothes in repair must be undertaken. Minor repairs should be made by the pupils on the sewing machine under the guidance of the teacher.

Choice of material must be made from the point of view that the girls are to learn those techniques which are most useful in life and to master them up to a certain degree of facility. As in every type of instruction, progress is to be made from the easier to the more difficult tasks. In *Untersekunda* the greater number of hours for freer activities on the part of the girls and the artistic treatment of the problem will serve to good advantage, but primarily to make possible further extension of study in the problems of sociology and political economy. Certain external conditions must be fulfilled in order to carry out the problems of instruction in needlework. This course necessitates a special room which must be equipped adequately with machines and observational material. In machine sewing at least one machine is necessary for every four girls. Since this machine can be used only alternately by the various girls, intervals in time are to be used for performing auxiliary duties and for discussions which serve the advancement of the whole class. The rooms and collections of materials should be placed under the supervision of a technically trained teacher.

When there are more than twenty girls the needlework period demands a double teaching staff, and the sections should be taught separately.

### PHYSICAL TRAINING

The following suggestions apply to physical training in secondary schools for boys. The publication of a special plan for physical training for girls is in prospect. Until then regulations of the *Principles of Physical Training for Girls,* Berlin, Cotta, 1913-16, remain in force.[1]

*Aim.* The important position which physical education takes in the whole plan of the secondary school is determined by its double objective. It has to bring about the practical cultivation of health which the youth need in these critical years of their physical development, in order to attain the endurance and efficiency necessary for life and vocation. More important still is the function of contributing on its own part and with means suitable to it to the training of character and personality. Its ideal goal is the man, healthy in body and soul, joyful and full of life, efficient, and harmoniously developed, possessing the desire to find his place in the community and thus educated for obedience, as well as for leadership.

Of course, this goal is only to be attained when the principle gains more and more acceptance that the practice of physical exercises is a general and important function of the whole school, and when all teachers feel the obligation of supporting the work of the physical training instructor. Manifold opportunity to this end is at hand in the daily practice of health in the school, on the play afternoons and excursion days, in the council of the pupils' associations and in the festivals for gym-

---

[1] This has now been issued by Decree of May 21, 1926.

nastics, sports, and games. In keeping with the principle that the education and training to be accomplished by the secondary school demands an organic integration of all subjects, and that the harmonious development of personality is only possible in a common educational endeavor which reaches out over the individual subjects, it is a clear requirement that the notions of the necessity and of the importance of regular physical training and culture be considered in the other phases of instruction. In natural science instruction this would be the case in the study of the human body and in German and history, in classical and modern languages, especially in connection with a discussion of the educational ideals of the various ages. The activity in the gymnasium and on the playground can provide much valuable stimulation for the instruction in drawing, while physical training and hiking will supplement the work in singing in that the store of German folk and *Wanderlieder* becomes the full and permanent possession of the people.

*Remarks on Method.* 1. Two physical training periods a week in all classes are available for the required work in physical training and one required play afternoon, during which time there are no lessons. In addition to this there is one excursion day every month.

2. Physical training is only able, then, to fulfill its especial hygienic and educational aim if it is carried on according to a unified plan. This holds for the physical training periods as well as for the activity on the play afternoon. The selection and sequence of the exercises must be adapted, out of reasonable consideration of youthful peculiarities, to the present condition of the physical, intellectual, and spiritual development of the different stages of life and is determined by the need of exercise and the aims and means of education. The objective of physical training is not that the class shall learn as many exercises as possible, but that the individual pupil be advanced in health, vivacity, elasticity and efficiency, and in independence, courage, and endurance up to the point which can be reached by him.

3. In the activity and exercise plan, which every school must organize for itself, it is recommended to lay down a definite amount of required or core material for each individual class. The proposed instructional topics are to indicate merely points

of direction. In particular, in the case of variety of sectional and local conditions as well as of the physical characteristics of the pupils, a certain degree of freedom and flexibility is desirable and necessary in the selection of material.

4. The numerous and many-sided exercises which are used in physical training and instruction can be organized in three groups according to their importance for the physical and intellectual development of the pupil. In the *Körperschule* the forms of exercises are grouped together which are particularly adapted for training the body and developing the constitution, and those which are suited to attaining good posture, deep and sufficient breathing, and a light, elastic step. In this group are also assembled the walking, running, and posture exercises to the widest degree. To the second group, efficiency exercises, belong the exercises in jumping and throwing and the so-called "ground exercises," wrestling, and the exercises on apparatus. These all contribute to a special degree in training for skill, endurance, courage, readiness, and self-control. Games from the simple running and ball games of the middle and lower sections up to the large competitive games of later youth comprise a third special group.

5. The method of instruction must correspond to the various ages and their development, and at the same time, the various forms of exercise must also be taken into consideration. Whereas in the *Grundschule* play predominated, or the exercises were clothed in a form of treatment which the child experienced spiritually, from the tenth year on the urge for many-sided activity and the intense need of movement are the factors which predominate, and the introduction to regular practice and habituation to discipline and order are necessary. Accordingly, this section of the school demands the use of a lively, severe, group exercise. This holds also for the stage of later childhood, which comprises in boys the ages from twelve to fifteen and represents that portion of development of the second great growth in stature, in which the lung and heart at the same time play an essential part. In the period of maturity, from fifteen on, in addition to group physical training, efficiency exercises in squads arranged according to skill are to be cultivated. In all sections, the pupils, even the weaker ones, are to experience

continually the joyous success of the exercise and of the increase of their ability and efficiency.

6. Calisthenics are usually carried on as group exercises. The command is solely for the purpose of regulating the quick execution of the exercise but never should it disturb the rhythm of the one exercising.

Natural exercises must not be analyzed too much into their parts. Errors are to be lessened by limitation of the amount of movement and are to be eliminated by auxiliary exercises. The introduction to movements which conserve strength and which take place according to the natural laws of movement is an important task of the teacher in all sections. Where the exercises themselves do not call forth the natural spirit of participation in the pupils, intellectual stimulation, such as reasons and arguments concerning the value and purpose of the work, will awaken interest and appreciation and thus will give the exercise a new stimulus.

7. In order to give consideration to the need of independence on the part of the pupils and to the variation in their accomplishment, elective gymnastics of a well-ordered nature are occasionally to be introduced as early as the lower section. In the upper section, this is to be practiced frequently and in freer forms, according to the demands of the activity instruction.

8. Only when the physical training teacher, with inner participation and joy, works as the comrade of his pupils and at the same time as their leader, will he secure educative results. He will be able to impress upon the youth, most naturally and impressively, in the gymnasium, at play, and on excursions, the need of regulated care of the body and of systematic inurement, the necessity of a reasonable mode of life and the importance of abstinence from alcohol and nicotine, especially if he, by his own conduct as an example, makes an effort in that direction.

9. Each physical training period must be used to the fullest. It should proceed strictly and in a lively manner; it should be varied in plan and stimulative in many directions. The selection and arrangement of the exercises must be made from the point of view that a complete and thorough work-out of all pupils is assured in every physical training period.

10. The period of exercise begins with an exercise calculated to stimulate quick transfer from seat-work and study of the

preceding periods to physical activity and relaxation by the pupils; for example, with a short run, or in the lower section with imitative movements, or with a short march with singing.

Posture exercises of the modern type belong to the fixed content of the *Körperschule* of every period of instruction. They meet, if limited to forward and backward bending, the physiological demands and youthful peculiarities more than the varied posture and movement exercises, and are preëminently fitted to make the whole body wiry and strong, especially the musculature of the trunk. They counteract faults in posture. Usually about six exercises are to be put into an exercise group and are to be repeated from eight to sixteen times, according to the difficulty of the exercise and the age of the pupil. In order to permit those practicing the possibility of executing the movement in the particular rhythm characteristic to them, it is recommended that not every individual repetition be executed with counting. In a trained class, where the exercise has been demonstrated and explained, it is preferable if free exercise is permitted until the teacher gives the command to stop. To the regular work of every physical training period which is carried on out of doors, running exercises also belong on account of their importance in developing the heart and lungs. They, like the other popular exercises, are to be regularly practiced as a rule in the more favorable seasons, and in the winter also if the weather at all permits.

Exercises for skill on the apparatus are carried on in the middle and lower sections as class exercises, and in the upper section in squads. In this work all the pupils are to be active continuously in so far as the available apparatus and possibility of sufficient supervision permit. It is not a question here of practicing the most difficult exercises possible, but rather an effort is made that the pupils seek to execute the simpler exercises with correct application of strength, with full mastery of the body, and in good posture.

While smaller games, especially in the lower section, form the happy conclusion of the physical training period, large group and competitive games represent the chief part of the play afternoon. On play afternoons posture exercises also, when a purpose is thus served, are undertaken, and, when there is opportunity, running, jumping, and throwing exercises are to be provided.

In all exercises, especial attention is to be devoted to breathing.

11. It is a fundamental principle to carry on physical training exercises out of doors. If the gymnasium must be used, careful attention should be given to its cleaning and ventilation.

12. Clothing used in the physical training instruction should be light and adapted to the purpose. In the warmer season open-air physical training exercises in short exercising trunks is of special hygienic value.

13. It is in keeping with the sense of education for the full and harmonious development of personality to cultivate the ability of each individual pupil to the highest degree of performance. To this end, every program fixes standards of performance in the various measurable exercises. They serve not as class standards, but as a standard of the attainment to be reached in the individual case. The standard in the individual classes, so far as possible, is to be divided according to the various years. Tables of standards are to be posted in order that the pupils themselves may check continually the progress they make.

14. In addition to the demand for maximum performance, the contest is an important educative means for the youth and meets their desires and needs. In the lower section it is limited to a happy, friendly comparison. Individual and group competitions in sport form are matters of the upper section. In this matter excess is to be absolutely avoided. The participation of the pupils in competitive games and matches should be limited generally to festivals for physical training and play supported by the school, which are to-day very frequent, and perhaps to the greater public exhibitions such as the Federal Athletics for Youth or the Prussian Ball Games.

15. After free activity and free exercise outside of the physical training period, consideration can be given best to the gymnastic and sport interests and wishes of the pupils in pupil gymnastic and sport associations. The closest possible connection with the school and the participation of the teachers and other pupils in the undertakings of such associations best assure their success on the one hand, and on the other guarantee the real purpose of these associations by supplementing

on their part the work of the school and by preventing harmful excess and too great participation in competitive undertakings outside the school. Like all pupil associations, the gymnastic and sport associations must be as independent as possible and conducted and administered by the pupils themselves. In addition to training for independence and leadership, to its tasks belong also the cultivation of a friendly community life through association during practice hours in gymnastics and sport with voluntary excursions, evening drills, and bivouac.

# VI

## COURSES OF STUDY FOR ALL TYPES OF SCHOOLS

### 1. CORE SUBJECTS

To a great extent the same units of instruction arise in all schools from the core subjects which are the chief supports of the German cultural unity and supply organic connection between the varied secondary schools (see p. 326). In the distribution of the work, especially with reference to subjects peculiarly characteristic of the individual types of schools, special additional units of instruction are assigned in these subjects and are to receive consideration in the distribution of the material. However, in the same topics the cultural ideal, characteristic of the individual school type, will develop primarily in the spirit and in the inner organization of the instruction. Likewise the sex of the pupils will be an essential determining factor in the treatment of the same subject matter as far as the type and method of instruction are concerned.

### EVANGELICAL RELIGION

#### VI

Review and more extended treatment of the Old Testament stories studied in the *Grundschule*. Bible stories of the New Testament, in groups related in content, up to the story of Whitsuntide. Use of suitable works of German art. Passages from the Bible, if possible in connection with the Bible stories. Church hymns with the melody, in connection with the church festivals. Summary and expansion of the theses of the Catechism studied in the *Grundschule*, in connection with the Bible stories.

The local church, its houses of worship and architectural monuments, its organization and feast customs.

A Bible history which contains the Bible stories, if possible in Luther's language, and the necessary memoriter material as instructional aids. A special district edition, or a supplement of the Bible history reader, which furnishes local information, is desirable.

1

In girls' schools are selected especially the family stories from the Old Testament and other idyllic stories; in boys' schools preferably hero stories.

## V

Stories from the lives of the Apostles and the Old Church. Quotations and church hymns as in class VI. Concluding summary of the catechism with thorough drill on the first three main sections without Luther's explanation.

Individual illustrations from the spread of Christianity in Germany, with special reference to the local community and the district. Important religious personalities of Germany from all centuries, with particular consideration of the home and the local district. In association with the work in German the continuance of the old German religion in present-day popular beliefs and especially those of the local community. Observation of churches and religious institutions.

In boys' schools specific emphasis on the bold, world-conquering character of Christian missions; in girls' schools, on the deep sympathy with all human need, brought into the world with the origin of Christianity.

## IV

Introduction to the religion of the Old Testament. Geography of Palestine in conjunction with the work in geography. Backward look upon the pre-prophetic literature of the Old Testament with regard for the religious-historical material already known to the pupils from their history work. The history of the patriarchs, particularly the life of Abraham because of its religious importance. The mission of Moses; view of the world religions of the time, important for the comprehension of the Old Testament. The periods of heroes, prophets, and kings. Special emphasis on the reading of valuable portions of the prophetic and devotional literature adaptable to this age. The contact of Judaism with the Greek religion and the Maccabees' struggle for freedom. The continuance of the Old Testament piety in the Christian religion, morality, and art. The first chapter and the first article of Luther's explanation. Bible quotations, important passages from the Psalms, prophets, and church hymnology as in class VI.

A Bible reader which contains all of the New Testament and all of the essential parts of the Old Testament in closest possible connection with Luther's classical language, serves as an instructional aid from class IV on.

The lives of great women from Hebrew history are of essential importance for the girls' schools.

## U III

The story of Jesus based on the reading of the gospel of Mark. The second and third chapters with explanations. Bible quotations and important portions from the Gospels, also church hymns as in VI. Only so much from the Old Church history as is necessary for the comprehension of German church history.

From German church history about as follows: The conversion of Germany by Irish-Scotch and Anglo-Saxon monks. The German Imperial Church. The Cluniac reform. The struggle between the Papacy and the Empire. The Crusades. The conversion of the North. The conversion of the East by the *Cistercians* and the *Premonstratensians*. The home missions of the mendicant orders. Innocence III and St. Francis. Pre-Reformation movements.

In the discussion of the Middle Ages, especially in girls' schools, the important place which the woman assumed in medieval culture and religion must be shown in individual illustrations. Medieval morality is likewise to be evaluated from this point of view.

In gymnasial schools the strong influence of antiquity in the medieval church will be especially considered—borrowed ecclesiastical terms. In the other schools the instruction will devote more time to the activity of the British missionaries as the first representatives of the British urge for explorations and missions. Wycliffe, among the early reformers, will be considered as the representative of the national independence of the English church. In connection with the French instruction, the Crusades and the Sermon on the Mount, with the use of Bible materials,

## O III

The teaching work of Jesus with special study of the parables and the Sermon on the Mount, with the use of Bible materials, especially from the prophets and the Psalms, which are important for understanding. The third chapter along with Luther's interpretation. Important portions of the teachings of Jesus.

The Reformation through the biography of Luther, Zwingli, and Calvin. The Bible of Luther, the Evangelical hymnal, the Evangelical Church ritual, and the Evangelical symbolical books. Illustrations from the periods of the Counter Reformation, Pietism and the Enlightenment. Protestant ecclesiastical art in church architecture, poetry and religious music. Church hymns as the expression of religious life of the Reformation and post-Reformation periods. Various outstanding women of the period of Pietism must be discussed in girls' schools.

In gymnasial schools the influence of Humanism upon the Reformation must be particularly considered.

In *Real* institutions Calvin will be treated intensively as the founder of Western European Protestantism; also the Counter Reformation; and here is the opportunity to acquaint the pupils with some of the spiritual leaders of this movement.

## U II

Interpretation of important life problems of the present time from the viewpoint of the New Testament, especially in the light of the teachings of Jesus and those portions of Paul's Epistles which come into consideration.

Selected passages from the church history of the nineteenth century; also from the history of the Evangelical Church constitution. Illustrations from the religious-ecclesiastical life of Germany from the religious revival since the beginning of the nineteenth century until the present time. Anglo-Saxon Christianity and its world importance. The Catholic Church in the nineteenth century. Ecclesiastical coöperative movements, home and foreign missions, Christian socialism, free churches and sects, religious tendencies. Summary of religious instruction materials in the form of a short study of the church.

In girls' schools the problems of the woman are especially considered and therefore problems of personal life are preferred for discussion. In church history the numerous representatives of feminine religious life since the period of Romanticism are exhaustively considered. The important work of Christian women in the fields of home and, to a certain extent, of foreign missions, social activities, and the like, are brought up.

In gymnasial schools the New Testament discussions take up somewhat more time than they do in other schools; isolated, easy passages can be read in Greek. In all other schools the emphasis is placed upon discussion of the religious life of the nineteenth century.

*Lyzeum U IIb.* The third hour is devoted especially to preparing the young girls for the religious and social life of the woman of the present day. Of first importance in accomplishing this purpose are activities which acquaint the girls with the practical work, but theoretical instruction is also useful.

## O II

The rise of Christianity with the background of the religious history of the declining ancient world. The preparation in Judaism—Prophecy, Apocalypse—Jesus' work and the original church. Development of the world mission by Paul and the condition therefor in the Greek-Roman world. The founding of the old Christian Church, in constitution and doctrine. Monasticism. The difference between oriental and occidental piety.

The character of occidental Christianity. The position of Augustine on worldly politics. The educational work of the Church with the Roman-German peoples. The idea of the World Church and the Papacy. The struggle between the Papacy and the Empire. The medieval monasticism. Scholasticism and mysticism. Romanesque and Gothic architecture. The political and spiritual conflict between Christianity and Islam. Reform movements in the late medieval church.

In girls' schools it must be developed that, in the Christian Church from the beginning on, woman has stood on an equal footing with man as helper, saint, and martyr. Otherwise the principles set up for U III apply for the special selection of subject matter in girls' schools.

In gymnasial schools there will be greater emphasis upon the Old Church history. The conflict between Christianity and Hellenism, the doctrine in its relation to Greek philosophy, monasticism in its relationships to similar phenomena of the late classical period, are more fully treated.

The other schools will place chief emphasis upon the Middle Ages and especially upon the source of Roman Catholic tradition which gives to medieval Europe a striking uniformity— Augustine, the Vulgate, Benedict, Gregory the Great, with illustrations from particular writings.

# I

Conclusion of church history. Renaissance and Humanism. The German Reformation, especially the work of Luther, employing appropriate thoughts from St. Paul and special works of Luther. Calvin and the universal importance of Calvinism. Council of Trent and Catholicism subsequent thereto. Pietism and the Enlightenment. The rise of the modern world. German idealism and romanticism and their relationship to Christianity. The importance of the church for political and social life. Protestantism outside Germany and its influence upon Germany. Evaluation of modern Catholicism.

The permanent importance of the person of Jesus for the faith, with particular use of the gospel of John. A comparison of Christianity with non-Christian religions, especially with the religions of India, with non-Christian views of life and ideals, with the intellectual and social tendencies of the present. Problem of the philosophy of life—both personal and social—which affects the pupils.

The religious instruction in *Prima* performs its function in cooperation with the other core subjects and consciously takes account of the different arrangements of problems and the possibilities of intensive development in the different schools. Thus the gymnasial schools are able, with the use of the original text, to go deeply into the problems of the New Testament literary history and to clarify the relations between religion and science. The modern language instruction in the other schools will furnish an opportunity to understand more thoroughly Calvinism on the one hand and the Counter Reformation on the other; while the problems of the period of the Enlightenment can be handled more intensively in the *Oberrealschule*. Likewise in the comparison with the non-Christian views of the world and ideals of life it will be possible to correlate the different historical periods in the various types of schools.

*Oberlyzeum.* The third hour will be used chiefly to give girls a picture of what woman has done in the Christian Church in the course of the centuries and what she can do and is to do to-day in the Evangelical Church.

## CATHOLIC RELIGION
### BOYS' SCHOOLS

## VI

In organic connection with the curriculum of the *Grundschule* and in view of the aim of the secondary school, the function of *Sexta* is as follows: Intensification and extension of the elementary ideas. The instruction begins with a practical introduction into the life of prayer—divine worship at school. With this is associated short liturgical instruction—church, altar, holy mass, instruments, and vestments. Review of the most important parts of the confession and communion instruction. In connection with the ecclesiastical year, drill upon prayers and songs. The Bible stories from the Old Testament—with the exception of those with little relationship to the story of the gospel—show God and His characteristics, sin and its consequences, the preparation for salvation. Catechism instruction begins with the second chapter and treats the most important duties toward God and one's neighbor. From *Sexta* on, emphasis is placed upon the positive building of a Christian life by a study of ethics and by instruction in the practice of virtues.

By reason of the integrated instruction dealing with the study of the home, an introduction to the church organization and church life of the immediate community, suitable to the child's age, shall afford an insight into the organization of God's kingdom of the church. Religious customs and memorials in the life of the people are discussed in connection with the more important holidays. Group visits to the churches and objects of interest are intended to build up an understanding and love for religious art and life. Pictures of Christian heroes, primarily from the Old Church, are intended to arouse enthusiasm for the greatness of the Catholic religion.

## V

In connection with the Bible instruction of class VI the instruction in the catechism—first chapter—treats the creed, God and His qualities, Christ, the Church—foundation, organization, and purpose—consecration and perfection of man.  The Bible instruction—New Testament as far as the Resurrection—connects itself as closely as possible with the ecclesiastical year: youth and public work of Jesus—miracles and the simpler parables—suffering and death, with special development of the two chief facts: Redemption and foundation of God's kingdom. Drill on prayers and hymns as in VI.

Study of the local religious community is to afford views of periods and personalities in medieval and modern times.  Excursions to church buildings and discussions of religious customs and events of the immediate vicinity are continued.  In detail the following are presented.  Introduction of Christianity into the local community.  Boniface.  A Benedictine cloister.  Francis of Assisi.  St. Francis Xavier and his missionary work.  The patrons of youth: Aloysius, Stanislaus Kostka, Johannes Berchmanns.  Local saints, especially name patrons.

## IV

Bible stories from the Resurrection of the Lord to the deaths of the Apostles.  The following topics especially are to be developed:  The effect of the Resurrection, meaning of Whitsunday, biographical sketches of the Apostolic princes.  As supplementary to and deepening of the Bible instruction of class V: Christ the divine teacher—Sermon on the Mount, parables.  The catechism instruction—third chapter—treats intensively the means of grace, primarily the atonement, sacrament of the altar, and prayer.  In connection therewith a more thorough introduction to the liturgy—ecclesiastical year, sacramental offerings, ceremonies, celebration of the holy mass, pericopes for Sundays. More prayers and hymns.

Biographical and cultural sketches of Christian antiquity make up the subject matter of Church history.  Christendom is made clearer in its importance for world and cultural history by means of short discussions correlated with profane history, which deal with Greek and Roman theism, of the religious position of the Hebrews and their neighbors during the time of Jesus.  The following are treated in detail: Peter, the first head of the Church, missionary work of the apostle among the nations, God's wrath upon the Jews.  Persecution of the Christians. Catacombs.  Constantine and the victory of the Cross.  Great church hymns.  Life of the first hermits.  Cloister life.  Character and nature of the Catholic Church will be developed through all discussions.

## U III

Intensified treatment of the Old Testament in conjunction with Bible history. Cultural and religious historical questions—history of prehistoric times; the Bible and science, monotheism; religious personalities—Abraham, Moses, the Prophets. The Old Testament as a guide to Christ. Prefigurations and prophecies in summarized form: the hope for a Messiah among the Jews. Selected passages from the Old Testament. Bible study and Bible geography. The catechism instruction, the second chapter, with constant consideration of the spiritual condition of the beginning years of puberty. The following are to be emphasized: jeopardy of faith due to reading and association. Modern superstition. Consecration of the Sabbath. Relation of the home and school. Authority and freedom. Good example and temptation. Purity. Meaning and protection of property. Love of truth and honor. This portion deals with treatment of sin and its causes as well as with a portrayal of the ideals of Christian perfection. Drill upon liturgical prayers and songs.

In connection with the cultural phases of the integrated instruction (*Gesamtunterricht*) the importance of the Catholic Church for the German peoples, especially in the German Middle Ages, is considered. According to the time available the following topics are studied: The importance of the migration of the Western peoples for the spread of the Church. The Benedictine Order on German soil. Charlemagne. Separation of the Eastern Church from Rome. The migration of the Arabic races and the threat of Islam to Christendom. The Crusaders and their importance for the Church and civilization. The mendicant orders in the body of the Church. The picture of the penetration of the entire life of this period by the Church is completed in the sections dealing with the Church and school, the Church and medieval art, the Church and charity. Premonitions of church division. Luther and the separation of the churches. The discussion of the separation of the churches is to create a deeper appreciation for the differences between the Catholic Church and the chief forms of Protestantism. Spread of the Reformation in Germany and the Northern countries. The Council of Trent and its importance for the regeneration of the Church— Karl Barromaeus. Order of Jesuits. The missionary work of the Church from the age of discoveries until the death of Francis Xavier. St. Vincent de Paul, the apostle of brotherly love.

## O III

Proceeding from a summarizing review of the life and teaching activity of our Lord in connection with Bible history, the Bible instruction treats the Kingdom of God in the New Testament. The Kingdom of God as a new conviction, trust in God, humility, a helping and a forgiving love. The position of the modern man toward civilization—labor, capital, state, and family. The Kingdom of God as the visible church. Drill upon the important passages to be learned.

The aim of the catechism instruction is to conclude the presentation and assimilation of the subject matter of the first and third chapters of the catechism. Selected portions of the creed. Writing and tradition. The secrets of faith: The Trinity, the Incarnation, and the Redemption. The effect of the Holy Spirit in the church and in man's soul. The religious man. Faith and works. Sacraments. The service of God through a life of work and of asceticism. More detailed presentation of the liturgy of Holy Mass (*Ordo missae*).

Church history from the end of the Thirty Years' War to the beginning of the nineteenth century in contemporary pictures. It is important to keep external events more in the background and to present the spiritual tendencies of the time within and without the Church, according to the ability of the child of this age to understand. Church and Protestantism in German states. Protestant sects. The Catholics in Great Britain, Ireland, and Holland. Royal absolutism. Josephinism. Enlightenment and unbelief. Freemasonry. The French Revolution and its consequences for the Church.

## U II

The creed of the Church. The divinity of the Church proved by its origin, its preservation, its fruits, its unity. The Catholic Church the Church of Christ. All of the characteristics given by Christ have proved themselves in it: primacy, apostolicity, unity, holiness, catholicity, indestructibility. Churches of the Orient. Church organizations in the Reformation.

The Church as the living Christ. Teaching office: organs, infallibility, free investigation, heresy. Preaching office: intermediary activity of the Church in sacrifice, sacrament, prayer; the general priesthood; the spiritual character of Catholic piety. Pastoral office: training to holiness; the Church the mother of the saints. Ecclesiastical legislation. Expurgatory index. Punishments of the Church. Ecclesiastical administration. Importance of parish life.

Necessity of the Church for salvation. The salvation of the non-Catholics. Home and foreign missions. The Church and churches—converts, efforts toward union, tolerance and Christion love. The Church and society. The Church and the family. The Church and the state—the religious consecration of authority. The Church and economic life—the religious and moral forces in their importance for economic life. The Church and education. The Church and art. Catholic literature. Reading of Apostolic history is to introduce the rise and spirit of the original church.

Since, with the completion of *Untersekunda,* many pupils enter practical life, there appears to be essential an apologetic treatment of the foundations of the faith which will correspond to the standpoint of that stage of development. Existence of God; divinity of Christ. Some comprehensible reasonable proofs for the existence of God. Brief discussion of the divinity of Christ, the founder of the Church.

Church history of the nineteenth century to the present time, with special consideration of the development of Germany. The presentation of the leading personalities to be worked out as far as possible in vivid pictures. New organization of ecclesiastical relationships in Germany. Diocesan division. Awakening of new Catholic life—Bernhard Overberg, Leopold Stolberg, Sailer, Clemens Hofbauer, Görres. The disorders in Cologne. Social problems—Ketteler, Kelping. The Vatican Council. The cultural struggle—*Kulturkampf*—Mallinckrodt, Windthorst. The recent Popes. The Catholic coöperative organizations. New orders and societies. The World War and the Church. Excursions and visits are, as opportunity offers, to furnish a glimpse into the development of the religious art of modern and recent times.

## O II

Christ—His personality and work: The personality and work of Christ are to be presented in a form which corresponds to the need and problems of the present. In particular the following topics are to be treated: Heathen, Jewish, and Christian sources for the life of Jesus. Reliability of the Christian source. The Messianic and the divine personal testimony of Jesus. The spiritual dignity of Jesus. His Gospel of the adoption by God, of God's kingdom. His prophecies. The moral perfection of Jesus—innocence and virtue. The miracles of Jesus and science. Resurrection of Jesus. The history of His work. The dogma of God incarnate connected therewith. Christ, the second person in the Godhead. The work of redemption. Jesus' death for atonement. Christ and Paul. The reëstablishment of the destroyed supernatural order. Means of grace through the Church. Doctrine of grace and the sacrament, especially the sacrament of the altar. Christ the head of the Church. The root of the vine and the vine. (See letters to the Ephesians and Colossians.) Christ's kingdom. The Lawgiver and the Judge of the world. The worship of Christ—historical view. The succession of Christ. Mary the Mother of Jesus and our Mother. Forms of the crucifix.

Typical representations of Christ in art: Poetry dealing with Christ. Reading of one of the synoptic gospels.

Church history in connection with instruction in secular history. Ecclesiastical antiquity and the Middle Ages to Boniface VIII are treated. Complete presentation is not striven for. Christendom is to be recognized first in its religious and constructive values as contrasted with the pagan types of religion of antiquity. A view on the methods, value, and errors of comparative religious history. The unfolding of the doctrine of the Church in the doctrinal struggles of the first centuries. Development of old Christian literature. Important doctrine of the Eastern and Western Church for theology and ecclesiastical life. The changed face of the world and the intermingling of the old Christian-Latin with the national German factors of civilization. Benedict and his Order. The Empire and the Church from Charlemagne to Innocence III. Byzantine State Church. Islam and its opposition during the Crusades. Catholic intellecttual and artistic life in the Middle Ages. Thomas Aquinas and the importance of scholasticism. Bonaventura and mysticism. Outstanding German mystics. The Church and popular education. Medieval piety. The development of the idea of Orders. The nobility and the German Church. Lights and shadows of medieval times.

## U I

The Christian conception of God: God in the light of reason. Mankind's belief in God. The experience and proof of God. God and the world,—the explanation of the world without God,—monism; the explanation of the world without a personal God—pantheism. The theory of evolution. Man and animal. Spirituality and immortality of the soul.

God in the light of revelation. The conception, possibility, necessity, and character of the revelation. Nature and qualities of God. The dogma of creation. Story of creation. Divine providence. Trinity.

God as the Creator of supernatural order. Original sin. Redemption. Predestination. The riddle of the universe and Christendom's solution. Pessimistic and optimistic views of the world. God the Eternal. The ideal of truth, morality, and beauty. True piety. Belief in God. Happiness. Belief and unbelief.

Reading of selected passages on the idea of God from the Psalms and the prophecies. Gospel of John in selected passages.

Church history from Boniface VIII to the French Revolution. The disintegration process in the Middle Ages. State and Church at the end of the Middle Ages. The religious and moral condition of the German people. Humanism and the Renaissance. Ecclesiastical reform movements. Luther's religious development. The Protestant reform of Germany. The three chief forms of Protestantism. The Council of Trent and the Reform of the Church. The era of the Saints. Life in the orders of missionary activity. Development of the State Church Law. The Enlightenment and unbelief. The importance of the Enlightenment as an experiment in shaping life without God and the supernatural. The position of the German classicists toward religion and the Church. The inner development of Protestantism since 1555. Religious and moral conditions in Germany and France on the eve of the Revolution. The aim of this instruction is to understand how modern civilization develops as a result of the effect of humanism, criticism, natural science theories, and subjectivism.

## O I

Introduction to the great personal and public problems of the Catholic. The religious foundation of moral life: theonomy not autonomy; doctrine of law and of conscience. Conflict of conscience. The training of the will in education and self-guidance and freedom of the will. Duty and inclination. Virtue. Virtue and happiness. Sin and redemption from sin.

The special fields of duty: religious duties in the narrower sense. The doctrine of faith and doubt. Belief, faith, and knowledge. Private and Church life of prayer, concluding technical and practical treatment of literature. The Catholic and his Church. The Catholic of reality. The Catholic family ideals: unity, indissolubility, and holiness of marriage. The ecclesiastical marriage laws. Sexual problems. Authority and freedom in education. The Church and the modern youth movement. Duties toward the State, State and Church, State and school, State and religious freedom, Catholic ideal of the State, nationalism, the Catholic and human society. Protection of life. Duels. Alcohol question. Secular calling. Choice of vocation. Professional ethics. Renunciation of the world and overcoming the world. Life and industry. The Church and the social problem. Personal and community economy. The Catholic and education. The ideal of personality, truth, moral freedom, love. The religious consecration of personality.

Old and New Testament texts on ethics. Reading and explanation of Paul's Epistles—first Epistle to Corinthians.

Church history from the French Revolution to the present. The French Revolution and its reactions on the Church. Secularization. Reconstruction of the ecclesiastical orders. The Concordats. The reawakening of the Catholic consciousness until 1848. Struggle of State, Church, and liberalism. The State and Church in Prussia in 1850-1870. The importance of the Vatican. The *Kulturkampf*. The Papacy since 1870. Leo XIII. Catholic charity in the nineteenth century. The Church and educational questions. World missions. Present condition of the Church in the most important civilized countries.

Modernism. The Greek-Eastern Churches. Tendencies in modern Protestantism. Occultism. The Church and the World War. Current Church history.

## VI

In connection with the diocesan hymn and prayer-book, practical and detailed introduction to prayer and participation in the divine service at school. Explanation of some of the devotional exercises of the Church calendar, as they are used in the school and parish divine services of the high feasts. Some Church songs. Observation of the Church and its inner arrangements. The parish community. Its relation to the diocese and to the whole Church. Religious customs and the life of the people of the community.

Bible history: Old Testament. Selection of reading on the basis of their importance for moral life.

Catechism: Moral instruction. The virtuous life must be cultivated and must be presented in the heroes of virtue which are especially honored in the community. Name patrons.

## V

Extension of the religious observational instruction beyond the home community. The Catholic Church in Germany: Dioceses, orders, church societies, missions. Diaspora. The society of St. Boniface.

Bible history: The New Testament until the Resurrection of Jesus, in connection with the Church year. Easier pericopes.

Catechism. The creed.

Illustrations from Church history: The spread, establishment, and effect of the Catholic faith in Germany presented in biographies, chiefly of German saints: Boniface, Lioba—Benedictine monastery,—Mathilde, Henry, Francis of Assisi, Dominicus, Elizabeth, Peter Canisius, German missionary bishops.

## IV

Bible history: Apotheosis of Jesus, the Church filled with the Holy Spirit spreads beyond the German Empire. The activity of the Apostles in Jerusalem, Judea, Samaria, and even unto the ends of the earth.

Church history: The history of antiquity. The moral of the religious conditions of the Jews and Medes. External and internal reasons for the spread of Christianity. The fall of Jerusalem. Persecution of the Christians. The martyrs. The catacombs.

The life of the first Christian. Constantine and Helena. Athanasius. Nicaea. Augustine and Monica. An old Christian divine service. Benedict and Scholastica. Leo I and Gregory I.

Catechism: The doctrine of grace and the sacraments. Liturgy of the holy sacrament and of holy mass.

For Sundays the remaining pericopes in which Jesus appears as a teacher.

### U III

The Old Testament story of the revelation in its inner development under God's direction and in its preparatory character for the coming of Jesus Christ—prefigurations, prophecies. In the course of this presentation attention to the sacred books as the sources of the same. Reading of special passages from the teachings of prophetic books and the school Bible. Liturgy of the Old Testament realized in the New Testament. Development of the Old Testament thought in the life of the Church—prayer, song, liturgy, art.

Moral instruction: Conscience, moral law, its observance (good conduct, virtue, perfection, transgression, sin, temptation). Treatment of the individual commandments according to the catechism. Effort is always made toward practical exercise of these principles. Herein emphasis is ever laid upon the necessity of grace and means of grace for worthy works, holiness, and final persistence.

Church history: Christianization of Europe and especially of the German people; migration of the peoples; Clovis, Boniface, Lioba, Benedictines, Charlemagne. The ecclesiastical state. Penetration of all civilization by the leaven of Christianity. Saintly women. Charity. Life in Orders. Islam. Crusades. Papacy and the Empire. Premonitions of the Church division in Germany. Luther and the division of the faith. Principles of difference. The Church at the time of the Council of Trent. The Jesuit orders. Francis Xavier. Peter Canisius. St. Angela. St. Vincent de Paul. Charity.

### O III

Life of Jesus: His teaching, preaching, and pastoral office. His survival and influence in the Church.

Catechism: God and His qualities. Trinity. Creation. Man and his soul. Sin and Redemption. Jesus Christ. The Holy Ghost and the Church eschatology.

Discussion of the liturgical book as introduction to prayer in the Church during the Church year.

Church history: The Church and Absolutism. The Church in defense against the Enlightenment and unbelief. Freemasonry. French Revolution.

## U II

*Untersekunda* serves on the one hand as a concluding class of the *Lyzeum* for preparation for life; on the other hand for preparation for the higher classes.

Some proofs of God which are easily comprehensible. Brief proof of the divinity of Christ, the founder of the Church.

The doctrine of the Church: The divinity of the Church proved by its origin, its preservation, its fruits, and its unity. The Catholic Church, the Church of Christ. All of the qualities and characteristics of this Church as given by Christ prove themselves in its primacy, apostolicity, unity, holiness, catholicity, indestructibility. Churches of the Orient. Church organizations in the Reformation. The living Christ in the Church. Teaching office: organs, infallibility, pronouncement of doctrine, free investigation, heresy. Preaching office: mediation of the Church in sacrifice, sacrament, prayer; the general priesthood; the religious character of Catholic piety. Pastoral office: education for holiness; the Church, the mother of the saints; ecclesiastical legislation; index; ecclesiastical punishments; ecclesiastical administration; the importance of parish life.

Necessity of salvation in the Church. The doctrine of the body and soul of the Church. Salvation of non-Catholics. Home and foreign missions. Converts. Efforts toward consolidation. Tolerance and Christian love. The Church and society. The Church and the family. The Church and the State. Religious consecration of authority. The Church and economic life; religious-moral forces and their importance for economic life. Church charity. The Church and education. The Church and art. Catholic literature.

Reading of the history of the Apostles: introduction to the spirit of the early Church.

Church history of the nineteenth century to the present with special reference to its development in Germany. This presentation will develop here, as far as possible, vivid pictures of outstanding personalities. New organization of Church relationships in Germany. Division of the dioceses. Awakening of new Catholic life—Countess Gallitzin, Bernhard Overberg, Leopold von Stolberg, Sailer, Görres, Clemens Hofbauer; the disturbances in Cologne. The social question—Ketteler, Kolping. Struggle of the Church against anti-religious and anti-Christian movements. Syllabus. The Vatican Council. The cultural struggle—Mallinckrodt, Windhorst, missionary bishops. The recent popes, the present condition of the Church missionary system. Catholic system of societies. New Orders. The World War and the Church. The Church and the Revolution.

Excursions and visits where possible are to afford a view into the development of ecclesiastical art of modern and recent times.

## O II

Natural and supernatural knowledge and worship of God: Their sources and direction.

The natural knowledge of God: The idea of religion developing out of religious historical observation. Differences among religions according to the difference in the conception of God. The true conception of God as the eternal perfect, personal being, separated from the world and originating in Himself,— the source, the foundation, and purpose of all things. Detailed proof of God. The different ways to God.

Supernatural knowledge of God: through the self-revealing God. The fact of the Revelation is vouched to us by the Church as God's foundation. The nature, the necessity, the obviousness, and the blessings of the Revelation for mankind—rationalism, the Enlightenment. The infallible acceptance of the Revelation by the Church. The sources of the Revelation accepted by the Church: The Holy Scripture—inspiration, the canon of the Old and New Testaments; original texts and translations, especially the Vulgate; the reading of the Holy Scripture, its explanation by the Church and under its supervision; content of the Holy Scripture. Ecclesiastical traditions—the Catholic rule of faith.

Church history: The ecclesiastical antiquity and the Middle Ages to Boniface VIII treated in connection with the history instruction. Completeness is not the aim. Christendom first to be made known in its religious and constructive values as opposed to the pagan religions of antiquity. View of the methods, values, and errors of comparative religious history. The development of the Church doctrine in the doctrinal struggles of the first centuries. Development of old Christian literature. Development of Eastern and Western Church doctrine for theology and life. The changed places of the world and the intermingling of old Christian-Latin with the national German factors of civilization. Benedict and his Order. Empire and Papacy from Charlemagne to Innocent III. Byzantine State Church. Islam and its opposition to the Crusades. Intellectual and artistic life in the Middle Ages. Thomas Aquinas. The meaning of scholasticism. Bonaventura and mysticism. Outstanding German mystics. The Church and popular education. Medieval piety. Development of the idea of orders. Catholic charity. Lights and shadows of the medieval times.

## U I

God's nature and work: God as a source, prototype, and guide to supernatural existence. Character and qualities of God— pantheism, monism, the mystery of the Trinity. God as the creator of the world. The purpose of the creation. The preservation and government of the world. Divine providence—deism. Six days' work. The spiritual world. Man. Nature of man. Qualities of the human soul, its spirituality and immortality. Freedom of the will. Supernatural gifts of man. The elevation of man to supernatural existence. The conception of the supernatural. Its lofty dignity—naturalism.

Catholic ethics as a way of man to his goal. God as the highest lawgiver. Attempts of morality without God. Law as the external guide of moral conduct. The division of the Law. Its sanctity. The conscience as the inner guide of moral conduct. The morally good work. Virtue. Perfection. Sin. Vice. Temptation. Duties of man toward God: faith, hope, love, honor, supplication, sacrifice. Worship and supplication of the saints as indirect approach to God. Duty toward God's representatives—parents, Church, faith. Duties with reference to the life of the body and the soul. Charity and public welfare. The duties of chastity. Duty toward property of others. Irrational theories concerning property. The duty and value of work. The social problem. Duty with reference to truth and honesty. The sanctity of daily labor. The sanctity of family life. The education of the child for God and for eternal life. Evangelical councils.

Reading of important speeches and parables of Jesus and sections from the doctrinal books of the Old and New Testaments.

Church history: From Boniface VIII to French Revolution. The disintegrating process of the Middle Ages. The religious-moral condition of the German people at the end of the Middle Ages. Humanism and the Renaissance. Ecclesiastical reform movements. The Protestant reform of Germany. Three chief forms of Protestantism. Council of Trent. The reform and the Church. The era of the saints. Life in Orders. Missionary activity. Charity. Development of the State Church law. Enlightenment and unbelief. Importance of the Enlightenment as an attempt at direction in life without God and the supernatural. Attitude of the German classicists toward the Church. Religious and moral conditions in France and Germany on the eve of the Revolution.

The purpose of this instruction is to know how modern civilization developed in consequence of the effect of humanism, criticism, natural science theories, and subjectivism.

## O I

Departure of man from his purpose and his return through Christ and the Church. The destruction of the supernatural and the wounding of the natural in man by the original sin. The nature of the original sin. Its consequences. The plan and promise of redemption. Jesus the promised Redeemer. Jesus

Christ.  Man and God.  Sources of the life of Jesus.  The secret of the incarnation.  Dignity and merit of the God in man.  Nature of Jesus Christ.  The worship of Jesus.  The divine heart of Jesus.  Jesus our life ideal.  The kingdom of Jesus.  Jesus and public life.  Jesus Christ in art and literature of the centuries, especially in the nineteenth century.  The Mother of God.  Her priority of grace.  The new Eve.  Worship of the woman in Mary.  Jesus, the new Adam.  Jesus' work of redemption.  Resurrection of Jesus.  His ascension.  His heavenly life.  The fruits of Jesus' work of redemption:  Jesus' grace, the holy sacraments, holy mass.  Liturgy of the holy sacraments, especially of holy mass.  The Church of Christ as a mediator of the fruits of redemption.  The constitution of the Church.  The effect of the Holy Ghost in the Church and in man's soul.  The infallibility of the ecclesiastical ministry and its officials.  Pastorship of the Church.  The holy orders.  Community of saints.  Mystical body of Jesus Christ.  Our life in Christ as the safest assurance of reaching our goal.  Man's consummation; eschatology.  The reading of the Gospel of John.

Church history:  From the French Revolution to the present.  French Revolution and its reaction upon the Church.  Secularization.  Reorganization of the ecclesiastical orders.  Concordats.  Rebirth of the Catholic consciousness in the first half of the nineteenth century.  Struggle against State, Church, and liberalism.  The State and the Church in Prussia from 1850 to 1870.  The importance of the Vatican.  The *Kulturkampf*.  The Papacy since 1870.  The recent popes.  Catholic charity in the nineteenth century.  The Church and educational questions.  World missions.  Present condition of the Church in the most important civilized countries.  Modernism.  The Greek-Eastern church communities.  Tendencies in modern Protestantism.  Occultism —theosophy.  Church and the World War.  Current Church history.

In concluding reviews and in free reports, the girls are to try to summarize the most important facts and ideas concerning the origin and struggle of God's Kingdom of the Church through the whole course of Church history, both in cross-sections and in developmental views.

## JEWISH RELIGION

A special course is laid out for Jewish religious instruction.

## GERMAN

## VI

*Phonetics.*  Practice in correct formation of sounds in connection with music and foreign language instruction.  Comparison of the sounds in dialect, everyday language and High German.

*Etymology and Syntax.* Kinds and classes of words. The most important facts on the inflection of the nouns, adjectives, and verbs. Distinction between strong and weak forms. Extension of vocabulary upon the basis of the pupil's observation in daily life and the whole of the instruction.

The simple sentence, its chief parts and their expansion. Word agreement, sentence accent. The most important facts about punctuation as a means of clarification of sentence structure.

Thorough drill upon the grammatical terminology which has to be introduced in the school.

*Style.* In connection with the reading material and with the oral exercises, modes of language expression—primarily adjectives and verbs—are sought to describe noises, color effects, movements, sensations of smell and taste, natural phenomena and other observations. Sound-descriptive force of vowels and consonants. Terminology for the tools and activities of the working people.

*Oral Exercises.* Exercises in thoughtful reading, narration and recitation of poetry. Reports on what has been experienced and observed, read, or heard. Short performances of what has been written by the pupils themselves or memorized.

*Written Exercises.* Short written reports dealing with what has been experienced, thought out, related, and read—with the exception of paraphrasing and analyzing poems in prose. Exercises in etymology and syntax. Spelling.

*Literature.* From the reader. Introduction to the local environment and its forms of life. Custom and usage. The classes and their work. Biographical material of famous men and women of the home and district. Fairy tales, animal stories, stories about children, also stories from recent literature. Suitable stories of adventure. Humor and pathos in home and neighborhood, rounds, and riddles. Fairy tales, ballads, short poems. Stories and anecdotes in local dialect.

Art appreciation with preference for the objective and in connection with reading material and poetry—Schwind, Richter, Spitzweg, etc.

In the *Gymnasium* and the *Realgymnasium* and in the girls' schools there is a reduction of the reading material in view of the somewhat smaller number of hours. In the girls' schools the selection depends on special points of view. Special emphasis will be laid upon the biography of women of the community and the work of women in the home. Fairy tales and nature stories are to be preferred to stories of adventure. Children's stories and children's rounds retain their charm longer for girls than for boys.

V

*Phonetics.* Exercises in correct formation of sounds as in class VI. Change of sound, gradation, change and modification. Accent in word and sentence. Syllabication—language and speech syllables.

*Etymology and Syntax.* The parts of speech, as to form and meaning. Important groups of substantives. Personal names, names of things. Designation of activities and conditions. Extension and fixation of inflected forms. Word compounds, logical relation of root and modifier. Importance of structural syllables—prefix and suffix. Enlargement and refinement of the vocabulary as in VI. Related words.

Review and expansion of the simple sentence. Sentence combination. The simpler coördinate conjunctives. The most important facts concerning the subordinate clause, its character; the classification of subordinate clauses according to their connectives. All with consideration of word placement, accent, and punctuation and in close connection with foreign language instruction.

*Style.* As in VI. Personification. Personification of natural forces. Concrete content of abstract and worn-out expressions. Original meaning of prepositions and conjunctions. Explanation of popular idioms and proverbs. Folk-lore in the language.

*Oral Exercises.* As in VI with stronger emphasis on High German purity.

*Written Exercises.* Short written exercises as in VI. Short exercises at home from the field of the child's experience and thought—continuation, paraphrases and imitations of fairy tales. Full treatment of a theme which has been assigned or found by the pupil himself. Exercises in grammar and spelling as in VI.

*Literature.* From the reader. Remains of early Germany with special reference to the home community. Nature experience and German feeling for nature. German mythology as it still continues to exist in the life of the people; belief in spirits, witches, elves, werwolves, dwarfs, giants. Memorials of early times in the popular superstitions. German forms of life in their provincial differences. German life abroad. German economy. German activity in history and at the present time. Legal customs, festival customs, humor in the life of the common people. Songs, proverbs, riddles. Customs and games of youth. Art study within the limits of the whole cultural instruction of the class, especially study of German cities and villages, fountains and gates, castles, churches, markets, and streets.

In the *Gymnasium* and the *Realgymnasium* a limitation of the reading material with reference to a somewhat smaller number of hours; still essentials must not be omitted from the materials which belong to the whole cultural instruction of the class. In girls' schools a slight shift of emphasis in reading as in class VI.

*Story-telling.* Not in special hours. Stories are best given as "life pictures" which assure the pupils an insight into the important phases of national history; for example, Arminius and the old Germans; Theodoric and the migrations of nations; Boniface and the conversion of Germany; Charlemagne and the Western Empire; Henry I and the founding of the German Empire; Otto of Bamberg and the Christianization of the East; Frederick Barbarossa, the high point of medieval imperial power; Maximilian, the last knight; Luther, Charles V and the period of the Reformation; Gustavus Adolphus, Wallenstein and the Thirty Years' War; Frederick the Great and the rise of Prussia; Bismarck and the founding of the new German Empire; Hindenburg and the World War.

## IV

*Phonetics.* Exercises in correct formation of sounds within the limits of reading, speaking, and declamation.

*Etymology.* Summary and development of the classes of words. Conclusion of the declensions, with inclusion of proper names and the most common foreign words. Conclusion of the conjugations. Change of tenses, principles of the formation of verbs. Continuation of the exercises to increase the vocabulary.

*Syntax.* Sentence structure. Principles of subordinate clauses: the importance of subjective, objective, attributive, and adverbial clauses, with exercises in changing clauses into phrases and phrases into clauses; their form; their position; development of subordination from coördination; the most important subordinate conjunctions. Exercises in the different possibilities of expression of sentence relationship, also from the point of view of style. The inner connection of punctuation with sentence structure.

*Style.* As in class V. Change of meaning—expansion, contraction, degeneracy, and improvement; transfer of meaning from one field of thought to another, from the concrete to the abstract.

*Oral Exercises.* As in classes VI and V, with special treatment of easy description.

*Written Exercises.* Short written exercises in school and at home as in class V, with the addition of easy description. Occasional grammatical and spelling exercises, especially for the purpose of understanding sentence structure and punctuation.

*Literature.* In the reader. Continuation and extension of the subject-matter fields of class VI and V. Additional subject matter corresponding to the educational objective of the class. Antiquity. Myths from the Greek and Roman world. In the introduction to the culture of Greece and Rome easily understood passages from the ancient poets and writers are to be studied in artistically important translations and occasionally simpler selections from the technical literature dealing with antiquity. In the study of art attention is to be given to the remains of Greek and Roman culture upon German soil.

Since in the *Gymnasium* and *Realgymnasium* the Latin instruction supports the German in dealing with the subject matter of the ancient world, in spite of the reduced number of hours the general humanistic materials must not be crowded out.

In girls' schools the heroines of the Greek myths and important women of Greek and Roman history will be especially considered. Within the limits of the general reading slight shifting of emphasis as in VI and V.

*Poetry.* From class IV on, the German instruction seeks to develop an appreciation of artistic form,—at first only the most important from verse, strophe and rhyme. Training of pupils in tone color, melody, and rhythm. The poetic technique, however, must be discussed in connection with the individual masterpiece only in so far as it is necessary for its comprehension.

## U III

*Phonetics and Etymology.* Ancient forms and words in the language of to-day. Introduction to the origin and life of sounds and words. Native words, borrowed words, and foreign words; cultural-historical meaning of borrowed words. Cultural history in dialects and proverbs. Popular etymology. Names of persons and places; district, river, and mountain names of the immediate vicinity.

*Syntax and Style.* Review and development of syntax with special study of punctuation. Indirect speech. Word placement, sentence accent.

Occasional consideration of the grammatically correct from the point of view of the grammatically beautiful.

*Oral Exercises.* As in IV.

*Written Exercises.* Delineation is added to description. Occasional exercises in the arrangement of a subject and in analysis of reading selections.

*Literature.* In the reader and in simple classics. Survey of the civilization of the old German based upon portrayals which have literary value. Selected portions of the *Edda*, the *Nibelungen, Hilde and Gudrun*, the *Dietrich* myths—in random samples from the original text in translations or in paraphrased form. Myths of the Lombards, Franks, and Vandals. Tales of Arthur. German folk literature. Anecdotes, Christmas games, and other spiritual plays. Cultural, historical novels and tales. Also autobiographies and letters—heroes of labor. Ballads, songs, and lyrics. Scientific literature for insight into heroic German life and its struggles and objectives in all walks of life.

In girls' schools the heroines of German mythology, also women of Nordic mythology, are especially treated. In addition to heroes of labor, heroines of labor and their patience must not be forgotten.

*Art Study.* Primarily records of the German Middle Ages. Pictures which have artistic value for German mythology and history.

*Poetry.* Continuation of the work of class IV. Reference to the composition of a rather long poetic masterpiece, the ballad to begin with.

## O III

*Etymology.* New forms and disappearance of words. Words created at the present time through the war, technology, and trade. Backward view upon the change of meaning and the imaginative content of the German language. The foreign word and the struggle for purity in language.

*Syntax and Style.* Occasional extensions of the work.

*Oral Exercises.* As before.

*Written Exercises.* Systematic introduction to the observation and description of events, conditions, and men, with increasing demand for accurate and concrete reproduction. Descriptions with careful use of the reading materials and subject matter of other subjects. Short summaries and technical outline reports of what has been read. Exercises in organization.

*Literature.* In the reader and in individual classics. Portrayals from the history of the German people with stress upon the economic and social aspects, natural science and technology. Sketches from the colonization of the German East, from Germanism in the lost states and in foreign lands. Descriptions of voyages of discovery, sea travels. History of the modern state as mirrored in the short story, also in the lighter historical novel. Some of the lighter dramas. The ballad up to the present time. Lyrics as in U III.

In girls' schools the position of the German woman in the nation and in culture will be treated more intensively, corresponding to the importance of woman for German civilization with the beginning of the seventeenth century; for example, woman as the wife and mother of important men; woman as a heroine, as a missionary, doctor, pioneer of civilization in the colonies. In addition worthwhile examples of poetry by women.

*Art Study.* With reference to the whole objective of the class, especial consideration of monuments of the German Renaissance and the German Baroque.

*Poetry.* Deepening of the insight into the nature of the ballads, with consideration of the means of expression characteristic of the different ballad writers.

## U II

*Phonetics, Etymology, and Syntax.* Only occasional additional lessons.

*Rhetoric.* Study of literary works from the artistic point of view—keenness of thought, emotional content, sound pointing, cadence, and images. Continuation of exercises to develop acute feeling for language.

*Oral Exercises.* As before. Especially exercises in extemporaneous speech relying only on key words. Exercises in oral reproduction of literary works with increasing care in the choice of words and in sentence structure suitable to and in keeping with the sentiment contained.

*Written Exercises.* Particularly short written exercises for the development of style in different directions; concrete reproduction of observations, short descriptions of objects and processes. Descriptive reports, with emphasis upon the essentials. Moods of nature, impressions of works of art. Simple characterizations. Composition subjects from the same points of view. Composition based upon experience, the subject to be the free choice of the pupil. Exercises in organization.

*Literature.* In the reader and in individual classics, for the purpose of comprehending the nineteenth century and the present. Novels and short stories which are characteristic and suitable to the stage of development of the class. For dramatic reading preferably masterpieces which deal with political ideas and the relation of the individual to people and society. The age as reflected in the lyric. The home in proverb, song, and local art.

Scientific literature for the purpose of becoming acquainted with worthwhile personalities of the age through letters, speeches, and daily life; also biographies for the sake of introduction to characteristic German personal life. Artistically worthwhile descriptions on the subject of nature and the spiritual world, and modern economic and social life.

In girls' schools sketches from lives of women, as in O III. In addition the woman in public life. Study of worthwhile women's literature in the *Studienanstalten,* with the limitations required by the reduced number of hours.

*Art Appreciation.* Art of the nineteenth century. Tendencies in art of the present, especially in architecture, street, and city planning. The aim of artistic expression of the present in technology and industrial arts.

*Poetry.* Awakening of the first insight into the inner artistic form of the drama. Introduction to the composition of the novel and short story.

## O II

*Grammar.* Summary and development of the previous language instruction by using the different possibilities in the various schools for increasing the knowledge of the facts in the history of the language. Survey of the historical development of the German language and the German dialects by means of the language atlas. Introduction to Middle High German upon the basis of the reading materials, with occasional use of selection from the Gothic and Old High German. Additional study of the principles of change of meaning with reference to cultural historical development, with the use of the German dictionary.

*Style.* As in U II. Perhaps with Luther as an example, introduction to the style of an outstanding creator of language. Continuation of the exercises to increase the feeling for language.

*Oral Exercises.* More exercises in linguistically artistic reading, declamation, and extemporaneous speech.

*Written Exercises.* Short written exercises as in U II. Also composition in the form of essays, with as many-sided treatment as possible of the very varied problem of German composition.

*Literature.* Upon the gymnasial institutions, and especially upon the classical language instruction, falls the problem of establishing the relationships of classic literature to German intellectual life. At the end of this school year, on the other hand, the effect of Shakespeare's works upon the German intellectual life is shown in connection with the reading of some of his important works. In all other school types, in connection with the history in the first quarter of the year, some works from Greek literature, from the time of Homer to the tragedians, will be studied primarily from the point of view of their importance for German intellectual history; also the Greek tragedy as an introduction to the history of the theater.

In all schools emphasis is laid upon the introduction to medieval intellectual life, especially its poetry and its art. In addition, it is to be considered that the various types of schools stand for various degrees of thoroughness in the facts of cultural history.

Rise of the whole epoch from Germanic antiquity and Christianity; its golden age and its decline. Art and literature of the migrations of the peoples with an outlook upon Nordic intellectual life—*Edda* and saga. The Latin medieval age under the Carolingians and the Ottos in a selection of characteristic translations,—in institutions studying Latin in the original in connection with the Latin instruction.

In connection with the French instruction: longer selected portions from the most important poetry of the Middle High German classical period; folk epics, classic epics, minstrelsy, folk lyrics. The purpose is to create understanding for the poetic character and literary form of the works read, which can be attained also without translation by means of thoughtful and accurate reading. Worthwhile translations of artistic value and transcriptions serve to extend and round out this reading. Prose of the Middle Ages in connection with the religious instruction, especially examples from the mystics. The rise of civic city culture; popular plays, anecdotes, Meistersinger; the period of the Renaissance and the Reformation; German humanists, Luther.

The scientific literature considers also the other phases of the life of medieval culture, law, economy, and morals.

*Archæology.* Prehistoric remains upon German soil. German antiquities and their influences, which are to be noted in connection with art appreciation, especially from the period of the migrations of the peoples.

*Art Appreciation.* Art appreciation seeks, in conjunction with religion, history, and drawing, primarily to make clear the artistic expressions of the attitudes toward life and the ideas of the ecclesiastical, chivalric, and civil Middle Ages; also in its difference from the Greek artistic tendency. Architectural principles of Romance, Gothic, and Renaissance style. Some characteristic paintings of German medieval times.

*Poetry.* Upon the basis of the reading, a summarizing characterization of the folk and literary epic, minstrelsy and folk poetry.

# I

*Grammar.* With application of facts from the history of language, which have previously been gathered, discussions in the field of philology. Language differences as the expression of the spiritual character of the peoples. Essays of important philologists and language creators.

*Style.* Introduction to the style of outstanding creators of the language in constant connection with the reading. Style and personality, style and content, style and nationality; the rhetorical means of the language for the different purposes of language, in business, in public life, in art.

*Oral Exercises.* Systematic exercises in extemporaneous speech, in debate, and in formal speech.

*Written Exercises.* As in O II. Also longer essays as a substitute for compositions written at home.

*Literature.* In accordance with the objective of the class. The revival of German intellectual civilization in connection with the rise of the modern spirit after the debacle in the

Thirty Years' War. The period of the Enlightenment in connection with the other courses. The work of Klopstock, Lessing, and Herder in connection with the tendencies in the whole of European culture. The Storm and Stress period, especially in connection with the young Goethe and the young Schiller. The age of German idealism, primarily represented by Goethe and Schiller, also their whole influence reaching out over Germany. Romanticism as a second characteristic form of German idealism. From the superabundance of literature following Goethe careful selection must be made. The continuing influence and the persistence of earlier motifs can be demonstrated; civic drama from Lessing to Hauptmann—from world-citizen to state-citizen; Schiller, Hebbel, Gottfried Keller. Likewise in cross-sections of subjects and problems the steps in the development of the literature of the nineteenth century will have to be considered—Austrian, Swiss, Low German poets, young Germany and political poetry, artistic realism, impressionistic and expressionistic art, social lyric, the appearance of new motifs. References to the tendencies of the times—realism, naturalism, impressionism, expressionism—and to corresponding literary tendencies in foreign countries are desirable.

*Scientific Literature.* In *Prima* scientific literature is to be given especial attention, especially in the choice of the prose writings of the authors. Artistically worthwhile works selected from particular phases of modern life, which are illustrative of the character and development of the German intellect, are to be studied. This task demands especially systematic integration of all subjects of instruction and consideration of the type of school concerned.

*Art Appreciation.* Primarily in connection with drawing, Baroque architecture, chiefly in Germany, and Classicism, the period of the would-be gentlemen. The revival of German painting in the nineteenth century. Present-day painting, pictorial art, and architecture.

*Poetry.* In connection with literature, German poetic art in its characteristic form.

Along with systematic summarizing of the material previously developed, the formal elements of poetry will be discussed from a historical and fundamental viewpoint: its classes and tendencies with special consideration of the various types of æsthetic poetry, particularly tragedy and comedy.

In the gymnasial schools, in connection with Greek and Latin, the effect of the classics upon German poetry is considered.

The other types of schools will give more attention to the tendencies of entire Europe which have had an effect upon the German intellect; primarily the French and English influence,—particularly the influence of Shakespeare, but also that of Milton, Shaftesbury, and Rousseau.

In the *Oberrealschule* the connection of the Enlightenment with the mathematical, mechanical conception of nature is emphasized. The naturalistic contributions of Goethe and of Romanticism in the further course of the nineteenth century,—especially realism, and naturalism and impressionism in connection with the natural-scientific attitude of the time,—natural science, technical and social problems in the literature of the nineteenth century to the present.

In girls' schools in the choice of artistic material attention must be paid to the problems of women.

## HISTORY AND CIVICS

### V

For the content see German (p. 460).

### IV

*From the Early Greek Period to the Fall of the Western Roman Empire (476)*. Sketches from the early Greek period and the middle Greek period: Troy, Mycenæ, Crete; migrations. Greek cultural unity: Olympus and Delphi; colonization. Old Sparta and Athens. Heroes from the period of the Greek war of liberation. Athens at the time of Pericles. Philip, Alexander. Sketches from the age of Hellenism. In connection with religion and geography the historical fact of world importance from oriental civilization,—if possible along with the study of Alexander.

Views of civilization from early Roman times; rule of the aristocracy and class struggles. Important personalities from the period of the Punic Wars. The century of civil wars. The age of Augustus. The Roman Empire through some of its characteristic representatives—Tiberius, Nero, Trajan, Hadrian, Diocletian, Constantine.

For insight into the subject matter presented from a civic point of view: development of the essential types of constitutions, interaction of political and economic forces. Peaceful expansion, migrations, racial intermingling.

Myths and tales from antiquity in connection with the German instruction. In connection with geography, relationship between the Mediterranean country and the history of Greek and Roman states. In the gymnasial and realgymnasial institutions, the Latin instruction supports the history instruction by description of the life of ancient times.

### U III

*From the Early German Period to the Peace of Westphalia.* Sketches from the political, economic, and social phases of life among the Germans. The migrations only in their chief outlines. The German state within the limits of the Roman Empire. Influence of Roman civilization upon the Germans. Germanism and Christianity. The monk and the cloister. Clovis and the Frankish kingdom. The conflict with Islam. Charlemagne. The German Empire through its most important representatives. The Empire and the Papacy. Connection between the wide extent of the German Empire, natural economy, dependency, and imperial weakness. Cultural and economic importance of the Crusades. Knighthood and medieval military system. The towns and middle classes. Rise of the princely power. Expansion of Germanism toward the East. Hansa and the Teutonic Order. Founding and importance of the dynastic policy of the Hapsburgers and Luxemburgers. Most important inventions and discoveries. Luther, the Reformation and Charlemagne. The Peasants' War. Sketches from the period of the Counter-Reformation and of the Thirty Years' War. Imperial power and particularism. Mercenary system.

Cultural discussion in connection with religion. German and drawing. In the gymnasial schools: Cæsar's wars with the Gauls and with the German tribes in combination with the Latin. In the *Real* institutions sketches from French and English history.

Reasonable reduction of the subject matter if the number of lesson periods is reduced.

## O III

*From the Peace of Westphalia to the Congress of Vienna.* Rise of Austria as a great power; its importance in world history as a bulwark against the Turks. Sketches from the history of Absolutism: Tudors and Stuarts; Louis XIV; The Great Elector; Frederick the Great; Frederick II and Maria Theresa; the Silesian wars; Joseph II. The nature of the absolute state: its policy of economy, population, taxation and civilization; the standing army; the professional official; protective tariff and free trade. Mercantilists and physiocrats. England's struggle for world domination from Cromwell to the Congress of Vienna. The decision in India and North America. Rise of the United States.

Causes and course of the French Revolution in its main outline. German and civil rights; constitution and popular representation, the citizens' army. The age of Napoleon. Stein, Hardenberg, Scharnhorst. The struggle for freedom in Prussia and Germany. Congress of Vienna. The Holy Alliance.

The cultural materials in connection with religion and German literature. English and French history with reënforcement through the reading in modern language.

Reasonable reduction of subject matter if the number of lesson periods is reduced.

In the gymnasial institutions: From the Peace of Westphalia to the founding of the Empire. Reduction of the subject matter primarily in the treatment of the military history and the history of England and France. The elimination of subject matter, however, must not lead to a summary treatment of the work at the expense of its treatment upon the principles of activity instruction.

In the existing parallel classes in the *Gymnasium*, the pupils leaving school with promotion to *Obersekunda* can be grouped in one class which is taught according to the course of *Real* institutions.

## U II

*From 1815 to the Present.* National efforts and movements for independence in Europe, with special reference to Germany. The Customs' Union and Frederick List. The German Revolution. Constitutional and parliamentary government reform. The reaction. The emergence of the capitalistic system of economy in Germany about 1850 and its consequences for the social reorganization of the people.

The German wars for unification. Bismarck and the founding of the Empire. The imperial constitution of 1871. Development of agriculture and industry. Manchester school, Marxism, revisionism, and land reform. Agricultural and industrial middle class. Bismarck in the struggle against the clerics and social democracy. Workmen's protective legislation. Labor unions and trusts.

The division of the world's territory. The Triple Alliance and international trade and international trade dependencies. The World War in its high points. The political and economic results of the peace treaties, especially in Germany. Survey of Germany abroad.

The Constitution of Weimar. Federal state and independent state. The Prussian constitution. Rights and duties of the citizen in the republic. Different forms of suffrage. Organization of state administration. Principles of the legal system.

The cultural materials in connection with religion. German and geography.

In the gymnasial institutions, in the first half year—twenty school weeks: From the development of the Empire to the present; work essentially the same as in the other schools in U II.

In the second semester: History of ancient times to the Second Punic War (201). The Greek middle period in the history instruction: the political and social economic side—natural economy, aristocracy, feudal system. In the Greek instruction:

its religion and culture—Homer, lyrics, tragedy. Greek constitutional history: Sparta and the problem of state socialism; Athens and the nature of the democracy. Chief events of the political history of Greece: Age of Pericles. The epoch of Hellenism; also the sphere of civilization of Egypt and Asia Minor in so far as it stands in organic connection with the history of Greece. National state and world citizenship. Services of Greece of world importance in the various fields of human activity: scientific thought, fundamental interrogations of philosophy, the highest creations of art.

From the early period of Roman history: The relation of Rome to the Etruscan kingdom; the aristocracy and the class struggles—from about the fifth century on; spread of Rome's dominion over Italy. The Punic Wars and their importance for the development of the foreign policy, the political and social life of the Romans.

Problems for the purpose of understanding the political side of the subject matter. Confederations. Classes and their political rights. Titular offices, elective office, civil service office. The Greek and the barbarian. Money system and plutocracy. Slavery question. The importance of the family and the tribe, especially among the Romans. Public land. The ancient class state. Ancient and modern democracy. City-state and rural-state. World empire and city organization. The Romans and the provincials.

In organizing the courses of study in the gymnasial institutions, there should be agreement concerning the topics from the political and cultural history of the Greek and Roman ancient world which the classical language instruction will take over partly or entirely from the history instruction—first in a preparatory manner, later intensively. (See also the course of study for Latin and Greek.)

## O II

*History of the Ancient World and the Middle Ages.* The history of the ancient world with constant references to the work of the Greeks, in the intellectual field and in art, to that of the Romans in politics and law, so far as they have had formative effect upon the Middle Ages and modern times. The development of the state, economy; society of the Greeks in its classical forms. More intensively only the Age of Pericles and Hellenism and its importance for the Roman Empire and Christianity. The development of Rome into a world empire, only in its broad outlines. More intensively the period of Augustus and the events of the imperial period important for the formation of the Middle Ages. Christianity and the ancient state. The fall of Rome.

*In the second semester—twenty school weeks: From the Early
German Period to the End of the Hohenstaufens.* The Germanic
peoples' migrations in broad outline; the Ostrogoths, Franks
and Lombards. Political and economic conditions in the early
German period. The impact of the Germans with Rome and
Christianity. Byzantium—Justinian, Islam and its importance
for the civilization of the West. The age of Charlemagne. The
revival of the Roman Empire. Cloistral life. The German Empire: natural administrative feudal system, and kingship; the
Ottoman system; Henry III and the Cluniac movement; Henry
IV and Gregory; the age of the Hohenstaufens; knighthood.
The Crusades and the cultural and economic importance for
western and middle Europe. Scholasticism and mysticism. Culture in the cities. Colonization of the East. The Hansa.

Problems for the purpose of the political interpretation of the
subject matter; family and kindred among the Teutons. The
Teutonic-German spirit of coöperation. Tribal duchies and particularism. The German legal system. Common freedom, seign-
orial rights, constitution of the feudal service court. Cities,
knights, and princes. Hereditary and occupational classes of
society. Trade in kind in Germany; money control in Italy.
Principles of the divine state and theocracy.

The treatment of the medieval civilization in connection primarily with religion and German; in connection with the modern foreign languages. The foundations of the western European states and their relations to Germany.

*Work of the gymnasial schools in the first semester—twenty
school weeks: From the Fall of Carthage to the Fall of Rome—
476.* Golden age of the Republic and the expansion of the
Roman Empire. The century of civil wars. The age of Augustus. The imperial period, despotism and enlightened absolutism with its less characteristic representatives. The foreign
policy of the emperors vacillating between the urge for conquest
and defense of the Empire. Reorganization of the Empire by
Diocletian and Constantine. Christianity and the Roman state.
The decline of ancient civilization.

Problems for political interpretation of the subject matter:
Landed proprietorship and its part in the political collapse.
Ancient communism and socialism. Principality and monarch.
Civil army and professional army. Spread of state control to
other phases of life. Humanitarian provisions. Coinage and
precious metals. Monetary administration and bureaucracy.

In connection with Latin: The political and economic development, and especially the Hellenizing of Rome. In connection
with religion: Eastern influences on Rome and the relation between Hellenism and Christianity.

*In the second semester: From the Early German Period to
the End of the Hohenstaufens.* The work is the same as in other

types of schools. In the activity group with the Latin reading, more thorough consideration of the early German cultural conditions of the Carolingian and the Ottonian renaissance.

## U I

*From the End of the Middle Ages to the End of the Period of the French Revolution.* Importance of the policy of national power of the Hapsburg dynasty and the Luxemburgers, with the sovereignty gradually growing stronger. Popular culture, early capitalism; universities and reception of Roman law. Inventions and discoveries. The economic importance of the new route of trade for middle Europe. Reform movements in the late medieval church. The Renaissance and Humanism in Germany and Italy. The rise of national states in Spain, France, and England.

The period of the Counter-Reformation, Calvinism, and the Thirty Years' War. The struggle of the great powers for the leadership in Europe and on the Mediterranean; its reaction upon Germany. Struggle for the control of the Baltic.

Absolutism in France and England. The rise of Prussia since 1640. The colonial empires and the French-English struggle. The American Revolution. European Enlightenment—in connection with the modern foreign languages. The French Revolution—in connection with the French reading. The reorganization of Germany in the revolt against Napoleon. The Congress of Vienna.

Problems for political interpretation of the subject matter: Mercantilism; state administration; officialdom, the standing army, and serfdom. Absolutism and state citizenship. State controlled by police, and state controlled by law. Natural right and social contract; human and civil rights. Mercenary army control system; national army. Direct and representative democracy. The three divisions of authority in the state. The prefect system and self-government according to Stein's plan. Protective tariff and free trade. The physiocratic doctrine. Adam Smith.

The whole cultural objective of the class in connection with the Latin reading, a more thorough knowledge of the civilization of the Renaissance and of humanism; in connection with French and English, the national independence-seeking democratic movements in England and in France and their cultural results.

## I

*From the Congress of Vienna to the Present.* Period of the Holy Alliance and the Restoration. The struggle for a constitutional national state. Conservatism and liberalism in France,

England, and Germany—in connection with the modern foreign languages. The economic efforts for unity in Germany. The revolution in middle and western Europe, especially in Germany. The Prussian constitution.

Bismarck and the struggle for German unity. The imperial constitution of 1871. The settlement with Austria. Constitutional and parliamentary forms of government.

Capitalism and its sociological antitype, socialism, in England, France and Germany—in connection with the modern foreign languages. Agricultural and industrial middle class. The parties in the Empire. Bismarck and the opposition. The development of the Empire: financial and tariff policy. Army and taxation systems. Uniformity in law.

The Bismarckian policy of alliances. Russia, the Balkan question, and eastern Asia. The development of international trade and the dependence of Germany's domestic economy upon the world markets. The Triple Alliance and the Triple Entente. The international struggle for the world markets; international imperialism; the World War. The economic and political results of the peace treaties; the German in foreign countries and in the surrendered territories. The constitution of Weimar; the Prussian constitution.

Problems for political interpretation of subject matter. Comparison of important foreign constitutions with the German constitution. International law and the League of Nations. The problem of pacifism. The idea of nationality. Forms and importance of colonial policy. The will of the individual and the will of the people. Different forms of the suffrage. Principles of civil and criminal law. Organization of the state administration. The more important political theories; the parties and their relation to the state. The social strata of the German people. Employees and workers' organizations. Buyers' and producers' associations. Money and capital. Natural and legal monopoly. Bankers and the stock exchange system. Land reform and domestic colonization.

The tendencies in the intellectual field of the nineteenth and twentieth centuries, in connection with religion and German. The connections between German domestic economy and politics and their geographic postulations, in conjunction with geography. In the corresponding school types in combination with the modern foreign languages, a thorough understanding of the English, French, and American world policies; of political organization; of social and economic development; of the culture of England, France, and America.

GEOGRAPHY

## VI

Concrete introduction to the home community for the purpose of understanding simple geographical phenomena and for drill upon the topographical description of the home province or a corresponding area with natural boundaries. A very short view beyond the boundaries of the home to the German fatherland, Europe, and the world.

Orientation in the open country by sun and compass. The apparent path of the sun in connection with the length of days and seasons in the home district.

Introduction to map study through the making of a map of the school grounds and the neighborhood, if possible with the aid of an aërial picture. First introduction to reading enlarged sections of the surveyor's map of the home community on which chiefly the tracts of open country are to be seen. Transition from the large scale map to the wall map and to the synoptical table of the home community in the atlas.

Introduction to the fundamental geographical principles by means of observation of simple, comprehensible forms of land, water, weather, colonization, husbandry, and trade, and expansion of these ideas by means of pictures and observations gained on trips.

## V

The German Republic and the German-speaking districts, especially German-Austria, also Switzerland and Holland, in concrete individual sketches. Working out of topographical relations with the atlas and map and drill upon a definite stock of names and comparative figures. The political divisions of middle Europe with special emphasis upon the organization of the German Republic. Sketches from the life of Germans in border countries.

Development of geographical principles; for example, metropolitan city, harbor, moors, agriculturally developed country, industrial region, secondary chain of mountains, primary mountain district. Simple exercises in summarizing related geographical phenomena—perhaps the rivers of the north German plain, the German coasts, vine-culture in Germany, coal regions of Germany.

Continuation of map reading exercises on the surveyor's chart and introduction to the local map of the official map of the German Republic (1:100,000).

Simple astronomical observations—clouds, position of the sun, phases of the moon, polar stem.

First lessons in the study of the globe—parallels and meridians on the globe and map.

## IV

Geographical study of Europe—except Germany, German-Austria, Switzerland and Holland, beginning with the Mediterranean countries, with a view of Asia Minor and North Africa, proceeding over western Europe to northern and eastern Europe, with special emphasis upon the Mediterranean countries and the country whose language is the first modern language to be studied in the school. After careful consideration for all of the cultural studies in the curriculum of the particular school, the study of eastern Europe also may be assigned to U III. In conclusion a survey of the physical and political appearance of Europe.

With respect to the type of school concerned, transmission of the primary ideas, also of the dependence of foreign cultures upon the conditions of life of peoples in the past and in the present. Survey of the German world in Europe outside of Germany.

Development of typical regions for the purpose of enriching the general principles; for example, the artificially watered region in southern Europe, Vesuvius as the volcanic type, Paris and London as world-cities, the fiord region.

## U III

The continents of the East: Asia, Africa, Australia—with Oceania; the Indian Ocean. Germany in these parts of the earth with emphasis upon the cultural activity of the German people in its former colonies. The chief events of the history of discovery, in combination with the history instruction. The geographical distribution of the world religions. Some facts of ethnology.

Extension of the general principles of geography by means of new regional types; for example, deserts, steppes, savannas, tropical forests regions, cultivated areas in the different latitudes.

Mathematical geography: The apparent paths of the sun in other latitudes. The daily and yearly movements of the earth. Time belts and date lines. Eclipses of the sun and moon. The tilted position of the earth's axis and the cause of the seasons.

Use of official maps upon excursions; orientation by means of the watch.

In the *Gymnasium* and in the girls' schools the mathematical geography may be distributed to cover *Untertertia* and *Obertertia*.

## O III

The western continents with the oceans which confine them. Arctic and Antarctic. The economic, political, and cultural relations of Europe to America and other parts of the world, with special emphasis upon Germanism in the world. Continuation of ethnology. Chief routes of world trade.

Continued exercises in map reading upon excursions.

Schools in which one hour of history is dropped out begin in the course of the second semester with the study of Germany.

## U II

Geographical study of middle Europe, with special emphasis upon the causal relationships between natural environment and civilization. The national, religious, and political organization of middle Europe. Germany's part in world trade and commerce.

Study of selected sheets from the official atlases.

Survey of the geology of Germany and introduction to the comprehension of the geological map.

Note for the upper section: The subject matter of the three upper classes forms a natural, integrated unit; it progresses from the study of the natural facts of the earth, by means of a study of their economic, political, and cultural-geographical effects, to a picture of the earth to-day.

## O II

Selected topics of general geography on the earth as a unit and the home of man, with constant emphasis on their importance for man.

Shape and age of the earth; the most common geographical projections.

The forms of the earth's surface and their explanation by means of the structure of the earth's crust and the effect of natural forces. The covering of water and air. The climate zones of the earth. The regional zones on the earth's surface and their cultural-geographical importance as shown by a summarizing survey of all natural conditions, as well as of the plant and animal world. Here it is recommended to place the Mediterranean region at the beginning of this study, and to spend more time on this in the gymnasial schools.

Evolution and spread of the human race. The human races and their distribution. The stages of human civilization found on the earth to-day and their dependence upon the character of the natives of the region. Forms of colonization.

## U I

The economic conditions of the earth; regions of food and raw products, export markets; world routes of trade and maritime commerce.

Some facts from general geographical political economy. A selection from states or federations; for example, the British world empire, France and its colonies, United States of America, Latin-America, Japan, China. Other smaller states can also be studied from the viewpoint of their typical character. Naturally, however, the countries whose civilization is especially important for the type of school in question must receive thorough cultural-geographical treatment.

## O I

Cultural geography of Germany. The German soil as the basis of the appearance of the landscape and its transformation by means of the industry of the German people. The German colonies. The various forms of German economic life.

The ethnographic and political relations of middle Europe. The relation of German economic life with the neighboring states and the rest of the world. Such cultural-geographical influences of Germany upon other people as can be comprehended. Germany in the world.

Thorough study of the home district.

A final, synoptical study, made by a short survey of the whole, shows the present geographical picture of the world.

## 2. Aesthetic Subjects

### Music

## VI

Conception, representation, discovery, and writing of simple rhythmic movements in binary and non-binary measure; in addition thereto, introduction to punctuated rhythm, employment of note and rest values as far as the sixteenth, of syncopation, and the triplet, of the bar as indication of emphasis of time signatures, and of the most common signs of expression.

Comprehension, discovery, and writing of rhythmic melody movements.

Development of the major scale by harmonic derivation from third-fifth related chords and by melodic composition from second-fifth related tetrachords. When vocal music offers motive for it, formation of cadence with the dominant seventh chord. In addition C-major, also F-major or G-major. Occasional exercises in transposition. Introduction to a knowledge of modulation.

One-part and, if possible, also two-part singing in connection with the exercises serving to develop the musical talents; also awakening of a knowledge of the form-building elements of melody, motif, imitation, inversion, phrasing, and the like. Occasional singing of canons.

In direct connection with the singing, an introduction to the appreciation of instrumental music by listening to music, and exercises in understanding short instrumental types, such as marches, dances, and slow, lyrical instrumental compositions.

## V

Homophonic and polyphonic two-part singing. In connection with this, elements of consonance and dissonance; rhythmic exercises; exercises in comprehension and writing of chords and short connected chords in series, gradual extension of range of keys in the major to A and E flat major; singing of the scales but not from the key-notes only; derivation of minor scales from the corresponding major scales; conception of their principles of formation from their key-note; and distinction of the major and minor chords.

Continuation of original exercises. Instrumental music as in the other class.

## IV

Review of the most important facts from the principles of music of the lower section; continuation of the original exercises and musical dictation. Singing in one or several parts, if possible with accompanying instruments. In boys' schools introduction also to the bass key system.

Increased use of instrumental music by means of music demonstration and discussion of pieces in more complicated form of song—the minuet, the adagio, and short roundelays; introduction to simple polyphonic instrumental selections—imitation, canon, fugue.

## U III

One and several part singing with or without instruments; in boys' schools interchangeable use of tenor and bass key; in addition, in connection with the German instruction, occasionally a song related to a Teutonic legendary cycle, for example, Faroese *Sigurdlied*, Icelandic *Götterdämmerung*, later *Hildebrandslied*, *Roland* and *Gotelinde*, or the study of a ballad composition of Loewe. Also continuation of the original exercises and of the musical dictation in variation of two or more part cadences, and in more complicated form.

In the instrumental music a study of classical examples of forms of variations—Ciaconne or Passacaglia, Doubles, variations of Haydn, Mozart, Beethoven, and some of Bach's compositions.

## O III

Objective treatment of the development of our notation system. In singing, examples of historical songs,—in boys' schools also of soldiers' songs,—also examples of the chorals in original form and a study of their sources; examples of the simple, accompanied artistic song of the seventeenth and eighteenth centuries. Occasional exercises in original melodies and in musical dictation.

In the instrumental music, examples of piano-suites, the prelude and the fugue as well as of the transition style in piano music—Bach.

In abbreviated school types: also examples of the minstrel's song—Neidhart von Reuenthal; the important facts concerning the position of music in the Catholic religious service—*Ordinarium missae* and *Requiem*—and in the Protestant service; in addition, study of one of Bach's church cantatas. An oratorio by Händel.

## U II

Besides the folk songs, examples of the artistic songs of the nineteenth century. Occasional exercises in making original melodies and in musical dictation.

In instrumental music, examples of the classical sonata—Haydn, Mozart, Beethoven, and in connection with examples of songs something of the history of piano music of the nineteenth century. Study of one of Beethoven's symphonies and of one opera of the Romantic period, possibly the *Freischütz*; also discussion of the composition of the orchestra and the arrangement of the orchestral score.

In all schools except the *Gymnasium*, in connection with biology, the most important facts concerning the hygiene and functions of the human vocal organs.

In abbreviated types of schools, also the explanation of pure and modified pitch. Study of Bach's *Passion of Matthew*.

## O II

Besides the other folk songs, cultivation of the pre-Reformation religious folk-song and the minstrel song. Occasional exercises in making original melodies and in music dictation.

In connection with the instruction in ancient history, survey of the development of the European musical system from the Greeks to the evenly modulated pitch. The idea of the musical drama in the Renaissance opera, primarily in Gluck—study of one of Gluck's operas. Reference to Richard Wagner's idea of reform.

In connection with religion, the position of music in the Catholic religious service, especially the *Ordinarium missae* and *Requiem*—these in the Latin schools in connection with Latin. Study of concert mass of Mozart and Beethoven.

In the instrumental music, examples of the older organ, piano, and chamber music down to Händel and Bach.

In the *Gymnasium,* also in connection with biology, the most important facts concerning the functions and hygiene of the human vocal organs.

## U I

Occasional exercise in writing original music and in musical dictation. Singing: Locheimer Song Book, Folk-song of 1530. Easier duets of the later Dutch and great German masters of the sixteenth and seventeenth centuries. Examples of the artistic songs of the eighteenth century, especially of the compositions of Klopstock, poems of Gellert and Goethe,—Gluck, Mozart, Beethoven, Reichardt and Zelter, and of the music from Mozart's works which can be sung.

In connection with the instruction in religion, the music in the Protestant religious service, especially in the time of Bach. Study of a religious cantata and Bach's *Passion of Matthew.*

In connection with German, the struggles for a German opera in the seventeenth century. In addition, study of something like the *Entführung* by Mozart.

In connection with the history instruction, examples of Italian music in the sixteenth and seventeenth centuries, examples of English vocal and instrumental music in the time of Elizabeth. Short characterizations, illustrated with examples of the music at the courts of Louis XIV and Frederick the Great.

In instrumental music besides the subject matter already named, works of Händel and Bach.

## O I

In addition to the folk music, examples of the artistic songs of the nineteenth century with special consideration of the compositions of important poets known and easily accessible to the pupils, especially compositions of Schubert, Schumann, Hugo Wolf (based on poems of Goethe), Eichendorf, Heine, and Mörike.

Occasional continuation of the original music exercises and exercises in musical dictation.

Study of the Wagnerian musical drama, if possible in connection with the German instruction; also the study of the German *Requiem* by Brahms.

In the instrumental music selected works of the Vienna classicists, of the Romanticists, and of the younger generations: sonata, symphonies, and symphonic composition. Illustrations from the musical literature of the nineteenth century: E. T. A. Hoffmann, Schumann, Wagner, Nietzsche. The struggle for a new musical style at the beginning of this century.

The course of study given here, in the number of hours now available, can give the music teacher hints only as to the direction which he will have to take in the construction of a working plan adapted to the conditions of his institution. Especially in schools with only four music hours in *Quarta* to *Prima*, considerable restriction of the subject matter cannot be avoided. In the other schools also the music teacher, each according to the local conditions, will have to limit or eliminate some parts of the entire subject matter in favor of other parts. For the purpose of introducing as much of the detailed course of study as possible, the hours available for music are to be assigned primarily for class instruction, in which all pupils must take part; combinations of the various years' work are to be avoided so far as it is possible. Under present conditions only one hour a week at the most can be employed for choral singing, and never more than two. In boys' schools, which, departing from the distribution of hours recommended below, have one hour's practice a week for soprano and alto, and a second for tenor and bass, the whole chorus is to be combined occasionally in one of these hours for common practice. Practice for the instrumental group, where there is not a special practice period available for it, must occur within the limits of the class hours. Every pupil with the proper ability to participate in the chorus or in the instrumental group may be required by the music teacher to do so.

DISTRIBUTION OF HOURS WHICH CAN BE RECOMMENDED TO THE VARIOUS SCHOOLS FOR CLASSES IV TO I

A. BOYS' SCHOOLS

1. Single complete schools:
    Each 1 hour: IV to U III, O III to U II, O II to I
        chorus.

2. Double complete schools:
   *a.* Each 1 hour: IV, U III, O III, U II, O II, U I, O I, chorus.
   *b.* Each 1 hour: IV, U III, O III, U II, O II, I, chorus, instrumental groups.
3. Single partial schools:
   *a.* Each 1 hour: IV, U III, U II, chorus.
   *b.* Each 1 hour: IV to U III, O III, U II, chorus.
4. Double partial schools:
   *a.* Each 2 hours: IV, O III, U II; each 1 hour: U III, chorus.
   *b.* Each 2 hours: IV, U II; each 1 hour: U III, O III, chorus and instrumental group.

### B. GIRLS' SCHOOLS

1. Single complete schools:
   1 hour chorus: O II to I, with pupils coöperating optionally from IV to U II; each 1 hour: IV, U III, O III, U II, O II to I; in gymnasial *Studienanstalten* U II takes part in the combined class instruction and choral singing of O II to I.
2. Double complete schools:
   *a.* 1 hour chorus: O II to I with elective pupils from IV to U II; each 2 hours: IV, U III, O III, U II, O II; 1 hour, I; in gymnasial *Studienanstalten* U II and O II together 2 hours.
   *b.* 1 hour chorus (O III with U II, with elective pupils from the other classes; each 1 hour for the gifted pupils of O III and U II; 1 hour for the less gifted of O III and U II; each 2 hours: IV, U III, O II, I.
3. Single partial schools:
   Each 1 hour: IV, U III, O III, U II. Every class forms a class chorus from its best singers; the class choruses are combined to form a school chorus upon special occasions. In U IIb also 1 hour for intensifying and increasing class work.
4. Double partial schools:
   1 hour chorus: U II with elective pupils from IV to O III; 2 hours each: IV, U III, O III; 1 hour, U II. In U IIb also 1 hour as in single partial schools.

### C. AUFBAUSCHULEN

   *a.* 2 hours in U III, 1 hour each in O III, U II, O II, I, chorus, instrumental groups.
   *b.* Each 2 hours in III, II, I; each 1 hour chorus, instrumental group.
   *c.* 2 hours in U III; 1 hour each: O III, U II, O II, U I, O I, chorus.

## DRAWING AND ART EDUCATION

The following course of study is to indicate only possibilities for the organization of the drawing and art instruction within the limits set for it by the Notes on Method.

### VI TO IV

*Free-hand Drawing.* Free composition of impressions and experiences from the environment and in the age-world of the child through drawing, painting, cutting, pasting, modeling, weaving, and the like. Exercises in simple decorative writing —ancient, and in black and white and color representations of plane surfaces. In time, according to the intellectual growth of the pupil and the motives which arise from free composition, transition to conscious observation and to reproduction of objects in nature from memory.

*Mechanical Drawing.* Projective representation of simple articles of use, from paper, cardboard, cloth, and the like. Transition to the use of rule, tape, and compass.

*Art Appreciation.* For enlivenment and intensification of the pupil's work, use of pictures, drawings, prehistoric and primitive illustrative and ornamental art, of simple local architectural types and industrial products.

### U III TO U II

*Free-hand Drawing.* Free composition of impressions and experiences from the pupil's widened experience, without the constraint of imaginative creation, however, when no longer any inclination therefor is at hand. Greater emphasis upon observation and upon the direct as well as the memoriter reproduction of objects in nature. Exercises in black and white and color representation of solids and surfaces. Continuation of the exercises in decorative writing—cursive, Gothic, and block letter —and space distribution and arrangement. Simple problems for definite purposes, also with application of simple printing; for example, invitations, programs, resolutions, notebook and book covers, book marks, and the like.

*Mechanical Drawing.* Projective representation of simple utensils, tools, apparatus, containers, parts of buildings—columns, pillars, moldings, roofs, windows, gates—with special reference to local architectural forms and industrial products. Sketching of simple objects and development of the working-drawing in connection with the manual training instruction and, especially in U IIb of the *Lyzeum,* with sewing.

*Art Appreciation.* In connection with the exercises in space representation: study of buildings as examples of space treatment conditioned by purpose and material—dwellings, castles, cloisters, school buildings, railway stations, factories, and the like; also in connection with the exercises in composition: study of works of art and handicraft which show how periods with a set feeling of style have influenced living rooms, house furnishings, clothing, writing and printing, handicraft and trade marks.

## O II TO O I

*Freehand Drawing.* Free composition and solution of problems in drawing which the pupils must set for themselves to an ever-increasing degree. In connection therewith, studies in nature—animals, man, architecture, street scenes, and landscape, and memoriter reproduction of pictures, statues, and buildings from different points of view—structure, treatment of line, distribution of mass, choice and distribution of color, dimensions, rhythm, dynamics, and the like. Decorative exercises for definite purposes, especially for the school and the pupils' own organization.

*Mechanical Drawing.* More difficult problems in projectional representation of utensils, tools, apparatus, containers, parts of buildings and whole structures with preference given to architectural memorials and products of handicrafts of the home community and of the peoples to whose civilization the school leads. In the representation of buildings, application of pictorial perspective and shadow construction.

*Art Appreciation.* Introduction to problems of graphic, plastic and architectural composition and their solution in different times and countries—including the present. Acquaintance with the most important graphic and reproductive technique. Survey of the development of the forms of expression of German art and the art of the nation to whose culture the school leads, with especial consideration of outstanding artists.

## SEWING

## VI

Making of articles of simple form from thread—crocheting or close woven material—sewing. Darning stockings.

(*a*) Crocheting: For example, shawl, cap, bodice, overjacket, little bag.

(*b*) Sewing: For example, serviette bag, apron, straight bodice, petticoat.

Principles of materials and equipment: cotton, wool, spinning and twisting, weaving, crocheting needle.

## V

Making of articles of somewhat more difficult form from thread—knitting—or from materials with threads that can be counted.

(*a*) Knitting, in which the preliminary exercises learned in the *Grundschule* can be used: socks or half-hose, footing of stockings, mittens, baby's jacket, bag, coffee-warmer.

(*b*) Sewing in materials which offer the basis for cross-stitch, hemstitching or other decorative stitches: For example, smock, under-bodice, apron, collar, pillow, work-bag.

Materials and implements: Securing and unpacking of yarns, open yarns. Simple fastenings on the weaving board. Sewing and knitting needles.

## IV

Making of articles from finer materials: Patching and darning of laundry and articles of clothing. Repair of knitted articles with mesh-darning. Crocheting of collars, covers, and the like; also crocheting on smaller articles, such as handkerchief, collar, or bag.

Principles of materials: Linen, flax; carded, stamped, and interwoven materials. Silk, artificial silk, finer yarns. Weaving experiments with the different fastenings on the weaving looms of the folk art.

## U III

Making of washable articles upon the sewing machine; for example, pillow covers, corset bodice, petticoat and the like, ornamented by means of techniques already known or with the addition of embroidery.

Principles of materials and implements: Instruction concerning the sewing machine, its care and repair. Discussion of the materials most useful for the preparation of the articles of clothing. Criteria and prices of good materials.

## O III

Continuation of sewing of washable clothes; for example, shirt, nightshirt, union suits, wash blouse, also with use of embroidery upon linen with white yarn, with the preparatory preliminary exercises. Darning of the laundry upon the machine.

Principles of materials: Nettle, hemp, jute. Compositions of all sorts of raw materials, preparation of small collection of materials. Embroidery cottons.

## U IIb

Making of clothing and washable articles, in fine materials and of delicate construction—handsewing. Trimming articles according to choice.

Principles of materials and implements: Clothing, materials, experiments in dyeing. Instruction concerning special parts of the machine, exercises in the hand-weaving loom.

## U II. Elective

Making of articles of clothing; for example, blouse, dress, or slip-over, bloomers. Articles finished as desired.
Instruction as in U IIb.

## PHYSICAL TRAINING

### GYMNASTICS, GAMES AND SPORTS

## VI TO IV

### 10 to 12 Years of Age

1. *Body Exercises.*

1. Exercises in walking of all kinds, with singing and to music. Marching, walking on the toes, hopping and jumping, walking with knees high, goose-step, straddle walk, walking on balance-poles.

2. Running exercises: Training in running for systematic practice of racing: 50 to 75 meter dash, distance running up to 2,000 meters, relay races.

3. Exercises for posture: Life types of freest sort and school types.

    *a.* Imitation of animal's movements: Running like dogs, cats, horses; walking like a bear; hopping like a frog; flying like birds, and so on.

    *b.* Movements imitating work: Chopping wood, sewing, mowing, bell-ringing, swinging the arms, rolling the wheel barrow, crawling exercises with riders, rowing, tag, pirouette, and the like.

    *c.* Simple systematic exercises in relaxation; expansion, stretching, especially for the purpose of making the trunk pliant and strong and for the adjustment of faults in posture, standing, sitting, kneeling and lying. Body-bending and stretching, squatting, body rotating, body rotating with arm and leg exercises. Simple exercises in balancing; standing on one leg and with use of balancing pole. Posture exercises on horizontal bar and parallel bars.

II. *Efficiency Activities.*

1. Jumping and throwing: Broad jump, 1.40 meters to 4.2 meters; and running high jump, 6 meters to 1.25 meters. Free jumps and mixed jumps over fixed obstacles. Baseball

throwing, 12 to 40 meters, and throwing at a mark, exercises in catching and batting the ball. Running: See section on ''body exercises.''

2. Exercises on apparatus for strength, courage and skill. Climbing, also pole climbing races, climbing on ladders.

The horizontal bar: Swing with the knee up over the horizontal bar, circling the horizontal bar, grinder backwards, circling the horizontal bar backwards.

The parallel bars: Different sitting postures, change of seat, vaulting, rear vault.

Horse: Straddle vaults.

3. Floor exercises: Falling and getting up, sitting and rising with partner, somersault forwards and backwards, short hand stands at the wall, pushing and pulling games, tug of war, cat and mouse, obstacle race, obstacle crawl.

### III. *Games.*

The simple running and ball games of the *Grundschule:* Old Bear, people's ball, hunters' ball, wander ball, and others; baseball with simplified rules.

## U III TO U II

### 13 to 15 Years of Age

### I. *Body Exercises.*

1. Walking exercises as in the lower section.

2. Running, and running exercises with increased standards. Dash to 100 meters in 13 to 17 seconds. Starting exercises: form the crouching position: Distance running up to 3,000 meters in 12 to 15 minutes. Relay races, cross-country races.

3. Posture exercises as in the lower section. Light bending, also sideways and backwards in the upper part of torso, trunk rotation. Leaning-rest exercises, instep exercises, balancing exercises, also some use of balancing poles, ladders, horizontal and parallel bars. Exercises on stall bars.

### II. *Efficiency Activities.*

1. Jumping and throwing. Running broad jump, 2.20 to 4.50 meters; running high jump, .75 to 1.35 meters.

Baseball throwing, 20 to 60 meters, and throwing at a mark. Hammer (1 to 1½ kilogram) throwing, 14 to 36 meters. Shot-put (2½ kilograms) 4 to 7.5 meters; 5 kilogram shot, 3.5 to 7.5 meters.

Running: See running exercises above.

2. Exercises for strength, courage, skill, on apparatus. Climbing and swinging on poles and ropes.

Horizontal bar: Swing on knee up to bar and circling the horizontal bar from swinging in bent arm and hanging position, hanging by knees and pulling up to sitting position with weight on the arms, pull knees up to bar and turn around, side vault, back vault, kneeling on the bar, straddle.

Parallel bars: Straddle, scissors, vault, back vault, flank vault, screw, rolling from straddle position to straddle position. Shoulder stand from sitting position. Arm bending and stretching in cross lying position. See-saw.

Horse: Various jumps.

3. Floor exercises. Somersault with partner, hand stand with support, comic exercises, preliminary exercises for wrestling.

### III. *Games.*

Games of the lower section: Prisoner's base, baseball, handball, football.

## O II TO O I

### 16 Years Upwards

### I. *Body Exercises.*

1. Racing and running exercises with increased standards. 100 meter dash, in 12 to 15 seconds; distance race up to 3,000 meters, in 12 to 15 mintues; relay, cross-country and hurdle races.

2. Posture exercises. Body exercises with and without helper as before with thorough working out of the whole body. Leaning-rest exercises with arm and leg movements, balancing, resistance exercises with or without partner.

### II. *Efficiency Activities.*

1. Jumping and throwing. Running broad jump, 2.5 to 5 meters; running high jump, .90 to 1.50 meters; pole-vault for height and distance.

Baseball throwing, 30 to 70 meters and throwing at a mark. Hammer throw (1 to 1½ kilogram) 18 to 40 meters. Shot-put (5 kilograms) 4 to 8 meters, (7.5 kilogram) 3.5 to 8 meters. Javelin throw (800 kilograms) 15 to 20 meters. Discus throwing.

Running: See running exercises above.

2. Exercises for strength, courage, and skill on apparatus. Climbing and hanging on poles and ropes.

Horizontal bar: Turning over the horizontal bar, pulling up with even and uneven arms, under swing, circling the bar from swinging position, up-start, swinging rest.

Parallel bars: Hand swing with balancing, forearm swing forwards and backwards, shoulder or upper arm stand from

swinging position. Swing and balance, swing, rest. Tumbling
forwards and backwards. Side vault, flank vault, back vault,
squatting vault for the side rest.

Horse: Jumps and swings from rest.

Rings: Exercises without swing and with swing.

3. Floor exercises. Wrestling, comic stunts, folk dances.

III. *Games.*

Prisoner's base, baseball, handball, football, volley ball.

### Tramping

Regularly in all classes on the monthly tramping days,—at
first half days; from 12 years on, whole day excursions. In the
upper section, as the opportunity offers, once a year an excursion (hike) of several days' duration. Observation-exercises for
quickening the powers of perception, map reading, open country
games, cultivation of tramping and folk songs. The distances
walked must not be overdone. On whole day trips, 12 to 18
kilometers are sufficient for the lower section, 16 to 24 for the
middle section, and 20 to 30 for the upper section.

### Swimming [1]

In one physical training period a week and on play afternoons
generally, where opportunity is offered. To fulfill the requirement that no healthy child is to leave school without having
learned to swim, preparatory "dry-swimming" exercises from
*Sexta* on, and swimming training in *Quarta* and U III. In the
upper section also the different types of swimming, simple dives
and introduction to life-saving and first aid.

### Rowing [2]

With the participation of as many pupils as possible in student rowing clubs and squads, where there is opportunity for it.
Rowing trips with camping, cooking, and the like. Competitive
rowing only in the upper sections after scientific training and
with the coöperation and supervision of a physician and a teacher
trained in sports.

Skating, snow-shoeing, and tobogganing on play afternoons.

Orthopedic school gymnastics, where arrangements have been
made for them, with compulsory attendance of the pupils designated by the school physician.[3]

[1] *Min-Erlass vom 3 Mai, 1924.*
[2] *Min-Erlass vom 8 Juli, 1924.*
[3] *Min-Erlass vom 29 September, 1924.*

# CURRICULUM CONTENT FOR THE INDIVIDUAL SCHOOL TYPES

## Boys' Schools

### A. GYMNASIUM

#### The Educational Objective of the *Gymnasium*

Within the limits of the whole problem of the secondary school, a certain portion falls to the *Gymnasium*. It is to prepare the youth of to-day for a life of vigorous individuality, through the special employment of the cultural values inherent in the classics and through their inner connection with those values of our own civilization, thus providing a humanistic training. The unity of complete humanistic training shall proceed out of the organic connection between the core subjects and the subjects peculiar to each school, and the interplay with the other branches of instruction, which give the supplementation necessary for training and education.

Herein special problems arise for the Greek and Latin instruction as the subjects peculiar to the *Gymnasium*. While the study of the classical languages themselves is able to clarify and fortify the mind and widen its horizon to an unsuspected extent and at the same time deepen the appreciation of the history and nature of the mother tongue, the ever-constant problem of conceiving thoughts expressed in another language far removed from one's own, and reproducing them in one's native speech will be a strict discipline for the mind; at the same time one becomes thus accustomed to a method of work which can be applied to other materials in a like manner. The effort to re-experience with understanding and feeling the original form of the great classical creations in literature must train and enrich the spirit in a special way. The contact with the creative thoughts of the Greeks, the immersion in the great works of

Hellenic and Roman art and science, the participation in the labor and fate of outstanding personalities of antiquity should awaken in the adolescent youth forces through which he can develop into an independent personality, but one which pays honor reverentially to the great. A knowledge gained from direct observation of the community life of antiquity and of the classical political conception in their perfection or weakness, must increase the understanding of life's problems in one's own community. The feeling for form and style can be developed greatly by reliving certain epochs of Greek and Roman culture noted for their unity in style—as the age of Pericles and of Augustus—and by study of individual works of the pictorial arts which are rigorous in form. Greek physical training, whose ideal was the harmonic development of body and mind, must also be the ideal for the students of the *Gymnasium*. The indication, however, of the connection between ancient days and the present, the proof of the terrible struggle of the Roman mind with the Greek, of the German mind with that of the classical period upon the most widely divergent fields can awaken an inkling of the effects of the forces which have created European culture, and will thereby deepen the comprehension of the intellectual history of the German people.

## LATIN

### VI

Prepared for and supported by the German grammar instruction: Simple etymology, that is, the *a-, d-, u-, e-,* consonantal and *i-*declensions; the most necessary pronouns; the so-called regular comparison; the *a-, e-, i-,* and the consonantal conjugations (the latter as early as possible on account of the great number of its verbs, without, however, the so-called deponents) in their most important examples and without the forms which are lacking in German. Thorough assimilation of a primary vocabulary as a preparation for later reading; a reading and exercise book, which, proceeding from the experience of the child, must offer as soon as possible original Latin sentences and very early must bring out the connection between the present day and Roman civilization. Elementary translation of Latin sentences and selections into German; thoughtful reading; oral translation of German sentences and passages according to previous construction. Conjugation exercises, primarily in short sentences, also with conjunctions; from the beginning correct distinction between the imperfect and perfect tense; exercises in the recognition of form—development and practice of some elementary syntactical rules, also of such as deal with word position, in constant comparison with the modes of expression in the mother tongue. Short oral speech exercises, also occasionally in connection with a pictorial presentation. Transposition and development of given Latin sentences; short Latin tales reproduced. Drill upon quotations, also some in verse form. All with as great use as possible of the blackboards. Frequent dictations and translations into the foreign language in the practice book. The class-written exercises consist in this section of rather long practice exercises, whose number is fixed by the teachers' activity group of the faculty. At times, the review of a translated passage as a home assignment.

## V

At the time of the review of the subject matter of *Sexta:* The so-called irregular comparison of the adjectives; of the numerals —the cardinal and ordinal numbers—the others occasionally in vocabulary; the principles of the adverb. The most important special cases in declension. Compounds of *esse.* The *u-*, and *i-*, conjugation—considered as belonging to the third conjugation— this as early as possible. More detailed principles of the gender of words, also drill upon certain combinations of nouns and adjectives, for example, *sermo Latinus,* but limited to the most necessary items. More detailed principles of the verb and drill upon the most necessary root forms of such verbs as appear frequently in later reading—in the sequence: present infinitive, perfect active, and supine stem, also the so-called irregulars and deponents. In connection with the German grammar instruction, extension of their stock of syntactical rules in connection with the reading, also, among other things, the linguistic-historical explanation of the use of cities' names and the explanation of the accusative with the infinitive and of the participial construction as phrases or clauses and also elementary exercises in their use. The reading book supplements also, by means of its stories, the history instruction of the class. Speech exercises, transpositions, translation exercises, drill upon quotations as in VI. Review and extension of the vocabulary learned in *Sexta,* also by means of systematic classification and grouping.

Written exercises as in *Sexta.*

## IV

*Grammar.* Rounding out and conclusion of etymology, also extension of the principles of pronouns—also the pronominal adjectives, indefinite pronouns, correlative pronouns, and pro-

nomial adverbs which are most important for reading, and more
detailed principles dealing with the infinitive, participle, gerund,
and gerundive. Review and extension of the previously acquired
vocabulary in systematic classification and review of verb roots
which have been learned. In connection with the reading, the
most important facts about tense and mode as well as the theory
of case—most of this by means of vocabulary. Oral translation also of longer selections with the use of the blackboards.
Additional speech exercises and transposition, especially of short,
simple, direct discourse address into indirect Latin, reproduction of the content of selections read. Occasional thorough construction of the more difficult Latin passages for the correct
comprehension of the dependent relationships of the subordinate clauses. Memoriter material as in *Quinta*.

*Written Exercises.* As in *Quinta,* in practice exercises, also
first efforts in written Latin reproduction of stories.

*Reading.* From the reading book especially such tales and
descriptions of life as can be made serviceable at the same time
for the work in ancient history, keeping as close as possible to the
original form.

## U III

*Grammar.* In connection with school grammar, systematic
treatment of the principles of syntax and word formation, beginning with the foreign word as well as with the mother tongue;
with limitation to that which is most essential; review of the
previously acquired vocabulary and verb root forms.

Oral translations and other language exercises as in *Quarta.*
Written exercises as in *Quarta;* as home work, occasionally the
completion of the translation of a passage which has only been
prepared for in school—see Notes on Method.

*Reading.* Selection from Cæsar's *Bellum Gallicum,* from the
historical point of view as far as possible, reading portions and
stories suitable to the stage of development and to the language
ability acquired, for example, I 1-29; II, 1-15, 16-33; III, 7-16;
IV, 20-36; also the building of the bridge over the Rhine, after a
preliminary translation by the teacher or with the aid of a German translation. Presentation of the organization, tendency, and
historical importance to the world of the work as well as
reading of the struggles with the Germans and description
of their customs are best reserved for *Obersekunda.* Review,
extension, and classification of the material in proverbs and
poetical quotations previously learned; also some especially valuable metrical inscriptions.

## O III

*Grammar.* Review and conclusion with extension of syntax;
also comparison with that of German and Greek and of that

modern language known to the pupil. Review of vocabulary previously acquired and of the root verb forms. Oral translation exercises, other language exercises and written work as in U III; in class, occasionally a written translation from the Latin with considerable assistance from the teacher.

*Reading.* Wider selection from Cæsar's *Bellum Gallicum* from the same points of view as in U III; for example, V, 24-58; many selections from VII; for comparison, Cæsar in Meyer's *Ballads,* or selections from the *Historiæ Alexandri* of Curtius Rufus as a contrast to Xenophon's *Anabasis.* Phædrus selected with glimpses into other literature of the fable; some fable or other in Latin to be learned by heart. Everything in oral activity instruction. From this section on retranslation can be replaced to an increasing degree by thoughtful reading.

## U II

*Grammar.* Review as needed from all phases of school grammar. Written and oral exercises in the translation of a German text, perhaps also of an easy, narrative, original text into the Latin, and additional exercises in reproducing in Latin of passages read. Exercises in writing a Latin letter.

*Reading.* In connection with the ancient history introduced in the second semester, a selection is to be made from the first books of Livy and from his study of the Second Punic War, which will consider rather the great personalities and events than the individual incidents of the war. For variety: Ovid's *Fasti* and other elegiac poems; also one book of the *Metamorphoses.* In the course of the year first efforts in preparatory reading at home with the guidance of the teacher and after introduction to the use of the lexicon.

*Written Class Work.* About every four weeks a written composition, mostly a translation into Latin or a reproduction; occasionally a translation from Latin, especially from the latter portions of Livy, with adequate assistance from the teacher.

## O II

*Grammar.* Apart from the necessary reviews, it limits itself in the upper classes to occasional summarizing grammatical and lexicographical discussion and written analysis—from sentences and word forms, in connection with the reading. These discussions and analyses are to serve for better comprehension, and in addition will be limited to a study of style acquired through the reading itself (see Notes on Method).

*Reading.* Ancient history, German history, later, and, if possible, in close connection with these subjects:

1. A valuable source work from the revolutionary period— Sallust's *Bellum Jugurthinum* or *Bellum Catilinæ,* besides one

of Cicero's orations against Catiline or another rather easy political speech of Cicero or a selection from Cicero's letters; especially valuable also are the fragments of speeches of the Gracchi and of Cornelia's letters.

2. Tacitus' *Germania*, 1-27, besides selections from the second part; also with use of the different German translations—best is an edition which also contains other information concerning the Teutons; also continuation and conclusion of the reading of Cæsar—see U III—along with outside reading.

3. One or more Latin works of the Carolingian or Ottonian Renaissance; *i.e.*, *Einhard* and *Notker* or Ekkehard's *Waltharius*, and valuable selections from Latin hymnology and minstrelsy—some of these poems selected for memorization.

*Written Class Work.* About every four weeks a translation from the Latin, if possible in close connection with the reading, under systematic guidance—also assignment of home work. Material: Latin in its natural form to be translated into suitable German form. Also regularly written explanations of some Latin sentence constructions and individual forms are to be required; occasionally also a textual explanation.

# I

The problem of *Prima* is to learn to know the men and works in which Roman character appears in its typical form, especially in its political aspects, and at the same time to comprehend the transformation of the Hellenic cultural values into a new culture. Also, in connection with the other subjects, to attempt to show the historical importance of Rome to the world and its integration into the intellectual history of Europe by means of individual examples; such as Cicero and his effect upon French and English oratory. Of special importance as an illustration is the way the idea of the humanities found ideal incorporation in the group around Terence, Cicero, and Augustus; connection also with the German. In detail, particular attention is to be paid to the influence of Horace upon Lessing, whose *Vademecum* is recommended for reading, of Virgil upon Schiller, of Lucretius, Horace, and Propertius upon Goethe, and of Tibullus upon Mörike.

*Method.* Reading, grouped around a point of emphasis, from which as a center a more inclusive sequence can be surveyed, using outside reading and reports of individual pupils (see Notes on Method) and translations. There still remains undiminished the problem of penetrating deeply into the foreign language itself, of seeing the individual thoughts sharply, and of recognizing the characteristic literary form of the work as the author's tools of artistry. For grammar, see O II. Extension of the reading through a study of works of the pictorial arts, especially architecture and portraiture.

The following may serve as points of emphasis in the reading, from which as a starting point the instruction is to be built up in each class according to the individuality and desire of the teacher and of the class.

1. The Roman comedy—Plautus' *Mostellaria* to be recommended primarily; under certain conditions also a selection from Terence, either *Andria* or *Adelphæ*.

2. Catullus and Lucretius in suitable selections.

3. Cicero as an orator—either *Pro Roscio Amerino*, or an oration against Verres or a Phillipic; selections from *De Oratore;* also selections from Quintilian.

4. The Ciceronian group—Cicero's *Letters*, chosen from personal points of view.

5. The Age of Augustus: Livy's *Proœmium; Monumentum Ancyranum;* Suetonius' *Augustus;* Virgil, selections from the *Æneid,* with reference to Ekkehard—and the *Georgics;* selections from Horace from the point of view of reading these lyric and epic poems in which the Romanism of his time comes to its purest expression; Tibullus, selections; and a little from Propertius.

6. Roman (Greek) philosophy: Lucretius; Cicero, some selections from *De Deorum Natura* and *De Republica;* selections from Seneca's moral works.

7. Tacitus and the Younger Pliny: *Annales*—introduction; selections from the history of Tiberius, with supplementary work from Velleius Paterculus; Suetonius' *Tiberius,* Dio Cassius; selected passages from history of Nero; *Historiæ,* The Year 69; the Batavia Rebellion; Book V as a contrast to the *Germania; Agricola;* selected letters of Pliny.

It is assumed that every pupil will learn some songs of Catullus, some of the most valuable of the odes of Horace, and a portion of a connected story by Tacitus.

Written work as in *Obersekunda.* In case of special interest of the pupils, a rather long home assignment in German, on a theme in connection with the Latin instruction, as a substitute for one or more compositions.

Free "activity groups" (at the election of the teacher and pupils): Exercises in translation into Latin of a difficult original German selection or supplementation of the class work with consideration of works not read in class, or the extension of this reading by means of the following possible themes: Valuable metrical and prose inscriptions; Roman satirists—selections from Petronius and Martial; a tragedy of Seneca in comparison with the Greek and later drama; Roman law, selections from Roman juristic literature; Christian Roman authors, Minucius Felix, selections from Augustine; Rome and Germany, more detailed treatment of the influence of the Roman language and culture upon the German, also illustrations of the language of the Catholic Church; reading of the *Mosella* of Ausonius, works of medieval and Renaissance Latin; also reading of neo-Latin composition, completion of neo-Latin inscriptions.

See Notes on Method with reference to the free German compositions.

### GREEK

### U III

The Greek alphabet; also its importance in the history of civilization. The so-called regular etymology of the Attic dialect—in constant comparison with the Latin, down to and including the *verbum liquidum*. (See Notes on Method for the principles of accent.) Learning of the syntactical rules in connection with the reading, in which the chief value is to be placed upon a knowledge of the characteristic differences among the Greek, Latin, and German, together with drill upon model examples. Drill upon the vocabulary—with simple principles of word formation and language exercises as in the beginning of Latin instruction; from the first, however, the starting-point is to be taken more from the foreign language. The best introduction to the language is afforded by beginning the reading of Xenophon's *Anabasis* as early as possible after finishing a short preparatory course; beginning at the same time with Xenophon or even with Homer is not to be excluded, but the formation of sentences in "Homeric prose" is to be avoided.

*Written Exercises.* Especially dictations, as in beginning Latin instruction; occasional home papers consist in copying neatly a Greek text (with accents) which has been studied with or without translation and in review of German sentences already translated.

### O III

*Grammar.* The verbs in *v* and the most important irregular verbs of the Attic dialect. Connected treatment of prepositions and particles, with constant drill upon fundamental meanings. Review and extension of the acquired vocabulary and extension of the stock of syntactical rules in combination with the reading and in comparison with the German, Latin, and occasionally the modern language method of expression.

*Language Exercises.* As in U III; in addition, every quarter, a short translation from the Greek under the guidance of the teacher.

*Reading.* Continuation and conclusion of the reading of the *Anabasis;* development of the historical, cultural-historical, and geographical importance of the work. Some of Æsop's fables—

in connection with the reading of the *Phædrus*. Occasionally a principle of Euclid in Greek in connection with the instruction in mathematics. Everything in oral "activity instruction."

## U II

*Grammar.* Review of etymology, especially of the root verb forms studied. Treatment of syntax, with limitation to the most essential facts, in comparison with the methods of expression of the other languages already known to the pupil. With the aid of the instruction in Homer, and perhaps in Herodotus, occasional observations of the development of the Greek language in word and sentence formation.

*Reading.* Odyssey: Introductory books in their most valuable parts, especially books, $\varepsilon$, $\zeta$, $\eta$, also association with Schiller's *Cassandra* and *Siegesfest;* later discussion of Goethe's *Nausikaa*. Prosody and the Homeric colloquial usage are taught inductively and clarified by occasional summaries. The use of printed, scientifically arranged vocabulary lists is to be recommended; drill upon words from the Greek. Prose reading which has value for history and for the history of culture: Selections from Herodotus, especially from the first books, or from the Athenian Constitution of Aristotle, particularly from the history from Solon to Cleisthenes; or from Xenophon's *Hellenika,* particularly Books I and II, or the *Memorabilia,* or, for specially gifted pupils, from Arrian's *Anabasis*. The reading, even in Homer, is organized to prepare for and assist in the ancient history instruction which is begun in the second semester. For this purpose, here as in the history instruction, translations are to be employed; for example, from the dates of Herodotus dealing with the Persian wars, and of the messenger's report of the *Persae*. Drill upon historically and artistically worthwhile epigrams. Survey of the *Anabasis* and its historical importance; retrospect upon the *History of Alexander* by Curtius Rufus. The reading of Homer and of the prose does not follow in succession but is interchanged for valid reasons. Everything in the oral "activity instruction."

*Written Work.* Practice exercises as in O III; as class work approximately every four weeks, alternately a translation into the Greek and one from the Greek; these with abundant help from the teacher.

## O II

*Grammar.* See remarks on the Latin instruction in *Obersekunda*.

*Reading.* First theme: Early Greek World. Odyssey, the most valuable portions of the later books, possibly the conclusion of $\theta$, $\iota$-$\lambda$, selections from $\nu$ and $\tau$, conclusion of $\varphi$, parts of $\chi$ and $\psi$; summary of the organization of the work and of the world of

the Odyssey; comparison with the *Gudrunlied*. Reading of
some parts of Hauptmann's *Bogen des Odysseus*. In case the
reading of the Odyssey is greatly curtailed, selected Greek
elegiac and lyric poets. In addition novels of Herodotus, if not
in U II, or one of Plutarch's *Lives*, as possibly that of Themis-
tocles or Aristides. Support of the instruction in literature by
means of the pictorial arts, particularly with works from vase
painting in connection with the drawing instruction. Second
theme: Preparation for reading Plato in *Prima*. Selection from
Xenophon's *Memorabilia*, if not read in U II, Plato's *Apologia*
required, perhaps also *Crito;* comparison of the characterization of Socrates by Plato, Xenophon, and Aristophanes; under
certain circumstances a court speech of Lysias as a contrast.
First attempts in reading preparation done at home, under the
guidance of the teacher and after introduction to the use of the
lexicon.

*Class Work.* About every four weeks a translation from the
Greek. Compare here the principles for translations from the
Latin in the upper section of the *Gymnasium* (p. 492).

## I

The aim in *Prima* is to cause to live anew the eternal present
values of the works and thoughts of the Greek mind and
to set forth vividly their productive after-effects, primarily upon
the intellectual life of the German people in the period of Romanticism and Idealism.

The remarks for Latin instruction in *Prima*, p. 496, apply to
the method. An increased importance is attached to philosophical study and art appreciation (see Notes on Method).

The *Iliad*, tragedy, Plato, and Thucydides occupy the chief
place in the instruction.

The reading of the *Iliad* limits itself to the most valuable
parts—possibly *A*, a little from *B* and *Γ, Z, I, Π, Σ, Φ-Ω;* however, with the assistance of translations and lectures, the artistic
structure of the whole work, as the world of the *Iliad* in contrast to that of the *Odyssey*, must be brought to attention; also
comparison with the Middle High German epic. Summarizing
observations on the types of style employed in the Greek epic.
Lessing's and Goethe's position with respect to Homer deserves
especial presentation. Occasional comparative criticism of the
various German translations of Homer.

From the Greek tragedy, if possible, three works are to be read
from two or three different poets; from Æschylus those especially adapted are *Prometheus, Perseus, Eumenides*, as the most
important examples of the tragic, religious festive play; from
Sophocles: *Œdipus Rex, Antigone, Philoctetus, Aias, Electra;*
from Euripides: *Heracles, Hippolytus, Medea, Alcestis, Bac-*

*chus,* the *Iphigenia* in translation. It is assumed that every pupil will learn to read the *Oresteia* in translation and *Œdipus Rex* and *Antigone* in the original or in translation. In connection with the German, French, drawing and art instruction the importance of the Greek tragedy for the later theory and the later dramatic poetry, as well as for the pictorial arts, for example, Feuerbach's, is to be made clear.

From Plato admirably adapted are: *Symposium,* selections suitable to bring out clearly the progression of thought and structure; *Gorgias,* whose rhetoric is best discussed only with reference to content; *Phædo,* particularly the introduction and conclusion with reference to the *Apologia* and the portions dealing with the theory of knowledge; *The Republic,* in selections which contain the introduction to Book VII. In addition, possibly *Meno, Laches, Euthyphro,* parts of the *Phædrus,* or of the *Theætetus,* or of the *Protagoras.* It is expected that at least one dialogue will be treated as a whole. For the philosophical penetration of the instruction in Plato, see Notes on Method.

*Thucydides:* The fundamental explanation of the first book and the outbreak of the war; the Sicilian expedition. Also comparison with other ancient historians read—Herodotus, Livy, Sallust, and explanation of the nature of historical investigation and presentation. The address of Pericles on those fallen in battle, as the most effective conclusion of the whole Greek instruction; in addition Plutarch's *Pericles* in translation.

In addition the following are to be considered for class reading: Demosthenes, either one Olynthian oration, a part of the third Philippic oration, or the speech *On the Crown;* comparison also with Cicero. For additional reading see the free activity groups. For private reading see Notes on Methods. Especially worthwhile at this point is the reading of essays from scientific literature dealing with the classical period and its relation to German cultural and intellectual life.

For written class exercises and free home exercises, see the remarks on page 497.

*Free Activity Groups.* At the election of the teacher and pupils extension of the class instruction with consideration of the works not read in class or the intensification and extension of the class reading, somewhat along the following lines: For the purpose of deepening the instruction in philosophy, more detailed reading of the fragments of the pre-Socratic philosophers or parts of Aristotelian ethics and politics or form. Marcus Aurelius or Epictetus—in the Wilamowitz reader; for the purpose of increasing the knowledge of Greek poetry, reading of the Aristotelian works on the art of poetry or a comedy of Aristophanes—either *Frogs* or *Birds;* in connection with Latin instruction, one of Plutarch's *Lives,* either the *Gracchi,* with supplementary material from Appian, or *Cicero* and *Cæsar;* in connection with the other subjects, reading of such portions of the Wilamowitz reader as present the accomplishments of the Greeks in the field of mathematics, crafts, natural sciences, or the views of early Christian writers.

## FRENCH

### IV TO U II

*Pronunciation.* What was said for French as the first foreign language in the *Reformrealgymnasium* applies here as the situation requires.

*Grammar.* As in the Realgymnasium, with French as the first modern language, but with the reduction of work required by the smaller number of hours—9 hours as against 15 hours. The conclusion of a study of the principles in *Untersekunda* can be only very provisional.

*Reading.* At the beginning use of the reader—see *Realgymnasium;* connected reading, from about the middle of the second year's instruction; easy stories, lively descriptions, and historical sketches.

*Oral Exercises, Vocabulary.* What was said for French as the first foreign language in the *Reformrealgymnasium* applies here as the situation requires.

*Written Exercises.* Dictations, transpositions, and easy compositions in connection with experiences and observations as well as with reading; descriptions of pictures and the like.

### O II TO O I

*Grammar.* Extension and fixation of the knowledge and ability gained in the middle section; in connection with the history of language, explanations of grammatical phenomena by comparison with the Latin. In word study, insight into etymological relationships, especially on the basis of the Latin and Greek.

*Reading.* A drama of the classical period; examples from the prose writers of the seventeenth and eighteenth centuries, especially such as have reference to the classical period in content or spirit; chapters from important historians; outstanding works of the modern narrative literature; examples of lyric poetry.

*Written Exercises.* Similar to the middle section; many exercises in translation from the French.

## ENGLISH

### IV TO U III

*Pronunciation.* What was said with reference to English as the first foreign language in the *Reformrealgymnasium* applies here as the situation requires.

*Grammar.* As in the *Realgymnasium,* with English as the first foreign language; but with the reduction of work required by the smaller number of hours—9 hours as against 15 hours. The conclusion of a study of the principles in *Untersekunda* can be only very provisional.

*Reading.* At the beginning use of the reader—see *Realgymnasium;* connected reading, approximately from the middle of the second year's instruction on; easy stories, lively descriptions, historical sketches from such writings as Dickens, Child's *History of England;* Collar, *An Industrial and Social History of England.*

*Oral Exercises and Vocabulary.* What was said with reference to English as the first foreign language in the *Reformrealgymnasium* applies here as the situation requires.

*Written Exercises.* Dictations, transpositions, and simple compositions in connection with the pupil's experiences and observations as well as with reading; description of pictures and the like.

### O II TO O I

*Grammar.* Extension and fixation of the knowledge and ability acquired in the middle section; occasional explanation and comparison with the German, Greek, and Latin, from the point of view of the history of language. In word study insight into the etymological relationships on the basis of the German, Latin, and Greek.

*Reading.* Selections from Shakespeare, especially the Roman dramas; selections from Milton with reference to German, Greek, and Latin poems; worthwhile stories; chapters from historical treatises; comparison of English and Roman politics; the *Empire* and the *Imperium;* parliamentary speeches with reference to political oratory in Greece and Rome; illustrations from lyric poetry.

*Written Work.* Similar to that in the middle section; numerous exercises in translation from the English.

## MATHEMATICS

### VI

The four fundamental operations with integral abstract numbers, simple and compound denominate numbers. The German measures, weights and coins. Exercises in writing decimals and in the simplest decimal calculations. Applications to the home and the community. Concrete treatment of special forms, especially with reference to the needs of the instruction in geography.

## V

Continued exercises with concrete decimal numbers. Divisibility of numbers. The four fundamental operations with common fractions. Making numbers concrete by means of lines and surfaces. Solution of easy problems in proportion by reducing to unity or to a common measure. Applications to community or state management. Further consideration of space forms.

## IV

The four fundamental operations with decimal fractions: Changing common fractions to decimal fractions and the reverse. Short-cuts in calculation. Simplest cases of percentage, discount, interest, and other problems from daily life, with applications of simple and compound proportion. Making number series concrete by lines and surfaces. Arithmetical calculation of selected tables, especially calculation of averages and proportions. Applications to the management of the community, state, and nation.

*Geometry.* Concrete development of the fundamental geometric principles; sides and angles of the triangle; simplest triangle constructions; principles of congruency.

*Geometrical Drawing and Measurement.* Exercises in the correct use of the rule, the triangle, and compasses. Drawing of parallels, erection of perpendiculars, dropping of perpendiculars with the two triangles. Drawing of the outline of the cube, rectangular tetrahedron, octohedron. Perpendicular projection of the cube and rectangular parallelepiped standing upon the board. Construction of the diagonals of these solids. Constructions of the prism and pyramid and their graticulations. Measuring of straight lines and angles.

## U III

*Algebra.* Introduction to literal calculation. The four fundamental operations with absolute, relative, integral, and fractional numbers. Illustration on counting frames and machines. Calculation with tables by given formulæ. Simple equations of the first degree with one unknown in connection with calculation operations in the field of rational numbers. As opportunity presents itself, introduction of the linear function. Drawing of curves.

*Geometry.* Continuation of the principles of the triangle, and construction of triangles. Principles of the quadrilateral, espe-

cially the parallelogram and trapezium. Calculation of areas
and comparison of surfaces,—Pythagorean Theorem. Extension
of geometrical study and calculation of volume to space.

*Geometrical Drawing and Measurement.* Projection of the
points, straight lines, the plane, triangle, in any position in
space. Altitude and slope of the plane. Angle of incidence of a
straight line and a plane toward the drawing board. Straight-
line intersection of two planes which are defined by the section
and by the angle of inclination. The triangular pyramid. The
quadrilateral pyramid and the polygonial pyramid. In addition
to measurements of lines and angles, exercises in estimation out-
of-doors.

## O III

*Algebra.* Equations of the first degree with one or more unknowns; easy applications, especially from practical life. Introduction to graphic representations on the basis of empirical functions; representation of linear functions, the linear function as
a straight line and its use in solving equations of the first degree.
The function $y = m \cdot x$; proportionality factor. Introduction to
use of millimeter paper.

*Geometry.* Theory of the circle; chords and angles on the
circle. Extension of study of space.

*Geometrical Drawing and Measurement.* Oblique cones. Simple oblique solids. Measurement of lines, angles, and surfaces
out-of-doors.

## U II

*Algebra.* Powers with positive and negative integral exponents. The function $y = x^n$, when $n$ is a positive or a negative
number; and its graphic representation, especially the graphs of
the general function of a parabola and the equilateral hyperbola.
Calculation with radical expressions, powers with fractional exponents and their graphs. Calculation of square root. Exponential and logarithmic functions. The four-place logarithmic
table and logarithmic calculation. Explanation of the slide-rule.
Quadratic equations with one unknown.

*Geometry.* Proportion of straight lines; theory of similarity.
Application to the circle and right triangle. Circumference and
area of the circle. Something from the history of geometric
problems; for example, the squaring of the circle. Calculation
of the simplest solids.

*Geometrical Drawing and Measurement.* The perpendicular
coördinates in space; the regular bodies in stereometric representation. Plotting of curves in connection with algebra. Approximate constructions, circles. More exact measurement—
Nonius. Exercises in surveying in connection with the theory
of similarity.

## O II

*Algebra.* Easy integral and rational functions. Simple equations and simultaneous equations which can be solved by use of the quadratic equations, in arithmetric and graphic treatment. Arithmetic progressions of the first order and geometric progressions. The infinite geometric progression. Compound interest and annuities with applications from business life; economic arithmetic. Binomial theorem for positive integral functions.

*Geometry.* The trigonometric functions. Easy calculations of triangles. Goniometry. Theory of the periodic function. Continuation of the calculation of solids.

*Geometrical Drawing and Measurement.* Projection of the circle. Constructions for trigonometric problems; also for those whose limits do not lie in a plane. Plotting of curves in connection with algebra. Easy exercises in surveying and leveling.

## I

*Algebra.* Introduction to infinitesimal calculation, definition of differential quotients, its geometric and physical meaning, and its application to the treatment of rational and possibly also of the trigonometric functions, especially for calculating maximum and minimum roots, points and tangents of inclination, and the like. Simple calculations of the area of surfaces and content of solids by means of integration; for example, the sphere, the paraboloid, and the like. Structure of the number system from the positive integral to the complex number. Easy illustration by means of functions of complex variables.

*Geometry.* Survey of curves plotted thus far and introduction to analytic geometry up to the summarizing treatment of conic sections. Additional work from stereometry—sphere. Line and plane in space. Plane and axis. Fundamental principles of spherical trigonometry, principles of the sine and cosecant. Applications to mathematical geography and astronomy.

*Geometrical Drawing and Measurement.* Fundamental problems on point, line, plane; conic sections; projection of the sphere. Simple astronomical observations with exercises in measurement and calculation.

Survey from historical and philosophic points of view.

## NATURAL SCIENCES
### SURVEY OF COURSES IN SCIENCE

| | VI | V | IV | U III | O III | U II | O II 1 Se-mester | O II 2 Se-mester | U I | O I | Total |
|---|---|---|---|---|---|---|---|---|---|---|---|
| Physics .... | | | | 2 | 2 | | | 2 | 2 | 2 | 10 |
| Chemistry .. | | | | | | 2 | | | | | 2 |
| Biology .... | 2 | 2 | 2 | | | | 2 | | | | 8 |

## PHYSICS

### U III AND O III

*Introduction to Physics.* Experimental treatment of simple phenomena from the different fields of physics. With adherence to the order, the following topics serve as a standard to be attained.

*Mechanics of Solid Bodies.* Absolute and specific weight. The so-called simple machines and balance. The theory of work. Elementary theory of uniform and non-uniform motion. Projection. Centrifugal force. Pendulum.

*Mechanics of Fluid Bodies.* Connected vessels. Archimedes' principle and its applications. Hydraulic machines.

*Mechanics of Gases.* Atmospheric pressure, water and air pump. Expansibility of the air. Balloon and airships.

*Acoustics.* Fundamental phenomena of the theory of sound. Structure of the ear and of the human vocal organs.

*Principles of Heat.* Expansion. Melting and evaporation. Fusion temperatures of water. Heat machines. Frictional heat. Radiation of heat. Survey of the simplest meteorological phenomena.

*Principles of Magnetism and Electricity.* Fundamental laws of phenomena of magnetism. Magnetic field of the earth. The simplest phenomena in electrostatic fields. The electric current, its heat, light, chemical and physiological effects. Electromagnetism and its applications. Ohm's law and the most common electrical units. Telephone.

*Theory of Light.* Reflection and refraction of light. Prism and lens. Prismatic diffraction of light. Simplest optical instruments. The eye.

### O II

Extension of the material treated in the middle section, especially from the field of the theory of electricity; induction, principle of the dynamo, cathode and Röntgen rays. Survey of the theory of electro-magnetic eddies.

### I

Intensive treatment of one well-rounded portion of the field, which does not necessarily fall in with a phase of the work according to the traditional division of the subject. Outside of mechanics and the theory of light or electricity, the theory of oscillation or the group of phenomena which lay the foundation for and support the atomic theory are treated. The sound conception of physical processes is to be attained on the basis of such an example. Summarizing survey of the whole field of physics from the point of view of the conversion of energy.

Elements of astronomical mechanics.  Copernican universe with
the laws belonging thereto; distance, size, and physical qualities
of the planets and stars.  The world of modern physics.

## CHEMISTRY

### U II

Development of the fundamental notions, mixture and compound, element, chemical process, analysis, structure, reciprocal
replacement of elements, oxidation, and reduction, acid, base,
salt, on the basis of chemical processes.  Introduction to chemical
terminology.  Continued consideration of the chemistry of daily
life and of the importance of chemical technology for science
and art.

For illustrative purposes the following are recommended for
study without restriction as to order or choice:  Sulphur, water,
air, carbonic acid; oxidation, burning, heating, breathing, roast-
ing, and steps in oxidation.  Nitrogen and fertilizers.  Anthracite coal, illuminating gas.  Production of iron.  Lime and building materials.  Aluminum.

## BIOLOGY

### VI

Introduction to a knowledge of the important phanerogamous
plants and vertebrates of the locality.  Some foreign vertebrates.
Introduction to the fundamental principles in biology by observation of simple and noticeable biological phenomena from the
environment of the child by means of observations and easy experiments.  Development of an appreciation of the connection
between form and manner of life of plants and animals and of
the characteristics of life in general.  Useful plants, weeds, and
poisonous plants.  The external parts of the human body and
their functions.  Skin, bones, muscles.  Their structure and care.

The development of some life system.

Simple and natural plant groups.  Influence of light, air,
water, and soil.  Relation of animals to their environment.

### V

Comparative study of individual blossoming plants of Germany; also study of such plants with a more complex and less
discernible blossom structure, with consideration of local grains
and vegetables.

The parts of the plant in their mutual relationships and their
relation to the environment.

The human digestive, respiratory, and circulatory systems and
the hygiene of these organs.

Structure and life of articulata, especially of insects.

Simple and more difficult interdependent plant and animal groups in Germany.

Organization of ecologic, physiologic, and systematic groups with employment of the instructional material of *Sexta*.

Extension of the knowledge of plants and animals.

## IV

Selected representatives of the gymnospermo and lower plants; causes of plant diseases, worms, mollusks, echinodermata, nematophorans and protozoans, with emphasis upon the processes of nutrition and reproduction.

The simplest facts from the theory of the cell and its life. Human nervous system and sense organs and their hygiene.

Comparative study of the chief groups of the plant and animal kingdoms for the purpose of securing an insight into the fundamental characteristics of the system with incorporation of the paleontological facts from plant and animal geography. Foreign plants and animals and plant associations; for example, Mediterraneon Sea section; tundras.

## O II

The cell and its life phenomena. One-celled animal system. Colonization of one-celled animals and plants. Structure of animal and plant bodies from cells and tissue.

The most essential facts concerning the nutrition of plants and the life processes associated therewith.

Development of the many-celled animal from the one-celled animal. Care of offspring and heredity. Structure and life of the human body. Hygiene and prophylaxis, alcohol, nicotine, and other narcotics. Sexual hygiene. Importance of physical training, play, and sport.

The human organs are treated primarily from a physiological point of view.

## B. REALGYMNASIAL SCHOOLS

The Educational Objective of the *Realgymnasial* Schools

Within the common German educational objective of all schools, *realgymnasial* institutions have the special function of making clear to the German youth culture as founded on Roman civilization and Christianity in its historical contrast with western civilizations and in its formation likewise through mathematical-scientific thinking. The human and national values and formative forces appearing in this development are to be made fruitful for their personal life and their activity in the world and in the homeland.

For this purpose the young student will have to live over the epochs of German intellectual history in which the German mind, in conscious contrast with the French, English, and classical civilizations, welded its creative power into a unit which was fundamental for further development even until to-day when this development broke new trails.

This educational objective gives special importance to the modern language instruction in the *realgymnasial* institutions. By means of a thorough study of the French and English languages, to which the Latin gives aid and support, the youthful mind is clarified and made keen. The constant contrast and comparison of German, English, French, and Latin modes of expression will lead to a broader introduction' to language in general as an organic whole. Only the reading of foreign literature in the original permits this to be understood in its entire depth and formative power. Familiarization with the creative thoughts of the west-European mind, delving into its great literature, into the works of its most important writers and thinkers, will be of enormous importance for the historical, political, and humanitarian training of the youth. In connection with the core subjects, language instruction promotes a comprehension of German culture as it has developed, in adjustment and in contrast, as a special national mold of the western European mind. From this there develops for the youth a deeper appreciation of the problems of their people within the European world.

Since mathematics and the natural sciences in the *realgymnasial* institutions also serve to fulfill the whole cultural objective of these types of schools, it will become clear to the pupil to what extent these sciences have contributed materially to the development of the modern European thought by their methods of investigation and research, and to what extent they have become especially clear forms of expression of this thought. Deeper penetration into these subjects, especially if it takes into consideration the psychological points of view, will show our youth in what manner also German thought in its characteristic way has advanced and influenced these subjects; and thus in its own way will assist in awakening and strengthening national feeling.

## I. Realgymnasium

### Latin

### VI to IV

Common foundation with the *Gymnasium*.

### U III

*Grammar.* In connection with the text in grammar, summary and supplementary review of syntax and etymology, proceeding chiefly from the foreign language. Review of the earlier vocabulary and of the root verb forms.

*Oral Translation and Written Exercises.* As in *Quarta*, in both of which systematic exercises in translating the Latin expression into the corresponding German expression.

*Reading.* In connection with the French and history instruction, selections from Cæsar's *Bellum Gallicum* according to points of view set forth on page 510; or, in connection with the history instruction, worthwhile selections of medieval Latin, suitable for this section; for example, *The Legenda Aurea.* This would be best accomplished through a source reader.

### O III

*Grammar.* Continuation of the work of U III; always beginning, however, with the foreign language.

*Written Exercises.* As in U III, always, however, in the form of translations from the Latin, with sufficient help from the teacher.

*Reading.* In connection with the French, further selections from Cæsar's *Bellum Gallicum*, especially from Books VI, and VII (see page 513); in connection therewith perhaps something also from the *Bellum Civile.* Selection from *Phædrus* in connection with the modern literature of the fable.

### U II

*Grammar.* Occasional reviews from syntax and etymology, these especially in comparison with forms of expressions from the mother tongue and from both of the modern foreign languages with which the pupils are acquainted. Observations with reference to usage and characteristics of style of the authors that have been read.

*Reading.* Selected letters of Pliny. A selection from Roman technical natural science writers—Pliny the Elder, Vitruvius, Seneca,—in an anthology. With a gifted class, instead of this either Sallust's *Bellum Catalinæ* or *Bellum Jugurthinum.* For variety, Ovid's *Fasti* or other elegiac poems; also one of the tales of the *Metamorphoses.* Some of Martial's epigrams.

*Written Class Exercises.* Every four weeks a translation from the Latin under the direction of the teacher as to the method of the correct use of the lexicon.

## O II

*Grammar.* In connection with German and history, presentation of the effect of the Latin language and civilization upon the German from the early German period down into the Middle Ages. Summary of words derived, and foreign words taken from the Latin. Rhetoric in the upper section as in *Untersekunda.*

*Reading.* In connection with German and history, reading of Tacitus' *Germania* from the points of view set forth on page 510. One or more Latin works of the Carolingian-Ottonian renaissance (see above), or Otto von Freising's *Gesta Friderici.* In addition to these, worthwhile illustrations from Latin hymnology and minstrelsy. Some poems selected by pupil to be learned by heart. Constant use of translations which serve to supplement and round out the picture. Review of the reading in *Untertertia.*

*Written Class Exercises.* As in *Untersekunda,* if possible in connection with the reading. Grammatical and objective explanations as in the class exercises of *Obersekunda* of the *Gymnasium.*

## I

In connection with the instruction in religion, either Minucius' *Felix* or selections from Augustine's *Confessions,* or valuable selections of Renaissance Latin in connection with the history, of the later letters of the humanists and reformers, or selections from Copernicus' *De revolutionibus orbium cœlestuim.* More's *Utopia.* The language of the Catholic Church represented by characteristic illustrations, including recent times. Occcasionally a portion of philosophical and mathematical Latin of the eighteenth or nineteenth century. Collection of new Latin inscriptions.

As the high point of the Latin instruction generally: Some works of Roman literature of especially strong character and of importance for later ages: A comedy of Terence, *Andria* or *Adelphœ;* some poems of Catullus or Horace; Cicero's *De Republica,* VI, or Cicero's *Letters,* selected from personal viewpoints and compared with the letters of Pliny, or some read in modern language instruction; *Monumentum Ancyranum;* selected portions from the philosophical works of Seneca or the historical writings of Tacitus (see above); selection of Roman juristic literature.

It is assumed that every pupil will learn some of the poems of Catullus and some of the most valuable poems of Horace.

*Written Class Exercises.* As in *Obersekunda.*

Free "activity groups" are to serve to extend and enrich the class reading according to the points of view which are set up for the instruction in *Prima.*

### French as the First Modern Foreign Language

#### IV to U II

*Phonetics.* What is said concerning the middle section of the *Reformrealgymnasium* applies here, subject to the requirements of the situation.

*Reading Material.* Reading book the first year: Tales, descriptions from the environment of the pupil, French life, poems, proverbs and other types of material; at the latest from the middle of the second year's instruction forward, connected reading, which is supplemented by further use of a reading book organized from the point of view of the content, and a collection of poems. The points of view named for the middle section of the *Reformrealgymnasium* apply in the selection of the reading material. The survey of France to-day and of the course of French history there required will naturally be less complete in the *Realgymnasium* and will have to be enlarged in the upper section.

*Oral Exercises and Vocabulary.* As in the *Reformrealgymnasium.*

*Grammar.* Etymology and syntax with careful use of the pupil's grammatical knowledge and insights which have already been acquired in the German and Latin instruction. The provisional conclusion of regular work in grammar can be attained only at the end of *Untersekunda;* supplementing and rounding out must be reserved for the upper section.

Proposal for the distribution of the subject matter in grammar:

In IV: Nouns; conjunction of the most commonly used verbs in the organization designated in the Notes on Methods; chief types of pronouns.

In U III: Conclusion of conjugation; transitive, intransitive, reflexive, and impersonal verbs.

In O III: Use of tenses; use of conjunctions; infinitive, gerund, participle.

In U II: Article and substantive, adjective; pronouns; position of words.

*Written Exercises.* As in the *Reformrealgymnasium.*

#### O II to O I

The same points of view apply as in the *Reformrealgymnasium* but with recognition of the essentially smaller number of hours of French in the *Realgymnasium* as contrasted with the *Reformrealgymnasium*, 27 against 44.

## French as the Second Modern Foreign Language

### U III to U II

In general as in the *Reformrealgymnasium*. The difference in the number of hours—11 against 14—will be counterbalanced largely by the possibility of coördinating with Latin.

### O II to O I

In general as in the *Reformrealgymnasium*.

## English as First Modern Foreign Language

### IV to U II

*Phonetics.* The requirements for the lower section of the *Reformrealgymnasium* apply here as the situation directs.

*Reading Material.* Reading book the first year: Tales, descriptions from the pupil's environment and from English life, poems, proverbs, and the like, connected reading which is supplemented by wider use of a reader organized from the point of view of the content, and of a collection of poems. For the selection of reading material the points of view which were named for the middle section of the *Reformrealgymnasium* apply. The survey of England to-day and of the course of English history there demanded will naturally be less complete in the *Realgymnasium* and will have to be supplemented in the upper section.

*Oral Exercises and Vocabulary.* As in the *Reformrealgymnasium.*

*Grammar.* Etymology and syntax with careful use of the grammatical knowledge and insights which have already been acquired in the German and Latin instruction. The provisional conclusion of regular work in grammar can be attained only at the end of *Untersekunda;* supplementing and rounding out must be reserved for the upper section.

Proposal for the distribution of the subject matter in grammar.

In IV: Etymology including the verbs arising in the reading and in the speech exercises; elements of syntax in connection with the etymology.

In U III: Conclusion of the etymology; defective verbs, word position; passive voice; moods and progressive forms; use of auxiliary verbs.

In O III: Use of tenses; use of the subjunctive; infinitive; gerund and infinitive.

In U II: Article and substantive; adjective; relative clauses; prepositions.

*Written Exercises.* As in the *Reformrealgymnasium.*

## O II TO O I

The same points of view hold here as in the *Reformrealgymnasium,* with adaptation, however, to the essentially smaller total number of hours, 24 against 41.

### ENGLISH AS THE SECOND MODERN FOREIGN LANGUAGE

#### U III TO U II

In general as in the *Reformrealgymnasium,* with a certain reduction of demands, however, in view of the smaller number of hours, 11 against 14.

#### O II TO O I

In general as in the *Reformrealgymnasium,* with regard, however, for the smaller total number of hours, 20 against 23.

### MATHEMATICS

#### VI TO IV

As in the *Gymnasium.*

#### U III

*Algebra.* As in the *Gymnasium.* In addition there are the following topics: The linear function, the function $y = m \cdot x,$—proportionality factor. Continuation of exercises in arithmetic, —which were begun in earlier classes, and have to do with economic conditions.

*Geometry.* Completion of the study of the triangle. Continuation of the construction of triangles. Theory of the quadrilateral, especially the parallelogram and trapezoid. Introduction to theory of the circle, chords and angles on the circles. Extension of geometrical motives to space.

*Geometrical Drawing and Measurement.* As in the *Gymnasium.* In addition to this the oblique cone. Easy inclined bodies and road plans. Exercises in exact and accurate execution of constructions.

## O III

*Algebra.* Equations of the first degree with one or more unknowns. Easy applications, especially to problems of practical life. Introduction to graphical representation on the basis of empirical functions. Representations of linear functions—the linear function as a straight line—and their employment in solution of equations of the first degree. Introduction to the use of millimeter paper. Powers with positive integral exponents; representation of the function $y = x^n$ for positive integral values for $n$. Extraction of square roots.

*Geometry.* Further study of the circle. Calculation and comparison of areas.

*Geometrical Drawing and Measurement.* The perpendicular coördinates in space. The regular solids in axonometric representation. Plotting of curves in connection with algebra. Graphical representation of area by means of millimeter paper. Practical measurement of distances, angles, and areas.

## U II

*Algebra.* Powers with negative integral exponents. The function $y = x^n$ for negative integral values for $n$. The calculation of radical expressions. Exponential and logarithmic functions; inversion of a function. Reflection of the exponential function. Four-place logarithmic table and slide rule. Logarithmic calculation. Quadratic equations with one unknown.

*Geometry.* Proportion of lines; theory of similarity; application to the circle. Harmonic points and rays. Circumference and area of the circle. Calculation of the simplest solids. Some facts from the history of geometric problems.

*Geometric Drawing and Measurement.* Perpendicular projection of the circle, representation of solids in connection with stereometry. Plotting of curves in connection with algebra. Approximate constructions—circle. More exact measurements —Nonius. Surveying exercises in connection with the theory of similarity.

## O II

*Algebra.* Integral and rational functions. Simple equations and simultaneous equations which can be solved by means of equations of the second degree. Conic sections. Arithmetic progressions of the first order and geometric progressions. The infinite geometric progressions. Compound interest and annuities with applications to economic life. Binomial theorem for positive integral exponents.

*Geometry.* The trigonometric functions. Simple calculations of triangles. Goniometry. Principle of the periodic function. Straight lines and planes in space. Continuation of calculation of solids.

*Geometrical Drawing and Mensuration.* In connection with trigonometry: Constructions of problems whose data do not lie in a plane. For stereometry: Systematic development of fundamental problems dealing with the point, straight line, and plane. Continuation of the constructions of solids, especially of the sphere. Plotting of curves in connection with algebra. Simple exercises in surveying and leveling.

## I

*Algebra.* Organization of the number system from the positive integral number to the complex number. Review treatment of the integral, partial, algebraic and indeterminant functions which have been studied in the course. Introduction to infinitesimal calculation—definition of differential quotients, their geometric and physical importance, and their application to the treatment of rational and some indeterminant functions—the trigonometric, cyclometric, logarithmic and exponential functions; study of related curves. Approximate calculation of indeterminant functions by means of development of series. Simplest cases of integration with application to the solution of curves, areas, and volumes. Concrete treatment of the law of averages. The theory of equations, especially approximate solutions and percentage of error. Simple diagrams by means of functions of complex variables.

*Geometry.* Fundamental principles of spherical trigonometry —principle of the sine and cosecant. Application to mathematical geography and astronomy. Geometry of coördinates. Review treatment of conic sections.

*Geometrical Drawing and Measurement.* Constructions for spherical trigonometry; map drawing. Conic sections as plane sections on the cylinder and cone. Introduction to projection on two planes in some examples. Constructions with the aid of altitude lines of the first and second type in place of trace lines. Introduction to perspective, central projection. Perspective of the circle. Simple astronomical observations with exercises in measurement and calculation.

Review from historical and philosophical points of view.

## NATURAL SCIENCES

### SURVEY OF COURSES

| | VI | V | IV | U III | O III | U II 1st Sem. | U II 2nd Sem. | O II 1st Sem. | O II 2nd Sem. | U I | O I | Total |
|---|---|---|---|---|---|---|---|---|---|---|---|---|
| Physics ... | | | | 2 | 2 | 2 | | | 3 | 2 | 2 | 13 |
| Chemistry . | | | | | | | 2 | | | 2 | 2 | 6 |
| Biology ... | 2 | 2 | 2 | | | | 2 | 3 | | | | 11 |

## PHYSICS

### U III TO U II

As in the lower section of physics in the *Gymnasium*, with the extension of the particular and especially suitable fields and with the inclusion of practical exercises.

### O II TO O I

As in the upper section of physics in the *Gymnasium*, with the extension of the particular fields and the inclusion of pupil exercises.

## CHEMISTRY

### U II

As in the *Gymnasium*.

### U I

Oxygen, hydrogen, sulphur, nitrogen, halogen, phosphorus, arsenic, silica, light metals, heavy metals, carbon compounds. Related discussion of the following ideas: Analysis, synthesis, substitution, atomic weight, combining weight, valence. Foundation of the atomic theory and of Avogadro's Law. Emphasis upon the qualities of families of elements. Fundamentals of the natural system of elements. The importance of the elements and their compounds from the purely chemical, biological, technological, economic, mineralogical, and geological standpoints. Thorough treatment of chemical terminology.

### O I

More complicated chemical changes in natural and artificial salts and their acids. Summary of whole group of chemical changes by introduction to the nature of solutions and to the ionic theory. Structure and characteristics of organic compounds which are simple in their composition and which are important in technology, economic life, public food and health. Summarizing review of the whole field of chemistry.

## BIOLOGY

### VI TO IV

As in the *Gymnasium*.

## U II

As in the *Obersekunda* of the *Gymnasium*.

## O II

Intensive treatment of plant and animal ecology; that is, of their relations to the surrounding inorganic environment and to each other. Derivation of the conditions of the emergence of plants and animals into the life regions of the earth. Plants and animals as factors in civilization, in connection with geography. See Notes on Methods under Concentration.

The influence of man upon the dispersion of the other life systems of the earth.

## II. REFORMREALGYMNASIUM

### LATIN

#### U II

In connection with the reader,—whose content is organized around the subject matter in history in *Obersekunda* and which contains, as early as possible, original Latin, prose and poetry text, also of the late Latin,—the so-called regular etymology. Particular irregularities are derived from the reading. Observation of the most important syntactical phenomena and acquisition of a vocabulary, which is organized carefully upon the basis of the later reading with systematic use of linguistic knowledge already acquired. The instruction can also from the very beginning be connected with Cæsar's *Bellum Gallicum*.

The whole language instruction from the beginning is organized for the main and ultimate purpose of translating from the Latin. Only the fundamental elements of the Latin language, especially the etymology,—apart from the more important exercises in recognition of forms—must be practiced by means of translation of German sentences into the foreign language.

The translation from the foreign language takes place with as literal a translation as is possible, followed by a free reproduction of the thought. In passages which offer rich instructional opportunity, analysis of sentences.

*Written Class Exercises.* About every four weeks a translation from the Latin, at first with considerable help from the teacher, then, after introduction to the use of the Latin lexicon, gradually with greater independence on the part of the pupils.

#### O II

*Grammar.* Review and fixation of the subject matter of *Untersekunda.* Drill upon the most essential portions of the

so-called irregular etymology, especially of the verb. Extension
of the knowledge of syntax, primarily that of the sentence structure. The dependent clause; principle of inner dependence.
Regular development of the vocabulary.

*Reading.* In the course of the year, beginning of the connected
reading: Cæsar's *Bellum Gallicum,* especially those portions
dealing with the Teutons; in addition Tacitus' *Germania* in
translation. Some of the sources for the history of Charlemagne
—Einhard and Notker. Some examples of the Latin hymnology
and wandering students' songs.

*Written Class Exercises.* As in *Untersekunda;* in these exercises regular written explanations of some Latin sentence constructions and individual forms.

# I

*Grammar.* Review of elementary grammar according to need.
Summarizing treatment of the cases in syntax observed in the
reading and some of the simpler problems of style. Fixing and
developing the vocabulary. Summarizing treatment of the persistence of classical language in the mother tongue.

*Reading.* In connection with the history instruction, some
worthwhile selections from the Latin Renaissance literature,
possibly letters of the humanists and reformers. The language
of the Catholic Church illustrated by characteristic examples,
also of the modern period. Summary of new Latin inscriptions
from Roman literature. The following may be selected: Phædrus, in connection with the literature of the fable; some songs
of Catullus and *Elegies* of Ovid; selections from Cicero's *Letters;*
Pliny's *Letters;* perhaps also Tacitus' *Agricola* in connection with
English. Selections from the technical-natural science writers in
an anthology—something from Pliny the Elder, Vitruvius,
Seneca.

*Written Class Exercises.* As in *Obersekunda.*

## FRENCH AS THE FIRST MODERN FOREIGN LANGUAGE

### VI AND V

*Phonetics.* Training in listening and practice with the sounds
in connection with words and shorter sentences; oral exercises.
Reading exercises from phonetic script and from orthographic
copy; in the reading and oral exercises observation of the sentence tone and inflection; speaking in concert; singing of songs,
memorization of poems and short prose selections, phonetic exercises with use of the phonetic charts.

*Reading Material.* Illustrations from the environment of the
school, home, community, industry, and the like; fairy tales,
stories, description of nature; poems, songs, and proverbs.

*Oral Exercises.* In connection with the processes and incidents of daily life, the reading material, simple pictorial illustrations and other objective materials.

*Vocabulary.* Summary of the words which have appeared in the reading and oral exercises, grouped according to form and meaning; word relationships and simplest derivatives.

*Grammar.* Drill in the forms with simultaneous practice in the syntactical applications,—for example, personal pronouns in connection with verbs.

Proposal for the distribution of the subject matter in grammar:

In VI: The noun; the most common verbs in the present and imperfect; numerals; chief types of pronouns.

In V: Formation of the adverb; comparison of the adjective and adverb; the verbs according to type, in the historical perfect and in the future; transposed verb forms; subjunctive in special cases; other types of pronouns.

*Written Exercises.* Exercises in spelling from dictation and from memory; rearranging sentences; filling in missing parts of sentences; sentence development; simple reproduction of stories and easy descriptions; answering of questions; translation of easy German sentences for the purpose of fixing and drilling in grammatical knowledge. Frequent exercises in the class. The class exercises in this section consist of rather long practice exercises whose number is fixed by the teachers' activity group. From time to time there is also written work to be done at home.

## IV TO U II

*Reading Material.* At the beginning a reading book which is organized from the point of view of content; at the latest beginning with U III connected reading which is supplemented by a reader and a collection of poems. The connected reading covers tales which have content and formal value, for example, from Maupassant, Daudet, Bazin, Theuriet, Mérimée, Margueritte, Anatole France, Moselly, Jammes; biographical sketches of leading personalities. Individual sketches in lively form from French life or French history or from French heroic myths; for example, an abridgment of the works of Gaston Paris, in *Untersekunda,* a lighter drama, possibly Molière's *Bourgeois Gentilhomme,* Sandeau's *Mademoiselle de la Seiglière.* Dry, didactic accounts of historical, geographical, economic, and technical type as well as artistically valueless light reading are excluded. In the selection of the connected reading and also of the sections of the reader, attention is to be given if possible to the whole educational objective of the class and to the topics of instruction of the other courses. At the end of the middle section the pupils must have a gradually acquired picture of the course of French history in its chief epochs and events.

*Speech Exercises.* In connection with the reading material, with the occurrences of daily life, with the topics of the other subjects of instruction and the like as much conversation among the pupils of the class as possible; recitations before the class.

*Vocabulary.* Development of the vocabulary in connection with reading and independently thereof in connection with oral exercises of all types. Constant reorganization and systematic development of the range of meanings of words; synonyms and phraseology; continually deeper penetration into word relationships and principles of word formation.

*Grammar.* Conclusion of etymology; syntax to be concluded mainly in *Obertertia* and to be supplemented in *Untersekunda* through special cases.

Proposals for the distribution of the subject matter in grammar:

In IV: Conclusion of conjugation; summary of the forms within the single verb; transitive, intransitive, and reflexive verbs; impersonal verbs.

In U III: Use of tenses; use of subjunctive; infinitive; gerund; participle.

In O III: Article and substantive; adjective; pronouns; position of words.

In U II: Summary. Supplementation and intensification of the individual topics, especially the theory of prepositions.

*Written Exercises.* Dictation as exercises in understanding and reproducing a shorter or longer connected passage in the foreign language; free reproduction; statements and reports of all sorts in connection with the reading, with observations and experiences or with instruction in other subjects; descriptions of pictures and natural scenes; letters; free translation of German texts, at the beginning on the basis of oral preparation in the class, but later independently; grammatical exercises, for example, rearranging sentences, combination of sentences, and the like. Numerous written exercises; up to and including *Obertertia*, class exercises consist of rather long practice exercises whose number is determined by the activity group of teachers; in *Untersekunda* a written class exercise about every four weeks.

## O II to O I

*Grammar and Etymology.* More thorough comprehension of the laws of grammar by means of a historical review of the Latin and a contrast with the German and English; fixation of the fundamental characteristics of the French language with reference to clearness, accuracy, and logic upon the one hand, and to euphony and rhetorical effect upon the other; evaluation of striking individual characteristics of syntax, as for example the preference for transitive verbs and avoidance of the passive voice; observations of sentence rhythm and sentence inflection in connection with the syntax—word position; style in close connection with syntax. In etymology: synonyms, etymology, change of meaning; the Germanic and academic Latin in the vocabulary. History of language in connection with cultural history.

*Reading and Study of Culture.* In *Obersekunda*, in flexible transfer over into *Unterprima*, as close connection as possible with history and German: Perhaps even in this class a classical tragedy by Racine or Corneille; correlation with ancient history and German, persistence of the classical in the history of modern drama. Accounts from French medieval history; French knighthood and French Gothic; view of old French poetry possibly in connection with Gaston Paris or Bédier; illustrations from Victor Hugo, *Notre Dame de Paris* or *La Légende des Siècles.*

In *Prima*: 1. Classicists of the seventeenth century. Corneille: his relation to the Renaissance, his connection with the political movements of his time (Richelieu, *Fronde*), the Stoic element of his ethics—reference to Schiller; his importance for the development of French ethics, especially of patriotism; his antithetic, sententious style as expression of the French type of mind; the *Esprit français* of de la Rochefoucauld down to modern times. Racine: his relation to Port-Royal; his relation to the classical period in comparison to that of the German classicists—in connection with German; his language as expression of French feeling of beauty. Racine and Corneille: two types of artistic writing in relation to statement of problem, language, composition; development of this theme by means of similar contrasts, such as Goethe–Schiller, Raphael–Michelangelo, in connection with German and art—Molière: the theater as rhythmic play, changing relation and position of persons to one another; the figures of his comedies as characters of the period; illuminations by La Bruyère and La Fontaine, possibly also Taine, *La Fontaine et ses Fables;* types of comedy; nature and types of the comic element in connection with German and English—the form of the classical drama; its importance for the German drama, in connection with German; Lessing. Rounding out of the cultural picture of French classicism by means of examples from literature in memoirs and letters; essays of Sainte-Beuve, Anatole France and Brunetière. In connection with music and art, the royal-aristocratic culture of Paris and Versailles, possibly in contrast to popular culture in the German city in earlier centuries. Poetry and linguistic culture of the classical period; Boileau and the academy; linguistic culture and cultivation of language in service of the national state; related

phenomena both in England and in Germany; contrary movements in France.

2. The great pulpit orators of the seventeenth century.
French and German pulpit orators, in connection with religion
and German; the oration as art, in connection with Latin, German and English; survey of the history of theological thought
and religious life in Germany; Gallicanism; survey of related
developments in other countries, in connection with religion and
history.

3. Philosophical thinkers of the seventeenth, eighteenth, and
nineteenth centuries. Descartes; his relation to his time; rationalism and classicism; the interlacing of the mathematics-
natural science problem with the problem of the theory of
knowledge and metaphysics; survey of history of mathematical-
physical thought in France by means of illustrations from
d'Alembert, Laplace, H. Poincaré and others, in connection with
the mathematics-natural science instruction, English, German,
and the activity group in philosophical reading; Descartes as
representative of a fundamental mode of thought especially
prominent in France; need of supplementation of this intellectual position, in connection with English, German, activity
group in philosophical reading—Malebranche; his relation to
mysticism; his importance for the philosophical movement of
the seventeenth and eighteenth centuries; the metaphysical
characteristic of French thought.—Pascal; his relation to the
history of mathematics; his connection with Port-Royal; his
position in the history of Catholic thought; his method in apologetics, in connection with religion; the fundamental characteristics in the French nature down to the modernists.—Rousseau;
his relation to the mysticism and Calvinism; the conflict of the
Germanic and Roman nature in him; survey of the irrational-
istic movement in modern European intellectual history, in
connection with German and English; the problem of culture
and civilization; survey of the different modern attempts at
solution, in connection with history and German; natural
right and positive right, in connection with history.—
Voltaire; survey of the tendencies of the Enlightenment, in connection with history and German; the French
intellectual clearness in contrast perhaps to that of
Lessing, Schiller, Goethe, in connection with German; the skep-
tical-ironical strain in the French intellectual pattern from
Montaigne to Anatole France; Gallic wit and German humor.—
Proudhon and Saint-Simon; survey of the history of the social
movement, in connection with history and English; the Utopian
and historical socialism; Christian socialism, especially in
France, Sillon.—Maine de Biran; idealistic philosophy in
France, in connection with German and the activity instruction
in philosophical reading.—Taine; the importance of external

factors for intellectual activity; historical outlooks; value and limits of the natural science method in the mental sciences; Taine and naturalism.—Bergson; his connection with German thought; his importance for modern France; vitalism; philosophy and life; survey of various solutions of this problem.

4. Historians and statesmen. Primarily such historical presentations as give insight into the development of civilization, as Duruy, Michelet, Rambaud, the Goncourt, Lavisse, Sorel, and such as opened up the view upon the whole Western development,—such as Guizot, Taine, Seignobos. In connection with history, especially in the study of the Revolutionary period: the Revolution as a movement of ideas in connection with Montesquieu, Helvetius, Voltaire, Rousseau, and others; counter movements, also in France, De Maistre, Bonald, Constant; the foundations of the idea of the state with rationalistic, romantic, and religious thinkers, in connection with history and German; relation of political ideas of the Revolution with the classical period; the course of the Revolution in connection with a historian of more profound type, as De Tocqueville, Taine, Aulard; speeches of Mirabeau; psychological and ethical illumination of the events of the Revolution by means of such novels as France's *Les Dieux ont Soif*—while from the English, Dickens' *Tale of Two Cities* should come in for consideration; the figure of Napoleon possible in connection with Taine, Chateaubriand, or Stendhal; Revolution and Empire as historical memories of France; the Napoleonic cult down to Rostand's *L'Aiglon;* period of the Revolution and the Middle Ages as the two chief sources of French national feeling; survey of the political and spiritual struggles between these two tendencies in modern France.

5. Narrative writers and dramatists of the nineteenth and twentieth centuries to be read uninterruptedly in the class, or as private reading. Rich illumination of French characteristics, of cultural and spiritual association from a historical viewpoint, for example, Stendhal and Mérimée: the Renaissance ideal in artists and thinkers of the nineteenth century, in connection with history and German; Balzac and Flaubert: the French middle classes in the nineteenth century; Anatole France: his intellectual position. Irony and goodness as the French contrast to German humor; Anatole France as the intellectual heir of Voltaire and the eighteenth century; the humanitarian idea in French thought; Anatole France and Flaubert: observations of the style of artistic prose, in connection with German and English; Romain Rolland: German and French art contrasted and supplemented, in connection also with music instruction.

6. Victor Hugo. Examples of his dramatic, epic, and lyric creations and his critical prose; his relation to Romanticism, his importance as representative of French character; power of

the traditional idea. Magic of the word; Hugo's phantasy in comparison with that of the German poets, possibly Heinrich Heine.

7. Lyric poets of the nineteenth and twentieth centuries; in connection with reading of tales, dramas, philosophical and critical prose as well as observation of works of the pictorial arts. Survey of the development of French art and French thought from the period of Romanticism on; relation of the political, social, and intellectual development in the nineteenth century, in connection with history, German, and English; survey of the various tendencies in French intellectual life which contend with one another even until the present time; rationalism and irrationalism, skepticism and dogmatism, folk origins and cultural forms, survey of Western conditions in general. Paris and the provinces in the intellectual picture of France; importance of the Flemish and German elements in French cultural life, Verlaine, Verhæren, Maeterlinck.

8. Theoretical writers of the present and past. Primarily such portrayals and essays as present in intellectually rigid form the technical, sociological, scientific, artistic problems ·of the present and give higher points of view for the training of judgment, as, for example, Maeterlinck, *Vie des Abeilles;* Fabre, *Souvenirs Entomologiques.*

The suggestions are only to furnish hints as to how certain relationships which have to do with the development of culture and civilization can be surveyed from various high points; naturally the majority of these relationships can be viewed from other points of view, since their circles cut one another in many places. For every school generation a selection from the possibilities mentioned above shall be made, in which the determining factor shall be primarily the whole educational objective of the instruction—see Notes on Methods. It will be the especial function of the "free activity groups" to advance further and to bore deeper in one direction or the other.

*Written Work.* Dictation as exercises in understanding and reproducing longer passages in the foreign language; French compositions in connection with selections from French writers read or presented by the teacher; free reproduction upon the basis of German or French text which has been read or recited; retranslation following a good German translation; free translation of easy original German text into French; translations from the French into German; French compositions of all sorts in connection with the reading and instruction, upon the basis of experiences and events. Eight to ten class exercises during a year. Translations and reproductions from the French in connection with the reading and instruction are considered also as exercises in German style and composition.

### French as the Second Modern Foreign Language

#### U III to U II

*Phonetics.* What was said for French as the first modern language in the *Reformrealgymnasium* applies here as the situation demands.

*Reading Material, Oral Exercises, Vocabulary.* In general as in the *Realgymnasium,* when French is the first modern language.

*Grammar.* Etymology and syntax with careful employment of the grammatical knowledge and insights which the pupil has already acquired in the German and English instruction.

Proposal for distribution of the grammar subject matter:

In U III: Nouns; conjugation of the most common verbs in arrangement indicated in the Notes on Methods; chief types of pronouns.

In O III: Conclusion of etymology; transitive, intransitive and reflective verbs, impersonal verbs; use of tenses; use of the subjunctive.

In U II: Infinitive; gerundive; participle; article and substantive; adjectives; pronouns; word position; supplementing and rounding out of the grammatical system are reserved for the upper section.

*Written Exercises.* As when French in the *Reformrealgymnasium* is the first foreign language.

#### O II to O I

The same points of view apply here as when French in the *Reformrealgymnasium* is the first foreign language; however, the essentially smaller total number of hours must be considered, —26 against 44.

### English as the First Modern Foreign Language

#### VI and V

*Phonetics.* Training to listen and drill upon the sounds in connection with words and rather short sentences—oral exercises. Reading exercises from phonetic script and orthographic copy; in reading and oral exercises observation of the sentence tone and inflection; speaking in concert; singing of songs; memorizing poems and short prose selections; phonetic exercises with the help of a phonetic chart.

*Reading Material.* Descriptions from the environment of the child; school, home, community, family, industrial life and the like; fairy tales, stories, and descriptions from nature; poems, songs, and proverbs.

*Oral Exercises.* In connection with the processes and incidents of daily life, the reading material, simple pictorial illustrations and other objective material.

*Vocabulary.* Summary of words, which appear in the reading or oral exercises, grouped as to form and meaning; word relationships and simplest derivatives.

*Grammar.* Drill upon the forms with simultaneous practice in the syntactical application,—for example, transposed forms of the verb, position of the personal pronouns.

Proposal for distribution of the grammar subject matter as follows:

In VI: Nouns; the portions of conjugation which are necessary for practical use; numerals; chief classes of pronouns; comparison of the adjective.

In V: Conclusion of conjugation; transitive, intransitive, reflexive verbs; other types of pronouns; adverb.

*Written Exercises.* Exercises in spelling from dictation and from memory; remodelling of sentences; filling in missing parts of sentences; sentence development; simple reproductions of stories and easy descriptions; answering of questions; translation of easy German sentences for drill and fixation of grammatical knowledge. Frequent practice exercises in the class. The class exercises in this section consist of rather long practice exercises, the number of which is to be determined by the teachers' "activity group." From time to time also written assignments to be prepared at home.

## IV to U II

*Reading Material.* At first a reader which is organized from the point of view of subject matter; later beginning with U III connected reading which is supplemented by the reader and collections of poetry. The connected reading includes tales, worthwhile as to content and form; for example, Marryat, Hughes, Dickens, Wilde, Jerome, Stevenson, Kipling, Irving, Poe, Twain, Hawthorne; it includes also descriptions from English life and history which are written in lively style; for example, Collar, *An Industrial and Social History of England*, biographies, travel, and lighter drama. Dry, didactic essays of historical, geographical, economic, or technical nature, as well as light reading of no artistic value, are not permitted. In the selection of the connected reading, and also of the portions of the reader, attention is to be paid, if possible, to the whole educational objective of the class and to the topics in the other subjects. By the end of the middle section the pupils must possess a gradually developed idea of the organization of the

British Empire and of the course of English history with reference to its chief epochs and events.

*Oral Exercises.* In connection with the reading material, the events of daily life, the topics in the other subjects of instruction; as much conversation as possible among the pupils; speeches before the class.

*Vocabulary.* Extension of the vocabulary in connection with the reading and independently thereof in connection with oral exercises of all sorts; constant development and systematic extension of the range of meanings of words; synonyms and phraseology; continually more thorough study of word relationship and principles of word formation.

*Grammar.* Syntax, the main portions to be concluded in *Obertertia* and supplemented by details in *Untersekunda*.

Proposal for the distribution of grammar subject matter as follows:

In IV: Word position; passive voice; defective verbs; elementary facts about the infinitive, gerund, and participle.

In U III: Use of auxiliary verbs; infinitives, gerund, participle, relative clauses; elementary facts with reference to the article and numeral.

In O III: Use of tenses; progressive forms and moods; articles, numerals, case; adjective; pronouns, adverbs.

In U II: Summary, supplementation, and further study of the individual topics, especially the use of prepositions.

*Written Exercises.* Dictations as exercises in understanding and reproducing a longer or shorter connected passage in the foreign language; free reproduction of what has been read or heard; compositions and reports of all sorts in connection with the reading, with observations and experiences or with instruction in other subjects; descriptions of pictures and landscapes; letters; free translation of German texts, at first only on the basis of oral preparation in the class,—later independently; grammar exercises, for example, recasting of sentences, combining sentences and the like. Numerous written exercises; the class exercises consist, up to and including *Obertertia,* of rather long practice exercises, whose number is determined by the teacher's activity group; in *Untersekunda* a written class exercise about every four weeks.

## O II TO O I

*Grammar and Etymology.* Historical foundation of the phonetic and etymological character of English, especially by means of comparison with the German and French; summary and systematic extension of the notion which appeared in the lower and middle sections; history of syntax, primarily in connection with reading in Shakespeare; observation of the vital nature and characteristic phenomena of the language, its analytical character, its tendency toward abstract expression; observation of sentence rhythm and sentence inflection in connection with the syntax—word position; rhetoric in close connection with syntax. Word formation and change of meaning in close connection with the German language; the Teutonic element in the grammar; history of the language in connection with history of culture; the assimilative power of the English language; insight into accentuation from its historical background.

*Reading and Cultural Studies.* In *Obersekunda,* in preparation to pass easily into *Unterprima,* very close connection with history and German. Works on the foundations of the English Constitution, legal and social organization, selections from older English history; English ballads of ancient and modern times; narratives which bring out concretely the Germanic element in the English people, or which are particularly akin to German point of view, as those of Scott and Dickens.

In *Prima*: 1. Shakespeare. At least a complete drama, also excerpts from other works in a Shakespeare reader; Shakespeare; position in the history of English culture, possibly in connection with Creighton; his relation to English nationality—fairy tales, myths, ballads, songs. The following topics in connection with German, based upon extended reading of translations: Shakespeare's personality; his art and mode of thinking; his conception of the work and humanity; the mystic element of his poetry with reference to Nordic poetry in general; in further connection wth history and art, Shakespeare's art in light of the Renaissance and of the Baroque; by contrast of his art with classical, French and German dramatic poetry,—possibilities of artistic form; in connection with Carlyle or Emerson,—Shakespeare as one of the spiritual leaders and pioneers— in connection with German and religion.

2. Milton. Examples of his prose and poetry; Milton as typical representative of English ethics; survey of the development of the ecclesiastical-religious life down to Newman and the Oxford movement,—in connection with religion; survey of the history of English national feeling; criticism of English nationalism by English writers, for example, Meredith or Shaw; Puritanism in its after-effect upon English and American national character. Milton as a Christian poet and as a poet of the Renaissance,—in connection with German.

3. Lyric and epic poets of the eighteenth and nineteenth centuries. Burns and the English folk-song in connection with music; the artist's love of the lowly in Burns in connection with German and Dutch art. In Moore, Wordsworth, Coleridge, Byron, Shelley, Keats, Scott and others and in connection with German, French, music, and art: the romantic movement in its manifold forms; from this as a beginning a survey of the Vic-

torian poetry and its many relationships with English and American literature of the recent past and present.

4. Narrative writers and dramatists of the modern period, to be read in class without discussion, or as private reading. Rich illumination of English characteristics, phases of cultural and intellectual development, for example, in Dickens, survey of English, American, and German humorists and satirists; life and ideals of the English middle and lower classes—cockney, the social problem, especially in England; artistic simplification of reality by means of idealization and caricature,—Chesterton, Shaw, and Wilde: the importance of the Celtic element in English and American intellectual life.

5. Historians and statesmen. Primarily such historical accounts as open up the greater vistas in the history of culture and develop the feeling for history and politics. In connection with the history instruction possibly the following topics: Struggle between feudalism and monarchy—Shakespeare reading; the rise of the middle class in the seventeenth century; development of English democracy upon an aristocratic basis; advantages and disadvantages of English and American democracy; liberal and conservative thought in England in respect to politics, economics, religion, and ethics, by contrasting leading personalities, as Disraeli and Gladstone, Joseph Chamberlain and Lloyd George; illustration from their writings, parliamentary speeches and editorials; survey of the conditions in the rest of Europe, especially in Germany,—history of the British Empire, or the personal and material forces incorporated in Seeley or Dilke; the spiritual aspect of British imperialism, as found in Froude, Kipling, Wells; the British Empire as a fact of world history; comparison with the Roman Empire; internal and external difficulties of the empire to-day, possibly as found in editorials. Essential facts from American history, as found in Lecky, *The American War of Independence,* or Spark's, *The Life of George Washington;* modern America in connection with geography; Americanism as an idea, as illustrated in Ford or Carnegie; opposition to this idea in America, Emerson and others; criticism of America as found in English writers, for example, Dickens or Shaw.

6. Philosophers and thinkers of the eighteenth and nineteenth centuries. Shaftesbury; his ideal of personality in light of the German classicists, in connection with German; the ideal of the German gentleman; survey of the English educational system; limits, dangers and types of degeneracy of the "gentleman ideal," as viewed in Locke, Hume, Thackeray, Wilde, Shaw. Survey of the history of the theory of knowledge, in connection with German and French, and the activity group in philosophical reading; relation to the Enlightenment, in connection with history and French; relation to a fundamental tendency in

thought appearing especially in England; additional tendencies, also in England; Berkeley and spiritualism, in connection with German, religion, French, and the activity group in philosophical reading. Adam Smith, survey of the history and the forces of modern economic life, in connection with history and geography; different systems of political economy, in connection with history and German; the Manchester school in the past and present; relation to social and ethical problems; the social and ethical reaction in the nineteenth century in connection with Carlyle, Ruskin, sociological novels and poetry; survey of the history and importance of the English labor movement, in connection with editorials or modern dramas, for example, Galsworthy's,—John Stuart Mill, in his essay *On Liberty,*—the idea of freedom, in connection with religion, German, and the activity group in philosophy. Herbert Spencer; metaphysical, ethical, sociological problems from the point of view of natural sciences; value and limitations of this method of study, in connection with the natural sciences and the activity group in philosophy. William James, survey of pragmatism, especially as a tendency in American and English thought; philosophy and life; survey of the various solutions of this problem.

7. Theoretical writers of the present and recent times. Primarily such works and essays as present a thoroughly intellectual treatment of technical, economic, scientific, and artistic problems of the present day and furnish for training of judgment higher points of view, for example, chapters from Darwin or various writings of Wells.

These guiding principles furnish hints only as to how certain cultural and intellectual problems can be surveyed from various points of view. Naturally, most of these problems permit of treatment from other standpoints, since the fields intersect one another at many points for each school generation. A choice is to be made from the possibilities cited above in which primarily the whole educational purpose of the curriculum is the determining factor. It will be the especial function of the free activity groups to advance further and to penetrate more deeply in one direction or another.

*Written Exercises.* Dictations as exercise in understanding and reproduction of rather long, connected passages; written reports in English in connection with selections from English which are read or delivered by the teacher; free reproduction of German or English text and material which has been delivered or read to the pupils; retranslation from a good German translation; free translation of simple original German text into English; translation from English into German; sketches in English of all sorts in connection with the reading and instruction, upon the basis of experiences and events. Eight to ten class exercises during the year. Translations from the English and sketches in connection with the reading and instruction are counted also as exercises in composition and rhetoric.

### ENGLISH AS SECOND MODERN FOREIGN LANGUAGE

#### U III TO U II

*Phonetics.* What was said for English as the first foreign language applies in the *Reformrealgymnasium* as far as the situation permits.

*Reading Material, Oral Exercises, and Vocabulary.* In general, as in the *Realgymnasium,* when English is the first modern foreign language.

*Grammar.* Etymology and syntax, with careful utilization of the pupil's knowledge and insight in grammar which have already been gained in German and French.

Proposal for the distribution of the subject matter in grammar:

In U III: Etymology and elements of syntax in connection with it.

In O III: Position of words; passive; use of tense; infinitive; gerund; participle; mood and progressive forms; use of auxiliary verbs.

In U II: Article; number and case; adjective; pronouns; preposition.

*Written Exercises.* As in the case where English in the *Reformrealgymnasium* is the first foreign language.

#### O II TO O I

The same points of view obtain as in the case where English in the *Reformrealgymnasium* is the first foreign language; however, the essentially smaller total number of hours—23 against 41—is to be considered.

### MATHEMATICS

#### VI AND V

As in the *Gymnasium* and *Realgymnasium.*

#### IV

As in the *Gymnasium* and *Realgymnasium;* in addition elements of literal expression of numbers; calculation of tables by means of formulæ; application of everyday and simple commercial arithmetic, and use of tables. Stock exchange, economic system.

## U III TO O I

As in the *Realgymnasium.*

### NATURAL SCIENCES

#### SURVEY OF COURSES

| | VI | V | IV | U III | O III | U II | | O II | | U I | | O I | | Total |
|---|---|---|---|---|---|---|---|---|---|---|---|---|---|---|
| | | | | | | 1st Sem. | 2nd Sem. | 1st Sem. | 2nd Sem | 1st | 2nd | 1st | 2nd | |
| Physics ... | | | | 2 | 3 | | | | | 3 | 3 | | 3 | 14 |
| Chemistry . | | | | | | 3 | | | | 3 | | 3 | | 9 |
| Biology ... | 2 | 2 | 2 | | | | 3 | 3 | | | | | | 12 |

### PHYSICS

As in the *Gymnasium.*

### CHEMISTRY

As in the *Realgymnasium* with reduction of the individual topics.

### BIOLOGY

### VI TO IV

As in the *Gymnasium.*

### U II

In general, as in *Obersekunda* in the *Gymnasium,* the increased number of hours is used for the purpose of more intensive work in the fields of work indicated there.

## C. *OBERREALSCHULE*

Educational Objective of the *Oberrealschule.*

As all secondary schools, so the *Oberrealschule* seeks to bring its pupils to a historically developed conception of the present and of Germany's cultural problems. The position given to mathematics and natural sciences as the characteristic subjects is in no way to stamp the *Oberrealschule* as a technical school, but to serve to develop in an all-round way the possibilities residing in these subjects for intellectual, philosophical, humanitarian, and historical training and to make these opportunities useful in solving the entire educational problem.

The intensive study of mathematics and natural sciences accustoms the youthful mind to clearness, logical thinking, accuracy and appreciation of the truth, acquaints him with methods of thinking whose application reaches far out beyond the mathematics-natural science field—functional thought and inductive process. The connection between mathematics-natural science and philosophic problems turns the attention to an increasing degree from the individual to the whole and makes it possible to objectify general problems in definite form. Retracing the route along which mathematical and natural science thinking has arrived at its present results, position and methods awakens an appreciation for the earnestness and magnitude of intellectual work and respect for creative personalities. The pupil will become aware of the deeper unity of the human intellect as shown by the enthusiastic exchange and rapid mutual understanding among the various peoples in the fields of mathematics-natural science investigation,—where insight into the special accomplishments of German science and technology will strengthen patriotic feeling, and study of the conditions and technical processes will deepen the social understanding.

In constant integration with the instruction in the core subjects and the modern languages the mathematics-natural science instruction promotes the educational objective of the *Oberrealschule*. The active rôle of mathematics-natural science thinking in the whole structure of modern intellect and its history, and not least of all in classical German cultural epoch from Leibnitz to the period of romanticism, will be emphasized here especially.

From the activity group working in the mathematics-natural science subjects there arise special problems in subject matter and method for the instruction in the core subjects as well as in the modern languages in the *Oberrealschule*. The stronger emphasis upon the present justifies also the freedom given the *Oberrealschule* of electing in place of English or French another modern language, according to the necessities of the various districts and educational situations.

### French as the First Modern Foreign Language

#### VI to U II

In general as in the *Reformrealgymnasium;* in U II reduction of one hour will necessitate a slight restriction of subject matter, while in the choice of reading matter, in written and oral exercises, and finally in grammar in the whole middle section certain variations will arise on account of the nature of the whole course—see Notes on Methods.

### O II TO O I

What was set forth for the middle section above applies in the upper section to an increased degree. In the study of the language the historical factor, as contrasted with the logical-systematic nature of the language, must not occupy such a prominent place; in the reading and in the study of French civilization, the stronger emphasis upon the present time will occasion the omission of many points in their intellectual history. Especially in the selection of the private reading recommended for the various pupils consideration must be shown to the altered point of view. Further, the objectives will have adapted themselves to the smaller number of hours for French in the *Oberrealschule* as contrasted with the *Reformrealgymnasium*—in the upper section, 9 against 12. With these limits, what was said for the *Reformrealgymnasium* applies here.

### FRENCH AS THE SECOND MODERN FOREIGN LANGUAGE

### U III TO U II

In general as in the *Reformrealgymnasium,* with the variation in the selection of reading material occasioned by the whole nature of the instruction.

### O II TO O I

The same points of view hold as in the case where French is the first foreign language, with regard, however, to the essentially smaller total number of hours—22 against 40.

### ENGLISH AS THE FIRST MODERN FOREIGN LANGUAGE

### VI TO U II

In general as in the *Reformrealgymnasium;* in U II the one less hour per week necessitates a slight restriction of subject matter; while in the selection of reading material, in written and oral exercises, and finally in the study of grammar in the whole middle section, certain variations will arise from the whole nature of the instruction—see Notes on Methods.

## O II to O I

What was said for the middle section applies to an increased degree in the upper section. In the reading and in the study of English civilization, the greater emphasis upon the present will occasion the omission of many topics in the history of civilization. Particularly can consideration be given to the change in the point of view in the selection of the private reading recommended to the various pupils.

## English as the Second Modern Foreign Language

## U III to U II

In general as in the *Reformrealgymnasium,* with such modifications of reading material selected as are demanded by the whole character of the instruction.

## U III to U II

The same points of view apply as in the case where English is the first foreign language; however, the essentially smaller total number of hours must be taken into consideration—22 hours as compared to 40.

## Mathematics

## VI to O III

As in the *Realgymnasium.*

## U II

*Algebra.* Powers with negative integral exponents. The function $y = x^n$ for negative integral values of $n$. Calculation with radical expressions. The function $y = \sqrt[n]{x}$. Quadratic equations with one unknown. The function $y = x^2 + ax + b$. Exponential function and the logarithmic function, inversion of a function, reflection of the exponential function. Four-place logarithmic table and the slide rule. Logarithmic calculation. Integral and rational functions.

*Geometry.* Proportionality of straight lines; principles of similarity and application to the circle; harmonic points and rays; the trigonometric functions. Simple calculations of triangles. Representation and calculation of simple solids. Some facts from the history of geometric problems.

*Geometrical Drawing and Measurement.* Plotting of curves in connection with algebra. Graphical interpolation. Approx-

imate construction,—division of the circle, squaring the circle.
Drawing of simple solids in oblique parallel perspective and
horizontal-perpendicular projection.    More exact measurements—Nonius.    Easy exercises in surveying and leveling.

## O II

*Algebra.*    Arithmetic progressions of the first order and geometric progressions.    The infinite geometric progression.    Compound interest and annuities with illustrations from business
life.    Binomial theorem for positive integral exponents.    Organization of the number system from the positive integral
number to the complex number; the fundamental operations
with complex numbers; Moivrian principle; binomial equations.
Derivation of integral and rational functions; maximal and
minimal values; points of inflection and stationary tangents of
related curves.    The functions sin $x$ and cos $x$ and their derivatives.

*Geometry.*    Straight lines and planes in space; continuation
of the calculation of solids.    Goniometry.    Continuation of the
calculation of triangles and rectangles.

*Geometrical Drawing and Measurement.*    Plotting of curves
in connection with algebra.    Horizontal and perpendicular projection.    Continued exercises in surveying and leveling.

## I

*Algebra.*    Fundamental principles of the theory of probability.
The theory of equations, especially approximate solutions; the
solution of simple systems of quadratic equations with two unknowns.    Some transcendental functions and their derivations,
—the trigonometric and the cyclometric functions, the logarithmic and exponential functions.    Objective treatment of
law of averages in connection with approximations and
calculation of error.    Convergence and divergence of infinite
series.    The binomial theorem.    The development of transcendental functions in power series and their application to the
calculation of trigonometric values, logarithms, and of the numbers $\varepsilon$ and $\pi$.    Simplest cases of integration applied to computation of curves, areas, and volumes.    Survey of the development
of the number concept and the concept of function.    Simple
illustrations by means of functions of complex variables.

*Geometry.*    Spherical trigonometry; mathematical geography
and astronomy.    Analytical geometry of straight lines and the
circle.    Plane sections through the cylinder and cone, in connection with the locus definition of the conic sections,—Dandelinian spheres.    Elementary geometrical and analytical treatment of conic sections.    The conic sections as perspective representation of the circle.    Pascal's and Brianchon's laws.

*Geometrical Drawing and Measurement.* Plotting of curves in connection with algebra and geometry, especially approximate constructions of conic sections. Representation of parts of the spherical surface. Fundamental principles of central perspective and shadows and simple applications. Measurements and calculations from mathematical geography and astronomy. Survey from historical and philosophical points of view.

## NATURAL SCIENCE

### SURVEY OF COURSES

| | VI | V | IV | U III | O III | U II | | O II | U I | | O I | | Total |
|---|---|---|---|---|---|---|---|---|---|---|---|---|---|
| | | | | | | 1st Sem. | 2nd Sem. | | 1st | 2nd | 1st | 2nd | |
| Physics ... | | | | 2 | 3 | 3 | | 3 | 3 | | 3 | | 17 |
| Chemistry . | | | | | | | 3 | 3 | | 3 | | 3 | 12 |
| Biology ... | 2 | 2 | 2 | | | | 3 | | 3 | | 3 | | 15 |

## PHYSICS

### U III TO U II

As in the lower section of physics in the *Realgymnasium,* with additional work and accompanying pupil exercises.

### O II

Principles of heat with applications to meteorology. Magnetism and electricity with special emphasis upon the newer theories and applications.

### I

Theory of motion. Principle of the conservation of energy. Mechanics of heavenly bodies. Principles of sound and light. Additional work and summary.

## CHEMISTRY

### U II

As in the *Gymnasium* with more intensive study from the physicochemical side and additonal work in a biochemical direction. Correlated practical exercises.

### O II

Introduction to quantitative relationships in chemical changes. Atomic theory and its historical development. Intensive study of chemical symbols. Valence. Mineralogical and geological studies in connection with their chemical compounds. Technical processes which are important for economic life, such as the utilization of coal, production of sulphuric acid, utilization of nitrogen from the air, extraction of iron; glass, clay products, cement, porcelain, depending upon local conditions.

## I

Development of the various fields. Characteristics of families of elements. Survey of the periodic system. Theory of ionization and dissociation. Structure and characteristics of the organic compounds which are most important for technology and economic life and for national food supply and public health.

### BIOLOGY

#### VI TO IV

As in the *Gymnasium*.

#### U II

As in O II of the *Gymnasium*, with the addition of the work of U II of the *Reformrealgymnasium*.

#### U I

As in O II of the *Realgymnasium*.

#### O I

Development of the knowledge acquired in U II of plant and animal physiology by comparative observation concerning mechanical structure, assimilation of food,—in connection with chemistry,—growth, reproduction, sensitiveness and movements.

In connection with a survey of the evolution of the earth and its inhabitants, the development of an appreciation for the scientific basis of evolution.

## Girls' Schools

*Educational Objective of the Girls' Schools.* Fundamentally the instructional objective and courses of study of the corresponding schools for boys apply with reference to the various types of schools for girls. A special educational objective can scarcely be set up for the *Lyzeum*. It remains the basis of all secondary schools for girls. The *Oberlyzeum* as the modern language school fulfills essentially the educational function of the *Realgymnasium*.

Again, the girls are to be educated to a more objective attitude of mind through an introduction to scientific work, and they are to comprehend the German civilization which has arisen from contact and interchange with the other western civilizations. Finally, they are to be prepared for university entrance by the method of work employed throughout all of the instruction.

Within the limits of the common educational objective of the higher school, however, the special characteristics and life purposes of girls must receive special consideration. They must learn to recognize that they are destined some day to work as women of education and solid moral character in the further development of civilization, either in the family, in a vocation, or in some other place in the interests of general welfare. Therefore the school must afford them primarily an education which yields its value by setting, as its objective, intellectual maturity as well as fitness for life. The cultivation of art and technical courses and greater emphasis upon the core subjects in the *Oberlyzeum* are to aid in the accomplishment of the special problems of these schools.

In the selection of subject matter, primarily in the core subjects, those periods of time are to be studied chiefly in which woman has been one of the outstanding factors in civilization. Problems of women are discussed in the German and foreign language reading. The legal position of woman in the family, in society, and in the state is to be made clear, with historical illustrations as a basis. It is, however, always to be kept in mind that it is not so much the subject matter itself as its presentation and assimilation that determine the success of the instruction. The finer mutual relationships that exist between teachers and pupils cannot at all be fixed by the course of study.

In view of the very early receptivity of girls for instruction concerning moral, ethical, and religious problems, it is the duty of the teachers so to clarify that which has been sensed through the emotions that points of view develop therefrom which will become the basis of moral conduct.

Provision is made by the organization of U IIb of the *Lyzeum*, of the *Frauenschule*, and of courses connected with these schools for the special educational needs of those girls whose inclination and endowment are directly bent toward activities exclusively of interest to women.

## A. LYZEUM

### French or English as the First Modern Foreign Language

In general as in the *Oberrealschule* from VI to U II. There are, however, only 27 hours available as compared to 31 hours.

In the lower section, in VI and in V, approximately the same work is to be covered for the reasons set forth in the case of the *Oberlyzeum*,—see page 546. Since the first observational material is to be provided by the nearer and more remote environment of the pupils, there is no objection to the use of a uniform elementary book for boys' and girls' schools. Each teacher will be able easily to provide for special cases.

In classes IV, U III, O III, and U II, heed must be given to the smaller number of hours by a most rigorous limitation of exercises and subject matter. However, neither the thorough assimilation of the language forms, nor the demands of the reading content must be lessened. Also the girls in U II must read at least a work from the classical French literature or a lighter Shakespearean drama. In U IIb it will suffice to put time upon good modern reading matter in which skill in quick comprehension of the text is especially sought for.

### French or English as the Second Modern Foreign Language

In general as in the *Oberrealschule*, VI to U II. Total number of hours, 12 as compared to 13 hours.

### Mathematics

### VI

*Arithmetic.* The four fundamental operations with whole abstract numbers, and with simple and compound denominate numbers. The German measures, weights, and coins, and applications. Exercises in writing decimals and in the simplest decimal calculations. Simple exercises in proportion. Applications to housekeeping. Objective treatment of simple geometric forms.

## V

*Arithmetic.* Continuation of the exercises with denominate-decimal numbers. Divisibility of numbers. The four fundamental operations with common fractions. Objective representation of numbers by means of lines and surfaces. Solution of simple problems from proportion by solving for unity or a common measure. Application to community financial problems. Further study of geometric forms.

## IV

*Arithmetic.* The four fundamental operations with decimal fractions; changing from common fractions to decimal fractions and vice versa. Short cuts in calculation. Simplest cases of percentage, discount, and interest and other problems from daily life with application to simple and compound proportion. Representation of number series by means of lines and surfaces. Summary of problems which have been solved with the use of letters instead of concrete numbers. Arithmetic calculation of prepared tables, especially the calculation of averages and ratios. Application to financial problems of the state and country.

*Geometry.* Concrete development of fundamental geometric principles. Principles of straight lines and angles. Sides and angles of the triangle. Simplest construction of triangles. Principles of congruency. Geometrical problems.

*Geometrical Drawing and Measurement.* Exercises in the correct use of the rule, scale, protractor, compass and drawing triangle. Execution of simple constructions. Measurement of lines and angles.

## U III

*Algebra.* Review and further study of the subject treated in arithmetic with introduction to the use of letters for figures. Calculation from tables by means of formulæ. The four fundamental operations with absolute and relative, integral and fractional numbers. Objective representation on the number frame. Simple equations of the first degree in connection with arithmetical operations in rational numbers. Graphic representation of functions presented in tabular form. The linear function. Plotting of curves. Continuation of exercises in arithmetic calculations in connection with business problems.

*Geometry.* Continuation of the theory of triangles. Continuation of construction of triangles. Principles of the quadrilateral, especially the parallelogram and trapezium. Introduction to study of the circle,—chords and arcs on the circle. Solid bodies.

*Geometrical Drawing and Measurement.* Exercises in accurate and exact execution of constructions. Measurement of lines and angles. Exercises in estimating measurements out-of-doors.

## O III

*Algebra.* Equations of the first degree with one or more unknowns; simple applications especially from practical life. Elements of graphical representations on the basis of empirical functions. Representation of linear functions and their value in solution of equations. The function $y = m.x$,—proportionality factor. Powers with positive integral exponents. Representation of the function $y = x^n$ for positive integral values of $n$. Extraction of square roots.

*Geometry.* Continuation of the study of the circle. Calculation and comparison of areas. Simple solids.

*Geometrical Drawing and Measurements.* Plotting of curves in connection with algebra. Graphical determination of area by means of millimeter paper and other processes. Measurement of lines, angles, and surfaces. Also such measurements out-of-doors.

## U II

*Algebra.* Principles of powers and roots, with graphical representations of the functions $y = x^n$ and $y = \sqrt[n]{x}$. Calculations with radical expressions. Continued exercises in practical arithmetic, especially in short cuts. Quadratic equations with one unknown. The function $y = x^2 + ax + b$.

*Geometry.* Proportional lines. Principles of similarity. Applications to the circle; harmonic points and rays. Circumference and area of the circle. Representation and calculation of the simplest solids. Introduction to the trigonometric treatment of the right angle triangle by means of practical exercises; by means of graphically projected tables of some values of functions.

*Geometrical Drawing and Measurement.* Plotting of curves in connection with algebra. Approximate constructions,—circle. Exact measurements,—Nonius. Surveying exercises in connection with the study of similarity. Correct representation of solid figures.

## U IIb

*Arithmetic.* Problems from household and political economy with elementary explanations. Business arithmetic.

*Algebra.* Simple equations of the second degree with one unknown. Graphic solution of the quadratic equation. Reviews.

*Geometry.* The regular polygon. Measurement of the circumference and area of the circle. Measurement of volume.

## NATURAL SCIENCES

### SURVEY OF COURSES

| | VI | V | IV | U III | O III | U II | | Total |
|---|---|---|---|---|---|---|---|---|
| | | | | | | 1st Sem. | 2nd Sem. | |
| Physics ........... | | | | 2 | 3 | | | 5 |
| Chemistry ......... | | | | | | 3 | | 3 |
| Biology ........... | 2 | 2 | 2 | | | | 3 | 9 |

## PHYSICS

### U III

Fundamental physical principles. Simplest phenomena of the principle of equilibrium, of solid, fluid, and gaseous bodies, and also of the principles of heat, without following any definite order.

### O III

Selected exercises from study of sound and light and also of magnetism and electricity.

## CHEMISTRY

### U II

Development of fundamental principles of chemistry—decomposition of matter elements, chemical process, structure of matter, mixtures and chemical compounds—by means of investigation of natural bodies and observation of process in nature and in natural life. The following topics are adapted to this study: Water, air, coal, and carbonic acid, sulphur, useful metals, lime, petroleum, oxidation including burning, heating, breathing, reduction, assimilation, acid, base salt. Study of molecular weights.

## BIOLOGY

### VI TO IV

As in the *Gymnasium*.

### U II

In general as in O II in the *Gymnasium*, with the additional topic: the growing human body, its care and protection.

## *B. OBERLYZEUM*

### French or English as the First Modern Foreign Language

The objective of the *Oberrealschule* applies here. The small difference in the number of hours, 39 as compared to 40, will be taken care of by the greater ease which girls are accustomed to show in acquisition of a foreign tongue and in oral exercises. While the course of instruction and the objective are the same as in the boys' school, attention is to be paid in the selection of material to the interest of women as far as is necessary. This holds especially in the selection of the reading material which has to do with historical points of view. Thus, for example, in Shakespeare, instead of the historical works, one of his comedies would better be chosen, and from Molière the *Femmes Savantes* would be selected before the others, since they represent the turning point of the history of the education of women.

See the corresponding regulations in the *Lyzeum* for the lower and middle sections.

In the upper section twelve hours are available as compared to nine in *Oberrealschule*. The excess will be of particular advantage in a wider selection of reading which makes possible for the more mature students a more exhaustive type of instruction in the history of civilization. Likewise language study basing its work upon knowledge and skill previously acquired will go deeper, and especially will it enable the pupil to carry a systematic comparison with the mother tongue and the second foreign language.

### French or English as the Second Modern Foreign Language

In general as in the *Oberrealschule,* with the total number of hours 24 as compared to 22 hours.

### Mathematics

#### VI to U II

As in the *Lyzeum.*

#### O II

*Algebra.* Exponential function and logarithmic function. Four-place logarithmic table and slide rule; logarithmic calculation. Arithmetic progression of the first order and geometric progression. Compound interest and annuities with illustrations from business life. Binomial theorem for positive integral exponents. Structure of the number system from the positive integral to the complex number; the complex number; binomial equations.

*Geometry.* The trigonometric functions. Simple calculations of triangles. Goniometry. The principle of the periodic function. Straight lines and planes and space. Continuation of the calculation and representation of solids.

*Geometrical Drawing and Measurement.* Plotting of curves in connection with algebra. Representation of simple solids in oblique parallel projection and in horizontal perpendicular projection. Simple exercises in surveying and leveling.

## I

*Algebra.* The theory of equations, especially approximate solutions. The integral and the rational functions and their derivatives; maximal and minimal values. The solutions of simple systems of equations of the second degree with two unknowns. Some transcendental functions and their derivatives,—the trigonometric, cyclometric, logarithmic, and exponential functions. Approximate calculation of transcendental function by means of the development of a series. Simplest cases of integration with application to the calculation of curves, areas, and volumes.

*Geometry.* Necessary facts from spherical trigonometry which are of importance for mathematical geography and astronomy. Coördinates. Review of conic sections.

*Geometrical Drawing and Measurement.* Drawings from conic sections. Central perspective. Graphic representation of spherical surfaces. Skeleton map. Simple astronomical observations with exercises in measurement and calculation.

Survey from historical and philosophical points of view.

### NATURAL SCIENCES

#### SURVEY OF COURSES

| | VI | V | IV | U III | O III | U II 1st Sem. | U II 2nd Sem. | O II 1st Sem. | O II 2nd Sem. | U I 1st Sem. | U I 2nd Sem. | O I 1st Sem. | O I 2nd Sem. | Total |
|---|---|---|---|---|---|---|---|---|---|---|---|---|---|---|
| Physics ... | | | | 2 | 3 | | | | | 3 | 3 | | 3 | 14 |
| Chemistry . | | | | | | 3 | | | | | | | | 6 |
| Biology ... | 2 | 2 | 2 | | | | 3 | 3 | | | | 3 | | 15 |

### PHYSICS

#### U III and O III

As in the *Lyzeum.*

#### O II

Heat. Thermometry and calorimetry. Equation of condition of gases; absolute temperature. The changes of the form species (types of strain). Work value of the heat unit. Kinetic theory of heat. Caloric machines. Mineralogy.

## U I

Theory of sound. Vibrating strings. Color tone. Transmission of sound on the wave theory. Breaking and interference of sound. Vibratory columns of air. The human ear and its functions.

Theory of light. Refraction of light and its application in optical instruments. Wave theory in light. Spectrum and spectrum analysis. Transmission of light. Interference. Thermal and chemical effects of light rays.

## O I

Theory of electricity. The basic phenomena of static electricity and the principles of electrical mass, potentiality, capacity, electric field of force, field strength, lines of force. Tension and electric current. Transformation of current energy into heat and chemical energy. Induction. Electrical machines. Electric rays. Electric oscillation.

Mechanics. Selected portions from the theory of motion. Cosmic mechanics. Physical characteristics of planets. Summarizing survey of the whole field of physical phenomena. The physical universe.

### CHEMISTRY

#### U II

As in the *Lyzeum.*

#### U I

Supplementation and further study of the work of U II. Additional work with attention paid to the subject matter of great importance on account of its appearance in nature and its economic value. Work from organic chemistry with preference given to the subject matter and phenomena which are of greatest value for life processes and nutrition as well as for agriculture and industry.

### BIOLOGY

#### VI to IV

As in the *Lyzeum.*

#### O II

As in O II of the *Realgymnasium.*

## O I

As in the *Oberrealschule*.

## C. OBERLYZEUM

## MODELED ON THE OBERREALSCHULE

FRENCH OR ENGLISH AS THE FIRST MODERN FOREIGN LANGUAGE

In general as in the *Oberrealschule,* keeping in mind, however, the smaller total number of hours, 36 as compared with 40 hours.

FRENCH OR ENGLISH AS THE SECOND MODERN FOREIGN LANGUAGE

In general as in the *Oberrealschule;* the total number of hours is 21 as compared with 22.

### MATHEMATICS

### VI to U II

As in the *Lyzeum*.

### O II

Exponential and logarithmic functions. Four-place logarithmic table and slide rule. Logarithmic calculation. Arithmetical progressions of the first order and geometrical progressions. Compound interest and annuities with applications in business life. Binomial theorem for positive integral exponents. Structure of the number system from the positive integral number to the complex number; the fundamental operations with complex numbers; Moivrian law; binomial equations; the integral function and its derivation; maximal and minimal values; points of inflection and stationary tangents of related curves. The functions sin $x$ and cos $x$ and their derivatives.

*Geometry.* The trigonometric functions. Easy calculations of triangles. Goniometry. Straight lines and planes in space. Continuity of calculation of solids.

*Geometrical Drawing and Measurement.* Plotting of curves in connection with arithmetic. Cross and vertical sections. Exercises in surveying and leveling.

### I

*Algebra.* Fundamental principles of the theory of probability. The theory of equations, especially approximate solutions. The rational function and its derivation. The solution of simple systems of quadratic equations with two unknowns. Some transcendental functions and their derivatives,—the trigonometric, cyclometric, logarithmic, and exponential functions. Approximation of transcendental functions by development of a series. Simplest cases of integrations with application to calculation of curves, areas, and volumes. Survey of the development of the number and function concept.

*Geometry.* Spherical trigonometry. Mathematical geography and astronomy. Analytical geometry of straight lines and of the circle. Plane sections through the cylinder and the cone, in connection with the locus of conic sections—Dandelinian spheres. Elementary geometrical and analytical treatment of conic sections.

*Geometrical Drawing and Measurement.* Plotting of curves in connection with algebra and geometry, especially approximate construction of conic sections. Representation of sections of the spherical surface,—cartography. Central perspective and theory of shadows with simple applications. Measurement and calculations from mathematical geography and astronomy. Survey from historical and philosophical points of view.

## NATURAL SCIENCES

### SURVEY OF COURSES

| | VI | V | IV | U III | O III | U II | | O II | U I | | O I | | Total |
| --- | --- | --- | --- | --- | --- | --- | --- | --- | --- | --- | --- | --- | --- |
| | | | | | | 1st Sem. | 2nd Sem. | | 1st Sem. | 2nd Sem. | 1st Sem. | 2nd Sem. | |
| Physics ... | | | | 2 | 3 | | | 2 | 2 | | | 3 | 12 |
| Chemistry . | | | | | | 3 | | 2 | | 3 | | 2 | 10 |
| Biology ... | 2 | 2 | 2 | | | | 3 | | 3 | | 2 | | 14 |

## PHYSICS

### U III to O III

As in the *Lyzeum.*

### O II to O I

As in the *Oberlyzeum,* with the incorporation of exercises for the pupils and further work especially in electricity and mechanics.

## CHEMISTRY

### U II

As in the *Lyzeum.*

### O II to O I

As in the *Oberrealschule,* with limitation of some of the topics.

## BIOLOGY

### VI to IV and U II

As in the *Lyzeum*.

### I

As in the *Oberrealschule* with such limitation of the subject matter as is required by the smaller number of hours.

## D. REALGYMNASIAL STUDIENANSTALT

### LATIN

### U III to O III

The regulations for the *Gymnasial Studienanstalt* apply here as far as the situation permits. The smaller number of hours will permit only in exceptional cases connected reading, aside from Phædrus.

### U II

*Grammar.* See the regulation for U II of the *Gymnasial Studienanstalt.* In place of the translations into the Latin there appear from this stage on systematic exercises in translation from the foreign tongue.

*Reading.* Selections from Ovid's *Metamorphoses, Fasti,* and other elegaic poetry. Selections from the ancient history of Livy or Sallust's *Bellum Catilinæ,* as well as one of Cicero's orations against Catiline in translation or selections from Pliny's *Letters.*

*Written Class Exercises.* See the regulations for the *Realgymnasium.*

### O II to O I

The regulations for the *Realgymnasium* apply here as far as the situation permits.

### FRENCH AS THE FIRST MODERN FOREIGN LANGUAGE

Lower and middle section as in the *Lyzeum;* still the Latin being begun in U III will make possible a general increase in the amount of work. For the upper section, of course, the course and general purpose of the instruction will apply as in the *Reformrealgymnasium.* However, regard is to be paid in the selection of subject matter to the much smaller number of hours, 36 as compared with 44.

### FRENCH AS THE SECOND MODERN FOREIGN LANGUAGE

In the *Untersekunda* etymology, which is to be finished in *Obersekunda.* Also, syntax, which is to be expanded in I and which is to be intensified through historical and comparative study. In general, the same points of view obtain for the reading and the study of the culture (of France) as in the *Reformrealgymnasium* for boys. However, a decided limitation of subject matter is required by the essentially smaller number of hours, 16 as compared with 26, as well as a corresponding lessening in efficiency demanded.

### ENGLISH AS THE FIRST MODERN FOREIGN LANGUAGE

In the lower and middle sections as in the *Oberlyzeum* with a course like that of the *Oberrealschule*. The course of the *Reformrealgymnasium* applies to the upper section, however, keeping in mind the smaller total number of hours, 36 as compared with 41.

### ENGLISH AS THE SECOND MODERN FOREIGN LANGUAGE

In U II there is etymology, which is finished in O II. In O II there is syntax, which is to be expanded in I and intensified by historical and comparative study. In general, the same points of view apply for the reading and the study of the English culture as in the *Reformrealgymnasium* for boys. However, regard must be paid to the smaller total number of hours, 16 as compared with 23.

### MATHEMATICS

### VI to U II

As in the *Lyzeum*.

### O II to O I

As in the *Oberlyzeum*.

### NATURAL SCIENCES

#### SURVEY OF COURSES

| | VI | V | IV | U III | O III | U II 1st Sem. | U II 2nd Sem. | O II 1st Sem. | O II 2nd Sem. | U I 1st Sem. | U I 2nd Sem. | O I 1st Sem. | O I 2nd Sem. | Total |
|---|---|---|---|---|---|---|---|---|---|---|---|---|---|---|
| Physics .. | | | | 2 | 2 | 2 | | | 3 | 3 | 3 | | 3 | 13 |
| Chemistry | | | | | | | | 3 | | | | | | 8 |
| Biology .. | 2 | 2 | 2 | | | | 2 | | | | | 3 | | 11 |

### PHYSICS

### U III and O III

As in the *Lyzeum* with less of certain topics.

O II to O I

As in the *Oberlyzeum.*

## CHEMISTRY

### U II

As in the *Lyzeum* with limitation on the subject matter.

### O II

As in the *Oberlyzeum,* which is organized as the *Oberreal-schule,* with limitation of subject matter.

### U I

Study of organic chemistry with emphasis upon subject matter and phenomena which are of greatest importance for life processes and nutrition, and also for agriculture and industry.

## BIOLOGY

### VI to IV and U II

As in the *Lyzeum.*

### O I

As in the *Oberrealschule.*

## E. GYMNASIAL STUDIENANSTALT

### LATIN

#### U III

The following topics based on a reasonable application of the suggestions given for beginning Latin instruction in the *Gymnasium:* The so-called regular etymology of nouns, pronouns, and verbs and the most important rules of syntax; acquisition of a first vocabulary, but in systematic sequences. All of this is to be carried on always in connection with the modern foreign language with which the pupils are acquainted. The reading book in its selection of material is of service to the German and history instruction of the class. Oral exercises and written work as in the corresponding class of the *Gymnasium.*

#### O III

*Grammar.* Conclusion of the work in etymology in accordance with the same principles as in U III. In connection with the school grammar, systematic study of the sentence and of word forms, which is limited to the essential. Review and further development of the vocabulary and root verb forms previously acquired.

*Oral and Written Exercises.* As in the corresponding class of the *Gymnasium.*

*Reading.* Selections from Phædrus, with some attention to other fables; memorizing of a Latin fable. Selections from Curtius Rufus or from Cæsar's *Bellum Gallicum*, primarily Book VII, as preparation for the history work of U II.

## U II

*Grammar.* Review and final advanced work in syntax, also in comparison with German syntax and the syntax of the modern foreign language with which the girls are acquainted. Review of the vocabulary and root verb forms previously drilled upon. Oral and written translation and other language exercises as in O III.

*Reading.* The principles set up for U II of the *Gymnasium* apply here. Additional importance is attached to the reading of Ovid.

*Written Class Exercises.* See the regulations for the *Gymnasium.*

## O II to I

The regulations of the *Gymnasium* apply here.

## GREEK

## U II

The following topics based on a reasonable application of the suggestions given for beginning Greek instruction in the *Gymnasium:* Etymology down to and including the verbs in *M;* the fundamental rules of syntax.

The instruction can also be based upon a reading and exercise book which offers very early original Greek sentences and passages, such as maxims, apophthegms, fables, and easy tales, or based upon Homer's *Odyssey* or Xenophon's *Anabasis.* The instruction endeavors to be of assistance at the same time to the work in ancient history.

Abundant work in copying, dictation, exercises in the recognition of form, translations to be put in the exercise book. About every four weeks a translation into the Greek as a class exercise.

## O II

*Grammar.* Conclusion of the work in etymology. Finish drill upon root verb forms, the knowledge of which is necessary for the reading. Systematic study of syntax; which begins always with the expression in the foreign language and with constant comparison with methods of expression in the languages which are known to the children.

*Reading.* As early conclusion as possible of reading the *Anabasis*, in case it is chosen in U II. Otherwise the regulations which are set forth for O II of the *Gymnasium* apply. The reading of the *Odyssey* is appropriately concluded in this year, while the reading of the *Apology* can be reserved for U I.

*Written Class Exercises.* About every four weeks a translation at first into the Greek, then from the Greek. These are to be done with opportune grammatical explanation.

## I

*Grammar.* According to need review and drill upon etymology. Further study of syntax.

Otherwise the regulations given for the *Gymnasium* apply. Especial importance is assigned in the reading of Greek tragedy to the dramas, *Antigone, Electra, Hippolytus, Medea, Alcestis.* The reading of Menander is also recommended.

### FRENCH

In the lower and middle sections in general as in the *Lyzeum*. The smaller number of hours, 24 as compared with 27, is to be counterbalanced by the Latin introduced in U III. The same points of view apply for the upper section as in the *Gymnasium;* however, the essentially greater total number of hours, 30 as compared with 15, makes possible a considerable raising of the instructional objectives, especially as regards the range and the selection in the reading.

### ENGLISH

In the lower and middle sections as in the *Lyzeum*. The same points of view apply in the upper section as in the *Gymnasium;* however, the essentially higher total number of hours, 30 as compared to 15, makes possible a considerable raising of the instructional objectives, especially as regards the range and the selection in the reading.

### MATHEMATICS

#### VI to O III

As in the *Lyzeum.*

#### U II

*Algebra.* Theory of powers and roots. Calculation of radical expressions. Quadratic equations with one unknown.

*Geometry.* Proportionality of lines; theory of similarity; their applications to the circle. Circumference and area of the circle. Calculation and representation of the simplest solids. Introduction to the trigonometric treatment of right-angled triangles on the basis of practical problems which make use of graphically constructed tables of some functional values.

*Geometrical Drawing and Measurement.* Plotting of curves in connection with arithmetic. Approximate construction,— circle. Accurate representation of solid figures. Easy exercises in surveying in connection with the theory of similarity.

## O II

*Algebra.* Exponential and logarithmic functions. Four-place logarithmic table and slide rule; logarithmic calculation. Organization of the number system from the positive integral number to the complex number; the four fundamental operations with complex numbers.

*Geometry.* The trigonometric functions. Simple computation of triangles. Goniometry. Straight lines and planes in space. Continuation of the computation and representation of solids.

*Geometric Drawing and Measurement.* Plotting of curves in connection with algebra. Vertical and cross sections. Easy exercises in surveying and leveling.

## I

*Algebra.* Arithmetic progressions of the first order, and geometric progressions. Compound interest and annuities with illustrations from business life. Binomial theorem for positive integral exponents. Elements of infinitesimal computation,— definition of differential quotients; their geometric and physical importance—and its application to the treatment of rational and trigonometric functions, especially for the calculation of maximal and minimal values, points of inflection and stationary tangents and the like. Simplest calculation of areas and volumes with the aid of integration, for example, sphere, paraboloid, and the like.

*Geometry.* Fundamental principles of spherical trigonometry, —principle of the sine and cosecant; applications to mathematical geography and astronomy. The geometry of coördinates. Summary study of conic sections.

*Geometrical Drawing and Measurement.* Drawings from conic sections. Central perspective. Representation of sections of the spherical surface,—cartography. Simple astronomical observations with exercises in measurement and computation.

Survey from historical and philosophical points of view.

## NATURAL SCIENCES

### SURVEY OF COURSES

| | VI | V | IV | U III | O III | U II | | O II | U I | | O I | | Total |
| | | | | | | 1st Sem. | 2nd Sem. | | 1st Sem. | 2nd Sem. | 1st Sem. | 2nd Sem. | |
|---|---|---|---|---|---|---|---|---|---|---|---|---|---|
| Physics ... | | | | 2 | 2 | | | 2 | | 2 | | 2 | 10 |
| Chemistry . | | 2 | | | | 2 | | | 2 | | | | 4 |
| Biology ... | 2 | 2 | 2 | | | | 2 | | | | 2 | | 10 |

## PHYSICS

### U III and O III

As in the Realgymnasial *Studienanstalt*.

### O II to O I

As in the *Oberlyzeum*, with postponement of the theory of sound to O II and the theory of static electricity to U I. The whole subject matter is to be shortened, owing to the smaller number of hours.

## CHEMISTRY

### U II

As in the *Lyzeum*, with selections.

### U I

As in the *Oberlyzeum*, with selections.

## BIOLOGY

### VI to IV and U II

As in the *Lyzeum*.

### O I

As in the *Oberrealschule*, with less subject matter, as neces sitated by a smaller number of hours,

## Section IV

## The Deutsche Oberschule and Aufbauschule

### I

### MEMORANDUM CONCERNING THE FUNDAMENTAL *DEUTSCHE OBERSCHULE* [1]

The idea of the *Deutsche Oberschule,* born in the souls of great thinkers, scholars, and educators of our German past, was strengthened first in the days of hope of victory, and then so intensified in the days of defeat that the creation of *Deutsche Oberschulen* became a cultural and political necessity. Rudolf Hildebrand, who has thought through this idea most deeply and expressed it most clearly, recognized therein the great principle of the life of nations,—that they must seek themselves anew if they wish to be born again. For such a self-regeneration from one's own strength and thought into new life is from time to time an ever-recurring duty of the highest import, a great life principle for individuals as well as for nations.

In opposition to the depreciation of German culture by our enemies during the War, parrying the cultural propaganda of foreign peoples on our frontiers, in the feeling of a community of culture with Germans in the lost states and in foreign countries, and finally in conscious rejection of the point of view that our culture is already sterile for the world and has lost its inner spiritual force, faith in the cultural force and in the vitality of German culture has become so strong in important classes of society that it is justified in demanding that it be developed in a special form of secondary school.

The fullness and diversity of German life afford room for different types of schools, which in their variety are still all German. The term *Deutsche* in this new form of school will be no criterion of value but will only emphasize its chief subject

[1] *Denkschrift vom 18. 2. 1922—U II N 11 II, Zentralblatt, Heft 6, Beilage.*

of instruction.  Therein it comprehends under *Deutsche* a group of subjects which fuse into a unity: religion, German, philosophy, history, geography, and art.  It places all of the subjects of instruction, however, at the service of the central notion, so that it develops in fact a wholly new form of school.  Its special nature allows the *Deutsche Oberschule*, more than the other schools, to consider itself as the natural continuation of the *Volksschule*.  This great thought of the inner cultural unity with the *Volksschule* finds its characteristic expression in the *Aufbauschule;* for here it will be recognized that the *Volksschule,* particularly in the country and in the small town, trains pupils who, through uninterrupted contact with the home and the community and saturated with the cultural values of the *Volksschule*, can henceforth with accumulated strength secure in six years a training equal in value and recognition to the other types of schools.  In this manner the gifted children in the village and small town will be able to secure a higher type of training without prematurely breaking away from their early environment and its influence.  But, more than this, the parents with elementary school training, because of the inner relationship of the *Deutsche Oberschule* with the *Volksschule,* will no longer have the painful impression that their children are being alienated from them at the secondary school, and that through their education they are being lost to their social group.  The *Deutsche Oberschulen* and the *Aufbauschulen* are rather in the ideal sense higher elementary schools; they are the bridges over that disastrous chasm which for centuries lay between national education and secondary education, which, as Fichte complained, separated the educated from the uneducated classes.

The recognition of the *Deutsche Oberschulen* and the *Aufbauschulen* as of equal rank with other secondary schools rests upon faith in the educative value of our own culture.  Only by very earnest work will this newest school type be able to prove its right to existence.  At the same time it must not take lightly the fears and the objections of very sincere friends of the fatherland and of educators.  It must demand that it be allowed really to develop itself fully in a manner corresponding to its special nature and that doubt as to its educative value should not lead to the point of forcing on it again other educational ideals and turning it into a sort of degenerate form of *Oberreal-schule.*

A school which places the culture of its own people consciously in the center of its educational activity will only conceive its own culture fundamentally, if it makes clear its independence of foreign influences, if it makes clear the formative forces of other cultures in our intellectual history, and if at the same time it is just toward the humanistic contributions of the community of nations. The *Deutsche Oberschule* differentiates itself herewith from the other types of schools materially in that it considers these interrelationships from the German development outward. It has for the same facts a fundamentally different point of view. From foreign sources only that is important for this school which has become the content and formative principle of the German. From this point of view, it considers the whole of German life and surveys all fields of culture. It extends the formerly customary materials of Germanism to a "natural history" of German society in the various periods of its development. It will consider carefully all important life phenomena of the German people, its law and its economy, forms of society, social classes, the state's civic sense and the relation of the individual to life situations surrounding him in their inseparable unity and in their developmental associations. But it must not overlook the guiding principle of Wundt that only philosophy, as it brings out the impulses which surge in the soul of a people to self-consciousness, will give a composite picture of the spiritual values of national culture, such as the individual fields afford merely in diffuse rays. Therefore instruction in philosophy, which for the decisive periods of German intellectual history shows the great thinkers as leaders of their time, becomes of essential importance for the *Deutsche Oberschule.* Hence it will be essential for this curriculum to break down the barriers that were formerly erected by subject-instruction between the subjects dealing with German culture, so that the educational objectives set for each class will be so treated that the indissoluble unity of life's activities will remain assured. Here the distribution to the various subjects of the mass of materials inherently united will be one of the most important tasks of the class teacher. Such an extended *German* instruction, as ultimately will have to give to history richer possibilities of development, will then really, as Paulsen hoped, be adapted to assume the position which Latin has held for centuries, that is, of bearing the chief burden for the literary-æsthetic, for the stylistic-rhetorical, for the dialectic-philosophical culture.

Mathematics and natural sciences set up in the *Deutsche Oberschule,* in addition to their technical purposes, tasks of a special nature dealing with a study of things German. Their powerful impulse to German intellectual history, their central position in German philosophy, their transforming and forward-driving ideas must press into the consciousness of the mature pupils so that these sciences become intelligible in the complex of the entire mental life and the importance of these subjects and the industry and technology dependent upon their principles will be recognized in German life of to-day. That finally art and music, the deepest expressions of the German soul, must be cultivated zealously in the *Deutsche Oberschule* needs no special emphasis.

The scholarly character of the Germanistic subjects is not doubted by him who knows the methodical investigations underlying them. To be sure, a superfluous amount of subject matter must be avoided just as must an excess of stimulation and emotional reactions. Here the restful culture in Goethe's sense of the word, deep-rooted in the classical periods of our people, will assert itself against those things which would press their way into the *Deutsche Oberschule,* whether it be erudition of antiquity or the chaotic fullness of the immediate present. Here pedagogical caution will have to protect the *Deutsche Oberschule* against false friends.

Its special position with reference to language instruction is of decisive importance for the *Deutsche Oberschule.* It can finally fully unfold the cultural forces of the German language because of its dialect, conversational speech, and written language, and because also it trains in the Middle High German more than the other schools to a deepened, historical understanding of the language of to-day. Obvious errors in German language instruction of the past shall no longer compete with the course of study of the *Deutsche Oberschule.* Indeed, they are overcome through the labors of German philology, and only because the secondary school did not have time to translate into school practice the facts dealing with the psychology, history, and philosophy of language, the secondary school, as Jacob Grimm already complained, has merely robbed the German language and allowed insipid results to develop. It is, in fact, time that at least in one secondary school German philology be permitted to develop as archæology and the philology of modern foreign languages are able to develop in other schools. It must be honestly granted that in German language instruction much in material and method has not been entirely proved. And yet the other languages are always contending about the right method and will always have something to contend about. In fact, without the lessons of varied, even unfortunate, experiments no subject has yet been able to develop itself. The theoretical principles for scholarly and educative instruction in German are established. The greater part is proved by practice. The value to the wide circles of society of this instruction, which cannot be replaced by any other subject, has become apparent since the time of Rudolf Hildebrand. It is time that the gold of German philology is coined in some special school.

The study of German culture and German language instruction demands a foreign language and a foreign culture as a contrast and a basis of comparison. According to Mommsen, only he is educated who can think and express himself in two languages. Which of the foreign languages and cultures best fulfill this aim in the *Deutsche Oberschule* may remain undecided, except that it must be the language of a people which has in the course of our history strongly influenced us. In the *Deutsche Oberschule* which is organized on the basis of the present, it will best be a modern language. It is certainly a thought worthy of consideration to build up the *Deutsche Oberschule* in closest connection with Anglo-Saxon culture and language, which, fundamentally related to ours but still essentially different, might be able to unfold to a depth not yet reached. Not less worthy of respect, however, are the arguments made for French. The greater span between the German and the Roman character, the contrast between German freedom and French cultivation of form, the greater difference of a modern language which is based upon Latin, argue for the introduction of French, which is also supported by the practical reason of possibilities of transfer to *Reform-* and *Realschulen*.

For the development of its special character the *Deutsche*

*Oberschule* needs only one foreign language, but this, to be sure, developed to a high degree. The introduction of a second foreign language, which appears necessary to many for practical reasons, and to others for the sake of a full equivalence of the *Deutsche Oberschule*, might very easily injure the special character of the *Deutsche Oberschule* if it does not take its place on the periphery of the curriculum. However, in such a place it can indeed be valuable, because it can materially extend the further training of the pupil in his vocation or in his study. If it is a question, therefore, of learning for special needs, then freedom in the choice of this language, which is to be studied receptively, seems desirable in the sense that here the various foreign languages represent the elective subjects. Certainly for many fields of study Latin must not be lacking. Others will not wish to miss English. But indeed Russian, Polish, Spanish, Italian, Danish, and other languages may each be necessary according to the conditions for various schools. The very position of this second foreign language on the margin of the curriculum favors this freedom of election, since the nucleus of the course is not disturbed. If, then, the pupils are able to elect according to special conditions a language especially valuable to them, it may be assumed that they will be able to acquire sufficient training in the language in a smaller number of hours.

Even if it cannot be admitted that this Germanistic group of subjects does not afford by itself training for scholarly thinking, still an influential place is to be assigned to mathematics and natural sciences in the *Deutsche Oberschule*, not only because of their importance for human culture, as has already been mentioned, but also because of their value for abstract thinking and for training the mental faculties. Secure knowledge of facts, independent observation, and investigation in methodical development of principles of activity become the central aim of the natural science instruction. On account of the natural associations of biology with sociology, ethics, physical health, and political economy, the *Deutsche Oberschule* cannot do without biology instruction even up through the highest class.

Wide circles in the German woman's world will see in the *Deutsche Oberschule* the ideal *Mädchenschule*, since this school combines a strong sense of reality and earnest scholarly work without æsthetic sentimentality with the whole range of that

German humanity of which the German woman has always borne the burden.

The curriculum of the *Deutsche Oberschule* for girls will be able to adapt itself to the characteristic developmental curve of girls without lowering the objectives of the school.

In consequence of the close relationship between the *Volksschule* and the *Deutsche Oberschule,* it may be hoped that the *Aufbauschule* will attain the objectives of the *Deutsche Oberschule* in six years, if it accepts after careful examination only really gifted pupils from the *Volksschule.* The *Aufbauschule* will demand of the teachers and pupils the very highest efforts and attainments, but the friends of the German *Volksschule* believe firmly in the possibility of achieving the instructional goals set up within six years' time.

# II

## MEMORANDUM CONCERNING THE *AUFBAUSCHULE*[1]

The *Aufbauschule* builds on the seventh year of the *Volks-schule* a six-year secondary school which leads to the leaving examination (*Reifeprüfung*) and gives the same privileges as the *Deutsche Oberschule* and the *Oberrealschule*. The whole duration of school attendance of its pupils will hereafter cover the same time as in the case of the other secondary schools, that is, thirteen years.

It is to be understood that many experts who consider a nine-year school necessary look upon the *Aufbauschule* with mistrust and fear: with mistrust because they are doubtful about the equivalence of a six-year secondary school; with fear because they are afraid that the new type of school, on account of its greater cheapness, will supplant the old types of nine-year schools.

If the economic motive alone were the deciding factor in the establishment of the *Aufbauschule*, then, indeed, would mistrust and fear be justified.

The economic point of view is, indeed, to-day totally unavoidable. But in reality the idea of the *Aufbauschule* was conceived out of cultural-political purposes. It was recognized that the advancement of gifted children of the village and the small town was restricted and held down through our school system. But advancement out of these valuable classes of society is, in the first place, not so necessary for the future of the children themselves as it is at present of compelling cultural-political necessity for the whole nation.

In the village and small town our people not only possess latent, unused forces, the spring out of which it can ever create anew the pure streams of its national genius, but it possesses here forces of a very different, indeed, of a fundamentally opposite kind from those which are effective in the life of the

[1] See note on p. 558.

large city and which are operative upon the city dweller of all classes.

Sociology and social psychology have clearly recognized and sharply formulated this contrast between the country-born and the city-born. They have designated it as community and society, as organic and mechanical life, as simplicity and sophistication, as custom and convention, as inner connectedness and the mere contiguity of "naked persons," as the faith of the fathers and as the uncurbed freedom of the individual.

This antithesis, which Wundt brought to the formulation of voluntaryism and intellectualism from romanticism and the enlightenment, has made the country-born and the city-born into human types in people of fundamentally different structure, the more the spirit of the large city has disseminated itself among us.

The present demands, however, that these forces of health, of instinctive security, of national life in the village and in the small town come into their own in our higher culture so that the intellectual upper class will not entirely succumb to the spirit of the great city.

But these forces of betterment of our rural classes can develop only in the soul of the child in quiet, silent growth. The children must root themselves deep in the natural and community forms of their environment so they they may grow into instinctively sure motive power and into non-reflective certainty; for these powers develop not in the form of subject matter but only as life forms.

A premature uprooting of these children from the native soil of their community life means, therefore, the breach of a natural development which is dangerous, because the transplanting into the entirely different life of the great city robs them of the benefit of their early childhood without being able to give them in return therefor the different powers of the city child. Such children then easily represent an unsatisfactory middle type that is threatened with degeneration.

Formerly normal preparatory schools and normal schools have rendered these children a beneficial service. Accordingly, there have flowed into the elementary school teaching profession rather than into the other professions the powers of the country-born which have given it that inner association with the people which has made the educative work of the teacher in the village and small town beneficial far beyond the actual work of the school-room. Justice demands at this moment, when these schools are being abolished, to acknowledge gratefully this effect of their work.

As, on the one hand, the future elementary school teachers are to be brought into close contact with all classes of society by attendance on all forms of secondary schools, so the rural children, who formerly were the most valuable source of recruits for the elementary teaching profession, will more frequently than before enter into the higher callings. The duties previously borne by the normal schools can be taken over by none of the existing secondary schools. For pedagogical, cultural-political, and economic reasons this can be done only by the six-year *Aufbauschule,* which fills the gap left by the abolition of the normal school. The *Aufbauschule* will give to other vocations those values which the normal school was able to give only to the elementary school teachers.

The *Aufbauschule* is founded on the conviction that the *Volks-schule* in seven years of undisturbed work trains not a small number of its pupils so that these are able, in spiritual and physical health, and in the uninterruptedness of their curve of growth, to work up in a shorter time to the full completion of a secondary school. This, to be sure, only the really gifted pupils will be able to do. For all who do not reach the goal of this school pay too high a price for this life experiment. We have, indeed, no lack of men who through half-education are alienated from their class and are not fully trained for other classes. For this reason the *Aufbauschule* must from the beginning organize its instruction toward the objective of the leaving examination.

Whether the *Aufbauschule* is able to survive will depend upon the feeling of responsibility of those men who undertake this selection. In no case must pupils be taken for the purpose of proving the ability of the school to exist in a community. *Auf-bauschulen* must not be organized in unsuitable places because they are cheaper than other schools. This real danger, which might turn the blessing of the *Aufbauschule* for the rural class into a curse to the other classes of society, must be avoided, and the educational administration will always have to examine very

carefully the problem of whether the conditions for the organization of *Aufbauschulen* are really present.

The *Aufbauschule* will be and is to be no easy school. Only
pupils of pronounced talent, in vigorous health, in undisturbed
application to school work, in an atmosphere with as little confusion and distraction as possible, are able to acquire in six
years a training equal to that given in the nine-year institutions, if the criterion adopted is not the same amount of knowledge quickly acquired but the same scholarly capacity for
work.

In the organization of *Aufbauschulen* for girls, care will have
to be taken that only the really gifted and physically vigorous
girls, indeed those who in the period of development may need
no special freedom from work, can be considered for the *Aufbauschule.*

In suitable places and for suitable boys and girls the *Aufbauschule* can unfold and develop its power then, when it remains
thoroughly conscious of its connection with the *Volksschule,* and
also when in its entire make-up it takes into consideration the
special intellectual character and special spiritual needs of its
pupils. Here the educational purpose of the *Aufbauschule* is
in closest connection with the educational tendency of the
*Deutsche Oberschule.* The memorandum on the *Deutsche Oberschule,* therefore, can and must consider both school types as in-
trinsically belonging together. Not much more need be said
here concerning the *Aufbauschule* fashioned after the type of
the *Deutsche Oberschule* except that the *Aufbauschule* of the
*Deutsche Oberschule* type will have to afford its pupils by means
of agricultural and gardening activities the possibility of continuing in school the native occupations which have been cher-
ished, and of thus preserving a sympathetic association with
their class; with the help of the instruction in biology, which
is particularly meaningful for this school, it should enable its
pupils to pursue with knowledge and understanding the great
problems of the rural population and agriculture. Thus educated men and women will fight and overcome this regrettable
separation between country and city in whatever calling they
continue to be active.

But the *Aufbauschule* is not to be limited to the type of work
of the *Deutsche Oberschule.* Indeed, according to its whole

nature the *Oberrealschule* is possible as the *Aufbauschule*. The limitation to two foreign languages, the strong emphasis upon German, the more fully developed organization of natural science and geography all permit it, indeed, to appear also as a school type related to the *Oberrealschule*. A gymnasial or a realgymnasial type of *Aufbauschule* is not contemplated at the present time. The humanistic *Gymnasium* will only with great difficulty be able to dispense with the linguistic training of the classes from *Sexta* to *Quarta*. In its educational content it stands in too great contrast to the *Volksschule* to consider the fifth to seventh years of the *Volksschule* as its lower section. Where, however, conditions and needs would permit an *Aufbauschule* of the gymnasial type to appear as desirable, suitable experiments will be sanctioned. The *Realgymnasium*, with the variety of its subjects, can now fulfill its very diversified purposes in nine years only with the use of all its resources. An attempt to do this in six years would lead to a qualitative overburdening of a corresponding *Aufbauschule*.

Finally, it must be stated here, without possibility of misunderstanding, that the *Aufbauschule* stands in no other relationship to the training of elementary school teachers than do the other secondary schools. To be sure, the friends of the *Aufbauschule* hope that the special values of this school will have a strong attraction for many future elementary school teachers, especially those who come from the rural classes. The rural and the small-town teacher in particular must not stand aloof from the development of the particular ideals of the *Aufbauschule*, if in his later calling he is to enjoy the full possibility of entering sympathetically into the spiritual life of the parents and pupils.

But it must be insisted just as plainly that we need, none the less, elementary school teachers who through the educative forces of the other secondary schools have acquired intimate associations with the other educated classes.

# III

## SUGGESTIONS FOR A CURRICULUM OF THE *DEUTSCHE OBERSCHULE* AND THE *AUFBAUSCHULE*

### I. Cultural Subjects

#### *Introduction*

In order to carry out the educational ideas set forth in the Memoranda of the Ministry for Science, Art, and Popular Education bearing upon the fundamental *Deutsche Oberschule* and the *Aufbauschule,* issued February 18, 1922, U II 11 II, the *Oberschule* and its corresponding *Aufbauschule* combine the cultural subjects in such unity that a definite educational objective, which is to be attained by the common effort of all courses and subjects, is set for each class. *Sexta* and *Quinta* as the conclusion of childhood (period of primary experience), *Quarta* to *Untersekunda* as the age of boyhood (period of intuitive knowledge), and *Obersekunda* to *Oberprima* as the age of maturity (period of reflective thought) are to be sharply distinguished in education and instruction one from another from the standpoint of adolescent psychology. Careful consideration shall be given at this point to the special problems of education for girls.

1. Corresponding to the variety and diversity of German life in the different parts of the country, all of the instruction, especially in the lower and middle classes, must be adapted with great freedom to the many-sidedness of our cultural resources. The individual programs of study of the various schools will, therefore, adapt themselves to the special conditions here more than in the case of other schools with respect to the model set forth in the official programs. In this selection the faculty will decide, after earnest consideration, which objectives it may undertake with the prospect of success. The distribution of the subject matter among the various subjects of instruction will occur through grade conferences, in which also the amount of

time for accomplishing this work is determined according to the needs of the entire field of instruction. Only if the teachers of a class group themselves together into a working unit will the instruction as a whole be successful. Viewed from such standpoints the program of studies is left open as to which subject matter teacher the reading in philosophy and instruction in civics are assigned. The same naturally holds true of art appreciation, history of music, and other subject matter fields. Likewise the activity groups (*Arbeitsgemeinschaften*) can be assigned, each according to the nature of the case, to the service of the most varied subject matter interests. The assignment of a special instructional problem to a particular subject does not free the other subjects, however, from the obligation of serving the objective concerned as much as their strength permits. This holds true especially of the civic, philosophical, and art elements in the organization of all subjects. The assignment of an objective in the curriculum to a definite class, of course, does not prevent satisfactory preparation in early grades being made for this purpose, and assumes, as a matter of course, further study and intensification in later grades.

2. In addition to these points of view, the special programs of study will consider further, in the selection of subject matter, to what fields of study in the school the principles of "activity instruction" are directly applicable. Since cultural instruction more than instruction in the other subjects can bring the previous experiences of the pupil to full consciousness through self-activity, preliminary steps even in the lowest classes are especially favorable to fruitful "activity instruction." Therefore, in no class may excessive curricular demands limit such "activity instruction" in its quiet and undisturbed development. Through earnestness of performance the danger of purely whimsical instruction will be avoided.

3. The "integrated instruction" (*Gesamtunterricht*) in cultural subjects must consider foreign *Kultur* intensively (in all subjects and in coöperation with the foreign language work) in which the nature of the German is considered in its counterpart; and, on the other hand, the foreign language instruction must take into consideration in a similar manner the corresponding cultural forms of German life. Therefore, all of the language instruction must be correlated with the knowledge of lan-

guage forms used in German and with the technical expressions there developed. So long as there are still no general regulations on these points, these will be left to the individual institutions to come to an agreement with reference to a uniform terminology.

4. The "Instructional Objectives" and "Notes on Method" in the Curricula of May 29, 1901, and of August 18, 1908; and for the Evangelical religious instruction the regulations of April 18, 1917, apply also for the *Oberschule* and the *Aufbauschule*.

## VI

### EVANGELICAL RELIGION

### 3 hours

Bible stories of the New Testament as far as Pentecost. These stories should be taught along with a study of appropriate works of German art. A moderate number of selections for memorization should include verses from the Bible stories, church hymns, and individual verses of songs with appropriate music. This should be done as far as possible in connection with church festivals. Bible stories should also be supplemented with catechism. Special attention should be paid to the Ten Commandments and the Second Article—without Luther's explanations. The Lord's Prayer and the meaning of prayer in connection with the stories of Jesus. In organic connection with the objective of the class with reference to local informational studies, should go a knowledge of the local church, its places of worship and its monuments, its institutions, and its festivals. In natural connection with this should follow stories and biographical sketches from local church history and the surrounding country that are suited to the age of the children. Illustrations will be drawn from German poetry, in which local coloring should be considered.

### CATHOLIC RELIGION

### 3 hours

The work of *Sexta*, continuing upon the foundation laid in the lower grades and bearing the aims of the upper grades in mind, should be a deepening and an expansion of the fundamentals of religion. The instruction begins with a practical introduction to a life of prayer through divine service at school. This is followed by instruction in liturgy, church, altar, holy vessels, vestments, holy mass. Review of the most important

facts of confession and communion. In connection with the
church year, learning prayers and hymns. The Bible stories of
of the Old Testament teach of God and His nature, sin and its
consequence, the plan of salvation. Instruction in catechism
begins with the Second Article and treats of the most important
duties toward God and one's neighbor. *Sexta* should stress the
positive side of the Christian way of life through the teaching
of ethics and morals.

In keeping with the age and the interests of the children, a
suitable introduction to the ecclesiastical organization and life
of the local church should be given. Religious customs and
sacred memories dear to the folk mind will be discussed in connection with the more important holidays of the community.
An understanding and love for art in church and church life
through group excursions to places of worship and points of
interest in connection with the church. Pictures and paintings
of heroes, especially of the ancient church martyrs, should be
used as a stimulus to admiration of the greatness of the Catholic
Church.

## GERMAN

### 6 hours

*Phonetics.* Exercises in the formation of sounds in connection with reading, recitation, and public speaking generally
prescribed for German, the foreign languages, and singing.
Comparison of sounds in the dialect, colloquial German and
High German. The essentials of syllabication for spelling.

*Etymology and Syntax.* Parts of speech and word groups
according to meaning and inflection. The most important sub-
divisions of nouns, adjectives, numerals, and verbs. The most
important facts about the inflection of the noun, adjective, and
verb. Distinction between weak and strong forms. Enlargement of vocabulary based upon the pupil's observations from
life and the general curriculum. Distinction between related
words with regard to dialect. Content and spirit of treatment
according to Rudolf Hildebrand.

The sentence and its parts, position of words in it, its intonation; its punctuation in order to clarify the structure and content.

*Reading, Recitation, Public Speaking.* Exercises in dialect
and High German in thoughtful reading, story-telling, and natural rendering of poetry. Reports on experiences and observations. Reproduction of readings and oral narratives, sometimes in paraphrased form.

*Written Exercises.* Written exercises in connection with etymology and syntax. Spelling exercises in conjunction with
grammar without too much attention to subtleties, especially

small or capital letters, homophones, and foreign words. Dictations, essentially as practice exercises. Brief exercises on the
lesson taught or out of the experience of the child. Original
expositions, title to be chosen by the pupil, as written class
exercises, in the form of reports, letters, narratives.

Introduction to the use of the school dictionary in order to
avoid errors.

*Literature.* The reader, German in spirit and adapted to the
mind of the child, should contain valuable, well-written material
for all the subjects of the class, especially of the country and
life about them: customs and traditions, trades, professions and
their work. Biographical sketches of the famous men and women
of the immediate vicinity and the district. Fairy tales dealing
with folk, art, and nature. Animal stories. Children's stories
from recent literature. Appropriate stories of adventure.
Humorous and serious tales at home and in the community.
Roundelays and riddles. Fairy ballads. Short poems, stories,
and anecdotes in local dialect. Careful selections and worthwhile memorization of songs and poems. Stimulation to voluntary memorization of poems of their own selection. Sympathetic
appreciation of the experiences expressed in songs, especially
lyric folk songs, in connection with vocal music. Songs that
foster a better understanding of human nature, the seasons, the
festivals, etc., with constant correlation with religion, history,
song, gymnastics, scouting, and games. The objective study of
art in poetry and prose; for example, Busch, Hey, Liebermann,
Reinick, Richter, Speckter, Schwind, Spitzweg, Thoma. Stimulation of pupils to collect appropriate pictures.

*Historical Tales.* Tales and legends from the local community,
the neighborhood, and the surrounding country, so far as
possible in connection with memorials of the past in the broadest
sense. Names, streets, trades, buildings. The most beautiful
German legends.

### GEOGRAPHY

#### 2 hours

Home geography and development of geographical concepts.
Orientation on the plane of the horizon, directions, daily and
annual course of the sun, apparent course of the sun; compass,
clock. Exercises in the school yard and in the vicinity. Measurement and estimation of distances. Elements of map study by
comparison of nature, relief, and the drawing of maps.

Elementary geography on the basis of the pupil's own observations; character of the land, the rivers, the weather. Hand
in hand with this work goes a study of water-works plants, irri-
gation, the building of homes and streets, agriculture, and
forestry.

Knowledge of the home town in connection with German and history. History of one's native town as shown by map and public buildings. The immediate community as a part of the more remote districts. The most important facts of German topography based on the study of maps. The horizontal and vertical structure of Europe in the rough. The oceans and continents in connection with the first orientation on the globe.

## V

### EVANGELICAL RELIGION

#### 2 hours

Stories from the lives of the apostles with a continual retrospect to the life of Christ. Verses and catechism in connection with Bible stories. The Third Article of Faith without Luther's commentaries. Church hymns and special verses as in *Sexta*. In connection with other cultural subjects the religion of the old Germans and its continuation in German national faith. The spread of Christianity in Germany with biographical sketches of its most important saints and martyrs. Important legends concerning the saints. Luther and the other great personalities in the German church. Study of home and foreign missions and of German evangelical life in foreign lands. The study of art in relation to the church as in *Sexta*.

### CATHOLIC RELIGION

#### 2 hours

In connection with the Bible instruction of *Sexta*, the catechism (First Article) treats of faith; God and His nature; Christ; the Church, its origin, organization, and purpose; sanctification and perfection of man. Instruction in Bible (New Testament up to the Ascension) is given as far as possible in conjunction with the church year. Youth and public ministry of Jesus; miracles and the simpler parables; suffering and death of Jesus, with special treatment of two main facts, redemption and origin of the Kingdom of God. Memorization of prayers and hymns as in *Sexta*. Study of local church affairs and history should include a few sketches and biographies of the Middle Ages and of recent times. Visits to church memorials and discussions of ecclesiastical customs and traditions of the locality are continued. To specify, the following topics should be discussed: Introduction of Christianity into the locality. Boniface. A Benedictine cloister. Francis. Francis Xavier and missionary work. The patron saints for youth: Aloysius,

Stanislaus Kostka, Johannes Berchmans.  Saints of the local community, especially patron saints.

## GERMAN
### 5 hours

*Phonetics.*  Continuation of the rules pertaining to vowel change; weakening (*Schwächung*), lengthening, shortening, and omission.  In connection with syntax, phonetic aspects of the sentence.  Sentence rhythm and accentuation.  Comparison with local dialect and High German.

*Etymology and Syntax.*  Parts of speech, as to form and meaning: inflection, substantive, adjective, verb, participle.  Groups of nouns: proper, common, designations for activities and conditions.

Syllabication.  Root words and derivations, compounds; the simpler syllables.  Meaning, kind and accent of compounds, especially of the verb.  Grouping of word families according to form and meaning.  Enlargement and refinement of the vocabulary through observation, class instruction, and reading material as in *Sexta*.

Review and development of the simple sentence.  Chief parts of the sentence.  The kinds of sentences.  The coördinate connectives of main clauses.  All this keeping in mind word order and sentence accent and in connection with further study of punctuation.

*Reading, Recitation, Public Speaking.*  As in *Sexta* with greater emphasis upon High German as against the dialect and colloquial German.  The distinct differences of peculiarities between the dialect and High German should be noted by means of the phonetic chart.

*Written Exercises.*  Spelling and dictation exercises as in *Sexta*, but also in order to furnish drill in punctuation.  Written exercises in grammar, especially with regard to the teaching of sentence structure.  Brief written compositions upon the basis of subject matter treated.  Writing of imaginary stories, also reproductions of fairy tales, fables, and other reading.  This is to be supplemented by original compositions as in *Sexta*.

*Literature.*  The reader, as in *Sexta*, takes cognizance of the general objective of the course of study of the class, the home in relation to the Fatherland.  It offers, therefore, without neglecting the study of the local community, materials from German culture in general.  Nature and the German's appreciation of it.  German mythology, in so far as it still persists in popular belief: spirits, witches, elves, werewolves; dwarfs, giants.  Traces of former days common in popular beliefs.  German manners and customs in different parts of the country.

German life in foreign lands. German capital and labor, both past and present. Judicial customs. In connection with other subjects, a study of festive customs, humor among the common people, folk songs, proverbs, riddles. Customs and games among the youth. Memorization of poems and songs as in *Sexta*. Materials from German antiquities in close coördination with history, geography, and scouting trips. Every exercise should make appropriate use of works of art, especially pictures of German cities and hamlets, castles and churches, markets and streets, from the entire vast field of German culture.

### HISTORY

### 2 hours

General aim as in German; the home in relation to the Fatherland. Complete cultural and historical accounts from national legend and history will be vividly portrayed to the pupil in lectures by the teacher, who will employ concrete illustrative material and develop the characteristics of the period. Struggles with the Roman Empire. The heroic age of the great migration, as pictured in the ancient sagas, also in connection with German. German theology, the coming of Christianity, in connection with the instruction in religion. The great emperors of the early Middle Ages. The golden age of knightly culture. Pictures from the burgher and peasant life. Age of the Reformation. The Thirty Years' War. Frederick the Great. The War of Liberation. The establishment of the German Empire. The World War and the present age. All instruction is in close connection with geography and occasional references are made to local economic and civic conditions. The aim of the instruction is to pave the way for the child's first knowledge of public institutions and their organization and to lead him gradually to a knowledge of human coöperation and society.

### GEOGRAPHY

### 2 hours

*Geographical Knowledge of Germany.* Thorough study of the map of Germany and the central German States. In addition, study of mineral deposits, names of places, and landscape forms. Attention is devoted to the essential types of soil, economic life, problems of trade and population, and the chief types of communities. In the study of climate the relation between location and the effect upon man, animal, and plant life is emphasized. The fundamentals of geology are studied in close connection with geography. Comparative figures with regard to distances, areas, and altitudes are given. The main German

States and the Prussian provinces are studied. In connection with the general educational aims of the class, the various provinces, races, and countries with their characteristic traits and their mutual relationships. Always upon the basis of the pupil's observations, further development of the basic principles of mathematical geography throughout the school year. Included in the pupil's observations are the apparent movement of the stars, the moon and its phases, and the polar star. Maps made by pupils showing regional features and outlines. Longitude and latitude for orientation purposes.

## IV

### EVANGELICAL RELIGION

#### 2 hours

In connection with other cultural subjects a few facts from the religion of the ancients,—Egyptians, Babylonians, Persians. Coördinate with history instruction pictures from the religious life of the Greeks and Romans. The chief aim of the class is, however, the introduction to the religion of the Old Testament. Materials of the lower grades are continued and supplemented, down to the time of the prophets. Important passages suited to the age of the pupils, from prophetic and devotional literature. Memorization of significant passages from the Prophets, the Psalms, and Ecclesiastes. In connection with Bible readings, the First Article in the Catechism with Luther's commentary. The persistence of Old Testament piety in the Christian religion, in morals, in art, and especially in the German hymnology. Occasional memorization of hymns.

### CATHOLIC RELIGION

#### 2 hours

Bible stories from the resurrection of the Lord to the death of the Apostles. Special attention should be given to the ministry of the risen Lord, meaning of Pentecost, biographical sketches of the great Apostles. To supplement and enrich the Bible instruction in *Quinta,* Christ as the divine teacher should be studied—Sermon on the Mount, parables. Catechism (Third Article) treats of the means of grace, especially penitence, sacraments, and prayer. In direct connection with this, a thorough study of the liturgy—church year, the sacramental host, ceremonies, celebration of holy mass, pericopes for Sunday. Additional prayers and hymns.

*General Notes about the Instruction in Church History for the Middle Section.* Social and cultural studies should elicit a vivid understanding of the Church itself and its great task of the present day. As preparation for the instruction in church history in the *Oberstufe* the most important phases and dates of certain periods are studied.

The instructional material in church history for *Quarta* consists of biographical and cultural sketches of Christian antiquity. Christianity is studied in its cultural and world-wide influence. It is correlated with secular history through discussions of Roman religion and theology, the religious condition of the children of Israel and their neighbors at the time of Christ. Specifically, the following topics are treated: Peter, the first head of the Church. The missionary enterprise of the Apostle Paul. God's punishment of the children of Israel. Christian persecutions. Catacombs. Constantine and the victory of the Cross. Great Church fathers. Lives of the first hermits; life in the monasteries. The genius and nature of the Catholic Church are brought out in all discussions.

## GERMAN

### 5 hours

*Phonetics.* Exercises in organic connection with reading, recitations and extemporaneous speaking by use of the phonetic chart. Clear comparisons should be made, showing the relation between spoken and written sounds.

*Etymology and Syntax.* A recapitulation and supplementing of word families. Use of tenses. Declension of proper nouns and current foreign words. Discrimination between weak and strong declension as in gender of nouns. Regard should always be shown for differences in dialect. Continued practice in enlarging the vocabulary.

Sentence structure. Principles of dependent clauses. Subordination, meaning, form, value, position. Development of the subordinate clause from the coördinate clause. Expressing phrases as sentences and *vice versa*. Origin and nature of the subordinate conjunction. Exercises showing different possible ways of expressing ideas, as regards sentence relationships, particularly from standpoint of style. The relation of punctuation to sentence structure.

*Reading, Recitation, and Extemporaneous Speaking.* As heretofore, only greater insistence upon purity of sound, meaning, and expression. Continued use of and reference to the phonetic chart. Besides narratives and reports, simple descriptions. On festive occasions and field trips short original performances or pieces that have been memorized.

*Written Exercises.* Occasional exercises in spelling and dictation. Continued drill in punctuation. Grammatical exercises for better understanding of the subordinate clause. Brief exercises in all subjects as in *Quinta*. Short themes—about six a year—are based on the lessons taught in the school, but especially upon the pupil's own observation of his environment, to the study of which he is stimulated. Simple description as added to the earlier content. Type of essays as before. Occasionally an essay as a home exercise.

*Literature.* To supplement the work of *Sexta* and *Quinta* the reading is organized around the cultural problem of the class; namely, the ancient world. Sagas and legends of the Greek-Roman world. In treating ancient civilization it is well to use suitable passages from ancient poets and writers in translations of artistic values. Primarily in coöperation with religious instruction, occasional selections from the cultural landmarks of other ancient peoples; also simpler selections from scientific literature covering the entire field of antiquity.

In conjunction with history and geography, classical studies and art appreciation will consider also the cultural objective of the class, with emphasis upon the elements of Greek and Roman civilization which are still present upon German soil, and with reference to the persistence of classical tendencies in German art and architecture.

Home reading takes on larger proportions. It is prepared and directed in class.

*Theory of Poetry.* As German instruction, in coöperation with music, has limited itself to the pure joy of the child in melody, rhythm, and rhyme, it tries from *Quarta* on to develop conscious appreciation for artistic form in so far as this serves to disclose the poetic value and to provide artistic enjoyment. In no case must the theory of poetry be considered apart from the individual masterpiece. The training of the senses also for tone color, melody, and rhythm in prose, in connection with reading exercises and art of speaking.

## HISTORY

### 3 hours

*Preliminary Note for the Middle Section.* History instruction in the middle section—*Quarta* to *Untersekunda*—strives by means of biographical and cultural sketches to afford an objective knowledge of German history, its foundation in ancient history, and its relationship to world history. This work has at the same time the problem of preparing for the instruction in the upper class—*Obersekunda* to *Prima*—by the mastery of a secure body of facts. In *Quarta* the ancient world, as the general objective of the class, is of service in showing the forces derived from classical periods which are operative to-day in German civilization. For this reason political history, in so far as it does not concern itself with training for citizenship, gives way to the study of the history of civilization. Complete cultural and biographical studies as in *Quinta*. Ancient sagas in connection with the instruction in German. Clear portrayal of the early times and the Middle Ages in Greece: Troy and Mycenæ, Crete and old Sparta, Olympia and Delphi. Heroes from the period of the Greek wars of independence. A short statement of the Athens of Pericles. Somewhat more explicit, the deeds of Alexander; a cultural portrayal of the Hellenistic age, also some facts about daily life of that age. In connection with the instruction in religion and geography and in the treatment of the Persian wars, a few touches of oriental culture.

Reading selections from Roman history from the same points of view. A careful choice of cultural sketches from the early period. Great personalities from the age of the Punic Wars. The century of civil wars. The most important Roman emperors. The struggle with the Germans. In connection with the reading materials in German an introduction to an understanding of Roman culture and its effect upon the Germans. As in *Quinta* a political treatment of materials is presented; special development of constitutional forms, the interaction between political, economic, and cultural tendencies, social wars and revolutions, changing forms in state and economical affairs, colonization, peaceful expansion, immigrations, racial mixtures.

## GEOGRAPHY

### 2 hours

The Mediterranean country and Asia Minor, with a view to India and Eastern Asia. The class instruction aims at as clear an understanding as possible of the typical countries of this continent and compares them with countries of middle Europe which have different climatic conditions. The difference in peoples according to race, religion, and their historical destiny is also developed. The definite knowledge which comes from concrete observation of actual situations is also of great value. The simple explanation of the geographical character of different nations must always take into consideration the relationship of the subject matter of the class in history and German, and must explain the origin of ancient cultures in connection with the characteristic economic, political, artistic, and religious life which developed earlier. A comparison between the present and past civilization of this geographical area will aid the student to distinguish between the cross currents of this ancient civilization and to note the relationship between climate and civilization.

Continuation of the elements of mathematical geography. First introduction to the real movements of the solar system. Rotation and revolution of the earth. Place, time, and hour zones, orbit and zodiac planes, parallels and meridians. In connection with the study of meteorology of countries within the limits of geography, the question of mean temperature of day and year is taken up. The courses of isotherms in comparison with parallels of latitude are studied.

## U III

### EVANGELICAL RELIGION

### 2 hours

Biographical and cultural sketches taken from the history of Christianity from its beginning to the Reformation. In connection with the cultural material of *Quarta,* development of the significance of Jesus and of Christianity in the early Church. The Second and Third Articles with commentaries. Source readings from the New Testament and from a church history reader. The object here is to make clear the message of the great religious teachers for our time and particularly for the youth of to-day. These sketches, in connection with the general cultural course, should make clearly evident what Christianity accomplished for the different epochs and in the various spheres of life. The main objective of the course is the teaching of German church history. Origin of the papacy. St. Augustine and his significance for the Middle Ages. Characteristic glimpses from the history of monasticism to show what it accomplished in the different epochs. Boniface and the Frankish church. In conjunction with history, study of the struggle between the Empire and the Papacy; the Crusades. In connection with German and drawing, Christianity in the poetry and pictorial art of the Middle Ages. St. Francis and Innocent III. Pre-Reformation efforts. The Reformation from biographies of Luther, Zwingli, and Calvin. The Lutheran Bible, the origin of the evangelical hymn book and symbolic books, especially the shorter catechism. Sketches from the time of the Counter-Reformation. Reading and memorization of the more important hymns as an expression of the piety and of the religious life of the outstanding poets of the epochs under consideration.

### CATHOLIC RELIGION

### 2 hours

Critical analysis of the Old Testament in connection with biblical history. Historical problems of a social and religious nature, as the Creation, the Bible and science, monotheism. Outstanding religious leaders, as Abraham, Moses, and the prophets. The Old Testament as a guide to Christ. Symbols and prophecies in comprehensive exposition: longings of the Jews for the Messiah. Selected passages from the Old Testament. Bible study and geography of the Bible. Instruction in the Catechism is based on the Second Article, with constant regard for the spiritual status at the beginning of puberty. Especially to be emphasized are dangers to faith from questionable readings and associations. Modern superstition. Sanctity of the Sabbath. Relation of school and home. Authority and freedom. Good examples and corruption. Modesty. Meaning and protection of property. Love of truth and honor. Finally, a consideration of sin and its sources, as also an exposition of the Christian ideal of perfection. Drill upon liturgical prayers and hymns.

In connection with the general cultural courses, the significance of the Catholic Church for the German people, especially in the Middle Ages, will be evaluated. According to the time available, the following will be treated: The meaning of the western migrations for the extension of the Church. Benedictine orders in Germany. Boniface, the German apostle. Charlemagne. Separation of the Eastern Church from Rome. The Arabian migrations and the danger of Islam for Christianity. The Crusades and their significance for the Church and civilization. Mendicant orders in the organism of the Church. A brief study of these topics,—the Church and the school, the Church and medieval art, and the Church with its ministrations of charity,—will establish the conception of the penetration by the church into the whole life of the epoch. Forerunners of church schisms. Luther and the church schism. The discussion of this point should result in an understanding of the differences between the Catholic Church and the principal Protestant denominations. Spread of the Reformation in Germany and the Northern countries. The Council of Trent and its influence in the revival of the Church—Carl Borromæus. The Jesuit orders. The missionary work of the church from the age of discoveries to the death of Francis Xavier. St. Vincent de Paul, the apostle of brotherly love.

## GERMAN

### 5 hours

*Phonetics.* The study of phonetics in connection with instruction in foreign languages and singing. Comparative study of phonetic values in the dialect, colloquial language, and High German. Exercises in pure High German with the aim of eradicating errors of speech. Survey of the Indo-Germanic languages.

Phonetic changes in language development, especially of German and particularly with reference to the influence of different dialects and of foreign languages.

*Etymology and Syntax.* In the study of words, further development of the objectives of *Quarta,* with especial reference to historical insight into the origin and dissemination of words. Words taken from other languages and foreign words in relation to cultural and political history; influence on our language of Greek and Roman culture. Vocabulary of Christianity and of the Church. Old word forms and words in the language of today. Variations in speech usages. More intense study of related words as to meaning, emotional content, and acceptance in the dialect. Obsolescent and new language values. New forms. Folk etymology. As in *Quarta,* exercises for enlarging the vocabulary, with careful avoidance of all foreign words.

Different kinds of subordinate clauses. Refinement in the use of pronouns. Forms of the verb and rules for their formation. Word order, sentence stress, and importance of position in the sentence. Punctuation.

*Reading, Declamation, and Extemporaneous Speech.* Reading with correct enunciation and emphasis, constant exercises in impromptu speaking. Participation in short performances,— theatrical, declamatory, etc.

*Written Exercises.* Exercises in syntax. Exercises in all subjects as in *Quarta;* themes based on observations as in *Quarta.* Reports, descriptions, and portrayals prepared for by means of oral exercises and also by use of materials taken from other courses. Encouragement of writing of imaginative themes, allowing free choice of materials. Occasional exercises in outlining a subject and in analyzing selections read. About ten themes a year, of which four should be home work. Composition writing in class should not exceed two hours.

*Literature.* Legends relating to the great migration, sagas of Dietrich, the Nibelungen cycle, Hilde and Gudrun; legends of the Lombards, Franks, and Vandals. In connection with the other cultural courses, a survey of the old German civilization, based on the best literary accounts. Selections from the *Edda.* German folk romances (tales). Artistic literature in correlation with all subject matter of the class, especially with history. Historical novels and tales and other classics of the earlier and later poets selected to suit the needs and abilities of the class. Utilization of outside readings. Representative historical ballads. Rural lyrics. Poems in local and occasionally other dialects. Memorization of a considerable number of poems. Encouraging the pupil to learn poems of his own choice. Occasional selections from the older dramas,—farces, Christmas and religious plays.

Scientific writings for a deeper appreciation of the heroic in

German life, its struggles and conquests in all spheres of existence. Also autobiographies and letters,—heroes of labor. Studies in art in relation to other subjects, particularly drawing; above all, pictures illustrating legends and history. Selected monuments of art of the German Middle Ages.

*Theory of Poetry.* As in *Quarta,* with special reference to ballads and to the characteristic methods of expression employed by the different ballad writers. Verse forms and marks of different schools of thought are secondary to the poet's conception of the purpose of his art as shown by the inner unity of his material, his personal experience and form of expression.

## HISTORY

### 3 hours

Biographical and cultural sketches in German history from the earliest times to the Treaty of Westphalia, with careful use of appropriate source material and classical accounts, all unified within the cultural studies. In this treatment only such significant historical characters are examined closely as can be made vividly real to the pupils. The appreciation of characteristic types of the Middle Ages should be essentially enriched by this study of German history. For the first time in the period of great inventions and discoveries, the relationships with foreign history are more sharply emphasized as the result of the changed condition of the world. Sketches from German history further civic education and furnish also a clear understanding of the political and business methods of the Middle Ages: types of constitutions among the Germans, feudal system, German Empire at the time of the great emperors, contacts with foreign cultures as a result of the Crusades, German towns, and princely sovereignty.

The expansion of German culture toward the East and its special forms in the borderlands will receive careful attention. The cultural studies, in connection with religion and drawing, furnish a clear picture of all the more important life activities of each epoch, especially of its high points, as: early German times; cultural conditions in France; evolution of knighthood, of the army, of the administration of justice, and of the middle class and peasantry.

## GEOGRAPHY

### 2 hours

Western Europe. The Teutonic and Germanic neighbors of the German Empire in the south, in the northwest, in the north and in eastern Europe. States and provinces whose boundaries are determined by natural physical features and those determined by economic and historical conditions. Instability, divergence, and unification of boundaries of states, language spheres, nationalities and religious faiths. Alterations of German boundaries in the course of time. German peoples in Europe dwelling outside the Fatherland. Chief regions for agriculture, mining, and great industries; centers of population. Chief lines of travel and principal trading centers. At this point the political and economic geography is to be developed upon the basis of the physical geography of this region.

By means of repeated use of appropriate factual material derived from the courses presented in *Quinta* and *Quarta*, extension of the fundamental concepts of geography will be coördinated with the geographical content of this class. Gradually there will arise a more comprehensive survey of the atmosphere (climatic zones, air pressure, isobars, winds, rainfall); the water (the ocean and its movements, subterranean waters, rivers, and lakes); and the earth's crust (stratification of the rocks, faults and breaks, weathering by heat and moisture, tearing down and building up processes; volcanoes and earthquakes, ice and glaciers).

Review and further extension of knowledge of mathematical geography. Astronomical and solar day, length of year, the seasons, the calendar.

## O III

### EVANGELICAL RELIGION

#### 2 hours

History of Jesus in connection with the synoptic gospels. A more thorough treatment of the parables and the Sermon on the Mount, with constant application of their lessons to the present. Especially important passages should be memorized. The Lord's Prayer with commentaries from the Third Article of the Catechism.

As a part of the general work of the class, vivid portrayals of the life of the time of the pietists, and of the Enlightenment, using for this original sources with a thorough study of the larger unifying forces and the predominating spiritual trends. Protestant church art, as seen in church structures, religious poetry, and church music. Evangelical religious service and its significance for the religious life of the individual as well as of the community.

### CATHOLIC RELIGION

#### 2 hours

Beginning with a comprehensive review of the life and teaching of the Lord in connection with Bible history, the Bible instruction should treat of the kingdom of God in the New Testament. The kingdom of God as a new attitude, faith in God, humility, and a helping and forgiving charity. The attitude of the new man toward culture (labor, riches, state, and family). The kingdom of God as the visible church. Drill upon the more important passages.

The aim of instruction in catechism is the final exposition and assimilation of the catechetical material of the First and Second Articles. Selected chapters of the Creed. Scripture and tradition. The secrets of faith; the Trinity. Incarnation and salvation. The work of the Holy Spirit in the church and in the human soul. The religious man: faith and works. The sacraments. Worship of God in life through work and asceticism. More detailed exposition of the liturgy of the Holy Mass —*ordo missæ*.

Church history from the end of the Thirty Years' War to the beginning of the nineteenth century, presented in epochal sketches. The main point is to allow external events to take a more subordinate position and to present the spiritual tendencies of the time within and without the church in a manner corresponding to the intellectual development of the age group: The Church and Protestantism in German countries. Protestant sects. Catholics in Great Britain, Ireland and Holland. Princely absolutism. Josephinism. The Enlightenment and unbelief. Free-masonry. The French Revolution and its consequences for the Church.

## GERMAN

### 5 hours

*Phonetics.* Integration and completion of phonetics through occasional references to the history of the language—phonetic mutations in High German. Recapitulation and integration, according to the phonetic chart, by a comparison of dialects; pure High German and foreign languages, with references also to instruction in singing. Occasional references to other German dialects.

*Etymology and Syntax.* In the review a summary of the principles of transition between classes of words. Fuller discussion of the principles of root syllables and compound word forms. A survey of changes in meanings. Imagery content of the German language. Luther's German in connection with instruction in history and religion. The effect of cultural derivatives in light of borrowed and foreign words: the French and Italian influence; borrowing of words in our time in every field of culture—scientific foreign words, art expressions, and economic, military, and political terms. Examples from the history of Germanization. A glimpse at vocational terminology. Geography of language considered in connection with geography and history, emphasizing the dialects, German in foreign lands, and the Germanic languages. Changes in language boundaries, language "islands"—isolated groups using a different tongue. A survey of the development of German spelling.

*Rhetoric.* Refinement of feeling for language as contrasted to newspaper and book German. Exercises in recasting defective paragraphs, especially examples taken from newspapers and daily life, following the rules of logic and style.

*Reading, Declamation, and Impromptu Speaking.* Exercises in extemporaneous speaking and declamation, as in *Untertertia.* Free discussions in class.

*Written Exercises.* Grammatical exercises with special reference to an artistic application of syntactic materials. Conversion of independent clauses into dependent clauses. Short themes in all subjects as before. A systematic introduction to the observation and reporting of events, conditions, and people, with increasing demands for an exact reproduction of essential points. Descriptions with wise use of what has been read and studied in other subjects. Short compositions and exact reports on readings, and also summarizing statements of content. Exercises in analysis from standpoint of logical unity. The number, kind, and length of themes as in *Untertertia.*

*Literature.* As in *Untertertia,* the following points based on historical materials as assigned to the general problem of instruction of this class: Germany in relation to other European peoples up to the time of the French Revolution. First-hand experiences of the lower classes will be transformed into concrete knowledge by a greater use of important literature of scientific and artistic value. Clearer emphasis upon economic and social conditions; conquest of nature by means of technology and science. Glimpses at the economic, historic, and cultural past of the German people. Also sketches from the history of music of the corresponding epochs in connection with instruction in singing. Colonization of the German East. Germanization in denationalized regions and in foreign countries. Voyages of discovery, sea voyages. History as reflected in the modern short story and the lighter historical novel. A survey of the history of countries in worthwhile German writings and translations. A systematic use of home reading for this purpose. The same point of view obtains also in the choice of poems, with constant review and extension of the stock of poetry of earlier classes. Ballads down to the present time; idylls, and short epics. Memorizing of poems as in *Untertertia.* An introduction to the drama stresses a more direct and intuitive understanding of the thing represented than an insight into its technique. The comprehension of the drama will be enhanced by attending performances and by occasional retrospects to the history of the theater. The most famous writers of poetry which have been read. Something about the best known compilers of folk songs. Art study considers here also the educational objective of the class through a study of characteristic art and architecture of periods discussed; from time to time modern plays dealing with corresponding stages of culture. The effect of foreign influences on German art is not to be overlooked.

*Theory of Poetry.* A clearer understanding of the nature of the ballad is to be aimed at through a stronger emphasis of the historical folk song and outstanding representative poets. In the short story, novel, and drama the form and technique of art are to be gradually introduced for the sake of æsthetic appreciation.

### HISTORY

### 3 hours

The period from 1648 to 1815 portrayed in biographical and cultural sketches, greater use being made of original sources. According to the age and understanding of the pupils, the instruction begins to emphasize more sharply the larger relationships and the formative ideas. German history should awaken an appreciation of the rise of Austria as a great power and picture the rise of Prussia since the Great Elector; Frederick the Great; participation of Prussia in the struggle against Napoleon. In connection with German history a fuller consideration of the relationships between the European powers and their changes: period of Louis XIV; struggle of England for world domination from the time of Cromwell to the Congress of Vienna; age of the French Revolution; rise of the United States; East European events. In the history of wars, general political and economical considerations take precedence over war technique as such. Therefore, except for a few chapters from the wars of Frederick the Great and the wars of liberation, the general course and events of wars are to be considered only so far as they may be important for an understanding of the world's history. The thirst of youth for hero worship will be satisfied by a study of heroic achievements of individuals and races. The most essential facts in the development of the several countries and especially of the Prussian state are to be presented, according to the age of the students, from the standpoint of the transformation of the economic, political, and cultural phases of life. The history of the people whose language is studied as the fundamental foreign language should be pursued by way of comparison. Along with this should go a progressive consideration of the following from the civic and economic points of view: the nature of the absolute state, social organizations of a people in the eighteenth century, mercantilism and materialistic ambitions; setting and fundamental ideas back of the French Revolution, the Stein-Hardenberg reforms, and the doctrine of free trade. In connection with this a simple, concrete treatment of such concepts as constitution, legislative and executive powers, popular representation, self-government, domestic colonization, taxes, and customs.

## GEOGRAPHY

### 2 hours

The geography of non-European countries. Chief events of the epoch of the great discoveries and the Europeanization of the world. The essential location of native civilizations—Egypt, Asia Minor, India, and East Asia are reviewed. Peculiarities of fauna and flora of the tropical forests, of the ancient forest zones of the north, of the steppes and wastelands, and of the tropical, sub-tropical, and northern cultivated areas. The countries in active political and economical relationship with Germany are to be studied more in detail. Special emphasis will be given to German settlements in foreign lands and to the former German colonies. The colonial possessions of foreign powers are to be studied in connection with their history and emphasized according to their political and economic importance. Some facts from ethnology. Distribution of world religions. Regions of dense and sparse population, of the production of raw materials and manufactured materials. In connection with instruction in civics, markets, and world trade routes.

Amplification of mathematical geography. Variation of earth's form from that of a sphere; eclipses of moon and sun, planets, comets, and meteors. On excursions and trips introduction to the use of the surveyor's table.

## U II

### EVANGELICAL RELIGION

### 2 hours

The study of the New Testament. Reading of selected portions of the New Testament for religious edification and illustration of more important life problems of the present, giving preference to the writings of St. Paul.

In connection with the whole educational problem of the class, selected portions of the church history of the nineteenth century as revealed in biographies, letters, and other sources, particularly such as deal with religious church activities in Germany at the present time and with a survey of the status of Christianity in the more important foreign countries. Church

doctrine and regulations in connection with civic instruction.
Church organizations. Home and foreign missions. Social significance of Christianity. The free churches and sects. Religious tendencies of the present. Through home reading and
in correlation with the corresponding subjects of study, attention
to religious materials in recent literature, in pictorial art, and
especially in religious lyrics, music, and painting.

## CATHOLIC RELIGION
### 2 hours

*General Preliminary Remarks for Introduction in Sekunda
and Prima.* In *Sekunda* and *Prima* the faith of the Church
should be set forth in its vigorous unity and impressive majesty
and made fruitful for the development of personalities, happy
in their belief and unswerving in their moral stability. The
authenticity of Catholic truths must always be fundamentally
demonstrated by constant reference to the struggle in the field
of scientific and spiritual ideas; the Catholic dogma must be
brought home to the understanding in a deeper, clearer, and
more convincing manner, while emphasis must be repeatedly
laid upon the interrelation of divine works and human necessity. The pupils should, as far as conditions will permit, learn
to express themselves in impromptu discussion on important
topics. Special problems will be treated in open discussion
between pupils and teacher. The self-activity of the pupils
will be provided for in harmony with the principle of learning
by doing.

Rejecting systematic apologetics, necessary apologetic questions in the doctrine of God, Christ, and the Church will be
linked together.

The Bible reading in the New Testament should, by a careful
distribution of time and choice of material, contribute a vivid
insight into the thought life of Jesus and his apostles, and
also that of the spirit of the early Church. The first aim should
not be merely a mass of historical knowledge, but rather a deeper
understanding of the teachings of the Church, based on a happy,
heart-felt recognition of the authority of the Church. Preliminary and textual criticisms should be reduced to a minimum. The aim is an independent reading of God's word that will
bear fruit in the unfolding of the Christian life.

In *Untersekunda,* Church doctrine. The divine origin of the
Church as proved by its founding, its preservation, its fruits,
and its unity (see *Vaticanum,* Chap. 3, *de fide*). The Catholic
Church as the Church of Christ. All the characteristics given
by Christ revealed themselves in it: primacy, apostolicity, unity,
holiness, catholicity, indestructibility. The Eastern Church.
Types of the churches of the Reformation.

The Church of the living Christ. Teaching office—organization, infallibility, teaching and preaching, free investigation, heresy. Priesthood—mediatory activities of the Church in sacrifice, sacraments, prayer; the general priesthood; the religious character of Catholic piety. Pastoral office: education for righteousness; the Church as the mother of the saints; Church legislation; the Index. Church penalties; Church government; the meaning of pastoral life.

Necessity of the salvation of the Church. The doctrine of the soul and body of the Church. Salvation of the non-Catholic. Home and foreign missions. The Church and churches,—converts, efforts at union, tolerance, and Christian love. The Church and society; the Church and the family; the Church and the state,—religious consecration of authority. The Church and economic life,—moral and religious forces and their significance in economic life. The Church and education. The Church and art; Catholic literature. The reading of the history of the apostles should serve as an introduction into the growth and spirit of the early Church.

Since many pupils leave school to enter practical life at the end of *Untersekunda,* an apologetic treatment of the fundamentals of faith,—the existence of God, divinity of Christ,—in keeping with the age of the pupils, appears indispensable.

Church history of the nineteenth century to the present time, with special reference to its development in Germany. The exposition will aim at the most vivid portrayal possible of the leading personalities. New regulation in Church relationships in Germany. Diocesan distribution. Awakening of new Catholic life in Germany,—Bernhard Overberg, Leopold von Stolberg, Sailer, Klemens Hofbauer, Görres. Church agitations in Cologne. Social questions (Ketteler, Kolping). The Vatican Council. The *Kulturkampf* (Mallinckrodt, Windthorst). The recent popes. Present condition of the Church. Missionary system. Catholic organizations. New religious organizations. The World War and the Church. Excursions and sight-seeing trips, where possible, should afford insight into the development of the church art of modern and most recent times.

## GERMAN

### 5 hours

*Phonetics.* In connection with the elements of Middle High German.

*Etymology and Syntax.* Etymology, likewise in connection with Middle High German, from the standpoint of the history of the language, making use of the German dictionary. Comprehensive review of material from the history of the language.

Modes of speech, proverbs, legal language. Introduction to the study of names. Language movements of our times. Effect of mechanical inventions and trade relationships on the language. Historical insights and fundamental principles in the struggle against language deterioration and slang. Introduction to Middle High German in close connection with the readings from Middle High German and from historical language materials already studied.

*Rhetoric.* Study of selections from the standpoint of rhetoric, —clearness of thought, content, tone painting, cadence, word pictures. Continuation of exercises for intensifying language feeling.

*Reading, Declamation, and Extemporaneous Speech.* Exercises in oral reproduction of literature, with increasing demand for apt and accurate choice of words and sentence structure. Continuation of school dramatics.

*Written Exercises.* Short themes having for their object the development of great versatility in style: literal reproduction of situations observed, short description of objects studied, outline reports emphasizing essentials, moods of nature, impressions of art works. The choice of topics for essays follows similar lines, drawing on private reading, and on class reading in other subjects. Themes based on experiences and impressions, but only with subjects selected by students. Not over nine themes, of which five are class exercises (these last not over three hours). Exercises in analysis as in *Obertertia.*

*Literature.* Scientific and artistic literature will be discussed here with constant reference to the whole instructional objective of the class in the social and cultural subjects. Understanding of the nineteenth century. For the epoch under consideration well chosen fiction and novels, suited to the comprehension of the pupils, down to the present time, without absolutely excluding works originating in earlier times, on the basis of a well graded plan for private reading. The dramatic reading prefers classics which deal with political science, the relation of the individual to race, state, and society. The age as revealed in the lyric, especially such lyrics as deal with the great crises of history. The home as expressed in proverb, in song, and in local art.

Scientific writings, in connection with history, will aim at an understanding of worthwhile personalities of the age, through their letters, speeches, and diaries; also biographies as an introduction into characteristic German personal life. In combination with geography and civics, the most important accounts, from the standpoint of literary art, of modern economic and social life, particularly in Germany. Worthwhile essays, also from the field of natural science, and their relation to individual and social welfare.

In connection with language instruction in Middle High German, easier passages of Middle High German literature, especially from popular epics.

Art study as in *Obertertia,* but in relation to the nineteenth century. Present-day tendencies in art, also in architecture, city and street planning. The urge for artistic expression as seen in industrial art and crafts will occupy a part of the time assigned to drawing and manual instruction.

*Theory of Poetry.* Completely avoiding the dramaturgical and technical approach, disclose to the understanding the inner artistic form of the drama by a study of specially appropriate selections. In the study of lyric poems only so much should be said about the nature of the lyric as may yield a sharper grasp of the artistic content and reveal more clearly the art peculiar to each lyric poet.

## HISTORY

### 2 hours

History of the more recent times, from 1815 to the present. Outstanding features of the political history of this period: National and patriotic aspirations, with especial reference to Germany. The partitioning of the world, in broad outlines, especially the growth of the English and Russian world empires, and the rise of Japan and the United States. Rebirth of French imperialism. The creation of the new German empire by Bismarck. Origin and policy of the Triple Alliance and the understanding between England, France, and Russia. The World War in its outstanding points. The political transformation of Europe as a result of the treaties of Versailles and St. Germain: territorial losses of Germany; economic consequences of the treaty of peace. A survey of the condition of German culture in foreign countries. In the materials presented the war history must be strictly limited to the decisive facts of the war for German unity and the World War. The inner transformation of economic life and the social upheaval of the nineteenth century demand thorough treatment, and the development of industry, technology, inventions, world trade and commerce, in connection with the achievements of leading men. Changed labor conditions of agriculture and the forms of German economic life in relation to Germany's economic advance since 1870. Capitalism and socialism. The social classes, peasantry and working class, industrial middle classes, and agricultural class, and their significance for state and society. The formative forces of present-day life are studied as far as possible in connection with excursions and sight-seeing trips and made concrete by studying monuments of the times.

## CIVICS

### 1 hour

The study of civics in organic relation to the general cultural subjects, especially history and geography, aims to unify in *Untersekunda* the results of the instruction heretofore given in civics, in order to make intelligible the historic evolution of the state and society of to-day, and to impress upon the pupil that these constitute for him the most important field of moral action. In this task, school life serves magnificently as a preparatory training for civic participation by giving a clear notion of fundamental historical and political concepts and by developing a corresponding predisposition of the will. At a point of departure for this instruction stand the constitutions of Germany and Prussia. A comparison of the constitutions of 1849 and 1871 brings out the most significant constitutional concepts, such as monarchy, republic, one and two house system, parliamentarianism, house of commons (*Reichstag*), the diet (*Landtag*), federal state (*Bundesstaat*), federal council (*Bundesrat*), and senate (*Reichsrat*). This comparison will further emphasize the underlying ideas, especially fundamental rights and duties of the German people, contained in the Weimar constitution. As a conclusion of the instruction in the middle classes, there should be a survey of the most important governmental agencies, the legal system, the army for defence (*Wehrmacht*), and financial and taxation systems.

## GEOGRAPHY

### 2 hours

General information on middle Europe, including the German Empire, Netherlands, Belgium, Luxemburg, Alsace and Lorraine, Switzerland, Austria, Bohemia, Western Poland, Danzig, Memel, the Baltic. As far as the ability of the class will permit, the instruction aims to bind together the separate facts into greater unities, from the standpoint of objective reality. It emphasizes the accomplishments of the German people in rendering arable uncultivated areas, the maintenance and development of German soil and water control in swamps, rivers, lakes, and on the sea coast. This instruction includes tribal origins and conditions determining settlements through an investigation of city plans, styles of architecture, and building materials.

In combination with history and civics special emphasis is laid upon economic, cultural, and political affairs. Connection of dense settlements and the founding of cities with mining districts. Characteristics of agricultural areas and industrial zones; dependence of commerce on production, geographical location, and transportation facilities.

Amplification of the elements of general geography acquired up to this point by a survey of the chief periods in geological history with reference to Germany, whose soil furnishes typical examples of different formations. Introduction to use of the map of Germany (scale, 1: 100,000) and geological maps, which are to be utilized in geography instruction, and for reference during scout hikes and study excursions.

## O II

### EVANGELICAL RELIGION

### 2 hours

In combination with the general instruction in the social sciences, religious instruction derives from the history of religion, including the great world religions and the spiritual legacy of the Greco-Roman world, certain groups of biblical truths and fundamental rules of Christian living. For this purpose, through reasonable employment of readings from original sources in religious history, as, for example, selections from the Vedas, discourses of Buddha, the Koran, and also selections from Greek philosophy (Plato, the Stoic), the religious content of the Old Testament, as well as a series of the most significant religious and moral truths of the New Testament, are to be developed. Reading of the Gospel of St. John (selections) should bring to the pupils the full meaning of Jesus.

Following the course in history, religious instruction should strive primarily to give a very complete understanding of the religion of the Middle Ages, especially its fundamental ideas and life forces, whose influence continues down to the present time. Keeping purely historical facts in the background, and foregoing all notion of logical completeness, the significance of the religious world of the Middle Ages is made clear by a longitudinal as well as a cross-sectional study of its most important points. The character of Western Christianity, the place of St. Augustine in world history, the educational work of the church among the Roman and German peoples, the idea of a universal church, the idea of a world church and the papacy, conception and essential character of the church, the struggle between the empire and the papacy, scholasticism and mysticism, and finally the urge for artistic expression in the Middle Ages.

The influence of Islam on the Middle Ages. Upheaval and reconstruction in the wake of individualism. Reading of Middle-Age source material in connection with German and history.

## CATHOLIC RELIGION

### 2 hours

Christ, the Man, and His work. These are to give a form of expression adequate to the needs and critical attitude of the present generation. Such topics as heathen, Jewish, and Christian sources on the life of Jesus. Credibility of Christian sources. Divine and messianic proofs of Jesus. The spiritual majesty of Jesus. His gospel of the adoption by God, of the kingdom of God. His prophecies. The moral perfection of Jesus (innocence and virtue). The miracles of Jesus and science. His resurrection. The triumph of His works. The dogma of the God-man is to be tied up with this. Christ, the second person of the Trinity (*unio hypostatica*). Salvation. Atonement through the death of Jesus. Christ and Paul. Restoration of the disorganized supernatural order. Means of grace through the Church. Doctrine of grace and the sacraments, especially the sacrament of the altar (Lord's Supper). Christ as the head of the Church (vine and branch, *vid.* epistles to the Ephesians and Colossians). The kingdom of Christ. The law-giver and judge of the world. Adoration of Jesus (historical retrospect; worship of the Heart of Jesus). Imitation of Christ. Mary, the mother of Jesus and our mother.

Typical representations of the image of Christ in art. Poetry dealing with Christ. Reading of one of the synoptic gospels.

*Church History—Preliminary Remarks for the Upper Section.* With the knowledge acquired in the middle grades as a starting-point the instruction aims at a critical examination of the subject matter and a clear comprehension of predominant spiritual tendencies. In this way the position of the Church in the spiritual struggle of the centuries will be placed in sharp relief, the lines of development in church life will be made more apparent, and the significance of the Church for the solution of the many burning questions of the present will be better recognized. The pupils should learn to express themselves in impromptu discussions on various important questions, in harmony with sources and longer treatises. The first great aim of the course in church history is the education of men true to their convictions and inspired by a love for the Church in present-day life.

In *Obersekunda* the early Church (and the Middle Ages to Boniface VIII) will be studied in connection with history. No effort will be made at completeness of presentation. Above all, the religious and edifying values of Christianity should be recognized in contrast with heathen forms of religion. A survey of methods, values, and errors of comparative religious history. The evolution of church doctrine in the struggle concerning creed in the first centuries. Growth of early Christian literature. Meaning of Eastern and Western church doctrine for theology and church life. The changed conception of the world and the coalescence of the old Latin Christianity with German national cultural factors. St. Benedict and his order. The Empire and the priesthood from Charlemagne to Innocent III. The Byzantine state church. Islam and its counter-influence during the Crusades. Spiritual and artistic life of the Catholic Middle Ages. Thomas Aquinas and the meaning of scholasticism. Bonaventure and mysticism. Outstanding German mystics. The Church and popular education. Piety of the Middle Ages. Development of the idea of church orders. Higher nobility of the German Church. Lights and shadows of the Middle Ages.

## GERMAN

### 5 hours

*Phonetics.* Review and amplification of the theory of phonetics on the basis of language history, with constant reference to examples from the Gothic and Old High German and especially Middle High German. A more thorough consideration of German dialects. Distribution, displacement, and disappearance of dialects. Exercises in oral language technique.

*Etymology and Syntax.* Development of the knowledge of Middle High German by emphasis on syntactical facts for historical appreciation of New High German syntax, always in connection with reading. Survey of historical development of Teutonic languages and German dialects, based on use of language atlas. Territorial spread of words, their migrations. Creation and reconstruction of words. Intensive study of theory of changes of meaning with reference to cultural development, making use of the German dictionary. Word compounds and syntactical facts from the standpoint of rhetoric.

*Rhetoric.* Introduction to the style of important creators in language; in constant correlation with reading. Style and personality, style and dialect (*Stammesart*), style and subject matter, style and nationality. Struggle against faulty style.

*Reading, Declamation, Impromptu Speaking.* Further exercises in classical readings and orations, and in the tricks of oratorical art in improvised speaking.

*Written Exercises.* Short themes as in *Untersekunda*. Essays in the form of discussions, with thorough consideration of the manifold requirements of the German essay. Occasional independent work from sources. Employment of private reading. Not over eight essays, of which at least four should be done in class.

*Literature.* In correlation with history, materials from the Greco-Roman culture which are the most valuable for German intellectual life; especially readings from the Greek tragedies. Development of the Greek mind from Homer to Euripides. Selections from Greek philosophy (Plato). Also worthwhile essays from scientific literature on antiquity and its relation to German culture and intellectual life.

The whole instructional objective of the class is to attain the best all-round understanding possible of the culture of the Middle Ages in its different life manifestations. This imposes upon the teaching of German the special task of an introduction into the spiritual life of the Middle Ages, its poetry and its art. It traces this development from the origin of the whole era in German and ancient sources and from Christianity down to the unfolding of the great Renaissance and the dissolution of the Middle Ages. The art and the literature of the great migrations, with a résumé of the intellectual life of the Northern peoples,—eddas, sagas. The Latin Middle Ages under the Carolingians and Ottos, in a selection of representative translations. Some literary monuments (fragments), according to their artistic worth. Longer selections from the more important poetry of the Middle High German Renaissance: popular epics, classical epics, minnesongs, and popular lyrics. The aim is to create an understanding of the poetic peculiarities and modes of expression of the works read. This can be done by careful grammatical and logical reading without translating. Good literary translations and paraphrases will serve to amplify and round out the readings. Prose selections from the Middle Ages in connection with religion and especially samples from the mystics. The rise of the civic culture of the towns; the folk theater; farces; meistersongs. The age of the Renaissance and the Reformation; German humanists, Luther.

*Scientific Literature.* Should deal with the remaining aspects of the life and culture of the Middle Ages; chiefly, German mythology, jurisprudence, husbandry, morals.

*Private Readings.* In the summer, should cover the continuation and influence of antiquity in modern poetry; in the winter, the continuous recurrence of Old German and medieval materials, particularly in the age of Romanticism.

*Archæology.* Remains of prehistoric civilizations found on German soil. German antiquities and influences which are to be observed, especially in the period of the great migrations, in correlation with the study of art. German racial studies.

*Art Study.* This aims to develop the Greek feeling for form through a few but typical examples of architecture and sculpture. Above all, it strives to make plain the artistic expression and modes of life and the imagery of the church and knight errantry of the Middle Ages; also its divergences from the attitude and conception of the Greeks. Architectural principles underlying the Roman, the Gothic, and the Renaissance styles.

Characteristic sculptures of the German Middle Ages. The outstanding German painters from the Cologne masters to Dürer and Grünewald. Flemish painting. A contrast of German and Italian painting of the fifteenth and sixteenth centuries will be helpful in working out the characteristic style in German art.

*Theory of Poetry.* In connection with literature, German poetic art in accordance with its own peculiar rules. The history of its development from alliterative verse to *Opitz.* On the basis of readings, the formulation of the general characteristics of the popular and classical epics, the minnesongs, and popular poetry.

## HISTORY

### 4 hours

*Preliminary Remarks for the Upper Section.* On the basis of the objective knowledge already acquired and of the information gained in the middle section, the instruction in the higher classes rises to more thoughtful penetration and abstract formulation of historical problems. In this process of formulating the subject matter, emphasis will be laid upon important crucial points of development which are to be presented in their decisive significance in the general progress of events. This thoughtful consideration will lead to a discussion of historical and philosophical questions at suitable points. Thus this material relating to the history of civilization, in so far as it may not have been integrated with other cultural subjects into an organic unity with the general course in history, is to form an intimate part of national history in order to impress the fact that the state is a phase of civilization inseparable from the other fields of human culture. In accordance with the methods of activity instruction appropriate source readings will make clear to the pupils how the facts in a given case are derived from original documents and how historical judgments and principles are arrived at. Well chosen selections from the best historical writings will reveal the spirit and method of the great historical investigators. In addition to this, pupils should be encouraged to make independent studies which should prove valuable in class instruction. In this way "free activity groups" making coöperative studies will be kept in intimate relationship with the work of the class.

*Subject Matter for the Obersekunda.* History of antiquity and the Middle Ages to the downfall of the Hohenstaufens.

The treatment of antiquity will be limited to the essentials of Greek and Roman history, with special emphasis on such points as had direct effect upon subsequent epochs, and especially upon the German and Romance peoples. Therefore only the Periclean age and the epochs of Hellenism are to be studied in detail in Greek history, while in Roman history only the world domination of Rome from the golden period of the Republic to the downfall of ancient culture. In the choice of subject matter preference should be given to accomplishments of the Greeks which are of greatest significance for world culture in philosophy and art, and among the Romans those relating to statecraft and law. For a clear understanding of the fundamental political principles, a study of the political and social phases of Greek and Roman life in their transparent simplicity will be found of the greatest value. In this connection such topics as: the meaning of family and race; a unified popular consciousness in customs, language, literature, art, and religion; chief characteristics of the ancient state in its classical forms.

The principal aim of the instruction is an introduction to the early German times and the culture of the early Middle Ages in Germany, in organic unity with the development of political economy and social institutions of this epoch. Especially to be worked out are German characteristics and contributions to the general culture of the Middle Ages. Nor is the meaning of Arabian civilization for an understanding of this epoch to be overlooked. In the study of the subject matter in political history, the development of the state out of social conditions of the Middle Ages will occupy the foreground, as also that of the church as its sociological counterpart; in the study of civics, attention will be called on the one hand to the differences between the modern state and that of the Middle Ages, and on the other hand to the continuity of special Middle-Age characteristics and institutions down to the present time. For a survey of the forms of society in the Middle Ages, it will be best to emphasize, in the earlier times, the social freedom; in the Frankish epoch, the seigniorial landownership and its economic and social consequences; and in the time of the emperors, feudalism and the characteristics of knighthood.

## GEOGRAPHY
### 2 hours

*Preliminary Remarks for the Upper Section.* The course in geography in the higher classes calls for a correlation with mathematics and the natural sciences and with history and the humanities. The groups of problems to be treated in geography are, therefore, in their selection and orderly sequence dependent, in the main, on the subjects and material of these courses. Geographical instruction will, therefore, in reciprocal relation with mathematics, physics, and biology, and even with civics and history have for its special task: to show how civilization is deep-rooted in nature and demonstrate, by appealing to the universality of law, how culture has been built upon nature in accordance with her processes; to mature the judgment of the pupils for functional thinking; to train them to a genetic understanding of things; and finally to deepen and vitalize their civic consciousness through an accurate representation of the relation between soil and state, between the earth and mankind. The final course in geography does not, therefore, consider as its most important task a mere extension of the subject matter of the middle sections, but rather to substitute for the study of the several countries in their geographical groups a consideration of the social, economic, and political organizations of their peoples and their reciprocal influences, by means of a cross-sectional study and comparison of their morphological or climatic conditions, their ethnographic or cultural status, their economic and commercial conditions, and also their political organization. For this purpose such problems as: man's dependence on the earth and his dominion over it; stages and forms of economic development; types of colonization; production and manufacture of raw materials; and dependence of market values upon supply and demand. Advancement and retardation of peoples due to physical peculiarities of their country or to their own natural endowments. Relation between the state and the soil; natural and historical boundary lines; natural and artificially developed settlements; evolution of world traffic and its thoroughfares. Later the course should give the pupil, by means of a clear-cut presentation, a comprehensive view of the world, and organize for him the terrestrial bodies and their movements as to their place in the universe. Finally, it should introduce him to the history of geography and, by reading worthwhile essays and other appropriate works, prepare him in the cultural "activity groups" to develop thoroughly geographical problems. After all, the following distribution of subject matter represents only one of many possibilities.

*Obersekunda.* Geographical knowledge in harmony with the preliminary suggestions, preference being given to the most important of the great powers and leading economic and commercial centers of the world; namely, the United States of North America, Spanish-speaking countries, and British and French world empires.

## I

### EVANGELICAL RELIGION

### U I AND O I

### 2 hours each

*Unterprima.* In organic continuation of the course of the *Obersekunda,* and using similar methods, the salient and crucial points of religious development from the end of the Middle Ages down to the end of the eighteenth century. The chief objective of the class is the understanding of Protestantism in its religious, cultural, and intellectual meaning. The dissolution of the world of the Middle Ages in the age of Renaissance. The German Reformation, especially the work of Luther, with a detailed reading of characteristic passages from his writings and a comparison of corresponding passages from the Pauline letters. Lutheranism, Calvinism, and Tridentine Catholicism in their characteristic differences and enduring significance. The rise of the modern conception of the world and the adjustment of Protestantism to the ideas of the "Enlightenment." Constant use of sources. The final consideration of the questions arising at this point, when presented under the constant stimulus afforded by the other subjects, will bring home to the pupil the Christian and Evangelical truth of the New Testament.

*Oberprima.* As a part of the general problem of the class, religious instruction in common effort with German and philosophy, brings about an inner adjustment of Christianity with German idealism, either by source readings, as from Herder and Schleiermacher, or by working out various religious truths of Christianity through a study of corresponding fields of thought from philosophy and poetry, as well as from tendencies which are hostile to Christianity. By using historical and civic instruction, the meaning of Christianity and the Church for the political and social life will be brought out, either in connection with history or in the discussion of individual problems and questions of the day. In the same manner will be treated questions relating to one's personal life, for the purpose of awakening a keen sense of responsibility. The cultural "activity group" in the social sciences will also make it possible, in religious instruction, for the pupil to investigate individual problems of special interest to him. Likewise will religious instruction make use of private readings serviceable for its scientific and educative task. In this way will the relation of religion to poetry and pictorial art be made especially apparent.

## CATHOLIC RELIGION

### 2 hours

*Unterprima.* The Christian conception of God. God in the light of reason. Humanity's belief in God. Experiencing God and proof of God (*Vatic.* III, c. i.). God and the world: explanation of the world without God—monism. Explanation without a personal God—pantheism. Theory of evolution. Man and animal. Spirituality and immortality of the soul.

God in the light of revelation. Conception, possibility, necessity as characteristics of revelation. Being and qualities of divinity. The dogma of creation. The account of creation. Divine providence. The Trinity.

God as creator of the supernatural order. Original sin. Salvation. Predestination. The riddle of the universe and Christianity's solution. Pessimistic and optimistic world views. God as infinite. The ideal of truth, morality, and beauty. True religiousness. Belief in God and joy in life. Faith and unbelief. Readings selected from the Psalms and prophets that deal with the idea of God. Selected passages from the gospel of St. John.

*Church History.* From Boniface VIII to the French Revolution. The dissolution process of the Middle Ages. State and Church in the last days of the Middle Ages. The religious and moral condition of the German people. Humanism and the Renaissance. Efforts at church reform. Luther's religious development. Conversion of Germany to Protestantism. Three chief forms of Protestantism. The Council of Trent and the reform of the Church. The era of saints. Life among the orders and missionary activity. Development of the law of the state church. The Enlightenment and disbelief. The meaning of the Enlightenment as an effort to account for the world without God and the supernatural. The attitude of the German classical writers toward religion and the Church. The inner development of Protestantism since 1555. Religious and moral status of Germany and France on the eve of the Revolution. The aim of this course is to show how modern culture arose as a consequence of the effect of humanism, criticism, theories of natural science, and subjectivism.

*Oberprima.* Introduction to the important personal and public duties of Catholics.

Religious foundation of moral life: theonomy not autonomy. The doctrine of law and conscience. The conflicts of conscience. The training of the will in education and in self-education. Freedom of the will. Duty and inclination. Virtue. Virtue and happiness. Sin and salvation from sin.

The various individual obligations. Religious duties in the narrower sense. The doctrine of faith and doubt. Belief and knowledge. The life of prayer in private and in the Church. Final academic and practical treatment of the liturgy. The Catholic and his church (*sentire cum ecclesia*). The Catholic of action. The ideal Catholic family: unity, inseparability and sanctity of marriage. The law of the Church with respect to marriage. The sex problem. Authority and freedom in education. The Church and the modern youth movement. Duties toward the state: State and church. State and schools. State and religious freedom. The Catholic state ideal. Nationalism. The Catholic and human society: Protection of life. Duels. The alcohol question. Spiritual and secular callings. The choice of a vocation. Loyalty to one's calling. Withdrawal from and overcoming of the world. Industrial life. The Church and the social question. Individual and community affairs. Catholicism and education. The ideal of personality: Truthfulness, moral freedom, love. Consecration of personality.

Old and New Testament texts for instruction in morality: Reading and explanation of one of the Pauline letters—I Corinthians.

*Church History.* From the French Revolution to the present time. The French Revolution and its reaction on the Church. Secularization. Restoration of the ecclesiastical order. Concordats. Reawakening of Catholic consciousness up to 1848. The struggle between the state church and liberalism. State and Church in Prussia from 1850 to 1870. Meaning of the Vatican. The social *Kulturkampf.* The papacy since 1870. Leo XIII. Catholic charity in the nineteenth century. The Church and the education question. World missions. The present-day status of the Church in the most important enlightened countries. Modernism. The church organizations of the Eastern Greek churches. Trends in modern Protestantism. Occultism. The Church and the World War. For a final review, and as material for the impromptu discussions, the pupils should strive to sum up, by means of a longitudinal and cross-sectional study extending through the entire period of church history, the ideas and events most significant for the existence and struggles of the kingdom of God in the Church.

## GERMAN

## U I AND O I

### 4 hours each

#### Philosophical Readings: U I and O I—Each 1 Hour

*Philology.* In the utilization of the language history materials already developed, studies from the fields of the psychology, the philosophy, and the æsthetics of language, in connection with the foreign languages. Differences in language as an expression of the intellectual character of peoples. Ethics of language: The adequacy of German for accomplishing things in the different fields of culture. Essays of outstanding language scholars and creators. Something about the history of research in the German language. The most important points in the development of German script.

*Rhetoric.* The adaptability of German style to the different aims and uses of language: in business, in public life, in art.

*Reading, Declamation, and Impromptu Speaking.* Regular exercises in extemporaneous speaking in debate, and in a carefully prepared declamation. Speech technique in relation to the physiology of the voice and from hygienic and æsthetic standpoints.

*Written Exercises.* Written work as in *Obersekunda*, allowing the pupil the greatest possible freedom. As a substitute for the home essays, even more elaborate treatises on topics from the entire field of human culture, based on independent use of source materials—student investigation. Not over eight essays, of which four should be class essays.

*Literature.* The study of German in *Prima* considers German idealism as the classical educational epoch of German life, and therefore regards it as the central point of its educational effort. It strives to comprehend it from its intellectual and historical presuppositions, points out its fundamental meaning for all the fields of life, strives to penetrate as deeply as possible into its great poets and thinkers, and throws a bridge from classical times to the understanding of the present.

*Unterprima* has the special task of acquainting the pupils with the restoration of German intellectual culture in connection with the rise of the modern spirit. The collapse at the time of the Thirty Years' War and some of the characteristic representatives of that epoch. The age of the "Enlightenment" and its countercurrents, in connection with other cultural subjects. The entire works of Klopstock, Lessing, and Herder will be considered in relation to the trends of European culture in general. Likewise "storm and stress," especially the youthful Goethe and Schiller. In connection with the reading of dramas, a survey of the history of the German theater.

*Oberprima* aims to present clearly German idealism as the perfection and unification of these intellectual movements and to see to it that its chief representatives are understood, primarily Goethe and Schiller in their combined accomplishments reaching throughout the German world. The instruction must not, therefore, be limited to the reading of individual poems, but must compass the several poems in their connection with the personal life of the writers and the entire epoch. Romanticism in its organic relation to German idealism. Transition from world citizenship to the national state; Heinrich von Kleist. Further, relationships between literature, pictorial art, and music; between the drama and the stage.

Literature after Goethe will in general be treated as a continuation and extension of the epochs previously studied—political drama from Lessing to Hauptman; from world citizenship to state citizenship: Schiller, Hebbel, Gottfried Keller. The variations in the development of the literature of the nineteenth century and of the present must be considered in cross-sections and according to the problems and materials taken up: Austrian poets; young Germany and political poetry; classical realism;

art as impression and expression. Especially in the required and voluntary private reading, in free "activity groups," in the longer elective readings, and in the regular lectures, the feeling of the pupil for modern literature will be awakened and made fruitful for the regular work. A brief survey of the principal trends in the literature of foreign countries will be required in this connection. But in no case must German idealism lose its place as the central point in class instruction.

Scientific writings should be especially cultivated in *Prima*, with selections from works of the great writers. Appropriate excerpts and complete works in all fields of modern life wherein the natural sciences, economic life, political and social problems can be presented effectively in securing an understanding of the nineteenth century and of the present age should also be included. This task requires a carefully planned correlation of all subjects of study.

A special task devolves upon philosophical readings. When prepared beforehand and reënforced by a philosophical treatment of all courses in the higher classes, these readings contribute to the whole educational problem of the class. By using selected chapters and shorter works, especially of the greater German philosophers, who express the dominating thought of the corresponding age, they round out the complete picture of national culture, and in the continuity of their operation show clearly how the present grew out of the past. It is imperative to choose, as far as possible, self-explanatory chapters from the great intellectual composite of German idealism, at the central point of which stands Kant.

*Folk Lore and Antiquity.* Psychology of fairy tales, sagas, myths, and folk songs. Racial influences in the time of classicism and romanticism and in the present time.

*Art Study.* In harmony with the objective of the class in *Unterprima*, style of baroque architecture, especially in Germany. Development of Dutch art to Rembrandt and Reubens. In *Oberprima*, modern classicism. The renaissance of German painting in the nineteenth century. Present tendencies in art.

*Theory of Poetry.* Along with regular review of previous work comes a historical and critical study of the formal elements of poetry, its types and tendencies, with special consideration of trends in style and of the different kinds of æsthetics, especially the tragic and comic.

## HISTORY

### U I AND O I

### 3 hours each

*Unterprima.* From the beginning of the Middle Ages to the end of the period of the French Revolution. The choice of subject matter from political history is made with the aim of providing an appreciation of the modern state as a product of the political development of Western peoples. German development is therefore to be made clear in relation to the history of other great powers. The overthrow of medieval social ideals through the triumph of lay culture, the breakdown of individualism, and the development of a national consciousness. Rise and first growth of power of the middle class, establishment of the national state—Spain, France, and England; growth of German territories. The Renaissance, Humanism, and the Reformation. Accomplishments of absolutism. The struggle of the great powers for world domination and its reaction on Germany. The empire of the Hapsburgs. The struggle for the control of the Baltic—Poland, Denmark, Sweden, Russia. The rise of Prussia. The colonial empire; the American Revolution. The French Revolution and the transformation of Germany in its defense campaign against Napoleon.

In correlation with the other social sciences, the creative ideas of each epoch studied and the participation of the different peoples in the development of the modern spirit, especially at the time of the Enlightenment, must be made clear and their meaning for Germany carefully worked out. To history, in connection with geography, belongs especially the explanation of economic relationships, of social conditions and movements: overthrow of medieval natural economy through the use of money and business intercourse; organization and characteristics of manual industries; rise of middle class wealth and capitalistic system; mercantilism in theory and practice. History of social movements, especially struggles between sovereign princes; the nobility and the cities; guilds and apprentices; diminution of rights of peasants; vassalage and hereditary submission.

## CIVICS

### U I AND O I

#### 1 hour each

The course in civics selects certain problems of history for special study, and develops them particularly by using suitable source material. A thorough consideration of such problems as: restoration of Roman law; nature of the absolute state; rise of the modern army; officialdom; codification of laws; state craft; taxes. Theory of natural rights and social contracts; human rights. Beginnings of the national constitutional state. Secularization; concordats.

*Oberprima.* From the Congress of Vienna to the present. As a continuation of the course of the *Unterprima,* comes the development of the national constitutional state as the central point of political history. Era of the restoration and of liberalism; the revolutions in west and middle Europe, primarily in Germany. The struggles for national unity in Italy and Germany. Solution of the German question in the restricted sense and the work of Bismarck. Armed peace for the preservation of the European balance of power. The inner political development of Germany since 1870 is to be studied from all angles: development of the constitution and legislative power; the army; justice; social legislation; financial legislation concerning traffic and trade; state and church. The significance of the great German parties and commercial organizations. Colonial policy. Imperialism and political alliances; the Triple Entente and the Triple Alliance. The main facts of the World War and the Treaty of Versailles. The Revolution and the new order in Germany.

The predominant intellectual tendencies of the nineteenth century are to be made as concrete as possible in coöperation with the social sciences as a whole. Economic history treats primarily the transformation of the state and society in connection with the rise of modern political economy. Banks and exchanges, trade, commerce, industry, agriculture. German political economy and world markets. History of German labor movements in connection with the labor movements of England and France.

The modern state stands as the central topic in the study of civics. The German and Prussian constitutions will be studied thoroughly as to their most essential parts in comparison with the constitutions of the most advanced foreign countries. The course selects comprehensive problems and points out either their solution in the course of historical development or their effect on existing law. Such groups of problems as: Personal freedom; fundamentals of penal law; individual problems of civil rights; relation between the people, popular representation and executive power; individual will and popular will. Different forms of the elective franchise. Unitarianism and federalism. Self-government and bureaucratic government. Conservatism, liberalism, democracy, socialism, communism. Popular rights, supra-state organizations; League of Nations. As an introduction to the political and national economic theories of philosophers, politicians and economists, selections from their works and from speeches, party platforms, manifestoes, and newspapers are to be abundantly drawn upon.

## GEOGRAPHY

### U I AND O I

2 hours each

*Unterprima.* Conclusion of the geography of the different countries: the Balkan states; Italy and the Near East with a glance at the Far East; Russia and her related republics; Germany's neighbors and the German state. Corresponding to the whole work of the class, special attention is given to choosing the points of view of especial value to the study of civics. The relations of the several countries and their peoples to the German Republic are to be kept in the foreground. Special attention is given to German culture in foreign countries. The influence of German civilization on other peoples, and the linking up of German capital with German commercial industry and German agriculture with other world areas are given detailed consideration.

Selected topics from astronomical geography. The most important geographical projections and their mathematical foundation. Some facts from surveying.

*Oberprima.* On the basis of the course in geography and the several problems that have already been treated, a systematic survey of general geography, drawing upon the whole mathematical, physical, and scientific knowledge of the pupils. The terrestrial bodies and their movements in the universe. The physical and mathematical properties of the air, water, and earth's surface. The earth as the home and source of sustenance of animal life, especially of man. The coöperation and the reciprocal dependence of matter and energy. Historical-geological development of the inorganic and the organic world. The stages of cultural and political life still observable. Comparison of prehistoric and ethnological facts. Changes in the earth's surface in the course of time. Awakening of a consciousness, on the one hand, for the interdependency of mankind in causal relationships, and on the other, for freedom in determining the goal and course of future developments. The significance of geographical problems for questions of ethics and philosophy of life, in relation to the other cultural subjects, especially philosophy.

## II. FOREIGN LANGUAGES

### A. FUNDAMENTAL FOREIGN LANGUAGES

*Preliminary Remarks.* Instruction in foreign languages under the nine-year plan aims at an all-round, thorough knowledge of the languages and at an introduction to the culture of the foreign peoples concerned, on the basis of an intensive study of the most important works. In correlation with the cultural subjects the meaning of the foreign culture for German culture will be brought out, as well as its principal differences from the German.

The pupils should be made to grasp the special characteristics of the foreign language in the matter of vocabulary, syntax, and style, by a constant comparison with the mother tongue; to understand more fully the nature of linguistic phenomena; and by means of a variety of practice, to acquire a certain degree of facility in oral and written expression. This mastery of and general insight into language should enable them to work on by themselves and even learn other languages independently, and, through their understanding of the spirit of foreign peoples, to participate personally in the history of the time. The readings are therefore to be selected with the aim of utilizing the knowledge gained through the foreign language to form a well founded idea of the part the people whose language is being studied has had in the general development of civilization. These readings should also thoroughly cover all cultural manifestations of life in literature, pictorial art, politics, economic and social development, philosophy and religion, so as to follow more thoroughly certain lines of growth in the most varied fields. In this, as in the study of the cultural subjects, no attempt is made to attain a logically complete presentation. By means of a clearer understanding of the forces which, in gradual evolution, have created present conditions and continue to operate, the instruction aims to give a picture of present-day England, France, and America. For special consideration are the epochs and inventions of foreign peoples which have exerted an influence upon the development of our own culture.

*Fundamentals of Method.* The need for an intimate relationship between the instruction in foreign languages and the cultural studies must be the determining point of view in the selection and distribution of subject matter. This holds for the actual language teaching as also for the reading and the insight afforded by it.

1. *Pronunciation.* The development of the idiomatic pronunciation is best accomplished through untiring, exact pro-

nunciation by the teacher, repetition by individual pupils, by groups, and by the class. Phonetics should especially enable the teacher to suggest to his pupils practical means for aiding them in producing the sounds correctly. Above all, in those parts of the country where local dialects are strongly intrenched (as, for example, failure to discriminate between voiced and merely aspirated sounds), definite instruction and drill are necessary. This is generally necessary in the case of those sounds which are not found in German; for example, the French nasal sounds, the English *th*, and in High German territory the English *r, l;* also the soft blending of the voice, slurring of vowel groupings, and the like. Along with a correct pronunciation, proper inflection in continuous reading and in impromptu speaking is to be required.

Many of the exercises called for here, especially the strict articulation in French that must be acquired, will also be found helpful in German pronunciation.

Along with the pronunciation, must be practiced also the historical methods of writing.

2. *Oral Exercises.* These exercises are helpful to the whole process of language learning. They adapt themselves to the perceptive and imaginative capacities of the pupils and cover the various fields of experience, until they pass over into the simpler abstract concepts. On the basis of the progressive readings, a brief comparative study can be made of German with foreign culture. In the higher classes, where the study of foreign civilizations is made more intensive in connection with reading, the conversational exercises are adapted naturally to the more abstract fields of thought, without thereby losing either in clarity or in the full significance of the thought content.

Above all, these oral exercises serve the purpose of acquiring as large a number as possible of new forms of expression and of impressing them so they may not be forgotten. The textbooks of the first years should provide, in the main, the words and expressions which must be integrated with a vocabulary ready for immediate use. In the successive classes this is to be enriched constantly in all directions, and the oral exercises are to make sure that the pupils always have a definite choice of words ready for use.

3. *Reading.* The most important part of foreign language

instruction, the reading, takes into consideration as far as possible the intimate connection of the content with the cultural objective of the class concerned, in that it strives for a vivid conception of the mutual relationships and of the corresponding phases of the cultural life of the foreign people.  Hence, a discussion of Shakespeare, Shaftesbury, and others; of the French Middle Ages, French classicism, different trends in the nineteenth century; of scientific prose of all kinds, especially appropriate historical and cultural accounts; while especially capable pupils may be assigned portions of the works of the philosophers, —all these will serve to supplement the reading of *belles lettres.* In all these fields the characteristics of the foreign people are to be compared with our own.  Connected readings of entire works or selections from the larger works should begin as early as possible and become the chief feature of language study in the third or fourth year in the case of the fundamental language, and in the second language by the second year at the latest, especially in the case of the more mature students.

The history of literature is not to be systematic, but is to be carried on in connection with reading of complete works or separate portions of the larger works.  For example, the relation of a given work to the complete writings of an author should be pointed out, as also his place in the intellectual life of his time. In this way the main characteristics of each age will be summed up again in the development of its literature and culture as a whole.  In like manner a historical insight will be obtained in connection with the reading of historical materials.  In order to complete the picture secured by the reading of entire works, selections from good anthologies will be found invaluable.  In like manner the understanding of foreign literature may be deepened by using appropriate translations as material for private reading.

4. *Grammar.*  The fundamental principles of grammar, after they have been presented in their general aspects by the teachers of German, are to be illustrated and fixed in mind by a comparison with the mother tongue.  The grammar should point out and explain the nature of foreign modes of expression, and in so doing clear up the differences between the foreign and the mother tongue, but should by no means consist of rules for translation.

The grammar work is fundamentally inductive and, therefore, is to be worked out on the basis of familiar language materials. The learning of ready-made rules is useless. Only after previous acquaintance with a sufficient number of individual cases should an attempt be made to formulate the rule. From the particular, one arrives through coöperative activity at the universally valid, and thus recognizes the fundamental principle underlying the individual phenomena. For example, it is not a question of learning by heart the rules for the subjunctive and infinitive, but rather, by continuous observation of the foreign modes of expression, of securing a clear feeling and notion of what mood means in the foreign language that is being studied or what function each verb form serves. The German language is to be used primarily in grammar instruction.

In a case where, as in French, phonetic rules can be derived from the modern language, or where a relation to the German language is evident, as in English, it will be possible to awaken an understanding of the history of phonetics, without presupposing on the part of the pupil any considerable knowledge of the history of language. Nor should the teacher forego the psychological explanation of syntactical phenomena, whenever an opportunity offers. To feel called upon to give an explanation at any cost leads not to comprehension but rather to confusion. Whenever a simple explanation is not to be found, one should be satisfied to formulate the rule according to meaning and circumstance.

5. *Written Exercises*. In the first years the written exercises must be based closely on the readings. They consist of dictations, recasting from the standpoint of grammar and style, free reproduction of what has been read, and finally translations into the foreign language. One arrives at an independent use of the foreign tongue only through continued and varied elaboration of material learned upon the basis of good example. There is no need for a special exercise book for translations into the foreign tongue. The exercises in the class are to be carried on in an animated dialogue between teacher and pupils, based upon the reading. Later, when systematic translations into the foreign tongue are the rule, it will be found best not to use artificial materials, but rather original German selections. As a goal to be reached in this case it will be permissible to trans-

late a simple German text. Otherwise the aim is a voluntary piece of work, consisting either of an essay or of the reproduction of a German text read aloud in class, which is within the scope of materials developed in the reading.

### Course of Study

The subject matter to be taught in the three sections—lower, middle, and higher—is carefully circumscribed. The distribution of these materials to the respective classes is left to the individual course of study of the school.

### ENGLISH

### VI to IV

### 6 hours each

*Phonetics.* Training the ear, and drill upon phonetics. Reading and oral exercises. Memorization of poems, easy prose tales, and short dialogues. Singing of songs. Reading with attention to accentuation of words and sentence inflection.

*Vocabulary.* The acquisition of a vocabulary which is based primarily upon the immediate environment of the pupil, upon the simplest relationships in a larger realm of life—house, family, city, upon vocational activities and life in the country and the city, and the like.

*Grammar.* Drill on forms with simultaneous practical exercises in syntactical applications; pronouns are always to be practiced in connection with verbs. Understanding of elements of meaning and relationship is to be awakened early.

*Written Exercises.* Exercises in spelling, dictation, and recasting. Reproduction of short prose selections, also translation from German to fix the knowledge developed in the class.

*Reading Matter.* Fairy tales and stories, descriptions of nature, and elementary English history. In *Quarta,* connected readings.

### U III and O III

### 5 hours each

### U II

### 4 (3) hours

*Vocabulary.* The vocabulary is to be developed from the readings, with constant review of what was learned in the lower section; regular conversations are to be used to fix the new words.

Economic conditions, accounts of travel, letters of the most varied kinds. Some business letters must be used, since some pupils at the regular promotion to *Obersekunda* leave school to enter a vocation.

*Grammar.* Syntax; transition to rhetoric. Short study of synonyms. Survey of the relationship with German.

*Reading.* Nineteenth century prose with historical and geographical content to be studied in connection with actual events and conditions in England. Biographical sketches of leading personalities. Essays; transition to the novel. Ballads and some outstanding classical poetry. A comedy, a historical drama, or one of the easier tragedies of Shakespeare. In U II, the first attempt to form a cultural picture of present-day England as it arises from all the materials of study for the lower and middle sections.

## O II TO O I

### 4 hours each

*Grammar.* Broader knowledge of grammatical phenomena, likewise psychological and historical treatment of grammatical facts, so far as this treatment can be accomplished without auxiliary aid from the older language epochs. Practical work in composition; short essays.

*Reading.* Serious dramas from Shakespeare. Selections from the more thoughtful classical poetry down to the present time. Social problems in novels and dramas—Galsworthy, Shaw; in controversial works—Burke, Carlyle, Ruskin. Rise of the British world empire through a study of serious works of history and travel—Seeley, Froude. Something of the literature and history of Shakespeare, his stage, his predecessors, and his influence on later generations, also among us; of Dickens, Thackeray, and the development of the longer novel; of the thought movement seen in J. Stuart Mill; of the pre-Raphaelites; and the like. Attempt to formulate a comprehensive picture of present-day England. Main points of the history of the United States, with special reference to Emerson, Carnegie, and Münsterberg.

## FRENCH

### VI TO IV

### 6 hours each

As to phonetics, vocabulary, reading matter, grammar, and written exercises, the directions given under English apply as the case permits.

## U III AND O III

### 5 hours each

## U II

### 4 (3) hours

*Vocabulary.* As in the corresponding grade for English.

*Grammar.* Fixation, amplification, and intensification of the knowledge of word forms in connection with the study of syntax.

*Reading.* At first lighter prose readings, of a narrative and historical character. Stories like Daudet's *Le Petit Chose,* novels by Daudet, Margueritte, Theuriet, Paul Arène, Töpffer, and others. Historical accounts from such works as Lavisse, *Récits de l'Histoire de France,* D'Hombres and Monod, *Biographies,* Monod, *Allemands et Francais,* Michelet, and others. With the more mature pupils, somewhat harder prose; from poetical readings, principally La Fontaine's *Fables,* and epic poetry of the nineteenth century. As to dramas—in U II—such as: Sandeau, *Mlle de la Seiglière,* Augier, *La Pierre de Touche,* and others.

## O II TO O I

### 4 hours each

*Grammar.* In reviewing the inflectional forms and the syntax to gain a broader and more exact knowledge, the pupils should acquire a general notion of the fundamental rules of the French language. To develop an appreciation of the differences in style between the French and the German, the judgment must be trained by urging pupils to observe for themselves.

*Reading.* Some French classical works of the seventeenth century will be drawn upon as indispensable to an understanding of the development of German literature—Lessing. Also extracts from Pascal, La Rochefoucauld, La Bruyère, Bossuet; some of the letters of Mme. de Sévigné and La Fontaine's *Fables,* which can be adapted to each grade of the school.

From the eighteenth century, at least Montesquieu, Voltaire, and Rousseau must be brought within the scope of the pupil's consideration, either in extracts or by use of anthologies.

The chief point is the reading of the masterpieces of the nineteenth and twentieth centuries, so chosen as to furnish a picture of the intellectual development of the times. To this end, primarily along with selections from the most important poetic works of diverse tendencies, some of the greatest story tellers of the nineteenth century, from Balzac to Anatole France, and Romain Rolland should be read. Their influence upon the development of German and European literature is to be pointed out. As historical and philosophical writers are to be considered, Taine, Aulard, Hanotaux, De Tocqueville, and others, and also such works dealing with the history of culture as those of Goncourt and Seignobos. Worthy of recommendation also are collections of longer, independent extracts of the more important historical works; further, for completing the literary-historical survey, selections of a good anthology with such writers as Chateaubriand, Mme. de Staël, George Sand, Victor Hugo, Guizot, Michelet, Sainte-Beuve, Ernest Renan. With a class interested in philosophy selections can be read from Jouffroy, Victor Cousin, and others, and with a class which shows an appreciation of political questions, the pamphlets of Paul-Louis Courier, for example, can be used.

In the lyric poetry, the pupil must secure a more exact knowledge of the period of Romanticism through a study of its diverse representatives—Lamartine, Vigny, Victor Hugo; that of the Parnassians—Leconte de Lisle, Heredia, Sully-Prudhomme and Baudelaire; and also selections from the works of the modern poets, who, like Paul Verlaine, Verhæren, and others, stand in close relation to German poetry.

The above selections will serve merely as examples. In view of the great wealth of appropriate works, the teacher will choose freely the works he believes best adapted to the inclination and capacity of his pupils.

### B. THE SECOND FOREIGN LANGUAGE

*Introductory Remarks.* Instruction in the second foreign language will equip the pupils with the linguistic knowledge that will enable them to read worthwhile books and later to work independently.

1. Thoroughgoing explanations of the better literary works will lead naturally into the cultural life of the people concerned; at the same time, in keeping with the general task of the higher school, they will make this foreign culture serve as an aid to an understanding of our own.

2. The remarks on methods made for the fundamental foreign language will, in general, be found applicable to the second modern language, but even more apropos will be the foundation laid in German instruction.

### French or English as the Second Foreign Language

In cases where French or English, as the second foreign language, has only a four-year course, it must be seen to that the pupils, making use of the abilities and knowledge they have acquired from the first language—pronunciation, general grammar—not only attain in the first two years accuracy in pronunciation, but also a thorough foundation in grammatical forms in connection with syntax. Even in the second year, the reading of the easier authors can occupy first place. For grammar, which is to be learned inductively and through illustrations taken as far as possible from the readings, an extra hour a week is to be used. In the third and fourth years, the most important of the works mentioned in connection with the required language will be studied.

### FRENCH

### U II

#### 5 hours

*Phonetics.* Reading and oral exercises, with application of the elementary principles of phonetics.

*Grammar.* The regular conjugation in connection with the personal pronouns; the remaining parts of speech in their principal forms, especially the pronouns.

*Vocabulary.* To be acquired from reading and observation.

*Written Work.* Dictation, imitation, translation.

### O II

#### 4 hours

*Grammar.* The irregular conjugation with application of phonetic rules and in connection with similar phenomena in nouns. Syntax, especially mood and tense.

*Reading.* Prose readings, mostly of a historical type; stories.

*Written Work.* Dictations and easy, free reproductions.

### U I AND O I

#### 3 hours each

*Grammar.* More extensive study of syntax.

*Reading.* Especially suitable works of the eighteenth century and from the poetry of the nineteenth century. The intellectual and political relations with Germany are primarily to be developed, wherever the readings furnish opportunity for such study.

*Written Work.* Free reproduction of short German selections.

## ENGLISH

### U II

#### 4 (5) hours

*Phonetics.* In connection with simple conversations.
*Grammar.* Elements of inflection; sentence structure.
*Vocabulary.* Of school language and of simple daily life.
*Reading.* Stories and travel.
*Written Work.* As in the preliminary study of the first foreign language.

### O II

#### 3 (4) hours

*Grammar.* Completion of etymology. Syntax.
*Reading.* Historical material. Prose dramas. Ballads.
*Written Exercises.*

### U I

#### 3 (4) hours

*Grammar.* Transition from syntax to study of style.
*Reading.* One comedy from Shakespeare with an introductory study of his age. Historical prose. Novels like *Ivanhoe, Christmas Carol, Silas Marner.*

### O I

#### 3 (4) hours

*Grammar.* Reviews for the purpose of extending the knowledge of the subject. Exercises in style; short essays.
*Reading.* One tragedy from Shakespeare. Survey of English domestic and foreign history in the nineteenth century, with appropriate readings.

## III. LATIN

1. The instruction seeks, upon the basis of a thorough knowledge of elementary grammar, to attain an appreciation of the simpler works of Latin literature. To this end, it presupposes a combined text and reader that offers both shorter and longer selections from Latin literature. It must insure a sufficient number and variety of selections, and, at the same time, it must offer the pupil the possibility of learning the language chiefly by a study of written works of approximately the same epoch and linguistic form.

2. *Grammar, Vocabulary, Written Exercises.* The teaching of grammar has from the first the avowed purpose of translation from Latin, and therefore limits itself to the most characteristic things and the ones that are met oftenest in Latin. It discriminates sharply between occasional explanations for the understanding of a passage and what is to be a permanent possession of the pupil. As to the methods of teaching Latin grammar, the fundamental principles laid down for the fundamental foreign language hold good. The more mature age of the pupils and the training they have had in language learning make it possible in the Latin course to point out vividly the profound respect which the Romans had for law as revealed in their language, and also the movements in the development of their intellectual life out of which their language grew. The more gifted pupils may in this manner have their attention called to the linguistic peculiarities of individual writers or even of whole epochs. The drill upon a reasonable vocabulary must go forward methodically. Of even greater value than the especially prepared and printed vocabularies are those which first the teacher and later the pupils work out independently. The fundamental facts of Latin grammar and especially its etymology must first be learned by translating sentences into Latin. It is also recommended, in a paragraph of the foreign language, to have pupils determine word forms, and also recognize the forms of the sentence. In the gradual transition to the translation of texts from the Latin, a grammatical analysis of separate sentences and phrases, or an exact determination of forms, should be required. Only after such preliminary practice can a free translation be thought of. The written exercises are to be adapted to this method.

3. *Reading.* In the selection of reading matter the tastes and capacities of the pupils in the different years are to be consulted. The selections of the reader must be complete in themselves and must give a general notion of the work from which they are taken. Good German translations will serve to round out the general understanding of a larger work, bring to the attention of pupils the content of the works they have not read, and sharpen their feeling for language by a comparison of different results obtained in the translation of definite passages read. Stimulation to private reading, as in the cultural studies.

It is not permissible to read several authors at the same time. Grammatical explanations are to be limited to what may be necessary to an understanding of the text. The paragraphs are first to be translated in the school under the direction of the teacher and then assigned for retranslation. Only in the *Prima* are passages to be assigned as regular home work to be prepared independently. The pupils are to be taught how to use an un-abridged dictionary. Only a variation in the teaching process will satisfy the various objectives of the reading. This recognizes a great number of degrees, from a detailed explanation and the attempt at an artistic translation to the finished product, a free rendition of the content, with emphasis upon certain characteristic passages. The written work which is to be done in class will adapt itself to these different possibilities.

## U II
### 5 (4) hours

*Grammar.* Regular etymology. Various irregularities found in the reading and exercise material. In connection with the reading and exercise book, consideration of the most important facts of syntax, and at the same time acquisition of a vocabulary carefully developed as to range and selection.

*Reading.* The reading and the exercise book make use of the vocabulary of the prose writers of the so-called classical Latin period. Original Latin texts are to be taken up as early as possible. Instruction can even be based from the beginning on suitable prose writings, such as the parts of Cæsar's *Bellum Gallicum* that are most significant for earliest German history.

In the vocabulary exercises careful attention should be given to the etymological relationships of words, also relationship to the required foreign language and the mother tongue. Especial emphasis should be laid from the first on good pronunciation. The teacher's example and much reading for expression are of the highest importance.

About every three weeks a written exercise.

## O II
### 3 hours

*Grammar.* Review and fixing of what was taught in U II. Emphasis upon the most necessary of the irregular forms, especially of the verb. Extension of the knowledge of syntax, primarily with regard to sentence structure. Conception of inner dependence; indirect discourse. Systematic development of the vocabulary.

*Reading.* Cæsar's *Bellum Gallicum,* in selections. Excerpts from other ancient prose writers, as Cicero—for example, *Lædius;* Valerius Maximus; and Tacitus—*Germania,* Ch. 1 to 27; Ovid.

A written exercise about every three or four weeks.

## U I and O I

### 3 hours

*Grammar.* According to need and in connection with the reading. Review and intensification of the elements of grammar. Summarizing treatment of syntax and the simpler facts of style observed in the reading. Fixing and extension of the vocabulary; direction of observation to changes in the meanings of words and the persistence of certain words and language phenomena,—borrowed words and foreign words.

*Reading.* Along with appropriate prose writers, also later and medieval Latin writers, the use of selections from Latin poetry. In no case is it permissible to go into unusual stylistic or metrical refinements. Selections worth recommending are: Cæsar's *Bellum Civile;* Sallust; Cicero—*De Legibus, De Republica;* Suetonius—especially *Vita Augusti; Monumentum Ancyranum;* Seneca; Pliny's *Letters;* Tacitus.

Ovid, Catullus, Tibullus, Horace; also Phædrus.

Of the later literature the following are considered: Minucius Felix; Augustinius, *Confessiones* (perhaps also, *De Civitate Dei*); Thomas More's *Utopia;* Einhardt's *Vita Caroli Magni,* and other German literature in the Latin language, and selections from Latin student songs.

Every four or five weeks a translation from Latin.

## IV. Mathematics and Natural Sciences

### A. MATHEMATICS

*Preliminary Remarks*

1. *General Teaching Aim.* Accuracy and skill in manipulation of positive numbers, especially in mental calculation and in the application of these skills to everyday life. Training in the proper conception and comparison of quantities. Development and assimilation of thorough mathematical knowledge which will convince the pupils that mathematics is a valuable science, well ordered and capable of being built up independently of other sciences, and of great importance in practical life and to many other sciences. The aim is to develop

the capacity to recognize mathematical facts according to form, size, and number in the objects and facts of the environment, and to use this acquired knowledge independently; especially the development of the capacity for spatial concepts and a sense for mathematical appreciation of the mutual dependence of variable quantities. Training in logical reasoning and proof and a thorough understanding of the philosophical content and meaning of mathematics from the point of view of the history of intellectual development.

*Fundamental Principles of Method*

A.  *General.*  1.  Mathematical knowledge on the basis of a clear understanding can be attained best by suiting the work to the capacity of the pupil, by stimulating his initiative in the sense of "activity instruction," and by absolutely foregoing all memorization of explanations, theorems, rules, and, above all, proofs. The subject matter, therefore, which has been customary up to this time must be thoroughly sifted so as to afford a more thorough treatment of particular fields of knowledge. Only theorems and processes that are necessary for thorough connection and practical application are to be emphasized. However, memoriter materials which are to be limited to what is absolutely essential are to be assured by constant review.

2.  The solution of problems as the most important means for mastering the subject matter leads to mathematical thinking, especially if in so doing the pupils are directed also to the discovery of geometrical and arithmetical theorems, are trained in reasoning and proofs, and are continually encouraged to more and more intellectual self-activity.

3.  Practical problems should at the same time serve to give a better understanding of life. They should, therefore, take into consideration the other branches of study and the environment of the pupil, and strive thus at securing actual information, especially of economic conditions in purposeful correlation with the other studies. Actual practice in calculation, however, should not on that account be forced into the background.

4. The pupil can be trained in the habit of self-criticism by rough estimates or graphic outline before the exact execution of the work, by discussing the possibility of solution, and the num-

ber of possible solutions, and by actual proof after the solution has been completed.

5. The insight which has already been gained in the middle section into the limits of exactitude in calculations, which are closely related to measurements, will be increased in the upper classes to an estimation of the accuracy of the final results in all suitable cases.

6. Special attention should be given in all grades to the habit of clear, lucid expression.

7. The history of mathematics should receive consideration where it appears relevant in the development of the subject matter and in the assignment of work. In this way its connection with the general development of culture is deeply impressed upon the minds of the pupils. The pupils of the upper classes should be encouraged to read the works of mathematicians of historical importance.

B. *Arithmetic.* 1. Instruction in number strives not only for accuracy and speed in calculation with positive numbers, but demands primarily a comprehension of the measurement of numerical values. For training in computation in number, oral and written calculation is to be practiced continually in the geometry and algebra instruction. Oral arithmetic is to be cultivated to a certain extent in all classes.

2. Exercises in short methods of calculation, approximately from *Quarta* on, are best correlated with measurements which afford an appreciation of the folly of too great exactness.

3. Even in the lower classes, the use of lines and surfaces is to be taken advantage of, where possible, for the purpose of making clear relationships of values. For the representation of particular numerical values one will, from *Quinta* on, permit the use of geometrical representation of number series. Great value is to be placed upon an understanding of the practical meaning of such illustrations. They lead later to the graphic representation of empirical functions and still later form the beginning point for the graphic treatment of analytic functions.

C. *Arithmetic, Algebra, and Analytics.* 1. After a scientific summary of the knowledge gained in the number work, the concrete number is gradually replaced by the literal quantity. The inductive method of proof is replaced by the deductive, after the arithmetic instruction of the lower classes has summarized a simple rule by means of an algebraic formula.

2. The idea of function, which in the beginning appears in concrete form, is to be conceived more sharply during the course of instruction and is to be treated in general form in the upper section. In *Obertertia* the introduction to the fundamental principles of graphic representation is developed through practical examples. In connection therewith the pupils are acquainted purely on an observational basis with the more important characteristics of empirical functions, continuity, inclination, and area. In order that a clear differentiation of the concepts "variable" and "function" be arrived at, however, graphic representation in the right-angled coördinate system must be studied for the first time following equations of the first degree with several unknowns. In all classes, especially those in the middle section, care is to be taken in using graphic representation that the construction of the graphs is not the chief purpose, but only a means of ascertaining the course of the function, and that in addition the other means, the table, must likewise be employed.

3. In the upper section the pupils are introduced to infinitesimal computation, in which the instruction must maintain a balance between justifiable demands for scientific rigidity and the required consideration for practical needs, and will use freely geometrical representation as an auxiliary means.

D. *Geometry*. 1. Elementary instruction developing from the study of simple solids trains the power of observation, develops ability in geometrical abstraction, cultivates correct description of geometrical forms, and drills the pupils in estimation, measurement, and construction of models, and in the first use of compasses and rule.

2. This instruction affords an insight into the systematic organization of geometry and leads from geometrical information to geometrical insight in that it proceeds from empirical formulation to a logical-deduction method of study and thus trains the pupils in the need of proof.

3. Even in the lower section the variation of plane and solid figures is to be employed freely and the effect of the variation of the several dimensions of a figure upon the value of the others is to be determined. Further, axial and central symmetry, ro-

tation, displacement, and superposition of geometric forms deserve special attention.

4. By using in plane geometry suitable illustrations from real life the connection with spatial relationships is to be made as vivid as possible.

5. In the interest of clearness special attention is to be given to correct and careful construction of figures, and to the use of cross-hatching and color. The use of models must not militate against the development of the power of observation, since the power of spatial observation must develop gradually into the power of space conception.

6. Geometrical facts, especially in the problem work, are to be taught with emphasis on their applications.

7. In geometrical construction problems, which are to be especially fostered, aids from mechanical drawing may be used and approximate constructions considered. Likewise, attention is to be given occasionally to unfavorable relationships of position. So-called analysis must primarily give attention to the thought processes by which one arrives at the solution. The more skilled pupils are to be led to a critical comparison of the different methods of construction. All artificial constructions selected from unusual topics are to be avoided.

8. Geometry and trigonometry are limited to the simplest geometrical formulæ and the fundamental principles of the plane and spherical triangles. After the elements of geometric functions, next the computation of their values is to be taught and thoroughly drilled according to the short methods of calculating decimal fractions.

9. The introduction to stereometry, begun first upon a purely objective basis, is carried on simultaneously both arithmetically and graphically and then proceeds gradually to a systematic, scientific method of instruction which, limited to the more important principles, clothes the fundamental notions and laws in concrete form.

10. From the lowest classes up, geometrical drawing presents the geometrical facts to the pupil, shows their practical application, and brings to him thus gradually and more clearly the close connections between the observation, the conception, and the representation of space.

11. Likewise, value is to be assigned from the beginning to

the execution of measurements whereby the exactitude of the measurements is to be increased gradually by more refined means until finally a notion is attained of the extraordinary difficulties involved in exact execution of geodetical and astronomical measurements.

### Course of Study

#### VI

#### 4 hours

The four fundamental operations with integral, abstract and simple and compound concrete numbers. The German measures, weights and coins. Exercises in writing decimals and in the simplest decimal calculations. Applications of household and community economy. Study of space forms in so far as they are used in the geography and natural science work of this section.

#### V

#### 4 hours

Exercises with concrete decimal numbers continued. Divisibility of numbers. The four fundamental operations with common fractions. Representation of numbers by means of lines and areas. Solution of simple problems in proportion by solving for unity or a common measure. Applications to the business of the community and of the state. Further consideration of space forms.

#### IV

#### 4 hours

*Arithmetic.* The four fundamental operations with decimal fractions; conversion of common fractions to decimals and *vice versa.* Short methods in computation. Simplest cases of percentage, discount, interest, and other problems from daily life with applications of simple and compound proportion. Objectification of numbers by means of lines and areas. Arithmetical manipulation of prepared tables, especially calculation of averages and ratios. Applications to the business of the community, state, and nation.

*Geometry.* Objective development of the fundamental geometrical principles. Principles of straight line, angles, and triangles.

*Geometrical Drawing and Measurement.* Figures made up of lines and arcs. Measurement of lines and angles.

## U III

### 4 hours

*Algebra.* Elementary literal calculations. The four fundamental operations with absolute, relative, integral, and fractional numbers. Objectification by means of number lines and of number diagrams. Computation from tables by means of formulæ. Simple equations of the first degree with one unknown in connection with the operations in the rational number system. Proportion. Continuation of the exercises in number work begun in earlier classes, with reference to economic conditions.

*Geometry.* Theory of the quadrilateral, especially of the parallelogram and trapezium. Elements of the theory of the circle. Chords and angles on the circle.

*Geometrical Drawing and Measurement.* Exercises in exact and accurate execution of constructions. Measurement of lines and angles. Estimation exercises out-of-doors.

## O III

### 4 hours

*Algebra.* Equations of the first degree with one or more unknowns. Simple applications, especially from practical life. Introduction to graphic representation on the basis of empirical functions. Representation of linear functions and their employment in the solution of equations. Powers with positive integral exponents. Representation of the function $y$ equals $x^n$ for positive integral values of $n$. Extraction of square roots.

*Geometry.* Further study of the circle. Computation and comparison of areas. Pythagorean Theorem.

*Geometrical Drawing and Measurement.* Plotting of curves in connection with algebra. Graphic determination of area by means of millimeter paper and other procedures. Measurement of lines, angles, and areas, also out-of-doors.

## U II

### 4 hours

*Algebra.* Theory of powers and roots, with graphic representation of the functions of $y$ equals $x^n$ and $y$ equals $\sqrt[n]{x}$. Computation of radical expressions. Continued exercises in practical arithmetic, especially by means of short processes. Quadratic equations with one unknown. The function $y = x^2 + ax + b$.

*Geometry.* Proportional lines. Theory of similarity. Applications to the circle. Harmonic points and rays. Circumference and area of the circle. Representation and calculation of the simplest solids.

*Geometrical Drawing and Measurement.* Plotting of curves in connection with algebra. Approximate constructions, circle. More exact measurements. Surveying exercises in connection with the theory of similarity. Correct representation of solid figures.

## O II

### 4 hours

*Algebra.* Exponential and logarithmic functions. Logarithmic tables, and slide rule. Logarithmic computation. Simple algebraic functions of the second degree. Simple equations and equation systems which can be solved by the aid of the quadratic equation. Conic sections in empirical method of study.

*Geometry.* The trigonometric functions. Easy computation of triangles. Geometry. Notion of the periodic functions. Straight lines and planes in space. Continuation of the computation and representation of solids.

*Geometrical Drawing and Measurement.* Plotting of curves in connection with algebra. Representation of simple solids in oblique parallel projection and by the vertical-horizontal projection process. Simple exercises in surveying and leveling.

## U I AND O I

### 4 hours each

*Algebra.* Arithmetic progressions of the first degree and geometric progressions. Compound interest and annuities with applications from business life. Binomial theorem for positive integral exponents. Mathematical probability. Organization of the number system from the positive integral number to the complex number. Review of the rational, integral, fractional, algebraic and transcendental functions which have been studied. Discussion of such functions together with the means of infinitesimal computations, especially maximal and minimal values. Approximate solution of equations. Survey of the development of the number concept and the notion of function.

*Geometry.* Fundamental principles of spherical trigonometry, principle of the sine and the tangent. Applications to mathematical geography and astronomy. Geometry of coördinates. Summarizing treatment of conic sections. Review with addition of historical and philosophical points of view.

*Geometrical Drawing and Measurement.* Drawings from conic sections. Central perspective. Illustrative treatment of the surface of the sphere. Simple astronomical observations with exercises in measurement and calculation.

*Introduction*

I. *General Instructional Aim.* Knowledge of the most important physical phenomena, of their laws and the ways in which we have arrived at these laws. Insight into the theories fundamental to a comprehensive study of nature and to the acquisition of a picture of the physical world. Acquaintance with the technical applications of physics in so far as they are important for daily life or important in an economic connection.

II. *Fundamental Principles of Method.* 1. The instruction in physics, proceeding from the observation of natural phenomena, is based as far as possible upon exercises and experiments by the pupils themselves or upon observations directly at hand. If time is limited the pupils are also to be trained through home study to think over the method of carrying out an investigation. The experiment, which receives the major emphasis in all sections, forms the starting-point in the inductive process and furnishes the conclusive proof in the deductive procedure.

2. The selection of subject matter, which is especially essential in physics, takes into consideration in the preparatory work only those simpler natural phenomena important for an understanding of the environment. In the upper section some topics can be treated more briefly if the pupils obtain a well-rounded picture from the point of view of theoretical knowledge from the other branches of physical science. More important than the acquisition of a mass of physical facts is a thorough insight into the method of investigation in physics which has been developed through the pupil's own activity.

3. The mathematical formulation of physical laws will have to consider that mathematics is for physics simply a means to knowledge. It must avoid primarily pseudo-mathematical derivations, and, rather than an artificial, apparent proof, give the ready-made formula, with a statement of the reason why it cannot be proved by an elementary method.

4. In all stages of the instruction the pupils must create a clear image of the dimensions of the physical units which are useful in the experiments and discussions.

5. In physics instruction great importance is assigned to the historical method of study. Not only does this method bring a

closer relationship of mathematics-natural science subjects with other subjects that is highly desirable, but it frequently is best studied to introduce the pupils to an appreciation of the whole field of study, affording them a more thorough knowledge of the various problems. One may use to advantage, for example, the historical organization in "activity instruction" in that one may permit discoveries and invention made long ago to be discovered and invented once more. This historical approach is absolutely necessary when, as in *Prima*, it is a question of discussing the great fundamental principles, and of tying up the work with formulation of questions and systems of thought which influence the world. In the discussion of decisive physical theories in the development of the intellectual training of the pupils, one must go back from historical knowledge to the beginning of philosophy. One must also point out to the *Primaner* that physical problems merge finally into metaphysical problems. If the pupils, in their discussions of the historical development of great physical hypotheses, secure a conception of what limits are generally set to our knowledge, then they will be convinced that the great problems only begin where the mere senses believe everything is best explained.

### Course of Study

### U III

### 2 hours

Experimental treatment of simple fundamental phenomena from the mechanics of solid, liquid, and gaseous bodies, and from the theory of heat, with observations from daily life and simple experiments by the pupils.

### O III

### 2 hours

Simple and important phenomena from the theory of magnetism and electricity, acoustics, optics, with experimental treatment.

### U II

Twenty hours are assigned. The physical facts already learned are used and fixed in the introduction to chemistry; for example, in the discussion of the properties of water, air, common salt, and carbon.

## O II

### 2 hours

First scientific introduction to mechanics,—velocity and acceleration, gravitation, force and mass, work and energy, conservation and transformation of energy. Theory of heat,—degree of heat and expansion, latent and specific heat, changes of condition in gases and liquids, mechanical equivalent of heat, heatpower machines, phenomena of atmospheric heat.

## U I AND O I

### 2 hours each

Mechanics of rigid bodies. Moment of inertia, conditions of equilibrium, Newton's laws, centrifugal motion, harmonic vibration, pendulum, and the most essential facts from cosmographic physics.

Mechanics of liquids and gases,—laws of Archimedes, Pascal, Torricelli, Bernoulli, Boyle, Laplace. Wave theory, progressive waves and stationary vibrations,—Huygen's law. Acoustics,—velocity of sound, theory of vibratory strings and pipes. Magnetism,—Coulomb's law, field of force, strength of field, lines of force, earth's magnetism. Electricity, laws of Coulomb, Ohm, Joule, Volta, Kirchhoff, Oersted, Biot-Savart, Faraday, Arrhenius, and Maxwell; electrical units, direct, alternating and three-phase machines, transformers, transmission of energy. Optics, —hypotheses concerning the nature of light, theory and practice of optical instruments, interference and refraction, connection with light, heat and electrical waves, radio-activity, and structure of the atom.

### C. CHEMISTRY

*Introduction*

I. *General Instructional Aim.* Knowledge of the most important chemical phenomena, in so far as they are important for an appreciation of organic and inorganic nature and for the home and public economy. Acquaintance with the laws which lie at the basis of these phenomena, and insight into the theories which disclose an understanding of these laws. Knowledge of the most important minerals and rocks with reference to their technical, economic, and geological importance.

II. *Principle of Method.* 1. The statements on method as regards physics apply here in so far as the situation permits.

2. The practical exercises of the pupils are to be brought

into closest connection with the class instruction; they must in no way be used solely as exercises in analysis.

3. The minerals are to be studied in connection with the treatment of the elements found in them, together with an evaluation of their economic values and their geological importance. The study of crystal forms can be assigned to geometrical drawing.

4. Short studies from the history of chemistry will make clear at suitable places the chief features of its historical development and will work out by means of particular illustrations the development of an idea or the effect of an individual.

5. Instructional excursions provide understanding of natural processes, give a view into the great chemical industry, and show the great value of chemistry for the home and public health.

6. The fundamental principles of selection of subject matter in chemistry are to be carried by shortening or completely eliminating various phases of the subject. Renouncing comprehensiveness, the course of study seeks in the most important parts of the subject to give a deeper insight into the methods of chemical study, relates in systematic fashion the topics studied with one another and with related topics in the other natural sciences, and gradually shows the great interrelationships of all natural processes.

### Course of Study

### U II

### 2 hours

Preparatory course in chemistry: Experimental treatment of easy and important chemical processes and principles,—properties of air, water, sulphuric acid, sodium chloride, carbon, element, compound, mixture, oxidation, reduction, affinity, and base and salt. Establishment of the law of simple and compound proportion. Elements of chemical symbols.

### O II

### In Combination with Botany and Zoology

### 3 hours

The instruction is given in both subjects by the same teacher who can divide the three hours available between chemistry and biology as needs dictate.   Usually two hours will be given to chemistry and one to biology.

In the systematically organized course in chemistry:  Hydrogen, oxygen, sulphur, halogens, and in this connection discussion of conceptions such as analysis, synthesis, substitution, atomic weight, combining weight, valence.   Establishment of the atomic theory and Avogadro's hypothesis.

## U I AND O I

### In Combination with Biology

### 3 hours each

Discussion of the metalloids and their most important compounds.   In this connection the technology of the most powerful acids, bituminous coal, and illuminating gas.   The alkali metals, especially their salts, as to their geologic and technical importance.   The other light metals and the most important heavy metals, with special reference to their extraction and technology.   Survey of the periodic system of the elements.   Ionic and dissociation theories, structure and properties of the organic compounds which are of greatest importance for technology and economic life, food, and public health.

### D. NATURAL HISTORY

I. *General Instructional Aim.*   Knowledge of the most important life processes in plants and animals, their organization, and the relationships existing between their structure and manner of life.   Survey of the multiplicity of life systems, their immediate and remote kinship and their modifiability.   Knowledge of the chief groups of the plant and animal kingdoms.   Insight into the interaction between organism and environment, between organisms of the same and different class, with special reference to the place of man in nature and of the natural foundations of national economy arising therefrom.   Relation with the forces effective in the formation of the earth's surface. The most important kinds of rocks and soils.   The chief division of geology.   Insight into the importance of natural history for an appreciation of the great world and life problems.

II. *Principles of Method.*   1.   The chief aim of the natural history instruction, knowledge of life phenomena, is to be sought from the lowest class up essentially by means of observation of living plants and animals and of their own bodies.

2. By thoughtful application of the principles of method, as given for physics and chemistry, the pupils are to be led to the preparation and performance of experiments, and are to be encouraged to carry on personal observations and experiments in cultivation. Preparation of drawings and models, determination of plants and animals, as well as simple dissections, advance the self-activity of the pupils. Regular experiments by the pupils are necessary in the upper section.

3. According to the advancement of the class, the notions of species, germs, family, order, class, and branch are to be developed upon the basis of concrete examples, and thus, without aiming at a knowledge of classification, acquaint the pupil with the principles of classification. The leaf, blossom, and fruit forms, and the various forms of inflorescence are discussed only to such an extent as is necessary for a knowledge of life phenomena and for the determination of plants and animals. Regular instruction in classification is not given.

4. From the lowest class up, the pupils are to learn to recognize the living organism in its development. Observations of the development of plants, amphibia, some insects and snails are to be carried on by the pupils themselves in pots, aquaria, and terraria.

5. In the selection of subject matter species of animals and plants important to the local region and civilization are emphasized. However, the most important cultivated plants and animals characteristic of foreign lands and oceans must not be omitted. Extinct animals and plants also are occasionally discussed.

6. The economic importance of biology is to be illustrated by means of suitable examples.

7. Instruction in hygiene is not to be limited to instruction in physiology in U II.

8. In conjunction with geography, biology as well as the other natural science subjects aims at insight into the inherent connection of all natural phenomena and natural laws and into the control and regulation of man and his civilization exercised by life and nature.

9. The discussion of the theory of evolution affords the pupils an insight into the value of the doctrine of the origin of the species as a working hypothesis. The problems of monism, dual-

ism, mechanism, vitalism, are to be presented to the pupils, in which final, one-sided decisions and dogmatic judgments are to be avoided. The teacher must not be denied, however, the privilege of indicating his own personal opinion.

## Course of Study

### VI

#### 2 hours

*Botany.* The chief parts of plants: root, leaf, blossom, fruit, seed. Shooting forth of winter buds, tubercles, and bulbs. Germination, importance of seminal leaves, dependence of plants upon light, air, water, and soil foods. The most important trees of the vicinity. Fruit trees and grains. Some important mushrooms. Natural and artificial plant communities: meadow, woodland, field, forest, and park.

*Physiology.* The chief parts of the human body and their functions.

*Zoölogy.* Structure and life habits of selected local animals with consideration of their relationships to their environment and to man. The most important domestic animals. Some naturally related groups: beasts of prey, rodents, ruminants.

*Geology.* The most important kinds of soils and rocks of the immediate vicinity.

### V

#### 2 hours

*Botany.* Review and extension of the subject matter of *Sexta* Important leaf and blossom forms as well as types of inflorescence, explained by means of characteristic plants of the vicinity. Important vegetables. Some grasses, ferns, mosses, and mushrooms. Comparison of related types in order to secure a conception of species and genus.

*Zoölogy.* Continuation of the subject matter of *Sexta* by means of a study of some especially important foreign species, through consideration of selected species of local anthropoids, mollusks, and helminthes (reptilia and vermes) and by development of some systematic notions, as species and genus.

*Geology.* Influence of water upon the formation of soil.

### IV

#### 2 hours

*Botany.* Structure of the blossom, pollination, and fertilization. Wind and insect flowers. Comparative study of selected types of especially characteristic plant families for the purpose of acquiring systematic ideas, especially relating to the concept of family.

*Zoölogy.* Selected insect groups as to structure and method of life. Comparative treatment to develop the concept of order. Importance of insects in the whole scheme of nature, especially in relation to plant kingdom.

*Geology.* Relation between the soil and the living world.

## U III

### 2 hours

*Botany.* Selected representatives of the chief group of the plant kingdom in ascending series to gain insight into the principles of classification. The different types of plant feeding and reproduction.

*Zoölogy.* Selected representatives of the lower group of animals in ascending series, protozoa, nematophoras, helminthes, and mollusks, to gain insight into the principles of classification. The different types of animal feeding and reproduction.

## O III

### 2 hours

*Zoölogy.* Selected representatives of echinodermata, anthropoids, and vertebrates in ascending series, to acquire notions of systematic classification.

*Geology.* Reasons for the hypothesis of a continual change of the earth's surface. The earth's transforming forces, water, air, tectonic processes, volcanism. The most important rocks and rock-forming minerals. The chief portions of the earth's history.

## U II

### 2 hours

*Biology.* The organization of the plant and animal bodies from cells and tissues. Unicellular organisms. Development of multicellular bodies from the unicellular. Dissection of selected representatives of various animal groups. Structure and life of the human body.

## O II

### Together with Chemistry

### 3 hours

Relationships of organisms to environment. Means of dispersion of animals and plants.

## U I and O I

### Together with Chemistry

### 3 hours

Comparative observation of metabolism, movement, susten-tacles, sensitivity, and reproduction in the plant and animal world. Survey of the development of the earth and its inhabi-tants. Place of man in the natural world. Selected portions from physiological psychology.

## V. Music, Drawing, and Manual Training

### A.  music

"The course of study for music instruction in secondary schools for boys,"[1] which will soon appear, will be applicable to the *Deutsche Oberschule* and *Aufbauschulen.*

### B.  drawing

*General Instructional Aim.* Cultivation of drawing and painting as a manifestation of emotional experience and of the natural desire for expression as well as a means of explanation and expression for artistic, scientific and technical purposes. In conjunction with all of the cultural instruction, an introduc-tion to an appreciation of the pictorial arts, especially of local architectural and art monuments.

## VI to IV

### 2 hours each

Free exercises which afford the pupils an opportunity to ex-press their own impressions and experiences through drawing and painting. In this connection exercises in free-hand draw-ing and cutting from a subject and from memory. The drawing exercises are also to be executed upon the blackboard. Exercises in color work upon surfaces. Exercises in pasting. Beginning of painting. Upon suitable occasions study of good pictures. Measurement and representation of simple flat objects. Writing exercises according to Sutterlin.

## U III to U II

### 2 hours each

In connection with the free pupil exercises, exercises in spatial representation from an object and from memory. Repro-

[1] *Min. Erl. zur Musikreform vom 14. April 1924.*

duction of phenomena of perspective and light and shadow. These exercises are to be carried out also on the blackboard. Exercises in color distribution on surfaces. Painting from nature and from memory. Pasting exercises. Cutting with scissors. Cutting in linoleum. Exercises in easy decorative script. Blocking out and representation of simple solids, utensils, and parts of buildings from various positions with sections and arrangements. Study of works of art in connection with exercises in drawing and painting.

## O II TO O I

### 2 hours each

Studies from nature, sculpture, and local examples of architecture and art. Free exercises in various techniques, also decorative writing. In connection with the study of works of art, the pupils are introduced to the technical foundations of the pictorial arts and to the position of local art in the development of art in Germany and in western countries. Principles of pictorial perspective and shadow construction. Projective and perspective representation of utensils, buildings, and parts of buildings. Sketching of landscapes.

### C. MANUAL TRAINING AND MECHANICAL DRAWING

*A. General Aim.* This is constructive manual work. It serves not only the intellectual and physical training of the pupils but also the needs of the school, in the spirit of the regulation of April 9, 1921,[1] especially through the construction and repair of instructional materials and equipment.

*B. Special Aims of Instruction.* (a) *Woodwork, Cardboard Work, Metal Work, Mechanical Drawing:*

## VI

The instruction covers easy work in wood. Its purpose is to enable the pupils to prepare, by means of the simplest sort of tools, playground apparatus, toys, and small useful articles. The articles are carved by hand or constructed from planed lumber. In the course of the construction the pupils are instructed as to the nature of woods and tools.

## V

The light woodwork is continued and extended to more difficult problems. The form of the objects is to be very simple,

[1] *Erlass vom 9. April 1921.*

and the outline limited to the straight line, right and obtuse angles, the circle and parts of the circle. Elements of mechanical drawing. Instruction about materials and tools.

### IV

The instruction takes in cardboard work. Its purpose is to enable the pupils to construct useful articles from cardboard and to cover such articles with decorative paper. Carefulness and cleanliness are to be especially cultivated. The work is limited to simple forms; outlines with sharp and distorted angles are to be avoided. The more advanced pupils can be introduced to bookbinding. This work should be restricted to simple, easy bindings. Imitations of wood, leather, and other materials are not to be employed as media. The pupils are acquainted in the simplest way with the manufacture of paper and should learn the preparation and use of adhesive substances.

### U III

The instruction in cardboard work and bookbinding is continued. In given cases, instead of this, work in joinery may be begun. The instruction in joinery is to enable the pupils, after previous construction of the customary joints, such as the dovetail, to make simple, useful articles with saw and plane from rough boards. The finished work can be oiled or stained. Every article is to be sketched by the pupil himself in the simplest form possible. The sketch is to be developed into a working drawing in natural dimensions. The pupils in the course of the work are to be instructed with reference to the kinds of work, its occurrence, its production, and manufacture as well as concerning the tools which they use.

### O III

The work covers joinery and includes working drawings. It corresponds to the work in U III. The problems can be more difficult; the size of the individual piece of work, however, must not exceed a certain easily managed size. Pupils, who are especially adapted therefor, can continue bookbinding instead of woodwork.

### U II

The instruction now includes metal work. Its purpose is to enable the pupils to execute the easy problems in wire and sheet-metal which arise occasionally in every home or which can serve the purpose of the instruction. Where possible the pupils are to learn also to make small articles from brass and copper. In the course of the work they are to be taught concerning the oc-

currence and production of the metals, their artificial compounds, and their distinguishing characteristics as well as the
tools which are used in their manufacture or reduction.

### O II to O I

The instruction in metal work can be carried further with
the forge and metal lathe. Fine mechanical exercises, with the
addition of work in glass, enable pupils to construct physical
and chemical apparatus for school use.

(b) *Sewing and Pattern Drawing.* The courses for *Lyzeum*
and *Frauenschulen* of August 18, 1908, apply in these fields.

### VI. Physical Training

The courses of study of 1901 apply to physical training.

### The Aufbauschulen

1. The *Aufbauschule* with the goal of the *Deutsche Oberschule*
or the *Oberrealschule,* for which essentially the same instructional objectives are set as for the nine-year school, will in the
selection of subject matter have to avoid mechanical condensa-
tion of the subject matter of the nine-year school into six years.
Rather, it must increase the power of its pupils by a form of activity instruction which deals with truly educative materials and
rejects compendial perfection and completeness and thus must
give its attention to the organic development of the subject
matter.

2. Corresponding to the many-sidedness of the *Volksschule*
the *Aufbauschule* must consider the attainments brought from
the *Volksschule* and systematically plan to extend them. The
development of the materials will be connected as organically
as possible in the nine-year school with the problem of the class
concerned. By a more refined selection of subject matter, which
will have to give attention to special local conditions, time will
be secured for this work. The instructional problems of the
corresponding classes of the nine-year school are the foundations
in other respects for the *Aufbauschule,* wherein immaterial displacement or exchange of subject matter is not impossible. The
suggestions given in the courses of study for the *Deutsche Oberschule* can also find application in the *Aufbauschule* modeled

after the *Oberrealschule*.  However, in this matter the characteristic difference in the educational ideal of the *Deutsche Oberschule* and the *Oberrealschule* must not be destroyed.

3. The courses of study to be set up in accordance with these
points of view must regard the following suggestions in particular:

(*a*) *Religion*.  In religion, the instructional materials of
*Quarta*, necessary for an appreciation of the history of Christianity, can be made up in *Untertertia* by limitation to essential
facts, since it can be assumed that the other topics in religion in
this class have been done by the pupils of the *Volksschule*.

(*b*) *German*.  The chief problem of German instruction in
*Untertertia* is to increase and intensify greatly the materials of
the *Volksschule* in favor of the grammar instruction of the foreign languages.  Primarily, the syntax must be adapted to the
special needs of the secondary school.  In phonetics, regular
exercises in pure High German are frequently necessary for the
purpose of overcoming deeply rooted impurities of speech.  In
etymology the objective of the *Volksschule* must be carried
further in the direction of historical insight into the origin and
history of words.

(*c*) *History*.  The history instruction must see primarily that
at suitable places facts from ancient history necessary for an
appreciation of German civilization and literature are inserted.
Particularly in *Untertertia*, reference must be thus made to
Roman history.

(*d*) *Geography and Civics*.  Since the objectives in the "Suggestions for the Organization of Courses of Study for the Upper
Years of the *Volksschule*" correspond in essentials to the course
of study of the *Oberschule* in geography and civics, the *Aufbauschule* will be able to follow the courses of study of the *Oberschule*, and keep in mind the distribution of subject matter in
the *Volksschule*.

(*e*) *English or French*.  In English or French also the same
objective generally is to be set in the *Aufbauschule* as in the
fundamental type of school.  In essentials it will suffice in the
distribution of subject matter to consider U III and O III as the
lower section, U II and O II as the middle section, and U I
and O I as the upper section.  By use of the general educative
materials developed in the *Volksschule*, however, a more rapid

advancement may usually be possible than in the lower and middle sections of the nine-year schools; thus for the first foreign language even in *Obersekunda* the selection of reading materials and the treatment of language values may be built on the forms provided for the same level in the fundamental type of school. The language material is from the beginning to be adapted to the more advanced age of the pupil. It is especially important in the *Aufbauschule* to have a systematic selection of reading material in order that the general educational objectives of the type of school in question may be attained in spite of the necessary restrictions.

(*f*) *Mathematics.* In consequence of the presupposedly great, but often mechanical, skill found in many pupils of the *Volksschule* in dealing with fractions and decimals numbers, calculation with positive numbers can be raised to abstract knowledge by means of algebraic treatment of the fundamental operations. This introduction to algebra will thus combine unequally trained pupils into a uniform activity group.

### AUFBAUSCHULE WITH OBJECTIVE OF THE OBERSCHULE

It is the purpose of the courses of study of the undivided schools to distribute the topics of the *Oberschule* from *Quarta* to *Untersekunda* to the classes *Untertertia* to *Untersekunda* of the *Aufbauschule,* wherein in *Untertertia* the topics from arithmetic of *Quarta* are to be made up.

### AUFBAUSCHULE WITH OBJECTIVE OF THE OBERREALSCHULE

#### U III

#### 6 hours

Arithmetic, algebra, geometrical drawing and measurement as in the *Aufbauschule* with the objective of the *Oberschule.*

Geometry in connection with the objective study of simple geometric forms which have been drilled upon in the *Volksschule:* theory of the triangle and the quadrilateral, especially the parallelogram and the trapezium. Theory of the circle.

#### O III

#### 6 hours

*Algebra.* Equations of the first degree with one or more unknowns; simple applications, especially from life. Introduction to graphic representation, empirical functions, linear functions and their application in the solution of equations. Powers with positive and negative integral exponents. The function $y = x^n$ for positive and negative integral values of $n$. Principle of roots; calculations with radical expressions. The function $y = \sqrt[n]{x}$. Continued exercises in arithmetic, especially with short methods.

*Geometry.* Calculation and comparison of area,—Pythagorean theorem. Proportion of lines; theory of similarity. Applications to the circle; harmonic points and rays. Position and points of similarity.

*Geometrical Drawing and Measurement.* Continued exercises in execution of construction. Graphic calculation of area by means of millimeter paper and by other processes, also out-of-doors. Plotting of curves in connection with algebra; graphic and arithmetic interpolation. More exact measurement of lines, angles, and areas. Nonius.

## U II

### 5 hours

*Algebra.* Quadratic equations with one unknown. The function $y = x^2 + ax + b$. Exponential and logarithmic functions. Logarithmic table and slide rule; logarithmic calculation.

*Geometry.* Circumference and area of the circle. Representation and calculation of simple solids. The trigonometric functions. Easy calculation of triangles.

*Geometrical Drawing and Measurement.* Plotting of curves in connection with algebra. Approximate constructions,—division of circle; squaring of circle. Drawing of simple solids in oblique parallel projection and in vertical-horizontal section. Simple exercises in surveying and leveling.

## O II

### 5 hours

*Algebra.* Arithmetic progressions of the first order; geometric progressions. Compound interset and annuities, with applications from business life. Structure of the number system from positive integral to the complex number; the fundamental operations with complex numbers. Moivrian theorem; binomial equations. The rational integral function and its derivation; maxima and minima, points of deflection of $x$ and $\cos x$ and their derivatives.

*Geometry.* Straight lines and planes in space; continuation of computation of solids. Goniometry. Continuation of computation of triangles and quadrilaterals.

*Geometrical Drawing and Measurement.* Plotting of curves
in connection with algebra. Drawing of geometric forms by
vertical-horizontal section process. Continued exercises in surveying and leveling.

### U I AND O I

#### 5 hours each

*Algebra.* Fundamental principles of the calculation of probability. Calculation of insurance. The theory of equations, especially of approximate equations. Simple rational non-continuous
functions and their derivatives; discovery of related curves.
Simple algebraic functions and their derivatives; solutions of
simple systems of equations of the second degree with two unknowns. Some transcendental functions and their derivatives,
trigonometric, cyclometric, logarithmic, and exponential functions; discovery of related curves. Convergence and divergence
of infinite series. The binomial theorem. Development of the
transcendental functions in exponential series and their application in the calculation of trigonometric values, logarithms and
the quantities $\varepsilon$ and $\pi$. Simplest cases of integrations with
application to the computation of length of arcs and area of
surfaces and content of solids. Survey of the development of
the number concept and the idea of function.

*Geometry.* Spherical trignometry; mathematical geography
and astronomy. Analytic geometry of the straight line and the
circle. Plane sections through the cylinder and cone. Relation
with the definition of locus of the conic sections,—Dandelinian
spheres. Synthetic geometry of conic sections. Conic sections
as the perspective representation of the circle; laws of Pascal
and Brianchon. Survey of the development of conic sections by
means of projective series of points and pencil lines.

*Geometrical Drawing and Measurement.* Plotting of curves
in connection with algebra and geometry, especially approximate
construction of conic sections. Representation of parts of
spherical surface,—cartography. Fundamental principles of
central perspective and theory of shadows; easy applications.
Measurements and computations from mathematical geography
and astronomy.

Survey with employment of historical and philosophical points
of view.

(*g*) *Physics.* In the *Aufbauschule* with the objective of the
*Oberschule* as in the corresponding classes of the *Oberschule*.
In the *Aufbauschule* with the objective of the *Oberrealschule* in
classes U III, O III and U II as in the corresponding classes of
the *Oberschule*. In O II, U I and O I, each 3 hours a year,

essentially the same subject matter as in the upper section of the *Oberschule*. The greater part of the instructional time is to be primarily for laboratory exercises in which the instruction given in class is worked out thoroughly and supplemented by a more intensive treatment of the more difficult topics. Among such topics, perhaps, are the mechanical theory of heat, kinetic theory of gases, spectral analysis, polarization and double refraction, modern phenomena of rays, theory of the composition of the atom.

(*h*) *Chemistry*. As in the *Oberschule*.

(*i*) *Natural History*.

### U III

#### 2 hours

*Botany*. Review of flowering plants with consideration of their life relationships and in reference to the organization of the plant kingdom. Useful plants in agriculture and forestry.

*Zoölogy*. Review of vertebrates and insects with consideration of life processes and with regard to the division of the animal kingdom. Some facts with reference to animal husbandry, hunting and their economic importance.

*Geology*. Effect of water upon soil formation. Relation between soil and life.

### O III

#### 2 hours

*Botany*. Selected representatives of all groups of the plant kingdom in ascending order for the development of the systematic fundamental ideas.

*Zoölogy*. Selected representatives of all groups of the animal kingdom in ascending order to attain an insight into the organization of the animal kingdom.

*Geology*. The forces operating to transform the earth. Chief sections from the earth's history.

From U II to O I as in the corresponding classes of the *Oberschule*.